Meta Learning With Medical Imaging and Health Informatics Applications

The Elsevier and Miccai Society Book Series

Advisory Board

Titles

'Dalca, A.V., et al., Imaging Genetics, 9780128139684.

Depeursinge, A., et al., Biomedical Texture Analysis, 9780128121337.

Munsell, B., et al., Connectomics, 9780128138380.

Pennec, X., et al., Riemannian Geometric Statistics in Medical Image Analysis, 9780128147252.

Wu, G., and Sabuncu, M., Machine Learning and Medical Imaging, 9780128040768.

Zhou S.K., Medical Image Recognition, Segmentation and Parsing, 9780128025819.

Zhou, S.K., et al., Deep Learning for Medical Image Analysis, 9780128104088.

Zhou, S.K., et al., Handbook of Medical Image Computing and Computer
Assisted Intervention, 9780128161760.

Tian et al., Radiomics and Its Clinical Application, 978-0-12-818101-0.

MICCAI

Meta Learning With Medical Imaging and Health Informatics Applications

Edited by

Hien Van Nguyen
Ronald Summers
Rama Chellappa

ELSEVIER

ACADEMIC PRESS
An imprint of Elsevier

Academic Press is an imprint of Elsevier
125 London Wall, London EC2Y 5AS, United Kingdom
525 B Street, Suite 1650, San Diego, CA 92101, United States
50 Hampshire Street, 5th Floor, Cambridge, MA 02139, United States
The Boulevard, Langford Lane, Kidlington, Oxford OX5 1GB, United Kingdom

Notices

Knowledge and best practice in this field are constantly changing. As new research and experience broaden our understanding, changes in research methods, professional practices, or medical treatment may become necessary.

Practitioners and researchers must always rely on their own experience and knowledge in evaluating and using any information, methods, compounds, or experiments described herein. In using such information or methods they should be mindful of their own safety and the safety of others, including parties for whom they have a professional responsibility.

To the fullest extent of the law, neither the Publisher nor the authors, contributors, or editors, assume any liability for any injury and/or damage to persons or property as a matter of products liability, negligence or otherwise, or from any use or operation of any methods, products, instructions, or ideas contained in the material herein.

ISBN: 978-0-323-99851-2

For information on all Academic Press publications
visit our website at https://www.elsevier.com/books-and-journals

Publisher: Mara Conner
Acquisitions Editor: Tim Pitts
Editorial Project Manager: Aera F. Gariguez
Production Project Manager: Sojan P. Pazhayattil
Cover Designer: Mark Rogers

Typeset by VTeX

Working together to grow libraries in developing countries

www.elsevier.com • www.bookaid.org

Contents

CHAPTER 11   Smart task design for meta learning medical image analysis systems **185**
Cuong C. Nguyen, Youssef Dawoud, Thanh-Toan Do, Jacinto
C. Nascimento, Vasileios Belagiannis, and Gustavo Carneiro

Contributors

Xavier Amatriain
Curai, Palo Alto, CA, United States

Yogesh Balaji
NVIDIA, San Jose, CA, United States

Stefan Bekiranov
University of Virginia, Charlottesville, VA, United States

Vasileios Belagiannis
Universität Ulm, Ulm, Germany

Anas-Alexis Benyoussef
Ophthalmology Department, CHRU Brest, Brest, France

Gustavo Carneiro
Australian Institute for Machine Learning, University of Adelaide, Adelaide, SA, Australia

Manish Chablani
Curai, Palo Alto, CA, United States

Cheng Chen
Department of Computer Science and Engineering, The Chinese University of Hong Kong, Hong Kong, China

Hyun Jae Cho
University of Virginia, Charlottesville, VA, United States

Jingyuan Chou
University of Virginia, Charlottesville, VA, United States

Béatrice Cochener
Ophthalmology Department, CHRU Brest, Brest, France

Pierre-Henri Conze
IMT Atlantique, Brest, France

Youssef Dawoud
Universität Ulm, Ulm, Germany

Thanh-Toan Do
Department of Data Science and AI, Monash University, Clayton, VIC, Australia

Qi Dou
Department of Computer Science and Engineering, The Chinese University of Hong Kong, Hong Kong, China

Azade Farshad
Technical University of Munich, Munich, Germany

Chi-Wing Fu
The Chinese University of Hong Kong, HKSAR, China

Abhijit Guha Roy
Ludwig Maximilian University of Munich, Munich, Germany

Pengfei Guo
Johns Hopkins University, Baltimore, MD, United States

Pheng-Ann Heng
Department of Computer Science and Engineering, The Chinese University of Hong Kong, Hong Kong, China
The Chinese University of Hong Kong, HKSAR, China

Hieu Hoang
Department of Computer Science, VNUHCM-University of Science, HCM, Viet Nam

Shanshan Jiang
Johns Hopkins University, Baltimore, MD, United States

Yueming Jin
University College London, London, United Kingdom

Anitha Kannan
Curai, Palo Alto, CA, United States

Jieum Kim
Hanyang University, Seoul, South Korea

Mathieu Lamard
Univ Bretagne Occidentale, Brest, France
Inserm, UMR 1101, Brest, France

Ngan Le
Department of Computer Science & Computer Engineering, University of Arkansas, Fayetteville, AR, United States

Patrick Le Callet
Nantes Université, Centrale Nantes, CNRS, LS2N, Nantes, France

Alexandre Le Guilcher
Evolucare, Le Pecq, France

Xiaomeng Li
The Hong Kong University of Science and Technology, HKSAR, China

Suiyi Ling
Nantes Université, Centrale Nantes, CNRS, LS2N, Nantes, France

Quande Liu
Department of Computer Science and Engineering, The Chinese University of Hong Kong, Hong Kong, China

Pascale Massin
Ophthalmology Department, Lariboisiére Hospital, APHP, Paris, France

Sarah Matta
Univ Bretagne Occidentale, Brest, France
Inserm, UMR 1101, Brest, France

Aryan Mobiny
Department of Engineering & Computer Engineering, University of Houston, Houston, TX, United States

Jacinto C. Nascimento
Institute for Systems and Robotics, Instituto Superior Técnico, Lisbon, Portugal

Nassir Navab
Technical University of Munich, Munich, Germany
Johns Hopkins University, Baltimore, MD, United States

Cuong C. Nguyen
Australian Institute for Machine Learning, University of Adelaide, Adelaide, SA, Australia

Hien Van Nguyen
Department of Engineering & Computer Engineering, University of Houston, Houston, TX, United States

Andreas Pastor
Nantes Université, Centrale Nantes, CNRS, LS2N, Nantes, France

Vishal M. Patel
Johns Hopkins University, Baltimore, MD, United States

Angshuman Paul
Imaging Biomarkers and Computer-Aided Diagnosis Laboratory, Radiology and Imaging Sciences, National Institutes of Health Clinical Center, Bethesda, MD, United States

Sebastian Pölsterl
Ludwig Maximilian University of Munich, Munich, Germany

Viraj Prabhu
Georgia Tech, Atlanta, GA, United States

Gwenolé Quellec
Inserm, UMR 1101, Brest, France

Murali Ravuri
Curai, Palo Alto, CA, United States

Vincent Ricquebourg
Evolucare, Le Pecq, France

Jean-Bernard Rottier
Centre Médico Chirurgical du Mans, Le Mans, France

Swami Sankaranarayanan
MIT, Cambridge, MA, United States

Thomas C. Shen
Imaging Biomarkers and Computer-Aided Diagnosis Laboratory, Radiology and Imaging Sciences, National Institutes of Health Clinical Center, Bethesda, MD, United States

Shayan Siddiqui
Ludwig Maximilian University of Munich, Munich, Germany

David Sontag
MIT, Cambridge, MA, United States

Ronald M. Summers
Imaging Biomarkers and Computer-Aided Diagnosis Laboratory, Radiology and Imaging Sciences, National Institutes of Health Clinical Center, Bethesda, MD, United States

Qiuling Suo
University of Virginia, Charlottesville, VA, United States

Yu-Xing Tang
Imaging Biomarkers and Computer-Aided Diagnosis Laboratory, Radiology and Imaging Sciences, National Institutes of Health Clinical Center, Bethesda, MD, United States

Minh-Triet Tran
Department of Computer Science, VNUHCM-University of Science, HCM, Viet Nam

Viet-Khoa Vo-Ho
Department of Computer Science & Computer Engineering, University of Arkansas, Fayetteville, AR, United States

Christian Wachinger
Ludwig Maximilian University of Munich, Munich, Germany

Puyang Wang
Johns Hopkins University, Baltimore, MD, United States

Lei Xing
Stanford University, Palo Alto, CA, United States

Kashu Yamazaki
Department of Computer Science & Computer Engineering, University of Arkansas, Fayetteville, AR, United States

Yousef Yeganeh
Technical University of Munich, Munich, Germany

Lequan Yu
The University of Hong Kong, HKSAR, China

Pengyu Yuan
Department of Engineering & Computer Engineering, University of Houston, Houston, TX, United States

Chongzhi Zang
University of Virginia, Charlottesville, VA, United States

Aidong Zhang
University of Virginia, Charlottesville, VA, United States

Jinyuan Zhou
Johns Hopkins University, Baltimore, MD, United States

Introduction to meta learning

Learning to learn in medical applications

A journey through optimization

1

Azade Farshad[a], Yousef Yeganeh[a], and Nassir Navab[a,b]
[a]Technical University of Munich, Munich, Germany
[b]Johns Hopkins University, Baltimore, MD, United States

1.1 Introduction

Meta learning has many different definitions, but it is generally known as learning to learn. This term was first introduced in 1987 by Jürgen Schmidhuber in [1]. Works in the field of meta learning focus on different problems such as few-shot learning, neural architecture search; however, most of these works have something in common: the use of prior data to improve the learning capability of the model. This prior knowledge [2] can be obtained from: 1. the similarity or distance of the data points 2. the learning algorithm, e.g., for fast adaptation of the parameters or learning an optimal update rule 3. the data, using automated augmentations or learning from the data statistics.

Deep learning advances initiated with supervised learning using a labeled set of data, which made it a hot topic in many fields such as medical imaging. Most of the early proposed works are, nevertheless, dependent on large amounts of labeled data as the depth of the model increases. Even though it is a difficult task to gather and annotate data in most fields, it is a much more challenging task in the medical field as it needs the expert knowledge of the physicians.

Meta learning is generally used for the few-shot learning problem similar to transfer learning by pretraining (metatraining) a model on a set of tasks and fine-tuning on the limited labeled data. We present a taxonomy of the works in meta learning, discussed in this chapter in Fig. 1.1.

This chapter first goes through the background and notations in meta learning and the well-known works on this topic. Then, we delve into the task construction problem and representation learning for meta learning. We go through a few works on unsupervised learning for meta learning. After that, we explore some applications of meta learning in medical imaging and other related domains such as few-shot segmentation and few-shot image generation. Later, we discuss the relation of meta learning to federated learning and review several ideas that could also benefit meta learning. Finally, we conclude the chapter and discuss the outlook of this field.

1.2 Problem statement

In few-shot classification, for an N-way-K-shot problem, each task τ of the total T tasks consists of support set S with N classes of K samples each. The support set is used for learning how to learn the task. The query set Q includes more examples of the same classes for evaluation of the task.

Meta Learning With Medical Imaging and Health Informatics Applications. https://doi.org/10.1016/B978-0-32-399851-2.00008-9

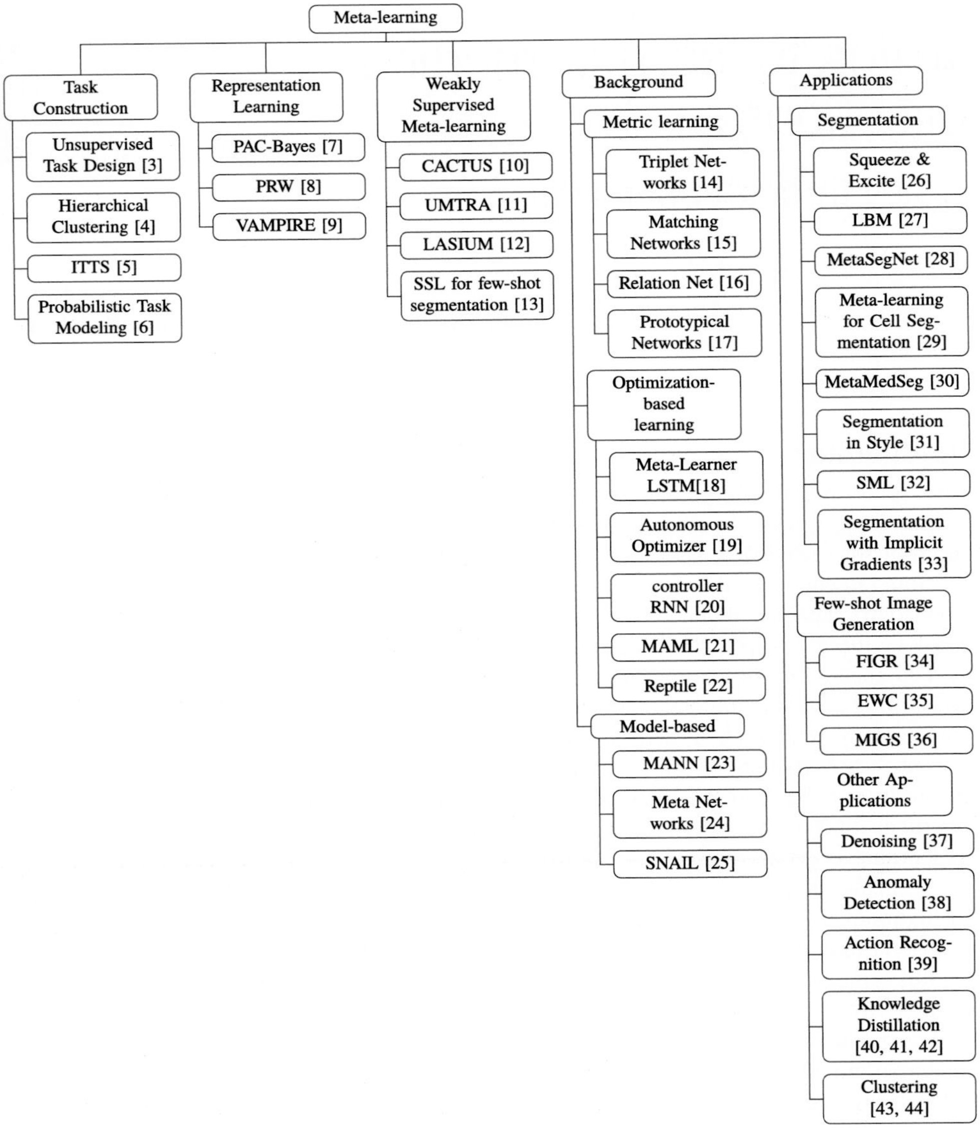

FIGURE 1.1

A Taxonomy of Meta learning and its Applications.

The model is meta-trained for a total of E steps and then fine-tuned given the few-shot data. At each meta-training step i, a task τ_i is randomly sampled from the set of all training tasks. The loss $\mathcal{L}$

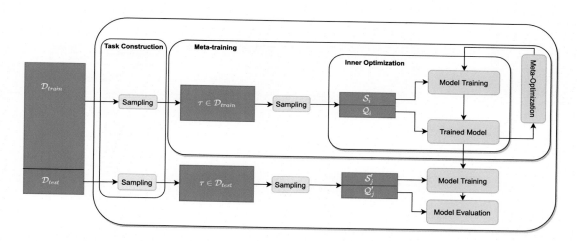

FIGURE 1.2 A general meta learning pipeline.

Given a dataset $\mathcal{D}$, the data is first split into training and testing subsets, $\mathcal{D}_{train}$ and $\mathcal{D}_{test}$ respectively. The meta learning tasks are constructed by sampling from the train and test subsets. Each sampled task τ_i consists of a support and a query set. The model is optimized on the support set and its performance on the query set is used to optimize the metatrainer. Finally, the model is evaluated on $\mathcal{D}_{test}$ by training on each $\mathcal{S}'_j$ and testing on its corresponding query set $\mathcal{Q}'_j$.

is usually defined by the performance of the classification on $\mathcal{Q}$ trained on $\mathcal{S}$. Training in this manner helps the model generalize well to newly seen tasks in each training episode. Therefore, the final meta-trained model is able to adapt fast to previously unobserved data. A general meta learning pipeline is demonstrated in Fig. 1.2.

1.3 Background

Earlier meta learning works [1,44,45,17], aim at learning update functions or learning rules. Recent works in meta learning are more diverse in the usage of prior knowledge and are generally grouped into the following categories [46]:

1. Metric learning, which takes the similarity or dissimilarity of classes into account
2. Optimization-based, which optimizes the training task using a learning algorithm
3. Model-based, which is based on the architecture design of the model

In this section, we go through these categories and the well-known works on each topic.

1.3.1 Metric learning

Metric learning is based on a metric that measures similarities or dissimilarities of the data. In this area, contrastive learning focuses on learning from the data similarity between different classes. The goal is

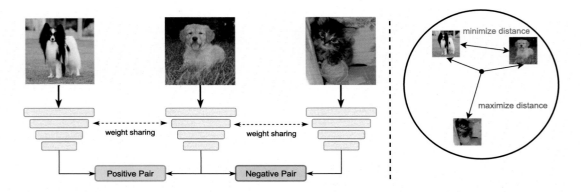

FIGURE 1.3

In metric learning approaches, the goal is to minimize the distance in the latent space for the images belonging to the same class (positive pair) and to maximize the distance between a negative pair (from different class categories).

to learn separated and disentangled embeddings for different classes from training tasks. This enables us to separate unseen classes with few amounts of data.

The first work in this category is the Siamese Network along with contrastive loss, which is first proposed in [47]. Pairs of randomly selected images (x_1, x_2) are passed to two identical networks sharing the same parameters θ, and based on the assumption that these are from two different classes, we try to maximize their distance in the embedding space. A one-shot learning approach using the Siamese architecture has been proposed in [48]. The contrastive loss is shown in Eq. (1.1):

$$\mathcal{L}_\theta(x_1, x_2, y) = (1 - y)E_\theta(x_1, x_2) + y\max(0, m - E_\theta(x_1, x_2)) \tag{1.1}$$

$$E_\theta(x_1, x_2) = \|G_\theta(x_1) - G_\theta(x_2)\| \tag{1.2}$$

Where Eq. (1.2) defines the energy function E_θ which computes the $L1$ distance between the embeddings of the data pairs using the embedding function G_θ. y denotes a binary flag of 0 for a negative pair and 1 for a positive pair. The network parameters are denoted by θ, and m is a constant margin.

The triplet loss [49] in Eq. (1.3) brings in an anchor data point. The positive pair embeddings similarities are maximized, while the negative pair embeddings are diverged based on their distance to the anchor point x_a.

$$\mathcal{L}_\theta(x_p, x_n, x_a) = \max(0, m + d(G_\theta(x_a), G_\theta(x_p)) - d(G_\theta(x_a), G_\theta(x_n))) \tag{1.3}$$

Where x_p, x_n, d, and G_θ are the positive data points, the negative data points, the distance metric, and the embedding function, respectively.

Triplet networks [13] on the other hand, are similar to Siamese Network. Instead of a pair of networks sharing the same weights, triplet networks have three instances of the same network with a similar objective to the triplet loss. Fig. 1.3 shows a simple visualization of the triplet networks.

Matching Networks [14] rely on an attention mechanism applied to the learned embeddings of the input from the support set for predicting the classes for the points in the query set. Then, the sum of labels from the support set weighted by an attention kernel is computed to predict the class. The attention kernel for two data points is defined in its simplest form as the cosine similarity of their corresponding embeddings.

$$a(\hat{x}, x_i) = \frac{e^{c(f(\hat{x}), g(x_i))}}{\sum_{j=1}^{k} e^{c(f(\hat{x}), g(x_j))}} \tag{1.4}$$

Eq. (1.4) shows the attention kernel, where $\hat{x}$ is a test example, $f(.)$ and $g(.)$ are embedding functions that could potentially be equal, i.e. $f = g$. The embedding functions can be a simple neural network or an LSTM (Long Short Term Memory [50]) for complex scenarios. The final objective is:

$$\mathcal{L}_\theta(\hat{x}) = -\log \sum_{i=1}^{k} a(\hat{x}, x_i) y_i \tag{1.5}$$

Where $a(.)$ is the attention kernel from Eq. (1.4), and $\hat{x}$ is the test data sample.

Prototypical Networks [16] are proposed for the problem of few-shot classification. An embedding function f_θ is used to encode each input x_i to its corresponding features. For each class k in the training set, a prototype feature vector c_k is defined by averaging the embeddings of the data samples in that class from the support set, i.e., $\mathcal{S}_k$:

$$c_k = \frac{1}{|\mathcal{S}_k|} \sum_{(x_i, y_i \in \mathcal{S}_k)} f_\theta(x_i) \tag{1.6}$$

The classification is done by calculating the Euclidean distances to the prototype vector of each class:

$$\mathcal{L}_\theta(x, y) = -\log \frac{\exp(-d(f_\theta(x), c_k))}{\sum_{k'} \exp(-d(f_\theta(x), c_{k'}))} \tag{1.7}$$

Where k is the ground truth class and $d(.)$ is the distance function. This method has been shown to perform well in zero-shot learning as well.

Similar to [48], Relation Network [15] is based on an embedding module and a similarity measure. The Relation Net consists of two modules: 1. The embedding network, generating feature representation from the input 2. A relation module, computing a relation score based on the similarity of its inputs. The support and query data points are passed to the embedding module to acquire their corresponding feature embeddings. Finally, for the few-shot classification task, the embeddings from each support data sample $x_i \in \mathcal{S}$ are concatenated with the embeddings from the query sample $x_j \in \mathcal{Q}$ and passed to the relation module to classify whether the support and query samples are from the same class or not, by producing a similarity score between 0 and 1.

$$r_{i,j} = g_\phi(concat(f_\theta(x_i), f_\theta(x_j))) \tag{1.8}$$

The relation score $r_{i,j}$ is defined in Eq. (1.8) as the relation score between the data points x_i and x_j, and $g_\phi(.)$ is the relation module. The objective function is the mean square error (MSE):

$$\mathcal{L}_\theta(\mathcal{Q}) = \sum_{(x_i, x_j, y_i, y_j \in \mathcal{Q})} (r_{i,j} - 1_{(y_i = y_j)})^2 \tag{1.9}$$

1.3.2 Optimization-based learning

The optimization-based learning methods focus on the fast adaptation of models to newly seen data by modifying the optimization steps towards gradients that would help the fast adaptation and better generalization, given a few examples of data.

One of the well-known early works in meta learning is "Optimization as a Model for Few-shot Learning" [17]. The "learner" M parameterized by θ, which is the primary neural network classifier, is trained in the few-shot setting by an LSTM-based metalearner network R to optimize the learner. The metalearner learns the update rule for training the learner. The parameters of the learner are assigned to the cell state of the LSTM. This method is formulated as a bi-level optimization approach, where the first level focuses on quick learning for each separate task and the second level on slower learning across all tasks.

$$\mathcal{L}_\theta^\tau(\mathcal{S}) = \mathcal{L}_\theta(M(x), y) \tag{1.10}$$

where $\mathcal{L}_\theta$ is the average negative log-probability assigned by M to the correct class and $\mathcal{L}_\theta^\tau$ is the task-specific loss which is optimized by the metalearner.

Another work using reinforcement learning for better convergence is "Learning to Optimize" [18]. In this work, the algorithms that converge quickly are rewarded, and the ones that do not converge are penalized; therefore, the optimization problem is formulated as finding the optimal policy, which is solved using reinforcement learning.

Another approach in meta learning is automating the update rule design for optimization methods. [19] tackles this problem by using a recurrent neural network (RNN) as a controller for generating an update function for the optimizer. The controller's objective is to train the primary model optimally. The controller is optimized using reinforcement learning for maximizing the accuracy of the primary model. In this work, two new update rules, namely PowerSign and AddSign, and a new learning rate annealing scheme, linear cosine decay, are presented, which are discovered by the proposed method.

MAML [20] or model-agnostic meta learning is the first optimization-based work in the field of meta learning for few-shot learning in recent years. Unlike the previously mentioned works, MAML focuses on optimizing the model weights for fast adaptation. MAML does the optimization in two steps, an inner loop and an outer loop which makes it a second-order optimization problem. In order to overcome the computation complexities of second-order optimization, Reptile [21] and First-order MAML (FOMAML) [20] are proposed as first order approximation of MAML which are simpler to train. A visual comparison of MAML and Reptile is presented in Fig. 1.4.

1.3.3 Model-based learning

Model-based learning is a class of meta learning frameworks with models that are specifically designed for fast learning.

Meta learning with Memory-Augmented Neural Networks [22] (MANN) is one of the initial works in meta learning. It is proposed as a solution for the one-shot learning problem. In this work, Neural Turing Machines (NTMs) allow it to encode and retrieve new information quickly.

In Metanetworks [23] the architecture is designed for fast adaptation by proposing fast and slow weight layers. The fast weights are produced by processing the metainformation from gradients using an LSTM network. It consists of two objectives: 1. The embedding loss, which applies the contrastive loss in a similar manner to Eq. (1.1) to the output of a representation module and the support label

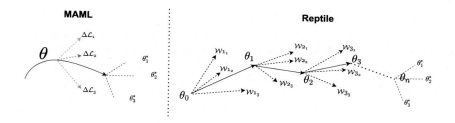

FIGURE 1.4

MAML [20] and Reptile [21] are examples of optimization-based meta learning. While MAML uses second-order derivation for model optimization, Reptile simplifies this by averaging the model parameters over the different tasks.

y. The representation module takes slow weights as input and produces fast weights. 2. The task loss, which optimizes the base learner using the slow weights.

Simple Neural AttentIve Learner (SNAIL) [24] formalizes meta learning as a sequence-to-sequence problem. The main idea of this work is the combination of temporal convolution layers with causal attention layers. This allows the metalearner to aggregate contextual information from past experience.

1.4 Task construction in meta learning

The construction of tasks is an essential part of meta learning since it can directly affect the optimization process. Generally, the tasks are defined from randomly selected classes with no overlap, i.e., n distinctive classes are chosen for the support set, and m classes with no overlap with the support set are chosen for the query set. Commonly, the tasks are hand-designed [51]; however, some works are focusing on automating the task construction problem that we discuss in this section.

An unsupervised task design approach for few-shot medical image classification has been proposed in [3]. They apply deep clustering methods to the dataset and get pairs of data samples from different clusters (e.g., data from clusters 1 and 3 or 2 and 5). Then, the network is optimized for the classification problem given the clustered data pairs. They show that the proposed task design can outperform other methods for the breast cancer classification task. Similarly, [4] performs meta learning by hierarchical clustering of the tasks.

An effective way of task selection has been explored in [5]. They demonstrate that if the training tasks are selected appropriately, learning can be faster and more effective in terms of better performance in the test tasks. To select the tasks, they take task difference and task relevance of the training tasks into account. This is performed in the reinforcement learning setting.

Here, the task difference is the average KL divergence of the respective policies over the states of the validation tasks, and the relevance of task τ_i to task τ_j is the expected difference in entropy of the policies before and after learning over the states of the validation tasks with regard to the on-policy distribution. The on-policy method aims at improving the policy that is used for action selection.

A probabilistic task modeling for meta learning is first proposed in [6]. The probabilistic modeling makes it possible to quantitatively measure task uncertainty for the goal of active task selection in meta learning. Initially, a variational autoencoder (VAE) [52] is adapted to reduce the data dimensionality and acquire the feature embeddings. These inferred embeddings are employed to model each task as a mixture of Gaussians using LDA (Latent Dirichlet Allocation) [53]. In contrast to the standard LDA, the embedding space of VAE is continuous; therefore, the categorical word-topic distributions in LDA are replaced by Gaussian task-theme distributions.

1.5 Representation learning in meta learning

This section focuses on studies that attempt to learn better representations or distributions using meta learning or for meta learning.

PAC-Bayes [54] framework, in which PAC stands for probably approximately correct, is a variational/generalization error bound for i.i.d. (independent and identically distributed) data. It was initially used in lifelong learning that is very similar to the meta learning setting in [55]. The framework permits a quantitative assessment of the data quality of transferred information by comparing the expected loss on a future learning task to the average loss on the observed tasks. The agent is enforced to identify prior knowledge from the information in the observed tasks to improve the performance on new, unobserved tasks. This framework is intended for solving single-task problems. [56] explore the same problem in meta learning for deep neural networks. They provide a tighter bound in the PAC-Bayes setting by taking the union of multiple single-task bounds. Nguyen *et al.* [57] assert that the generalization errors have not been well investigated for unseen tasks, resulting in limited generalization guarantee. Furthermore, they argue that variational functions may not correctly represent the underlying distributions; therefore, they use implicit modeling of both the prior and posterior distributions using a deep generator network. The proposed approach does not directly use the KL divergence term; instead, it uses an estimation of it by employing a probabilistic classification approach. Using the new estimation approach, they provide a tighter bound on the PAC-Bayes framework.

In an attempt at semisupervised few-shot learning, [7,58] build on top of Prototypical Networks [16]. A prototypical random-walk semisupervised loss (PRW) is proposed for learning compact and well-separated representations through a similarity graph between the prototypes and the embeddings of the unlabeled points. The random walker matrix is defined in a way that each $T_{i,j}$ entry denotes a walk starting at prototype i and ending at prototype j. Given this notion, the probabilities of the walker returning to the starting prototype would be at the diagonal entries of the T matrix. Since the objective for the walker is to return to the prototype it started from; the loss aims at maximizing the probabilities of the diagonal entries in T. The walker loss is then computed as the cross-entropy between the matrix T and the identity matrix I. As it is preferred to have the walker visit as many unlabeled points as possible, the visitor loss computes the overall probability that each point would be visited when walking from prototypes to the points. The final PRW loss is a sum of visitor and walker losses. Their proposed method is robust to labeled/unlabeled class distribution mismatch due to its resistance to unlabeled data not belonging to any of the training classes. This resistance results from the random walker avoiding the distractor points and not attracting them to the class prototypes.

Variational Agnostic Modeling that Performs Inference for Robust Estimation (VAMPIRE) [8] uses uncertainty in MAML using variational inference. VAMPIRE aims to learn a probability distribution of model parameters before the few-shot learning by approximating the task-specific parameters using

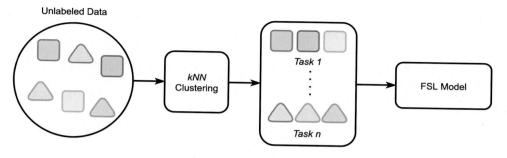

FIGURE 1.5

Few-shot learning approaches require data from a set of tasks with label information. This is solved in unsupervised meta learning approaches [9,10] using pseudo-labels generated by clustering or data augmentation. The generated tasks from unlabeled data are later used for standard few-shot learning models such as MAML [20], and Prototypical Networks [16].

a variational distribution. In contrast to MAML, which has fixed values for parameters, the goal here is to have probability distributions for metaparameters for more robust learning.

1.6 Unsupervised / self-supervised meta learning

Although meta learning makes it easier to learn with few data, some labeled data still needs to exist for pretraining. Several approaches are proposed to use unlabeled data in the pretraining step and a few labeled data for the fine-tuning step to overcome this issue.

The first method in this line of work is unsupervised learning using meta learning [9] or CACTUS. CACTUS constructs tasks from unlabeled data automatically by clustering the feature embeddings from data points and using the cluster IDs as pseudo labels for the metatraining step as shown in Fig. 1.5. It is shown that even using a simple task construction method, such as clustering the embeddings, leads to performance improvement on different sets of tasks. Different meta learning approaches such as MAML [20] and Prototypical Networks [16] are applied in the metatraining step to evaluate the few-shot classification performance.

On the same topic, Khodadadeh *et al.* propose UMTRA (Unsupervised Meta learning for Few-shot Image Classification) [10]. Instead of using cluster IDs as pseudo labels as presented in CACTUS, UMTRA takes each data sample and applies different augmentations to the data sample. The task is constructed by assigning the same label to each data sample and its augmentations. They use the AutoAugment [59] approach for augmentation of images on mini-Imagenet and random augmentation such as random flip or crop on Omniglot. Similar to CACTUS, UMTRA uses its proposed task construction method with different meta learning frameworks.

In follow-up work, LASIUM (Latent-Space Interpolation in Unsupervised Meta learning) [11] focuses on automatic task construction using generative models. LASIUM is based on sampling data from generative models, such as GANs or VAEs, by modeling the data distribution and interpolating the latent space of the generative model for generating new data samples. The generated samples are then used for constructing tasks for pretraining.

Another direction towards less supervision is self-supervised learning (SSL). It is based on employing information in the underlying structure of the data for pretraining a model on a pretext task that is later used for a downstream task. A related SSL approach to meta learning is SSL for few-shot segmentation [12]. This work has three main components: 1. An adaptive tuning mechanism, 2. A self-supervised base, 3. A metalearner.

Initially, the features of input support and query images are obtained from a Siamese Network [48] with shared parameters. The distribution of the support features is tuned using the self-supervised module (SSM) from the underlying semantic information of the data. Then the similarity between the tuned feature map and the query features is measured using a deep nonlinear metric inspired from Relation Network [15]. The similarity metric is used to determine the regions of interest in the query image. Finally, a segmentation decoder network produces and refines the segmentation map results in the original image size. The self-supervised module performs by duplicating the support feature maps R_s, multiplying one with the corresponding segmentation mask, which gives us R_s' and applying cross-entropy loss between R_s and R_s'. The gradients from the later cross-entropy loss are used to update the SSM module. The optimization-based metalearner inspired by [15] is employed as the outer loop of the proposed framework for refining the segmentation results.

1.7 Meta learning applications

In this section, we explore some of the typical applications of meta learning, such as few-shot segmentation and few-shot image generation. After that, we go through other applications that would be less common.

1.7.1 Segmentation

Semantic segmentation is an essential task in the medical field for identifying different diseases or detecting anomalies in organs and pathology. Deep neural networks have achieved outstanding performance in semantic segmentation, but they usually need large amounts of labeled data. Hence, few-shot learning seems like a natural solution to this problem by learning new classes from only a few annotated data. U-Net [60] is a commonly used architecture for 2D semantic segmentation using pairs of data and segmentation labels. V-Net [61] is similar to U-Net, but for 3D volumes.

In this section, we list a number of the recent works in few-shot segmentation for medical applications.

Squeeze & excite guided few-shot segmentation of volumetric images [25]
One of the challenges in few-shot medical image segmentation is the scarcity of pretrained models compared to computer vision tasks and the difficulty of training on volumetric data. Roy *et al.* propose a few-shot learning framework [25] for segmentation of volumetric medical images with few annotated slices. Their proposed method enables stable training without relying on a pretrained model, which is usually unavailable for medical data. The proposed method consists of three building blocks:

1. A conditioner arm
2. Interaction blocks with their proposed 'channel squeeze & spatial excitation' (sSE) modules
3. A segmenter arm

The conditioner and segmenter arms are both encoder-decoder-based architectures with a few differences. The segmentation is performed by matching a few slices of the support volume to all the slices of the query volume. A task-specific representation is generated from the annotated support input using the conditioner arm. This task-specific representation models how a new semantic class looks in the image. The generated representation is fed to the segmenter arm for segmenting the new query image using the interaction blocks.

One of the main contributions of this work is the sSE module in the interaction block, which is based on Squeeze & excite blocks. These blocks are initially proposed in [62,63]. The goal of the sSE module is the efficient interaction between the conditioner and segmenter arms. sSE is a lightweight computational module with a low computational complexity which improves the gradient flow. These blocks are used between all the encoder, bottleneck, and decoder blocks in the network. sSE performs 'channel squeeze' on the obtained learned representation from the conditioner block to learn a spatial map. Subsequently, the learned spatial map performs 'spatial excitation' on the segmenter feature map.

The models are trained using 2D images and tested with 3D volume queries; hence, the support set needs to be selected from a diverse set of annotated slices. The proposed method is evaluated for organ segmentation on whole-body contrast-enhanced CT scans from the Visceral Dataset [64].

Learn to segment organs with a few bounding boxes [26]

This work [26] proposes a method for 3D medical segmentation in low-data setting. This method has two main modules: 1. prototype learner, and 2. segmenter. The prototype learner takes the input image and its corresponding label as input and provides a prototype as output. The prototype, along with the query images, is then fed to the segmenter model to predict segmentation maps. The prototype learning is optimized using the nearest neighbor loss, while the segmenter is trained using weighted cross-entropy. They also propose a semisupervised approach by providing weak supervision from bounding boxes, as it is easier to acquire than semantics segmentation labels. This method has been evaluated on the Visceral dataset [64].

Differentiable meta learning model for few-shot semantic segmentation [27]

Most methods in semantic segmentation target single object per image (1-way) segmentation problem. Nevertheless, this is not a realistic scenario. Tian *et al.* [27] propose a method for K-way multiobject few-shot semantic segmentation called MetaSegNet which is based on meta learning. Here, the few-shot segmentation task is formulated as a pixel-classification problem. They propose a differentiable metalearner which is based on ridge regression and an embedding network that is composed of two main components: 1. The feature extractor, and 2. The feature fusion module. The feature extractor provides local and global features for both support and query sets. The feature extractor is a slightly modified version of ResNet-9 with two branches, one for local and one for global context extraction, which are trained from scratch. The global and local features extracted by the feature extraction module are then passed to the feature fusion module, which fuses the latter by concatenating the local feature map and the unpooled global feature for better prediction of each pixel. After applying the L2 norm in each channel for normalization, the combined feature map is reshaped for pixel-wise classification. This approach can be applied to the multiorgan segmentation problem or other similar topics.

Few-shot microscopy image cell segmentation [28]

Cell segmentation in microscopy is a challenging task because of the limited amount of labeled data required for segmentation using deep neural networks. Meta learning makes it possible to have a well-generalized model by pretraining the model on a large amount of data from other domains and fine-tuning the model on the limited labeled data from the target domain. [28] focuses on this issue by proposing a meta learning-based algorithm for cell segmentation. They employ data from a different domain with different image appearance and cell types and transfer the knowledge to the target domain. They use Reptile [21] as the meta learning framework due to its simplicity in optimization compared to previous works. They implement two auto-encoder-based architectures for the segmentation task, 1. fully convolutional regression network (FCRN) [65], 2. U-Net. They slightly modify FCRN by replacing the bi-linear upsampling layers with transposed convolution layers and altering the heat-map predictions to sigmoid activation functions for better performance. They propose three loss terms for metatraining: 1. standard binary cross-entropy loss for segmentation 2. entropy regularization for moving the segmentation results away from the classification boundary 3. distillation loss for enforcing the learning of a common feature representation across different tasks.

SML: semantic meta learning for few-shot semantic segmentation [31]

Incorporating semantic information in the few-shot setting can be extremely beneficial. SML [31] proposes combining visual features with semantic information for improving class prototypes in prototypical learning [16]. Inspired by [66] that obtains better class prototypes using the class names into the base learner, the semantic information is acquired using existing pretrained language models such as Word2Vec [67], or FastText [68] by getting the attribute vectors given the class name. The image pixels in the support and query set belonging to the same class are enforced to have the same semantic representation using the obtained attribute vectors. SML has two main modules: 1. Feature extractor and 2. Attribute-injector. Given support images as input in each episode, the visual features are obtained from the feature extractor module that is a VGG-16 or Resnet-50 network pretrained on Imagenet. The background and foreground regions of the image, which are obtained from the segmentation masks, are used to compute the average foreground and background feature embeddings for each support image. The background and foreground feature embeddings combined with the attribute-injector module's semantic information using the support set's class names are then incorporated into the base-learner. The incorporation of the semantic information into the embeddings is done by ridge regression which effectively combines the class-level semantic information with the information from multiple images for prototype computation. After the metatraining is done, the final segmentation map prediction task is performed using the class prototypes, and background features are utilized. Although this work is not on medical applications, it can be used to process semantic information from medical reports and employ it for medical image segmentation.

Few-shot segmentation of medical images based on meta learning with implicit gradients [32]

In a work [32] proposed by Khadga *et al.*, implicit MAML (iMAML) [69] combined with the attention U-Net [70] is used for medical image segmentation. iMAML aims at removing the need for differenti-

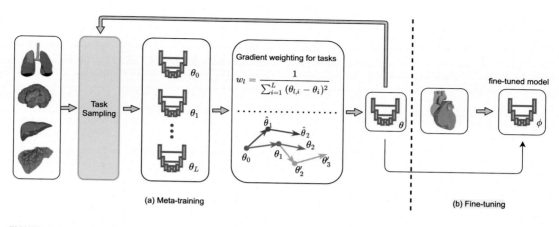

(a) Meta-training (b) Fine-tuning

FIGURE 1.6

Segmentation of medical images with limited labeled data is a challenging task which could be solved using meta learning. In MetaMedSeg [29], the model is first metatrained on a set of organs with high amount of labeled data available. Then the model is fine-tuned on the organ with limited data.

ating through the optimization path using an iterative optimization solver. The metatraining step is done on two datasets for the attention U-Net, then the metatrained network is fine-tuned on an unseen dataset for few-shot segmentation. In this work, conjugate gradients are used for optimizing the weights for computing the metagradients in the metatraining steps using iMAML. This method is applied to skin and polyp data for identifying cancerous data samples.

Segmentation in style [30]

Unsupervised segmentation can be performed by discovering knowledge from unsupervised models, such as Generative Adversarial Networks [71] or as done in [30] using a trained StyleGAN V2 [72] model. In this work, unsupervised segmentation is performed by clustering the latent space of the StyleGAN model into the number of segmentation classes. Some rare classes such as beard, hat, or glasses are not segmented by the model since they are not normally assigned to a specific cluster. Therefore, the data is augmented by manipulating the latent space using CLIP [73] and generating more samples of the rare classes. This approach can outperform semisupervised methods and is on par with fully supervised ones.

MetaMedSeg: volumetric meta learning for few-shot organ segmentation [29]

In our recent work on few-shot organ segmentation, we propose a meta learning framework for learning from broadly labeled organs to learn a model for organs with limited labeled data. The model performs segmentation of 2D slices, which are extracted from 3D volumes. The main contributions of this work are: 1. A volumetric task definition, where the images in a task are sampled from the same volume 2. An inverse distance weighting scheme for model parameter aggregation designed for the high cross-domain shift between the organs used for metatraining and the organs used for testing. An overview of this work is shown in Fig. 1.6.

1.7.2 Few-shot image generation

Another use case of meta learning is few-shot image generation. Generative Adversarial Networks (GANs) are commonly used for generating images or manipulating them [74]. These networks require large amounts of data for generating high-quality images. The few-shot image generation problem is first introduced by Cloûatre, and Demers in FIGR (Few-shot image generation with Reptile) [33], which combines the idea of GANs with meta learning using Reptile [21]. Similarly, MIGS (Metaimage Generation from Scene Graphs) [35] uses Reptile for few-shot generation of images from scene graphs and improving the image generation quality. Even though current works in few-shot image generation are not used in the medical field, this direction of research can help generate images as a way of augmentation for unbalanced datasets, e.g., cancerous vs. malignant [75].

Another attempt at few-shot image generation is made in [34], where the goal is to regularize the changes of the weights during the fine-tuning step while preserving the information and diversity of the source domain and at the same time adapting to the appearance of the target domain. To preserve the essential weights during the adaptation, they use a metric for quantifying the importance of the weights, namely Elastic Weight Consolidation (EWC) [76], which evaluates the importance of each parameter by estimating its Fisher Information relative to the objective likelihood.

1.7.3 Other applications

Meta learning has been used for many applications in medical imaging in recent years. We go through some of these works in this section.

1.7.3.1 Denoising

Noisy data are ubiquitous in medical datasets, such as in Electroencephalography (EEG) that can be affected by many conditions such as muscle movements in the face. Deep denoising approaches have been recently explored for noise removal from images or other data modalities. Few-shot Metadenoising [36] is a denoising approach that is based on meta learning shown in Fig. 1.7. Given a dataset of clean and noisy data, a deep network is trained for the denoising task. The network receives a noisy data sample and is enforced to output the clean data. However, the mentioned approach would be prone to overfitting if the training set is small, which is a typical scenario. Therefore, it is proposed in [36] to generate a large dataset with pairs of clean and synthesized noisy data samples for pretraining using a meta learning approach, namely Reptile [21]. The pretrained model is then fine-tuned on the small data with pairs of normal and real noisy samples as a few-shot learning task. The adoption of meta learning approaches makes it possible to have a careful design of training tasks to improve the method further with a potentially infinite amount of synthetic data in the training set. Unlike transfer learning, meta learning can provide a model that adapts fast to new data, even pretrained on synthetic data. This method is evaluated on CT-Scan [77] and ECG [78] denoising.

1.7.3.2 Anomaly detection

Anomaly detection in medical data is of high importance because of the unbalanced nature of diseases. In most medical datasets, there are many labeled data from healthy samples and only a few from unhealthy ones. It is also challenging to acquire data from diseases such as cancer that can be considered anomalies. To this cause, there have been a few works studying few-shot anomaly detection in medical scenarios. Standard anomaly detection methods generally intend to learn the normal image distribution,

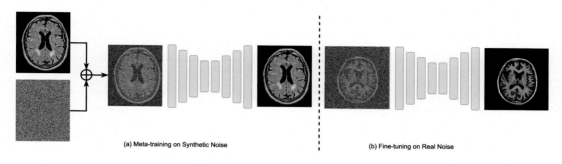

(a) Meta-training on Synthetic Noise   (b) Fine-tuning on Real Noise

FIGURE 1.7

Pairs of real noisy and denoised data are difficult to obtain. However, generating synthetic noise and adding it to normal data is an easy task that provides a large number of labeled data. This information is used in [36] for few-shot denoising of medical images.

i.e., healthy samples, and perform the anomaly detection during testing by detecting outlier samples, i.e., diseased samples which are far from the learned distribution. This can be useful in many cases, yet it is challenging for some medical scenarios such as colonoscopy images with a small polyp due to the sensitivity of the standard approaches to outliers that are close to the inliers distribution. To overcome this issue, few-shot anomaly detection for polyp frames from colonoscopy [37] is proposed.

In this work, a few-shot anomaly detection network (FSAD-Net) is trained on a highly imbalanced dataset for polyp detection in colonoscopy images. FSAD-Net has two main components: an encoder that, along with dimensionality reduction, maximizes the mutual information between the normal images from the training set and their corresponding embeddings, and a score inference network (SIN) [79] for classification of normal and abnormal images. The SIN network optimizes the features representation using a contrastive loss by pushing the anomaly score of the normal images close together and forcing the anomaly score of the anomalies farther from the normal ones. Since SIN suffers from the curse of dimensionality, the Deep Info Max (DIM) [80] method is used for dimensionality reduction of the images and mutual information maximization.

1.7.3.3 Action recognition

Action recognition is an important problem in robot-guided surgery and medical interventions. Acquiring labeled data for action recognition is an onerous task in normal domains; this becomes even harder in medical scenarios. A typical problem in medical settings is first-person action recognition. Due to the lack of large-scale labeled datasets, few-shot learning or transfer learning approaches are popular solutions to this problem. Coskun *et al.* propose a meta learning based method for few-shot first-person action recognition [38] in video frames. Their method has three components:

1. Visual cue extraction
2. Temporal module, trained from source domain videos
3. Transfer learning

The visual cue component extracts a-priori visual cues from object-object interactions, hand grasps, and motion within specific regions. These visual cues obtained from image-only datasets are extracted

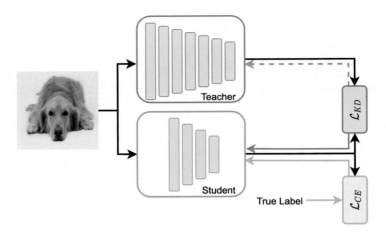

FIGURE 1.8

In knowledge distillation, the student not only learns from the true label information but also is trained using the soft labels from a deeper / more complex teacher network. In MetaDistill [41], the teacher also receives some feedback from the student and gets updated to provide more helpful information to the student.

to decouple the foreground and background context and have the method focus only on the hand and the objects that the hand is interacting with. The visual cues are then fed to the second component for training the temporal module, which consists of a bi-directional GRU network and attention layers. Here, the GRU network is considered a class-agnostic embedding network, and the attention layer acts as the classifier.

The third component is interdataset transfer learning. The transfer learning is performed by pretraining the model on one dataset and fine-tuning it on a new dataset with unseen samples. They introduce Attentive MAML (A-MAML), which is built on the MAML algorithm [20] combined with an attention mechanism for performance improvement on temporal sequences. As a result of observing convergence issues in MAML combined with the difficulties in optimizing the RNN network, they optimize the task-specific loss only over the attention layer parameters.

1.7.3.4 Knowledge distillation

Knowledge distillation (KD) [81] is a way of transferring knowledge from one or multiple neural networks to a new one, with a goal of either compressing a complex network into a small one or learning a more generalized model from an ensemble of other models [82,83] (see Fig. 1.8). The objective of KD is to train a student model using the output of a pretrained teacher model instead of the original labels from the training set. The goal is to enforce the student to output logits that look as similar as possible to the logits acquired from the teacher when the same input is fed to both networks.

Meta learning for knowledge distillation has been explored in several recent works. Pan *et al.* combine meta learning and KD for language model compression in [39]. Recently, a self-distillation method, "MetaDistiller" [40] is proposed using a label generator for soft targets. The label generator network is metatrained for fusing feature maps from deeper layers in a top-down manner. Due to the compatibility gap between the features of the soft targets from deep models with shallower models, these features may not be a good fit for supervision of the latter model. The goal of the label generator is to generate soft targets learned from intermediate feature maps of the model. The bi-level optimization scheme of the label generator is inspired by meta learning or learning to learn.

Differently, MetaDistil [41] focuses on enabling interaction between the teacher and student, allowing the teacher to "learn to teach." Contrary to standard KD methods, where the teacher model is frozen during the student optimization, in this method, the feedback from the student performance is utilized to improve the transfer of knowledge by having a trainable teacher network that improves its teaching skills. For this purpose, a "quiz set" is designed to assess student performance, from which the teacher can adjust its output. The proposed approach is less sensitive to hyperparameters and the capacity of the student.

1.7.3.5 Clustering

Using metainformation can be helpful for unsupervised learning methods such as clustering. An open problem in clustering is how to determine the number of clusters of unlabeled data systematically. [42] investigates this problem and introduces a way of predicting the number of clusters by learning a mapping from the features to Adjusted Rand Index. Meta-k [43] proposes a solution to this problem by using a network to predict the number of clusters in data and a metatrainer network that optimizes the prediction network using policy gradient optimization. The reward score for optimizing the predictor network is the silhouette score which is a measurement for clustering performance without labels.

1.8 Relation to federated learning

It is shown in [84] that the well-known federated averaging method in federated learning [85] and the Reptile meta learning algorithm [21] are in fact very similar and in some aspects the same algorithm. In both methods, either model gradients or model weights across different tasks or models are aggregated or averaged to get a global model with better generalization over different existing tasks or local models.

Federated learning has been mainly used for privacy concerns in multisite or multidevice problems. This raises its attractiveness in medical settings, essentially because the privacy of patients' data needs to be preserved. There have been many recent works on federated learning for medical imaging, such as brain segmentation [86], but here we focus on its aspects that are closer to meta learning.

One common problem between federated learning and meta learning methods such as Reptile is the aggregation of gradients or weight. In federated learning, we have a server and multiple clients. In each iteration of training, the global model weight from the server is sent to the clients. Each of these clients performs individual optimization on its private data and sends the model weights back to the server after a few iterations of optimization. Then, the new global model is aggregated from all of the models received from clients. The aggregation is usually done by averaging the model weights of different clients, but it can also be done by weighting each client by specific criteria. A weighting scheme for federated learning on non-i.i.d. data is first introduced in [87]. The proposed weighting method, IDA (Inverse Distance Aggregation), is based on the inverse distance of each local model from the global model, which is a metainformation that can be used for learning to learn. The aforementioned weighting method can also be applied to meta learning methods such as MAML [20] and Reptile [21] for gradient aggregation as done in [29].

A meta learning-based approach for federated learning [88], namely FedMeta, is proposed by Chen *et al.* as a way for personalization of the local models on the private data from the clients. Given a non-i.i.d. dataset, it would be challenging to have a model that generalizes well to different clients with diverse private data. Therefore, meta learning is a well-suited solution for fast adaptation and convergence of models to the personalized data of different clients. In this work, MAML [20] and MetaSGD [89] are used as meta learning frameworks incorporated into the federated setting. While in standard meta learning, the tasks are defined as pairs of support and the query set used for training and testing the same model, in this work, the global parameters are sent to the clients in each episode of metatraining. After the metatraining in each client is done, the test results on the query set are sent back to the server for updating the metalearner.

1.9 Discussion

We explored the recent works in meta learning and a few of its applications in general and medical data. Task construction, representation learning in meta learning, and unsupervised meta learning are a number of promising areas of research in meta learning, which can help advance the topic. A taxonomy of the presented works is shown in Fig. 1.1. Meta learning has shown great potential in few-shot learning problems, making it the natural option in many scenarios and an initialization alternative to transfer learning. Nevertheless, some works [90] argue that the episodic nature of few-shot learning tasks in current literature is in favor of meta learning methods, which would affect their applicability in more realistic scenarios and make them less competitive in cross-domain settings.

1.10 Conclusion and outlook

Meta learning has proven to be one of the leading ideas of recent years in automated machine learning. As a result of access to large amounts of unlabeled data over the past years, the amount of research in the unsupervised and self-supervised method has increased dramatically. With the recent advances in unsupervised and self-supervised learning, it is expected that meta learning methods will move in this direction. This would help achieve the final goal of artificial intelligence, which is artificial general intelligence or AGI.

References

[1] J. Schmidhuber, Evolutionary principles in self-referential learning, or on learning how to learn: the meta-meta-... hook, Ph.D. thesis, Technische Universität München, 1987.

[2] Research open source publications blog, https://www.borealisai.com/en/blog/tutorial-2-few-shot-learning-and-meta-learning-i/, 2019.

[3] G. Maicas, C. Nguyen, F. Motlagh, J.C. Nascimento, G. Carneiro, Unsupervised task design to meta-train medical image classifiers, in: 2020 IEEE 17th International Symposium on Biomedical Imaging (ISBI), IEEE, 2020, pp. 1339–1342.

[4] H. Yao, Y. Wei, J. Huang, Z. Li, Hierarchically structured meta-learning, in: International Conference on Machine Learning, PMLR, 2019, pp. 7045–7054.

[5] R.L. Gutierrez, M. Leonetti, Information-theoretic task selection for meta-reinforcement learning, arXiv preprint, arXiv:2011.01054, 2020.

[6] C.C. Nguyen, T.-T. Do, G. Carneiro, Probabilistic task modelling for meta-learning, arXiv preprint, arXiv:2106.04802, 2021.

[7] A. Ayyad, Y. Li, R. Muaz, S. Albarqouni, M. Elhoseiny, Semi-supervised few-shot learning with prototypical random walks, in: 35th AAAI Conference on Artificial Intelligence (AAAI), 2021.

[8] C. Nguyen, T.-T. Do, G. Carneiro, Uncertainty in model-agnostic meta-learning using variational inference, in: Proceedings of the IEEE/CVF Winter Conference on Applications of Computer Vision, 2020, pp. 3090–3100.

[9] K. Hsu, S. Levine, C. Finn, Unsupervised learning via meta-learning, arXiv preprint, arXiv:1810.02334, 2018.

[10] S. Khodadadeh, L. Boloni, M. Shah, Unsupervised meta-learning for few-shot image classification, Advances in Neural Information Processing Systems 32 (2019).

[11] S. Khodadadeh, S. Zehtabian, S. Vahidian, W. Wang, B. Lin, L. Boloni, Unsupervised meta-learning through latent-space interpolation in generative models, in: International Conference on Learning Representations, 2020.

[12] K. Zhu, W. Zhai, Z.-J. Zha, Y. Cao, Self-supervised tuning for few-shot segmentation, arXiv preprint, arXiv:2004.05538, 2020.

[13] E. Hoffer, N. Ailon, Deep metric learning using triplet network, in: International Workshop on Similarity-Based Pattern Recognition, Springer, 2015, pp. 84–92.

[14] O. Vinyals, C. Blundell, T. Lillicrap, D. Wierstra, et al., Matching networks for one shot learning, Advances in Neural Information Processing Systems 29 (2016) 3630–3638.

[15] F. Sung, Y. Yang, L. Zhang, T. Xiang, P.H. Torr, T.M. Hospedales, Learning to compare: relation network for few-shot learning, in: Proceedings of the IEEE Conference on Computer Vision and Pattern Recognition, 2018, pp. 1199–1208.

[16] J. Snell, K. Swersky, R. Zemel, Prototypical networks for few-shot learning, in: Proceedings of the 31st International Conference on Neural Information Processing Systems, 2017, pp. 4080–4090.

[17] S. Ravi, H. Larochelle, Optimization as a model for few-shot learning, 2016.

[18] K. Li, J. Malik, Learning to optimize, arXiv preprint, arXiv:1606.01885, 2016.

[19] I. Bello, B. Zoph, V. Vasudevan, Q.V. Le, Neural optimizer search with reinforcement learning, in: International Conference on Machine Learning, PMLR, 2017, pp. 459–468.

[20] C. Finn, P. Abbeel, S. Levine, Model-agnostic meta-learning for fast adaptation of deep networks, in: International Conference on Machine Learning, PMLR, 2017, pp. 1126–1135.

[21] A. Nichol, J. Achiam, J. Schulman, On first-order meta-learning algorithms, arXiv preprint, arXiv:1803.02999, 2018.

[22] A. Santoro, S. Bartunov, M. Botvinick, D. Wierstra, T. Lillicrap, Meta-learning with memory-augmented neural networks, in: International Conference on Machine Learning, PMLR, 2016, pp. 1842–1850.

[23] T. Munkhdalai, H. Yu, Meta networks, in: International Conference on Machine Learning, PMLR, 2017, pp. 2554–2563.

[24] N. Mishra, M. Rohaninejad, X. Chen, P. Abbeel, A simple neural attentive meta-learner, arXiv preprint, arXiv:1707.03141, 2017.

[25] A.G. Roy, S. Siddiqui, S. Pölsterl, N. Navab, C. Wachinger, 'Squeeze & excite' guided few-shot segmentation of volumetric images, Medical Image Analysis 59 (2020) 101587.

[26] A. Parida, A. Tran, N. Navab, S. Albarqouni, Learn to segment organs with a few bounding boxes, arXiv preprint, arXiv:1909.07809, 2019.

[27] P. Tian, Z. Wu, L. Qi, L. Wang, Y. Shi, Y. Gao, Differentiable meta-learning model for few-shot semantic segmentation, in: Proceedings of the AAAI Conference on Artificial Intelligence, vol. 34, 2020, pp. 12087–12094.

[28] Y. Dawoud, J. Hornauer, G. Carneiro, V. Belagiannis, Few-shot microscopy image cell segmentation, in: Y. Dong, G. Ifrim, D. Mladenić, C. Saunders, S. Van Hoecke (Eds.), Machine Learning and Knowledge Discovery in Databases. Applied Data Science and Demo Track, Springer International Publishing, Cham, 2021, pp. 139–154.

[29] A. Makarevich, A. Farshad, V. Belagiannis, N. Navab, MetaMedSeg: volumetric meta-learning for few-shot organ segmentation, arXiv preprint, arXiv:2109.09734, 2021.

[30] D. Pakhomov, S. Hira, N. Wagle, K.E. Green, N. Navab, Segmentation in style: unsupervised semantic image segmentation with stylegan and clip, arXiv preprint, arXiv:2107.12518, 2021.

[31] A.K. Pambala, T. Dutta, S. Biswas, Sml: semantic meta-learning for few-shot semantic segmentation, Pattern Recognition Letters 147 (2021) 93–99.

[32] R. Khadga, D. Jha, S. Ali, S. Hicks, V. Thambawita, M.A. Riegler, P. Halvorsen, Few-shot segmentation of medical images based on meta-learning with implicit gradients, arXiv preprint, arXiv:2106.03223, 2021.

[33] L. Clouâtre, M. Demers, Figr: few-shot image generation with reptile, arXiv preprint, arXiv:1901.02199, 2019.

[34] Y. Li, R. Zhang, J. Lu, E. Shechtman, Few-shot image generation with elastic weight consolidation, arXiv preprint, arXiv:2012.02780, 2020.

[35] A. Farshad, S. Musatian, H. Dhamo, N. Navab, MIGS: meta image generation from scene graphs, in: BMVC, 2021.

[36] L. Casas, A. Klimmek, G. Carneiro, N. Navab, V. Belagiannis, Few-shot meta-denoising, arXiv preprint, arXiv:1908.00111, 2019.

[37] Y. Tian, G. Maicas, L.Z.C.T. Pu, R. Singh, J.W. Verjans, G. Carneiro, Few-shot anomaly detection for polyp frames from colonoscopy, in: International Conference on Medical Image Computing and Computer-Assisted Intervention, Springer, 2020, pp. 274–284.

[38] H. Coskun, M.Z. Zia, B. Tekin, F. Bogo, N. Navab, F. Tombari, H. Sawhney, Domain-specific priors and meta learning for few-shot first-person action recognition, IEEE Transactions on Pattern Analysis and Machine Intelligence (2021).

[39] H. Pan, C. Wang, M. Qiu, Y. Zhang, Y. Li, J. Huang, Meta-kd: a meta knowledge distillation framework for language model compression across domains, arXiv preprint, arXiv:2012.01266, 2020.

[40] B. Liu, Y. Rao, J. Lu, J. Zhou, C.-J. Hsieh, Metadistiller: network self-boosting via meta-learned top-down distillation, in: European Conference on Computer Vision, Springer, 2020, pp. 694–709.

[41] W. Zhou, C. Xu, J. McAuley, Meta learning for knowledge distillation, arXiv preprint, arXiv:2106.04570, 2021.

[42] V.K. Garg, A. Kalai, Supervising unsupervised learning, arXiv preprint, arXiv:1709.05262, 2017.

[43] A. Farshad, S. Hamidi, N. Navab, Meta-k: towards unsupervised prediction of number of clusters, 2020.

[44] S. Bengio, Y. Bengio, J. Cloutier, J. Gescei, On the optimization of a synaptic learning rule, in: Optimality in Biological and Artificial Networks?, Routledge, 2013, pp. 281–303.

[45] M. Andrychowicz, M. Denil, S. Gomez, M.W. Hoffman, D. Pfau, T. Schaul, B. Shillingford, N. De Freitas, Learning to learn by gradient descent by gradient descent, in: Advances in Neural Information Processing Systems, 2016, pp. 3981–3989.

[46] L. Weng, Meta-learning: learning to learn fast, 2018.

[47] S. Chopra, R. Hadsell, Y. LeCun, Learning a similarity metric discriminatively, with application to face verification, in: 2005 IEEE Computer Society Conference on Computer Vision and Pattern Recognition (CVPR'05), vol. 1, IEEE, 2005, pp. 539–546.

[48] G. Koch, R. Zemel, R. Salakhutdinov, et al., Siamese neural networks for one-shot image recognition, in: ICML Deep Learning Workshop, vol. 2, Lille, 2015.

[49] K.Q. Weinberger, J. Blitzer, L.K. Saul, Distance metric learning for large margin nearest neighbor classification, in: Advances in Neural Information Processing Systems, 2006, pp. 1473–1480.

[50] S. Hochreiter, J. Schmidhuber, Long short-term memory, Neural Computation 9 (8) (1997) 1735–1780.

[51] G. Maicas, A.P. Bradley, J.C. Nascimento, I. Reid, G. Carneiro, Training medical image analysis systems like radiologists, in: International Conference on Medical Image Computing and Computer-Assisted Intervention, Springer, 2018, pp. 546–554.

[52] D.P. Kingma, M. Welling, Stochastic gradient vb and the variational auto-encoder, in: Second International Conference on Learning Representations, vol. 19, ICLR, 2014, p. 121.

[53] R. Das, M. Zaheer, C. Dyer, Gaussian lda for topic models with word embeddings, in: Proceedings of the 53rd Annual Meeting of the Association for Computational Linguistics and the 7th International Joint Conference on Natural Language Processing (Volume 1: Long Papers), 2015, pp. 795–804.

[54] D.A. McAllester, Pac-Bayesian model averaging, in: Proceedings of the Twelfth Annual Conference on Computational Learning Theory, 1999, pp. 164–170.

[55] A. Pentina, C. Lampert, A pac-Bayesian bound for lifelong learning, in: International Conference on Machine Learning, PMLR, 2014, pp. 991–999.

[56] R. Amit, R. Meir, Meta-learning by adjusting priors based on extended pac-Bayes theory, in: International Conference on Machine Learning, PMLR, 2018, pp. 205–214.

[57] C. Nguyen, T.-T. Do, G. Carneiro, Pac-Bayesian meta-learning with implicit prior and posterior, arXiv preprint, arXiv:2003.02455, 2020.

[58] A. Ayyad, N. Navab, M. Elhoseiny, S. Albarqouni, Semi-supervised few-shot learning with local and global consistency, International Journal of Computer Mathematics 91 (2019).

[59] E.D. Cubuk, B. Zoph, D. Mane, V. Vasudevan, Q.V. Le, Autoaugment: learning augmentation strategies from data, in: Proceedings of the IEEE/CVF Conference on Computer Vision and Pattern Recognition, 2019, pp. 113–123.

[60] O. Ronneberger, P. Fischer, T. Brox, U-net: convolutional networks for biomedical image segmentation, in: International Conference on Medical Image Computing and Computer-Assisted Intervention, Springer, 2015, pp. 234–241.

[61] F. Milletari, N. Navab, S.-A. Ahmadi, V-net: fully convolutional neural networks for volumetric medical image segmentation, in: 2016 Fourth International Conference on 3D Vision (3DV), IEEE, 2016, pp. 565–571.

[62] A.G. Roy, N. Navab, C. Wachinger, Concurrent spatial and channel 'squeeze & excitation' in fully convolutional networks, in: International Conference on Medical Image Computing and Computer-Assisted Intervention, Springer, 2018, pp. 421–429.

[63] A.G. Roy, N. Navab, C. Wachinger, Recalibrating fully convolutional networks with spatial and channel "squeeze and excitation" blocks, IEEE Transactions on Medical Imaging 38 (2) (2018) 540–549.

[64] O. Jimenez-del Toro, H. Müller, M. Krenn, K. Gruenberg, A.A. Taha, M. Winterstein, I. Eggel, A. Foncubierta-Rodríguez, O. Goksel, A. Jakab, et al., Cloud-based evaluation of anatomical structure segmentation and landmark detection algorithms: visceral anatomy benchmarks, IEEE Transactions on Medical Imaging 35 (11) (2016) 2459–2475.

[65] W. Xie, J.A. Noble, A. Zisserman, Microscopy cell counting and detection with fully convolutional regression networks, Computer Methods in Biomechanics and Biomedical Engineering: Imaging & Visualization 6 (3) (2018) 283–292.

[66] K. Wang, J.H. Liew, Y. Zou, D. Zhou, J. Feng, Panet: few-shot image semantic segmentation with prototype alignment, in: Proceedings of the IEEE/CVF International Conference on Computer Vision, 2019, pp. 9197–9206.

[67] T. Mikolov, K. Chen, G. Corrado, J. Dean, Efficient estimation of word representations in vector space, arXiv preprint, arXiv:1301.3781, 2013.

[68] A. Joulin, E. Grave, P. Bojanowski, T. Mikolov, Bag of tricks for efficient text classification, arXiv preprint, arXiv:1607.01759, 2016.

[69] A. Rajeswaran, C. Finn, S. Kakade, S. Levine, Meta-learning with implicit gradients, 2019.

[70] O. Oktay, J. Schlemper, L.L. Folgoc, M. Lee, M. Heinrich, K. Misawa, K. Mori, S. McDonagh, N.Y. Hammerla, B. Kainz, et al., Attention u-net: learning where to look for the pancreas, arXiv preprint, arXiv:1804.03999, 2018.

[71] I. Goodfellow, J. Pouget-Abadie, M. Mirza, B. Xu, D. Warde-Farley, S. Ozair, A. Courville, Y. Bengio, Generative adversarial nets, Advances in Neural Information Processing Systems 27 (2014).

[72] T. Karras, S. Laine, M. Aittala, J. Hellsten, J. Lehtinen, T. Aila, Analyzing and improving the image quality of stylegan, in: Proceedings of the IEEE/CVF Conference on Computer Vision and Pattern Recognition, 2020, pp. 8110–8119.

[73] A. Radford, J.W. Kim, C. Hallacy, A. Ramesh, G. Goh, S. Agarwal, G. Sastry, A. Askell, P. Mishkin, J. Clark, et al., Learning transferable visual models from natural language supervision, arXiv preprint, arXiv:2103.00020, 2021.

[74] H. Dhamo, A. Farshad, I. Laina, N. Navab, G.D. Hager, F. Tombari, C. Rupprecht, Semantic image manipulation using scene graphs, in: Proceedings of the IEEE/CVF Conference on Computer Vision and Pattern Recognition, 2020, pp. 5213–5222.

[75] C. Baur, S. Albarqouni, N. Navab, Generating highly realistic images of skin lesions with gans, in: OR 2.0 Context-Aware Operating Theaters, Computer Assisted Robotic Endoscopy, Clinical Image-Based Procedures, and Skin Image Analysis, Springer, 2018, pp. 260–267.

[76] J. Kirkpatrick, R. Pascanu, N. Rabinowitz, J. Veness, G. Desjardins, A.A. Rusu, K. Milan, J. Quan, T. Ramalho, A. Grabska-Barwinska, et al., Overcoming catastrophic forgetting in neural networks, Proceedings of the National Academy of Sciences 114 (13) (2017) 3521–3526.

[77] X. Yi, P. Babyn, Sharpness-aware low-dose ct denoising using conditional generative adversarial network, Journal of Digital Imaging 31 (5) (2018) 655–669.

[78] A.L. Goldberger, L.A. Amaral, L. Glass, J.M. Hausdorff, P.C. Ivanov, R.G. Mark, J.E. Mietus, G.B. Moody, C.-K. Peng, H.E. Stanley, Physiobank, physiotoolkit, and physionet: components of a new research resource for complex physiologic signals, Circulation 101 (23) (2000) e215–e220.

[79] G. Pang, C. Shen, A. van den Hengel, Deep anomaly detection with deviation networks, in: Proceedings of the 25th ACM SIGKDD International Conference on Knowledge Discovery & Data Mining, 2019, pp. 353–362.

[80] R.D. Hjelm, A. Fedorov, S. Lavoie-Marchildon, K. Grewal, P. Bachman, A. Trischler, Y. Bengio, Learning deep representations by mutual information estimation and maximization, arXiv preprint, arXiv:1808.06670, 2018.

[81] G. Hinton, O. Vinyals, J. Dean, Distilling the knowledge in a neural network, arXiv preprint, arXiv:1503.02531, 2015.

[82] L.J. Ba, R. Caruana, Do deep nets really need to be deep?, arXiv preprint, arXiv:1312.6184, 2013.

[83] V. Belagiannis, A. Farshad, F. Galasso, Adversarial network compression, in: Proceedings of the European Conference on Computer Vision (ECCV) Workshops, 2018.

[84] Y. Jiang, J. Konečný, K. Rush, S. Kannan, Improving federated learning personalization via model agnostic meta learning, arXiv preprint, arXiv:1909.12488, 2019.

[85] B. McMahan, E. Moore, D. Ramage, S. Hampson, B.A. y Arcas, Communication-efficient learning of deep networks from decentralized data, in: Artificial Intelligence and Statistics, PMLR, 2017, pp. 1273–1282.

[86] A.G. Roy, S. Siddiqui, S. Pölsterl, N. Navab, C. Wachinger, Braintorrent: a peer-to-peer environment for decentralized federated learning, arXiv preprint, arXiv:1905.06731, 2019.

[87] Y. Yeganeh, A. Farshad, N. Navab, S. Albarqouni, Inverse distance aggregation for federated learning with non-iid data, in: Domain Adaptation and Representation Transfer, and Distributed and Collaborative Learning, Springer, 2020, pp. 150–159.

[88] F. Chen, M. Luo, Z. Dong, Z. Li, X. He, Federated meta-learning with fast convergence and efficient communication, arXiv preprint, arXiv:1802.07876, 2018.

[89] Z. Li, F. Zhou, F. Chen, H. Li, Meta-sgd: learning to learn quickly for few-shot learning, arXiv preprint, arXiv:1707.09835, 2017.

[90] M. Boudiaf, H. Kervadec, Z.I. Masud, P. Piantanida, I. Ben Ayed, J. Dolz, Few-shot segmentation without meta-learning: a good transductive inference is all you need?, in: Proceedings of the IEEE/CVF Conference on Computer Vision and Pattern Recognition, 2021, pp. 13979–13988.

Introduction to meta learning

Pengyu Yuan and Hien Van Nguyen

Department of Engineering & Computer Engineering, University of Houston, Houston, TX, United States

2.1 History of meta learning

The traditional method for developing a machine learning model entails selecting a base model (for example, a deep network), an optimization algorithm, and training data for the model to optimize its parameters. The optimization usually starts from scratch with a random parameter initialization. This approach has been widely successful in many fields, including [5,6,7], particularly with recent advances in deep learning models. This approach, however, has fundamental limitations [8], such as the need for large amounts of training data and compute resources. Because of these limitations, machine learning models are inapplicable to many critical applications in medicine and healthcare, where data is inherently scarce and difficult to collect [9]. Furthermore, the acceleration toward mobile health necessitates energy- and computing-efficient methods of developing, adjusting, and executing machine learning models [10].

The way humans learn new skills may hold the key to solving these issues. Radiologists, for example, can learn to identify a new disease from just a few examples. Humans rarely learn anything from the ground up. They construct an effective process for performing a new task by building on prior experience, knowledge, and reasoning ability. We can say that humans learn how to learn across tasks in this way. This serves as motivation to create a novel approach to building machine learning models.

The term "meta learning" or "learning-to-learn" appears for the first time in [15]. The study advocated for self-referential learning, in which a machine learning model learns to learn. This method specifically trained neural networks to predict updates to their own parameters. The model was optimized using evolutionary algorithms. Meta learning was later adopted and expanded in a variety of topics. Bengio *et al.* [30,31] proposed learning biologically plausible learning rules. Schmidhuber *et al.* [32,33] further developed self-referential and meta learning. In [11], S. Thrun *et al.* elaborated on the definition of the term *learning to learn* and provided theoretical justifications for meta learning. Proposals for training meta learning systems using gradient descent and backpropagation were first made in 1991 [34]. In 2001, [4,35,24] summarized the literature body at the time. Meta learning was first applied to reinforcement learning in 1995 [36], and has since been extended [37,38]. Readers are referred to [60] for the discussion of how meta learning applies to diverse applications in other fields, including finance, economy, transportation, and climate science.

Meta learning aims to reuse knowledge from previous tasks in order to improve the efficiency and efficacy of future learning tasks. Meta learning, in other words, captures transferable knowledge to allow models to rapidly adapt to new tasks. Meta learning is an important step toward lifelong learning, [13,12,14] whose goal is to continuously learn many tasks over a long time horizon. S. Thrun *et al.* [11]

argued that this approach could result in a variety of benefits, including increased data and computing efficiency. As a result, meta learning is thought to be more consistent with human, and animal learning [12].

Recent advances in deep learning have sparked a surge of interest in meta learning technologies. This is due to the potential for meta learning to address several fundamental limitations of modern deep networks [8]. Neural networks, for example, are data-hungry, requiring thousands to millions of data samples to achieve competitive prediction accuracy. Deep networks need 100,000 images to compete with opthamopathologists in the referral of sight-threatening diseases. Image recognition [16,20], reinforcement learning [21], neural architecture search (NAS) [18,22,23], and hyperparameter optimization [17] have all seen success. The integration of feature and model learning is the key to deep networks' success. This is taken to the next level by meta learning, which aims to integrate feature, model, and learning algorithm.

2.2 Formal definition

There are different ways to formulate meta learning. This section examines supervised learning first, then broadens its definition to include meta learning based on the work of S. Thrun *et al.* [11].

2.2.1 Supervised learning

In supervised learning setting, we have a training dataset $\mathcal{D}^{tr} = \{(x_1, y_1), \ldots, (x_N, y_N)\}$ for optimizing the learning model's parameters, and a validation dataset $\mathcal{D}^{val} = \{(x_1, y_1), \ldots, (x_{N'}, y_{N'})\}$ for validating the trained model. We can train a predictive model $\hat{y} = f_\theta(x)$ parameterized by θ, by the carrying out maximum likelihood estimation with respect to parameters θ as follows:

$$\theta^* = \arg\min_\theta \mathcal{L}(\mathcal{D}; \theta, \phi) \tag{2.1}$$

where $\mathcal{L}$ is a loss function that measures the error between true labels and those predicted by $f_\theta(\cdot)$. The conditioning on ϕ denotes the solution's reliance on assumptions about how to learn, such as the optimizer for θ or type of function f. One can view ϕ as a set of hyperparameters for the learning model. Once trained, the classifier's generalization is assessed using $\mathcal{D}^{val}$. Note that in the deep learning literature, data are partitioned into a training set for optimizing model parameters, a validation set for hyperparameters selection, and a test set for evaluating the model's generalization. Here, we define supervised learning using two datasets (train and validation) to make the transition to meta learning easier to understand.

2.2.2 Meta learning

The conventional assumption is that the optimization in Eq. (2.1) is done *from scratch* for each new task $\mathcal{D}$. Moreover, ϕ is prespecified. However, the specification of ϕ can significantly impact the performance, such as accuracy or data efficiency. Meta learning attempts to improve these metrics by learning the learning algorithm itself rather than assuming it is prespecified and fixed. This is frequently accomplished by returning to the first assumption above and learning from the distribution of tasks rather than from scratch.

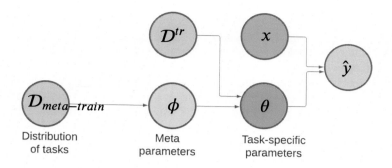

Distribution of tasks   Meta parameters   Task-specific parameters

FIGURE 2.1

Graphical model shows the dependency among meta learning components. Given a distribution of tasks, meta learning estimate metaparameters ϕ. These parameters enable efficient adaptation to novel tasks given a few training samples in $\mathcal{D}^{tr}$. With the task-specific parameters and input data x, the model predicts the corresponding label.

Formally, let us assume $\mathscr{D}_{meta-train} = \{(\mathcal{D}^{tr}_{meta-train}, \mathcal{D}^{val}_{meta-train})^{(i)}\}_{i=1}^{N}$ are N source tasks available in the metatraining stage, where each task has a training set $\mathcal{D}^{tr}_{meta-train}$ and validation set $\mathcal{D}^{val}_{meta-train}$. The training dataset consists of a few examples to help the model become familiar with the new task, while the validation dataset is to verify the model's performance. The train and validation datasets are frequently referred to as *support* and *query* sets. Fig. 2.1 shows the graphical model of meta learning. Metaparameters ϕ are acquired based on the metatraining set $\mathcal{D}_{meta-train}$. For a novel task $\mathcal{D} = \{\mathcal{D}^{tr}, \mathcal{D}^{val}\}$, metaparameters ϕ and its support set $\mathcal{D}^{tr} \in \mathcal{D}$ determine task-specific parameters θ. The probability of the ground truth label for a particular input $x \in \mathcal{D}^{val}$ is traditionally computed by maximum likelihood estimation as follows:

$$p(y|x, \mathcal{D}^{tr}, \mathcal{D}_{meta-train}) = \tag{2.2}$$

$$\operatorname*{argmax}_{\theta} \int_{\theta} p(y|x, \theta) p(\theta|\mathcal{D}^{tr}, \mathcal{D}_{meta-train}) d\theta \tag{2.3}$$

where $(x, y) \sim \in \mathcal{D}^{val}$, and θ the classifier parameters specific for the task $\mathcal{D}$. The above computation requires knowing the posterior distribution of θ conditioned on both the support set $\mathcal{D}^{tr}$ from that task, and the metatraining set $\mathcal{D}_{meta-train}$. The goal is to utilize metaknowledge acquired from $\mathcal{D}_{meta-train}$ to find a good set of parameters for the task $\mathcal{D}$. To better understand the role of metaknowledge, we further expand the posterior probability to incorporate metaparameters ϕ according to the graphical model in Fig. 2.1 as follows:

$$\log p(\theta|\mathcal{D}^{tr}, \mathcal{D}_{meta-train}) = \log p(\theta, \phi|\mathcal{D}^{tr}, \mathcal{D}_{meta-train})$$
$$= \log p(\theta|\phi, \mathcal{D}^{tr}, \mathcal{D}_{meta-train}) + \log p(\phi|\mathcal{D}_{meta-train})$$
$$= \log p(\theta|\phi, \mathcal{D}^{tr}) + \log p(\phi|\mathcal{D}_{meta-train}) \tag{2.4}$$

Note that we apply a logarithm function to the posterior probability to convert the product to an addition of two terms. The first equality in Eq. (2.4) is due to the fact that ϕ is a function of $\mathcal{D}_{meta-train}$, therefore, introducing ϕ does not change the posterior probability. The second equality comes from the observation that ϕ does not depend on $\mathcal{D}^{tr}$. Finally, the third equality comes from the assumption that task-specific parameters θ are conditionally independent of the metatraining datasets $\mathcal{D}_{meta-train}$ given the metaparameters ϕ. In other words, the learning process compresses all relevant information for estimating task-specific parameters into metaparameters, thus, eliminating the need for keeping $\mathcal{D}_{meta-train}$ around.

To maximize the likelihood probability in Eq. (2.3), we need to maximize the log posterior probability term in Eq. (2.4). This entails to solving a joint maximization of $\log p(\theta|\phi, \mathcal{D}^{tr})$ and $\log p(\phi|\mathcal{D}_{meta-train})$. The first term corresponds to the adaptation step (a.k.a. inner loop) that adjusts the model to a specific task, while the second term is equivalent to a meta learning step (a.k.a. outer loop) that extracts metaknowledge from a collection of tasks.

2.3 Meta learning formulation
2.3.1 Task distribution perspective

In the definition by T. Mitchell [2], *learning* involves the following elements:

1. a task
2. training experience
3. and a measure for the model's performance

Meta learning is commonly viewed as learning a general-purpose learning algorithm that can generalize across tasks. As more tasks become available, a new task can be learned better than the last. We can extend the definition of Mitchell for meta learning as follows:

1. a family of tasks
2. training experience for each task
3. performance measure for each task

We can access the performance of ϕ over a distribution of tasks $p(\mathcal{T})$. In this case, we define a task to be a dataset with the loss function $\mathcal{T} = \{\mathcal{D}, \mathcal{L}\}$. Learning how to learn thus becomes

$$\min_{\phi} E_{\mathcal{T}\sim p(\mathcal{T})}\mathcal{L}(\mathcal{D}, \phi) \tag{2.5}$$

where $\mathcal{L}(\mathcal{D}, \phi)$ measures the performance of a model trained using ϕ on dataset $\mathcal{D}$. 'How to learn', i.e. ϕ, is also known as *across-task* knowledge or *metaknowledge*. Let $\mathcal{D}_{meta-train}$ denote a finite number of source tasks sampled from $p(\mathcal{T})$. As discussed in Eq. (2.4), the *metatraining* can be viewed as the following maximum a posteriori probability (MAP) estimate:

$$\phi^* = \arg\max_{\phi} \log p(\phi|\mathscr{D}_{meta-train}) \tag{2.6}$$

The set of N' target tasks used in the metatesting stage is denoted as $\mathscr{D}_{meta-test} = \{(\mathcal{D}^{tr}_{meta-test}, \mathcal{D}^{val}_{meta-test})^{(i)}\}_{i=1}^{N'}$ where each task has both training and test data. The learned metaknowledge ϕ^*

is used to train the base model on each previously unseen target task i during the *metatesting* stage:

$$\theta^{*\,(i)} = \arg\max_{\theta} \log p(\theta | \phi^*, \mathcal{D}^{tr\,(i)}_{meta-test}) \qquad (2.7)$$

In contrast to supervised learning in Eq. (2.1), learning for a new target task i can use prior metaknowledge ϕ^* to improve the learning. ϕ^* can be the initialization of deep networks [16], or an entire learning model [25] or optimization strategy [57]. Modeling the posterior probabilities in Eq. (2.6) and Eq. (2.7) is currently an active research topic. The performance of $\theta^{*\,(i)}$ is evaluated on the validation split of each target task $\mathcal{D}^{val\,(i)}_{meta-test}$. Meta learning can suffer from *metaunderfitting* and *metaoverfitting*, analogous to underfitting and overfitting in supervised learning. Metaoverfitting is a problem in which the metaknowledge learned on the source tasks does not generalize to the target tasks. While overfitting in supervised learning is often due to a lack of training samples, overfitting in meta learning often happens when the number of training tasks is insufficient.

2.3.2 Meta learning from bilevel optimization view

The previous section formulates meta learning from the task distribution perspective. However, it is still not clear how to train the meta learning model in Eq. (2.6). In this section, we look at how to solve the metatraining step by casting it as a bilevel optimization problem [26]. Each optimization is coupled with another optimization as a constraint. Using this notation, we can specify the training step as follows:

$$\phi^* = \arg\min_{\phi} \sum_{i=1}^{M} \mathcal{L}^{meta}(\theta^{*\,(i)}(\phi), \phi, \mathcal{D}^{val\,(i)}_{meta-train}) \qquad (2.8)$$

$$\text{s.t. } \theta^{*(i)}(\phi) = \arg\min_{\theta} \mathcal{L}^{task}(\theta, \phi, \mathcal{D}^{tr\,(i)}_{meta-train}) \qquad (2.9)$$

Where $\mathcal{L}^{meta}$ and $\mathcal{L}^{task}$ refer to the outer and inner losses, respectively. In this case, the inner level optimization Eq. (2.9) is conditional on the learning strategy ϕ defined by the outer level. Moreover, the inner level optimization cannot change ϕ during its training. Here ϕ could represent an initial condition in nonconvex optimization [16], a hyperparameter like regularization strength [17], or even a parameterization of the loss function to optimize $\mathcal{L}^{task}$ [27]. The outer level optimization learns ϕ in such a way that it produces models $\theta^{*\,(i)}(\phi)$ that perform well after training on their validation sets.

Solving a bi-level optimization problem requires calculating Hessian vector products, which is computationally expensive. Various Hessian-free algorithms have been proposed to address this issue, including an optimization library that unifies meta learning algorithms [1] under a bi-level optimization framework. More generally, the above formulation can be viewed as a noncooperative game between two players [26].

2.3.3 Feed-forward model view

As we will see, there are several meta learning approaches that synthesize models in a feed-forward fashion, rather than through an explicit iterative optimization as in Eqs. (2.8)-(2.9) above. While the degree of complexity varies, it can be helpful to understand this family of approaches by instantiating the abstract objective in Eq. (2.5) to define a toy example for metatraining linear regression [28].

$$\min_{\phi} E \underset{\substack{\mathcal{T} \sim p(\mathcal{T}) \\ (\mathcal{D}^{tr},\mathcal{D}^{val}) \in \mathcal{T}}}{} \sum_{(\mathbf{x},y) \in \mathcal{D}^{val}} \left[(\mathbf{x}^T \mathbf{g}_{\phi}(\mathcal{D}^{tr}) - y)^2 \right] \tag{2.10}$$

In this case, we metatrain by optimizing across a distribution of tasks. A train and validation set is created for each task. The train set $\mathcal{D}^{tr}$ is embedded [29] into a vector $\mathbf{g}_{\phi}$ which defines the linear regression weights used to predict examples $\mathbf{x}$ from the validation set. Optimizing Eq. (2.10) leads to a function $\mathbf{g}_{\phi}$ that maps a training set to a weight vector. As a result, $\mathbf{g}_{\phi}$ should provide a good solution for novel metatest tasks $\mathcal{T}^{test}$ derived from $p(\mathcal{T})$. The complexity of the predictive model $\mathbf{g}$ used in this family varies, as does how the support set is embedded [29]. In theory, $\mathbf{g}_{\phi}(\cdot)$ can predict parameters of any model, and the general meta learning problem can be written as follows:

$$\min_{\phi} E \underset{\substack{\mathcal{T} \sim p(\mathcal{T}) \\ (\mathcal{D}^{tr},\mathcal{D}^{val}) \in \mathcal{T}}}{} \sum_{(\mathbf{x},y) \in \mathcal{D}^{val}} \mathcal{L}(f(\mathbf{x}; \theta^*), y) \tag{2.11}$$

$$\theta^* = \mathbf{g}_{\phi}(\mathcal{D}^{tr}) \tag{2.12}$$

where the linear regression is replaced by a general function $f(\mathbf{x}; \theta^*)$.

2.4 Meta learning taxonomy

Meta learning algorithms are commonly divided into three categories [39,40]. They are metric learning (or nonparametric) methods, optimization methods, and model-based (or black box) methods. More recent work [59] group meta learning algorithms based on choice of metarepresentation ϕ, metaoptimizer (i.e., how to optimize ϕ), and metaobjective.

Metric-Learning: The metaoptimization process learns an embedding network ϕ that transforms raw inputs into a representation suitable for recognition via simple similarity comparison between query and support instances [45,53,58,20] (e.g., with cosine similarity or Euclidean distance) This was accomplished using various modeling architectures, including siamese neural networks [49], matching networks [58], prototypical networks [20], relation networks [50], and graph neural networks [51]. Under this category, outer-level learning corresponds to metric learning. The goal is to find a feature extractor ϕ that adequately represents the data comparison. As previously explained, ϕ is learned on source tasks, then applied to target tasks. Metric learning can also be viewed as a subset of the feedforward models. For example, several approaches compute logits based on the inner product of the support and query images' embeddings [45,53]. In this case, the support image embeddings can be viewed as the generated 'weights' to make a prediction for the query example. This is similar to the feed-forward approach in 'hypernetwork' which generates a linear classifier for the query set. Other methods in this family were further improved by using task-conditional embeddings [54,52], learning more sophisticated comparison metric [50,51], or combining with the strength of gradient-based approaches [55].

Optimization: Optimization-based methods formulate the inner-level task (Eq. (2.9)) as an optimization problem. The goal is to capture metaknowledge ϕ that would increase the optimization performance. A notable example is model-agnostic meta learning (MAML) [16], which seeks an initialization

$\phi = \theta_0$, such that a few inner steps result in a classifier that performs well on validation data. The update step is done by truncated gradient descent. Alternatively, one can also learn step sizes [41,42] or train recurrent networks to predict steps from gradients [57,43,19]. Fundamental challenges of this approach include more complex gradient computation and higher memory requirements. Existing methods address these challenges by using the first-order approximation of gradients, and parameter sharing across gradient coordinates. Finally, [44] provides a unified framework for many gradient-based meta learning algorithms.

Model-Based: Model-based algorithms use feed-forward pass to model the inner learning step in Eq. (2.9) as seen in Eq. (2.11). The model encodes the current dataset $\mathcal{D}$ into an activation state which then serves as the input for predicting the task-specific parameters. Popular architectures for encoding $\mathcal{D}$ include recurrent networks [4,57], convolutional networks [25] or hypernetworks [45,56]. The inner-level learning is performed via the model's activation state, which is purely feed-forward. Memory-augmented neural networks [3] employ an external storage buffer and fall under model-based category [46,47]. Compared to optimization-based approaches, model-based algorithms enjoy simpler optimization without the need to compute second-order gradients. However, these methods are arguably less able to generalize to out-of-distribution tasks than optimization-based counterparts [48].

References

[1] Yaohua Liu, Risheng Liu, Boml: a modularized bilevel optimization library in python for meta learning, in: 2021 IEEE International Conference on Multimedia & Expo Workshops (ICMEW), IEEE, 2021, pp. 1–2.

[2] T.M. Mitchell, Machine Learning, McGraw-Hill International Editions, McGraw-Hill, 1997.

[3] Alex Graves, Greg Wayne, Ivo Danihelka, Neural Turing Machines, arXiv preprint, arXiv:1410.5401, 2014.

[4] Sepp Hochreiter, A. Steven Younger, Peter R. Conwell, Learning to learn using gradient descent, in: Artificial Neural Networks, ICANN 2001, Springer, 2001, pp. 87–94.

[5] K. He, X. Zhang, S. Ren, J. Sun, Deep residual learning for image recognition, in: CVPR, 2016.

[6] D. Silver, A. Huang, C.J. Maddison, A. Guez, L. Sifre, G. Van Den Driessche, J. Schrittwieser, I. Antonoglou, V. Panneershelvam, M. Lanctot, et al., Mastering the game of go with deep neural networks and tree search, Nature (2016).

[7] J. Devlin, M. Chang, K. Lee, K. Toutanova, BERT: pre-training of deep bidirectional transformers for language understanding, in: ACL, 2019.

[8] G. Marcus, Deep learning: a critical appraisal, arXiv e-prints, 2018.

[9] H. Altae-Tran, B. Ramsundar, A.S. Pappu, V.S. Pande, Low data drug discovery with one-shot learning, CoRR, 2016.

[10] A. Ignatov, R. Timofte, A. Kulik, S. Yang, K. Wang, F. Baum, M. Wu, L. Xu, L. Van Gool, AI benchmark: all about deep learning on smartphones in 2019, arXiv e-prints, 2019.

[11] S. Thrun, L. Pratt, Learning to learn: introduction and overview, in: Learning to Learn, 1998.

[12] H.F. Harlow, The formation of learning sets, Psychological Review (1949).

[13] J.B. Biggs, The role of meta-learning in study processes, British Journal of Educational Psychology (1985).

[14] A.M. Schrier, Learning how to learn: the significance and current status of learning set formation, Primates (1984).

[15] J. Schmidhuber, Evolutionary principles in self-referential learning, in: On Learning How to Learn: The Meta-Meta-... Hook, 1987.

[16] C. Finn, P. Abbeel, S. Levine, Model-agnostic meta-learning for fast adaptation of deep networks, in: ICML, 2017.

[17] L. Franceschi, P. Frasconi, S. Salzo, R. Grazzi, M. Pontil, Bilevel programming for hyperparameter optimization and meta-learning, in: ICML, 2018.

[18] H. Liu, K. Simonyan, Y. Yang, DARTS: differentiable architecture search, in: ICLR, 2019.

[19] M. Andrychowicz, M. Denil, S.G. Colmenarejo, M.W. Hoffman, D. Pfau, T. Schaul, N. de Freitas, Learning to learn by gradient descent by gradient descent, in: NeurIPS, 2016.

[20] J. Snell, K. Swersky, R.S. Zemel, Prototypical networks for few shot learning, in: NeurIPS, 2017.

[21] F. Alet, M.F. Schneider, T. Lozano-Perez, L. Pack Kaelbling, Meta-learning curiosity algorithms, in: ICLR, 2020.

[22] E. Real, A. Aggarwal, Y. Huang, Q.V. Le, Regularized evolution for image classifier architecture search, in: AAAI, 2019.

[23] B. Zoph, Q.V. Le, Neural architecture search with reinforcement learning, in: ICLR, 2017.

[24] R. Vilalta, Y. Drissi, A perspective view and survey of meta-learning, in: Artificial Intelligence Review, 2002.

[25] N. Mishra, M. Rohaninejad, X. Chen, P. Abbeel, A simple neural attentive meta-learner, in: ICLR, 2018.

[26] H. Stackelberg, The Theory of Market Economy, Oxford University Press, 1952.

[27] Y. Li, Y. Yang, W. Zhou, T.M. Hospedales, Feature-critic networks for heterogeneous domain generalization, in: ICML, 2019.

[28] G. Denevi, C. Ciliberto, D. Stamos, M. Pontil, Learning to learn around a common mean, in: NeurIPS, 2018.

[29] M. Zaheer, S. Kottur, S. Ravanbakhsh, B. Poczos, R.R. Salakhutdinov, A.J. Smola, Deep sets, in: NIPS, 2017.

[30] Y. Bengio, S. Bengio, J. Cloutier, Learning a synaptic learning rule, in: IJCNN, 1990.

[31] S. Bengio, Y. Bengio, J. Cloutier, On the search for new learning rules for ANNs, Neural Processing Letters (1995).

[32] J. Schmidhuber, J. Zhao, M. Wiering, Simple Principles of Meta-Learning, Technical report IDSIA, 1996.

[33] J. Schmidhuber, A neural network that embeds its own meta-levels, in: IEEE International Conference on Neural Networks, 1993.

[34] J. Schmidhuber, A possibility for implementing curiosity and boredom in model-building neural controllers, in: SAB, 1991.

[35] A.S. Younger, S. Hochreiter, P.R. Conwell, Meta-learning with backpropagation, in: IJCNN, 2001.

[36] J. Storck, S. Hochreiter, J. Schmidhuber, Reinforcement driven information acquisition in non-deterministic environments, in: ICANN, 1995.

[37] M. Wiering, J. Schmidhuber, Efficient model-based exploration, in: SAB, 1998.

[38] N. Schweighofer, K. Doya, Meta-learning in reinforcement learning, Neural Networks (2003).

[39] H. Yao, X. Wu, Z. Tao, Y. Li, B. Ding, R. Li, Z. Li, Automated relational meta-learning, in: ICLR, 2020.

[40] S.C. Yoonho Lee, Gradient-based meta-learning with learned layerwise metric and subspace, in: ICML, 2018.

[41] Z. Li, F. Zhou, F. Chen, H. Li, Meta-SGD: learning to learn quickly for few shot learning, arXiv e-prints, 2017.

[42] A. Antoniou, H. Edwards, A.J. Storkey, How to train your MAML, in: ICLR, 2018.

[43] K. Li, J. Malik, Learning to optimize, in: ICLR, 2017.

[44] E. Grefenstette, B. Amos, D. Yarats, P.M. Htut, A. Molchanov, F. Meier, D. Kiela, K. Cho, S. Chintala, Generalized inner loop meta-learning, arXiv preprint, arXiv:1910.01727, 2019.

[45] S. Qiao, C. Liu, W. Shen, A.L. Yuille, Few-shot image recognition by predicting parameters from activations, in: CVPR, 2018.

[46] A. Santoro, S. Bartunov, M. Botvinick, D. Wierstra, T. Lillicrap, Meta learning with memory-augmented neural networks, in: ICML, 2016.

[47] T. Munkhdalai, H. Yu, Meta networks, in: ICML, 2017.

[48] C. Finn, S. Levine, Meta-learning and universality: deep representations and gradient descent can approximate any learning algorithm, in: ICLR, 2018.

[49] G. Kosh, R. Zemel, R. Salakhutdinov, Siamese neural networks for one-shot image recognition, in: ICML, 2015.

[50] F. Sung, Y. Yang, L. Zhang, T. Xiang, P.H.S. Torr, T.M. Hospedales, Learning to compare: relation network for few-shot learning, in: CVPR, 2018.

[51] V. Garcia, J. Bruna, Few-shot learning with graph neural networks, in: ICLR, 2018.

[52] A. Antoniou, A. Storkey, Learning to learn by self-critique, in: NeurIPS, 2019.

[53] W.-Y. Chen, Y.-C. Liu, Z. Kira, Y.-C. Wang, J.-B. Huang, A closer look at few-shot classification, in: ICLR, 2019.

[54] B. Oreshkin, P. Rodríguez López, A. Lacoste, TADAM: task dependent adaptive metric for improved few-shot learning, in: NeurIPS, 2018.

[55] H.-Y. Tseng, H.-Y. Lee, J.-B. Huang, M.-H. Yang, Cross-domain few-shot classification via learned feature-wise transformation, in: ICLR, Jan. 2020.

[56] Spyros Gidaris, Nikos Komodakis, Dynamic few-shot visual learning without forgetting, in: Proceedings of the IEEE Conference on Computer Vision and Pattern Recognition, 2018, pp. 4367–4375.

[57] Sachin Ravi, Hugo Larochelle, Optimization as a model for few-shot learning, 2016.

[58] Oriol Vinyals, Charles Blundell, Tim Lillicrap, Daan Wierstra, et al., Matching networks for one shot learning, in: Advances in Neural Information Processing Systems, 2016, pp. 3630–3638.

[59] T. Hospedales, A. Antoniou, P. Micaelli, A. Storkey, Meta-learning in neural networks: a survey, arXiv preprint, arXiv:2004.05439, 2020.

[60] L. Zou, Meta-Learning Theory, Algorithms and Applications, Elsevier, 2022.

Metric learning algorithms for meta learning

Pengyu Yuan and Hien Van Nguyen

Department of Engineering & Computer Engineering, University of Houston, Houston, TX, United States

3.1 Siamese networks for meta learning

Siamese networks were initially introduced for signature verification task [29]. A siamese network takes in two inputs and uses two networks to process them to produce two vectors. Finally, the loss function enforces a certain relationship between these the two vectors. Koch *et al.* [26] adapted Siamese networks to one-shot image recognition, which is closely related to meta learning. The rest of this section will describe Koch's approach and set the foundation for subsequent metric learning approaches in meta learning.

3.1.1 Model architecture

Koch's model [26] is a siamese convolutional neural network with L layers each with N_l units, where $(h_{1,l}, h_{2,l})$ represents the hidden vector in layer l for the first and second twins, respectively. The model has multiple convolutional layers, each followed by a ReLU activation function. The final convolutional layer's output is flattened into a single vector, followed by a fully connected layer. The two networks' outputs then serve as the input to compute the following metric:

$$p = \sigma(\phi^T \|h_{1,l} - h_{2,l}\|) \tag{3.1}$$

where σ is sigmoid function. The function p serves as the similarity between two feature vectors. ϕ are additional parameters learned by the model during the training, weighting the importance of the component-wise distance. Fig. 3.1 shows the model configuration.

Let M denote the minibatch size, and i the i-th minibatch's index. Let $y(x_{1,i}, x_{2,i})$ be a length-M vector which contains the labels for the minibatch, where we assume $y(x_{1,i}, x_{2,i}) = 1$ whenever x_1 and x_2 come from the same class and $y(x_{1,i}, x_{2,i}) = 0$ otherwise. Koch's method imposes a regularized cross-entropy objective on our binary classifier of the following form

$$\mathcal{L}(x_{1,i}, x_{2,i}) = y(x_{1,i}, x_{2,i})\log p(x_{1,i}, x_{2,i}) +$$
$$(1 - y(x_{1,i}, x_{2,i}))\log(1 - p(x_{1,i}, x_{2,i})) + \lambda^T \|\phi\|^2 \tag{3.2}$$

Intuitively, siamese networks learn an embedding that transforms the inputs to vector space so that distances between two samples within the same class are small, and those coming from different classes are large.

Meta Learning With Medical Imaging and Health Informatics Applications. https://doi.org/10.1016/B978-0-32-399851-2.00010-7

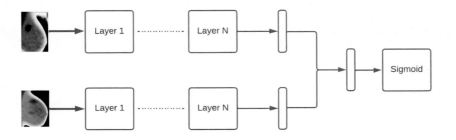

FIGURE 3.1

Architecture of a siamese network for signature verification.

3.1.2 Training and testing procedure

The training procedure samples *same* and *different* pairs from the training dataset then optimizes the loss function in (3.2) mini-batch gradient descent. Koch *et al.* uses Omniglot dataset [21] for few-shot image recognition tasks. Omniglot contains hand-written examples from 50 different alphabets, ranging from well-established international languages such as Latin and Korean to lesser-known local dialects. The dataset is split into a training set with 40 alphabets and a nonoverlapping test set with 10 alphabets. In addition, data augmentation methods like affine distortion are used to generate more copies of the original dataset. Once optimized, few-shot image recognition is straightforward. Let $\{x_k\}_{k=1}^{C}$ denote the given set of examples from C classes. We can perform inference for x as follows:

$$\hat{y} = \underset{k}{\mathrm{argmax}}\; p(x, x_k) \tag{3.3}$$

3.2 Matching networks

Matching networks [28] are another prominent metric-learning technique for rapidly learning from a few samples. This approach employs new modeling based on attention mechanisms. Second, it introduces the notion of episodic training to make the training phase more consistent with the test phase. The rest of this section will describe this method in detail.

3.2.1 Model architecture

Matching networks can be considered as a nonparametric approach to solving one-shot learning. It is based on two novel components. First, matching networks' architectures employ neural networks augmented with memory as shown in Fig. 3.2. Given a (small) support set $\mathcal{D}^{tr}$, the model maps this set to a classifier $\varphi_{\mathcal{D}^{tr}}: \mathcal{D}^{tr} \to \varphi_{\mathcal{D}^{tr}}(.)$. Second, matching networks employ a training strategy that is tailored for one-shot learning from the support set $\mathcal{D}^{tr}$.

Specifically, MNs map a small support set of k examples, denoted by $\mathcal{D}^{tr} = \{(x_i, y_i)\}_{i=1}^{k}$, to a classifier $\varphi_S(x)$. Given a new test example x, MNs define a probability distribution over outputs $\hat{y}$ using

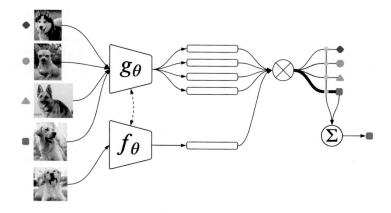

FIGURE 3.2

Matching Networks architecture [28].

the following formula:

$$\hat{y} = \sum_{i=1}^{k} a(x, x_i) y_i \qquad (3.4)$$

where x_i, y_i represent the samples and labels from the support set $\mathcal{D}^{tr} = \{(x_i, y_i)\}_{i=1}^{k}$, and a is an attention mechanism that measure the relevance of x_i to the query sample x.

The Attention Kernel The attention mechanism $a(., .)$ fully specifies the classifier given the support set $\mathcal{D}^{tr}$. For example, $a(., .)$ can be a softmax function over the cosine distance c similar to common attention models in the literature:

$$a(x, x_i) = e^{\varphi(f(x), g(x_i))} / \sum_{j=1}^{k} e^{\varphi(f(x), g(x_j))} \qquad (3.5)$$

in which embedding functions f and g are neural networks that encode x and x_i. Both f and g can share the same network architecture or even the weights. Specifically, f and g can be deep convolutional networks for image tasks or word embeddings for natural language tasks, respectively. f and g are analogous to two networks of a siamese network. We observe that, despite being related to metric learning, the classifier defined by Eq. (3.4) is discriminative. To correctly classify x with a given support set $\mathcal{D}^{tr}$, sample x must be closer to pairs $(x', y') \in \mathcal{D}^{tr}$ where $y' = y$ than to other pairs. This type of loss is also related to methods such as Neighborhood Component Analysis (NCA) [22], triplet loss [20], and large margin nearest neighbor [24]. However, the loss function of matching networks is consistent with the few-shot classification setting. This consistency between the training and testing phases leads to better performance compared to its counterparts. Moreover, the objective function is simple and differentiable, which can be trained in an end-to-end manner.

3.2.2 Full-context embeddings

The embedding functions f and g are similar to two branches of a siamese network. They map the two inputs to the feature space X so that the classification accuracy in Eq. (3.4) is maximized. Matching networks employ a novel modeling of the embedding functions f and g to make them dependent on the entire support set $\mathcal{D}^{tr}$.

Full-Context Embedding of f: While the classification strategy is fully conditioned on the whole support set through $P(.|x, \mathcal{D}^{tr})$, the embeddings f and g are myopic in the sense that each element x_i gets embedded by $f(x_i)$ and $g(x_i)$ independently of other elements in the support set $\mathcal{D}^{tr}$. Ideally, $\mathcal{D}^{tr}$ should be able to modify how we embed the test image x through f. With this realization, we use LSTM with read-attention over the whole set $\mathcal{D}^{tr}$, whose inputs are equal to x to model f so that the embedding depends on the set $\mathcal{D}^{tr}$:

$$f(x, \mathcal{D}^{tr}) = \text{attention-LSTM}(f'(x), g(\mathcal{D}^{tr}), K) \tag{3.6}$$

Here, $f'(x)$ denote the features extracted by CNN which then serves as the input to the LSTM recurrent network. K denotes the number of LSTM unrollings over time. $g(\mathcal{D}^{tr})$ is the embeddings of the support set that the model attends to. This modification to f enables the model to potentially ignore some elements in the support set $\mathcal{D}^{tr}$, and increases the richness of the attention mechanism. The output of attention-LSTM$(f'(x), g(\mathcal{D}^{tr}), K)$ is a vector h_K obtained from running the following processing K steps:

$$\hat{h}_k, c_k = \text{LSTM}(f'(x), [h_{k-1}, r_{k-1}], c_{k-1}) \tag{3.7}$$

$$h_k = \hat{h}_k + f'(x) \tag{3.8}$$

$$a(h_k, g(x_i)) = \text{softmax}(h_k^T g(x_i)) \tag{3.9}$$

$$r_k = \sum_{i=1}^{|\mathcal{D}^{tr}|} a(h_k, g(x_i)) g(x_i) \tag{3.10}$$

where LSTM(x, h, c) follows the same LSTM implementation defined in [23]. (x, h, c) respectively represent the input, the output, and the memory cell of LSTM. a is a content-based attention mechanism that produces the attention scores between the current activation h_k and samples in the support set x_i. The scores are used for computing embedding r_k. Both r_{k-1} and h_{k-1} are concatenated and input to LSTM to estimate the next hidden states h_k following Eq. (3.7).

Full-Context Embedding of g: Matching networks also use full-context embedding for g. Specifically, the embedding of a particular sample x_i depends on both x_i and its support set $\mathcal{D}^{tr}$, denoted by $g(x_i, \mathcal{D}^{tr})$. As a result, changing the support set will modify how g would encode x_i. To achieve this, matching networks use a bidirectional Long-Short Term Memory (LSTM) [19] to process the support set $\mathcal{D}^{tr}$ as a sequence of samples. This choice makes the embedding dependent on the order of samples in $\mathcal{D}^{tr}$, which is undesirable. Alternative solution would be using set-based deep networks [1,5,4]. Let $g'(x_i)$ denote a neural network for feature extraction. Then we define the conditional embedding as follows:

$$g(x_i, S) = \vec{h}_i + \overleftarrow{h}_i + g'(x_i)$$

$$\vec{h}_i, \vec{c}_i = \text{LSTM}(g'(x_i), \vec{h}_{i-1}, \vec{c}_{i-1})$$

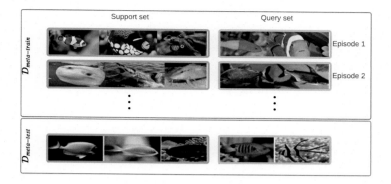

FIGURE 3.3

Episodic training and testing strategy for meta learning.

$$\bar{h}_i, \bar{c}_i = \qquad\qquad \text{LSTM}(g'(x_i), \bar{h}_{i+1}, \bar{c}_{i+1})$$

in which (x, h, c) are respectively the input, output, and memory cell of $\text{LSTM}(x, h, c)$ [23]. While the embedding still depends on the sample order in the support set, using bidirectional LSTM allows $g(x_i)$ to take into account information from all samples within $\mathcal{D}^{tr}$, instead of just samples prior to x_i (i.e., x_j, $j \leq i$).

3.2.3 Episodic training strategy

Matching networks introduced an episodic training procedure chosen carefully so as to match inference at test time as shown in Fig. 3.3. Let us construct a task $\mathcal{T}$ by uniform random sampling N unique classes, with k examples per class. This setting is called N-way and k-shot. In this case, a task will typically have $N \times k$ examples. Let $p(\mathcal{T})$ denote the distribution of tasks. A training "episode" is constructed by sampling a task $\mathcal{T} \sim p(\mathcal{T})$, then divide the data into nonoverlapping support set $\mathcal{D}^{tr}_{meta-train}$ and a validation set $\mathcal{D}^{val}_{meta-train}$. Note that both sets have the same number of classes. Given the support set $\mathcal{D}^{tr}_{meta-train}$, Matching Networks' parameters are then trained by minimizing the prediction errors on $\mathcal{D}^{val}_{meta-train}$. In other words, the training procedure explicitly learns to learn from a given support set to minimize a loss over a batch. The Matching Nets training objective is as follows:

$$\phi = \arg\max_{\phi} E_{\mathcal{T} \sim p(\mathcal{T})} \left[\sum_{(x,y) \in \mathcal{D}^{val}_{meta-train}} \log p_\phi \left(y | x, \mathcal{D}^{tr}_{meta-train} \right) \right]. \qquad (3.11)$$

This setting is consistent with the test phase, where only a few samples are given as support sets for new tasks. The trained model does not need any fine-tuning on the classes it has never seen due to its nonparametric nature. Obviously, as new tasks diverge far from the tasks used for learning ϕ, the model will not work.

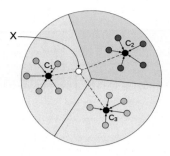

FIGURE 3.4

Prototypical networks for few-shot learning. Class-specific prototypes $\mathbf{m}_k$ are computed as the mean of embedded support examples for each class. A new data point (white circle) is classified via a softmax over distances to class prototypes [14].

3.3 Prototypical networks

Prototypical networks [14] are based on the idea that for each class, there exists an embedding where data samples tightly cluster around a prototype representation. To accomplish this, prototypical networks use a neural network to learn a nonlinear mapping of the input into an embedding space. Then a class prototype is computed by taking the mean of the embeddings of samples falling within this class. The nearest class prototype is then used to perform classification for an embedded query point as illustrated in Fig. 3.4. Because prototypical networks are simpler than most metric-learning-based meta learning algorithms, they are appealing for the few-shot learning setting.

3.3.1 Model architecture

Let us consider the standard few-shot learning setting where a small support set is given. We denote this set by $\mathcal{D}^{tr} = \{(\mathbf{x}_1, y_1), \ldots, (\mathbf{x}_N, y_N)\}$ in which $\mathbf{x}_i \in \mathbb{R}^D$ is the D-dimensional vector and $y_i \in \{1, \ldots, C\}$ is the corresponding label. $\mathcal{D}^{tr}_k$ denotes the set of examples labeled within class k. Let function $f_\phi : \mathbb{R}^D \to \mathbb{R}^M$ denotes an embedding function with parametrized by ϕ. Prototypical networks estimate a *prototype* defined as an M-dimensional vector $\mathbf{m}_k \in \mathbb{R}^M$ for each class by computing the mean vector of the embedded support samples within the class as follows:

$$\mathbf{m}_k = \frac{1}{|\mathcal{D}^{tr}_k|} \sum_{(\mathbf{x}_i, y_i) \in \mathcal{D}^{tr}_k} f_\phi(\mathbf{x}_i) \tag{3.12}$$

Given a distance function $d : \mathbb{R}^M \times \mathbb{R}^M \to [0, +\infty)$, prototypical networks compute a probabilistic prediction for a query point $\mathbf{x}$ by applying softmax over distances from the query point's embedding to the prototypes:

$$p_\phi(y = k \mid \mathbf{x}) = \frac{\exp(-d(f_\phi(\mathbf{x}), \mathbf{m}_k))}{\sum_{k'=1}^{C} \exp(-d(f_\phi(\mathbf{x}), \mathbf{m}_{k'}))} \tag{3.13}$$

Algorithm 3.1 Episodic training procedure in prototypical networks. N and C respectively denote the number of examples in the training set and number of classes. DRAWSAMPLE$(\mathcal{D}, n)$ denotes a set of n elements randomly drawn from set $\mathcal{D}^{tr}$ with no replacement. Algorithm is adopted from [14].

Require: Training set $\mathcal{D} = \{(\mathbf{x}_1, y_1), \ldots, (\mathbf{x}_N, y_N)\}$, where each $y_i \in \{1, \ldots, K\}$. $\mathcal{D}_k$ denotes the set of samples $(\mathbf{x}_i, y_i)$ in $\mathcal{D}$ satisfying $y_i = k$.
Ensure: Loss function $\mathcal{L}$ for each task

$\quad \mathcal{I} \leftarrow$ DRAWSAMPLE$(\{1, \ldots, C\}, n_c)$ {Indices of n_c randomly sampled classes}
$\quad$ **for** k in $\{1, \ldots, n_c\}$ **do**
$\qquad \mathcal{D}_k \leftarrow$ DRAWSAMPLE$(\mathcal{D}_{\mathcal{I}_k}, n_s)$ {Draw support samples}
$\qquad Q_k \leftarrow$ DRAWSAMPLE$(\mathcal{D}_{\mathcal{I}_k} \setminus \mathcal{D}_k, n_q)$ {Draw query examples}
$\qquad \mathbf{m}_k \leftarrow \dfrac{1}{n_c} \displaystyle\sum_{(\mathbf{x}_i, y_i) \in \mathcal{D}_k} f_\phi(\mathbf{x}_i)$ {Compute prototype from support examples}
$\quad$ **end for**
$\quad J \leftarrow 0$
$\quad$ **for** k in $\{1, \ldots, n_c\}$ **do**
$\qquad$ **for** $(\mathbf{x}, y) \in Q_k$ **do**
$$\mathcal{L} \leftarrow \mathcal{L} + \frac{1}{n_c n_q}\left[d(f_\phi(\mathbf{x}), \mathbf{m}_k)) + \log \sum_{k'} \exp(-d(f_\phi(\mathbf{x}), \mathbf{m}_k)) \right]$$
$\qquad$ **end for**
$\quad$ **end for**

The training is performed by minimizing the following negative log-probability using stochastic gradient descent method. Note that the log-probability is corresponding to the true label k of the sample x.

$$\mathcal{L}(\phi) = -\log p_\phi(y = k \mid \mathbf{x}) \tag{3.14}$$

The training procedure constructs episodes by randomly selecting N classes from the training set, then choosing a few examples from each class to serve as the support set and another few samples to serve as the query set. Algorithm 3.1 provides more details of the training procedure.

An interesting property of prototypical networks is that they are equivalent to performing mixture density estimation on the support if the distance function $d(., .)$ falls within the family of regular Bregman divergences [25].

3.3.2 Reinterpretation as a linear model

This section provides a simple analysis to reveal useful insight about the nature prototypical networks. Specifically, the model is equivalent to a linear model when Euclidean distance $d(\mathbf{z}, \mathbf{z}') = \|\mathbf{z} - \mathbf{z}'\|^2$ is used. Let us rewrite the term inside the exponent of Eq. (3.13) as follows:

$$-\|f_\phi(\mathbf{x}) - \mathbf{m}_k\|^2 = -f_\phi(\mathbf{x})^\top f_\phi(\mathbf{x}) + 2\mathbf{m}_k^\top f_\phi(\mathbf{x}) - \mathbf{m}_k^\top \mathbf{m}_k \tag{3.15}$$

The first term of the above equation is a constant for each class k, therefore, it can be removed without affecting the softmax probabilities. The remaining terms form a linear model with the weights $\mathbf{w}_k$, bias

b_k, and the feature $f_\phi(\mathbf{x})$ as below:

$$2\mathbf{m}_k^\top f_\phi(\mathbf{x}) - \mathbf{m}_k^\top \mathbf{m}_k = \mathbf{w}_k^\top f_\phi(\mathbf{x}) + b_k, \text{ where } \mathbf{w}_k = 2\mathbf{m}_k \text{ and } b_k = -\mathbf{m}_k^\top \mathbf{m}_k \qquad (3.16)$$

While this is similar to a linear model when $d(.,.)$ is a square Euclidean distance, the original papers show that prototypical networks are effective since the embedding function $f_\phi(\mathbf{x})$ can take care of nonlinearity within the data. Nevertheless, this interpretation is useful for understanding ProtoMAML method introduced in the later section, where the weights and bias of the classifier is fine-tuned for each new task via stochastic gradient descent.

3.3.3 Comparison to matching networks

In case there is only one sample for each class in the support set, prototypical networks are equivalent to matching networks [28]. However, the two approaches are generally different for the case of more than one sample per class in the support set. First, Matching networks [28] use a weighted nearest neighbor classifier, while prototypical networks employ a linear classifier when the distance function is squared Euclidean. Second, matching networks choose the cosine distance function. Prototypical networks mainly rely on square Euclidean distance, which falls within the family of regular Bregman divergence distance. As a result, prototypical networks have a theoretical property of being equivalent to mixture density estimation.

Vinyals et al. [28] and Ravi and Larochelle [27] construct episodes by choosing N classes and k support samples per class. The values of (N, k) should be consistent with those in the test phase. Specifically, if the test phase involves performing 5-way classification and 2-shot classification, then training episodes should have of $N = 5$, $k = 2$. Prototypical networks' training was slightly different in which a higher N is used during the training phase. The authors or prototypical networks found significant benefits with this training procedure. Having a bigger number of training classes in each episode could promote the networks to learn stronger and more generalizable features. In contrast, it is usually best to train and test with the same "shot" number. While the difference in the number of shot between the training and testing phases potentially leads to decreased performance, recent work demonstrated that training with a *random* number of shots in each episode make the classifier more robust to variable shots in the inference phase [2].

3.4 Relational networks

This section introduces Relation Networks (RN) for relational reasoning [31,15]. RNs were specifically designed for performing reasoning on a complex set of input data. In what follows, we describe the mathematical formulation of relation networks. We then go over how relational networks can be used for meta learning.

3.4.1 Model architecture

A relational network module (RN) is a neural network module with a structure optimized for relational reasoning. The RN design philosophy is to constrain a neural network's functional form so that it captures the essential capabilities required for relational reasoning. In other words, the ability to understand relations among data points is encoded into the RN architecture without the need for training. This is similar to baking the ability to reason about spatial, translation invariant properties into CNNs, or the ability to reason about sequential dependencies into recurrent neural networks. RNs have the following mathematical form:

$$\text{RN}(O) = g_\phi \left(\sum_{i,j} f_\varphi(x_i, x_j) \right), \tag{3.17}$$

where $X = \{x_1, x_2, ..., x_n\}$ is the input set, $x_i \in \mathbb{R}^m$ is the vector representation i^{th} objects within the set. g_ϕ and f_φ are functions parameterized by ϕ and φ, respectively. For example, g_ϕ and f_φ can be two deep neural networks. The output of f_φ is called *relation* that describes how two objects are related to each other. Function g_ϕ summarizes pairwise relations into the final prediction. RNs enjoy three important strengths, which are baked-in relation reasoning capability, high data efficiency, and ability to operate on a set of input with an arbitrary size. The form of RNs ensures that the final output takes into account all relations among samples. One can think of RNs as learning both the existence and implication of data relations. Since RNs use a single function f_φ to score all object pairs, it can generalize better and enjoy higher data efficiency. Given n samples at the input, there are n^2 pairs for optimizing f_φ. This large number of pairs prevent the function f_φ from overfitting to a particular data pairs. In contrast, using a single neural network to replace both g_ϕ and f_φ would be inefficient. The neural network must learn to encode n^2 relations within its parameters, which quickly become intractable and prone to overfitting. Finally, the summation in Eq. (3.17) makes RNs invariant to the order of samples within the input set.

3.4.2 Relation networks for meta learning

This section shows how to modify relation networks for meta learning under the few-shot setting as done in [18]. Specifically, let us consider a RN with two modules: an *embedding* module f_φ and a *relation* module g_ϕ. Fig. 3.5 provides an overview of the learning architecture. The function f_φ embeds x_j in the query set $\mathcal{D}^{val}$, and samples x_i in the support set $\mathcal{D}^{tr}$ to a feature space $f_\varphi(x_i)$ and $f_\varphi(x_j)$, respectively. These features $f_\varphi(x_i)$ and $f_\varphi(x_j)$ are concatenated, and denoted by $\mathcal{C}(f_\varphi(x_i), f_\varphi(x_j))$.

The relation module g_ϕ maps the concatenated features to a scalar value within 0 to 1. This score is called relation score, measuring the similarity between x_i and x_j. For example, in the N-way one-shot setting, there will be N relation scores $r_{i,j}$ between one query input x_j and sample within the support set x_i,

$$r_{i,j} = g_\phi(\mathcal{C}(f_\varphi(x_i), f_\varphi(x_j))), \quad i = 1, 2, ..., N \tag{3.18}$$

For k-shot where $k > 1$, we element-wise sum over the embedding module outputs of all samples from each training class to form this class' feature map. This pooled class-level feature map is combined with the query image feature map as above. Thus, the number of relation scores for one query is always N in both one-shot or few-shot settings. The training is performed by minimizing the mean square error loss in Eq. (3.19) to obtain optimal networks' parameters. The objective is to force the relation score

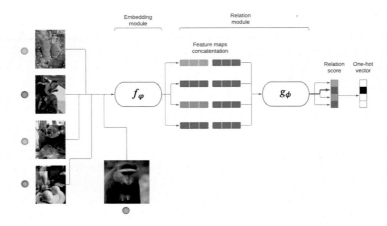

FIGURE 3.5

Relation Network architecture for a 5-way 1-shot problem with one query example [18].

$r_{i,j}$ to be close to 1 for matched pairs and the 0 for mismatched pairs.

$$\varphi, \phi \leftarrow \underset{\varphi,\phi}{\operatorname{argmin}} \sum_{i=1}^{m} \sum_{j=1}^{n} (r_{i,j} - \mathbf{1}(y_i == y_j))^2 \qquad (3.19)$$

While this training procedure considers individual labels for each relation, an alternative setting is to map all relations to one label with a set deep network [1,5,4].

3.4.3 Relationship to existing models

Related works in the literature, such as Matching Networks and Prototypical Networks, use predefined distance metrics such as Euclidean or cosine distance to perform classification [28,17]. These studies can be viewed as distance metric learning, where all the learning occurs in the feature embedding function, and the classification is done with a fixed distance function. Another metric learning approach [3] employs Mahalanobis distance with fixed feature representation. In contrast, RNs learn deep feature embedding and a distance metric. This approach is flexible and able to discover a good metric in a data-driven manner instead of relying on the manual choice of metric simultaneously.

3.5 Graph neural networks

Meta learning can be viewed as a supervised interpolation problem on a graph, in which nodes correspond to data samples, and edges are given by a trainable similarity function. This section introduces a simple graph-based few-shot learning model that implements a task-driven message passing algorithm [16]. Graph neural networks naturally apply to this setting. Specifically, graph neural networks allow end-to-end training and can capture metaknowledge across tasks. In what follows, the procedure of adapting graph neural networks to meta learning tasks will be discussed in detail.

3.5.1 General setup

We first introduce the general setup and notations, and then describe the meta learning setting. Let us consider input-output pairs $(\mathcal{T}_i, Y_i)_i$ drawn i.i.d. from a distribution P of partially-labeled image collections.

$$\mathcal{T} = \left\{ \{(x_1, y_1), \ldots (x_s, y_s)\}, \{\bar{x}_1, \ldots, \bar{x}_t\} \right\}; \tag{3.20}$$

$$y_i \in \{1, C\}, x_i, \bar{x}_j \sim \mathcal{P}_l(\mathbb{R}^d), \tag{3.21}$$

$$Y = (\bar{y}_1, \ldots, \bar{y}_t) \in \{1, C\}^t, \tag{3.22}$$

for arbitrary values of s, t, and C. In this case, (s, t, C) are respectively the number of labeled samples, the number of samples to classify, and the number of classes. Let $\mathcal{P}_l(\mathbb{R}^d)$ denote a class-specific image distribution over $\mathbb{R}^d$. In our context, Y_i correspond to the ground truth labels of images $\bar{x}_1, \ldots, \bar{x}_t$ that we need to estimate. Given a collection of tasks $\{(\mathcal{T}_i, Y_i)_i\}_{i \leq L}$, we formulate the learning under standard supervised setting as follows:

$$\min_{\phi} \frac{1}{L} \sum_{i \leq L} \mathcal{L}(\gamma(\mathcal{T}_i; \phi), Y_i) + \mathcal{R}(\phi),$$

the choice of $\gamma(\mathcal{T}; \phi) = p(Y \mid \mathcal{T})$ will be discussed in Section 3.5.2. $\mathcal{R}$ is a regularization term. For the q-shot, C-way learning setting, label appears exactly q times for each class in $\mathcal{T}$.

3.5.2 Model architecture

This section first describes how the input data are embedded into a graphical representation, then goes over the architecture, and finally demonstrates how this model generalizes a variety of previously reported few-shot learning designs [16].

Graph Input Representations: The input $\mathcal{T}$ is represented by a collection of labeled and unlabeled images. Note that this is slightly different from the task definition introduced in previous sections, where tasks do not involve unlabeled data samples. The goal is to use graph neural networks as a tool for propagating label information from labeled samples towards the unlabeled query image. This propagation of information can be viewed as a posterior inference over a graphical model specified by the input images and labels.

Formally, let us define a task $\mathcal{T}$ using a fully-connected graph $G_{\mathcal{T}} = (V, E)$ where vertices/nodes correspond to both labeled and unlabeled data samples. This is similar to recent works which formulate the posterior inference problem under message passing with neural networks over graphs [10,32,7]. Note that this approach does not specify a fixed similarity metric between two vertices. Instead, the similarity function is learned in a discriminative fashion using siamese neural networks.

Graph Neural Networks: Graph Neural Networks were first introduced in [8,10] and further improved in [30,32,11]. These networks are based on local operators of a graph $G = (V, E)$, where V denote the set of vertices and E the set of edges as shown in Fig. 3.6. Readers are referred to the recent survey [6] for recent works and applications of graph neural networks.

Given an input signal $\mathbf{x} \in \mathbb{R}^{|V| \times d}$ on the vertices of a graph G, a simple version of GNNs utilizes a family $\mathcal{A}$ of graph intrinsic linear operators that transform the data locally. One example is *adjacency operator* $A : \mathbf{x} \to A(\mathbf{x})$ defined as follows:

$$(A\mathbf{x})_i := \sum_{j \sim i} w_{i,j} \mathbf{x}_j , \tag{3.23}$$

where $\mathbf{x}_j$ is the jth row of $\mathbf{x}$, $i \sim j$ iff an edge between the two vertices $(i, j) \in E$ is present, and $w_{i,j}$ its associated weight. This operator essentially updates the feature vector at each vertex by taking the weighted average of neighboring features. A graph neural network's layer GNN(.) receives as input a signal $\mathbf{x}^{(l)} \in \mathbb{R}^{V \times d_l}$ and produces $\mathbf{x}^{(l+1)} \in \mathbb{R}^{|V| \times d_{l+1}}$ as below. Here, l is the layer's index in GNNs.

$$\mathbf{x}_l^{(l+1)} = \text{GNN}(\mathbf{x}^{(l)}) = \rho \left(\sum_{A \in \mathcal{A}} A\mathbf{x}^{(l)} \phi_{A,l}^{(l)} \right) , \; l = d_1 \ldots d_{l+1} , \tag{3.24}$$

where $\phi_A^{(l)} \in \mathbb{R}^{d_l \times d_{l+1}}$, are trainable parameters and $\rho(\cdot)$ is a element-wise nonlinear rectifier like a 'leaky' ReLU [13] function. Increasing the number of GNN layers will lead to higher expressibility.

Learning edge features and weights: Recent works employ message-passing algorithms, [9,7] to enable GNNs to learn edge features from the node hidden representation. In a similar spirit, we can formulate the problem of learning edge weights as follows:

$$\tilde{A}_{i,j}^{(l)} = \varphi_{\tilde{\phi}}(\mathbf{x}_i^{(l)}, \mathbf{x}_j^{(l)}) , \tag{3.25}$$

where $\tilde{A}_{i,j}^{(l)}$ denotes the adjacency score of the edge corresponding to i-th and j-th vertices in l-layer. φ is a symmetric function parametrized with a neural network. The form of φ is defined in Eq. (3.26), where a multilayer neural network is applied on the absolute difference between two hidden node representations.

$$\varphi_{\tilde{\phi}}(\mathbf{x}_i^{(l)}, \mathbf{x}_j^{(l)}) = \text{NN}_{\tilde{\phi}}(abs(\mathbf{x}_i^{(l)} - \mathbf{x}_j^{(k)})) \tag{3.26}$$

Here, φ is a learned metric that satisfies distance properties such as *Symmetry* $\varphi_{\tilde{\phi}}(a, b) = \varphi_{\tilde{\phi}}(b, a)$ and *Identity* $\varphi_{\tilde{\phi}}(a, a) = 0$. The adjacency scores are then normalized using a softmax along each row to produce the edge weights $w_{i,j}$ and store them in a kernel matrix $A^{(l)} = \text{softmax}(-\tilde{A}^{(l)})$. We obtain node features' update rules by inserting the edge feature kernel $A^{(l)}$ into the operator family $\mathcal{A} = \{A^{(l)}, \mathbf{1}\}$ and applying the operation in Eq. (3.24). The identity matrix $\mathbf{1}$ represents self-edges and allows GNN to aggregate information from a vertex's own features. This is similar to adding a skip connection. Learning adjacency metric is beneficial for applications where the input set with geometric structure, but information about similarity metric is not known in advance.

Construction of Initial Node Features: The input collection $\mathcal{T}$ is mapped into node features as follows. For sample $x_i \in \mathcal{T}$ with known label y_i, the one-hot encoding of ground truth label is stacked with the feature vector to form the input of the GNN.

$$\mathbf{x}_i^{(0)} = (\phi(x_i), h(y_i)) , \tag{3.27}$$

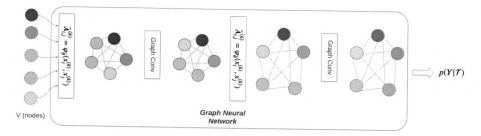

FIGURE 3.6

Illustration of a Graph Neural Network (GNN). Each task provides a set of labeled and unlabeled samples as the inputs to the network. GNN propagates information over several layers before computing the prediction of unknown labels [16].

where $h(y)$ is a one-hot encoding of the label, and ϕ a convolutional neural network. For sample $\bar{x}_j$ with unknown label $\bar{y}_i$, the model initially assigns a constant value to all classes to account for the uncertainty. This is done by replacing $h(y)$ with the uniform distribution over the C-simplex

$$V_j = (\phi(\bar{x}_j), C^{-1}\mathbf{1}_C) \tag{3.28}$$

3.5.3 Graph neural networks for meta learning

This section explains how GNNs can be configured for the few-shot learning setting. The goal is to predict the label Y corresponding to the image to classify $\bar{x} \in \mathcal{T}$, associated with node $*$ in the graph. To this end, we can configure the final layer of the GNN with softmax function to map the node features to the C-dimensional output. The model is trained using cross-entropy loss evaluated at an unlabeled node $*$:

$$\mathcal{L}(\gamma(\mathcal{T}; \phi), Y) = -\sum_k y_k \log P(Y_* = y_k \mid \mathcal{T}).$$

Note that the graph G differs from task to task. However, all tasks share the adjacency operators, edge similarity function, and classification layer. These are the metaknowledge captured by GNNs that generalize across tasks.

3.5.4 Relationship with existing models

Popular meta learning models in the literature can be viewed as special cases of GNNs with a certain configuration of the similarity function and adjacency operator.

Siamese Networks: Siamese Networks [26] is equivalent to a single layer GNN model. The initial node embedding is a concatenation of features and one-hot encoding label, which is the same as in general GNNs. In contrast, the edge similarity function is fixed. The following GNN configuration will make it equivalent to Siamese Networks:

$$\mathbf{x}_i^{(0)} = (\phi(x_i), h(y_i)), \tag{3.29}$$

$$\varphi(\mathbf{x}_i, \mathbf{x}_j) = \|\phi(x_i) - \phi(x_j)\| , \tag{3.30}$$

$$A^{(0)} = \text{softmax}(-\varphi) , \tag{3.31}$$

and the label prediction is given by:

$$\hat{Y}_* = \sum_j A^{(0)}_{*,j} \langle \mathbf{x}^{(0)}_j, u \rangle ,$$

where the dot product $\langle \mathbf{x}^{(0)}_j, u \rangle$ selects the label field from $\mathbf{x}$. The model essentially just performs learning of image embeddings $\phi(x_i)$ so that the Euclidean distances among these embeddings are aligned with their label similarities.

Prototypical Networks: Prototypical networks [17] extend Siamese networks by computing a prototype (i.e., mean of features) within each cluster corresponding to all nodes with the same label. The following GNN settings can give rise to a similar operation:

$$A^{(0)}_{i,j} = \begin{cases} q^{-1} & \text{if } y_i = y_j \\ 0 & \text{otherwise,} \end{cases}$$

where q is the number of samples in each class, and

$$\mathbf{x}^{(1)}_i = \sum_j A^{(0)}_{i,j} \mathbf{x}^{(0)}_j , \tag{3.32}$$

where $\mathbf{x}^{(0)}$ is defined as Eq. (in (3.29)). We then compute the edge similarity kernel $A^{(1)} = \text{softmax}(\varphi)$ for $\mathbf{x}^{(1)}$. The class label predictions are obtained by:

$$\hat{Y}_* = \sum_j A^{(1)}_{*,j} \langle \mathbf{x}^{(1)}_j, u \rangle \tag{3.33}$$

Here, u selects the label field from $\mathbf{x}^{(1)}_j$ as before.

Matching Networks: Matching networks [28] use a set representation for a collection of samples in $\mathcal{T}$. This is closely related to graph neural network model. The attention mechanism behind the set representation is similar to the edge feature learning in GNNs. However, Matching Networks' attention mechanism always operates on the same node embeddings, as opposed to multilayer adjacency learning in GNNs. In this case, GNNs are closer to [12] where the attention mechanism operates on a different embedding at each layer. Specifically, matching networks employs attention mechanisms of the form $A^{(k)}_{*,j} = \varphi(\mathbf{x}^{(k)}_*, \mathbf{x}^{(T)}_j)$, where $\mathbf{x}^{(T)}_j$ are the embeddings for the elements of the support set. These embeddings are computed by feeding the support to bidirectional LSTMs, and fixed afterward. In this case, the support set embedding is performed independently of the target image. Moreover, Matching Networks treat labels and data separately in the computation, except in the final step where labels are aggregated linearly. GNNs operate jointly on labels and data, which potentially enable the models to leverage rich dependencies between the two input fields.

References

[1] Juho Lee, Yoonho Lee, Jungtaek Kim, Adam Kosiorek, Seungjin Choi, Yee Whye Teh, Set transformer: a framework for attention-based permutation-invariant neural networks, in: International Conference on Machine Learning, PMLR, 2019, pp. 3744–3753.

[2] Pengyu Yuan, Aryan Mobiny, Jahandar Jahanipour, Xiaoyang Li, Pietro Antonio Cicalese, Badrinath Roysam, Vishal M. Patel, Maric Dragan, Hien Van Nguyen, Few is enough: task-augmented active meta-learning for brain cell classification, in: International Conference on Medical Image Computing and Computer-Assisted Intervention, Springer, 2020, pp. 367–377.

[3] Thomas Mensink, Jakob Verbeek, Florent Perronnin, Gabriela Csurka, Metric learning for large scale image classification: generalizing to new classes at near-zero cost, in: European Conference on Computer Vision, Springer, 2012, pp. 488–501.

[4] Samira Zare, Hien Van Nguyen, Picaso: permutation-invariant cascaded attentional set operator, arXiv preprint, arXiv:2107.08305, 2021.

[5] Manzil Zaheer, Satwik Kottur, Siamak Ravanbakhsh, Barnabas Poczos, Ruslan Salakhutdinov, Alexander Smola, Deep sets, arXiv preprint, arXiv:1703.06114, 2017.

[6] Michael M. Bronstein, Joan Bruna, Yann LeCun, Arthur Szlam, Pierre Vandergheynst, Geometric deep learning: going beyond Euclidean data, IEEE Signal Processing Magazine 34 (4) (2017) 18–42.

[7] Justin Gilmer, Samuel S. Schoenholz, Patrick F. Riley, Oriol Vinyals, George E. Dahl, Neural message passing for quantum chemistry, arXiv preprint, arXiv:1704.01212, 2017.

[8] M. Gori, G. Monfardini, F. Scarselli, A new model for learning in graph domains, in: Proc. IJCNN, 2005.

[9] Steven Kearnes, Kevin McCloskey, Marc Berndl, Vijay Pande, Patrick Riley, Molecular graph convolutions: moving beyond fingerprints, Journal of Computer-Aided Molecular Design 30 (8) (2016) 595–608.

[10] Franco Scarselli, Marco Gori, Ah Chung Tsoi, Markus Hagenbuchner, Gabriele Monfardini, The graph neural network model, IEEE Transactions on Neural Networks 20 (1) (2009) 61–80.

[11] Sainbayar Sukhbaatar, Rob Fergus, et al., Learning multiagent communication with backpropagation, in: Advances in Neural Information Processing Systems, 2016, pp. 2244–2252.

[12] Ashish Vaswani, Noam Shazeer, Niki Parmar, Jakob Uszkoreit, Llion Jones, Aidan N. Gomez, Lukasz Kaiser, Illia Polosukhin, Attention is all you need, arXiv preprint, arXiv:1706.03762, 2017.

[13] Bing Xu, Naiyan Wang, Tianqi Chen, Mu Li, Empirical evaluation of rectified activations in convolutional network, arXiv preprint, arXiv:1505.00853, 2015.

[14] J. Snell, K. Swersky, R.S. Zemel, Prototypical networks for few shot learning, in: NeurIPS, 2017.

[15] Adam Santoro, David Raposo, David G.T. Barrett, Mateusz Malinowski, Razvan Pascanu, Peter Battaglia, Timothy Lillicrap, A simple neural network module for relational reasoning, arXiv preprint, arXiv:1706.01427, 2017.

[16] V. Garcia, J. Bruna, Few-shot learning with graph neural networks, in: ICLR, 2018.

[17] Jake Snell, Kevin Swersky, Richard Zemel, Prototypical networks for few-shot learning, in: Advances in Neural Information Processing Systems, 2017, pp. 4077–4087.

[18] Flood Sung, Yongxin Yang, Li Zhang, Tao Xiang, Philip H.S. Torr, Timothy M. Hospedales, Learning to compare: relation network for few-shot learning, in: Proceedings of the IEEE Conference on Computer Vision and Pattern Recognition, 2018, pp. 1199–1208.

[19] S. Hochreiter, J. Schmidhuber, Long short-term memory, Neural Computation (1997).

[20] E. Hoffer, N. Ailon, Deep metric learning using triplet network, in: Similarity-Based Pattern Recognition, 2015.

[21] B.M. Lake, R. Salakhutdinov, J. Gross, J. Tenenbaum, One shot learning of simple visual concepts, in: CogSci, 2011.

[22] S. Roweis, G. Hinton, R. Salakhutdinov, Neighbourhood component analysis, in: NIPS, 2004.

[23] I. Sutskever, O. Vinyals, Q.V. Le, Sequence to sequence learning with neural networks, in: NIPS, 2014.

[24] K. Weinberger, L. Saul, Distance metric learning for large margin nearest neighbor classification, in: JMLR, 2009.

[25] Arindam Banerjee, Srujana Merugu, Inderjit S. Dhillon, Joydeep Ghosh, Clustering with Bregman divergences, Journal of Machine Learning Research 6 (Oct) (2005) 1705–1749.

[26] Gregory Koch, Siamese neural networks for one-shot image recognition, Master's thesis, University of Toronto, 2015.

[27] Sachin Ravi, Hugo Larochelle, Optimization as a model for few-shot learning, in: International Conference on Learning Representations, 2017.

[28] Oriol Vinyals, Charles Blundell, Tim Lillicrap, Daan Wierstra, et al., Matching networks for one shot learning, in: Advances in Neural Information Processing Systems, 2016, pp. 3630–3638.

[29] Jane Bromley, James W. Bentz, Léon Bottou, Isabelle Guyon, Yann LeCun, Cliff Moore, Eduard Säckinger, Roopak Shah, International Journal of Pattern Recognition and Artificial Intelligence (1993).

[30] Yujia Li, Daniel Tarlow, Marc Brockschmidt, Richard Zemel, Gated graph sequence neural networks, in: ICLR, 2016.

[31] David Raposo, Adam Santoro, David Barrett, Razvan Pascanu, Timothy Lillicrap, Peter Battaglia, Discovering objects and their relations from entangled scene representations, arXiv:1702.05068, 2017.

[32] David Duvenaud, Dougal Maclaurin, Jorge Aguilera-Iparraguirre, Rafael Gómez-Bombarelli, Timothy Hirzel, Alán Aspuru-Guzik, Ryan P. Adams, Convolutional networks on graphs for learning molecular fingerprints, in: Neural Information Processing Systems, 2015.

Meta learning by optimization

4

Pengyu Yuan and Hien Van Nguyen

Department of Engineering & Computer Engineering, University of Houston, Houston, TX, United States

Few-shot learning setting is challenging for gradient-based optimization for several reasons. First, popular gradient-based optimizers [11,10,9,33,34] are highly flexible with the updating rules applied to a large number of parameters. This property makes it prone to overfitting when there are only a few training samples. Since the loss function is nonconvex, these algorithms do not guarantee the speed of convergence, beyond the fact that they can converge to local optima after many iterations provided that the initialization and hyperparameters are selected correctly. Second, the network usually starts from a random parameter initialization for each new task, making it challenging to converge with only a few iterations. Transfer learning and domain adaptation techniques [1,2] can mitigate this problem by initializing parameters with those of a pretrained network from another task where more labels are available. However, the benefit of these approaches greatly decreases when the training and testing tasks diverge. Developing a systematic mechanism to benefit from common initialization while guaranteeing fast convergence is vital to dealing with few-shot learning setting. To this end, optimization-based meta learning algorithms seek optimal initialization that would enable knowledge transfer across tasks and fast convergence speed under a limited number of samples.

Optimization-based meta learning algorithms include those where the inner-level learning (Eq. (2.9)) is literally done by solving an optimization problem. These methods focus on extracting metaknowledge ϕ required to improve optimization performance. A famous example is MAML [3], which aims to learn the initialization $\phi = \theta_0$ (or a base model), such that a few gradient-based updating steps yield a classifier that performs optimally on validation data. More elaborate alternatives also learn step sizes [5,6] or train recurrent networks to predict steps from gradients [22,7,4].

4.1 Optimization as model

This section presents a method to address the weakness of neural networks' training procedure based on gradient-based optimization under a limited number of samples. The central theory is that a recurrent network can learn to optimize neural networks better than traditional gradient descent algorithms [22]. We call this recurrent network a metalearner, which is designed to capture both short-term knowledge within a task and long-term knowledge shared among all the tasks. During the training phase, the metalearner only uses a few samples in each task to optimize a task-specific network. This constraint forces the metalearner to capture the optimization knowledge required to enable fast convergence to good solutions under limited numbers of training samples.

4.1.1 Model architecture

Let $D = \{D^{tr}, D^{val}\} \in \mathcal{D}_{meta-train}$ define a training episode, and a task-specific neural network parametrized by θ to be optimized on D^{tr}. The traditional gradient descent procedure performs the following update:

$$\theta_t = \theta_{t-1} - \alpha_t \nabla_{\theta_{t-1}} \mathcal{L}_t \tag{4.1}$$

where (θ_{t-1}, θ_t) denote the network's parameters after $t - 1$ and t updates, respectively. α_t is the learning rate at time t, $\nabla_{\theta_{t-1}} \mathcal{L}_t$ is the gradient of the loss function $\mathcal{L}_t$ with respect to parameters θ_{t-1}. A key observation is that the update in (4.1) resembles the update for the memory cell in an LSTM recurrent network [36] as seen below:

$$c_t = f_t \odot c_{t-1} + i_t \odot \tilde{c}_t \tag{4.2}$$

where c_t is the memory cell state, $\tilde{c}_t$ the new candidate memory, (f_t, i_t) are respectively the forget and input gates. The input and forget gates are between 0 and 1. When setting $f_t = 1$, $c_{t-1} = \theta_{t-1}$, $i_t = \alpha_t$, and $\tilde{c}_t = -\nabla_{\theta_{t-1}} \mathcal{L}_t$, the LSTM update rule is identical to gradient descent procedure. Thus, we propose to use LSTM as our metalearner to learn an optimization strategy to train task-specific neural networks with the following configuration

$$c_t = \theta_t, \tag{4.3}$$

$$\tilde{c}_t = -\nabla_{\theta_{t-1}} \mathcal{L}_t, \tag{4.4}$$

$$i_t = \sigma(W_I . [\nabla_{\theta_{t-1}} \mathcal{L}_t, \mathcal{L}_t, \theta_{t-1}, i_{t-1}] + b_I), \tag{4.5}$$

$$f_t = \sigma(W_F . [\nabla_{\theta_{t-1}} \mathcal{L}_t, \mathcal{L}_t, \theta_{t-1}, f_{t-1}] + b_F) \tag{4.6}$$

Given that gradient is valuable for optimization, we set the candidate cell state to be the negative of gradient. The input gate and forget gate are computed from a rich set of information, including the gradient at the current time step, the loss value, the previous model's parameters, and the previous input and forget gate values. In this way, the metalearner is capable of extracting a sophisticated mechanism for adjusting the learning rate to achieve fast convergence and a good solution.

Finally, the initial value of the cell state c_0 for the LSTM is equivalent to the initialization in of the task-specific weights. Since a good initialization is critical, these parameters are also learnable during the training procedure. In this way, the optimization of the task-specific neural network begins from a good starting point that can facilitate fast convergence.

4.1.2 Parameter sharing and training strategy

Because we want our metalearner to create updates for deep neural networks, which have tens of thousands of parameters, we need to use parameter sharing to avoid an explosion of metalearner parameters. As in [9], parameters can be shared across learner gradient coordinates. In this way, each coordinate has its own hidden and cell state values, while the LSTM parameters are the same for all coordinates. This allows us to utilize a small LSTM model and has the added benefit of using the same update strategy for each coordinate, but one that is reliant on the respective history of each coordinate during optimization. The inputs to LSTM for i-th dimension are $(\nabla_{\theta_{t,i}} \mathcal{L}_t, \mathcal{L}_t)$.

Because the magnitudes of the gradients and losses might vary greatly, we must exercise caution while normalizing the values so that the metalearner can utilize them correctly during training. As a result, we discovered that the preprocessing strategy of [9] functioned effectively when applied to both the gradient and loss dimensions at each time step:

$$x \to \begin{cases} (\log(|x|)/p, \, sgn(x)), & \text{if } \|x\| \geq e^{-p} \\ (-1, e^p x) & \text{otherwise} \end{cases} \tag{4.7}$$

This preprocessing modifies the scale of gradients and losses while also segregating the magnitude and sign information. Empirical results show that [22] the value of $p = 10$ in the above formula worked well.

It is worth noting that the modeling of this approach implies that the learner's losses $\mathcal{L}_t$ and gradients $\nabla_{\theta_{t-1}} \mathcal{L}_t$ are dependent on the parameters of the metalearner. Gradients on the metaparameters learner's should generally account for this reliance. This, however, complicates the computation of the metagradients as seen in [9]. Thus, we use the simplistic assumption that their contributions to the gradients are insignificant and can be ignored, allowing us to avoid considering second derivatives, which is a costly process. Despite this simplifying assumption, metalearner can still be trained well in practice.

4.2 Model-agnostic meta learning

This section describes a task-agnostic meta learning (MAML) [15] technique that trains a model's parameters so that a minimal number of gradient updates results in quick learning on a new task. The central idea behind this strategy is to train the model's initial parameters so that the model performs optimally on a new job after the parameters have been modified using one or more gradient steps computed under a limited amount of data from that new task. Unlike previous meta learning methods that learn an update function or learning rule [30,27,26,29], this algorithm does not increase the number of learned parameters or impose constraints on the model architecture such as recurrent model [32] or a Siamese [28]. The approach easily applies to fully connected, convolutional, and a wide range of loss functions.

One can view MAML as learning a good initialization that is applicable for many tasks. Using this initialization, the model can obtain a good task-specific model using only a few gradient updates or even a single gradient update. The training procedure favors the initialization that can be fine-tuned rapidly while still producing good prediction results. One can also view this approach as maximizing the loss function's sensitivity to the parameters so that a little adaptation can significantly improve the results of new tasks.

From a feature learning approach, the process of training a model's parameters so that a few gradient steps may provide strong results on a new task can be considered as constructing an internal representation that is generically applicable to numerous tasks. If the internal representation is applicable for a wide range of tasks, a little fine-tuning of the parameters, such as altering the top layer weights in a feedforward model, can yield good results. In fact, our technique optimizes for models that are simple and quick to fine-tune, allowing adaptation to occur in the appropriate domain for rapid learning. From the perspective of dynamical systems, the learning process may be understood as increasing the sensitivity of the loss functions of new tasks to parameters so that tiny local changes to the parameters can lead to huge improvements in task loss.

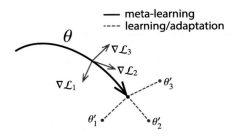

FIGURE 4.1

Diagram of our model-agnostic meta learning algorithm (MAML), which optimizes for a representation θ that can quickly adapt to new tasks. Figure is adopted from [15].

4.2.1 A model-agnostic meta learning algorithm

Unlike previous work, which focused on training recurrent neural networks [32,37] or feature embeddings [31,28], MAML proposes a way to learn the parameters of any standard model via meta learning in so that it is ready for fast adaptation. This technique is based on the assumption that some internal representations are more transferable than others. A neural network, for example, may acquire intrinsic characteristics that are widely relevant to all tasks in $p(task)$ rather than a single specific task. How might we promote the formation of such all-purpose representations? We adopt an explicit approach to this problem: because the model will be fine-tuned on a new task using a gradient-based learning rule, we will build a model in such a way that this gradient-based learning rule can make quick progress on new tasks selected from $p(\mathcal{T})$ without overfitting. In essence, we will seek model parameters that are sensitive to changes in the task so that minor changes in the parameters result in huge improvements in the loss function of any task chosen from $p(\mathcal{T})$ when changed in the direction of the gradient of that loss. This approach makes no assumptions about the model's architecture. It only requires that the loss function is smooth enough with respect to its parameters θ so that gradient can be easily computed.

Formally, we consider a model represented by a parametrized function f_θ with parameters θ. When adapting to a new task $\mathcal{T}_i$, the model's parameters θ become θ_i' as illustrated in Fig. 4.1. The updated parameter vector θ_i' is obtained with a few gradient descent updates on each task $\mathcal{T}_i$. For example, when using one gradient update,

$$\theta_i' = \theta - \alpha \nabla_\theta \mathcal{L}_{\mathcal{T}_i}(f_\theta).$$

The step size α may be fixed or learnable. For simplicity, the rest of this section will use notation for one gradient update. The model parameters are trained by optimizing with respect to θ the performance of tasks sampled from $p(\mathcal{T})$. The metaobjective is defined as follows:

$$\min_\theta \sum_{\mathcal{T}_i \sim p(\mathcal{T})} \mathcal{L}_{\mathcal{T}_i}(f_{\theta_i'}) = \sum_{\mathcal{T}_i \sim p(\mathcal{T})} \mathcal{L}_{\mathcal{T}_i}(f_{\theta - \alpha \nabla_\theta \mathcal{L}_{\mathcal{T}_i}(f_\theta)})$$

It is worth noting that the metaoptimization is done over the model parameters θ, while the loss function is calculated using the modified model parameters θ'. In essence, our proposed strategy seeks to improve the model parameters so that a small number of gradient steps on a new task results in the most

---

Algorithm 4.1 MAML Training Procedure.

Require: $p(\mathcal{T})$: distribution over tasks; gradient descent step size α, β for inner loop and outer loop
1: randomly initialize θ
2: **while** not done **do**
3:      Sample batch of tasks $\mathcal{T}_i \sim p(\mathcal{T})$
4:      **for all** $\mathcal{T}_i$ **do**
5:          Sample K datapoints $\mathcal{D} = \{\mathbf{x}^{(j)}, \mathbf{y}^{(j)}\}$ from $\mathcal{T}_i$
6:          Evaluate $\nabla_\theta \mathcal{L}_{\mathcal{T}_i}(f_\theta)$ using $\mathcal{D}$ and $\mathcal{L}_{\mathcal{T}_i}$ in Eq. (4.9) or (4.10)
7:          Compute adapted parameters with gradient descent: $\theta_i' = \theta - \alpha \nabla_\theta \mathcal{L}_{\mathcal{T}_i}(f_\theta)$
8:          Sample datapoints $\mathcal{D}_i' = \{\mathbf{x}^{(j)}, \mathbf{y}^{(j)}\}$ from $\mathcal{T}_i$ for the metaupdate
9:      **end for**
10:     Update $\theta \leftarrow \theta - \beta \nabla_\theta \sum_{\mathcal{T}_i \sim p(\mathcal{T})} \mathcal{L}_{\mathcal{T}_i}(f_{\theta_i'})$ using each $\mathcal{D}_i'$ and $\mathcal{L}_{\mathcal{T}_i}$ in Eq. (4.9) or (4.10)
11: **end while**

---

effective behavior on that task. The optimization of metaparameters is done via stochastic gradient descent (SGD) as follows:

$$\theta \leftarrow \theta - \beta \nabla_\theta \sum_{\mathcal{T}_i \sim p(\mathcal{T})} \mathcal{L}_{\mathcal{T}_i}(f_{\theta_i'}) \tag{4.8}$$

where β denote the metastep size. Algorithm 4.1 provides the full details of this algorithm.

In principle, the MAML metagradient computation requires second-order derivatives. However, [12] recent work shows MAML model can be trained well using only first-order approximation of this gradient.

4.2.2 Training strategy

Few-shot learning has received a lot of attention in the area of supervised tasks, where the objective is to learn a new function from only a few labeled data samples for that task, while utilizing past data from related tasks for meta learning. For example, the aim may be to categorize radiographs of a COVID-19 condition using a model that has previously seen many other pneumonia and a few samples of COVID-19 images. Similarly, after training on numerous functions with comparable statistical features, the aim of few-shot regression is to predict the outputs of a continuous-valued function from only a few data points taken from that function.

In supervised regression and classification problems, the task $\mathcal{T}_i$ generates K i.i.d. observations $\mathbf{x}$, and the task loss is represented as the difference between the model's output for $\mathbf{x}$ and the related target values $\mathbf{y}$ for that observation and task. Cross-entropy and mean-squared error (MSE), which we shall discuss below, are two popular loss functions used for supervised classification and regression; however, additional supervised loss functions may be employed as well. The loss for mean-squared error regression tasks is as follows:

$$\mathcal{L}_{\mathcal{T}_i}(f_\phi) = \sum_{\mathbf{x}_j, \mathbf{y}_j \sim \mathcal{T}_i} \| f_\phi(\mathbf{x}_j) - \mathbf{y}_j \|_2^2, \tag{4.9}$$

where $\mathbf{x}_j, \mathbf{y}_j$ represent an input/output pair sampled from job $\mathcal{T}_i$. For each K-shot regression task, K input/output pairings are presented for learning. Similarly, the loss for discrete classification jobs with a cross-entropy loss is as follows:

$$\mathcal{L}_{\mathcal{T}_i}(f_\phi) = \sum_{\mathbf{x}^j,\mathbf{y}^j \sim \mathcal{T}_i} \mathbf{y}^j \log f_\phi(\mathbf{x}^j)$$

$$+ (1 - \mathbf{y}^j) \log(1 - f_\phi(\mathbf{x}^j)) \tag{4.10}$$

K-shot classification tasks, according to standard few-shot learning setting, employ K input/output pairs from each class, for a total of NK data points for N-way classification. These loss functions may be immediately placed into the equations in Section 4.2.1 to conduct meta learning, as specified in Algorithm 4.1, given a distribution across tasks $p(\mathcal{T}_i)$.

4.2.3 Prototypical MAML

This section describes a metalearner that combines the complementary strengths of Prototypical Networks (simple inductive bias) and MAML (flexible adaptation mechanism). As explained by 3.3.2, Prototypical Networks can be re-interpreted as a linear classifier applied to a learned representation $g(\mathbf{x})$. The use of a squared Euclidean distance means that output logits are expressed as:

$$-||g(\mathbf{x}^*) - \mathbf{c}_k||^2 = -g(\mathbf{x}^*)^T g(\mathbf{x}^*) + 2\mathbf{c}_k^T g(\mathbf{x}^*) - \mathbf{c}_k^T \mathbf{c}_k = 2\mathbf{c}_k^T g(\mathbf{x}^*) - ||\mathbf{c}_k||^2 + constant$$

where *constant* is a class-independent scalar that may be disregarded because it does not impact the output probabilities. As a result, the k-th unit of the equivalent linear layer contains weights $\mathbf{W}_{k,\cdot} = 2\mathbf{c}_k$ and biases $b_k = -||\mathbf{c}_k||^2$, which are both differentiable with respect to θ as they are a function of $g(\cdot; \theta)$. We refer to (fo-)Proto-MAML as the (fo-)MAML model [25] in which the task-specific linear layer of each episode is started using the Prototypical Network-equivalent weights and bias established above and then optimized on the supplied support set using MAML algorithm. Proto-MAML allows gradients to flow through the Prototypical Network-equivalent linear layer initialization while computing the update for θ. While the change is minor, empirical results show that Proto-MAML [25] considerably improves model optimization and beats vanilla MAML by a wide margin.

4.3 Almost no inner loop meta learning

The MAML method described earlier has been demonstrated to be successful in few-shot learning. Recent work in the literature [8] investigates an important question: Is the efficacy of MAML mostly due to quick learning or feature reuse? This work divides a network into the *head* (final layer) of the network and the prior levels (the *body* of the network). Each few-shot learning task has a particular alignment of output neurons and classes. For example, in one task, the output neurons may correspond to the classes (pleural effusion, cardiomegaly, and nodule). In another task, they may correspond to the classes (COVID-19, non-COVID-19 pneumonia, fibrosis). This means that the head must change for each job in order to learn the new alignment. Therefore, we are primarily concerned in the behavior of the network's body to answer the quick learning versus feature reuse question. We return to this topic in greater depth in Section

We conduct two sets of experiments to investigate the impact of fast learning versus feature reuse. First, we assess few-shot learning performance when parameters are frozen after MAML training, and

Table 4.1 Freezing consecutive layers (which prevents inner loop adaptation) has little effect on accuracy, supporting the feature reuse hypothesis. The model's performance is measured when freezing a continuous block of layers at test time to determine the degree of feature reuse occurring in the inner loop adaptation. One can notice that freezing all four convolutional layers of the network (excluding the network head) has no effect on accuracy. Layers do not need to change much during adaption time since they already have good features from the metainitialization. Table is adopted from [8].

Freeze layers	MiniImageNet-5way-1shot	MiniImageNet-5way-5shot
None	46.9 ± 0.2	63.1 ± 0.4
1	46.5 ± 0.3	63.0 ± 0.6
1, 2	46.4 ± 0.4	62.6 ± 0.6
1, 2, 3	46.3 ± 0.4	61.2 ± 0.5
1, 2, 3, 4	46.3 ± 0.4	61.0 ± 0.6

no inner loop adaptation on new tasks. Second, we employ representational similarity analysis methods to study how much the network features and representations change as the effect of the inner loop adaptation. The experiments are performed using the MiniImageNet dataset and standard convolutional networks Finn et al. [15].

4.3.1 Freezing layer representations

After MAML training, a contiguous subset of the network's layers are fixed during the inner loop during test time to investigate the influence of the inner loop adaptation. The frozen layers, in particular, are not updated to the test time task at all, and must rely on the features learned by the metainitialization for performing a new task. The accuracy of few-shot learning when freezing is compared to the accuracy when inner loop adaptation is allowed.

Table 4.1 displays the results. Even when all layers in the network body are frozen, performance barely changes. This implies that the metainitialization has already learned sufficiently strong features that can be reused for any quick learning for new tasks.

4.3.2 Representational similarity experiments

This section describes experiments that investigate how much the neural network's latent representations change during the inner loop adaptation phase. Following [20,23,19,18,21,16,13], representation change can be quantified by applying Canonical Correlation Analysis (CCA) to the network's latent representations. CCA compares representations of two (latent) layers L_1, L_2 of a neural network, producing a similarity score between 0 (least similar) and 1 (most similar). See Raghu et al. [20], Morcos et al. [19] for further information on CCA analysis. In this experiment, L_1 denotes the layer preceding the inner loop adaptation steps, and L_2 the layer after the inner loop adaptation. CCA similarity between L_1 and L_2 is computed by averaging the similarity score over distinct random seeds of the model and different test time tasks.

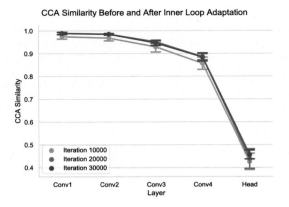

FIGURE 4.2

CCA similarity scores comparing network's representations before and after inner-loop adaptation are high for all layers except the head. Specifically, CCA similarity is almost 1 for all layers except the head. This result implies that these layers do not change much during adaptation, but instead mostly rely on feature reuse. The head of the network is expected to vary dramatically during adaptation, as seen by the much reduced CCA similarity. Figure is adopted from [8].

Fig. 4.2 (left panel) provides the result of this experiment. The representations in the network's body (the convolutional layers) are very similar (similarity scores of > 0.9). This result shows that the inner loop causes little to no functional change in representations. In contrast, the CCA similarity of the network's head does change dramatically in the inner loop (similarity score less than 0.5). To confirm this further, we compute CKA [17] (Fig. 4.2 right), another similarity measure for neural network representations that shows the same trend. These representational analysis findings strongly support the feature reuse hypothesis.

4.3.3 Feature reuse happens early in learning

After seeing that the inner loop has no effect on learned representations of trained networks, another experiment is conducted to study if the inner loop impacts representations and features early in training process. The same freezing experiments (as described in 4.3.1) are performed for MAML models saved at 10,000, 20,000, and 30,000 iterations. Representational similarities are then computed using the procedure described in 4.3.2).

Results in Fig. 4.3 show similar patterns from early steps in training. Specifically, CCA similarity between activations of the network body before and after the inner loop update on MiniImageNet-5way-5shot is extremely high. Table 4.1 shows freezing contiguous subsets of layers, or even all layers of the network body, have minimal impact on the test accuracy. This demonstrates that feature reuse takes place early in training, and the inner loop has little influence on final representations and features of new tasks.

The previous section shows that, with the exception of the neural network's head, the metainitialization learned by MAML's outer loop produces very good features that can be reused on new tasks. Even

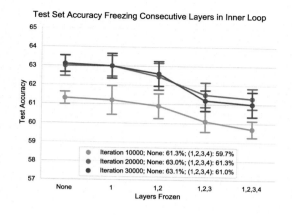

FIGURE 4.3

From the early phase of training, inner loop updates have minimal influence on learned representations. On MiniImageNet-5way-5shot, nearly equal performance were observed with or without adaptation at test time. The results suggest that feature reuse happens early in the training (iteration 10,000). Figure is adopted from [8].

Table 4.2 ANIL has comparable accuracy with MAML on few-shot image classification. Table is adopted from [8].

Method	Omniglot 20way-1shot	Omniglot 20way-5shot	MiniImageNet 5way-1shot	MiniImageNet 5way-5shot
MAML	93.7 ± 0.7	96.4 ± 0.1	46.9 ± 0.2	63.1 ± 0.4
ANIL	96.2 ± 0.5	98.0 ± 0.3	46.7 ± 0.4	61.5 ± 0.5

early in training, inner loop adaptation does not significantly alter the representations of these layers. This shows that the MAML method can be naturally simplified to an algorithm with almost no inner loop. The method is called ANIL (Almost No Inner Loop) algorithm [8]. ANIL removes the inner loop updates for the network body during training and testing, and applies inner loop adaptation to the head. The inner loop is required by the head in order for it to align to the various classes in each task.

Let $\theta = (\theta_1, ..., \theta_l)$ be the (metainitialization) parameters for the network's l layers. Let $\theta_m^{(i)}$ be the parameters for task $\mathcal{T}_i$ after u inner gradient updates. ANIL method uses the following update rule:

$$\theta_u^{(i)} = \left(\theta_1, \ldots, (\theta_l)_{u-1}^{(i)} - \alpha \nabla_{(\theta_l)_{u-1}^{(i)}} \mathcal{L}(f_{\theta_{u-1}^{(i)}}, \mathcal{T}_i) \right) \qquad (4.11)$$

That is, only the final layer receives inner loop updates. We then define the metaloss and compute the outer loop gradient update, as before. Table 4.2 compares the accuracy of ANIL to that of MAML. Because ANIL has almost no inner loop, it significantly accelerates both training and inference. An average speedup of 1.7x for each training iteration and a speedup of 4.1x for every inference iteration were observed.

Since MAML algorithm's effectiveness is largely attributable to feature reuse rather than quick learning, one can ask the same question in a broader context of meta learning paradigm. The support for feature reuse hypothesis for many other meta learning algorithms can be established by examining results published in previous work. One example is for the case of Matching Networks [35], which falls under metric learning category. Matching Networks' parameters are not directly optimized for the specific task on the support set. Instead, the model typically conditions its output on some representation of the task definition. One way to achieve this conditioning is to *jointly encode* the entire support set in the model's latent representation [35,24], enabling it to adapt to the characteristics of each task. This constitutes rapid learning for model-based meta learning algorithms.

One candidate for investigation is Matching Networks [35], which falls under the category of metric learning. Matching Networks' parameters are not directly optimized for the specific task on the support set. Instead, the model's output is often conditional on some representation of the task definition. This conditioning may be accomplished by jointly encoding the complete support set in the model's latent representation [35,24], allowing it to adapt to each task. If joint encoding improved test-time performance significantly more than nonjoint encoding, this would imply that rapid learning of the test-time task is taking place, since task-specific information is being used to impact the model's decision function.

However, based on previous research, this improvement appears to be minor. Indeed, in Matching Networks [35] with joint encoding achieves 44.2 percent accuracy on MiniImageNet-5way-1shot, whereas independent encoding achieves 41.2 percent. More refined models indicate that the gap is even narrower. For example, in Chen et al. [14], many one-shot learning methods were re-implemented and studied, and baselines without joint encoding achieved 48.24 percent accuracy in MiniImageNet-5way-1shot, whereas other models using joint encoding, such as Relation Net [24], achieved a very similar accuracy of 49.31 percent. As a result, we believe that the dominant mode behind these algorithms is "feature reuse" rather than "rapid learning". Feature reuse seems to be primarily responsible for the effectiveness of MAML, Matching Networks, and their variants.

References

[1] Sinno Jialin Pan, Qiang Yang, A survey on transfer learning, IEEE Transactions on Knowledge and Data Engineering 22 (10) (2009) 1345–1359.

[2] Vishal M. Patel, Raghuraman Gopalan, Ruonan Li, Rama Chellappa, Visual domain adaptation: a survey of recent advances, IEEE Signal Processing Magazine 32 (3) (2015) 53–69.

[3] C. Finn, P. Abbeel, S. Levine, Model-agnostic meta-learning for fast adaptation of deep networks, in: ICML, 2017.

[4] M. Andrychowicz, M. Denil, S.G. Colmenarejo, M.W. Hoffman, D. Pfau, T. Schaul, N. de Freitas, Learning to learn by gradient descent by gradient descent, in: NeurIPS, 2016.

[5] Z. Li, F. Zhou, F. Chen, H. Li, Meta-SGD: learning to learn quickly for few shot learning, arXiv e-prints, 2017.

[6] A. Antoniou, H. Edwards, A.J. Storkey, How to train your MAML, in: ICLR, 2018.

[7] K. Li, J. Malik, Learning to optimize, in: ICLR, 2017.

[8] A. Raghu, M. Raghu, S. Bengio, O. Vinyals, Rapid learning or feature reuse? Towards understanding the effectiveness of MAML, arXiv e-prints, 2019.

[9] Marcin Andrychowicz, Misha Denil, Sergio Gomez, Matthew W. Hoffman, David Pfau, Tom Schaul, Brendan Shillingford, Nando De Freitas, Learning to learn by gradient descent by gradient descent, in: Advances in Neural Information Processing Systems, 2016, pp. 3981–3989.

[10] John Duchi, Elad Hazan, Yoram Singer, Adaptive subgradient methods for online learning and stochastic optimization, Journal of Machine Learning Research 12 (7) (2011).

[11] Yurii E. Nesterov, A method for solving the convex programming problem with convergence rate o (1/k^ 2), Doklady Akademii Nauk SSSR 269 (1983) 543–547.

[12] Alex Nichol, Joshua Achiam, John Schulman, On first-order meta-learning algorithms, arXiv preprint, arXiv: 1803.02999, 2018.

[13] Anthony Bau, Yonatan Belinkov, Hassan Sajjad, Nadir Durrani, Fahim Dalvi, James Glass, Identifying and controlling important neurons in neural machine translation, arXiv preprint, arXiv:1811.01157, 2018.

[14] Wei-Yu Chen, Yen-Cheng Liu, Zsolt Kira, Yu-Chiang Frank Wang, Jia-Bin Huang, A closer look at few-shot classification, arXiv preprint, arXiv:1904.04232, 2019.

[15] Chelsea Finn, Pieter Abbeel, Sergey Levine, Model-agnostic meta-learning for fast adaptation of deep networks, in: Proceedings of the 34th International Conference on Machine Learning-Volume 70, JMLR. org, 2017, pp. 1126–1135.

[16] Akhilesh Gotmare, Nitish Shirish Keskar, Caiming Xiong, Richard Socher, A closer look at deep learning heuristics: learning rate restarts, warmup and distillation, arXiv preprint, arXiv:1810.13243, 2018.

[17] Simon Kornblith, Mohammad Norouzi, Honglak Lee, Geoffrey Hinton, Similarity of neural network representations revisited, arXiv preprint, arXiv:1905.00414, 2019.

[18] Niru Maheswaranathan, Alex H. Willams, Matthew D. Golub, Surya Ganguli, David Sussillo, Universality and individuality in neural dynamics across large populations of recurrent networks, arXiv preprint, arXiv: 1907.08549, 2019.

[19] Ari S. Morcos, Maithra Raghu, Samy Bengio, Insights on representational similarity in neural networks with canonical correlation, arXiv preprint, arXiv:1806.05759, 2018.

[20] Maithra Raghu, Justin Gilmer, Jason Yosinski, Jascha Sohl-Dickstein, SVCCA: singular vector canonical correlation analysis for deep learning dynamics and interpretability, in: Advances in Neural Information Processing Systems, 2017, pp. 6076–6085.

[21] Maithra Raghu, Chiyuan Zhang, Jon Kleinberg, Samy Bengio, Transfusion: understanding transfer learning with applications to medical imaging, arXiv preprint, arXiv:1902.07208, 2019.

[22] Sachin Ravi, Hugo Larochelle, Optimization as a model for few-shot learning, 2016.

[23] Naomi Saphra, Adam Lopez, Understanding learning dynamics of language models with SVCCA, arXiv preprint, arXiv:1811.00225, 2018.

[24] Flood Sung, Yongxin Yang, Li Zhang, Tao Xiang, Philip H.S. Torr, Timothy M. Hospedales, Learning to compare: relation network for few-shot learning, in: Proceedings of the IEEE Conference on Computer Vision and Pattern Recognition, 2018, pp. 1199–1208.

[25] Eleni Triantafillou, Tyler Zhu, Vincent Dumoulin, Pascal Lamblin, Kelvin Xu, Ross Goroshin, Carles Gelada, Kevin Swersky, Pierre-Antoine Manzagol, Hugo Larochelle, Meta-dataset: a dataset of datasets for learning to learn from few examples, arXiv preprint, arXiv:1903.03096, 2019.

[26] Marcin Andrychowicz, Misha Denil, Sergio Gomez, Matthew W. Hoffman, David Pfau, Tom Schaul, Nando de Freitas, Learning to learn by gradient descent by gradient descent, in: Neural Information Processing Systems (NIPS), 2016.

[27] Samy Bengio, Yoshua Bengio, Jocelyn Cloutier, Jan Gecsei, On the optimization of a synaptic learning rule, in: Optimality in Artificial and Biological Neural Networks, 1992, pp. 6–8.

[28] Gregory Koch, Siamese neural networks for one-shot image recognition, in: ICML Deep Learning Workshop, 2015.

[29] Sachin Ravi, Hugo Larochelle, Optimization as a model for few-shot learning, in: International Conference on Learning Representations (ICLR), 2017.

[30] Jurgen Schmidhuber, Evolutionary principles in self-referential learning. On learning how to learn: the meta-meta-... hook, Diploma thesis, Institut f. Informatik, Tech. Univ. Munich, 1987.

[31] Oriol Vinyals, Charles Blundell, Tim Lillicrap, Daan Wierstra, et al., Matching networks for one shot learning, in: Neural Information Processing Systems (NIPS), 2016.

[32] A. Santoro, S. Bartunov, M. Botvinick, D. Wierstra, T. Lillicrap, Meta-learning with memory-augmented neural networks, in: ICML, 2016.

[33] Matthew D. Zeiler, Adadelta: an adaptive learning rate method, arXiv preprint, arXiv:1212.5701, 2012.

[34] Diederik Kingma, Jimmy Ba, Adam: a method for stochastic optimization, arXiv preprint, arXiv:1412.6980, 2014.

[35] Oriol Vinyals, Charles Blundell, Tim Lillicrap, Daan Wierstra, et al., Matching networks for one shot learning, in: Advances in Neural Information Processing Systems, 2016, pp. 3630–3638.

[36] S. Hochreiter, J. Schmidhuber, Long short-term memory, Neural Computation (1997).

[37] Yan Duan, John Schulman, Xi Chen, Peter L. Bartlett, Ilya Sutskever, Pieter Abbeel, Rl2: fast reinforcement learning via slow reinforcement learning, arXiv preprint, arXiv:1611.02779, 2016.

Model-based meta learning

Pengyu Yuan and Hien Van Nguyen
Department of Engineering & Computer Engineering, University of Houston, Houston, TX, United States

5.1 Memory-augmented neural networks

5.1.1 Model architecture

The Neural Turing Machine (NTM) is made up of a controller, such as a feed-forward network or an LSTM, that communicates with an external memory module through a number of read and write heads [4]. Memory encoding and retrieval in an NTM external memory module is fast. These operations insert or retrieve vector representations out of memory at every time step. NTM is capable of both long-term storage via gradual weight updates and short-term storage via its external memory module. This capability makes the NTM an ideal option for meta learning. As a result, if an NTM can learn a general strategy to determine what to store in the memory and how to utilize them for predictions, it may be able to generate correct predictions for tasks with limited training samples.

In our model, the controllers are either LSTMs or feed-forward networks. The controller communicates with an external memory module through read and write heads, which respectively extract representations from memory and insert representations into memory. Given some input, $\mathbf{x}_t$, the controller generates a key, $\mathbf{k}_t$, based on the controller's hidden states:

$$\mathbf{k}_t = tanh(\mathbf{W}_{hk}\mathbf{h}_t + \mathbf{b}_k) \tag{5.1}$$

where $\mathbf{h}_t$ represent LSTM hidden states. The key is then used to update the information stored in a row of a memory matrix $\mathbf{M}_t$, or used to retrieve a particular memory $\mathbf{M}_t(i)$ from a row. When retrieving a memory, the cosine similarity measure is used to address $\mathbf{M}_t$,

$$K\left(\mathbf{k}_t, \mathbf{M}_t(i)\right) = \frac{\mathbf{k}_t \cdot \mathbf{M}_t(i)}{\parallel \mathbf{k}_t \parallel \parallel \mathbf{M}_t(i) \parallel}. \tag{5.2}$$

The algorithm then applies softmax on the cosine similarity K to compute each dimension of the read weights $\mathbf{s}_t^r$ as follows:

$$s_t^r(i) \leftarrow \frac{\exp\left(K\left(\mathbf{k}_t, \mathbf{M}_t(i)\right)\right)}{\sum_j \exp\left(K\left(\mathbf{k}_t, \mathbf{M}_t(j)\right)\right)}. \tag{5.3}$$

A memory, $\mathbf{r}_t$, is retrieved using this weight vector:

$$\mathbf{r}_t \leftarrow \sum_i s_t^r(i)\mathbf{M}_t(i). \tag{5.4}$$

Meta Learning With Medical Imaging and Health Informatics Applications. https://doi.org/10.1016/B978-0-32-399851-2.00012-0

This memory is concatenated with the controller's hidden vector to create the input to a classifier and input for the next controller state.

5.1.2 Least recently used access

MANN architecture employs a new memory access strategy called the Least Recently Used Access (LRUA) module. The LRUA module is a content-based memory writer that inserts new memories to the least utilized or most recently used memory location. This module focuses on the correct encoding of relevant information as well as pure content-based retrieval. New information is written into rarely-used areas (to better preserve recently encoded information) or to the most recently utilized location (to refresh memory with more relevant information). The differentiation between these two choices is achieved using an interpolation of past read weights and weights scaled according to usage scores s_t^u. At each time step, these use usage scores are updated as follows:

$$s_t^u \leftarrow \gamma s_{t-1}^u + s_t^r + s_t^w, \tag{5.5}$$

where γ is a decay parameter, and s_t^r is calculated as in Eq. (5.3). The *least-used* weights, s_t^{lu}, can then be computed for a given time-step based on s_t^u. Let $e(\mathbf{v}, n)$ denote the nth smallest element of the vector $\mathbf{v}$. Elements of s_t^{lu} are computed as follows:

$$s_t^{lu}(i) = \begin{cases} 0 & \text{if } s_t^u(i) > e(s_t^u, n) \\ 1 & \text{if } s_t^u(i) \le e(s_t^u, n) \end{cases}, \tag{5.6}$$

where n is set to equal the number of memory retrievals. The write weights s_t^w are obtained by a convex combination of previous read weights and previous least-used weights as follows:

$$s_t^w \leftarrow \sigma(\alpha)s_{t-1}^r + (1 - \sigma(\alpha))s_{t-1}^{lu}. \tag{5.7}$$

Here, $\sigma(\cdot)$ is a learnable sigmoid function, $\frac{1}{1+e^{-x}}$, and α is a scalar gate parameter controlling the contribution of two types of weights. Memory slots corresponding to least used indices are erased before the memory writing operation. Given the write weights, the new information is written to the memory according to the following rule:

$$\mathbf{M}_t(i) \leftarrow \mathbf{M}_{t-1}(i) + s_t^w(i)\mathbf{k}_t, \forall i \tag{5.8}$$

The external memory bank continuously changes as the model receives more samples. This operation makes the model depends on the order of the input sequence, even when samples in the support set do not have any natural order.

5.1.3 Training and testing procedure

The training proceeds as follows. First, the offset target label y_{t-1} and the input $\mathbf{x}_t$ is presented at each time step. In other words, the network sees the input sequence $(\mathbf{x}_1, \text{null}), (\mathbf{x}_2, y_1), \ldots, (\mathbf{x}_T, y_{T-1})$. At time t, the ground truth label corresponding to the previous data sample (y_{t-1}) is provided as input along with a new query $\mathbf{x}_t$. The network's task is to predict the label y_t for the input $\mathbf{x}_t$. Moreover, labels are shuffled from dataset to dataset to prevent the network from learning fixed sample-class bindings.

Instead, it must learn to keep data samples in memory until the relevant labels are supplied at the next time-step, at which point sample-class information may be bound and saved for later use. Thus, for a particular episode, optimal performance entails making a random guess for the first presentation of a class (since the proper label cannot be deduced from earlier episodes owing to label shuffling) and then using memory to attain perfect accuracy. Ultimately, the system aims at modeling the predictive distribution $p(y_t | D_{1:t}; \phi)$, where $D_{1:t} = \{(\mathbf{x}_1, \text{null}), (\mathbf{x}_2, y_1), \ldots, (\mathbf{x}_t, y_{t-1})\}$. The loss is measured as the difference between this predictive distribution and the ground truth information at each time step.

This task structure facilitates MANN to capture metaknowledge across tasks in the sense that the model learns to bind data representations to their labels despite (even when data representations and labels can change from task to task). Once trained, MANN does not require further parameter updates during the inference time. Given an unseen task, the network can predict the class labels from a limited number of labeled examples. For example, the network demonstrated good classification accuracy with very few examples (82.8% accuracy after the second presentation of class instances, 94.9% accuracy by the fifth instance, and 98.1% accuracy by the tenth).

Compared to optimization-based approaches, MANN allows for easier optimization without the need for second-order gradients. It has been argued, however, that model-based techniques are often less capable of generalizing to out-of-distribution tasks than optimization-based methods [5]. Furthermore, while MANN enjoys high data efficiency for few-shot learning, they have been criticized for being asymptotically weaker [5] because they struggle to incorporate a large training set into a rich base model.

5.2 Dynamic few shot visual learning
5.2.1 Problem setup

This section describes a dynamic network [7] capable of generating weights to classify new class labels given a few support samples. Let us assume that a dataset of C base categories is given as an input for training purposes:

$$D_{train} = \bigcup_{i=1}^{C} \{x_{i,j}\}_{j=1}^{N_i}, \tag{5.9}$$

where N_i and $x_{i,j}$ are respectively the number of training examples and j-th sample in the i-th category. The objective is to perform meta learning so that the system is able to classify novel classes while not forgetting the base ones. Fig. 5.1 provides an overview of this approach. There are two main components which are *Convolutional Network-based model* for classifying class labels, and a *weight generator* that dynamically creates weight vectors for new categories at test time.

The Convolutional Network-based model can be divided into (i) a feature extractor $e(.|\theta)$ that extracts a d-dimensional embedding $z = e(x|\theta_e) \in \mathbb{R}^d$ from an input x, and (ii) a classifier $f(.|\theta_f)$, where $\theta_f = \{\theta_{f,i} \in \mathbb{R}^d\}_{i=1}^{C}$ consists of C weight vectors, corresponding to C classes, that takes the feature embedding z to predict a K-dimensional vector containing the probability classification scores $p = f(z|\theta_f)$ of the C categories. Typically, the feature extractor is the body of a convolutional neural network (running from the first to the last hidden layer), and the classifier is the head (last layer) from

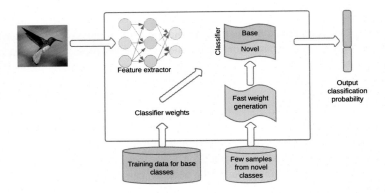

FIGURE 5.1

An overview of dynamic few-shot learning method. It is made up of (a) a Convolutional Network-based models for feature extraction and classification and (b) a few-shot weight generator. The weight generator accepts a few training data from a new category as well as classification weight vectors from base categories as input and generates a classification weight vector for this novel category. Figure is adopted from [7].

the same convolutional neural network. During our algorithm's single training phase, both embedding parameters θ_e and classification parameters $\theta_f = \{\theta_{f,i}\}_{i=1}^C$ are jointly optimized.

5.2.2 Few-shot classification weight generator

This algorithm is built around a few-shot classification weight generator $g(.,.|\phi)$. This function takes as input the feature embeddings $Z' = \{z'_i\}_{i=1}^{N'}$ of N' (typically small) training examples from a novel class, together with the base-class classification weights $\theta_f = \{\theta_{f,i}\}_{i=1}^C$, to generate new a classification weight vector $w' = g(Z', \theta_f|\phi)$ for that novel class. The rest of this section will describe two strategies to model the weight generator.

Cosine Similarity-Based Classifier. Conventional classification neural networks compute the raw classification score s_i of each category $i \in [1, C]$ using a dot-product between the input features and the classifier's weight vector:

$$s_i = z^{\mathsf{T}}\theta_{f,i} , \tag{5.10}$$

where z is the input features, $\theta_{f,i}$ is the weight vector of i-th class. The final probability is obtained with a softmax operator across all the C classification scores $p_i = softmax(s_i)$. In meta learning setting, weight vectors $\theta_{f,i}$ could be from the base classes or novel classes.

The procedures involved in learning those weights, however, are substantially different for the two cases. Starting from an initial condition, the base classification weights are gradually updated using SGD (i.e., slow learning). As a result, their magnitude varies slowly throughout the course of their training. The weight vectors generated for novel classes by g, on the other hand, dynamically predict (i.e., fast learning) the unique classification weights based on the input training feature vectors. Because of these variations, the weight values in those two scenarios (base and new classification weights) might be drastically different. This can negatively affect the training process. To address this critical issue, the cosine similarity function is used instead of the dot product to obtain raw classification scores:

$$s_i = \beta \cdot cos(z, w_i) = \beta \cdot \bar{z}^{\mathsf{T}} \bar{w}_i \, , \tag{5.11}$$

where $\bar{z} = \frac{z}{\|z\|}$ and $\bar{w}_k = \frac{w_k}{\|w_k\|}$ are the l_2-normalized vectors, and β is a learnable scalar value between $[-1, 1]$.

Because of the l_2 normalization, the absolute magnitudes of the classification weight vectors can no longer impact the value of the raw classification score. In addition to the aforementioned changes, the ReLU nonlinearity [6] after the feature extractor's last hidden layer is removed so that z can accept both positive and negative values. Aside from unifying weight vectors from both base and new classes, empirical results [7] show that the cosine-similarity-based classifier generalizes substantially better on novel categories than features learned with the dot-product based classifier.

Feature averaging based weight inference. A straightforward choice for the generator function is by averaging the feature vectors of the training examples from the novel class after they have been l_2-normalized:

$$\theta'_{avg} = \frac{1}{N'} \sum_{i=1}^{N'} \bar{z}'_i \, . \tag{5.12}$$

To increase the richness of the generated weight vector, we multiply the average feature with learnable scaling factors. The final weight vector has the following form:

$$\theta'_{f,avg} = \gamma_{avg} \odot \theta'_{avg} \, , \tag{5.13}$$

where $\odot$ is the Hadamard product, and $\gamma_{avg} \in \mathbb{R}^d$ is a learnable weight vector. *et al.* [8] previously presented a similar technique and achieved excellent results. However, this approach does not fully use the knowledge obtained by the convolutional network from the training phase with base classes. Furthermore, if the novel category only has a single training sample, feature averaging approach cannot derive an accurate weight vector.

Attention-based weight inference. We augment the earlier feature averaging process with an attention-based mechanism that composes novel weight vectors by borrowing the knowledge in base classification weight vectors $\theta_f = \{\theta_{f,i}\}_{i=1}^C$. Specifically, the novel weight vector is obtained as follows:

$$\theta'_{f,att} = \frac{1}{N'} \sum_{i=1}^{N'} \sum_{b=1}^{C} Attention(W_q \bar{z}'_i, k_i) \cdot \bar{\theta}_{f,i} \, , \tag{5.14}$$

where $W_q \in \mathbb{R}^{d \times d}$ is a learnable weight matrix that converts the feature vector $\bar{z}'_i$ to the query vector required for querying the memory. $Attention(.,.)$ is an attention mechanism based on cosine similarity function, followed by a softmax operation over the C base categories, and $\{k_i \in \mathbb{R}^d\}_{i=1}^C$ learnable keys (one per base category) used for indexing the memory. The final classification weight vector is calculated by weighting the weight vector based on feature averaging θ'_{avg} and the attention-based weight vector θ'_{att}:

$$w' = \beta_{avg} \odot \theta'_{f,avg} + \beta_{att} \odot \theta'_{f,att} \, , \tag{5.15}$$

where $\odot$ is the Hadamard product, and β_{avg}, $\beta_{att} \in \mathbb{R}^d$ are learnable scaling factors.

The base classification weight vectors capture representative feature vectors of their classes thanks to the cosine-similarity-based classifier. As a result, the base weight vectors encode visual similarity. For example, the classification vector of pneumonia related to one disease is similar to that of another disease's pneumonia than of a fibrosis condition. As a result, the classification weight vector of a novel category may be formed by linearly combining the base classification weight vectors most comparable to the few training samples of that novel category. This enables our few-shot weight generator to explicitly use the knowledge about the visual world (expressed through the base classification weight vectors) to improve few-shot recognition performance. This is a considerable improvement, particularly in the one-shot recognition situation, when averaging cannot yield an appropriate classification weight vector.

5.2.3 Training procedure

In order to learn the ConvNet-based recognition model (i.e. the feature extractor $\varphi(.|\theta_e)$ as well as the classifier $f(.|\theta_f)$) and the few-shot classification weight generator $g(.,.|\phi)$, we use as the sole input a training set $D_{train} = \bigcup_{i=1}^{C}\{x_{i,j}\}_{j=1}^{N_i}$ of C base categories. We split the training procedure into 2 stages and at each stage we minimize a different cross-entropy loss of the following form:

$$\frac{1}{C}\sum_{i=1}^{C}\frac{1}{N_i}\sum_{j=1}^{N_i}\mathcal{L}(x_{i,j}, y_j), \tag{5.16}$$

where $\mathcal{L}(x, y)$ is the negative log-probability $-\log(p_y)$ of the y-th category in the probability vector $p = f(\varphi(x|\theta_e)|\theta_f)$. The meaning of θ_f is different on each of the training stages, as we explain below.

1st training stage: During this stage we only learn the Convolutional Neural Network model without the few-shot classification weight generator. Specifically, at this stage we learn the parameters θ_e of the feature extractor $\varphi(.|\theta_e)$ and the base classification weight vectors $\theta_f = \{\theta_i\}_{i=1}^{C}$. This is done in exactly the same way as for any other standard recognition model. In this case θ_f is equal to the base classification weight vectors.

2nd training stage: During this step, the few-shot classification weight generator's parameters ϕ are trained jointly with classification weight vectors θ_f. The feature extractor does not change during this phase. To train the few-shot classification weight generator, we randomly select C_{novel} simulated novel categories from the base categories in each batch, which are treated the same way as the actual novel categories in the test time. Instead of using the classification weight vectors in θ_f for those simulated novel categories, we sample N' training examples (typically $N' \leq 5$) for each of them, compute their feature vectors $Z' = \{z'_j\}_{j=1}^{N'}$, and feed those feature vectors to the few-shot classification weight generator $g(.,.|\phi)$ to generate novel classification weight generators. For identifying the simulated new categories, the inferred classification weight vectors are applied. The whole training process is end-to-end. Classification vectors corresponding to the simulated novel categories are excluded from the base classification weight vectors used by a few-shot weight generator $g(.,.|phi)$. In this example, θ_f is the union of the simulated novel classification weight vectors created by $g(.,.|\phi)$ and the remaining base category classification weight vectors.

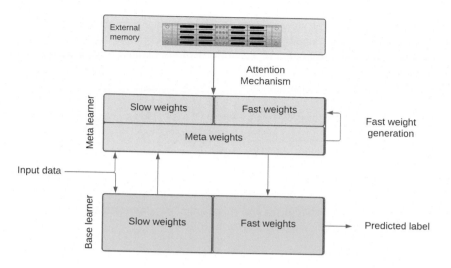

FIGURE 5.2

Overall architecture of Metanetworks. Figure is adopted from [9].

5.3 Metanetworks

By analyzing higher-order metainformation, MetaNet [9] learns to quickly parameterize underlying neural networks for rapid generalizations, resulting in a flexible AI model that can adapt to a succession of tasks with potentially varied input and output distributions. The model is divided into two major learning modules (Fig. 5.2). The first module is a metalearner responsible for quickly generating weights across tasks. The second module is a base learner that performs task-specific predictions. The produced fast weights are incorporated into both the base learner and the metalearner to modify the learners' inductive bias. To combine conventional slow weights and task-specific fast weights in a neural net, MetaNet offers a novel layer augmentation strategy.

The training procedure presented in Matching Networks Vinyals et al. [10] can be modified to train MetaNet. Specifically, the first step is to create a sequence of tasks, each consisting of a support set $\mathcal{D}^{tr}_{meta-train} = \{x_i, y_i\}_{i=1}^N$ and a validation set $\mathcal{D}^{val}_{meta-train} = \{x_i, y_i\}_{i=1}^L$. The class labels are consistent throughout both support and training sets of the same task but differ across tasks. Overall, MetaNet training consists of three primary procedures. That is, acquisition of metainformation, generation of fast weights, and optimization of slow weights, all of which are performed collaboratively by the base and metalearner. Testing of MetaNet is done by sampling a set of new tasks from a test dataset with unseen classes. The model is then used to categorize test cases based on their support set. During both training and testing, the assumption is that class labels for the support set are available.

5.3.1 Base learner

The base learner, denoted as f, is a function or a neural net that estimates the main task objective via a task loss $\mathcal{L}_{task}$. However, unlike standard neural nets, f is parameterized by slow weights W and example-level fast weights W^*. The slow weights are updated via a learning algorithm during training, whereas the fast weights are generated by the metalearner for every input.

The base learner uses a representation of metainformation obtained from a support set to provide the metalearner with feedback about the new input task. The metainformation is derived from the base learner in form of the loss gradient information:

$$\mathcal{L}_i = \mathcal{L}(f(x_i; \phi_f), y_i), \quad \text{where } (x_i, y_i) \sim \mathcal{D}^{tr}_{meta-train} \tag{5.17}$$

$$\nabla_i = \nabla_W \mathcal{L}_i \tag{5.18}$$

Where the loss function is represented by $\mathcal{L}$. The loss gradient with regard to parameters W is ∇, and that is our metainformation. We apply cross-entropy loss to train the classifier. The metalearner takes in the gradient information ∇_i for each input x_i and creates the fast parameters $\theta_f^{(i)}$ as shown in Eq. (5.20). The categorization is performed by the base learner as follows:

$$P(\hat{y}_i | x_i, \phi_f, \theta_f^{(i)}) = f(x_i; \phi_f, \theta_f^{(i)}) \tag{5.19}$$

where $\hat{y}_i$ is predicted output corresponding to $\{x_i\}_{i=1}^L$, both are drawn from the validation set $\mathcal{D}^{val}_{meta-train} = \{x_i, y_i\}_{i=1}^L$ for the task of interest. During training, given output labels $\{y_i\}_{i=1}^L$, we minimize the cross-entropy loss for few-shot learning.

5.3.2 Layer augmentation

This section describes the layer augmentation strategy for MetaNet. The key idea is that, for rapid generalization, a slow weight layer in the base learner is expanded with fast weights. Fig. 5.3 shows an example of the layer augmentation technique applied to a neural network. An augmented layer's input is initially modified by both slow and fast weights before being transformed by a nonlinear rectifier (i.e. *ReLU*), resulting in two distinct activation vectors. Finally, element-wise vector addition is used to aggregate the activation vectors. In the final *softmax* layer, the two transformed inputs are combined before being normalizing for classification prediction.

The fast and slow weights in the augmented layer can be viewed as feature detectors that operate at different domains. The use of a nonlinear rectifier transforms them into the same domain so that the activations can be combined and further processed. Although it is feasible to design the base learner using only fast weights, empirical results indicate that integrating both slow and fast weights with the layer augmentation strategy is critical for MetaNet model convergence. A MetaNet model based on a base leaner with only fast weights failed to converge, and its highest performance was not better than a trivial classifier that outputs the same label to every input.

5.3.3 Metalearner

The metalearner consists of a dynamic embedding function e, *sample-level* fast weight generation function w, *task-level* fast weight generation w', and a base classifier f. The weight generation functions w and w' are responsible for processing the metainformation and generating the sample-level and task-level fast weights, respectively. Let ∇_i denote the loss gradient derived from the base learner f

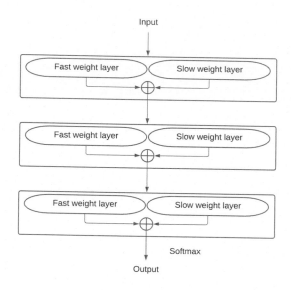

FIGURE 5.3

A layer augmented feed-forward neural network [9].

corresponding to the input $x_i \sim \mathcal{D}^{tr}_{meta-train}$. The function w learns the mapping from this loss gradient $\{\nabla_i\}^N_{i=1}$ to candidate sample-level fast weights stored in M:

$$M = \{w(\nabla_i; \phi_w)\}^N_{i=1} \tag{5.20}$$

where w is a neural network with parameter ϕ_w. The dynamic representation/embedding k_i for each input sample x_i is generated as follows:

$$\theta_e = w'(\{\nabla_i\}^T_{i=1}; \phi_{w'}) \tag{5.21}$$
$$k_i = e(x_i; \phi_e, \theta_e) \tag{5.22}$$

where the function w' is a neural network parameterized by $\phi_{w'}$ that accepts variable-sized input and produces a fixed-dimensional output θ_e, which are the task-level fast weights for the embedding function e. ϕ_e are the corresponding slow weights for e. MetaNet employs neural networks with augmented layers to model e so that both fast weights and slow weights are considered in one layer.

We sample T examples ($T \leq N$) from the support set $\{x_i, y_i\}^T_{i=1} \sim \mathcal{D}^{tr}_{meta-train}$ and obtain the loss gradient as metainformation. Then w' observes the gradient corresponding to each sampled data point and summarizes into the task-level parameters. MetaNet uses an LSTM recurrent network to represent w' although recent set-input deep networks [1,3,2] can also be used.

To classify each sample in the validation set $\mathcal{D}^{val}_{meta-train}$, MetaNet generates fast weights to modify the base learner f. Let $\theta^{(i)}_f$ denote the fast weights for a sample $x_i \sim \mathcal{D}^{val}_{meta-train}$. The model first embeds this sample into the feature space to obtain a dynamic representation k_i as in Eq. (5.22). The fast weights are computed based on the following soft attention mechanism:

$$a_i = attention(K, k_i) \tag{5.23}$$

$$\theta_f^{(i)} = norm(a_i)^\top M \tag{5.24}$$

where *attention* calculates similarity between the dynamic representation vectors from the training set $\mathcal{D}_{meta-train}^{tr}$ and the current input embedding k_i. *attention* is essentially based on cosine similarity, and *norm* is a normalization function based on *softmax*. The base learner with both fast weights θ_f and slow weights ϕ_f make prediction for each sample, which together with the ground truth labels create a task loss function. The training parameters of MetaNet consist of the slow weights $\phi = \{\phi_f, \phi_w, \phi_{w'}, \phi_e\}$ jointly updated via a training algorithm such as backpropagation to minimize the task loss.

References

[1] Juho Lee, Yoonho Lee, Jungtaek Kim, Adam Kosiorek, Seungjin Choi, Yee Whye Teh, Set transformer: a framework for attention-based permutation-invariant neural networks, in: International Conference on Machine Learning, PMLR, 2019, pp. 3744–3753.

[2] Samira Zare, Hien Van Nguyen, Picaso: permutation-invariant cascaded attentional set operator, arXiv preprint, arXiv:2107.08305, 2021.

[3] Manzil Zaheer, Satwik Kottur, Siamak Ravanbakhsh, Barnabas Poczos, Ruslan Salakhutdinov, Alexander Smola, Deep sets, arXiv preprint, arXiv:1703.06114, 2017.

[4] Alex Graves, Greg Wayne, Ivo Danihelka, Neural Turing machines, arXiv preprint, arXiv:1410.5401, 2014.

[5] C. Finn, S. Levine, Meta-learning and universality: deep representations and gradient descent can approximate any learning algorithm, in: ICLR, 2018.

[6] Vinod Nair, Geoffrey E. Hinton, Rectified linear units improve restricted Boltzmann machines, in: Icml, 2010.

[7] Spyros Gidaris, Nikos Komodakis, Dynamic few-shot visual learning without forgetting, in: Proceedings of the IEEE Conference on Computer Vision and Pattern Recognition, 2018, pp. 4367–4375.

[8] Jake Snell, Kevin Swersky, Richard Zemel, Prototypical networks for few-shot learning, in: Advances in Neural Information Processing Systems, 2017, pp. 4077–4087.

[9] Tsendsuren Munkhdalai, Hong Yu, Meta networks, in: International Conference on Machine Learning (ICML), 2017.

[10] Oriol Vinyals, Charles Blundell, Tim Lillicrap, Daan Wierstra, et al., Matching networks for one shot learning, in: Advances in Neural Information Processing Systems, 2016, pp. 3630–3638.

Meta learning for domain generalization

Swami Sankaranarayanan[a] and Yogesh Balaji[b]

[a]MIT, Cambridge, MA, United States
[b]NVIDIA, San Jose, CA, United States

6.1 Introduction

Existing machine learning algorithms including deep neural networks achieve good performance in cases where the training and the test data are drawn from the same distribution. While this is a reasonable assumption to make, it might not hold true in practice. Deploying the perception system of an autonomous vehicle in new environments not seen during training might lead to failure owing to the shift in the input data distributions. X-ray scans obtained from different laboratories can exhibit varied domain characteristics due to differences in camera parameters and image acquisition settings. Even strong learners such as deep neural networks are known to be sensitive to such domain shifts [5].

Two prominent approaches for addressing the issue of domain shift are domain adaptation and domain generalization. In domain adaptation, access to unlabeled target dataset is assumed during training. Models are then trained to minimize distributional distance between source and target feature distributions to make target representations look like source. However, access to target distribution is not always available, and it is beneficial to train robust models than can generalize to unseen target distributions. Domain generalization encompasses a class of techniques that can train models to achieve this goal of generalizing to novel target domains.

To accomplish this goal, domain generalization approaches typically make use of multiple source distributions during training. As shown in Fig. 6.1, models are trained using variations in multiple source domains so as to make them agnostic to the domain variations. A key challenge lies in how these models can be trained to enforce domain invariance. Over the recent years, meta learning has emerged as a promising approach to this problem.

Meta learning approaches for domain generalization begin by splitting the training domains into two nonoverlapping sets - one called the metatraining set and the other called the metatest set. Models are trained so that updates in metatraining set lead to a decrease in loss in the metatest set. These updates are then repeated over different samplings of the metatraining and metatest sets. Since, the updates taken by the algorithm minimize the loss in the unseen metatest set, the hope is that these models will lead to domain generalization in novel test domains. Different versions of the model updates lead to different training algorithms. We shall look at some of these algorithms in this chapter.

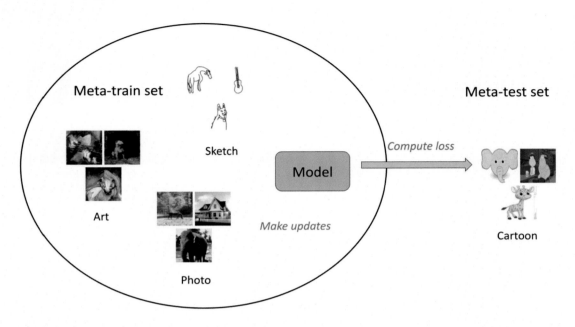

FIGURE 6.1 **Meta learning for domain generalization.**

Training domains are split into disjoint metatraining and metatest sets. Models are trained using samples from metatraining dataset so that these updates lead to a decrease in loss in the metatest set.

6.2 Related work

Over the recent years, several approaches have been proposed for domain generalization. Muandet et al. [14] propose a domain-invariant component analysis, a kernel-based optimization algorithm for minimizing the dissimilarity across domains. The use of multitask autoencoders for extracting domain-invariant feature representations has been explored in Ghifary et al. [6]. The method in [9] decomposes the parameters of a model (SVM classifier) into domain specific and domain invariant components, and uses the domain invariant parameters to make predictions on the unseen domain. Li et al. [12] extends this idea to decompose the weights of deep neural networks using multilinear model and tensor decomposition. Training models using several data augmentation strategies have also been explored. In [15], gradient-based domain perturbations are added to samples, while in [16], adversarial perturbations are used. Self-supervised pretext tasks such as solving jigsaw puzzles have also be effective for domain generalization as shown in [3].

The above approaches attempt to learn domain invariance either by explicit feature decomposition, or by using augmentation strategies. While these approaches show promising results, they would have to be tuned to specific datasets. For instance, when the type of dataset changes, the augmentation strategies used would have to be changed. Instead, in this chapter, we take a data-driven approach in which we learn the domain invariance by directly using variations in different input datasets.

6.3 Problem setup

We begin with a formal description of the domain generalization problem. Let $\mathcal{X}$ denote the instance space (which can be images, text, etc.) and $\mathcal{Y}$ denote the label space. Domain generalization involves data sampled from p source datasets and q target datasets, each containing data for performing the same task. In this chapter, we consider the classification task. Hence, $\mathcal{Y}$ is the discrete set $\{1, 2, \ldots n_c\}$, where n_c denotes the number of classes. Let $\{\mathcal{D}_i\}_{i=1}^{p+q}$ represent the $p + q$ input datasets, where each dataset $D_i = \{(\mathbf{x}_j^{(i)}, y_j^{(i)})\}_{j=1}^{n_i}$ contains samples drawn from the joint space $\mathcal{X} \times \mathcal{Y}$. In the rest of the paper, D_i is also referred to as the ith *domain*. Note that every D_i shares the same label space. In the domain generalization problem, each of the $p + q$ domains contain varied domain statistics. The objective is to train models on the p source domains so that they generalize well to the q novel target domains.

Let $M_\theta(\mathbf{x})$ denote the output of the neural network model $M(\cdot)$ acting on the input $\mathbf{x}$. On the ith domain, the network can be trained using the following cross-entropy loss

$$\min_\theta \quad \ell^{(i)}(\theta) := \mathbb{E}_{(\mathbf{x}, y) \sim \mathcal{D}_i}[-\mathbf{y}. \log(M_\theta(\mathbf{x}))] \tag{6.1}$$

Here $\mathbf{y}$ is the one-hot encoding of the label y. While this model could perform well on the ith domain, the performance on all other domains would be poor due to domain shift. One simple solution is to aggregate the data from all domains and train a classifier on the aggregated data. While this model could perform well on the in-domain datasets, there is no guarantee that it would generalize to unseen target domains, which is the objective of domain generalization.

To guarantee generalization to out of distribution data, we need to make updates to the model during training that lead to decrease in loss over unseen domains. Traditional classification loss in (6.1) does not satisfy this condition. Meta learning provides a framework to enforce this objective. More specifically, as shown in Fig. 6.1, the optimization updates involve samples from metatraining domains. The loss of the metatest set is measured using this optimized point. The model that operates on the metatraining set is updated so that the measured loss on the metatest set decreases. Different types of metaupdates lead to different training algorithms, which is explored over the next sections.

6.4 Meta learning Domain Generalization (MLDG)

The first algorithm we discuss here has a similar flavor to that of Model Agnostic Metaleaning (MAML) [4], where the initialization point in the optimization path is updated using the meta learning objective. More concretely, let us randomly choose a domain π from the p training domains as the metatest set, and use the other $p - 1$ training domains as the metatraining set. Define the metatrain and metatest losses as:

$$\ell_{mtr}(\theta) = \frac{1}{p-1} \sum_{d \in 1 \ldots p, d \neq \pi} \ell^{(d)}(\theta)$$

$$\ell_{mte}(\theta) = \ell^\pi(\theta)$$

Step 1: Starting from an initial point θ, a projection of the update is made using the metatrain loss. That is,

$$\theta' = \theta - \alpha \nabla_\theta \ell_{mtr}(\theta)$$

Step 2: From this one-step look-ahead projection of the metatrain update, the metatest loss, $\ell_{mte}(\theta')$, is measured.

The model is then updated using a combination of metatrain loss and the metatest loss

$$\min_\theta \ell_{mtr}(\theta) + \beta \ell_{mte}(\theta - \alpha \nabla_\theta \ell_{mtr}(\theta)) \tag{6.2}$$

The second term in the above equation has loss computed on the gradients of the metatraining loss. So, taking the gradient of the above loss function leads to second-order derivatives of the loss function. Once the above model is trained to convergence, it can be tested on the unseen domains. This algorithm, called MLDG, was initially proposed in [13].

We observe that this algorithm has similar flavor to that of MAML. However, the main difference lies in what is being considered as metatraining and metatest sets. In MAML, there are different tasks in metatraining and metatest sets. However, in MLDG, the metatraining and metatest sets contain the same classification task. Also, in MAML, since the objective is few-shot learning and that test tasks are different from training tasks, the final model is fine-tuned on the test tasks being evaluated. In domain generalization, however, we are not allowed to use any test samples. The final trained model is directly evaluated on the unseen test sets. The MLDG training algorithm is provided in Algorithm 6.1

Algorithm 6.1 MLDG training algorithm.

Require: n_{iter}: number of training iterations
Require: α, β: Hyperparameter
 1: **for** t in $1 : n_{iter}$ **do**
 2:     Sample a domain π from the p training domains as metatest set.
 3:     Metatrain set $\leftarrow$ Domains $\{1, 2, \ldots p\}\backslash\{\pi\}$
 4:     Obtain metatrain gradients $\nabla_\theta \ell_{mtr}(\theta)$
 5:     Obtain the projected metatrain update $\theta - \alpha \nabla_\theta \ell_{mtr}(\theta)$
 6:     Compute metatest loss from the projected update $\ell_{mte}(\theta - \nabla_\theta \ell_{mtr}(\theta))$
 7:     Update the network parameters as

$$\theta \leftarrow \theta - \nabla_\theta [\ell_{mtr}(\theta) + \beta \ell_{mte}(\theta - \alpha \nabla_\theta \ell_{mtr}(\theta))]$$

 8: **end for**

6.4.1 First order interpretation

To better interpret the training objective of Eq. (6.2), we can write the first order Taylor expansion of the metatest loss term. The first-order Taylor expansion of any function $f(\mathbf{x})$ can be written as

$$f(\mathbf{x}) = f(\mathbf{x}_0) + \nabla f(\mathbf{x}_0)^T (\mathbf{x} - \mathbf{x}_0)$$

The second term of the objective Eq. (6.2) can then be written as

$$\ell_{mte}(\theta - \alpha\nabla_\theta\ell_{mtr}(\theta)) = \ell_{mte}(\theta) + \alpha\nabla\ell_{mte}(\theta)^T[-\nabla\ell_{mtr}(\theta)]$$

Using this, the objective function of MLDG can be written as

$$\min_\theta \ell_{mtr}(\theta) + \ell_{mte}(\theta) - \alpha\beta\left[\nabla\ell_{mtr}(\theta)^T\nabla\ell_{mte}(\theta)\right]$$

We observe that MLDG objective minimizes both the metatraining and metatest loss, while maximizing the dot product between the metatraining and metatest gradients. That is, both metatraining and metatest losses are tuned in a coordinated way so that their gradients are aligned.

6.4.2 Sequential extension

Let us now look in detail of how the metatraining and metatest sets are sampled in the MLDG algorithm. First, from the p training domains, a random domain is chosen as the training set while the remaining $p - 1$ training domains are aggregated and used as training domains. This gives us p different configurations of metatrain metatest split. With a simple change in how the metatraining and metatest splits are constructed, we can get more diverse metatrain metatest samplings. In sequential variant of MLDG, training domains are considered in a sequence and meta learning is performed at each step of the sequence.

Consider a sequence of training domains $\pi_1, \ldots \pi_p$. Let $\ell(\mathcal{D}_{\pi_i}|\mathcal{D}_{1:\pi_{i-1}}, \theta)$ denote the metatest loss on the ith domain of the sequence given a model that is sequentially trained on $i - 1$ training domains. The models minimize this metatest loss with respect to initial parameters. The sequential metatraining loss can be written as

$$\min_\theta \ell(\mathcal{D}_{\pi_1}, \theta) + \beta\sum_{i=2}^{p}\ell(\mathcal{D}_{\pi_i}, \theta - \alpha\nabla_\theta\sum_{j=1}^{i-1}\ell_j)$$

Here, we use ℓ_i to denote the loss at the ith step of the sequence. That is, it is recursively defined as

$$\ell_1 = \ell(\mathcal{D}_{\pi_1}, \theta)$$
$$\ell_2 = \ell(\mathcal{D}_{\pi_2}, \theta - \alpha\nabla_\theta\ell_1)$$
$$\cdots$$
$$\ell_i = \ell(\mathcal{D}_{\pi_i}, \theta - \alpha\nabla_\theta\sum_{j=1}^{i-1}\ell_j)$$

We observe that for p domains, we obtain $p!$ different sequences, hence the number of metatraining metatest samplings have effectively been increased. This simple change to MLGD is shown to work effectively in improving the performance. The algorithm for sequential MLDG is given in Algorithm 6.2. This algorithm was proposed in [11].

Algorithm 6.2 S-MLDG training algorithm.

Require: n_{iter}: number of training iterations
Require: α, β: Hyperparameter
1: **for** t in $1 : n_{iter}$ **do**
2:     Sample a sequence of domains $\{\pi_1, \ldots \pi_p\}$.
3:     Sample mini-batches $\tilde{\mathcal{D}} = [\tilde{\mathcal{D}}_{\pi_1} \ldots \tilde{\mathcal{D}}_{\pi_p}]$ from the datasets $\{\mathcal{D}_{\pi_1}, \ldots \mathcal{D}_{\pi_p}\}$ respectively.
4:     $\tilde{\ell} = \ell(\tilde{\mathcal{D}}_{\pi_1}, \theta)$
5:     **for** i in $2 : p$ **do**
6:         $\tilde{\ell} \mathrel{+}= \beta \left(\ell(\tilde{\mathcal{D}}_{\pi_i}, \theta - \alpha \nabla \tilde{\ell}) \right)$
7:     **end for**
8:     Update $\theta \leftarrow \theta - \gamma \nabla \tilde{\ell}$
9: **end for**

6.5 Metaregularization

In the previous section, we looked at the MLGD algorithm, which is a direct extension of MAML for the domain generalization problem. This approach has the following limitations - the objective function of MAML is more suited for fast task adaptation for which it was originally proposed. In domain generalization however, we do not have access to samples from a new domain, and so a MAML-like objective might not be effective since we can't tune our model to the target task / domain. The second issue is scalability - it is hard to scale MLDG to deep architectures like Resnet-50 [8]. In this section, we look at MetaReg, an approach that attempts to tackle both these problems - (1) In Metareg [1], the objective of domain generalization is encoded in an episodic training procedure by using a regularizer to go from a task specific representation to a task agnostic representation at each episode. (2) The approach is made more scalable by freezing the feature network and performing meta learning only on the task network. This enables using Metareg for training deeper models like Resnet-50.

We are interested in training a parametric model $M_\Theta : \mathcal{X} \rightarrow \mathcal{Y}$ using data only from the p source domains. We decompose the network M into a feature network F and a task network T (i.e.) $M_\Theta(\mathbf{x}) = (T_\theta \circ F_\psi)(\mathbf{x})$, where $\Theta = \{\psi, \theta\}$. Here, ψ denotes the weights of the feature network F, and θ denotes the weights of the task network. The output of $M_\Theta(\mathbf{x})$ is a vector of dimension n_c with i^{th} entry denoting the probability that the instance $\mathbf{x}$ belongs to the class i. Standard neural network training involves minimizing the cross entropy loss function given by

$$\ell(\psi, \theta) = \mathbb{E}_{(\mathbf{x}, y) \sim D}[-\mathbf{y} . \log(M_\Theta(\mathbf{x}))] = \sum_{i=1}^{p} \sum_{j=1}^{N_i} -\mathbf{y}_j^{(i)} . \log(M_\Theta(\mathbf{x}_j^{(i)})) \qquad (6.3)$$

Here, $\mathbf{y}_j^{(i)}$ is the one-hot representation of the label $y_j^{(i)}$ and '.' denotes the dot product between two vectors. The above loss function does not take into account any factor that models domain shifts, so generalization to a new domain is not expected. To accomplish this, we propose using a regularizer $R(\psi, \theta)$. The new loss function then becomes $\tilde{\ell}_{reg}(\psi, \theta) = \ell(\psi, \theta) + R(\psi, \theta)$. The regularizer $R(\psi, \theta)$ should capture the notion of domain generalization (i.e.) it should enable generalization to a new distribution

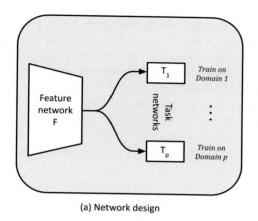 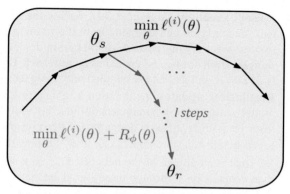

(a) Network design

(b) Learning a regularizer for generalizing from domain (i) to (j)

FIGURE 6.2 Illustration of Metareg framework.

Figure (a) depicts the network design - We employ a shared feature network F and p task networks $\{T_i\}_{i=1}^{P}$. Each task network T_i is trained only on the data from domain i, and the shared network F is trained on all p source domains. The figure on the right illustrates the optimization updates. At each iteration we sample a pair of domains (i, j) from the training set. The black arrows are the SGD updates of the task network T_i trained on domain i. From each point in the black path, we take l gradient steps using the regularized loss and the samples from domain i to reach a new point $*$. We then compute the loss on domain j at $*$. The regularizer parameters ϕ are updated so that this metaloss is minimized. This ensures that the task network T_i trained with the proposed regularizer generalizes to domain j.

with varied domain statistics. Designing such regularizers is hard in general, so we propose to learn it using meta learning.

6.5.1 Learning the regularizer

In Metareg, the regularizer R is modeled as a neural network parametrized by weights ϕ. Moreover, the regularization is applied only on the parameters θ of the task network to enable scalable meta learning. So, the regularizer is denoted as $R_\phi(\theta)$ in the rest of the chapter. We now discuss how the parameters of the regularizer $R_\phi(\theta)$ are estimated. In this stage of the training pipeline, the neural network architecture consists of a feature network F and p task networks $\{T_i\}_{i=1}^{P}$ (with parameters of T_i denoted by θ_i) as shown in Fig. 6.2. Each T_i is trained only on the samples from domain i and F is the shared network trained on all p source domains. The reason for using p task networks is to enforce domain-specificity in the models so that the regularizer can be trained to make them domain-invariant.

We now describe the procedure for learning the regularizer:

- **Base model updates:** We begin by training the shared network F and p task networks $\{T_i\}_{i=1}^{P}$ using supervised classification loss $\ell(\psi, \theta)$ given by Eq. (6.3). Note that there is no regularization in this step. Let the network parameters at the kth step of this optimization be denoted as $[\psi^{(k)}, \theta_1^{(k)}, \dots \theta_p^{(k)}]$.

- **Episode creation:** To train $R_\phi(\theta)$, we use the following episodic training procedure. Let a, b be two randomly chosen domains from the training set. Each episode contains data partitioned into two subsets - (1) m_1 labeled samples from domain a denoted as *metatrain* set and (2) m_2 labeled samples from domain b denoted as *metatest* set. The domains contained in both the sets are disjoint (i.e.) $a \neq b$, and the data is sampled only from the source distributions (i.e.) $a, b \in \{1, 2, \ldots p\}$.
- **Regularizer updates:** At iteration k, a new task network T_{new} is initialized with $\theta_a^{(k)}$ - the base model's task network parameters of the ath domain at iteration k. Using the samples from the *metatrain* set (which contains domain a), l steps of gradient descent is performed with the regularized loss function $\ell_{reg}(\psi, \theta)$ on T_{new}. Let $\hat{\theta}_a^{(k)}$ denote the parameters of T_{new} after these l gradient steps. We treat each update of the network T_{new} as a separate variable in the computational graph. $\hat{\theta}_a^{(k)}$ then depends on ϕ through these l gradient steps. The unregularized loss on the *metatest* set computed using T_{new} (with parameters $\hat{\theta}_a^{(k)}$) is then minimized with respect to the regularizer parameters ϕ. Each regularizer update unrolls through the l gradient steps as $\hat{\theta}_a^{(k)}$ depends on ϕ through the l gradient steps. This entire procedure can be expressed by the following set of equations:

$$\beta^1 \leftarrow \theta_a^{(k)}$$
$$\beta^t = \beta^{t-1} - \alpha \nabla_{\beta^{t-1}} \left[\ell^{(a)}(\psi^{(k)}, \beta^{t-1}) + R_\phi(\beta^{t-1}) \right] \qquad \forall t \in \{2, \ldots l\} \qquad (6.4)$$
$$\hat{\theta}_a^{(k)} = \beta^l$$
$$\phi^{(k+1)} = \phi^{(k)} - \alpha \nabla_\phi \ell^{(b)}(\psi^{(k)}, \hat{\theta}_a^{(k)})|_{\phi=\phi^{(k)}} \qquad (6.5)$$

Here, $\ell^{(i)}(\psi, \theta_{new}) = \mathbb{E}_{(\mathbf{x},\mathbf{y}) \sim D_i}[-\mathbf{y}. \log(T_{\theta_{new}}(F_\psi(\mathbf{x})))]$ (i.e.) the loss of task network T_{new} on samples from domain i, and α is the learning rate. Eq. (6.4) represents l steps of gradient descent from the initial point $\theta_a^{(k)}$ using samples from *metatrain* set, with β_t denoting the output at the tth step. Eq. (6.5) is the metaupdate step for updating the parameters of the regularizer. This update ensures that l steps of gradient descent using the regularized loss on samples from domain a results in task network a performing well on domain b. It is important to note that the dependence of ϕ on $\hat{\theta}_a^{(k)}$ comes from the l gradient steps performed in Eq. (6.4). So, the gradients of ϕ propagate through these l unrolled gradient steps.

Since the same regularizer $R_\phi(\theta)$ is trained on every (a, b) pair, the resulting regularizer we learn captures the notion of domain generalization. Please refer to Fig. 6.2 for a pictoral description of the metaupdate step. The entire algorithm is given in Algorithm 6.3

6.5.2 Training the final model

Once the regularizer is learnt, the regularization parameters ϕ are frozen and the final task network initialized from scratch is trained on all p source domains using the regularized loss function $\ell_{reg}(\psi, \theta)$. The network architectures consist of just one $F - T$ pair. In this chapter, we use weighted L_1 loss as our regularization function, (i.e.) $R_\phi(\theta) = \sum_i \phi_i |\theta_i|$. The weights of this regularizer are estimated using the meta learning procedure discussed above. However, our approach is general and can be extended to any class of regularizers (refer [1]). The use of weighted L_1 loss can be interpreted as a learnable weight decay mechanism - Weights θ_i for which ϕ_i is positive will be decayed to 0 and those for which ϕ_i is negative will be boosted. By using our meta learning procedure, we select a common set of weights that achieve good cross-domain generalization across every pair of source domains (a, b).

Algorithm 6.3 MetaReg training algorithm.

Require: n_{iter}: number of training iterations
Require: α_1, α_2: Learning rate hyperparameters
1: **for** t in $1 : n_{iter}$ **do**
2:     **for** i in $1 : p$ **do**
3:         Sample n_b labeled images $\{(x_j^{(i)}, y_j^{(i)}) \sim D_i\}_{j=1}^{n_b}$
4:         Perform supervised classification updates:
5:         $\psi^{(t)} \leftarrow \psi^{(t-1)} - \alpha_1 \nabla_\psi \ell^{(i)}(\psi^{(t-1)}, \theta_i^{(t-1)})$
6:         $\theta_i^{(t)} \leftarrow \theta_i^{(t-1)} - \alpha_1 \nabla_{\theta_i} \ell^{(i)}(\psi^{(t-1)}, \theta_i^{(t-1)})$
7:     **end for**
8:     Choose $a, b \in \{1, 2, \ldots p\}$ randomly such that $a \neq b$
9:     $\beta^1 \leftarrow \theta_a^{(t)}$
10:     **for** $i = 2 : l$ **do**
11:         Sample *metatrain* set $\{(x_j^{(a)}, y_j^{(a)}) \sim D_a\}_{j=1}^{n_b}$
12:         $\beta^i = \beta^{i-1} - \alpha_2 \nabla_{\beta^{i-1}} [\ell^{(a)}(\psi^{(t)}, \beta^{i-1}) + R_\phi(\beta^{i-1})]$
13:     **end for**
14:     $\hat{\theta}_a^{(t)} = \beta_l$
15:     Sample *metatest* set $\{(x_j^{(b)}, y_j^{(b)}) \sim D_b\}_{j=1}^{n_b}$
16:     Perform metaupdate for regularizer $\phi^{(t)} = \phi^{(t-1)} - \alpha_2 \nabla_\phi \ell^{(b)}(\psi^{(t)}, \hat{\theta}_a^{(t)})|_{\phi = \phi^{(t)}}$
17: **end for**

6.5.3 Summary of the training pipeline

The feature network is first trained using combined data from all source domains, and is kept frozen in the rest of training. The regularizer parameters are then estimated using the meta learning procedure described in the previous section. As the individual task networks are updated on their respective source domain data, the regularizer updates are derived from each point of this SGD path with the objective of cross-domain generalization (refer Algorithm 6.3). To learn the regularizer effectively at the early stages of the task network updates, replay memory is used where the regularizer updates are periodically derived from the early stages of the task networks' SGD paths. The learnt regularizer is used in the final step of the training process where a single $F - T$ network is trained using the regularized cross-entropy loss.

6.6 Experiments

In this section, we describe the experimental validation used for evaluating domain generalization algorithms. We perform experiments on the PACS dataset [12], a benchmark dataset for domain generalization. This dataset contains images from four domains - *Photo*, *Art painting*, *Cartoon*, and *Sketch*.

Table 6.1 Cross-domain recognition accuracy (in %) on PACS dataset using Alexnet architecture. For the baseline setting, the numbers on the parenthesis indicate the baseline performance as reported by [13].

Method	Art painting	Cartoon	Photo	Sketch	Average
Baseline	67.21	66.12	88.47	55.32	69.28
D-MTAE ([6])	60.27	58.65	**91.12**	47.68	64.48
DSN ([2])	61.13	66.54	83.25	58.58	67.37
DBA-DG ([12])	62.86	66.97	89.50	57.51	69.21
MLDG ([13])	66.23	66.88	88.0	58.96	70.01
MetaReg ([1])	69.82	70.35	91.07	59.26	72.62

A visualization is shown in Fig. 6.1. Each domain has varied style and background characteristics. Experiments are performed on four settings: In each setting, one of the four domains is treated as the unseen target domain, and the model is trained on the other three source domains.

In all experiments, *Baseline* setting denotes training a neural network on the aggregate of all source domains without performing any domain generalization. We compare the meta learning based approaches with the following methods: Multitask Autoencoders (MTAE) [6], Domain Separation Networks (DSN) [2], Artier Domain Generalization (DBA-DG) [12], CrossGrad [15] and Undo-Bias [9]. While some of these methods were originally proposed for domain adaptation, they were adapted to the domain generalization problem. Please refer to [13] for more details.

6.6.0.0.1 Alexnet

The first set of experiments is based on the Alexnet [10] model pretrained on Imagenet. For the MLDG algorithm, the meta learning is performed on the parameters of the entire network. For the Metareg algorithm, the feature network F comprises of the top layers of Alexnet model till $pool5$ layer, while the task network T contains $fc6$, $fc7$, and $fc8$ layers. Weighted L_1 loss is used as the regularization function (i.e.) $R_\phi(\theta) = \sum_i \phi_i |\theta_i|$, where ϕ_i are the parameters estimated using meta learning.

All models are trained using the SGD optimizer with learning rate $5e - 4$ and a batch size of 64. For the MLDG algorithm, α and β are set as 0.0005 and 1.0, while α_1 and α_2 for the Metareg algorithm is set as 0.001. Table 6.1 presents the results of meta learning based approaches along with other methods to compare. We observe that meta learning based approaches perform better than the baseline and yield good performance improvements.

6.6.0.0.2 Resnet

Next, we report the results on Resnet architecture. For the Metareg algorithm, we use the last fully connected layer as the task network, while the rest of the network is used as the feature network. Similar to the previous experiment, we used weighted L_1 loss as our class of regularizers. All models were trained using SGD optimizer with a learning rate of 0.001 and momentum 0.9. The hyperparameters α_1 and α_2 for Metareg are both set as 0.001. For the S-MLGD algorithm, α and β are both set as 0.002 and 1.85 respectively.

The results of the experiments on Resnet-18 model are reported in Table 6.2. We observe that meta learning based approaches (MLGD, Metareg, and S-MLDG) all perform better than the baseline, and

Table 6.2 Cross-domain recognition accuracy (in %) on PACS dataset using Resnet architectures.

Method	Art painting	Cartoon	Photo	Sketch	Average
	Resnet-18				
Baseline	77.6	73.9	94.4	70.3	79.1
DANN ([5])	81.3	73.8	94.0	74.3	80.8
CrossGrad ([15])	78.7	73.3	94.0	65.1	77.8
Undo-Bias ([9])	78.4	72.5	92.8	73.3	79.3
MLDG ([13])	79.5	77.3	94.3	71.5	80.7
Metareg ([1])	83.7	77.2	95.5	70.3	81.7
S-MLDG ([11])	80.5	77.8	94.8	72.8	81.5

Table 6.3 Cross-domain recognition accuracy (in %) on PACS dataset using Resnet architectures.

Method	Art painting	Cartoon	Photo	Sketch	Average
Baseline	85.4	77.7	97.8	69.5	82.6
Metareg ([1])	87.2	79.2	97.6	70.3	83.6

perform better or on par with other comparison methods. It is important to note that the baseline numbers for Resnet architectures are much higher than that of Alexnet. Even with such stronger baselines, meta learning based approaches achieve good performance improvement.

One disadvantage with meta learning based approaches is poor scalability since they require computing higher order derivatives, which is hard to compute and optimize for deeper models. However, this scalability issue is fixed in Metareg by performing meta learning only on the task network. The task network can be as small as one fully connected layer, which makes it easy to train this approach. To demonstrate this scalability, we repeat the domain generalization experiments on Resnet-50 model, which is a much deeper model compared to Resnet-18. The results are shown in Table 6.3. We observe that Metareg achieves good performance improvement compared to the aggregate baseline.

6.7 Conclusion

In this chapter, we looked at an interesting application of meta learning for the problem of domain generalization. The idea is to split the input domains into disjoint sets of metatraining and metatest splits. Then, meta learning is performed so that updates in metatraining set lead to a drop in performance in the metatest set. Two algorithms were discussed for the problem - MLGD, which extends the MAML algorithm for domain generalization and Metareg, which proposes a regularization framework for domain generalization. The effectiveness of these approaches is validated on the PACS benchmark in which meta learning approaches consistently improved performance over the aggregate baselines to yield better generalizable models. Recent work in domain generalization has created larger testbeds such as DOMAINBED [7] and new metrics that provide researchers the ability to develop algorithms that work at scale.

References

[1] Yogesh Balaji, Swami Sankaranarayanan, Rama Chellappa, Metareg: towards domain generalization using meta-regularization, Advances in Neural Information Processing Systems 31 (2018) 998–1008.

[2] Konstantinos Bousmalis, George Trigeorgis, Nathan Silberman, Dilip Krishnan, Dumitru Erhan, Domain separation networks, in: D.D. Lee, M. Sugiyama, U.V. Luxburg, I. Guyon, R. Garnett (Eds.), Advances in Neural Information Processing Systems 29, Curran Associates, Inc., 2016, pp. 343–351.

[3] Fabio M. Carlucci, Antonio D'Innocente, Silvia Bucci, Barbara Caputo, Tatiana Tommasi, Domain generalization by solving jigsaw puzzles, in: Proceedings of the IEEE/CVF Conference on Computer Vision and Pattern Recognition, 2019, pp. 2229–2238.

[4] Chelsea Finn, Pieter Abbeel, Sergey Levine, Model-agnostic meta-learning for fast adaptation of deep networks, in: Proceedings of the 34th International Conference on Machine Learning, ICML 2017, Sydney, NSW, Australia, 6–11 August 2017, 2017, pp. 1126–1135.

[5] Yaroslav Ganin, Victor Lempitsky, Unsupervised domain adaptation by backpropagation, in: International Conference on Machine Learning, PMLR, 2015, pp. 1180–1189.

[6] Muhammad Ghifary, W. Bastiaan Kleijn, Mengjie Zhang, David Balduzzi, Domain generalization for object recognition with multi-task autoencoders, in: 2015 IEEE International Conference on Computer Vision, ICCV 2015, Santiago, Chile, December 7–13, 2015, 2015.

[7] Ishaan Gulrajani, David Lopez-Paz, In search of lost domain generalization, arxiv preprint - under review ICLR 2021, 2021.

[8] Kaiming He, Xiangyu Zhang, Shaoqing Ren, Jian Sun, Deep residual learning for image recognition, in: Proceedings of the IEEE Conference on Computer Vision and Pattern Recognition, 2016, pp. 770–778.

[9] Aditya Khosla, Tinghui Zhou, Tomasz Malisiewicz, Alexei A. Efros, Antonio Torralba, Undoing the damage of dataset bias, in: Proceedings of the 12th European Conference on Computer Vision - Volume Part I, ECCV'12, 2012.

[10] Alex Krizhevsky, Ilya Sutskever, Geoffrey E. Hinton, Imagenet classification with deep convolutional neural networks, Advances in Neural Information Processing Systems 25 (2012) 1097–1105.

[11] Da Li, Yongxin Yang, Yi-Zhe Song, Timothy Hospedales, Sequential learning for domain generalization, in: European Conference on Computer Vision, Springer, 2020, pp. 603–619.

[12] Da Li, Yongxin Yang, Yi-Zhe Song, Timothy M. Hospedales, Deeper, broader and artier domain generalization, in: IEEE International Conference on Computer Vision, ICCV 2017, Venice, Italy, October 22–29, 2017, 2017, pp. 5543–5551.

[13] Da Li, Yongxin Yang, Yi-Zhe Song, Timothy M. Hospedales, Learning to generalize: meta-learning for domain generalization, CoRR, arXiv:1710.03463 [abs], 2017.

[14] K. Muandet, D. Balduzzi, B. Schölkopf, Domain generalization via invariant feature representation, in: Proceedings of the 30th International Conference on Machine Learning, W&CP 28(1), JMLR, 2013, pp. 10–18.

[15] Shiv Shankar, Vihari Piratla, Soumen Chakrabarti, Siddhartha Chaudhuri, Preethi Jyothi, Sunita Sarawagi, Generalizing across domains via cross-gradient training, in: International Conference on Learning Representations, 2018.

[16] Riccardo Volpi, Hongseok Namkoong, Ozan Sener, John Duchi, Vittorio Murino, Silvio Savarese, Generalizing to unseen domains via adversarial data augmentation, arXiv preprint, arXiv:1805.12018, 2018.

PART

2

Meta learning for medical imaging

Few-shot chest x-ray diagnosis using discriminative ensemble learning

7

Angshuman Paul[a], Yu-Xing Tang[b], Thomas C. Shen, and Ronald M. Summers

Imaging Biomarkers and Computer-Aided Diagnosis Laboratory, Radiology and Imaging Sciences, National Institutes of Health Clinical Center, Bethesda, MD, United States

7.1 Introduction

In recent years, machine learning methods designed using deep convolutional neural networks (CNN) [23], have matched and surpassed human performance in different clinical tasks. These include breast cancer screening [28], skin cancer classification [5], diabetic retinopathy detection [53], wrist fracture detection [27], and age-related macular degeneration detection [36]. However, these algorithms generally rely on large volumes of training data with carefully curated annotations by experts. While several large-scale medical image datasets have been made publicly available in the last few years [17,18,55], only major diseases (or pathologies, clinical findings, and conditions) were extracted and labeled using natural language processing (NLP) techniques [37] in those datasets. In practice, annotating a sufficient number of image examples for rare diseases that have low population prevalence for large-scale training may be difficult. Dealing with this kind of long-tailed, imbalanced datasets, prevalent in real-world settings is challenging in both computer vision [19,31] and medical imaging [25]. In designing machine learning models using such datasets, overfitting can be a critical issue. Overfitting often results in poor generalization of the model. To alleviate class imbalance, researchers have used data augmentation [45], modification of the sampling weight per class in each batch [50] or assigning different weights to different classes in the loss function [55] to balance the under-represented classes in the training data. Once trained, these neural network models can not be readily adapted to unseen classes. Typically, such a model needs to be re-trained or fine-tuned with large annotated training sets of new classes.

A particularly appealing property of human vision and cognition is that human beings can learn new concepts from just a few examples. Few-shot learning (FSL) [46] is an exciting field of machine learning that tries to mimic this incredible ability of human vision. FSL provides alternative solution to training robust and discriminative classifiers from a limited amount of training data. In few-shot classification, we may train a classification model from a large labeled training set of base classes and aim to generalize it to novel classes not seen in the training set, given only a small number (e.g., five) of examples per novel class. However, the extremely limited number of training examples per class can

---

[a] The author is presently with the Department of Computer Science & Engineering, Indian Institute of Technology Jodhpur, Rajasthan, India.

[b] The author is presently with the PAII Inc., USA.

Meta Learning With Medical Imaging and Health Informatics Applications. https://doi.org/10.1016/B978-0-32-399851-2.00015-6

hardly represent the real distribution of the new data, making classification significantly challenging. In this context, FSL has attracted much attention from the computer vision community (see a survey paper in [57]) in recent times.

Radiology residents often require to transfer knowledge from what they have learnt previously to perform few-shot diagnosis in their rotating training programs [52], where only a few samples of each new disease or modalities are given. Towards advanced computer-aided detection (CADe) and computer-aided diagnosis (CADx), FSL may therefore play a crucial role, especially for the identification of rare diseases. However, applying FSL techniques for medical image diagnosis poses several compelling challenges. A major difficulty is on how to learn disease-specific, discriminative image features for novel classes from only a few examples. The high appearance similarity due to the chest anatomy and interclass disease similarity in chest x-rays may obstruct the learning of salient features for the target task.

In this chapter, we discuss a method proposed in [34] for the few-shot diagnosis of chest radiographs. This work builds on our preliminary work published in [35]. Our design philosophy is based on learning general characteristics of chest x-rays first and then extracting disease-specific characteristics to perform disease classification with only a few labeled training examples. Our method is capable of learning disease-specific characteristics from as little as five labeled training data. We design a two-step solution for few-shot learning from chest x-rays. The first step involves a CNN-based *coarse-learner* to learn the general characteristics of different chest abnormalities diagnosable from chest x-rays. In the second step, we introduce a *saliency-based classifier* to extract disease-specific salient features from the output of the coarse-learner and classify the disease. We propose a novel discriminative autoencoder ensemble to design the saliency-based classifier. Each autoencoder is assigned a weight based on its internal characteristics. Weighted voting is performed during inference to determine the class label for a query image. Our contributions in this work are as follows:

- We design a two-step solution consisting of a coarse-learner and a saliency-based classifier for few-shot diagnosis of chest x-rays.
- The saliency-based classifier is designed using an ensemble of discriminative autoencoders.
- We propose a novel intrinsic weight to be assigned to each autoencoder for weighted voting during inference.
- Our method can be trained with one dataset and can still be effectively applied to similar datasets (datasets of the same modality that contain images of the same diseases and conditions) from different sources.
- Rigorous experiments show significant improvement in F1 score compared to the baseline.

The rest of the chapter is organized as follows. We present the related works in Section 7.2 followed by the proposed method in Section 7.3. The details of the experiments and the results are presented in Section 7.4. Finally, we conclude the chapter in Section 7.5.

7.2 Related work

7.2.1 Deep CNN-based chest x-ray diagnosis

Chest radiography is one of the most common radiology imaging test worldwide. It is used for screening and monitoring various thoracic diseases [15,51]. Recent advances in deep learning and availability of large-scale chest x-ray datasets [17,18,55] provide scopes for improving automated interpretation and diagnosis of chest x-rays. In [22], the authors used an ensemble of deep CNN models to identify pulmonary tuberculosis on chest x-rays, achieving an accuracy of 96%. Nam *et al.* [30] designed a deep learning-based automated detection algorithm for the malignant pulmonary nodules on chest x-rays. Fourteen thoracic disease labels were text-mined from the associated radiology reports using NLP techniques [37] on the NIH ChestX-ray14 dataset [55] containing 112,120 frontal-view chest x-ray images. The authors trained a weakly-supervised CNN model for multilabel thoracic disease classification and localization, using only image-level labels. In [48], the authors incorporated disease severity level information extracted from radiology reports to facilitate curriculum learning in an attention-guided model for a more accurate diagnosis. Rajpurkar *et al.* and Zhou *et al.* improved classification and localization performance by training with Densely Connected Convolutional Networks [16,40,41,60] to make the optimization of such a deep network tractable. Li *et al.* [26] presented a unified network that simultaneously improved classification and localization with the help of additional bounding boxes indicating disease location used in the training stage. See [56] for an end-to-end deep learning architecture that learns to embed visual images and text reports for disease classification and automated radiology report generation. Guan *et al.* [12] proposed to ensemble the global and local cues into a three-branch, attention-guided CNN to better identify diseases. In order to alleviate data scarcity, [45,49] used variants of generative adversarial networks (GANs) [11] to synthesize chest x-ray images to augment training data for disease classification and pathological lung segmentation. For anomaly detection in chest x-rays, Tang et al. [47] proposed a one-class classifier based on the GAN architecture using only normal chest x-rays. In the present work, we exploit the few-shot learning principle for chest x-ray diagnosis, requiring only a few examples from each novel class. To the best of our knowledge, none of these previous works have been able to deal with merely a few training examples, as they usually need a large amount of data to avoid overfitting.

7.2.2 Few-shot learning

Recently, few-shot learning has become a hot topic [43,57–59] in the computer vision community. Major approaches include meta learning and metric-learning. Meta learning based algorithms [6,43,59] generally rely on transfer learning techniques and have two learning stages. In the first stage, a model is often trained with a set of classes containing a large number of labeled samples, called base classes. The objective of this stage is to enable the model to learn some transferable visual representations that are also useful for recognizing a different set of classes, called the novel classes. In the second stage, the model learns to recognize novel classes that are unseen during the first stage, using only a few training examples, typically 1 to 5 per class. In the second stage, the model learns to recognize novel classes that are unseen during the first stage, using only a few training examples, typically 1 to 5 per class. Few-shot classification is an instantiation of meta learning in the field of supervised learning.

Metric-learning based approaches [14,46,54] have been proposed to learn the best distance metric by comparing target examples and few labeled examples in an embedding space. The objective of metric learning is to learn a projection function that can map images to an embedding space (e.g., feature space) in which images from the same class are projected close to each other while images from different classes are projected far apart. The fundamental hypothesis behind this technique is that the learned feature representations from the base classes can be generalized to the novel classes. Our proposed method is related to meta learning where we learn a generic chest x-ray classifier for multiclass classification on base classes in the first stage. In the second stage, the learned model is generalized into the novel classes with only a few labeled samples.

Few-shot learning and self-supervised learning [9,10] tackle different aspects of the same problem: how to train a model with little or no labeled data. Self-supervised representation learning is a subset of unsupervised learning methods. Like few-shot meta learning methods, self-supervised learning approaches also have two stages. In the first stage, the visual feature representations are learned through the process of training deep neural networks with one or a few multiple predefined pretext tasks. These pretext tasks should be designed to favor the second stage in such a way that: 1) visual features need to be extracted by deep learning models to solve them, 2) models can be explicitly trained with automatically generated pseudo labels from unlabeled data. Examples of these tasks include image colorization, prediction of image rotations, prediction of the relative position of image patches, etc. In the second stage, the learned deep neural networks (usually lower layers) can be further transferred to downstream tasks, especially when only relatively small data is available, as pretrained models to overcome overfitting and improve performance.

There is a relatively small body of work on few-shot learning in the medical imaging domain. In [29], the authors utilized a GAN-based method for few-shot 3D multimodal brain MRI image segmentation. Puch *et al.* [38] proposed a few-shot learning model for brain imaging modality recognition based on Deep Triplet Networks [14]. They first metatrained the model with several tasks containing small metatraining sets, and then trained the model to solve the particular task of interest. Lacking pretrained models to start from, Roy et al. [44] designed 'channel squeeze and spatial excitation' blocks for aiding proper training of the volumetric medical image segmentation framework from scratch, with only a few annotated slices. However, it is difficult to find methods addressing the problem of few-shot medical image diagnosis. We introduce a first-of-its-kind discriminative autoencoder ensemble for few-shot diagnosis of chest radiographs. In the next section, we present the proposed method in detail.

7.3 Methods

A few-shot method is generally composed of metatraining and metatesting phases [42]. Both metatraining and metatesting phases involve a training and a testing (and/or a validation) phase. Hence, a dataset for few-shot learning is divided into metatrain set and metatest set each of which contains training data and test data (may also contain validation data). The metatest set must contain only a few labeled training data per class. Metatraining involves training and testing with the metatrain set while metatesting involves training and testing with the metatest set [6]. The class labels in the metatrain set do not overlap with the class labels in the metatest set.

We follow the aforementioned protocol to prepare metatrain and metatest sets for our experiments with chest x-rays. The disease labels in our metatrain and the metatest sets do not overlap. The metatest set contains diseases with only a few training examples per class. We design a few-shot learning method to diagnoses the diseases in the metatest set.

In few-shot learning, the lack of data points is the main prohibiting factor in drawing a good classification boundary in the feature space. Nevertheless, if we can represent the small amount of training data in a feature space that is highly discriminative w.r.t. the classes, it is still possible to draw a good classification boundary [57]. Based on this fact, we aim to design a few-shot learning technique that would perform classification using salient features which are class-discriminative. Different lung diseases af-

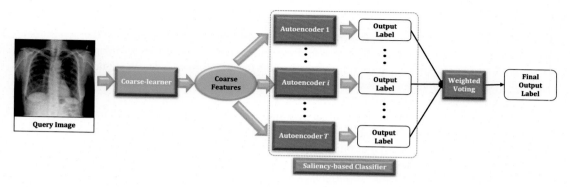

FIGURE 7.1

Pipeline of the proposed method. The saliency-based classifier is composed of T autoencoders.

fect different regions of the lungs. Therefore, to find the salient characteristics of different diseases, it is important to localize the affected regions from the chest x-rays. Localizing the affected regions often becomes difficult due to poor contrast. As a result, extraction of disease-specific salient features from chest x-rays is challenging.

Hence, we take an indirect approach to find the disease-specific salient features from the chest x-rays. We first extract coarse-level features from the entire chest x-ray without. This task is performed by a coarse-learner implemented using a CNN. Subsequently, we design a novel saliency-based classifier that extracts salient features from the coarse-level features and performs classification based on the salient features. We propose an ensemble of discriminative autoencoders with intrinsic weights to design the saliency-based classifier. Our design of the method adds several advantages discussed in Section 7.3.3.3. We train only the coarse-learner during metatraining while metatesting involves training of the saliency-based classifier. In the next few paragraphs we describe our method in details. The proposed architecture is presented in Fig. 7.1.

7.3.1 Coarse-learner

The coarse-learner is intended to extract imaging modality-based features from the images of a specific body part. For our application, the coarse-learner is expected to extract the common features of chest x-rays across different diseases and conditions. However, the coarse-learner may not extract disease-specific features for all the diseases.

7.3.1.1 Network architecture

Dense Convolutional Networks (DenseNet) [16] are capable of utilizing information in an effective manner through strengthening feature propagation and encouraging feature reuse. Furthermore, by allowing exhaustive connections from one layer to all of its subsequent layers, DenseNet can alleviate the vanishing gradient problem. Due to these qualities, DenseNet has been successfully used in the diagnosis of chest x-rays [41]. Being motivated from this success, the coarse-learner in our application is designed using 121-layer DenseNet (DenseNet-121) [16] architecture.

7.3.1.2 Training

We use the network design of [41] to implement the coarse-learner. The output from the penultimate layer of the network is used as the feature vector corresponding to an input x-ray image. The coarse-learner produces 1024 feature maps of dimension 7×7 in the penultimate layer. We flatten these feature maps to get the feature vector corresponding to an input image. Hence the dimension of the feature vector put out by the coarse-learner is 50,176 (i.e. $7 \times 7 \times 1024$).

We initialize the weights of coarse-learner with the weights of a DenseNet-121 model pretrained on ImageNet [4]. We further train this model to minimize the summation of weighted binary cross entropy losses [55] for multilabel and multiclass chest x-ray disease classification on the base classes. The Adam optimizer with the standard parameters ($\beta_1 = 0.9$ and $\beta_2 = 0.999$) [20] is used for training. We use a mini-batch size of 16 and an initial learning rate of 0.001. Following the protocol of [41], the learning rate is decayed by a factor of 10 whenever the validation loss reaches a plateau after an epoch. At the end of the training, we pick the model with the lowest validation loss.

Unlike [16], we train the coarse-learner with the training data from only the metatrain set. Thus, training of the coarse-learner is actually the training phase of metatraining. Consequently, the different class labels of the metatest set remain unseen to the coarse-learner during training. At the time of metatesting, we use the trained coarse-learner to extract feature vectors corresponding to the images of the metatest set. As a result, the extracted features from the x-ray images of the metatest set are likely to be noisy, redundant and not disease-specific. Hence, we look for a saliency-based classifier that can extract disease-specific salient features from the noisy feature vectors extracted by the coarse-learner and perform classification of the input data based on those features.

7.3.2 Saliency-based classifier

Design of the saliency-based classifier is challenging due to several reasons. First, the output of the coarse-learner is high dimensional (50,176 dimensions). Moreover, the coarse-learner is trained on the metatrain set. However, since at the time of metatesting, we use the trained coarse-learner to extract feature vectors corresponding to the images of the metatest set, the extracted features from the x-ray images of the metatest set are likely to be noisy and redundant. Most importantly, we deal with a few-shot learning problem where we have only a few training examples per class label in the metatest set. So, the problem boils down to finding salient features from high dimensional, noisy and redundant feature vectors with a small number (typically five) of labeled training data.

Autoencoders may be useful in finding salient features from input data [13] from which the input may be reconstructed. The vanilla autoencoder is trained by minimizing a reconstruction loss. However, the aforementioned simple autoencoder architecture can not effectively deal with noisy data. Hence, it is not a good solution for our problem. Furthermore, typical autoencoders may not produce class-discriminative feature space in the hidden layer. We make novel modifications in the autoencoder architecture that allow the autoencoder to deal with noise and produce a discriminative feature space in the hidden layer through training with a small number of training data. Towards that goal, we consider the following facts.

Ensemble learning is often useful in dealing with noisy features [2]. Each individual learner in an ensemble is termed as a 'weak-learner'. We introduce the idea of ensemble learning using discriminative autoencoders [32] with novel modifications as weak learners. Our model can produce a discriminative hidden feature space with salient features by training with small number of training data that may possibly be noisy.

In an ensemble learning scenario, each weak-learner may not be trained equally well [33]. These inferior weak-learners may adversely affect the performance of the ensemble. To handle the inferior autoencoders in the proposed ensemble, we assign weights to each autoencoder based on their quality of training. A weighted voting from the autoencoders is used during inference for classification. Next, we present the basics of autoencoders.

7.3.2.1 Autoencoders

An autoencoder [13] consists of an encoder and a decoder. The encoder maps an input to a hidden feature space and the decoder reconstructs the input from the hidden representation. The encoder may contain several linear layers of neurons with an activation.

Let X to be the input to an autoencoder. Assume that the linear layers of the encoder have weights $W_1, W_2, \ldots$ and so on. Then after the first linear layer followed by the first activation layer of the encoder, we have:

$$Z_1 = \phi_1(W_1 X). \tag{7.1}$$

Similarly, after the second linear layer, we have $Z_2 = \phi_2(W_2 Z_1)$ and so on. Eventually, at the end of the encoder, we have the hidden space representation Z corresponding to X. Considering an encoder of R layers, we have

$$Z = \phi_R(W_R Z_{(R-1)}) = \phi_R(W_R \ldots (\phi_2(W_2 \phi_1(W_1 X)))). \tag{7.2}$$

The decoder operates in the opposite fashion and produces a reconstructed output $\widehat{X}$ corresponding to the input X. For the decoder layer r, let us assume the decoder weight to be W_r' and activation function to be $\phi_r'(\cdot)$. Then the reconstructed input is for a decoder with R layers is

$$\widehat{X} = \phi_R'(W_R' \ldots (\phi_2'(W_2' \phi_1'(W_1' Z)))). \tag{7.3}$$

The typical objective function of the autoencoder is designed to minimize the reconstruction error. The objective function of a vanilla autoencoder [13] is given by:

$$J = \|\widehat{X} - X\| = \|\phi_R'(W_R' \ldots (\phi_2'(W_2' \phi_1'(W_1' Z)))) - X\|. \tag{7.4}$$

We modify the above objective function to design a discriminative autoencoder.

7.3.2.2 Discriminative autoencoders

Our application requires the hidden space representation Z to be class-discriminative. To that end, we modify the objective function of (7.4). Let $\mathbf{Z}^u$ and $\mathbf{Z}^v$ be the hidden space representations of input data points $\mathbf{X}^u$ and $\mathbf{X}^v$ respectively. To be discriminative, $\mathbf{Z}^u$ and $\mathbf{Z}^v$ should be closely spaced given $\mathbf{X}^u$ and $\mathbf{X}^v$ belong to the same class. Otherwise, $\mathbf{Z}^u$ and $\mathbf{Z}^v$ should be well-separated. We use an indicator function $I(\cdot)$ to incorporate the above fact in the autoencoder objective function. Let $I(u, v) = 1$ when data points $\mathbf{X}^u$ and $\mathbf{X}^v$ have the same class label and $I(u, v) = -1$, otherwise. Then modifying (7.4), the objective function of the discriminative autoencoder is given by

$$J_{\mathrm{D}} = J + \lambda \sum_{\forall \mathbf{Z}^u, \mathbf{Z}^v \in Z} I(u, v) \|\mathbf{Z}^u - \mathbf{Z}^v\|, \tag{7.5}$$

where λ is a predefined regularization constant. Minimization of (7.5) helps to condense data from same class and forces data from different classes to be away from each other in the hidden space.

The encoder in our model consists of an d'-dimensional input layer that maps the input to 1024 dimensions. Subsequent linear layers map the intermediate representations to 256, 128, 64, and 16 dimensions respectively. Each linear layer except the last layer is followed by a ReLU activation function [21]. The decoder has the same number of linear layers mapping the 16 dimensional representation to 64, 128, 256, 1024 and d' dimensions respectively. Each linear layer in the decoder except the last layer is followed by a ReLU activation as well. The last layer of the decoder is followed by a tanh activation. Next we show how to construct an ensemble of discriminative autoencoders and assign intrinsic weights to each of the autoencoders.

7.3.2.3 Ensemble of weighted discriminative autoencoders

An ensemble consists of weak-learners which in our case are the discriminative autoencoders. According to [2], when the weak-learners are trained with sufficient diversity, the probability of overfitting reduces and the classification accuracy improves. This fact is even more important when dealing with a small training dataset like the one we have. Therefore, it is required that the individual discriminative autoencoders are trained with sufficient diversity.

There are two ways to create diversity among the weak-learners during training. One is based on the data and the other is based on the features. We exploit both of these forms to create diversity in our training of the discriminative autoencoder ensemble. Furthermore, we want to train each autoencoder in the ensemble with class-discriminative features. However, the feature vectors extracted by the coarse-learner are likely to be noisy (as described in Section 7.3.1.2). Our mechanism of creating diversity in terms of the features comes with an additional benefit of mining class-discriminative features from the noisy feature vectors for training the autoencoders.

Assume that X is composed of N number of feature vectors from the coarse-learner. X is the input to the discriminative autoencoder ensemble. Let the ensemble be composed of T autoencoders. The training data for the ith ($i \in 1, 2, ..., T$) discriminative autoencoder is created through the following steps:

I. Generation of Bootstrap Sample: We want the training data for each autoencoder to be different from each other. To achieve this, we create bootstrap samples by randomly choosing N' training feature vectors (with replacement) from the pool of the N number of training feature vectors. Let B_i be the bootstrap sample for the ith autoencoder. We prepare the training data for the ith autoencoder using B_i.

II. Feature Selection: We employ a two-step quasirandom mechanism to bring in diversity in the features with which each autoencoder is trained. Assume that the dimension of each input feature vector in X is d. For the ith autoencoder, we first choose M number of random d'-dimensional feature subspaces. Then we select the best out of those subspaces. The best subspace is selected based on how well the data of different class labels are separated in the subspace. The details of the method for finding the best subspace are presented in Appendix 7.A. Thus the mechanism for selecting the best subspace helps to train each autoencoder with class-discriminative features from the noisy feature vectors extracted by the coarse-learner. Since the subspace selection process involves some degree of randomness, the best subspaces chosen for different autoencoders are likely to be different. Let the best subspace for the ith autoencoder is found to be $S^*(i)$. We prepare the training data for the ith autoencoder using $S^*(i)$.

III. Preparation of the Training Data: We project the bootstrap sample B_i into the best (out of M) subspace $S^*(i)$. Let this projection be B'_i. We use B'_i to train autoencoder i. The randomness involved in the process of generating bootstrap samples and choosing the best subspaces causes diversity in training. Due to the use of the best subspace, B'_i is expected to contain class-discriminative information. This separation is further enhanced by the discriminative autoencoder i in its hidden space representation. Thus, our method to create diversity in training the autoencoders also helps to create more class-discriminative hidden space representations.

7.3.2.4 Training the ensemble

For each discriminative autoencoder in the ensemble, we create the training data following steps I, II, and III. During feature selection for each discriminative autoencoder, we select the best subspace out of $M = 20$ random subspaces of dimension $d' = 40,000$ from the feature space of dimension $d = 50,176$. We minimize the objective function of (7.5) through back-propagation to train each autoencoder in the ensemble. Autoencoders are trained using the Adam optimizer [20] with a mini batch size of 16 and a learning rate of 0.001. The regularization constant λ is set to 0.001. An advantage of using the discriminative autoencoders is that the autoencoders are trained fast and can produce a salient discriminative hidden space representation in as few as fifteen epochs.

Due to the process of preparing the training data, each autoencoder ('weak-learner') is trained effectively with different training data leading to diversity among the trained autoencoders. It also makes each autoencoder explore feature subspaces that are likely to be different for different autoencoders. Furthermore, the use of the best subspace helps us to get rid of the noisy features to a great extent. All these factors lead to better classification by the ensemble. The training data for each autoencoder can be prepared independently. Therefore, each autoencoder can be trained independently as well. As a result, the time required to train the ensemble is the same as the time required to train one autoencoder. Furthermore, assume the time complexity of training one autoencoder to be $O\left(f(N')\right)$, where N' is the number of data points in the bootstrap sample for training an autoencoder. Therefore, the time complexity of training an ensemble of T autoencoders is $O\left(Tf(N')\right) = O\left(f(N')\right)$, since T is a constant. Thus, the time complexity of training the ensemble is the same as the time complexity of training one autoencoder. Once the ensemble is trained, we assign weights to individual autoencoders based on the test data. Hence the weight is dynamic in nature w.r.t. the test data. Note that we do not need to know the ground truth class labels of the test data to assign the weights to the autoencoders.

7.3.2.5 Assigning weights to the autoencoders

Due to the random nature of the input to the autoencoders, all the autoencoders are not exposed to the same data points or same feature subspaces. For example, some of the autoencoders are trained with a balanced (w.r.t. class labels) dataset while some others may be trained with a skewed one. The subspace that an autoencoder explores might not be as discriminative as the subspaces explored by other autoencoders. Hence, each of the autoencoders is not expected to be trained equally well. We assign an importance weight to each of the autoencoders based on the quality of the training. The formulation of the weight is derived from an intrinsic property of the autoencoder.

Consider an autoencoder with input X and output (reconstructed input) $\widehat{X}$. As an example, let there be two encoder layers E_1 and E_2, hidden layer H and two decoder layers D_1 and D_2. The outputs of layers E_1, E_2, H, D_2, and D_1 are Z_1, Z_2, Z, Z'_2, and Z'_1 respectively. Let there be C different class labels in the training data X. The projection of the training data X in the hidden layer H is Z. Assume

$Z(c)$ to be the projection corresponding to the training data of class label c. Let $\overline{\mathbf{Z}(c)}$ be the center of the projection. Similarly, we can find the center of the projections for all the other class labels. We can also find the center of the projections for different class labels at layers E_1, E_2, D_2, and D_1. Let the centers of the projections for class label c at layers E_1, E_2, D_2, and D_1 be $\overline{\mathbf{Z}_1(c)}$, $\overline{\mathbf{Z}_2(c)}$, $\overline{\mathbf{Z}'_2(c)}$, and $\overline{\mathbf{Z}'_1(c)}$ respectively. For an autoencoder with R encoding layers and R decoding layers, the centers of the projections would be $\overline{\mathbf{Z}_1(c)}$, $\overline{\mathbf{Z}_2(c)}$, ..., $\overline{\mathbf{Z}_R(c)}$, $\overline{\mathbf{Z}'_R(c)}$, ..., $\overline{\mathbf{Z}'_2(c)}$, and $\overline{\mathbf{Z}'_1(c)}$ respectively.

Now consider a test data point $\mathbf{X}^{\text{test}}$ at the input of the autoencoder i. Let the projections of $\mathbf{X}^{\text{test}}$ at layers E_2 and D_2 be $\mathbf{Z}_2^{\text{test}}$, and $\mathbf{Z}'_2^{\text{test}}$ respectively. Also, let the projection of $\mathbf{X}^{\text{test}}$ at the hidden layer H be $\mathbf{Z}^{\text{test}}$. Now we analyze the center of the projections corresponding to different class labels. Let the center of the projection closest to $\mathbf{Z}^{\text{test}}$ correspond to class label c_h. So, from the hidden space representation $\mathbf{Z}^{\text{test}}$, we may infer that the test data belongs to class label c_h. Similarly, let the center of the projections closest to $\mathbf{Z}_2^{\text{test}}$ correspond to class label c_2 and the center of the projections closest to $\mathbf{Z}'_2^{\text{test}}$ correspond to class label c'_2. Recall that $\mathbf{Z}_2^{\text{test}}$ and $\mathbf{Z}'_2^{\text{test}}$ are the projections of the test data at the layer before and after the hidden layer respectively. If the autoencoder is well-trained, each layer of the autoencoder is expected to contain some class-discriminative information about the test data. Therefore, we can expect to obtain the same class label for a test data if the projections of the test data at different layers (especially at the hidden layer and the layers close to the hidden layer) are used for classification of the test data. Thus, the better the autoencoder is trained, the more identical the class labels (obtained from the projections of the test data at different layers) are. Hence, after a good training of autoencoder i, we should get $c_h = c_2 = c'_2$. More generally, for an autoencoder with R number of encoder and decoder layers, if we consider k number of encoder layers and k number of decoder layers close to the hidden layer, a good training should yield

$$c_h = c_R = c'_R = c_{(R-1)} = c'_{(R-1)} = \ldots = c_{(R-k-1)} = c'_{(R-k-1)}. \tag{7.6}$$

Based on this fact, we formulate the weight of each individual autoencoder. Let the number of test data be N_{test}. Out of these, assume that $N(i)$ number of test data satisfies (7.6). Then the weight of the ith ($i \in 1, 2, \ldots, T$) discriminative autoencoder is computed as

$$\beta(i) = \frac{N(i)}{N_{\text{test}}}. \tag{7.7}$$

The weight of a discriminative autoencoder ($\beta(i) \in [0, 1]$) indicates the consistency of the different layers of a discriminative autoencoder in inferring the class labels of the test data points. Since the weights of the individual autoencoders are dependent on the test data, the weights are dynamic w.r.t. the test data. We use the weights of the individual autoencoders during the inference in few-shot learning as described next.

7.3.3 Few-shot learning

Most of the existing few-shot learning techniques require training the entire process pipeline during training phases of metatraining and metatesting. This incurs substantial overhead when one tries to include new class labels in the metatest set. We propose a novel scheme where the training phases of neither metatraining nor metatesting require training the entire pipeline. Instead, we need to train only a specific portion of the pipeline during the training phases of metatraining and metatesting. In fact, the training phases of metatraining and metatesting are architecturally disjoint in our method. This makes the training processes faster and adding new class labels in the metatest set easier. Next we discuss how to perform metatraining and metatesting in our model.

7.3.3.1 Metatraining

We train only the coarse-learner during metatraining. We use the metatrain set to train the coarse-learner in an end-to-end fashion. Hence, the training of the coarse-learner is not dependent on the saliency-based classifier by any means. We perform metatraining following the protocol of Section 7.3.1.2 and use the validation set of the metatrain set to find the best metatraining (coarse-learner) model.

7.3.3.2 Metatesting

The training phase of metatesting involves training the saliency-based classifier. For this, we first extract the feature vectors corresponding to the training images of the metatest set. We train the saliency-based classifier with these features vectors as described in Section 7.3.2.4. Each discriminative autoencoder inside the saliency-based classifier is trained during the above training process. The training is performed with $T = 15$ autoencoders considering $k = 1$, i.e., one encoder layer before the hidden layer and one decoder layer after the hidden layer for computing the weights of the autoencoders. Consider the ith ($i \in 1, 2, ..., T$) discriminative autoencoder. At the end of the training, we obtain the centers of projections in the different layers of the autoencoder i for each class label in the metatest set. Let the center of projection at the hidden layer for metatest class label c be $\overline{\mathbf{Z}(c)}$. Once the training phase of metatesting is complete, we obtain the weights of individual autoencoders using (7.7).

To test the performance of the proposed method, we use the test images of the metatest set. First, the feature vector corresponding to a test image Im^{test} is extracted by a coarse-learner. Let this feature vector be $\mathbf{X}^{\text{test}}$. When we apply $\mathbf{X}^{\text{test}}$ to the autoencoder i of the saliency-based classifier, we get the projection $\mathbf{Z}^{\text{test}}$ at the hidden layer. The class label corresponding to the nearest center of projection is assigned to the test image Im^{test} by autoencoder i. Therefore, the class label assigned to Im^{test} by autoencoder i is:

$$y^{\text{test}}(i) = \underset{c}{\text{argmin}} \, \|\mathbf{Z}^{\text{test}} - \overline{\mathbf{Z}(c)}\|. \tag{7.8}$$

In this way, each autoencoder in the ensemble assigns a class label to the input test image Im^{test}. Let $\beta(i)$ be the weight of autoencoder i. Then the final output class label, determined by our method is obtained by taking weighted votes from individual autoencoders in the ensemble. The total weighted vote for class label c is:

$$\gamma(c) = \sum_{\forall i: \, y^{\text{test}}(i)=c} \beta(i). \tag{7.9}$$

Consequently, we compute the final output class label by the proposed method to be the class label with the highest vote. Therefore, the output class label for Im^{test} using the proposed method is:

$$Y^{\text{test}} = \underset{c}{\text{argmax}} \, \gamma(c). \tag{7.10}$$

A pictorial representation of the metatraining and the metatesting phases are presented in Fig. 7.2.

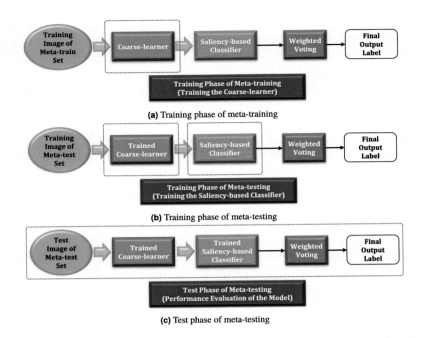

(a) Training phase of meta-training

(b) Training phase of meta-testing

(c) Test phase of meta-testing

FIGURE 7.2

Pictorial representation of metatraining and metatesting in our model. The block with the red dotted line is the block that is trained in a particular phase. A block with a green dotted line indicates a block that is already trained.

7.3.3.3 Comments on few-shot learning

Training (or even fine-tuning) the coarse-learner adds substantial computational overhead due to the very deep architecture of the coarse-learner. Whereas, training the saliency-based classifier is relatively simple due to the shallower structures of the autoencoders and also since the ensemble can be trained in parallel fashion. Now, suppose we try to include new class labels in the metatest set. Then we do not need to train the coarse-learner afresh (or do a fine-tuning) as long as the images of the new class labels are of same modality as that of the metatrain set. The coarse-learner extracts somewhat noisy features from the images of the new labels. We use these feature vectors to train only the saliency-based classifier. This makes the process of incorporating new metatest labels faster.

Furthermore, the characteristics that depend on the imaging modality (such as x-ray) are taken care of by the coarse-learner. However, to design the saliency-based classifier, we do not make any assumptions, specific to the imaging modality. As a result, if we want to use our model for the images from a different modality, we need to change the architecture of just the coarse-learner. This potentially makes our model portable across different modalities without requiring to change the architecture of the saliency-based classifier. However, note that with the change of imaging modalities, both the coarse-learner and the saliency-based classifier needs to be retrained.

7.4 Experiments & results
7.4.1 Dataset

In order to look into the robustness of our method, we perform experiments on chest x-ray datasets from two different sources: the NIH chest x-ray dataset [55] and the Open-i dataset [3] (frontal images). Note that we use only the NIH dataset [55] for training during metatraining and metatesting phases. The test phase of metatesting is performed on the test datasets from the above two sources (NIH and Open-i). Therefore, the results on the Open-i dataset also show the applicability of our training in the diagnosis of chest x-rays from a different source. The disease labels are extracted using a rule-based natural language processing method from the x-ray reports corresponding to the above images [55]. Any word or phrase that falls outside the scope of the rules may therefore lead to incorrect disease labels. Hence, our results indicate the usefulness of the proposed method in datasets with noisy labels.

Our datasets contain x-ray images corresponding to 14 thorax diseases or conditions. The diseases/conditions are atelectasis, consolidation, infiltration, pneumothorax, fibrosis, effusion, pneumonia, pleural thickening, nodule, mass, hernia, edema, emphysema, and cardiomegaly. If none of these diseases are present in an x-ray, we assign a label 'no finding' to that x-ray. Out of these 15 classes (14 disease classes+no finding), we randomly choose 12 classes without replacement to be the *base classes* and the remaining 3 classes to be the *novel classes*. We construct the metatrain set and the metatest set for metatraining and metatesting respectively.

The above datasets are multilabel datasets. While constructing the metatrain set, we make sure that each data point in the metatrain set has all the labels from the base classes only. This ensures that the metatrain set does not contain any information of the novel classes. On the other hand, few-shot learning requires the metatest set to be composed of data points from novel classes [57]. Therefore, each x-ray image in the metatest set must contain at least one of the novel classes as its label. That particular novel class is treated as the label for the corresponding x-ray image of the metatest set. If there is more than one novel class associated with an x-ray image of the metatest set, we randomly choose one of those classes as the label for the corresponding x-ray image. Thus, the metatrain set contains x-rays with only the base classes while the metatest set consists of x-rays with only the novel classes.

The training during metatesting is performed with five x-ray images corresponding to each of the novel classes in accordance with the requirements of few-shot learning [57]. The training data for metatesting is chosen randomly from [55] such that the training data and the test data for the novel classes in the NIH dataset never overlap. For our experiments on the Open-i dataset, the training phase of metatraining and the training phase of metatesting are performed using the NIH dataset while the test phase of metatesting is performed on the Open-i dataset. Recall that the training phase of metatraining involves training the coarse-learner and the training phase of metatesting involves training the saliency-based classifier. Therefore, we can say that for our experiment on Open-i dataset, we train the coarse-learner and the saliency-based classifier with the NIH dataset while the Open-i dataset is used to perform the test phase of metatesting.

We have 15 different classes in our dataset and we randomly select (without replacement) 3 disease classes as novel classes and rest as base classes at a time for our experiments. Hence we try five different combinations of the base classes and the novel classes. The novel classes in each of these combinations are presented in Table 7.1. Since we choose the novel classes (and hence the base classes also) without replacement, the novel classes chosen at each of the five combinations do not overlap. Consequently, the union of all novel classes in Table 7.1 becomes the full set of labels. The number of test data

Table 7.1 Novel classes for different combinations (with the number of test data points for different novel classes in the NIH, the Open-i datasets).

Combination	Novel Classes (#test data points in NIH, Open-i)
1	Fibrosis (308, 9), Hernia (61, 34), Pneumonia (85, 26)
2	Mass (723, 11), Nodule (575, 82), Pleural Thickening (344, 15)
3	Cardiomegaly (884, 262), Edema (735, 5), Emphysema (760, 80)
4	Consolidation (1270, 3), Effusion (2674, 44), Pneumothorax (954, 7)
5	Atelectasis (3260, 257), Infiltration (3032, 22), No Finding (9856, 2858)

points corresponding to different novel classes in the NIH and the Open-i datasets are also indicated in this table. We randomly select the training data from the NIH dataset for training the saliency-based classifier. To look into the effect of this randomness in training data selection, we repeat our experiments five times and calculate mean and standard deviation of different performance measures.

7.4.2 Performance measures & comparisons
7.4.2.1 Performance measures
The performance of our method is evaluated through F1 score for different diseases in novel classes. As presented in Table 7.1, we have five different combinations of novel classes. We evaluate the performance of different methods on each combination separately.

7.4.2.2 Competing methods
There is no existing baseline in the literature for few-shot chest x-ray diagnosis. So, we set the baseline method. Consider a combination of the base and the novel classes from Table 7.1. Towards setting the baseline, we extract feature vectors corresponding to the training data of the metatest set (i.e. the training data from each of the novel classes) using our coarse-learner. Subsequently, we find the cluster centers from the above training feature vectors corresponding to each novel class. At test time, we extract the feature vectors for the test data from the novel classes with the help of the coarse-learner. The class label corresponding to the nearest cluster center is assigned to each test data. These class labels are considered for evaluating the baseline performance. Therefore, the baseline method is same as the proposed method excluding the saliency-based classifier. However, the baseline method uses all the features extracted by the coarse-learner whereas the proposed method uses the benefit of feature selection. Therefore, we set a stronger baseline, denoted as *Baseline+* that uses the advantage of feature selection. The *Baseline+* method is same as the proposed method except the fact that we use vanilla autoencoder (with the loss function of (7.4)) instead of the proposed discriminative autoencoder to design the saliency-based classifier. Hence, the performance of the *Baseline+* method also helps to look into the roles of discriminative autoencoders.

Since we design an ensemble based few-shot learning technique, we compare the performance of the proposed method with other ensemble based approaches. In particular, we compare with random forest [2] (RF), AdaBoost [7] (Ada), and ExtraTree [8] (ET). We also compare with support vector machine [1] (SVM). Finally, we perform comparisons with several state-of-the-art few-shot learning methods. These methods include recent techniques such as MetaOptNet [24] (with SVM base learner) and ANIL [39], and well-known few-shot learning techniques such as MAML [6] and ProtoNet [46]. For all of the

Table 7.2 Performances of different methods in terms of F1 scores for fibrosis, hernia, and pneumonia as novel classes in the NIH dataset. *Bold fonts indicate the best values in each column.*

Method	Fibrosis	Hernia	Pneumonia
Ada	0.59±0.06	0.28±0.04	0.32±0.03
ET	0.14±0.03	0.26±0.03	0.19±0.03
RF	0.06±0.02	0.08±0.02	0.16±0.09
SVM	0.22±0.18	0.09±0.05	0.09±0.07
MAML	0.57±0.05	0.29±0.01	0.45±0.02
ProtoNet	0.56±0.08	0.21±0.02	0.39±0.04
MetaOptNet	0.41±0.06	0.15±0.03	0.23±0.02
ANIL	0.56±0.07	0.27±0.03	0.38±0.06
Baseline	0.52±0.05	**0.45±0.04**	0.42±0.04
Baseline+	0.63±0.06	0.35±0.04	0.45±0.03
Proposed	**0.63±0.04**	0.38±0.02	**0.49±0.02**

aforementioned competing methods, the metatraining phase remains the same as that of the proposed method. The coarse-learner is trained during metatraining. At the time of metatesting, each of the above models is trained with the training feature vectors corresponding to the different novel classes extracted by the coarse-learner. We train each of the competing methods with only five training examples from each of the novel classes. The performance of the competing methods is evaluated through F1 score on different novel classes.

7.4.2.3 Performance analysis

The performances of different methods for different combinations of base and novel classes in the NIH dataset are presented through Tables 7.2 to 7.6. The best value in each column is the one with the lowest standard deviation among the values with the highest mean. Notice that for most of the disease classes, the proposed method outperforms the competitors by a significant margin in terms of the F1 score. The superiority of the proposed method over state-of-the-art few-shot learning techniques such as MAML, ProtoNet, MetaOptNet, and ANIL shows the utility of our design for few-shot chest x-ray diagnosis. We also have noticeable improvement compared to the baseline and *Baseline+* in most cases. This shows the efficacy of the proposed method in few-shot diagnosis of chest radiographs. The superiority of the proposed method compared to the *Baseline+* method indicates the improvement due to the use of the discriminative autoencoders (used in the proposed method) instead of the vanilla autoencoders (used in *Baseline+*). However, it can be observed that for diseases like hernia and effusion, our method does not obtain the best results. In the following paragraphs we analyze the possible reasons.

There are a number of causes of pleural effusion that also cause lung consolidation. So, it is possible that one may have effusion and consolidation at the same time. Consequently, during the training at metatesting phase, the saliency-based classifier may be trained with x-ray images that contains both effusion and consolidation. Since our method deals with only one label for an x-ray image, the saliency-based classifier either learns the characteristics of effusion or consolidation (but not both) from such x-ray images. This learning causes confusion at the test time of metatesting phase resulting in poor

Table 7.3 Performances of different methods in terms of F1 scores for mass, nodule, and pleural thickening as novel classes in the NIH dataset. *Bold* **fonts indicate the best values in each column.**

Method	Mass	Nodule	Pleural Thickening
Ada	0.44±0.02	0.39±0.04	0.26±0.02
ET	0.04±0.01	0.09±0.05	0.09±0.09
RF	0.02±0.01	0.02±0.01	0.06±0.03
SVM	0.09±0.04	0.19±0.07	0.14±0.05
MAML	0.41±0.02	0.38±0.03	0.28±0.02
ProtoNet	0.37±0.11	0.38±0.02	0.28±0.08
MetaOptNet	0.28±0.01	0.31±0.03	0.22±0.03
ANIL	0.40±0.02	0.37±0.05	0.30±0.01
Baseline	0.30±0.04	0.31±0.08	0.22±0.07
Baseline+	0.41±0.02	0.41±0.06	0.28±0.02
Proposed	**0.45±0.02**	**0.48±0.01**	**0.33±0.01**

Table 7.4 Performances of different methods in terms of F1 scores for cardiomegaly, edema, and emphysema as novel classes in the NIH dataset. *Bold* **fonts indicate the best values in each column.**

Method	Cardiomegaly	Edema	Emphysema
Ada	0.40±0.06	0.44±0.04	0.36±0.03
ET	0.08±0.04	0.17±0.05	0.13±0.06
RF	0.01±0.00	0.04±0.01	0.13±0.03
SVM	0.04±0.03	0.08±0.04	0.10±0.08
MAML	0.39±0.02	0.56±0.01	0.44±0.04
ProtoNet	0.32±0.07	0.43±0.14	0.36±0.06
MetaOptNet	0.26±0.04	0.32±0.05	0.19±0.05
ANIL	0.40±0.02	0.49±0.03	0.46±0.05
Baseline	0.35±0.04	0.52±0.01	0.36±0.02
Baseline+	0.40±0.05	0.56±0.01	0.49±0.02
Proposed	**0.44±0.05**	**0.57±0.01**	**0.50±0.02**

classification performance. Similar values of F1 scores for consolidation and effusion (see Table 7.5) support the above claim.

In many occasions, a small hiatal hernia may appear as a gas-filled structure in the chest cavity. This often makes visual detection of hernias from chest x-rays a challenging task. Also, as evident from Table 7.1, hernia has the smallest number of test data points in the NIH dataset. As a result, only a few mis-classified data points may affect the performance. This is likely to be the cause of the inferior performance of the proposed method for hernia.

Our method is found to be superior compared to its competitors for datasets from different sources as well. The results of different methods on the Open-i dataset are presented in Fig. 7.3, Fig. 7.4, and

Table 7.5 Performances of different methods for in terms of F1 scores consolidation, effusion, and pneumothorax as novel classes in the NIH dataset. *Bold* **fonts indicate the best values in each column.**

Method	Consolidation	Effusion	Pneumothorax
Ada	0.33±0.02	**0.50±0.03**	0.28±0.01
ET	0.06±0.03	0.09±0.05	0.15±0.06
RF	0.09±0.05	0.03±0.02	0.10±0.05
SVM	0.09±0.05	0.09±0.12	0.12±0.06
MAML	0.44±0.02	0.44±0.04	0.38±0.00
ProtoNet	0.32±0.13	0.39±0.13	0.29±0.05
MetaOptNet	0.23±0.05	0.34±0.05	0.25±0.10
ANIL	0.44±0.02	0.48±0.03	0.38±0.01
Baseline	0.35±0.06	0.32±0.04	0.36±0.02
Baseline+	**0.44±0.01**	0.43±0.07	0.39±0.01
Proposed	0.44±0.02	0.47±0.03	**0.40±0.01**

Table 7.6 Performances of different methods in terms of F1 scores for atelectasis, infiltration, and no finding as novel classes in the NIH dataset. *Bold* **fonts indicate the best values in each column.**

Method	Atelectasis	Infiltration	No Finding
Ada	0.28±0.02	0.27±0.01	0.54±0.05
ET	0.06±0.02	0.04±0.00	0.16±0.18
RF	0.03±0.02	0.03±0.02	0.08±0.05
SVM	0.16±0.07	0.09±0.04	0.05±0.03
MAML	0.31±0.03	0.30±0.06	0.57±0.05
ProtoNet	0.27±0.06	0.28±0.08	0.45±0.10
MetaOptNet	0.24±0.03	0.20±0.03	0.18±0.13
ANIL	0.27±0.02	0.29±0.07	0.50±0.08
Baseline	0.23±0.04	0.29±0.02	0.43±0.05
Baseline+	0.30±0.02	**0.35±0.02**	0.60±0.02
Proposed	**0.33±0.02**	0.34±0.01	**0.62±0.02**

Fig. 7.5. For experiments on the Open-i dataset, we plot the mean and the standard deviation of F1 scores over five runs for different novel classes. Notice that for most of the diseases and conditions, our method outperforms the competing methods by a significant margin. The exception occurs in case of fibrosis where we have only 9 test data. Even a small number of mis-classifications significantly affects the performance when the number of test data is so small. This is the most probable cause behind our poor performance for fibrosis in case of the Open-i dataset. We have also evaluated the area under the ROC curve (AUROC) for different diseases and conditions in the NIH and the Open-i datasets using different methods. The AUROC using the proposed method ranges from 0.55 to 0.79 for different diseases and conditions (see the supplementary material for the details of AUROC values

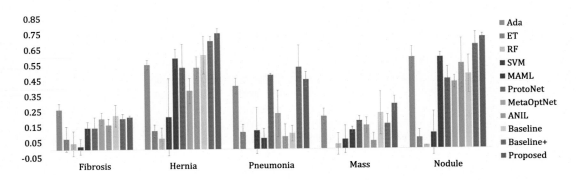

FIGURE 7.3

Comparative performances of different methods on the Open-i dataset in terms of the mean and standard deviation (presented through error bars) of F1 scores over five runs for fibrosis, hernia, pneumonia, mass, and nodule.

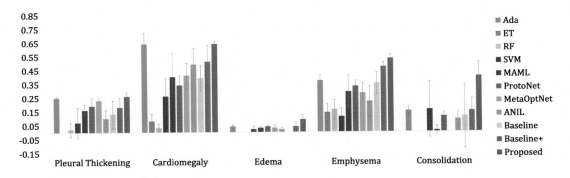

FIGURE 7.4

Comparative performances of different methods on the Open-i dataset in terms of the mean and standard deviation (presented through error bars) of F1 scores over five runs for pleural thickening, cardiomegaly, edema, emphysema, and consolidation.

using different methods). The comparative standing of different methods in terms of AUROC almost identically follows that in terms of F1 Scores.

As discussed in Section 7.2, in recent years, several methods have been successfully applied for automated diagnosis of chest radiographs. However, only a few of them report the F1 scores. In [41], an F1 score of 0.435 has been reported for diagnosis of pneumonia in the NIH dataset. F1 scores for diagnosis of different diseases in the NIH dataset have been reported in [40] as well. The F1 scores for atelectasis, cardiomegaly, consolidation, edema, effusion, emphysema, fibrosis, hernia, infiltration, mass, nodule, pleural thickening, pneumonia, and pneumothorax are 0.512, 0.47, 0.656, 0.672, 0.728, 0.125, 0.243, 0.374, 0.33, 0.662, 0.632, 0.52, 0.477, and 0.635 respectively. Recall that none of the above methods are few-shot learning methods and all of them are trained with a large number of training

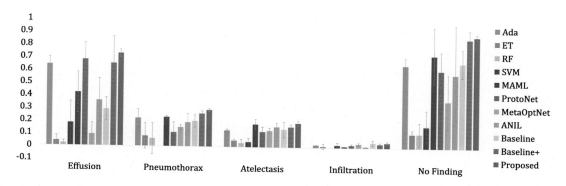

FIGURE 7.5

Comparative performances of different methods on the Open-i dataset in terms of the mean and standard deviation (presented through error bars) of F1 scores over five runs for effusion, pneumothorax, atelectasis, infiltration, and no finding.

images for each disease category. In contrast, our method is trained with only five images for each novel class. Furthermore, the experimental setups of the above methods are different from that of ours. Nevertheless, from Tables 7.2 to 7.6, notice that our method, in spite of being a few-shot learning method, has values of F1 scores that are comparable with those of [41] and [40] for different diseases. In fact, for diseases like pneumonia, emphysema, fibrosis, hernia, and infiltration the values of F1 scores obtained by the proposed method are higher than those of [41] and [40]. Although this is not a direct comparison of the performances, the values of the F1 scores obtained using the proposed method indicate the potential of our technique in few-shot chest x-ray diagnosis.

7.4.3 Ablation studies

We perform ablation studies to evaluate the role of different components in the proposed architecture. First, we look into the importance of the ensemble in comparison with a single autoencoder. Then we evaluate the role of assigning weights to individual autoencoders.

7.4.3.1 Importance of the ensemble

To evaluate the importance of the ensemble, we construct the saliency-based classifier with only a single discriminative autoencoder. The autoencoder takes the 50,176-dimensional feature vectors put out by the coarse-learner as input for few-shot classification. The training procedure of the saliency-based classifier remains exactly the same as that of the proposed method. This technique with a single autoencoder is abbreviated as SAE. The results of using SAE on the NIH and the Open-i datasets are presented in Fig. 7.6 and Fig. 7.7 respectively. Notice that for both of these datasets, our method outperforms SAE by a significant margin for most of the novel classes. This demonstrates the utility of the proposed ensemble for good classification.

The results for the Open-i dataset are especially interesting. Recall that for testing on the Open-i dataset, we train our coarse-learner and saliency-based classifier using the NIH dataset. From Fig. 7.6, it can be observed that for effusion in the NIH dataset, SAE obtains a far better result compared to the

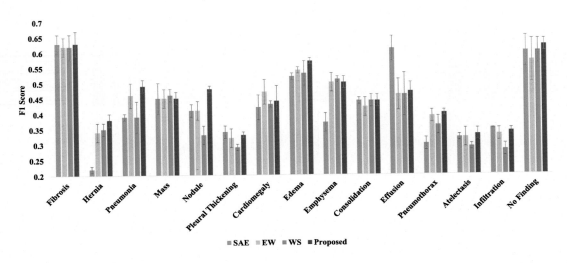

FIGURE 7.6

Results of ablation studies with single autoencoder (SAE), autoencoders with equal weights (EW) and without feature selection (WS) alongside the proposed method for NIH dataset in terms of the mean and standard deviation (presented through error bars) of F1 scores over five runs.

proposed method. However, when it comes to the Open-i dataset where the test data is from a different source than that of the training data, our method outperforms SAE for effusion. In case of the Open-i dataset, the proposed method obtains better or comparable performances for all the novel classes. Therefore, we conclude that the proposed ensemble helps in generalization across datasets.

7.4.3.2 Role of autoencoder weights

We have introduced weights for the autoencoders in Section 7.3.2.5. The output class label of a query x-ray images is computed in the proposed method through weighted voting, as explained in (7.9) and (7.10). In order to look into the role of the autoencoder weights in finding the class label, we run our method assigning equal weights to each of the autoencoders. This technique is abbreviated as EW. We present the results with EW alongside the proposed method for the NIH and the Open-i dataset in Fig. 7.6 and Fig. 7.7 respectively.

Notice that the proposed method outperforms EW for most of the novel classes in both the datasets. From the results, especially on the Open-i dataset, it can be observed that for diseases like pneumonia and consolidation, our method performs significantly better compared to EW. Also in case of infiltration, we achieve results that are comparable with the results using EW. These facts are of significant importance because consolidation, infiltration and pneumonia often cause similar lung opacity in chest x-rays making it difficult to find visually distinguishable features. The use of the autoencoder weights in our method tend to assign more importance to the autoencoders that learn the visual discrimination among the different classes in a better way. As a result, our method successfully handles the problem of visual similarity among the above diseases/conditions through the use of autoencoder weights. However, in case of the EW method, each autoencoder is assigned equal weight that results in failure to

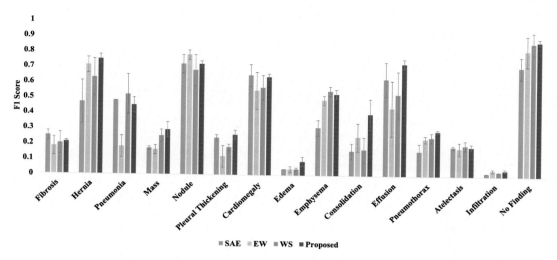

FIGURE 7.7

Results of ablation studies with single autoencoder (SAE), autoencoders with equal weights (EW) and without feature selection (WS) alongside the proposed method for the Open-i dataset in terms of the mean and standard deviation (presented through error bars) of F1 scores over five runs.

distinguish between visually similar diseases/conditions. This fact is evident from the results on consolidation, infiltration and pneumonia from Fig. 7.6 and 7.7. Hence, we conclude that use of autoencoder weights helps the proposed ensemble in discriminating between the visually similar classes.

7.4.3.3 Role of feature selection

While training the autoencoder ensemble, we have performed feature selection as described in Section 7.3.2.3. Each autoencoder has been trained with a feature subspace chosen in a quasirandom manner. We analyze the role of feature selection in the performance of the ensemble through the following ablation study. We train each autoencoder of the ensemble using the entire d-dimensional feature space instead of the d'-dimensional subspace. Therefore, each autoencoder is trained with the same set of features. This technique is abbreviated as WS (WS stands for **W**ithout **S**election of feature subspace). The results of WS alongside the result of the proposed method for the NIH and the Open-i dataset are presented in Fig. 7.6 and Fig. 7.7 respectively.

From the figures, it can be observed that for most of the novel classes, the proposed method yields better performance compared to WS. This indicates that feature selection plays an important role in the performance of the ensemble. There are two main reasons behind the improved performance due to feature selection in the proposed method. First, the proposed feature selection method is quasirandom that increases diversity among the autoencoders in training. Performance of an ensemble improves with this diversity [2]. Second, the feature vectors extracted by the coarse-learner are likely to be noisy (see Section 7.3.1.2). The feature selection helps us to choose class-discriminative feature subspaces from the noisy features which eventually leads to better training. However, for the ablation study WS, since there is no feature selection, the autoencoders in the ensemble are trained with noisy features resulting

Table 7.7 F1 Scores for different disease and conditions in the NIH dataset with varying number of discriminative autoencoders (T) in the saliency-based classifier. *Bold* fonts indicate the best values in each row.

T	5	10	15	20	25
Fibrosis	**0.74±0.03**	0.67±0.03	0.63±0.04	0.65±0.04	0.66±0.03
Hernia	0.32±0.03	0.32±0.04	**0.38±0.02**	0.38±0.04	0.37±0.04
Pneumonia	0.45±0.01	0.43±0.02	**0.49±0.02**	0.43±0.02	0.43±0.02
Mass	0.45±0.02	**0.48±0.03**	0.45±0.02	0.45±0.02	0.46±0.03
Nodule	0.42±0.02	0.42±0.03	**0.48±0.01**	0.44±0.02	0.40±0.03
Pleural Thickening	0.32±0.02	0.31±0.02	**0.33±0.01**	0.30±0.03	0.30±0.02
Cardiomegaly	**0.48±0.05**	0.44±0.03	0.44±0.05	0.45±0.04	0.46±0.02
Edema	0.55±0.01	0.54±0.02	**0.57±0.01**	0.54±0.02	0.54±0.01
Emphysema	0.48±0.03	**0.51±0.02**	0.50±0.02	0.50±0.02	0.51±0.03
Consolidation	0.44±0.02	**0.46±0.01**	0.44±0.02	0.44±0.02	0.43±0.05
Effusion	0.51±0.05	0.52±0.03	0.47±0.03	**0.54±0.02**	0.48±0.04
Pneumothorax	0.38±0.03	0.38±0.02	0.40±0.01	0.40±0.01	**0.40±0.0**
Atelectasis	0.31±0.04	**0.35±0.01**	0.33±0.02	0.34±0.03	0.32±0.04
Infiltration	0.30±0.02	0.31±0.02	**0.34±0.01**	0.31±0.03	0.32±0.02
No Finding	0.57±0.04	0.57±0.05	**0.62±0.02**	0.60±0.05	0.62±0.03

in inferior training. Therefore, we conclude that feature selection helps to improve the performance of the proposed method.

7.4.3.4 The number of autoencoders in the saliency-based classifier

We analyze the effect of the number of autoencoders in the performance of the saliency-based classifier. For this, we run the proposed method with different number of autoencoders in the saliency-based classifier. In particular, we take 5, 10, 20, and 25 autoencoders to evaluate the results. We have already reported the performance of our method with 15 autoencoders in the ensemble. Hence we now have the performance of the proposed method with 5, 10, 15, 20, and 25 autoencoders. F1 Scores for different disease and conditions in the NIH and the Open-i datasets with varying number of discriminative autoencoders (T) in the ensemble are presented in Table 7.7 and Table 7.8 respectively. From both of these tables, notice that with $T = 15$ autoencoders in the ensemble, we obtain the best results for more diseases and conditions across the NIH and Open-i datasets than we obtain with any other value of T. This justifies our choice of the number of autoencoders in the ensemble. Nevertheless, in a more flexible setting, different values of T may be chosen using Table 7.7 and Table 7.8 for different combinations of base and novel classes in different datasets.

As we start increasing the number of autoencoders in the ensemble, more feature subspaces are explored for disease-specific information. As complementary information is brought in with the addition of new autoencoders, the performance of the ensemble improves. However, after a certain number of autoencoders (when the feature space is sufficiently explored), further addition of new autoencoders only brings in redundant information. Hence, performance of the ensemble may not change (or may even degrade) with further addition of autoencoders. Nevertheless, for different diseases and conditions, the disease-specific information contained in the feature space varies. Therefore, we need different number

Table 7.8 F1 Scores for different disease and conditions in the Open-i dataset with varying number of discriminative autoencoders (T) in the saliency-based classifier. *Bold* fonts indicate the best values in each row.

T	5	10	15	20	25
Fibrosis	**0.25±0.01**	0.23±0.01	0.21±0.01	0.24±0.02	0.24±0.03
Hernia	0.65±0.02	0.71±0.07	0.75±0.03	0.70±0.08	**0.76±0.02**
Pneumonia	0.46±0.13	0.37±0.06	0.45±0.05	0.40±0.10	**0.48±0.18**
Mass	0.22±0.01	0.20±0.06	0.29±0.05	**0.29±0.02**	0.21±0.08
Nodule	0.64±0.09	0.72±0.06	**0.72±0.02**	0.70±0.06	0.70±0.08
Pleural Thickening	0.25±0.02	0.24±0.02	**0.26±0.03**	0.21±0.04	0.23±0.03
Cardiomegaly	0.69±0.12	**0.78±0.02**	0.64±0.02	0.77±0.02	0.74±0.07
Edema	0.01±0.02	0.00±0.00	**0.09±0.03**	0.02±0.02	0.03±0.01
Emphysema	0.45±0.03	0.45±0.02	**0.53±0.03**	0.44±0.02	0.42±0.01
Consolidation	0.14±0.07	0.13±0.04	**0.40±0.1**	0.11±0.07	0.05±0.06
Effusion	**0.77±0.06**	0.70±0.17	0.73±0.03	0.72±0.12	0.62±0.21
Pneumothorax	0.21±0.02	0.24±0.12	0.29±0.01	0.24±0.01	**0.30±0.05**
Atelectasis	0.22±0.01	0.21±0.02	0.19±0.02	0.23±0.02	**0.23±0.01**
Infiltration	0.02±0.00	0.02±0.01	**0.04±0.01**	0.02±0.00	0.02±0.00
No Finding	0.74±0.05	0.79±0.10	**0.88±0.02**	0.84±0.05	0.85±0.08

of autoencoders in the ensemble to sufficiently explore the feature space in order to find disease-specific information for different diseases and conditions. That is why, for different diseases and conditions, the best performance is obtained for different number of autoencoders in the ensemble.

7.4.4 Notes on clinical applications

Few-shot diagnosis opens up the possibility of automated detection of rare diseases since the training requires only a few image examples. For the purposes of performing a proof-of-principle research study, we have chosen common diseases for both the base and novel classes. From Tables 7.2 to 7.6, it can be observed that for almost all the novel classes in the NIH dataset, our method yields a low value of standard deviation. More interestingly, even in case of the Open-i dataset, the values of standard deviations of F1 score (see Fig. 7.3, Fig. 7.4, and Fig. 7.5) for different novel classes is ≤ 0.05 (except for consolidation with only 3 test data points). These are important observations in terms of repeatability of the results when clinical applications are concerned. Low values of standard deviations in the NIH and the Open-i datasets indicate that the proposed method yields consistent results not only for the test data from same source (test data of NIH dataset) but also for the test data from a different source (Open-i dataset). This makes our model applicable with good repeatability across different datasets.

Through the ablation studies, we have seen that our method can effectively diagnose diseases with similar visual appearance in chest x-rays. Such diseases include consolidation, infiltration and pneumonia. Therefore, our method can be helpful in scenarios where disease with visual similarities is to be identified even with a small number of training examples.

Furthermore, our model has a modular architecture. In order to add more disease categories, one needs to train only the saliency-based classifier that too with as few as five chest x-ray images of each disease category. This makes adding more diseases in our model easier and less time consuming. We have also explained in Section 7.3.3.3 that application of our model for modalities other than chest x-rays requires the modification of only the coarse-learner with a modality-specific suitable network. Hence, our model can potentially serve as the basis for the development of a method for the few-shot diagnosis of different diseases including the rare ones from the images of different modalities in a clinical setup.

7.5 Conclusions

We propose a method for few-shot diagnosis of chest x-ray images using a novel ensemble of discriminative autoencoders. Each autoencoder in the ensemble is assigned a weight based on its layer-wise consistency in classification. Rigorous experiments show the utility of the ensemble in making our method applicable across different datasets. Assignment of weights to the discriminative autoencoders enables us to detect even the visually similar diseases and conditions from x-ray images. This opens up the possibility of few-shot fine-grained disease classification using our technique. The proposed method has good repeatability even for a test dataset from a source which is different from the source of training data. These characteristics make our method potentially useful in a clinical setup. In the future, we would like to explore the possibility of end-to-end training and the use of attention models to improve the performance. We would also extend our method to multilabel few-shot diagnosis of images from different imaging modalities.

Acknowledgment

This project was supported by the Intramural Research Program of the National Institutes of Health, Clinical Center, and by a Cooperative Research and Development Agreement with PingAn. We thank NVIDIA for GPU card donation.

Appendix 7.A On feature selection for autoencoders

We find a d'-dimensional best subspace from the feature space of d dimensions for each discriminative autoencoder. We use the bootstrap sample B_i composed of N' feature vectors to find the best subspace for autoencoder i. For this, we first choose M number of randomly selected d'-dimensional subspaces. The best out of these M subspaces is selected based on the discrimination index, defined as follows. Assume that we have C number of different class labels in B_i. Consider a d'-dimensional subspace S_j. Let $\mathbf{X}^u$ and $\mathbf{X}^v$ be any two data points in subspace S_j. Consider $r(u, v)$ to be the distance between $\mathbf{X}^u$ and $\mathbf{X}^v$ in the above subspace. Let $L(u, v) = 1$ if the class labels of $\mathbf{X}^u$ and $\mathbf{X}^v$ are not same and $L(u, v) = -1$ otherwise. Then the discrimination index of subspace S_j is defined as

$$\alpha(j) = \frac{1}{r^*\binom{C}{2}} \sum_{\forall u, v \in N'} L(u, v)\, r(u, v), \tag{7.11}$$

where $r^* = \max\limits_{\forall u,v \in N'} (r(u, v))$ is the maximum possible distance between any two data points in the subspace S_j. From our formulation of discrimination index, it is evident that the discrimination index is higher if data with same class labels are closely spaced and data with different class labels remains distant from each other in the subspace. Hence, a high value of the discrimination index indicates a better separability of data from different classes. We choose the subspace with the highest discrimination index out of the M subspaces to be the best subspace $S^*(i)$ for the ith ($i \in 1, 2, ..., T$) autoencoder. The dimensions corresponding to the best subspace are used for preparing the training data for the autoencoder.

References

[1] B.E. Boser, I.M. Guyon, V.N. Vapnik, A training algorithm for optimal margin classifiers, in: Proceedings of the Fifth Annual Workshop on Computational Learning Theory, ACM, 1992, pp. 144–152.

[2] L. Breiman, Random forests, Machine Learning 45 (2001) 5–32.

[3] D. Demner-Fushman, M.D. Kohli, M.B. Rosenman, S.E. Shooshan, L. Rodriguez, S. Antani, G.R. Thoma, C.J. McDonald, Preparing a collection of radiology examinations for distribution and retrieval, Journal of the American Medical Informatics Association 23 (2015) 304–310.

[4] J. Deng, W. Dong, R. Socher, L.J. Li, K. Li, L. Fei-Fei, Imagenet: a large-scale hierarchical image database, in: 2009 IEEE Conference on Computer Vision and Pattern Recognition, IEEE, 2009, pp. 248–255.

[5] A. Esteva, B. Kuprel, R.A. Novoa, J. Ko, S.M. Swetter, H.M. Blau, S. Thrun, Dermatologist-level classification of skin cancer with deep neural networks, Nature 542 (2017) 115.

[6] C. Finn, P. Abbeel, S. Levine, Model-agnostic meta-learning for fast adaptation of deep networks, in: Proceedings of the 34th International Conference on Machine Learning-Volume 70, JMLR. org, 2017, pp. 1126–1135.

[7] Y. Freund, R.E. Schapire, A decision-theoretic generalization of on-line learning and an application to boosting, Journal of Computer and System Sciences 55 (1997) 119–139.

[8] P. Geurts, D. Ernst, L. Wehenkel, Extremely randomized trees, Machine Learning 63 (2006) 3–42.

[9] S. Gidaris, A. Bursuc, N. Komodakis, P. Pérez, M. Cord, Boosting few-shot visual learning with self-supervision, in: Proceedings of the IEEE International Conference on Computer Vision, 2019, pp. 8059–8068.

[10] S. Gidaris, P. Singh, N. Komodakis, Unsupervised representation learning by predicting image rotations, arXiv preprint, arXiv:1803.07728, 2018.

[11] I. Goodfellow, J. Pouget-Abadie, M. Mirza, B. Xu, D. Warde-Farley, S. Ozair, A. Courville, Y. Bengio, Generative adversarial nets, in: Advances in Neural Information Processing Systems, 2014, pp. 2672–2680.

[12] Q. Guan, Y. Huang, Z. Zhong, Z. Zheng, L. Zheng, Y. Yang, Thorax disease classification with attention guided convolutional neural network, Pattern Recognition Letters (2019).

[13] G.E. Hinton, R.R. Salakhutdinov, Reducing the dimensionality of data with neural networks, Science 313 (2006) 504–507.

[14] E. Hoffer, N. Ailon, Deep metric learning using triplet network, in: International Workshop on Similarity-Based Pattern Recognition, Springer, 2015, pp. 84–92.

[15] B. de Hoop, D.W. De Boo, H.A. Gietema, F. van Hoorn, L. Mearadji, L. Schijf, B. van Ginneken, M. Prokop, C. Schaefer-Prokop, Computer-aided detection of lung cancer on chest radiographs: effect on observer performance, Radiology 257 (2010) 532–540.

[16] G. Huang, Z. Liu, L. Van Der Maaten, K.Q. Weinberger, Densely connected convolutional networks, in: Proceedings of the IEEE Conference on Computer Vision and Pattern Recognition, 2017, pp. 4700–4708.

[17] J. Irvin, P. Rajpurkar, M. Ko, Y. Yu, S. Ciurea-Ilcus, C. Chute, H. Marklund, B. Haghgoo, R. Ball, K. Shpanskaya, et al., Chexpert: a large chest radiograph dataset with uncertainty labels and expert comparison, arXiv preprint, arXiv:1901.07031, 2019.

[18] A.E. Johnson, T.J. Pollard, S. Berkowitz, N.R. Greenbaum, M.P. Lungren, C.y. Deng, R.G. Mark, S. Horng, Mimic-cxr: a large publicly available database of labeled chest radiographs, arXiv preprint, arXiv:1901.07042, 2019.

[19] J.M. Johnson, T.M. Khoshgoftaar, Survey on deep learning with class imbalance, Journal of Big Data 6 (2019) 27.

[20] D.P. Kingma, J. Ba, Adam: a method for stochastic optimization, arXiv preprint, arXiv:1412.6980, 2014.

[21] A. Krizhevsky, I. Sutskever, G.E. Hinton, Imagenet classification with deep convolutional neural networks, in: Advances in Neural Information Processing Systems, 2012, pp. 1097–1105.

[22] P. Lakhani, B. Sundaram, Deep learning at chest radiography: automated classification of pulmonary tuberculosis by using convolutional neural networks, Radiology 284 (2017) 574–582.

[23] Y. LeCun, Y. Bengio, G. Hinton, Deep learning, Nature 521 (2015) 436–444.

[24] K. Lee, S. Maji, A. Ravichandran, S. Soatto, Meta-learning with differentiable convex optimization, in: Proceedings of the IEEE Conference on Computer Vision and Pattern Recognition, 2019, pp. 10657–10665.

[25] Z. Li, K. Kamnitsas, B. Glocker, Overfitting of neural nets under class imbalance: analysis and improvements for segmentation, in: International Conference on Medical Image Computing and Computer-Assisted Intervention, Springer, 2019, pp. 402–410.

[26] Z. Li, C. Wang, M. Han, Y. Xue, W. Wei, L.J. Li, L. Fei-Fei, Thoracic disease identification and localization with limited supervision, in: Proceedings of the IEEE Conference on Computer Vision and Pattern Recognition, 2018, pp. 8290–8299.

[27] R. Lindsey, A. Daluiski, S. Chopra, A. Lachapelle, M. Mozer, S. Sicular, D. Hanel, M. Gardner, A. Gupta, R. Hotchkiss, et al., Deep neural network improves fracture detection by clinicians, Proceedings of the National Academy of Sciences 115 (2018) 11591–11596.

[28] S.M. McKinney, M. Sieniek, V. Godbole, J. Godwin, N. Antropova, H. Ashrafian, T. Back, M. Chesus, G.S. Corrado, A. Darzi, et al., International evaluation of an ai system for breast cancer screening, Nature 577 (2020) 89–94.

[29] A.K. Mondal, J. Dolz, C. Desrosiers, Few-shot 3d multi-modal medical image segmentation using generative adversarial learning, arXiv preprint, arXiv:1810.12241, 2018.

[30] J.G. Nam, S. Park, E.J. Hwang, J.H. Lee, K.N. Jin, K.Y. Lim, T.H. Vu, J.H. Sohn, S. Hwang, J.M. Goo, et al., Development and validation of deep learning–based automatic detection algorithm for malignant pulmonary nodules on chest radiographs, Radiology 290 (2018) 218–228.

[31] W. Ouyang, X. Wang, C. Zhang, X. Yang, Factors in finetuning deep model for object detection with long-tail distribution, in: Proceedings of the IEEE Conference on Computer Vision and Pattern Recognition, 2016, pp. 864–873.

[32] A. Paul, A. Majumdar, D.P. Mukherjee, Discriminative autoencoder, in: 2018 25th IEEE International Conference on Image Processing (ICIP), IEEE, 2018, pp. 3049–3053.

[33] A. Paul, D.P. Mukherjee, Reinforced quasi-random forest, Pattern Recognition 94 (2019) 13–24.

[34] A. Paul, Y.X. Tang, T.C. Shen, R.M. Summers, Discriminative ensemble learning for few-shot chest x-ray diagnosis, Medical Image Analysis 68 (2021) 101911, https://doi.org/10.1016/j.media.2020.101911.

[35] A. Paul, Y.X. Tang, R.M. Summers, Fast few-shot transfer learning for disease identification from chest x-ray images using autoencoder ensemble, in: Medical Imaging 2020: Computer-Aided Diagnosis, International Society for Optics and Photonics, 2020, p. 1131407.

[36] Y. Peng, S. Dharssi, Q. Chen, T.D. Keenan, E. Agrón, W.T. Wong, E.Y. Chew, Z. Lu, Deepseenet: a deep learning model for automated classification of patient-based age-related macular degeneration severity from color fundus photographs, Ophthalmology 126 (2019) 565–575.

[37] Y. Peng, X. Wang, L. Lu, M. Bagheri, R. Summers, Z. Lu, Negbio: a high-performance tool for negation and uncertainty detection in radiology reports, AMIA Summits on Translational Science Proceedings 2018 (2018) 188.

[38] S. Puch, I. Sánchez, M. Rowe, Few-shot learning with deep triplet networks for brain imaging modality recognition, in: Domain Adaptation and Representation Transfer and Medical Image Learning with Less Labels and Imperfect Data, Springer, 2019, pp. 181–189.

[39] A. Raghu, M. Raghu, S. Bengio, O. Vinyals, Rapid learning or feature reuse? Towards understanding the effectiveness of maml, in: International Conference on Learning Representations, 2020.

[40] P. Rajpurkar, J. Irvin, R.L. Ball, K. Zhu, B. Yang, H. Mehta, T. Duan, D. Ding, A. Bagul, C.P. Langlotz, et al., Deep learning for chest radiograph diagnosis: a retrospective comparison of the chexnext algorithm to practicing radiologists, PLoS Medicine 15 (2018) e1002686.

[41] P. Rajpurkar, J. Irvin, K. Zhu, B. Yang, H. Mehta, T. Duan, D. Ding, A. Bagul, C. Langlotz, K. Shpanskaya, et al., Chexnet: radiologist-level pneumonia detection on chest x-rays with deep learning, arXiv preprint, arXiv:1711.05225, 2017.

[42] S. Ravi, H. Larochelle, Optimization as a model for few-shot learning, 2016.

[43] M. Ren, E. Triantafillou, S. Ravi, J. Snell, K. Swersky, J.B. Tenenbaum, H. Larochelle, R.S. Zemel, Meta-learning for semi-supervised few-shot classification, arXiv preprint, arXiv:1803.00676, 2018.

[44] A.G. Roy, S. Siddiqui, S. Pölsterl, N. Navab, C. Wachinger, 'Squeeze & excite' guided few-shot segmentation of volumetric images, Medical Image Analysis 59 (2020) 101587.

[45] H. Salehinejad, E. Colak, T. Dowdell, J. Barfett, S. Valaee, Synthesizing chest x-ray pathology for training deep convolutional neural networks, IEEE Transactions on Medical Imaging 38 (2019) 1197–1206.

[46] J. Snell, K. Swersky, R. Zemel, Prototypical networks for few-shot learning, in: Advances in Neural Information Processing Systems, 2017, pp. 4077–4087.

[47] Y. Tang, Y. Tang, M. Han, J. Xiao, R.M. Summers, Abnormal chest x-ray identification with generative adversarial one-class classifier, in: IEEE 16th International Symposium on Biomedical Imaging, 2019, pp. 1358–1361.

[48] Y. Tang, X. Wang, A.P. Harrison, L. Lu, J. Xiao, R.M. Summers, Attention-guided curriculum learning for weakly supervised classification and localization of thoracic diseases on chest radiographs, in: Machine Learning in Medical Imaging, Springer, 2018, pp. 249–258.

[49] Y.B. Tang, Y.X. Tang, J. Xiao, R.M. Summers, XLSor: a robust and accurate lung segmentor on chest x-rays using criss-cross attention and customized radiorealistic abnormalities generation, in: Proceedings of the 2nd International Conference on Medical Imaging with Deep Learning, PMLR, 2019, pp. 457–467.

[50] A.G. Taylor, C. Mielke, J. Mongan, Automated detection of moderate and large pneumothorax on frontal chest x-rays using deep convolutional neural networks: a retrospective study, PLoS Medicine 15 (2018) e1002697.

[51] N.L.S.T.R. Team, The national lung screening trial: overview and study design, Radiology 258 (2011) 243–253.

[52] J.H. Thrall, X. Li, Q. Li, C. Cruz, S. Do, K. Dreyer, J. Brink, Artificial intelligence and machine learning in radiology: opportunities, challenges, pitfalls, and criteria for success, Journal of the American College of Radiology 15 (2018) 504–508.

[53] D.S.W. Ting, C.Y.L. Cheung, G. Lim, G.S.W. Tan, N.D. Quang, A. Gan, H. Hamzah, R. Garcia-Franco, I.Y. San Yeo, S.Y. Lee, et al., Development and validation of a deep learning system for diabetic retinopathy and related eye diseases using retinal images from multiethnic populations with diabetes, JAMA 318 (2017) 2211–2223.

[54] O. Vinyals, C. Blundell, T. Lillicrap, D. Wierstra, et al., Matching networks for one shot learning, in: Advances in Neural Information Processing Systems, 2016, pp. 3630–3638.

[55] X. Wang, Y. Peng, L. Lu, Z. Lu, M. Bagheri, R.M. Summers, Chestx-ray8: hospital-scale chest x-ray database and benchmarks on weakly-supervised classification and localization of common thorax diseases, in: Proceedings of the IEEE Conference on Computer Vision and Pattern Recognition, 2017, pp. 2097–2106.

[56] X. Wang, Y. Peng, L. Lu, Z. Lu, R.M. Summers, TieNet: text-image embedding network for common thorax disease classification and reporting in chest x-rays, in: Proceedings of the IEEE Conference on Computer Vision and Pattern Recognition, 2018, pp. 9049–9058.

[57] Y. Wang, Q. Yao, Few-shot learning: a survey, CoRR, arXiv:1904.05046 [abs], 2019.

[58] J. Yoon, T. Kim, O. Dia, S. Kim, Y. Bengio, S. Ahn, Bayesian model-agnostic meta-learning, in: Advances in Neural Information Processing Systems, 2018, pp. 7332–7342.

[59] R. Zhang, T. Che, Z. Ghahramani, Y. Bengio, Y. Song, Metagan: an adversarial approach to few-shot learning, in: Advances in Neural Information Processing Systems, 2018, pp. 2365–2374.

[60] B. Zhou, Y. Li, J. Wang, A weakly supervised adaptive densenet for classifying thoracic diseases and identifying abnormalities, arXiv preprint, arXiv:1807.01257, 2018.

Domain generalization of deep networks for medical image segmentation via meta learning

8

Quande Liu, Qi Dou, Cheng Chen, and Pheng-Ann Heng
Department of Computer Science and Engineering, The Chinese University of Hong Kong, Hong Kong, China

8.1 Introduction

Recent years have witnessed remarkable achievement of deep learning methods in automated medical image segmentation [18,39,56]. However, the clinical deployment of existing models still suffers from the performance degradation under the distribution shifts across different clinical sites using various imaging protocols or scanner vendors. Recently, many domain adaptation [7,20] and transfer learning methods [15,21] have been proposed to address this issue, while all of them require images from the target domain (labeled or unlabeled) for model re-training to some extent. In real-world situations, it would be time-consuming even impractical to collect data from each coming new target domain to adapt the model before deployment. Instead, learning a model from multiple source domains in a way such that it can directly generalize to an unseen target domain is of significant practical value.

Previously studies have adopted data augmentation techniques to improve the model generalization capability [43,55], assuming that the domain shift could be simulated by conducting extensive transformations to data of source domains. Performance improvements have been obtained on tasks of cardic [6], prostate [55] and brain [43] MRI image segmentations, yet the choices of augmentation schemes tend to be tedious with task-dependence. Some other approaches have developed new network architectures to handle domain discrepancy [23,51], which even though achieve promising progress, rely on network designs, or introduce extra parameters thus complicating the pure task model. Model-agnostic meta learning [13] is a recently proposed method for fast deep model adaptation, which has been successfully applied to address the domain generalization problem [2,9,25]. The meta learning strategy is flexible with independence from the base network, as it fully makes use of the gradient descent process. However, existing DG methods mainly tackle image-level classification tasks with natural images, which are not suitable for the image segmentation task that requires pixel-wise dense predictions.

In this chapter, we study meta learning based methods to address domain generalization problem in medical image segmentation, and present solutions under two realistic scenarios, i.e., centralized training and decentralized federated training. Under the first scenario, we present a shape-aware meta learning scheme, which roots in the gradient-based meta learning to simulate domain shift with virtual metatrain and metatest during training, and further integrates two complementary metaobjectives to enhance the shape compactness and smoothness of the segmentations under simulated domain shift.

For the second scenario where the multicenter data are stored distributedly and cannot be shared due to privacy issue, we identify the problem of Federated Domain Generalization, which aims to learn a federated model from multiple decentralized source domains that can directly generalize to unseen target domains. We present a new method for this problem named Episodic Learning in Continuous Frequency Space, which enables each client to exploit multisource data distributions under the constraint of data decentralization, by transmitting the distribution information across clients from frequency space in a privacy-protecting way. The episodic learning paradigm is then established locally to expose the local learning to domain shfits, with particular feature regularization around the ambiguous boundary regions. The effectiveness of our method under the two scenarios has been demonstrated with superior performance over state-of-the-arts and in-depth ablation experiments on two medical image segmentation tasks.

8.2 Related work
8.2.1 Domain generalization

Among previous efforts towards the generalization problem [15,34,36,53], a naive practice of aggregating data from all source domains for training a deep model (called 'DeepAll' method) can already produce decent results serving as a strong baseline. It has also been widely used and validated in existing literature [6,10,52]. On top of DeepAll training, several studies added data augmentation techniques to improve the model generalization capability [43,55], assuming that the domain shift could be simulated by conducting extensive transformations to data of source domains. Performance improvements have been obtained on tasks of cardic [6], prostate [55] and brain [43] MRI image segmentations, yet the choices of augmentation schemes tend to be tedious with task-dependence. Some other approaches have developed new network architectures to handle domain discrepancy [23,51]. Kour *et al.* [23] developed an unsupervised Bayesian model to interpret the tissue information prior for the generalization in brain tissue segmentation. A set of approaches [1,42] also tried to learn domain invariant representations with feature space regularization by developing adversarial neural networks. Although achieving promising progress, these methods rely on network designs, which introduce extra parameters thus complicating the pure task model. This chapter studies meta learning based domain generalization methods, and explicitly integrate the shape-relevant characteristics in medical image segmentation to improve the model generalizability at unseen domains.

8.2.2 Federated learning

Federated learning [11,16,22,38,50] provides a promising privacy-preserving solution for multisite data collaboration, which develops a global model from decentralized datasets by aggregating the parameters of each local client while keeping data locally. Representatively, McMahan et al. [38] propose the popular federated averaging algorithm for communication-efficient federated training of deep networks. With the advantage of privacy protection, FL has recently drawn increasing interests in medical image applications [5,19,27,28,35,45,47,48]. Sheller et al. [47] is a pilot study to investigate the collaborative model training without sharing patient data for the multisite brain tumor segmentation. Later on, Li et al. [28] further compare several weights sharing strategies in FL to alleviate the effect of data imbalance among different hospitals. However, these works all focus on improving performance on

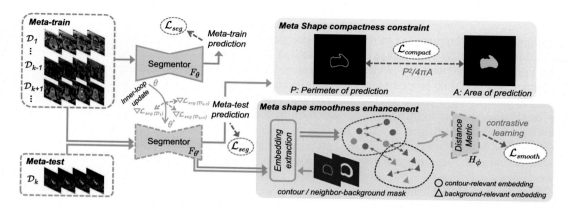

FIGURE 8.1

Overview of our shape-aware meta learning scheme. The source domains are randomly split into metatrain and metatest to simulate the domain shift (Sec. 8.3.1.1). In metaoptimization: (1) we constrain the shape compactness in metatest to encourage segmentations with complete shape (Sec. 8.3.1.2); (2) we promote the intra-class cohesion and interclass separation between the contour and background embeddings regardless of domains, to enhance domain-invariance for robust boundary delineation (Sec. 8.3.1.3).

internal clients, without considering the generalization issue for unseen domains outside the federation, which is crucial for wide clinical usability. Latest literature has studied a related problem of unsupervised domain adaptation in FL paradigm [30,44], whereas these methods typically require data from the target domain to adapt the model. In practice, it would be time-consuming or even impractical to collect data from each new hospital before model deployment. Instead, our tackled new problem setting of FedDG aims to directly generalize the federated model to completely unseen domains, in which no prior knowledge from the target domain is needed.

8.3 Domain generalization with shape-aware meta learning
8.3.1 Method

Let $(\mathcal{X}, \mathcal{Y})$ denote the joint input and label space in an segmentation task, $\mathcal{D} = \{\mathcal{D}_1, \mathcal{D}_2, ..., \mathcal{D}_K\}$ be the set of K source domains. Each domain $\mathcal{D}_k$ contains image-label pairs $\{(x_n^{(k)}, y_n^{(k)})\}_{n=1}^{N_k}$ sampled from domain distributions $(\mathcal{X}_k, \mathcal{Y})$, where N_k is the number of samples in the k-th domain. Our goal is to learn a segmentation model $F_\theta : \mathcal{X} \rightarrow \mathcal{Y}$ using all source domains $\mathcal{D}$ in a way such that it generalizes well to an unseen target domain $\mathcal{D}_{tg}$. Fig. 8.1 gives an overview of our proposed shape-aware meta learning scheme [33], which we will detail in this section.

8.3.1.1 Gradient-based meta learning scheme

The foundation of our learning scheme is the gradient-based meta learning algorithm [25], to promote robust optimization by simulating the real-world domain shifts in the training process. Specifically, at each iteration, the source domains $\mathcal{D}$ are randomly split into the metatrain $\mathcal{D}_{tr}$ and metatest $\mathcal{D}_{te}$ sets of domains. The meta learning can be divided into two steps. First, the model parameters θ are updated on data from metatrain $\mathcal{D}_{tr}$, using Dice segmentation loss $\mathcal{L}_{seg}$: 'where α is the learning-rate for this inner-loop update. Second, we apply a meta learning step, aiming to enforce the learning on metatrain $\mathcal{D}_{tr}$ to further exhibit certain properties that we desire on unseen metatest $\mathcal{D}_{te}$. Crucially, the metaobjective $\mathcal{L}_{meta}$ to quantify these properties is computed with the updated parameters θ', but optimized towards the original parameters θ. Intuitively, besides learning the segmentation task on metatrain $\mathcal{D}_{tr}$, such a training scheme further learns how to generalize at the simulated domain shift across metatrain $\mathcal{D}_{tr}$ and metatest $\mathcal{D}_{te}$. In other words, the model is optimized such that the parameter updates learned on virtual source domains $\mathcal{D}_{tr}$ also improve the performance on the virtual target domains $\mathcal{D}_{te}$, regarding certain aspects in $\mathcal{L}_{meta}$.

In segmentation problems, we expect the model to well preserve the complete shape (compactness) and smooth boundary (smoothness) of the segmentations in unseen target domains. To achieve this, apart from the traditional segmentation loss $\mathcal{L}_{seg}$, we further introduce two complementary loss terms into our metaobjective, $\mathcal{L}_{meta} = \mathcal{L}_{seg} + \lambda_1 \mathcal{L}_{compact} + \lambda_2 \mathcal{L}_{smooth}$ (λ_1 and λ_2 are the weighting trade-offs), to explicitly impose the shape compactness and shape smoothness of the segmentation maps under domain shift for improving generalization performance.

8.3.1.2 Metashape compactness constraint

Traditional segmentation loss functions, *e.g.*, Dice loss and cross entropy loss, typically evaluate the pixel-wise accuracy, without a global constraint to the segmentation shape. Trained in that way, the model often fails to produce complete segmentations under distribution shift. Previous studies have demonstrated that for the compact objects, constraining the shape compactness [12] is helpful to promote segmentations for complete shape, as an incomplete segmentation with irregular shape often corresponds to a worse compactness property.

Based on the observation that the prostate region generally presents a compact shape, and such shape prior is independent of observed domains, we propose to explicitly incorporate the compact shape constraint in the metaobjective $\mathcal{L}_{meta}$, for encouraging the segmentations to well preserve the shape completeness under domain shift. Specifically, we adopt the well-established Iso-Perimetric Quotient [29] measurement to quantify the shape compactness, whose definition is $C_{IPQ} = 4\pi A/P^2$, where P and A are the perimeter and area of the shape, respectively. In our case, we define the shape compactness loss as the reciprocal form of this C_{IPQ} metric, and expend it in a pixel-wise manner as follows:

$$\mathcal{L}_{compact} = \frac{P^2}{4\pi A} = \frac{\sum_{i \in \Omega} \sqrt{(\nabla p_{u_i})^2 + (\nabla p_{v_i})^2 + \epsilon}}{4\pi (\sum_{i \in \Omega} |p_i| + \epsilon)}, \tag{8.1}$$

where p is the prediction probability map, Ω is the set of all pixels in the map; ∇p_{u_i} and ∇p_{v_i} are the probability gradients for each pixel i in direction of horizontal and vertical; ϵ ($1e^{-6}$ in our model) is a hyperparameter for computation stability. Overall, the perimeter length P is the sum of gradient magnitude over all pixels $i \in \Omega$; the area A is calculated as the sum of absolute value of map p.

Intuitively, minimizing this objective function encourages segmentation maps with complete shape, because an incomplete segmentation with irregular shape often presents a relatively smaller area A and relatively larger length P, leading to a higher loss value of $\mathcal{L}_{compact}$. Also note that we only impose $\mathcal{L}_{compact}$ in metatest $\mathcal{D}_{te}$, as we expect the model to preserve the complete shape on unseen target images, rather than overfit the source data.

8.3.1.3 Metashape smoothness enhancement

In addition to promoting the complete segmentation shape, we further encourage smooth boundary delineation in unseen domains, by regularizing the model to capture domain-invariant contour-relevant and background-relevant embeddings that cluster regardless of domains. This is crucial, given the observation that performance drop at the cross-domain deployment mainly comes from the ambiguous boundary regions.

In this regard, we propose a novel objective $\mathcal{L}_{smooth}$ to enhance the boundary delineation, by explicitly promoting the intra-class cohesion and interclass separation between the contour-relevant and background-relevant embeddings drawn from each sample across all domains $\mathcal{D}$.

Specifically, given an image $x_m \in \mathbb{R}^{H \times W \times 3}$ and its one-hot label y_m, we denote its activation map from layer l as $M_m^l \in \mathbb{R}^{H_l \times W_l \times C_l}$, and we interpolate M_m^l into $T_m^l \in \mathbb{R}^{H \times W \times C_l}$ using bilinear interpolation to keep consistency with the dimensions of y_m. To extract the contour-relevant embeddings $E_m^{con} \in \mathbb{R}^{C_l}$ and background-relevant embeddings $E_m^{bg} \in \mathbb{R}^{C_l}$, we first obtain the binary contour mask $c_m \in \mathbb{R}^{H \times W \times 1}$ and binary background mask $b_m \in \mathbb{R}^{H \times W \times 1}$ from y_m using morphological operation. Note that the mask b_m only samples background pixels around the boundary, since we expect to enhance the discriminativeness for pixels around boundary region. Then, the embeddings E_m^{con} and E_m^{bg} can be extracted from T_m^l by conducting weighted average operation over c_m and b_m:

$$E_m^{con} = \frac{\sum_{i \in \Omega}(T_m^l)_i \cdot (c_m)_i}{\sum_{i \in \Omega}(c_m)_i}, \quad E_m^{bg} = \frac{\sum_{i \in \Omega}(T_m^l)_i \cdot (b_m)_i}{\sum_{i \in \Omega}(b_m)_i}, \tag{8.2}$$

where Ω denotes the set of all pixels in T_m^l, the E_m^{con} and E_m^{bg} are single vectors, representing the contour and background-relevant representations extracted from the whole image x_m. In our implementation, activations from the last two deconvolutional layers are interpolated and concatenated to obtain the embeddings.

Next, we enhance the domain-invariance of E^{con} and E^{bg} in latent space, by encouraging embeddings' intra-class cohesion and interclass separation among samples from all source domains $\mathcal{D}$. Considering that imposing such regularization directly onto the network embeddings might be too strict to impede the convergence of $\mathcal{L}_{seg}$ and $\mathcal{L}_{compact}$, we adopt the contrastive learning [8] to achieve this constraint. Specifically, an embedding network H_ϕ is introduced to project the features $E \in [E^{con}, E^{bg}]$ to a lower-dimensional space, then the distance is computed on the obtained feature vectors from network H_ϕ as $d_\phi(E_m, E_n) = \|H_\phi(E_m) - H_\phi(E_n)\|_2$, where the sample pair (m, n) are randomly drawn from all domains $\mathcal{D}$, as we expect to harmonize the embeddings space of $\mathcal{D}_{te}$ and $\mathcal{D}_{tr}$ to capture domain-invariant representations around the boundary region. Therefore in our model, the contrastive loss is defined as follows:

$$\ell_{contrastive}(m, n) = \begin{cases} d_\phi(E_m, E_n), & \text{if } \tau(E_m) = \tau(E_n) \\ (max\{0, \zeta - d_\phi(E_m, E_n)\})^2, & \text{if } \tau(E_m) \neq \tau(E_n) \end{cases}, \tag{8.3}$$

where the function $\tau(E)$ indicates the class (1 for E being E^{con}, and 0 for E^{bg}) ζ is a predefined distance margin following the practice of metric learning (set as 10 in our model). The final objective $\mathcal{L}_{smooth}$ is computed within mini-batch of q samples. We randomly employ either E^{con} or E^{bg} for each sample, and the $\mathcal{L}_{smooth}$ is the average of $\ell_{contrastive}$ over all pairs of (m, n) embeddings:

$$\mathcal{L}_{smooth} = \sum_{m=1}^{q} \sum_{n=m+1}^{q} \ell_{contrastive}(m, n)/C(q, 2), \qquad (8.4)$$

where $C(q, 2)$ is the number of combinations. Overall, all training objectives including $\mathcal{L}_{seg}(\mathcal{D}_{tr}; \theta)$ and $\mathcal{L}_{meta}(\mathcal{D}_{tr}, D_{te}; \theta')$, are optimized together with respect to the original parameters θ. The $\mathcal{L}_{smooth}$ is also optimized with respect to H_{ϕ}.

8.3.1.4 Technical and implementation details

We implement an adapted Mix-residual-UNet [54] as segmentation backbone. Due to the large variance on slice thickness among different sites, we employ the 2D architecture. The domains number of meta-train and metatest were set as 2 and 1. The weights λ_1 and λ_2 were set as 1.0 and $5e^{-3}$. The embedding network H_{ϕ} composes of two fully connected layers with output sizes of 48 and 32. The segmentation network F_{θ} was trained using Adam optimizer and the learning rates for inner-loop update and metaoptimization were both set as $1e^{-4}$. The network H_{ϕ} was also trained using Adam optimizer with learning rate of $1e^{-4}$. We trained 20K iterations with batch size of 5 for each source domain. For batch normalization layer, we use the statistics of testing data for feature normalization during inference for better generalization performance.

8.3.2 Experimental results

8.3.2.1 Datasets and evaluation metrics

We employ prostate T2-weighted MRI from 6 different data sources with distribution shift (cf. Table 8.1 for summary of their sample numbers and scanning protocols). Among these data, samples of Site A, B are from NCI-ISBI13 dataset [3]; samples of Site C are from I2CVB dataset [24]; samples of Site D, E, F are from PROMISE12 dataset [31]. Note that the NCI-ISBI13 and PROMISE12 actually include multiple data sources, hence we decompose them in our work. For preprocessing, we resized each sample to 384×384 in axial plane, and normalized it to zero mean and unit variance. We then clip each sample to only preserve slices of prostate region for consistent objective segmentation regions across sites. We adopt Dice score (Dice) and Average Surface Distance (ASD) as the evaluation metric.

8.3.2.2 Comparison with state-of-the-art generalization methods

We implemented several state-of-the-art generalization methods for comparison, including a data-augmentation based method (BigAug) [55], a classifier regularization based method (Epi-FCR) [26], a latent space regularization method (LatReg) [1] and a meta learning based method (MASF) [9]. In

Table 8.1 Details of our employed six different sites obtained from public datasets.

Dataset	Institution	Case num	Field strength (T)	Resolution (in/through plane) (mm)	Endorectal Coil	Manufactor
Site A	RUNMC	30	3	0.6-0.625/3.6-4	Surface	Siemens
Site B	BMC	30	1.5	0.4/3	Endorectal	Philips
Site C	HCRUDB	19	3	0.67-0.79/1.25	No	Siemens
Site D	UCL	13	1.5 and 3	0.325-0.625/3-3.6	No	Siemens
Site E	BIDMC	12	3	0.25/2.2-3	Endorectal	GE
Site F	HK	12	1.5	0.625/3.6	Endorectal	Siemens

Table 8.2 Generalization performance of various methods on Dice (%) and ASD (mm).

Method	Site A		Site B		Site C		Site D		Site E		Site F		Average	
Intra-site	89.27	1.41	88.17	1.35	88.29	1.56	83.23	3.21	83.67	2.93	85.43	1.91	86.34	2.06
DeepAll (baseline)	87.87	2.05	85.37	1.82	82.94	2.97	86.87	2.25	84.48	2.18	85.58	1.82	85.52	2.18
Epi-FCR [26]	88.35	1.97	85.83	1.73	82.56	2.99	86.97	2.05	85.03	1.89	85.66	1.76	85.74	2.07
LatReg [1]	88.17	1.95	86.65	1.53	83.37	2.91	87.27	2.12	84.68	1.93	86.28	1.65	86.07	2.01
BigAug [55]	88.62	1.70	86.22	1.56	83.76	2.72	87.35	1.98	85.53	1.90	85.83	1.75	86.21	1.93
MASF [9]	88.70	1.69	86.20	1.54	84.16	2.39	87.43	1.91	86.18	1.85	86.57	1.47	86.55	1.81
Plain meta learning	88.55	1.87	85.92	1.61	83.60	2.52	87.52	1.86	85.39	1.89	86.49	1.63	86.24	1.90
+ $\mathcal{L}_{compact}$	89.08	1.61	87.11	1.49	84.02	2.47	87.96	1.64	86.23	1.80	87.19	1.32	86.93	1.72
+ $\mathcal{L}_{smooth}$	89.25	1.64	87.14	1.53	84.69	2.17	87.79	1.88	86.00	1.82	87.74	1.24	87.10	1.71
SAML (Ours)	89.66	1.38	87.53	1.46	84.43	2.07	88.67	1.56	87.37	1.77	88.34	1.22	87.67	1.58

addition, we conducted experiments with 'DeepAll' baseline (i.e., aggregating data from all source domains for training a deep model) and 'Intra-site' setting (i.e., training and testing on the same domain, with some outlier cases excluded to provide general internal performance on each site). Following previous practice [9] for domain generalization, we adopt the leave-one-domain-out strategy, *i.e.*, training on K-1 domains and testing on the one left-out unseen target domain.

As listed in Table 8.2, DeepAll presents a strong performance, while the Epi-FCR with classifier regularization shows limited advantage over this baseline. The other approaches of LatReg, BigAug, and MASF are more significantly better than DeepAll, with the meta learning based method yielding the best results among them in our experiments. Notably, our approach (cf. the last row) achieves higher performance over all these state-of-the-art methods across all the six sites, and outperforms the DeepAll model by 2.15% on Dice and 0.60 mm on ASD, demonstrating the capability of our shape-aware meta learning scheme to deal with domain generalization problem. Moreover, Fig. 8.2 shows the generalization segmentation results of different methods on three typical cases from different unseen sites. We observe that our model with shape-relevant metaregularizers can well preserve the complete shape and smooth boundary for the segmentation in unseen domains, whereas other methods sometimes failed to do so. We also report in Table 8.2 the cross-validation results conducted within each site, i.e., Intra-site. Interestingly, we find that this result for site D/E/F is relatively lower than the other sites, and even worse than the baseline model. The reason would be that the sample numbers of these three sites are fewer than the others, consequently intra-site training is ineffective with limited generalization capability. This observation reveals the important fact that, when a certain site suffers from severe data scarcity for model training, aggregating data from other sites (even with distribution shift) can be very helpful to obtain a qualified model. In addition, we also find that our method outperforms the Intra-site model in 4 out of 6 data sites, with superior overall performances on both Dice and ASD, which endorses the potential value of our approach in clinical practice.

8.3.2.3 Ablation study

We first study the contribution of each key component in our model. As shown in Table 8.2, the plain meta learning method only with $\mathcal{L}_{seg}$ can already outperform the DeepAll baseline, leveraging the explicit simulation of domain shift for training. Adding shape compactness constraint into $\mathcal{L}_{meta}$ yields improved Dice and ASD which are higher than MASF. Further incorporating L_{smooth} (SAML) to encourage domain-invariant embeddings for pixels around the boundary, consistent performance im-

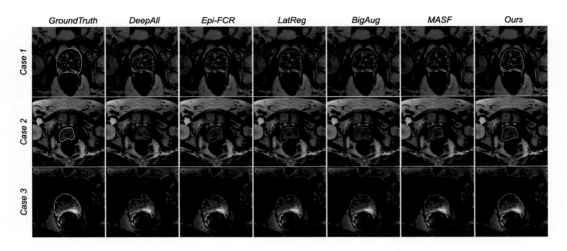

FIGURE 8.2

Qualitative comparison on the generalization results of different methods, with three cases respectively drawn from different unseen domains.

provements on all six sites are attained. Besides, simply constraining L_{smooth} on pure meta learning method (+ L_{smooth}) also leads to improvements across sites.

We further investigate the influence of training domain numbers on the generalization performance of our approach and the DeepAll model. Fig. 8.3 illustrates how the segmentation performance on each unseen domain would change, as we gradually increase the number of source domains in range [1, $K -$ 1]. Obviously, when a model is trained just with a single source domain, directly applying it to target domain receives unsatisfactory results. The generalization performance progresses as the training site number increases, indicating that aggregating wider data sources helps to cover a more comprehensive distribution. Notably, our approach consistently outperforms DeepAll across all numbers of training sites, confirming the stable efficacy of our proposed learning scheme.

8.4 Federated domain generalization with meta learning in continuous frequency space

8.4.1 Preliminary

Domain generalization typically requires aggregating multidomain data for model learning. However, such strong assumption may not always hold in practice, especially in medical field where the data sharing is highly concerned and sometimes prohibitive due to privacy issue. Fortunately, federated learning (FL) [22] has recently opened the door for a promising privacy-preserving solution, which allows training a model on distributed datasets while keeping data locally. The paradigm works in a way that each local client (e.g., hospital) learns from their own data, and only aggregates the model parameters at a certain frequency at the central server to generate a global model. Under the challenging constraint of

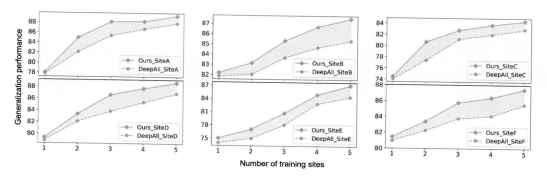

FIGURE 8.3

Curves of generalization performance on unseen domain as the number of training source domain increases, using DeepAll method and our proposed approach.

data decentralization, previous DG approaches, e.g., meta learning, usually lack feasibility as they are typically designed under the centralized setting and require to jointly access to multisource distributions in the learning process. In this part, we further identify the problem setting of Federated Domain Generalization (FedDG), which aims to learn a federated model from multiple decentralized source domains such that it can directly generalize to completely unseen domains. We propose a novel metabased approach, named as Episodic Learning in Continuous Frequency Space (ELCFS), by enabling each client to exploit multisource data distributions through exploring the information in frequency space, in order to promote the feasibility of meta learning under the challenging constraint of data decentralization.

8.4.2 Method

We start with the formulation for federated domain generalization and its challenges in medical image segmentation scenario. We then describe the proposed method *Episodic Learning in Continuous Frequency Space* (ELCFS) to explicitly address these challenges [32]. An overview of the method is shown in Fig. 8.4.

8.4.2.1 Federated domain generalization

Preliminaries: In FedDG, we denote $(\mathcal{X}, \mathcal{Y})$ as the joint image and label space of a task, $\mathcal{S} = \{\mathcal{S}^1, \mathcal{S}^2, ..., \mathcal{S}^K\}$ as the set of K distributed source domains involved in federated learning. Each domain contains data and label pairs of $\mathcal{S}^k = \{(x_i^k, y_i^k)\}_{i=1}^{N^k}$, which are sampled from a domain-specific distribution $(\mathcal{X}^k, \mathcal{Y})$. The goal of FedDG is to learn a model $f_\theta : \mathcal{X} \to \mathcal{Y}$ using the K distributed source domains, such that it can directly generalize to a completely unseen testing domain $\mathcal{T}$ with a high performance.

Standard federated learning paradigm involves the communication between a central server and the K local clients. At each federated round t, every client k will receive the same global model weights θ from the central server and update the model with their local data $\mathcal{S}^k$ for E epochs. The central server then collects the local parameters θ^k from all clients and aggregates them to update the global model. This process repeats until the global model converges. In this work, we consider the most popular

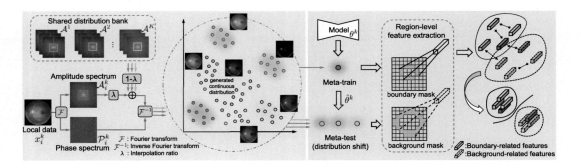

FIGURE 8.4

Overview of our proposed episodic learning in continuous frequency space (ELCFS). The distribution information is exchanged across clients from frequency space with an continuous interpolation mechanism, enabling each local client to access the multisource distributions. An episodic training paradigm is then established to expose the local optimization to domain shift, with explicit regularization to promote domain-independent feature cohesion and separation at the ambiguous boundary region for improving generalizability.

federated averaging algorithm (FedAvg) [38], which aggregates the local parameters with weights in proportional to the size of each local dataset to update the global model, i.e., $\theta = \sum_{k=1}^{K} \frac{N^k}{N} \theta^k$, where $N = \sum_{k=1}^{K} N^k$. It is worth noting that our method can also be flexibly incorporated to other FL backbones.

Challenges: With the goal of unseen domain generalization, a model is expected to thoroughly investigate the multisource data distributions to pursue domain-invariance of its learned latent space. However, the federated setting in the specific medical image segmentation scenario poses several challenges for that. *First*, the multisource data in FL are stored distributedly and the learning at each client can only access its individual local distribution, which constrains to make full use of the multisource distributions to learn generalizable parameters. *Second*, though FL has collaborated multisource data, the medical images acquired from different clinical sites can present large heterogeneity. This leads to distinct distributions among the collaborative datasets, which is insufficient to ensure domain invariance in a more continuous distribution space to attain good generalizability in complex clinical environments. *Third*, the structure of medical anatomises usually presents high ambiguity around its boundary region, raising challenge for previous DG techniques that typically lacks assurance for the domain-invariance of features in such ambiguous region.

8.4.2.2 Continuous frequency space interpolation

To address the restriction of decentralized datasets, the foundation of our solution is to exchange the distribution information across clients, such that each local client can get access to multisource data distributions for learning generalizable parameters. Considering that sharing raw images is forbidden, we propose to exploit the information inherent in the frequency space, which enables to separate the distribution (i.e. style) information from the original images to be shared between clients without privacy leakage.

Specifically, given a sample $x_i^k \in \mathbb{R}^{H \times W \times C}$ ($C = 3$ for RGB image and $C = 1$ for gray-scale image) from the k-th client, we can obtain its frequency space signal through fast Fourier transform [40] as:

$$\mathcal{F}(x_i^k)(u, v, c) = \sum_{h=0}^{H-1} \sum_{w=0}^{W-1} x_i^k(h, w, c) e^{-j2\pi(\frac{h}{H}u + \frac{w}{W}v)}. \tag{8.5}$$

This frequency space signal $\mathcal{F}(x_i^k)$ can be further decomposed to an amplitude spectrum $\mathcal{A}_i^k \in \mathbb{R}^{H \times W \times C}$ and a phase spectrum $\mathcal{P}_i^k \in \mathbb{R}^{H \times W \times C}$, which respectively reflect the low-level distributions (e.g. style) and high-level semantics (e.g. object) of the image. To exchange the distribution information across clients, we first construct a distribution bank $\mathcal{A} = [\mathcal{A}^1, ..., \mathcal{A}^K]$, where each $\mathcal{A}^k = \{\mathcal{A}_i^k\}_{i=1}^{N^k}$ contains all amplitude spectrum of images from the k-th client, representing the distribution of $\mathcal{X}^k$. This bank is then made accessible to all clients as shared distribution knowledge.

Next, we design a continuous interpolation mechanism within the frequency space, aiming to transmit multisource distribution information to a local client leveraging the distribution bank. As shown in the left part of Fig. 8.4, given a local image x_i^k at client k, we can replace some low-frequency component of its amplitude spectrum with the ones in distribution bank $\mathcal{A}$, while its phase spectrum is unaffected to preserve the semantic content. As an outcome, we can generate images with transformed appearances exhibiting distribution characteristics of other clients. More importantly, we continuously interpolate between amplitude spectrum of local data and the transferred amplitude spectrum of other domains. In this way, we can enrich the established multidomain distributions for each local client, benefiting from a dedicated dense space with smooth distribution changes.

Formally, this is achieved by randomly sampling an amplitude spectrum item $\mathcal{A}_j^n (n \neq k)$ from the distribution bank, then synthesize a new amplitude spectrum by interpolating between $\mathcal{A}_i^k$ and $\mathcal{A}_j^n$. Let $\mathcal{M} = \mathbb{1}_{(h,w) \in [-\alpha H : \alpha H, -\alpha W : \alpha W]}$ be a binary mask which controls the scale of low-frequency component within amplitude spectrum to be exchanged, whose value is 1 at the central region and 0 elsewhere. Denote λ as the interpolation ratio adjusting the amount of distribution information contributed by $\mathcal{A}_i^k$ and $\mathcal{A}_j^n$, the generated new amplitude spectrum interacting distributions for local client k and external client n is represented as:

$$\mathcal{A}_{i,\lambda}^{k \to n} = ((1 - \lambda)\mathcal{A}_i^k + \lambda\mathcal{A}_j^n) * \mathcal{M} + \mathcal{A}_i^k * (1 - \mathcal{M}). \tag{8.6}$$

After obtaining the interpolated amplitude spectrum $\mathcal{A}_{i,\lambda}^{k \to n}$, we then combine it with the original phase spectrum to generate the transformed image via inverse Fourier transform $\mathcal{F}^{-1}$ as follows:

$$x_{i,\lambda}^{k \to n} = \mathcal{F}^{-1}(\mathcal{A}_{i,\lambda}^{k \to n}, \mathcal{P}_i^k), \tag{8.7}$$

where the generated image $x_{i,\lambda}^{k \to n}$ preserves the original semantics of x_i^k while carrying a new distribution interacted between $\mathcal{X}^k$ and $\mathcal{X}^n$. In our implementation, the interpolation ratio λ will be dynamically sampled from [0.0, 1.0] to generate images via a continuous distribution space. As intuitive examples shown in Fig. 8.4, our interpolation operation allows the generated samples to bridge the intermediate space between distinct distributions across domains. Note that the method described above does not require heavy computations, thus can be performed online as the local learning goes on. Practically, for each input x_i^k, we will sample an amplitude spectrum A_j^n from the distribution bank for each external client $n \neq k$, and transform its image appearance as Eqs. (8.2)-(8.3). Through this, we obtain

$K - 1$ transformed images $\{x_{i,\lambda}^{k \to n}\}_{n \neq k}$ of different distributions, which share the same semantic label as x_i^k. For ease of denotation, we represent these transformed images as t_i^k hereafter, i.e. $t_i^k = \{x_{i,\lambda}^{k \to n}\}_{n \neq k}$. Furthermore, this approach does not violate the privacy concern since the phase spectrum containing core semantics are retained at each client throughout the whole process, and the raw images cannot be reconstructed with the amplitude spectrum alone [46].

8.4.2.3 Boundary-oriented episodic learning

The above constructed continuous multisource distributions at each local client provide the materials to learn generalizable local parameters. In the following, we carefully design a boundary-oriented episodic learning scheme for local training, by particularly meeting challenges of model generalization in medical image segmentation scenario.

Episodic learning at local client: We establish the local training as an episodic meta learning scheme, which learns generalizable model parameters by simulating train/test domain shift explicitly. Note that in our case, the domain shift at a local client comes from the data generated from frequency space with different distributions. Specifically, in each iteration, we consider the raw input x_i^k as meta-train and its counterparts t_i^k generated from frequency space as metatest presenting distribution shift (cf. Fig. 8.4). The meta learning scheme can then be decoupled to two steps. First, the model parameters θ^k are updated on metatrain with segmentation Dice loss $\mathcal{L}_{seg}$:

$$\hat{\theta}^k = \theta^k - \beta \nabla_{\theta^k} \mathcal{L}_{seg}(x_i^k; \theta^k), \tag{8.8}$$

where β denotes the learning rate for the inner-loop update. Second, a metaupdate is performed to virtually evaluate the updated parameters $\hat{\theta}^k$ on the held-out metatest data t_i^k with a metaobjective $\mathcal{L}_{meta}$. Crucially, this objective is computed with the updated parameters $\hat{\theta}^k$, but optimized w.r.t. the original parameters θ^k. Such optimization paradigm aims to train the model such that its learning on source domains can further fulfill certain properties that we desire in unseen domains, which are quantified by $\mathcal{L}_{meta}$.

Boundary-oriented metaoptimization: We define the $\mathcal{L}_{meta}$ with considering specific challenges in medical image segmentation. Particularly, it is observed that the performance drop of segmentation results at unseen domains outside federation often comes from the ambiguous boundary area of anatomies. To this end, we design a new boundary-oriented objective to enhance the domain-invariant boundary delineation, by carefully learning from the local data x_i^k and the corresponding t_i^k generated from frequency space with multisource distributions. The idea is to regularize the boundary-related and background-related features of these data to respectively cluster to a compact space regardless of their distributions while reducing the clusters overlap. This is crucial, since if the model cannot project their features around boundary area with distribution-independent class-specific cohesion and separation, the predictions will suffer from ambiguous decision boundaries and still be sensitive to the distribution shift when deployed to unseen domains outside federation.

Specifically, we first extract the boundary-related and background-related features for the input samples. Given image x_i^k with segmentation label y_i^k, we can extract its binary boundary mask $y_{i\_bd}^k$ and background mask $y_{i\_bg}^k$ with morphological operations on y_i^k. Here, the mask $y_{i\_bg}^k$ only contains background pixels around the anatomy boundary instead of from the whole image, as we expect to enhance the discriminability for features around the boundary region. Let Z_i^k denote the activation map extracted from layer l, which is interpolated with bilinear interpolation to keep consistent dimensions as y_i^k. Then the boundary-related and background-related features of x_i^k can be extracted from Z_i^k with masked average pooling over $y_{i\_bd}^k$ and $y_{i\_bg}^k$ as:

$$h_{i\_bd}^k = \frac{\sum_{h,w} Z_i^k * y_{i\_bd}^k}{\sum_{h,w} y_{i\_bd}^k}; \; h_{i\_bg}^k = \frac{\sum_{h,w} Z_i^k * y_{i\_bg}^k}{\sum_{h,w} y_{i\_bg}^k}, \tag{8.9}$$

where $*$ denote element-wise product. The produced $h_{i\_bd}^k$ and $h_{i\_bg}^k$ are single-dimensional vectors, representing the averaged region-level features of the boundary and background pixels. By further performing the same operation for K-1 transformed images t_i^k with different distributions transferred from the frequency space, we accordingly obtain together K boundary-related and K background-related features.

Next, we enhance the domain-invariance and discriminability of these features, by regularizing their intra-class cohesion and interclass separation regardless of distributions. Here, we employ the well-established InfoNCE [8] objective to impose such regularization. Denote (h_m, h_p) as a pair of features, which is a positive pair if h_m and h_p are of the same class (both boundary-related or background-related) and otherwise negative pair. In our case, the InfoNCE loss is defined over each positive pair (h_m, h_p) within the $2 \times K$ region-level features as:

$$\ell(h_m, h_p) = -log \frac{exp(h_m \odot h_p / \tau)}{\sum_{q=1, q \neq m}^{2K} \mathbb{F}(h_m, h_q) \cdot exp(h_m \odot h_q / \tau)}, \tag{8.10}$$

where $\odot$ denote the cosine similarity: $a \odot b = \frac{\langle a, b \rangle}{||a||_2 ||b||_2}$; the value of $\mathbb{F}(h_m, h_q)$ is 0 and 1 for positive and negative pair respectively; τ denotes the temperature parameter. The final loss $\mathcal{L}_{boundary}$ is the average of ℓ over all positive pairs:

$$\mathcal{L}_{boundary} = \sum_{m=1}^{2K} \sum_{p=m+1}^{2K} \frac{(1 - \mathbb{F}(h_m, h_p)) \cdot \ell(h_m, h_p)}{B(K, 2) \times 2}, \tag{8.11}$$

where $B(K, 2)$ is the number of combinations.

Overall local learning objective: The overall metaobjective is composed of the segmentation dice loss $\mathcal{L}_{seg}$ and the boundary-oriented objective $\mathcal{L}_{boundary}$ as:

$$\mathcal{L}_{meta} = \mathcal{L}_{seg}(t_i^k; \hat{\theta}^k) + \gamma \mathcal{L}_{boundary}(x_i^k, t_i^k; \hat{\theta}^k), \tag{8.12}$$

where $\hat{\theta}^k$ is the updated parameter from Eq. (8.8), γ is a balancing hyperparameter. Finally, both the inner-loop objective and metaobjective will be optimized together with respect to the original parameter θ^k as:

$$\arg \min_{\theta^k} \mathcal{L}_{seg}(x_i^k; \theta^k) + \mathcal{L}_{meta}(x_i^k, t_i^k; \hat{\theta}^k). \tag{8.13}$$

In a federated round, once the local learning is finished, the local parameters θ^k from all clients will be aggregated at the central server to update the global model.

8.4.2.4 Technical and implementation details

In the federated learning process, all clients use the same hyperparameter settings, and the local model is trained using Adam optimizer with batch size of 5 and Adam momentum of 0.9 and 0.99. The metastep size and learning rate are both set as $1e^{-3}$. The interpolation ratio λ in frequency space is randomly sampled within [0.0, 1.0], and we will investigate this parameter in the ablation study. The hyperparameter α is empirically set as 0.01 to avoid artifacts on the transformed images. The activation maps from the last two deconvolutional layers are interpolated and concatenated to extract the semantic features around boundary region, and the temperature parameter τ is empirically set as 0.05. The weight γ is set as 0.1 and 0.5 in the two tasks to balance the magnitude of the training objectives. We totally train 100 federated rounds as the global model has converged stably, and the local epoch E in each federated round is set as 1. The framework is implemented with Pytorch library, and is trained on two NVIDIA TitanXp GPUs.

8.4.3 Experimental results

8.4.3.1 Datasets and evaluation metrics

We employ **retinal fundus images from 4 different clinical centers** of public datasets [14,41,49] for optic disc and cup segmentation. For preprocessing, we center-crop a 800×800 disc region for these data uniformly, then resize the cropped region to 384×384 as network input. We further collect **prostate T2-weighted MRI images from 6 different data sources** partitioned from the public datasets [3,24,31,34] for prostate MRI segmentation task. All the data are preprocessed to have similar field of view for the prostate region and resized to 384×384 in axial plane. We then normalize the data individually to zero mean and unit variance in intensity values. Note that for both tasks, the data acquired from different clinical centers present heterogeneous distributions due to the varying imaging conditions. The example cases and sample numbers of each data source are presented in Fig. 8.5. Data augmentation of random rotation, scaling, and flipping are employed in the two tasks. For evaluation, we adopt two commonly-used metrics of Dice coefficient (Dice) and Hausdorff distance (HD), to quantitatively evaluate the segmentation results on the whole object region and the surface shape respectively.

8.4.3.2 Comparison with DG methods

Experimental setting: In our experiments, we follow the practice in domain generalization literature to adopt the leave-one-domain-out strategy, i.e., training on K-1 distributed source domains and testing on the one left-out unseen target domain. This results in four generalization settings for the fundus image segmentation task and six settings for the prostate MRI segmentation task.

We compare with recent state-of-the-art DG methods that are free from data centralization and can be incorporated into the local learning process in federated paradigm, including: **JiGen [4]** an effective self-supervised learning approach to learn general representations by solving jigsaw puzzles; **BigAug [55]** a method that performs extensive data transformations to regularize general representation learning; **Epi-FCR [26]** a scheme to periodically exchange partial model (classifier or feature extractor) across domains to expose model learning to domain shift; **RSC [17]** a method that randomly discards the dominating features to promote robust model optimization. For the implementation, we follow their public code or paper and establish them in the federated setting. We also compare with the baseline

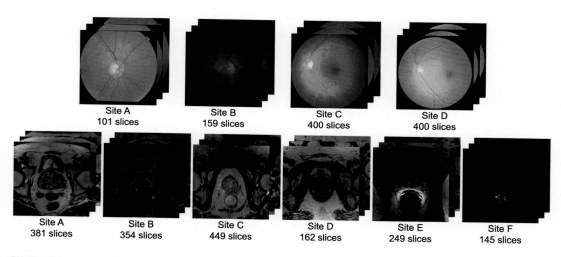

FIGURE 8.5

Example cases and slice number of each data source in fundus image segmentation and prostate MRI segmentation tasks.

setting, i.e., learning a global model with the basic **FedAvg [38]** algorithm without any generalization technique.

Comparison results: Table 8.3 presents the quantitative results for retinal fundus segmentation. We see that different DG methods can improve the overall generalization performance more or less over FedAvg. This attributes to their regularization effect on the local learning to extract general representations. Compared with these methods, our ELCFS achieves higher overall performance and obtains improvements on most unseen sites in terms of Dice and HD for both optic disc and cup segmentation. This benefits from our frequency space interpolation mechanism which presents multidomain distributions to local client. Specifically, for other DG methods, their local learning still can only access the individual distribution and fail to regularize the features towards domain-invariance in a diverse distribution space. In contrast, our method enables the local learning to take full advantages of the multisource distributions and explicitly enhances the domain-invariance of features around the ambiguous boundary region. In addition, our ELCFS achieves consistent improvements over FedAvg across all unseen domain settings, with the overall performance increase of 2.02% in Dice and 2.86 in HD.

For prostate MRI segmentation (c.f. Table 8.4), the comparison DG methods generally perform better than FedAvg, but the improvements are relatively marginal. Our ELCFS obtains the highest Dice across all the six unseen sites and HD on most sites. Overall, our method improves over FedAvg for Dice from 85.57% to 87.39% and HD from 12.42 to 10.88, outperforming other DG methods. Fig. 8.6 shows the segmentation results with two cases from unseen domains for each task. It is observed that our method accurately segments the structure and delineates the boundary in images of unknown distributions, whereas other methods sometimes fail to do so.

Table 8.3 Comparison of federated domain generalization results on Optic Disc/Cup segmentation from fundus images.

Task Unseen Site	Optic Disc Segmentation					Optic Cup Segmentation					Overall
	A	B	C	D	Avg.	A	B	C	D	Avg.	
	Dice Coefficient (Dice) ↑										
JiGen [4]	93.92	85.91	92.63	94.03	91.62	82.26	70.68	83.32	85.70	80.47	86.06
BigAug [55]	93.49	86.18	92.09	93.67	91.36	81.62	69.46	82.64	84.51	79.56	85.46
Epi-FCR [26]	94.34	86.22	92.88	93.73	91.79	83.06	70.25	83.68	83.14	80.03	85.91
RSC [17]	94.50	86.21	92.23	94.15	91.77	81.77	69.37	83.40	84.82	79.84	85.80
FedAvg [38]	92.88	85.73	92.07	93.21	90.97	80.84	69.71	82.28	83.35	79.05	85.01
ELCFS (Ours)	95.37	87.52	93.37	94.50	92.69	84.13	71.88	83.94	85.51	81.37	87.03
	Hausdorff Distance (HD) ↓										
JiGen [4]	13.12	20.18	11.29	8.15	13.19	20.88	23.21	11.55	9.23	16.22	14.71
BigAug [55]	16.91	19.01	11.53	8.76	14.05	21.21	23.10	12.02	10.47	16.70	15.39
Epi-FCR [26]	13.02	18.97	10.67	8.47	12.78	19.12	21.94	11.50	10.86	15.86	14.32
RSC [17]	19.44	19.26	13.47	8.14	15.08	23.85	24.01	11.38	9.79	17.25	16.16
FedAvg [38]	17.01	20.68	11.70	9.33	14.68	20.77	26.01	11.85	10.03	17.17	15.93
ELCFS (Ours)	11.36	17.10	10.83	7.24	11.63	18.65	19.36	11.17	8.91	14.52	13.07

Table 8.4 Comparison of federated domain generalization results on prostate MRI segmentation.

Unseen Site	A	B	C	D	E	F	Average
	Dice Coefficient (Dice) ↑						
JiGen [4]	89.95	85.81	84.06	87.34	81.32	89.11	86.26
BigAug [55]	89.63	84.62	83.86	87.66	81.20	88.96	85.99
Epi-FCR [26]	89.72	85.39	84.97	86.55	80.63	89.76	86.17
RSC [17]	88.86	85.56	84.36	86.21	79.97	89.80	85.80
FedAvg [38]	89.02	84.48	84.11	86.30	80.38	89.15	85.57
ELCFS (Ours)	90.19	87.17	85.26	88.23	83.02	90.47	87.39
	Hausdorff Distance (HD) ↓						
JiGen [4]	10.51	11.53	11.70	11.49	14.80	9.02	11.51
BigAug [55]	10.68	11.78	12.07	10.66	13.98	9.73	11.48
Epi-FCR [26]	10.60	12.31	12.29	12.00	15.68	8.81	11.95
RSC [17]	10.57	11.84	14.76	13.07	14.79	8.83	12.31
FedAvg [38]	11.64	12.01	14.86	11.80	14.90	9.30	12.42
ELCFS (Ours)	10.30	11.49	11.50	11.57	11.08	8.31	10.88

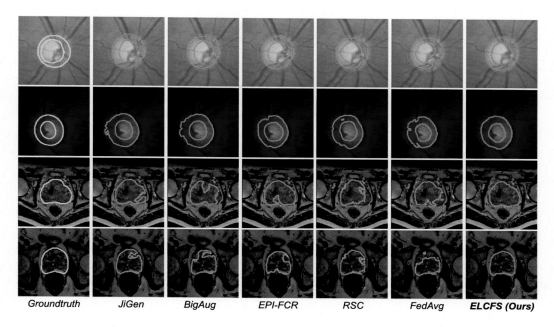

Groundtruth   JiGen   BigAug   EPI-FCR   RSC   FedAvg   **ELCFS (Ours)**

FIGURE 8.6

Qualitative comparison on the generalization results of different methods in fundus image segmentation (top two rows) and prostate MRI segmentation (bottom two tows).

8.4.3.3 Ablation analysis

We conduct ablation studies to investigate four key questions regarding our ELCFS: **1)** the contribution of each component to our model performance, **2)** the benefit of the interpolation operation and the choice of λ, **3)** how the semantic feature space around the boundary region is influenced by our method, and **4)** how the numbers of participating clients affect the performance of our method.

Contribution of each component: We first validate the effect of the two key components in our method, i.e. continuous frequency space interpolation (**CFSI**) and Boundary-oriented Episodic Learning (**BEL**), by removing them respectively from our method to observe the model performance. As shown in Fig. 8.7, removing either part will lead to decrease on the generalization performance in different unseen domain settings for the two tasks. This is reasonable and reflects how the two components play complementary roles to the performance of our method, i.e., the generated distributions from CFSI lays foundation for the learning of BEL, and the BEL inversely provides assurance to effectively exploit the generated distributions.

Importance of continuous interpolation in frequency space: To analyze the effect of continuous interpolation mechanism in ELCFS, we use t-SNE [37] to visualize the distribution of generated images in fundus image segmentation. As shown in Fig. 8.8 (a), the pink points denote the local data of a client, and other points denote the transformed data that are generated with amplitude spectrum from different clients. It appears that fixing λ (left) will lead to several distinct distributions, while the continuous

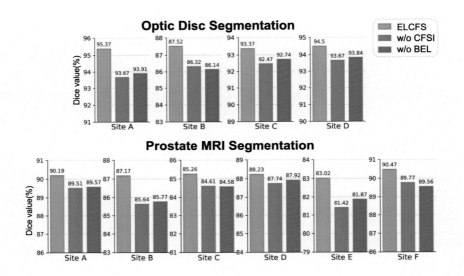

FIGURE 8.7

Ablation results to analyze the effect of the two components (i.e. CFSI and BEL) in our method.

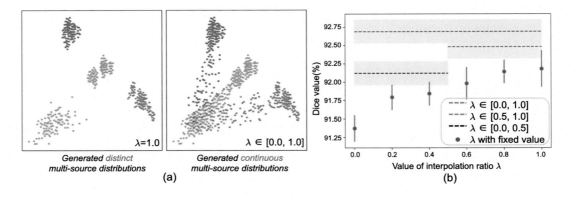

FIGURE 8.8

(a) Visualization of t-SNE [37] embedding for the original fundus images at a local client (pink points) and the corresponding transformed images with amplitude spectrum from different clients (green, yellow, and blue points); (b) Generalization performance on optic disc segmentation under different settings of interpolation ratio λ, with fixed value or continuous sampling from different ranges (with error bar from three independent runs).

interpolation mechanism (right) can smoothly bridge the distinct distributions to enrich the established multidomain distributions. This promotes the local learning to attain domain-invariance in a dedicated dense distribution space.

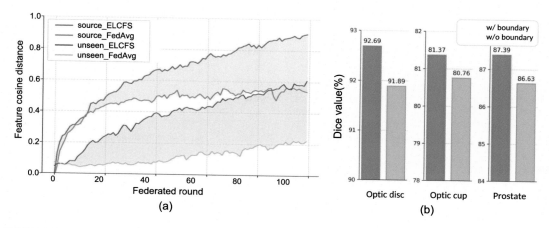

FIGURE 8.9

(a) Cosine distance between the boundary-related and background-related features; (b) Generalization performance of our method with or without the boundary-oriented metaobjective.

We then analyze the effect of the choice of λ on our model performance, for which we conduct experiments with fixed values from 0.0 to 1.0 with a step size 0.2, and continuous sampling in range of [0.0, 0.5], [0.5, 1.0], and [0.0, 1.0]. As shown in Fig. 8.8 (b), compared with not transferring any distribution information (i.e., λ = 0), setting λ > 0 as a fixed value can always improve the model performance. Besides, the continuous sampling can further improve the performance and the sampling range of [0.0, 1.0] yields the best results, which reflects the benefits of continuous distribution space for domain generalization.

Discriminability at ambiguous boundary region: We plot the cosine distance between the boundary-related and background-related features, i.e., $\mathbb{E}[h_{i\_bd} \odot h_{i\_bg}]$, to analyze how the semantic feature space around the boundary region is influenced by our method. In Fig. 8.9 (a), the two green lines denote the growth of feature distance in our ELCFS and the FedAvg baseline respectively, for samples drawn from the training source domains. We can see that ELCFS yields a higher feature distance, indicating that the features of the boundary and the surrounding background region can be better separated in our method. For the two yellow lines, sample features are drawn from the unseen domains. As expected, the distance is not as high as in source domain, yet our method also presents a clearly higher margin than FedAvg. We also quantitatively analyze the effect of $\mathcal{L}_{boundary}$ on the model performance. As observed from Fig. 8.9 (b), removing this objective from the metaoptimization leads to consistent performance drops on the generalization performance in different tasks.

Effect of participating client number: We further analyze how the generalization performance of our method and FedAvg will be affected when different numbers of hospitals participating in federated learning. Fig. 8.10 shows the results on prostate MRI segmentation, in which we present the generalization results on two unseen sites with the client number gradually increasing from 1 to $K - 1$. As expected, the models trained with single-source data cannot obtain good results when deployed to unseen domains. The generalization performance increases when more clients participating in the

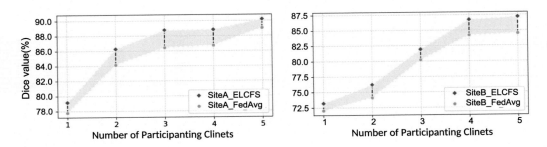

FIGURE 8.10

Curves of generalization performance on two unseen prostate datasets (i.e., site A and B) as the number of participating clients increases, using our proposed approach and FedAvg.

federated training, which is reasonable as aggregating data from multiple sources can cover a more comprehensive data distribution. Particularly, our ELCFS consistently outperforms FedAvg on all generalization settings with different client numbers, demonstrating the stable efficacy of our method to leverage distributed data sources to enhance the generalizability of federated learning model.

8.5 Conclusions

In conclusion, this chapter presents meta learning based methods to address domain generalizations problems in medical image segmentation. Solutions are established under two different realistic scenarios, i.e., centralized model training and decentralized federated training. In centralized training setting, the meta-based learning scheme is established by splitting the multidomain data into metatrain and metalearn to optimize the model towards simulated domain shift, with two shape-relevant metaobjectives proposed to enhance the model generalizability at unseen domains. For decentralized federated learning, a frequency-space interpolation mechanism has been devised to transmit the distribution information across clients in a privacy-protecting way. The meta learning scheme is then established locally with explicitly regularization for the features around ambiguous boundary regions to facilitate the generalization of federated models. Both application scenarios have demonstrated highly promising results on generalizing the deep models to the unseen target domains. Meanwhile, the proposed methods are general and can be extended to other scenarios in medical image computing to address model generalization issues.

8.6 Acknowledgment

These works were supported by the Hong Kong Innovation and Technology Fund (Project No. ITS/311/18FP and GHP/110/19SZ).

References

[1] S. Aslani, V. Murino, M. Dayan, R. Tam, D. Sona, G. Hamarneh, Scanner invariant multiple sclerosis lesion segmentation from mri, in: ISBI, IEEE, 2020, pp. 781–785.

[2] Y. Balaji, S. Sankaranarayanan, R. Chellappa, Metareg: towards domain generalization using meta-regularization, in: NeurIPS, 2018, pp. 998–1008.

[3] N. Bloch, A. Madabhushi, H. Huisman, J. Freymann, J. Kirby, M. Grauer, A. Enquobahrie, C. Jaffe, L. Clarke, K. Farahani, Nci-isbi 2013 challenge: automated segmentation of prostate structures, The Cancer Imaging Archive 370 (2015).

[4] F.M. Carlucci, A. D'Innocente, S. Bucci, B. Caputo, T. Tommasi, Domain generalization by solving jigsaw puzzles, in: Proceedings of the IEEE Conference on Computer Vision and Pattern Recognition, 2019, pp. 2229–2238.

[5] Q. Chang, H. Qu, Y. Zhang, M. Sabuncu, C. Chen, T. Zhang, D.N. Metaxas, Synthetic learning: learn from distributed asynchronized discriminator gan without sharing medical image data, in: CVPR, 2020, pp. 13856–13866.

[6] C. Chen, W. Bai, R.H. Davies, A.N. Bhuva, C. Manisty, J.C. Moon, N. Aung, A.M. Lee, M.M. Sanghvi, K. Fung, et al., Improving the generalizability of convolutional neural network-based segmentation on cmr images, arXiv preprint, arXiv:1907.01268, 2019.

[7] C. Chen, Q. Dou, H. Chen, J. Qin, P.A. Heng, Unsupervised bidirectional cross-modality adaptation via deeply synergistic image and feature alignment for medical image segmentation, IEEE Transactions on Medical Imaging (2020).

[8] T. Chen, S. Kornblith, M. Norouzi, G. Hinton, A simple framework for contrastive learning of visual representations, arXiv preprint, arXiv:2002.05709, 2020.

[9] Q. Dou, D.C. de Castro, K. Kamnitsas, B. Glocker, Domain generalization via model-agnostic learning of semantic features, in: NeurIPS, 2019, pp. 6450–6461.

[10] Q. Dou, Q. Liu, P.A. Heng, B. Glocker, Unpaired multi-modal segmentation via knowledge distillation, IEEE Transactions on Medical Imaging (2020).

[11] Q. Dou, T.Y. So, M. Jiang, Q. Liu, V. Vardhanabhuti, G. Kaissis, Z. Li, W. Si, H.H. Lee, K. Yu, et al., Federated deep learning for detecting Covid-19 lung abnormalities in ct: a privacy-preserving multinational validation study, NPJ Digital Medicine 4 (1) (2021) 1–11.

[12] R. Fan, X. Jin, C.C. Wang, Multiregion segmentation based on compact shape prior, IEEE Transactions on Automation Science and Engineering 12 (3) (2014) 1047–1058.

[13] C. Finn, P. Abbeel, S. Levine, Model-agnostic meta-learning for fast adaptation of deep networks, in: ICML, 2017.

[14] F. Fumero, S. Alayón, J.L. Sanchez, J. Sigut, M. Gonzalez-Hernandez, Rim-one: an open retinal image database for optic nerve evaluation, in: 2011 24th International Symposium on Computer-Based Medical Systems (CBMS), IEEE, 2011, pp. 1–6.

[15] E. Gibson, Y. Hu, N. Ghavami, H.U. Ahmed, C. Moore, M. Emberton, H.J. Huisman, D.C. Barratt, Inter-site variability in prostate segmentation accuracy using deep learning, in: MICCAI, Springer, 2018, pp. 506–514.

[16] T.M.H. Hsu, H. Qi, M. Brown, Federated visual classification with real-world data distribution, arXiv preprint, arXiv:2003.08082, 2020.

[17] Z. Huang, H. Wang, E.P. Xing, D. Huang, Self-challenging improves cross-domain generalization, in: ECCV, 2020.

[18] H. Jia, Y. Song, H. Huang, W. Cai, Y. Xia, Hd-net: hybrid discriminative network for prostate segmentation in mr images, in: MICCAI, Springer, 2019, pp. 110–118.

[19] G.A. Kaissis, M.R. Makowski, D. Rückert, R.F. Braren, Secure, privacy-preserving and federated machine learning in medical imaging, Nature Machine Intelligence (2020) 1–7.

[20] K. Kamnitsas, C. Baumgartner, C. Ledig, V. Newcombe, J. Simpson, A. Kane, D. Menon, A. Nori, A. Criminisi, D. Rueckert, et al., Unsupervised domain adaptation in brain lesion segmentation with adversarial networks, in: IPMI, Springer, 2017, pp. 597–609.

[21] N. Karani, K. Chaitanya, C. Baumgartner, E. Konukoglu, A lifelong learning approach to brain mr segmentation across scanners and protocols, in: MICCAI, Springer, 2018, pp. 476–484.

[22] J. Konečnỳ, H.B. McMahan, F.X. Yu, P. Richtárik, A.T. Suresh, D. Bacon, Federated learning: strategies for improving communication efficiency, arXiv preprint, arXiv:1610.05492, 2016.

[23] W.M. Kouw, S.N. Ørting, J. Petersen, K.S. Pedersen, M. de Bruijne, A cross-center smoothness prior for variational Bayesian brain tissue segmentation, in: IPMI, Springer, 2019, pp. 360–371.

[24] G. Lemaître, R. Martí, J. Freixenet, J.C. Vilanova, P.M. Walker, F. Meriaudeau, Computer-aided detection and diagnosis for prostate cancer based on mono and multi-parametric mri: a review, Computers in Biology and Medicine 60 (2015) 8–31.

[25] D. Li, Y. Yang, Y.Z. Song, T.M. Hospedales, Learning to generalize: meta-learning for domain generalization, in: AAAI, 2018.

[26] D. Li, J. Zhang, Y. Yang, C. Liu, Y.Z. Song, T.M. Hospedales, Episodic training for domain generalization, in: ICCV, 2019, pp. 1446–1455.

[27] D. Li, A. Kar, N. Ravikumar, A.F. Frangi, S. Fidler, Federated simulation for medical imaging, in: International Conference on Medical Image Computing and Computer-Assisted Intervention, Springer, 2020, pp. 159–168.

[28] W. Li, F. Milletarì, D. Xu, N. Rieke, J. Hancox, W. Zhu, M. Baust, Y. Cheng, S. Ourselin, M.J. Cardoso, et al., Privacy-preserving federated brain tumour segmentation, in: International Workshop on Machine Learning in Medical Imaging, Springer, 2019, pp. 133–141.

[29] W. Li, M.F. Goodchild, R. Church, An efficient measure of compactness for two-dimensional shapes and its application in regionalization problems, International Journal of Geographical Information Science 27 (6) (2013) 1227–1250.

[30] X. Li, Y. Gu, N. Dvornek, L. Staib, P. Ventola, J.S. Duncan, Multi-site fmri analysis using privacy-preserving federated learning and domain adaptation: abide results, arXiv preprint, arXiv:2001.05647, 2020.

[31] G. Litjens, R. Toth, W. van de Ven, C. Hoeks, S. Kerkstra, B. van Ginneken, G. Vincent, G. Guillard, N. Birbeck, J. Zhang, et al., Evaluation of prostate segmentation algorithms for mri: the promise12 challenge, Medical Image Analysis 18 (2) (2014) 359–373.

[32] Q. Liu, C. Chen, J. Qin, Q. Dou, P.A. Heng, Feddg: federated domain generalization on medical image segmentation via episodic learning in continuous frequency space, in: The IEEE/CVF Conference on Computer Vision and Pattern Recognition (CVPR), 2021.

[33] Q. Liu, Q. Dou, P.A. Heng, Shape-aware meta-learning for generalizing prostate mri segmentation to unseen domains, in: International Conference on Medical Image Computing and Computer-Assisted Intervention, Springer, 2020, pp. 475–485.

[34] Q. Liu, Q. Dou, L. Yu, P.A. Heng, Ms-net: multi-site network for improving prostate segmentation with heterogeneous mri data, IEEE Transactions on Medical Imaging 39 (9) (2020) 2713–2724.

[35] Q. Liu, H. Yang, Q. Dou, P.A. Heng, Federated semi-supervised medical image classification via inter-client relation matching, in: International Conference on Medical Image Computing and Computer Assisted Intervention, 2021.

[36] L. Luo, L. Yu, H. Chen, Q. Liu, X. Wang, J. Xu, P.A. Heng, Deep mining external imperfect data for chest x-ray disease screening, IEEE Transactions on Medical Imaging 39 (11) (2020) 3583–3594.

[37] L.v.d. Maaten, G. Hinton, Visualizing data using t-sne, Journal of Machine Learning Research 9 (Nov) (2008) 2579–2605.

[38] B. McMahan, E. Moore, D. Ramage, S. Hampson, B.A. y Arcas, Communication-efficient learning of deep networks from decentralized data, in: Artificial Intelligence and Statistics, 2017, pp. 1273–1282.

[39] F. Milletari, N. Navab, S.A. Ahmadi, V-net: fully convolutional neural networks for volumetric medical image segmentation, in: 3DV, IEEE, 2016, pp. 565–571.

[40] H.J. Nussbaumer, The fast Fourier transform, in: Fast Fourier Transform and Convolution Algorithms, Springer, 1981, pp. 80–111.

[41] J.I. Orlando, H. Fu, J.B. Breda, K. van Keer, D.R. Bathula, A. Diaz-Pinto, R. Fang, P.A. Heng, J. Kim, J. Lee, et al., Refuge challenge: a unified framework for evaluating automated methods for glaucoma assessment from fundus photographs, Medical Image Analysis 59 (2020) 101570.

[42] S. Otálora, M. Atzori, V. Andrearczyk, A. Khan, H. Müller, Staining invariant features for improving generalization of deep convolutional neural networks in computational pathology, Frontiers in Bioengineering and Biotechnology 7 (2019) 198.

[43] M. Paschali, S. Conjeti, F. Navarro, N. Navab, Generalizability vs. robustness: investigating medical imaging networks using adversarial examples, in: MICCAI, Springer, 2018, pp. 493–501.

[44] X. Peng, Z. Huang, Y. Zhu, K. Saenko, Federated adversarial domain adaptation, arXiv preprint, arXiv: 1911.02054, 2019.

[45] H.R. Roth, K. Chang, P. Singh, N. Neumark, W. Li, V. Gupta, S. Gupta, L. Qu, A. Ihsani, B.C. Bizzo, et al., Federated learning for breast density classification: a real-world implementation, in: Domain Adaptation and Representation Transfer, and Distributed and Collaborative Learning, Springer, 2020, pp. 181–191.

[46] H. Schomberg, J. Timmer, The gridding method for image reconstruction by Fourier transformation, IEEE Transactions on Medical Imaging 14 (3) (1995) 596–607.

[47] M.J. Sheller, G.A. Reina, B. Edwards, J. Martin, S. Bakas, Multi-institutional deep learning modeling without sharing patient data: a feasibility study on brain tumor segmentation, in: Brainlesion Workshop, MICCAI, Springer, 2018, pp. 92–104.

[48] S. Silva, B.A. Gutman, E. Romero, P.M. Thompson, A. Altmann, M. Lorenzi, Federated learning in distributed medical databases: meta-analysis of large-scale subcortical brain data, in: ISBI, IEEE, 2019, pp. 270–274.

[49] J. Sivaswamy, S. Krishnadas, A. Chakravarty, G. Joshi, A.S. Tabish, et al., A comprehensive retinal image dataset for the assessment of glaucoma from the optic nerve head analysis, JSM Biomedical Imaging Data Papers 2 (1) (2015) 1004.

[50] Q. Yang, Y. Liu, T. Chen, Y. Tong, Federated machine learning: concept and applications, ACM Transactions on Intelligent Systems and Technology (TIST) 10 (2) (2019) 1–19.

[51] X. Yang, H. Dou, R. Li, X. Wang, C. Bian, S. Li, D. Ni, P.A. Heng, Generalizing deep models for ultrasound image segmentation, in: MICCAI, Springer, 2018, pp. 497–505.

[52] L. Yao, J. Prosky, B. Covington, K. Lyman, A strong baseline for domain adaptation and generalization in medical imaging, in: MIDL, 2019.

[53] C. Yoon, G. Hamarneh, R. Garbi, Generalizable feature learning in the presence of data bias and domain class imbalance with application to skin lesion classification, in: MICCAI, Springer, 2019, pp. 365–373.

[54] L. Yu, X. Yang, H. Chen, J. Qin, P.A. Heng, Volumetric convnets with mixed residual connections for automated prostate segmentation from 3d mr images, in: AAAI, 2017.

[55] L. Zhang, X. Wang, D. Yang, T. Sanford, S. Harmon, B. Turkbey, B.J. Wood, H. Roth, A. Myronenko, D. Xu, et al., Generalizing deep learning for medical image segmentation to unseen domains via deep stacked transformation, IEEE Transactions on Medical Imaging (2020).

[56] Q. Zhu, B. Du, P. Yan, Boundary-weighted domain adaptive neural network for prostate mr image segmentation, IEEE Transactions on Medical Imaging 39 (3) (2019) 753–763.

Meta learning for adaptable lung nodule image analysis

Aryan Mobiny and Hien Van Nguyen
Department of Engineering & Computer Engineering, University of Houston, Houston, TX, United States

9.1 Introduction

Lung cancer is consistently ranked as the leading cause of cancer-related deaths all around the world in the past several years, accounting for more than one-quarter (26%) of all cancer-related deaths [1]. The stage at which diagnosis is made largely determines the overall prognosis of the patient. The five-year relative survival rate is over 50% in early-stage disease, while survival rates drop to less than 5% for late-stage disease [1]. Lung cancer screening of high-risk individuals, which is designed to detect the disease at an early stage, has been shown in the National Lung Screening Trial (NLST) to reduce lung cancer mortality by 20% [2]. The main challenge in lung cancer screening is detecting lung nodules [2,3]. Radiologist fatigue, increasing workload, and stringent turn-around-time requirements are just a few of the factors which negatively impact the detection rate for lung nodules. Many studies have documented the occurrence of diagnostic errors in clinical practice, caused by many different contributing factors which can generally be divided into person-specific (e.g. satisfaction of search, etc.), nodule-specific (e.g. small size, low density) and environment-specific issues (e.g. inadequate equipment, staff shortages, excess workload, etc.) [4], [5].

Computer-aided diagnosis (CAD) systems aim to improve the radiologist's performance in terms of diagnostic accuracy and speed [6]. The role of CAD systems in lung nodule detection and screening has been demonstrated over the years [7], as well as their role in distinguishing between benign and malignant nodules [6]. However, the automated identification of nodules from nonnodules is quite challenging mainly due to the large variation in size, shape, margins, and density of the nodules [8]. The nodules can also occur in different locations (such as peri-fissural, subpleural, endobronchial, perivascular), contributing to the diversified contextual environment around the nodule tissue [9].

In recent years, deep learning technology has attracted considerable interest in the computer vision and machine learning community [10,11]. Deep neural networks (DNNs) have an advantage of automatically capturing the image's higher-level features directly from the raw input data. This leads to powerful features tuned to specific tasks of medical image analysis [12,13,14,15]. Recent work has explored deep networks for detecting lung pathology [15,16]. In the context of pulmonary nodule classification in Computed Tomography (CT) images, Hua et al. [17] introduced models of a deep belief network and a convolutional neural network that outperforms the conventional hand-crafted features. Setio et al. [18] proposed a multiview convolutional network for lung nodule detection. Most recently, Ardila et al. [19] shows that deep networks, trained on a hospital-scale dataset of 42,290 computed tomography scans, achieve more than 94% area under the curve on the lung nodule detection task.

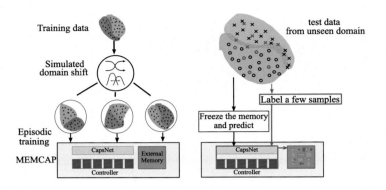

FIGURE 9.1

Overview of the episodic metatraining (Left) and metatesting (Right) of the MEMCAP for adaptive lung nodule classification. During the metatraining phase, the model learns to quickly encode and retrieve the required information about the new domain (task) using a small subset of annotated samples. During the metatesting phase, the model performance is evaluated on samples from never-before-seen target domains.

Machine learning models are typically trained under the assumption that training and test data are sampled from the same distribution. This assumption is often violated as conditions for data acquisition may change, and a trained system may fail to produce accurate predictions for unseen data affected by a domain shift. In medical imaging, images acquired at different sites can differ significantly in their data distribution, due to varying scanners, imaging protocols or patient cohorts, thus each new hospital can be regarded as a new domain [20]. However, it is impractical to collect data each time to update a trained system. In pulmonary nodule detection, while most of the existing work focuses on improving the classification accuracy for a static dataset, the problem of adapting a classifier to changes in lung CT data is largely under-investigated. There are many interpatient and intra-patient sources of variability in pulmonary CT scans that can affect classifier performance negatively; not only does each patient have unique characteristics, but each imaging scan utilizes different CT scanners with different imaging protocols which lead to large variations in image contrast and signal-to-noise ratio. The Hounsfield Unit (HU, a measure of radiodensity) differences observed between various CT scanners due to poor calibration can be significant, with the measured HU values of each scanner changing substantially with repeated use [21]. A possible solution is to use domain adaptation (DA) methods to narrow down the domain shift between the target and source domain [22,23].

Motivated by the above challenges, this chapter proposes a novel framework for the on-the-fly adaptation of a lung nodule classifier to changes in the data distribution using only a few labeled examples from the new domain. This removes the need for annotating many samples from the target domain, as well as re-training the whole deep model from scratch whenever the data distribution changes due to variation in sensing technologies or imaging protocols. Fig. 9.1 provides an overview of our approach. The proposed model takes sequential labeled samples one after the other, evaluates the performance enhancement in real-time, and stops when satisfied with the model prediction performance. Our chapter makes the following contributions:

- We develop an efficient meta learning method, called memory-augmented capsule networks (MEM-CAP), for rapidly adapting to target domains using only a few labeled samples. Our network is robust to various types of domain shifts including noisy data artifacts, variation of sensing technologies and patient populations.
- While traditional learning methods require multiple tasks (each task consists of data and labels) for training, we develop a domain shift simulation strategy to train our model using only one dataset. This contribution makes meta learning technology significantly easier to use in medical applications where annotations are expensive and difficult to obtain.
- We perform extensive experiments on three different lung nodule datasets to validate the proposed network. This includes the classification of incidental pulmonary lung nodules from contrast enhanced and noncontrast enhanced CT scans acquired with normal radiation dose. These nodules are detected during screening for another disease in patients with low-risk of lung cancer. Despite the changes in the lesion size, morphology image contrast and radiation dose, our model learns to incorporate the underlying information from the target domain and make accurate predictions for these complex cases.

The rest of this chapter is organized as follows: works related to domain adaptation and meta learning are presented in Section 9.2. Section 9.3 explains the proposed framework and training strategy in detail. Section 9.4 describes the three datasets used in this study. All the designed experiments and obtained configurations and results are presented in Section 9.5 and discussed in Section 9.6. Section 9.7 concludes the chapter with future research directions.

9.2 Related work

Domain Adaptation algorithms aim to train models that produce accurate predictions for unseen data with domain shift. Over the past 10 years, research in domain adaptation provides a number of effective techniques to mitigate the domain shift problem [24,25,26,27,28,29,30,31,32]. Donahue *et al.* showed that features of a deep network generalize well to unseen domains [29]. Nguyen *et al.* proposed a network of sparse representations for adaptation on multiple levels of the feature hierarchy [30]. In a similar spirit, Rusu *et al.* proposed a progressive network, by appending the source network to the target network, enabling the architecture to reuse both low-level and high-level features [31]. Some approaches have proposed to learn a target classifier regularized against the source classifier to facilitate adaptation when a limited amount of labeled data is available in the target domain [33,34]. Most of these domain adaptation techniques require a computationally intensive re-training process (e.g., hours to days) to find a good solution. Such a requirement will inevitably interrupt clinical workflows and cause a significant delay in diagnoses and treatments. Moreover, due to the small numbers of data samples from new domains, the re-training process is prone to poor generalization. It is also unrealistic to expect the user to collect many labeled data in each new domain [35,36]. In contrast, many clinical settings require real-time learning and inference from a small amount of data provided by physicians. This kind of flexible adaptation remains a major challenge for the existing approaches, including those using deep networks [37].

Meta learning (a.k.a. learning to learn) explores the training of a metalearner that learns to learn new tasks and skills quickly with a few training samples [38,39]. Model-agnostic meta learning (MAML) is a gradient-based procedure that incorporates an episodic training paradigm for the fast adaptation of models to new tasks and domains [40]. Santoro et al. [41] proposed a memory-augmented neural network (a recurrent network with an explicit storage buffer) with a set of modifications on the training set up and the memory retrieval mechanism which allows it to encode new information quickly and thus adapt to new tasks after only a few samples. While the meta learning approaches are significantly different in motivation and methodologies, their training requires the availability of multiple datasets [40,42]. In medical applications, this requires collecting and annotating data from different institutes which is often expensive and inefficient.

9.3 Methodology

9.3.1 Memory-augmented capsule network

We propose a network, called the Memory-Augmented Capsule Network (MEMCAP), for efficient adaptation of a classifier to unseen domains using only a few additional labeled samples. Our method makes no assumption about the form of the output $P_\theta(y|X)$, which is the probability of a data point X belonging to the class y. We denote input and output (label) spaces by $\mathcal{X}$ and $\mathcal{Y}$ respectively. MEMCAP is composed of two submodules; first, a feature extractor network $F_\theta : \mathcal{X} \to \mathcal{Z}$ extracts discriminative features from the large volumetric input images, where $\mathcal{Z}$ is the feature space of much lower dimension than $\mathcal{X}$. It then passes the embedding vectors to a task network $T_\phi : \mathcal{Z} \to \mathbb{R}^C$ where C is the number of classes in $\mathcal{Y}$. The final class predictions are given by

$$\hat{y} = p(y|\mathbf{x}; \theta, \phi) = \text{softmax}(T_\phi(F_\theta(\mathbf{x}))) \tag{9.1}$$

where $\text{softmax}(a) = e^a / \sum_i a_i$. The parameters θ, ϕ are optimized with respect to a classification ($\mathcal{L}_{\text{class}}$) and a task-specific ($\mathcal{L}_{\text{task}}$) objective function. We elected to use a deep capsule network architecture as the feature extractor network due to its ability to extract various invariant low-dimensional properties of the entities across domains; including different types of instantiation parameters such as position, size, orientation, etc. [43]. It then passes the abstract representations to the task network: a recurrent controller with an explicit storage buffer to rapidly encode and store the new information extracted from the labeled target examples, thus exploiting the underlying intrinsic information in the target domain for prediction [41]. Finally, we propose a self-supervised approach for simulating the domain shift during training and testing by applying random distortions to input and output data. The detailed information about the model architectures, the task set up and training strategies are provided in the following sections.

9.3.2 FastCaps++ as feature extractor network

Capsule networks (CapsNets) were proposed by Sabour et al. [43] as an alternative to convolutional neural networks (CNNs) that possess multiple desirable properties such as the ability to: generalize with fewer training examples, encode and compress a vast amount of information in short pose vectors and matrices, and being significantly more robust to adversarial attacks and noisy artifacts [16,44].

These properties prompted us to use a CapsNet with slight variations to encode input instantiation parameters into lower-dimensional feature vectors.

A CapsNet is composed of a cascade of capsule layers, each of which contains multiple capsules. A capsule is the basic unit of CapsNets and is defined as a *group of neurons* whose output forms a *pose* vector or matrix [43,44]. This is in contrast to traditional deep networks that use neurons as their basic unit. In this work, we elected to use matrix capsules as it helps with reducing the number of trainable parameters required by the transformation matrices [44] which eventually made our network less prone to overfitting. Let Ω_L denote the sets of capsules in layer L. Each capsule $i \in \Omega_L$ outputs a pose matrix P_i^L. Each element in the matrix characterizes the instantiation parameters (such as orientation, size, pose, etc.). The activation probability of a capsule a_i^L indicates the presence of an entity and is implicitly encoded in the capsule as the Frobenius norm of the pose matrix. The i-th capsule in Ω_L propagates its information to j-th capsule in Ω_{L+1} through a linear transformation $V_{ij}^L = W_{ij}^L P_i^L$, where V_{ij}^L is called a *vote* matrix. The pose matrix of capsule $j \in \Omega_{L+1}$ is a weighted combination of all the votes from child capsules: $P_j^{(L+1)} = \sum_i r_{ij} V_{ij}^L$, where r_{ij} are routing coefficients and $\sum_i r_{ij} = 1$. These coefficients are determined by the dynamic routing algorithm [43] which iteratively increases the routing coefficients r_{ij} if the corresponding voting matrix V_{ij}^L is similar to P_j^{L+1} and vice versa. Dynamic routing ensures that the output of each child capsule gets sent to the proper parent capsules. Through this process, the network gradually constructs a transformation matrix for each capsule pair to encode the corresponding part-whole relationship and retains geometric information of the input data.

We applied a few simple yet effective modifications to the Fast CapsNet proposed by Mobiny et al. [16] to make it scale properly to our high-dimensional volumetric inputs and improve its convergence speed and prediction performance while requiring a smaller number of trainable parameters. We called our model FastCaps++ whose architecture is depicted in Fig. 9.3. FastCaps++ is composed of an encoder and decoder path. The encoder path uses a 3D ResNet-20 [45] with three residual blocks as the base network, followed by a 1×1 convolution layer which outputs $A = 64$ feature maps. All the other layers are capsule layers starting with the primary capsule layer. The 4×4 pose matrix of each of the B primary capsule maps is a learned linear transformation of the output of all the lower-layer ReLUs centered at that location. The primary capsules are followed by two convolutional capsule layers with C and D capsule maps and kernels of size $K = 3$ and stride $s = 1$ and $s = 2$, respectively. We selected $B = C = D = 32$ for the capsule layers, and used a dynamic routing mechanism to route the information between the capsules. The last layer of convolutional capsules is linked to the final dense capsule layer which has only one capsule with an 8×8 pose matrix. The Frobenius norm of the pose matrices of the output capsule is used to determine the predicted class (nodule vs. nonnodule).

The decoder network then reconstructs the input from the final capsules, which will force the network to preserve as much information from the input as possible across the whole network. This effectively works as a regularizer that reduces the risk of overfitting and helps generalize to new samples. Inspired by [46] we used a convolutional architecture composed of three transposed convolution units (TCU) to reconstruct the input volume. Each TCU doubles the volume size and is composed of two 3D transposed convolution layers (with $K = 1, s = 1$ and $K = 3, s = 2$, respectively), each of which is followed by a ReLU nonlinearity. The final transposed convolution layer (shown as TC in Fig. 9.3) uses a kernel of size $K = 1$ and stride $s = 1$ with a sigmoid nonlinearity to map the values into the [0, 1] range.

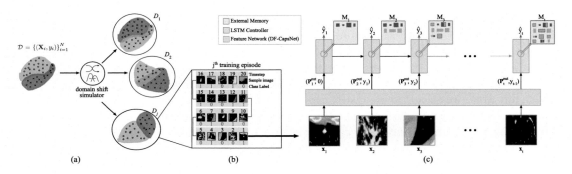

FIGURE 9.2

Overview of the proposed model-based meta learning approach for adaptive lung nodule classification. (a) Simulated domain shift, (b) Sampled sequence of images for the episodic training, (c) Architecture of the MEMCAP classifier, consisting of a feature network (a 3D Capsule Network named FastCaps++) and a task network (composed of an LSTM controller with an external memory bank). MEMCAP takes a few annotated inputs from the new domain and refines its decision function in real-time.

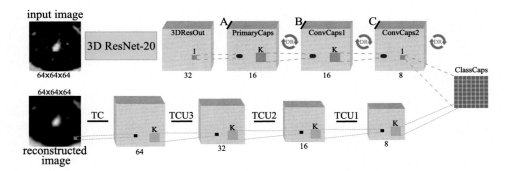

FIGURE 9.3

Illustration of the encoder (top) and decoder (bottom) paths of the FastCaps++ architecture. It outputs an 8×8 matrix of semantic features extracted from the high-dimensional input.

9.3.3 Memory-augmented task network

Due to the sequential nature of annotated feedback samples provided from each new target domain, and the need to encode and accumulate the information over time, neural networks with recurrent structures are a natural choice. They are equipped with an "internal memory" that captures information about what has been calculated so far. The long-short term memory (LSTM) model is introduced as a modification to vanilla recurrent networks (RNNs), which is capable of encoding long-term dependencies [47].

In the lung nodule detection problem, the model must be able to quickly encode and retrieve information, and modify its decisions to make accurate inferences by using a few annotated samples. This set of samples are provided as either information correction by the radiologist or brand-new samples from never-before-seen distributions. Thus the ideal model must learn to capture the cumulative expertise gained *across* domains and continuously adapt to never-before-seen distributions [48]. However, neural networks with internal memory capacity (such as LSTM) are not able to rapidly encode, store and access a significant amount of new information required at each step. Architectures such as memory networks [49] and Neural Turing Machines (NTMs) are developed as models that meet the requisite criteria. These are external-memory equipped networks capable of rapidly encoding new information and storing them in a stable, addressable representation that can selectively be accessed when needed. Inspired by [41], we use an LSTM architecture equipped with an external memory bank as the task network (as shown in Fig. 9.2) for sequentially processing the new information. The external memory bank interacts with the LSTM controller through reading and writing operations. The external memory is denoted by a matrix $\mathbf{M}_t \in \mathbb{R}^{k \times q}$ where k is the number of memory slots and q is the size of each slot. The model has an LSTM controller that reads and writes to the external memory at every time step (i.e. receiving each new annotated sample).

Reading: For a given input $\mathbf{x}_t$ and the memory matrix $\mathbf{M}_t$ with k rows (slots) of size q at time t, the controller will produce a key $\mathbf{k}_t$ computed as $\mathbf{k}_t = tanh(\mathbf{W}_{hk}\mathbf{h}_t + \mathbf{b}_k)$ from the controller hidden states ($\mathbf{h}_t$). $\mathbf{W}_{hk}$ and $\mathbf{b}_k$ are the corresponding weight matrix and bias values respectively. This key will be compared against each memory slot $\mathbf{M}_t(i)$ using the cosine similarity measure $C(.,.)$. This similarity is used to produce the read-weight vector $\mathbf{w}_t^r$:

$$\mathbf{w}_t^r = \text{softmax}\left[C(\mathbf{k}_t, \mathbf{M}_t(i))\right] \tag{9.2}$$

where softmax is used to get the normalized weight vector with its elements summing to one. This vector allows the controller to select values similar to previously-seen values, which is called content-based addressing. Finally, the reading operation is done by a weighted linear combination of all memory slots scaled by a normalized read-weight vector $\mathbf{w}_t^r$ as follows:

$$\mathbf{r}_t = (\mathbf{M}_t)^T.\mathbf{w}_t^r \tag{9.3}$$

Here, $\mathbf{r}_t$ is the content vector retrieved from the memory, and $\mathbf{w}_t^r \in \mathbb{R}^{k \times 1}$ is the read-weight vector which specifies how much each slot should contribute to $\mathbf{r}_t$.

Writing: To write into the memory, the controller will interpolate between writing to the most recently read memory rows and writing to the *least-used* memory rows. If $\mathbf{w}_{t-1}^r$ is the read-weight vector at the previous time step, and $\mathbf{w}_{t-1}^{lu}$ is a weight vector that captures the least-used memory location, the write weights $\mathbf{w}_t^w \in \mathbb{R}^{1 \times k}$ is then computed using a learnable sigmoid gate:

$$\mathbf{w}_t^w \leftarrow \sigma(\alpha_t)\mathbf{w}_{t-1}^r + (1 - \sigma(\alpha_t))\mathbf{w}_{t-1}^{lu} \tag{9.4}$$

where $\sigma(.)$ is the sigmoid function. α_t is a scalar computed as $\alpha_t = \mathbf{w}_\alpha\mathbf{h}_t + b_\alpha$ at each time step, and $\mathbf{w}_\alpha$ and b_α are trainable parameters learned discriminatively through back-propagation. This encourages information to be written into either rarely-used locations of the external memory to preserve recently encoded information, or the last used location to *update* the memory with newer, possibly more relevant information. The ith memory slot at time-step t, $\mathbf{M}_t(i)$, is then updated as:

$$\mathbf{M}_t(i) \leftarrow \mathbf{M}_{t-1}(i) + \mathbf{w}_t^w(i).\mathbf{a}_t \tag{9.5}$$

where $\mathbf{a}_t$ is the linear projection of the current hidden state followed by a *tanh* nonlinearity.

To create the least used weight vector $\mathbf{w}_t^{lu}$, the controller maintains a usage-weight vector $\mathbf{w}_t^u$ which gets updated after every read and write step as:

$$\mathbf{w}_t^u \leftarrow \beta \mathbf{w}_{t-1}^u + \mathbf{w}_t^r + \mathbf{w}_t^w \tag{9.6}$$

where $\beta \in [0, 1]$ is a scalar parameter used to determine how quickly previous usage values should decay. The least used weight vector $\mathbf{w}_{t-1}^{lu}$ is a one-hot-encoded vector generated from $\mathbf{w}_{t-1}^u$ by setting its minimum element to 1, and all other elements to 0. Finally, the concatenation of the read content vector and the hidden nodes $(\mathbf{r}_t, \mathbf{h}_t)$ is used to predict the output. The introduction of external memory enables the recurrent network to store and retrieve much longer-term information compared to LSTM. This frees up the main controller and increases its capacity to learn highly complicated patterns within the data.

9.3.4 Episodic training with simulated domain shift

Our learning procedure is an episodic training scheme meant to expose the model optimization to distribution mismatches. The idea of episodic training is inspired by human learning and evolution through generations [41,40]. Each training episode mimics a learner's lifespan where it learns to optimize its performance. The next episodes are like the next generation learners using the accumulated knowledge to solve a similar problem regardless of a possible shift in the data distribution. Given the labeled training data $\mathcal{D} = \{(\mathbf{x}_n, y_n)\}_{n=1}^N$, we synthetically generate samples from new domains $\mathcal{D} = \{\mathcal{D}_1, \mathcal{D}_2, ..., \mathcal{D}_K\}$ by altering the input/output data distributions. In our implementation, training on each sequence of images from the new domain $\mathcal{D}_k$ is called an *episode*.

Theoretically, any data transformation technique can be applied to slightly change the distribution of data. By increasing the diversity of the metatasks, the model can be well trained to extract useful features after adapting to training data in any task. We elected to synthetically enhance each metatraining task by using a variety of systematic transformations that equivalently alter the associated data and labels to simulate a new domain $\mathcal{D}_k = \{(\mathbf{x}_n^{(k)}, y_n^{(k)})\}_{n=1}^{N_k}$ where N_k is the number of labeled samples in the k-th domain. This is done by randomly applying affine transformations (scale, translate, shear), jittering the pixel intensities by applying Gaussian blurring and changing the contrast and/or brightness of the input images. This effectively simulates the domain shift in a real-world medical imaging scenario where differences in CT scanners, imaging protocols, and many other factors change the distribution of pixel intensity values [50]. Moreover, labels are randomly flipped from episode to episode (during training only). For example, nodules can be labeled as 1 in one episode and 0 in another. Note that labels are consistent within the same episode. This strategy helps prevent the MEMCAP from learning a fixed mapping from samples to their class labels, but a dynamic binding between image features and the provided labels. Consider the scenario where we do not flip the labels, the network can simply predict the ground-truth labels from input images instead of relying on the provided labels. This is undesirable as the model becomes insensitive to the new information from the target domain. This is inspired by the strategies used in other studies to learn dynamic mappings for different tasks [41,51]. Our extensive experiments show that introducing such synthetic domain shifts significantly improves the cross-domain transferability of the learned model.

Algorithm 9.1 summarizes the episodic training of the MEMCAP model. We first split the source domains $\mathcal{D} = \{\mathcal{D}_k\}_{k=1}^K$ into disjoint metatrain ($\mathcal{D}^{tr}$) and metatest ($\mathcal{D}^{te}$) sets. In the metatraining phase,

---

Algorithm 9.1 Episodic training with simulated domain shift.

Input: Source training domains $\mathcal{D} = \{\mathcal{D}_k\}_{k=1}^{K}$
Output: Feature extractor (F_θ) and task network (T_ϕ)

1: Randomly split $\mathcal{D}$ into disjoint $\mathcal{D}^{\text{tr}}$ and $\mathcal{D}^{\text{te}}$
2: **repeat**
3:     Randomly select a simulated domain $\mathcal{D}_k^{\text{tr}}$
4:     $\mathbf{M} \leftarrow 0$ ▷ Reset for each metatraining episode
5:     **for** $\mathbf{x}_t \in \mathcal{D}_k^{\text{tr}}$ **do**   ▷ for each labeled sample
6:         $\mathbf{P}_t^{\text{out}}, a_t = F_\theta(\mathbf{x}_t)$
7:         $\theta \leftarrow \theta - \alpha \nabla_\theta \mathcal{L}_{\text{class}}(y_t, a_t; \theta)$ ▷ update F_θ
8:         compute $\mathbf{k}_t, \mathbf{w}_t^r, \mathbf{w}_t^w, \mathbf{r}_t, \mathbf{a}_t$ ▷ Section 9.3.3
9:         $\mathbf{M}_t \leftarrow \mathbf{M}_{t-1} + \mathbf{w}_t^w \cdot \mathbf{a}_t$ ▷ update the memory
10:         $\hat{y}_t = T_\phi((\mathbf{P}_t^{\text{out}}, y_{t-1}); \mathbf{r}_t, \mathbf{h}_t)$
11:         $l \leftarrow l + \mathcal{L}_{\text{task}}(y_t, \hat{y}_t; \theta, \phi)$
12:     **end for**
13:     $(\theta, \phi) \leftarrow (\theta, \phi) - \gamma \frac{1}{|\mathcal{D}^{\text{tr}}|} \nabla l(\mathcal{D}^{\text{tr}}; \theta, \phi)$ ▷ update F_θ, T_ϕ
14:     $\mathbf{M} \leftarrow 0$ ▷ Reset for each metatesting episode
15:     $\hat{y}_{t'} = T_\phi(F_\theta(\mathbf{x}_{t'}))$ ▷ Evaluate for $\mathbf{x}_{t'} \in \mathcal{D}_j^{\text{te}}$
16:     $\mathcal{L} \leftarrow \frac{1}{|\mathcal{D}^{\text{te}}|} \sum_j \sum_{t'} \mathcal{L}_{\text{task}}(y_{t'}, \hat{y}_{t'}; \theta, \phi)$
17: **until** convergence

---

we train the system by sequentially feeding the input $\mathbf{x}_t$ from a new domain $\mathcal{D}_k^{\text{tr}}$ to FD-CapsNet (feature extractor network) to extract semantic features $\mathbf{P}_t^{\text{out}} \in \mathcal{Z}$, which will then be fed along with the time-delayed output y_{t-1} to the task network to predict the current label y_t (also shown in Fig. 9.2).

9.4 Dataset

We used three different sets of CT images in our experiments. These datasets are collected and preprocessed independently, and thus it is reasonable to consider their images as samples from different distributions. Fig. 9.4 shows examples of extracted candidates and the corresponding labels from all three sets. These images illustrate the highly challenging task of distinguishing nodules from nonnodule lesions. The first reason is that the pulmonary nodules come with large variations in shapes, sizes, types (solid, subpleural, cavitary, and ground-glass), etc. More complicated samples contain a mixed solid and ground-glass nodule with irregular margins. Other objects and tissues might also appear in the nodule samples, such as single or multiple blood vessels, chest wall, lung recess, etc. Moreover, one nodule image can also contain several nodules of different shapes and sizes. The second reason which hinders the identification process is the nonnodule candidates mimicking the morphological appearance of the real pulmonary nodules. Examples are calcification, short vessels, scarring, infection, vessels with motion artifact mimicking a ground-glass nodule, septal thickening. Some images might also contain a nodule while being centered on another tissue (such as a vessel) thus being labeled as

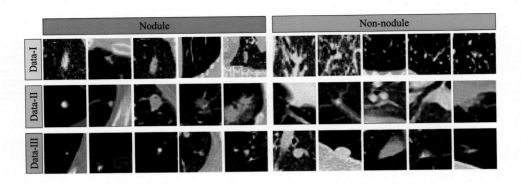

FIGURE 9.4

Sample images of nodules (Left) and nonnodules (Right) selected from Data-I (LUNA), Data-II (our dataset), and Data-III (incidental lung nodule). Each image is a slice along the 2D axial plane in the middle of the volume. Samples from Data-II are numbered and discussed in the text.

nonnodule. For all these reasons, the detection and classification of lung nodules is a challenging task, even for experienced radiologists.

9.4.1 Data-I: LUNA-16 lung nodule dataset

We use the candidate nodules provided by the LUNA-16 challenge [52] as the source data which is used for the initial metatraining and metatesting phases to train and evaluate the model. This dataset is a subset of LIDC-IDRI data [53], the largest publicly available reference database for lung nodules including a total of 1018 CT scans. It consists of low-dose CT scans collected from a wide range of scanner models and acquisition parameters from seven different participating academic institutions. LUNA-16 includes candidate nodules (of size ≥ 3 mm) generated from only 888 scans and labeled based on the criteria explained in [52]. This results in 750K candidate nodules of size $64 \times 64 \times 64$, containing about 1500 true nodules.

9.4.2 Data-II: collected lung nodule dataset

This dataset includes 226 unique CT Chest scans captured by General Electric and Siemens scanners at a single hospital on a single day. The data was preprocessed by an automated segmentation software in order to identify structures at the organ level. From within the segmented lung tissue, a set of potential nodule points is generated based on the size and shape of regions within the lung which exceeds the air Hounsfield Unit (HU) threshold. Additional filters, based on symmetry and other common morphological characteristics, are applied to decrease the false positive rate while maintaining very high sensitivity. Bounding boxes with at least 8 voxels padding surrounding the candidate nodules are cropped and resized to $64 \times 64 \times 64$ pixels. Each generated candidate is reviewed and annotated by board-certified radiologists. From all the generated images (about 7400 images), around 56% were labeled as nodules while the rest were labeled as nonnodules. The radius of the detected nodules ranges from 3 to 15 mm with an average of 5 (± 1.86) mm. The differences in scan protocol for the various chest studies yield slice thickness ranging from 0.625 - 2.5 mm. In each case, an attempt was made to get as close to isotropic as possible while adhering to slice thickness multiples of 0.625 mm. For example, most studies have an in-plane resolution of approximately 0.7×0.7 mm; in this case, linear interpolation was used to convert the data to 0.625 mm slice thickness (voxel dimension of $0.7 \times 0.7 \times 0.625$ mm).

9.4.3 Data-III: collected incidental lung nodule dataset

The incidental lung nodules on CT scans are usually small nodules (< 5 mm) detected incidentally on cross-sectional imaging studies performed for some other reason. Unlike low-dose CT lung cancer screening suggested by multiple trials and studies [54,2,55], this dataset is collected from either contrast or noncontrast enhanced CT scans with normal dose. This can make incidental lung nodules difficult to detect; the patient may have other abnormalities present in the scan that can mislead the radiologist or classifier. CT volumetry of lung nodules is an important quantitative imaging biomarker of cancer risk. Therefore, detecting them at the early stage and monitoring their growth over time can potentially help prevent them from developing into lung cancer in the future. Current lung nodule detection networks are typically trained on public low-dose CT datasets such as LUNA16 or NLST [52,56]. These models have shown inferior performance in identifying incidental lung nodules from normal dose CT scans. On the other hand, the size of the incidental lung nodules is comparatively smaller which can be considered another factor causing a shift in the data distribution for the detection problem.

Due to the unique nature of incidental lung nodules and the complexity involved in detecting and annotating them, this dataset is relatively small compared to the other two datasets, and consists of 94 CT scans; 55 of which have at least one nodule. The original CT slices are of size 512×512 pixels for all patients with varying numbers of slices for different patients. A resampling step is conducted to achieve an isotropic resolution of $1 \times 1 \times 1$ mm so that the networks do not need to learn zoom/slice thickness invariance. Normalization is also used to compress the HU values to be in the range of 0 to 255. Positive samples are created by cropping a volume centered on the nodule. Negative samples are created by collecting the false-positive nodules generated by a 3D Faster R-CNN network [57] pretrained on LUNA-16.

9.5 Experiments and results

9.5.1 Training procedure and implementations details

All baseline deep models were trained using an Adam optimizer with $\beta_1 = 0.9$ ($\beta_1 = 0.5$ for CapsNets), $\beta_2 = 0.999$, a fixed batch size of 16, and a learning rate of 10^{-3} which was decayed exponentially (every 1000 steps with a base of 0.97) to a minimum of 10^{-5}. CNNs were trained with cross-entropy loss while CapsNets were trained to minimize the margin loss [43] to enforce the output capsule to have a large activation a if and only if a nodule exists in the input image:

$$\mathcal{L}_{\text{class}} = y \max(0, m^+ - a)^2 + \lambda(1 - y) \max(0, a - m^-)^2] \tag{9.7}$$

where y is the ground truth label. Minimizing this loss forces a to be higher than m^+ if a nodule exists, and lower than m^- otherwise. In our experiments, we set $m^+ = 0.9$, $m^- = 0.1$, and $\lambda = 0.5$. The parameters of the recurrent task network are optimized through maximizing the cross-entropy between

Table 9.1 Prediction performance of deep networks trained on Data-I and tested on Data-I, Data-II, and Data-III. We performed 5-fold cross-validation on the source data (Data-I) and report the average (±std.) for each metric and dataset over the models.

Model	#param. (M)	Validation on different data (Data-I / Data-II / Data-III)			
		precision	recall	accuracy	AUROC
ResNet-20	0.8	90.7(±1.6) / 55.1(±1.8) / 9.5(±3.4)	59.7(±3.3) / 74.1(±2.1) / 80.9(±2.3)	86.7(±1.1) / 56.5(±2.4) / 37.4(±2.4)	78.6(±1.8) / 59.3(±2.7) / 57.3(±2.2)
ResNet-110	5.2	96.3(±1.4) / 58.1(±2.2) / 10.7(±2.8)	66.4(±4.3) / 86.5(±1.9) / 73.6(±2.1)	90.6(±2.8) / 61.9(±2.0) / 49.2(±1.8)	82.7(±2.3) / 67.7(±2.6) / 60.4(±2.0)
ResNet-1202	58.1	91.5(±1.7) / 72.1(±1.4) / 12.7(±2.1)	85.9(±2.7) / 64.5(±3.1) / 44.4(±4.0)	93.3(±1.4) / 69.6(±2.5) / 71.6(±2.0)	91.3(±1.8) / 69.7(±2.4) / 59.2(±2.3)
FastCapsNet	52.2	82.5(±2.0) / 63.5(±3.1) / 11.2(±3.2)	88.2(±2.9) / 90.6(±0.7) / 74.5(±1.8)	91.9(±1.7) / 69.1(±2.7) / 51.2(±2.3)	88.6(±1.8) / 69.0(±2.3) / 61.8(±1.9)
FastCaps++	2.4	96.2(±1.5) / 75.8(±2.1) / 11.6(±2.6)	87.0(±3.1) / 66.9(±2.6) / 69.3(±2.4)	95.3(±2.0) / 72.3(±2.5) / 55.8(±2.1)	92.8(±1.6) / 72.3(±2.4) / 62.0(±2.1)

predicted probabilistic scores and the ground truth labels. We train the MEMCAP model end-to-end using the ADAM optimizer with the same configuration as the baseline models. A random search is performed to find the best parameter values. The best validation results are achieved using 128 memory slots of size 40 and an LSTM controller with 200 hidden units.

For each episode, we randomly applied a combination of contrast, brightness, Gaussian blurring and affine transformations to the entire 3D space to generate samples from the new simulated domain (or task). The probability of each transformation being selected for a given simulated domain is 0.5. We used the Python Imaging Library (PIL) [58] to perform contrast, brightness and blurring transformations; parameters were selected in the range [0.1, 1.9] to allow for both low and high brightness and contrast values (where 1 outputs the original image) and a range of [0, 2] for blurring. We used TensorFlow [59] to apply affine transformations, including scaling ([0.5, 2], where 0.5 corresponds to half the image size in each dimension), translation (up to 20 pixels along each axis), and shear (with counterclockwise shear angle selected in the range [−0.5, 0.5] radians).

9.5.2 Baseline deep neural network performance

To understand the effects of domain shifts between training and testing data, we trained various 3D models on DATA-I (i.e. LUNA) and then evaluated performance on all three datasets. Table 9.1 shows the test performance on the three datasets. We observe significant drops in accuracy across various popular computer vision architectures when testing on data from a different domain (as shown in Table 9.1). This result was expected as these architectures are not explicitly designed to deal with the domain shift problem. This emphasizes the challenge of designing a framework that not only performs well on a provided set of samples, but also quickly adapts to a new domain by providing only a few samples without the need to retrain the whole system from scratch; especially in the medical imaging field where the annotation process is time-consuming, costly, and inconsistent.

9.5.3 Evaluation of adaptive classifier

To evaluate the domain adaptability of our memory-augmented architecture, we utilized an episodic training scheme with simulated domain shifts on Data-I. Note that the training and testing data subsets were disjointed to prevent data leakage. Fig. 9.5 shows a comparison of test performance with and without the external memory bank during the metatesting phase as a function of the number of training episodes. Each training episode consists of randomly sampling a few images from both classes and applying the simulated domain shift on all of them. We evaluated the adaptation performance of the model after every few episodes, during which no further learning occurred and the network predicts the class labels for samples pulled from a disjoint set. We drew labeled samples (from 2 to 30 samples) from the test data and evaluated the classifiers on the remaining data. The labeled samples effectively mimic the data that needs to be annotated by the human expert when adapting to the new domain. For example, the 2nd sample accuracy is the classification accuracy after labeling two samples for a given domain, while the 4th sample accuracy is the classification accuracy after the first four labeled samples, and so on. We generate 100 unique metatest tasks, each meant to mimic unique sample domains. We note that storing a single sample per class (yellow curve) allows the architecture to encode some relevant information which helps it exceed chance performance. The MEMCAP architecture achieves AUROC of 84.1% and 90.2%, after providing 10 and 30 labeled samples respectively (at 85,000 training episodes, as shown in Fig. 9.5).

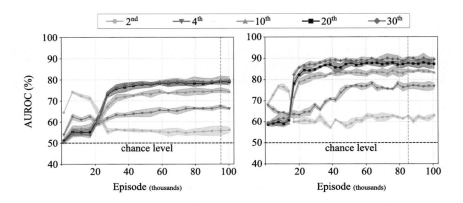

FIGURE 9.5

Comparison of the test prediction performance of the proposed framework with (right) and without (left) the external memory on the LUNA dataset. The average AUROC (±std.) is computed over 100 unique metatest tasks and after different numbers of labeled samples. The horizontal and vertical dashed line highlights the chance level and the best performance, respectively.

We then evaluated the proposed architecture's robustness to various domain shifts. To do this, we took the best model (MEMCAP trained for 85,000 episodes) and tested it in two different experiments. The first consisted of evaluating the model with three different simulated domain shifts (Contrast shifts, Gaussian blurring, and FGSM Adversarial attacks [60]) of various magnitudes. FGSM Adversarial attacks compute the gradient of the loss with respect to each pixel and then alter pixel intensity in the opposite direction of the gradient which is scaled by a single hyperparameter ϵ. We also compare with the results obtained from learning by association [61] and MAML [40]. We modify the baseline models to make the comparison fair. For associative learning, we train the network on the source domain (Data-I) to minimize the loss function (a combination of visit, walker and classification loss as explained in [61]). For MAML, the best performance was achieved when setting the inner and outer update learning rates as $\alpha = 10^{-3}$ and $\beta = 0.005$. The results presented in Fig. 9.6 demonstrates that the MEMCAP model trained with 30 labeled samples per domain significantly outperforms all other architectures after both mild and severe data distortions are applied.

The second experiment was conducted by simply evaluating the performance of the model on CT scan datasets derived from different institutions. This enables us to check the networks' adaptability and performance robustness in a more natural setting. Classification results of the different models are presented in Table 9.2. We also compare our results with those achieved using transfer learning in which the models trained on Data-I are fine-tuned to each respective target domain (i.e. Data II and III) [62,63]. After training the model on Data-I, we freeze the parameters of the convolutional layers and only fine-tune the parameters of the capsule layers to prevent overfitting on the small number of samples from Data-II and III. The initial learning rate is decreased to 10^{-4} and is decayed exponentially (every 1000 steps with a base of 0.97) to a minimum of 10^{-5}. For the domain adaptation with associative learning, we used the network that was pretrained under the associative learning regime and fine-tune it using a different number of labeled data from the target domain. Also note that a subset of 100 sam-

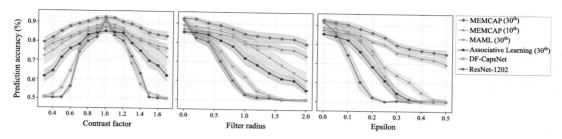

FIGURE 9.6

Quantitative comparison of the test classification performance of various models in response to applying different types of distortions to the input images; namely, contrast shift (left), Gaussian blurring noise (middle), and FGSM adversarial attack (right). The shaded areas depict the standard deviation of prediction AUROC over 100 randomly sampled episodes.

Table 9.2 Comparing the average test AUROC (%) achieved by different approaches over 100 runs with randomly selected annotated samples from the target dataset.

Model	AUROC with Labeled Samples (%)														
	Data-I					Data-II					Data-III				
	2nd	4th	10th	20th	30th	2nd	4th	10th	20th	30th	2nd	4th	10th	20th	30th
Transfer Learning	-	-	-	-	-	70.16	70.23	71.31	73.20	73.56	**62.04**	62.12	62.83	63.24	63.58
LSTM	56.45	68.86	73.22	79.54	80.33	60.33	67.01	75.40	81.00	81.31	59.42	61.33	67.81	72.91	74.68
Associative Learning	**67.29**	72.33	77.81	80.07	80.45	65.58	**73.01**	75.16	78.94	80.19	**62.10**	**64.21**	68.49	70.63	72.06
MAML	60.43	68.43	76.39	83.21	85.13	60.11	71.57	78.42	83.84	84.29	60.79	63.43	78.58	81.94	82.52
MEMCAP	62.77	**77.43**	**84.09**	**87.92**	**90.24**	64.17	73.07	**83.42**	**89.57**	**92.45**	61.23	**64.43**	**84.71**	**88.67**	**89.09**

ples from the remaining training data was randomly selected as the set of unlabeled samples required for this approach. For all three baseline approaches, we ran the fine-tuning for as many iterations as required and reported the best results achieved. We observed that MEMCAP significantly outperforms the other baseline methods, with larger labeled sample sets contributing to more substantial increases in performance.

9.6 Discussion

The adaptability of a CAD model to various different domains is fundamental to its feasibility in healthcare applications. This is due to the significant variation that can be seen across medical datasets; differences between patients, patient cohorts, and imaging centers can all contribute to potentially degraded CAD performance. In the context of Computed Tomography (CT) scans, we note that these variations are often caused by the use of unique CT scanners with varying Hounsfield Unit (HU) values [21]. The reason for scanning a patient can also contribute to these significant domain shifts; the dosage of radiation used for each disease can vary, which alters the image noise distributions. Even data derived from various different imaging centers (as is the case for the LUNA dataset) can not characterize all of the observable domain variations. This is reflected in our results presented in Table 9.1 which shows that deep neural networks trained on Data I do not generalize well to Data II, a similar sample set which was collected in a different institution. It is unrealistic to have physicians label data for each possible domain; even with a model trained on a large dataset, fine-tuning and retraining is required to match the new target domain. The use of domain adaptation methods is therefore warranted in the context of medical imaging tasks.

We propose MEMCAP, a deep neural network architecture trained with meta learning to perform domain adaptation in lung nodule classification from CT scans. It consists of a CapsNet feature network that extracts invariant low and high-level semantic structures across domains from the high-dimensional input volume. The output is then fed to the task network: a memory augmented recurrent network which learns to quickly store and retrieve domain-specific information from its external memory bank using a small number of labeled samples. MEMCAP is thus able to leverage the available labeled target examples to store and exploit the underlying intrinsic information in the target domain. To evaluate the performance of our proposed architecture, we compared our results with transfer learning, associative learning, and MAML. We simulated domain shifts by applying different types of distortions (contrast shift, Gaussian blurring, and FGSM adversarial attacks). From these results, we observe that MEMCAP was more robust to data distortions than the other evaluated methods. This suggests that MEMCAP was more resistant to domain shifts and was thus able to learn the underlying domain-independent information. We then evaluated the performance of the technique with data sets collected from unique institutions and with unique imaging settings. In Data II, the samples were collected from a single hospital and were then labeled by an independent group of experienced thoracic radiologists. We note that MEMCAP significantly outperforms the other techniques once enough labeled samples are provided; with just 10 labeled samples, MEMCAP achieves an 83.42% average AUROC, while MAML requires 20 labeled samples to achieve a similar level of performance. The performance disparity between MAML and MEMCAP is due to the inherent weaknesses of the MAML framework; while we observed stable performance across episodes in the MEMCAP model (as shown in the right panel of Fig. 9.5), we observed significant performance instability when training the MAML model. This can be the result of vanishing and exploding gradients that occur due to a lack of skip connections and the large depth of the unfolded network [64]. We also note that the performance of MAML depends heavily on finding the optimal hyperparameters across a large range of possible values (such as the α and β learning rates) for a given input dataset. MEMCAP is less susceptible to these limitations; it achieves its peak performance of 92.45% with 30 labeled samples, exceeding the performance of all baseline methods by a large margin.

We then evaluated the effectiveness of MEMCAP on the common occurrence of incidental lung nodules which are usually missed by radiologists and classifiers [65,66]. These are lung nodules that were incidentally detected while scanning for another disease; this means that either contrast or non-contrast enhanced scans could be used to image patients which generally have a low-risk of lung cancer. This makes the detection of incidental lung nodules challenging; while screening for lung nodules in a high-risk population primes the radiologist for the task at hand, the assessment of incidental lung nodules must be done simultaneously to detect the other intended abnormalities. This issue is exacerbated by the fact that incidental lung nodules are detected in both noncontrast and contrast enhanced scans with imaging protocols optimized for different organs other than the lung. This is especially limiting as a thin slice thickness is usually required to identify a small lung nodule. Unlike Data I and II, all samples generated in Data III were incidental. Moreover, due to the nature of these scans, the nodules are often smaller than the nodules observed in Data I and II. The results show that this significant domain shift is handled well by the MEMCAP framework when compared to the other baseline methods. We note that MEMCAP outperforms all other methods and achieves 84.7% and 89.1% accuracy for classifying incidental lung nodules after only 10 and 30 labeled samples, respectively. Given the resistance of MEMCAPS to domain shifts, we show that it is well suited to the task of assessing incidental lung nodules, and can be used effectively in a clinical setting.

9.7 Conclusion

This chapter systematically evaluates the adaptability of deep networks; we found that while deep neural networks achieve state-of-the-art performance on a set of data, they do not perform well in response to domain shifts. We propose a practical adaptive classifier called MEMCAP which is capable of taking a few annotated inputs from a new target domain to refine its decision making ability accordingly. This prevents the operator from having to re-train the network for each domain, as re-training requires a significant amount of time, computational resources, and human effort. Our experimental results have demonstrated that when the data distribution changes, the proposed classifier adapts almost perfectly in the lung nodule classification task while popular deep networks' performance decrease to chance with large domain shifts. Exploring the possibility of utilizing the proposed framework for the recognition of critical radiology findings from across the body (such as liver tumors, enlarged lymph nodes, and so on) as well as examining different optimization strategies to speed up the convergence of MEMCAP are promising directions for future work.

References

[1] R.L. Siegel, K.D. Miller, A. Jemal, Cancer statistics, 2017, CA: A Cancer Journal for Clinicians 67 (1) (2017) 7–30.

[2] N.L.S.T.R. Team, et al., Reduced lung-cancer mortality with low-dose computed tomographic screening, The New England Journal of Medicine 2011 (365) (2011) 395–409.

[3] N. Horeweg, Scholten, et al., Detection of lung cancer through low-dose ct screening (NELSON): a pre-specified analysis of screening test performance and interval cancers, The Lancet Oncology 15 (12) (2014) 1342–1350.

[4] A. Brady, R.Ó. Laoide, P. McCarthy, R. McDermott, Discrepancy and error in radiology: concepts, causes and consequences, The Ulster Medical Journal 81 (1) (2012) 3.

[5] A.P. Brady, Error and discrepancy in radiology: inevitable or avoidable?, Insights into Imaging (2016) 1–12.

[6] T.N. Shewaye, A.A. Mekonnen, Benign-malignant lung nodule classification with geometric and appearance histogram features, arXiv preprint, arXiv:1605.08350, 2016.

[7] K. Awai, K. Murao, A. Ozawa, M. Komi, H. Hayakawa, S. Hori, Y. Nishimura, Pulmonary nodules at chest ct: effect of computer-aided diagnosis on radiologists' detection performance, Radiology 230 (2) (2004) 347–352.

[8] Q. Dou, H. Chen, L. Yu, J. Qin, P.-A. Heng, Multilevel contextual 3-d cnns for false positive reduction in pulmonary nodule detection, IEEE Transactions on Biomedical Engineering 64 (7) (2017) 1558–1567.

[9] M. Firmino, A.H. Morais, R.M. Mendoça, M.R. Dantas, H.R. Hekis, R. Valentim, Computer-aided detection system for lung cancer in computed tomography scans: review and future prospects, Biomedical Engineering Online 13 (1) (2014) 41.

[10] Y. LeCun, Y. Bengio, G. Hinton, Deep learning, Nature 521 (7553) (2015) 436–444.

[11] A. Krizhevsky, I. Sutskever, G.E. Hinton, Imagenet classification with deep convolutional neural networks, in: Advances in Neural Information Processing Systems, 2012, pp. 1097–1105.

[12] Y. Xu, T. Mo, Q. Feng, P. Zhong, M. Lai, I. Eric, C. Chang, Deep learning of feature representation with multiple instance learning for medical image analysis, in: Acoustics, Speech and Signal Processing (ICASSP), 2014 IEEE International Conference on, IEEE, 2014, pp. 1626–1630.

[13] A. Mobiny, A. Singh, H. Van Nguyen, Risk-aware machine learning classifier for skin lesion diagnosis, Journal of Clinical Medicine 8 (8) (2019) 1241.

[14] H. Greenspan, B. van Ginneken, R.M. Summers, Guest editorial deep learning in medical imaging: overview and future promise of an exciting new technique, IEEE Transactions on Medical Imaging 35 (5) (2016) 1153–1159.

[15] Y. Bar, I. Diamant, L. Wolf, S. Lieberman, E. Konen, H. Greenspan, Chest pathology detection using deep learning with non-medical training, in: Biomedical Imaging (ISBI), 2015 IEEE 12th International Symposium on, IEEE, 2015, pp. 294–297.

[16] A. Mobiny, H. Van Nguyen, Fast capsnet for lung cancer screening, in: International Conference on Medical Image Computing and Computer-Assisted Intervention, Springer, 2018, pp. 741–749.

[17] K.-L. Hua, C.-H. Hsu, S.C. Hidayati, W.-H. Cheng, Y.-J. Chen, Computer-aided classification of lung nodules on computed tomography images via deep learning technique, OncoTargets and Therapy 8 (2015).

[18] A.A.A. Setio, F. Ciompi, G. Litjens, P. Gerke, C. Jacobs, S.J. van Riel, M.M.W. Wille, M. Naqibullah, C.I. Sánchez, B. van Ginneken, Pulmonary nodule detection in ct images: false positive reduction using multiview convolutional networks, IEEE Transactions on Medical Imaging 35 (5) (2016) 1160–1169.

[19] D. Ardila, A.P. Kiraly, S. Bharadwaj, B. Choi, J.J. Reicher, L. Peng, D. Tse, M. Etemadi, W. Ye, G. Corrado, D.P. Naidich, S. Shetty, End-to-end lung cancer screening with three-dimensional deep learning on low-dose chest computed tomography, Nature Medicine (2019), https://doi.org/10.1038/s41591-019-0447-x.

[20] Q. Wang, F. Milletari, H.V. Nguyen, S. Albarqouni, M.J. Cardoso, N. Rieke, Z. Xu, K. Kamnitsas, V. Patel, B. Roysam, et al., in: Domain Adaptation and Representation Transfer and Medical Image Learning with Less Labels and Imperfect Data: First MICCAI Workshop, DART 2019, and First International Workshop, MIL3ID 2019, Shenzhen, Held in Conjunction with MICCAI 2019, Shenzhen, China, October 13 and 17, 2019, Proceedings, vol. 11795, Springer Nature, 2019.

[21] A.M.A. Roa, H.K. Andersen, A.C.T. Martinsen, Ct image quality over time: comparison of image quality for six different ct scanners over a six-year period, Journal of Applied Clinical Medical Physics 16 (2) (2015) 350–365.

[22] A. Kumar, A. Saha, H. Daume, Co-regularization based semi-supervised domain adaptation, in: Advances in Neural Information Processing Systems, 2010, pp. 478–486.

[23] J. Hoffman, E. Tzeng, T. Park, J.-Y. Zhu, P. Isola, K. Saenko, A.A. Efros, T. Darrell, Cycada: cycle-consistent adversarial domain adaptation, arXiv preprint, arXiv:1711.03213, 2017.

[24] H. Daumé III, Frustratingly easy domain adaptation, arXiv preprint, arXiv:0907.1815, 2009.

[25] Y. Ganin, V. Lempitsky, Unsupervised domain adaptation by backpropagation, arXiv preprint, arXiv:1409.7495, 2014.

[26] S. Shekhar, V.M. Patel, H.V. Nguyen, R. Chellappa, Generalized domain-adaptive dictionaries, in: Proceedings of the IEEE Conference on Computer Vision and Pattern Recognition, 2013, pp. 361–368.

[27] K. Saenko, B. Kulis, M. Fritz, T. Darrell, Adapting visual category models to new domains, Computer Vision-ECCV 2010 (2010) 213–226.

[28] H. Van Nguyen, K. Zhou, R. Vemulapalli, Cross-domain synthesis of medical images using efficient location-sensitive deep network, in: International Conference on Medical Image Computing and Computer-Assisted Intervention, Springer, 2015, pp. 677–684.

[29] J. Donahue, Y. Jia, O. Vinyals, J. Hoffman, N. Zhang, E. Tzeng, T. Darrell, Decaf: a deep convolutional activation feature for generic visual recognition, in: International Conference on Machine Learning, 2014, pp. 647–655.

[30] H.V. Nguyen, H.T. Ho, V.M. Patel, R. Chellappa, DASH-N: joint hierarchical domain adaptation and feature learning, IEEE Transactions on Image Processing 24 (12) (2015) 5479–5491.

[31] A.A. Rusu, M. Vecerik, T. Rothörl, N. Heess, R. Pascanu, R. Hadsell, Sim-to-real robot learning from pixels with progressive nets, arXiv preprint, arXiv:1610.04286, 2016.

[32] J. Hoffman, E. Tzeng, J. Donahue, Y. Jia, K. Saenko, T. Darrell, One-shot adaptation of supervised deep convolutional models, arXiv preprint, arXiv:1312.6204, 2013.

[33] A. Bergamo, L. Torresani, Exploiting weakly-labeled web images to improve object classification: a domain adaptation approach, in: Advances in Neural Information Processing Systems, 2010, pp. 181–189.

[34] Y. Aytar, A. Zisserman, Tabula rasa: model transfer for object category detection, in: 2011 International Conference on Computer Vision, IEEE, 2011, pp. 2252–2259.

[35] K. Saenko, B. Kulis, M. Fritz, T. Darrell, Adapting visual category models to new domains, in: European Conference on Computer Vision, Springer, 2010, pp. 213–226.

[36] K. Saito, K. Watanabe, Y. Ushiku, T. Harada, Maximum classifier discrepancy for unsupervised domain adaptation, in: Proceedings of the IEEE Conference on Computer Vision and Pattern Recognition, 2018, pp. 3723–3732.

[37] G. Marcus, Deep learning: a critical appraisal, arXiv preprint, arXiv:1801.00631, 2018.

[38] J. Schmidhuber, Evolutionary principles in self-referential learning, or on learning how to learn: the meta-meta-... hook, Ph.D. thesis, Technische Universität München, 1987.

[39] S. Thrun, L. Pratt, Learning to learn: introduction and overview, in: Learning to Learn, Springer, 1998, pp. 3–17.

[40] C. Finn, P. Abbeel, S. Levine, Model-agnostic meta-learning for fast adaptation of deep networks, in: Proceedings of the 34th International Conference on Machine Learning-Volume 70, JMLR. org, 2017, pp. 1126–1135.

[41] A. Santoro, S. Bartunov, M. Botvinick, D. Wierstra, T. Lillicrap, One-shot learning with memory-augmented neural networks, arXiv preprint, arXiv:1605.06065, 2016.

[42] D. Li, Y. Yang, Y.-Z. Song, T.M. Hospedales, Learning to generalize: meta-learning for domain generalization, in: Thirty-Second AAAI Conference on Artificial Intelligence, 2018.

[43] S. Sabour, N. Frosst, G.E. Hinton, Dynamic routing between capsules, in: Advances in Neural Information Processing Systems, 2017, pp. 3856–3866.

[44] G.E. Hinton, S. Sabour, N. Frosst, Matrix capsules with em routing, in: International Conference on Learning Representations, 2018.

[45] K. He, X. Zhang, S. Ren, J. Sun, Deep residual learning for image recognition, in: Proceedings of the IEEE Conference on Computer Vision and Pattern Recognition, 2016, pp. 770–778.

[46] A. Mobiny, H. Lu, H.V. Nguyen, B. Roysam, N. Varadarajan, Automated classification of apoptosis in phase contrast microscopy using capsule network, IEEE Transactions on Medical Imaging 39 (1) (2019) 1–10.

[47] S. Hochreiter, J. Schmidhuber, Long short-term memory, Neural Computation 9 (8) (1997) 1735–1780.

[48] C. Giraud-Carrier, R. Vilalta, P. Brazdil, Introduction to the special issue on meta-learning, Machine Learning 54 (3) (2004) 187–193.

[49] A. Graves, G. Wayne, I. Danihelka, Neural Turing machines, arXiv preprint, arXiv:1410.5401, 2014.

[50] Q. Dou, D.C. de Castro, K. Kamnitsas, B. Glocker, Domain generalization via model-agnostic learning of semantic features, in: Advances in Neural Information Processing Systems, 2019, pp. 6447–6458.

[51] M. Woodward, C. Finn, Active one-shot learning, arXiv preprint, arXiv:1702.06559, 2017.

[52] A.A.A. Setio, A. Traverso, T. De Bel, M.S. Berens, C. van den Bogaard, P. Cerello, H. Chen, Q. Dou, M.E. Fantacci, B. Geurts, et al., Validation, comparison, and combination of algorithms for automatic detection of pulmonary nodules in computed tomography images: the LUNA16 challenge, Medical Image Analysis 42 (2017) 1–13.

[53] S.G. Armato, G. McLennan, L. Bidaut, M.F. McNitt-Gray, C.R. Meyer, A.P. Reeves, B. Zhao, D.R. Aberle, C.I. Henschke, E.A. Hoffman, et al., The lung image database consortium (lidc) and image database resource

initiative (idri): a completed reference database of lung nodules on ct scans, Medical Physics 38 (2) (2011) 915–931.

[54] A. Jemal, S.A. Fedewa, Lung cancer screening with low-dose computed tomography in the United States—2010 to 2015, JAMA Oncology 3 (9) (2017) 1278–1281.

[55] W.C. Black, I.F. Gareen, S.S. Soneji, J.D. Sicks, E.B. Keeler, D.R. Aberle, A. Naeim, T.R. Church, G.A. Silvestri, J. Gorelick, et al., Cost-effectiveness of ct screening in the national lung screening trial, The New England Journal of Medicine 371 (2014) 1793–1802.

[56] N.L.S.T.R. Team, The national lung screening trial: overview and study design, Radiology 258 (1) (2011) 243–253.

[57] S. Ren, K. He, R. Girshick, J. Sun, Faster r-cnn: towards real-time object detection with region proposal networks, in: Advances in Neural Information Processing Systems, 2015, pp. 91–99.

[58] F. Lundh, M. Ellis, et al., Python imaging library (pil), 2012.

[59] M. Abadi, P. Barham, J. Chen, Z. Chen, A. Davis, J. Dean, M. Devin, S. Ghemawat, G. Irving, M. Isard, et al., Tensorflow: a system for large-scale machine learning, in: 12th {USENIX} Symposium on Operating Systems Design and Implementation ({OSDI} 16), 2016, pp. 265–283.

[60] I.J. Goodfellow, J. Shlens, C. Szegedy, Explaining and harnessing adversarial examples, arXiv preprint, arXiv:1412.6572, 2014.

[61] P. Haeusser, A. Mordvintsev, D. Cremers, Learning by association-a versatile semi-supervised training method for neural networks, in: IEEE Conference on Computer Vision and Pattern Recognition (CVPR), vol. 3, 2017, p. 6.

[62] S.J. Pan, Q. Yang, A survey on transfer learning, IEEE Transactions on Knowledge and Data Engineering 22 (10) (2009) 1345–1359.

[63] J. Yosinski, J. Clune, Y. Bengio, H. Lipson, How transferable are features in deep neural networks?, in: Advances in Neural Information Processing Systems, 2014, pp. 3320–3328.

[64] A. Antoniou, H. Edwards, A. Storkey, How to train your maml, arXiv preprint, arXiv:1810.09502, 2018.

[65] R. Hossain, C.C. Wu, P.M. de Groot, B.W. Carter, M.D. Gilman, G.F. Abbott, Missed lung cancer, Radiologic Clinics 56 (3) (2018) 365–375.

[66] H. MacMahon, J.H. Austin, G. Gamsu, C.J. Herold, J.R. Jett, D.P. Naidich, E.F. Patz Jr, S.J. Swensen, Guidelines for management of small pulmonary nodules detected on ct scans: a statement from the Fleischner society, Radiology 237 (2) (2005) 395–400.

Few-shot segmentation of 3D medical images

Abhijit Guha Roy[a,d], **Shayan Siddiqui**[a,d], **Sebastian Pölsterl**[a,d], **Azade Farshad**[b,d], **Nassir Navab**[b,c,d], **and Christian Wachinger**[a,d]

[a]*Ludwig Maximilian University of Munich, Munich, Germany*
[b]*Technical University of Munich, Munich, Germany*
[c]*Johns Hopkins University, Baltimore, MD, United States*

10.1 Introduction

Fully convolutional neural networks (F-CNNs) have achieved state-of-the-art performance in semantic image segmentation for both natural [1–4] and medical images [5,6]. Despite their tremendous success in image segmentation, they are of limited use when only a few labeled images are available. F-CNNs are, in general, highly complex models with millions of trainable weight parameters that require thousands of densely annotated images for training to be effective. A better strategy could be to adapt an already trained F-CNN model to segment a new semantic class from a few labeled images. This strategy often works well in computer vision applications where a pretrained model is used to provide a good initialization and is subsequently fine-tuned with the new data to tailor it to the new semantic class. However, fine-tuning an existing pretrained network without risking overfitting still requires a fair amount of annotated images (at least in the order of hundreds). When dealing with an extremely low data regime, where only a single or a few annotated images of the new class are available, such fine-tuning based transfer learning often fails and may cause overfitting [7,8].

Few-shot learning is a machine learning technique that aims to address situations where an existing model needs to generalize to an unknown semantic class with a few examples at a rapid pace [9–11]. The basic concept of few-shot learning is motivated by the learning process of humans, where learning new semantics is done rapidly with very few observations, leveraging strong prior knowledge acquired from past experience. While few-shot learning for image classification and object detection is a well-studied topic, few-shot learning for semantic image segmentation with neural networks has only recently been proposed [7,8]. Making dense pixel-level high-dimensional predictions in an extremely low data regime is immensely challenging. However, at the same time, few-shot learning could significantly impact medical image analysis because it addresses learning from scarcely annotated data, which is the norm due to medical experts' dependence on manual labeling. This chapter discusses a few-shot segmentation framework designed exclusively for segmenting volumetric medical scans. A key to achieving this goal is to integrate the recently proposed 'squeeze & excite' blocks within the design of our novel few-shot architecture [12].

---

[d] The affiliations are for the time that the work was done.

Meta Learning With Medical Imaging and Health Informatics Applications. https://doi.org/10.1016/B978-0-32-399851-2.00018-1

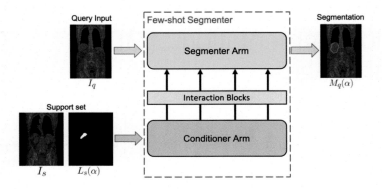

FIGURE 10.1

Overview of the few-shot segmentation framework. The support set consists of an image slice I_s and the corresponding annotation for the new semantic class $L_s(\alpha)$ (here α is the class liver). We pass the support set through the conditioner arm, whose information is conveyed to the segmenter arm via interaction blocks. The segmenter arm uses this information and segments a query input image I_q for the class α generating the label map $M_q(\alpha)$. Except for the support set, the few-shot segmenter has never seen annotations of a liver before.

10.1.1 Background on few-shot segmentation

Few-shot learning algorithms generalize a model to a new, previously unseen class with only a few labeled examples by utilizing the previously acquired knowledge from differently labeled training data. Fig. 10.1 illustrates the overall setup, where we want to segment the liver in a new scan given the annotation of the liver in only a single slice. A few-shot segmentation network architecture [7,8] commonly consists of three parts: (i) a conditioner arm, (ii) a set of interaction blocks, and (iii) a segmentation arm. During inference, the model is provided with support set $(I_s, L_s(\alpha))$, consisting of an image I_s with the new semantic class (or organ) α outlined as a binary mask indicated as $L_s(\alpha)$. In addition, a query image I_q is provided, where the new semantic class is to be segmented. The conditioner takes in the support set and performs a forward pass. This generates multiple feature maps of the support set in all the intermediate layers of the conditioner arm. This set of feature maps is referred to as *task representation* as they encode the information required to segment the new semantic class. The *task representation* is taken up by the interaction blocks, whose role is to pass the relevant information to the segmentation arm. The segmentation arm takes the query image as input, leverages the task information provided by the interaction blocks, and generates a segmentation mask M_q for the query input I_q. Thus, interaction blocks pass the information from the conditioner to the segmenter and form the backbone for few-shot semantic image segmentation. Existing approaches use weak interactions with a single connection either at the bottleneck or the last layer of the network [7,8].

10.1.2 Challenges for medical few-shot segmentation

Existing work in computer vision on few-shot segmentation processes 2D RGB images and uses a pretrained model for both segmenter and conditioner arm to aid training [7,8]. Pretrained models provide a strong prior knowledge with more robust features from the start of training. Hence, weak interaction between the conditioner and the segmenter is sufficient to train the model effectively. The direct extension to medical images is challenging due to the lack of pretrained models. Instead, both the conditioner and the segmenter need to be trained from scratch. However, training the network without pretrained models with weak interaction is prone to instability and mode collapse.

Instead of weak interaction, we propose a strong interaction between both arms at multiple locations. The strong interaction facilitates adequate gradient flow across the two arms, which eases the training of both arms without the need for any pretrained model. For effectuating the interaction, we propose our recently introduced 'channel squeeze & spatial excitation' (sSE) module [12,13]. Our previous works used the sSE blocks for adaptive self-recalibration of feature maps to aid segmentation in a single segmentation network. Here, we use the sSE blocks to communicate between the two arms of the few-shot segmentation network. The block takes the learned conditioner feature map as input and performs 'channel squeeze' to learn a spatial map. This is used to perform 'spatial excitation' on the segmenter feature map. We use sSE blocks between all the encoder, bottleneck, and decoder blocks. SE blocks are well suited for effectuating the interaction between arms, as they are lightweight and therefore only marginally increase the model complexity. Despite their lightweight nature, they can strongly impact the segmenter's features via recalibration.

Existing work on few-shot segmentation focused on 2D images, while here, we deal with volumetric medical scans. Manually annotating organs on all slices in 3D images is time-consuming. Following the idea of few-shot learning, the annotation should instead happen on a few sparsely selected slices. To this end, we propose a volumetric segmentation strategy by properly pairing a few annotated slices of the support volume with all the slices of the query volume, maintaining interslice consistency of the segmentation.

10.1.3 Contributions

In this work, we propose:

1. A novel few-shot segmentation framework for volumetric medical scans.
2. Strong interactions at multiple locations between the conditioner and segmenter arms, instead of only one interaction at the final layer.
3. 'Squeeze & Excitation' modules for effectuating the interaction.
4. Stable training from scratch without requiring a pretrained model.
5. A volumetric segmentation strategy that optimally pairs the slices of query and support volumes.

10.1.4 Overview

We discuss related work in Sec. 10.2, present our few-shot segmentation algorithm in Sec. 10.3, the experimental setup in Sec. 10.4 and experimental results and discussion in Sec. 10.5. We conclude with a summary of our contributions in Sec. 10.6.

10.2 Prior work
10.2.1 Few-shot learning

Methods for few-shot learning can be broadly divided into three groups. The first group of methods adapts a base classifier to the new class [9,14,15]. These approaches are often prone to overfitting as they attempt to fit a complex model on a few new samples. Methods in the second group aim to predict classifiers close to the base classifier to prevent overfitting. The basic idea is to use a two-branch network, where the first branch predicts a set of dynamic parameters, which are used by the second branch to generate a prediction [16,17]. The third group contains algorithms that use metric learning. They map the data to an embedding space, where dissimilar samples are mapped far apart, and similar samples are mapped close to each other, forming clusters. Standard approaches rely on Siamese architectures for this purpose [18,19].

10.2.2 Few-shot segmentation using deep learning

Few-shot image segmentation with deep neural networks has been explored only recently. In one of the earliest works, [20] leverage the idea of fine-tuning a pretrained model with limited data. The authors perform video segmentation, given the annotation of the first frame. Although their model performed adequately in this application, such approaches are prone to overfitting, and adapting to a new class requires retraining, which hampers the speed of adaptation. [7] use a 2-arm architecture, where the first arm looks at the new sample along with its label to regress the classification weights for the second arm, which takes in a query image and generates its segmentation. [21] extended this work to handle multiple unknown classes at the same time to perform multiclass segmentation. [8] took it to a challenging situation where supervision of the support set is provided only at a few selected landmarks for foreground and background, instead of a densely annotated binary mask. Existing approaches for few-shot segmentation were evaluated on the PASCAL VOC computer vision benchmark [7,8]. They reported low segmentation scores (mean intersection over union around 40%), confirming that few-shot segmentation is a very challenging task.

All of the papers mentioned above depend on pretrained models to start the training process. Although pretrained models are relatively easy to access for computer vision applications, no pretrained models are available for medical imaging applications. Moreover, they use 2D RGB images, whereas we deal with 3D volumetric medical scans. Few-shot segmentation of 3D volumetric images is more challenging than 2D because there is no established strategy to select and pair support slices with the query volume. This can lead to situations where the query slice can be very different from the support slice or may not even contain the target class at all.

In the domain of medical image segmentation, recently [22] Zhao et al. used a learned transformation to augment a single annotated volume heavily for one-shot segmentation. This differs from our approach in two aspects: (i) they use a single fully annotated volume, whereas we use annotations of only a few slices, (ii) they use a learned representation to highly augment the single annotated volume for segmentation, whereas we use a separate dataset with annotations provided for other classes. We follow the experimental setting defined in computer vision PASCAL VOC benchmarks by [7].

10.3 Method

In this section, we first introduce the problem setup, then detail the architecture of our network and the training strategy, and finally describe the evaluation strategy for segmenting volumetric scans.

10.3.1 Problem setup for few-shot segmentation

The training data for few-shot segmentation $\mathcal{D}_{\text{Train}} = \{(I_T^i, L_T^i(\alpha))\}_{i=1}^N$ comprises N pairs of input image I_T and its corresponding binary label map $L_T(\alpha)$ with respect to the semantic class (or organ) α. All the semantic classes α which are present in the label map $L_T^i \in \mathcal{D}_{\text{Train}}$ belong to the set $\mathcal{L}_{\text{Train}} = \{1, 2, \ldots, \kappa\}$, i.e., $\alpha \in \mathcal{L}_{\text{Train}}$. Here κ indicates the number of classes (organs) annotated in the training set. The objective is to learn a model $\mathcal{F}(\cdot)$ from $\mathcal{D}_{\text{Train}}$, such that given a support set $(I_s, L_s(\hat{\alpha})) \notin \mathcal{D}_{\text{Train}}$ for a new semantic class $\hat{\alpha} \in \mathcal{L}_{\text{Test}}$ and a query image I_q, the binary segmentation $M_q(\hat{\alpha})$ of the query is inferred.

Fig. 10.1 illustrates the setup for the test class $\hat{\alpha} = $ liver in a CT scan. The semantic classes for training and testing are mutually exclusive, i.e., $\mathcal{L}_{\text{Train}} \cap \mathcal{L}_{\text{Test}} = \emptyset$.

One fundamental difference of few-shot segmentation to few-shot classification or object detection is that test classes $\mathcal{L}_{\text{Test}}$ might already appear in the training data as the background class.

For instance, the network has already seen the liver on many coronal CT slices as part of the background class, although the liver was not a part of the training classes.

This potentially forms prior knowledge that could be utilized during testing when only a few examples are provided with the liver annotated.

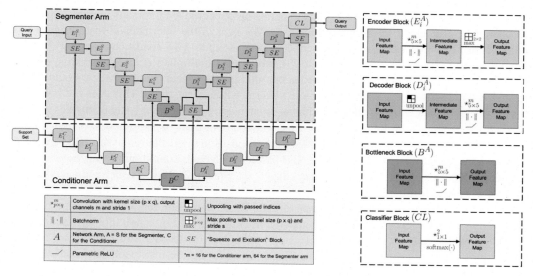

FIGURE 10.2

Illustration of the architecture of the few-shot segmenter. To the left, we show a block diagram with arrows illustrating the encoder-decoder based conditioner arm (bottom) and segmenter arm (top). Interaction between them is shown by SE blocks, which is detailed in Fig. 10.3. To the right, the operational details of the encoder block, decoder block, bottleneck block and the classifier block are provided.

10.3.2 Architectural design

As mentioned earlier, our network architecture consists of three building blocks: (i) a conditioner arm, (ii) interaction blocks with sSE modules, and (iii) a segmenter arm.

The conditioner arm processes the support set to model a new semantic class (organ) in an image. It efficiently conveys the information to the segmenter arm through the interaction blocks. The segmenter arm segments the new semantic class in a new query image by utilizing the information provided by the interaction blocks. Figs. 10.2 and 10.3 illustrate the architecture in further detail, which is also described below.

In our framework, we choose the segmenter and conditioner to have a symmetric layout, i.e., both have four encoder and decoder blocks separated by a bottleneck block. The symmetric layout helps in having a strong interaction between matching blocks, as feature maps have the exact spatial resolution. In existing approaches, conditioner and segmenter only interact via the final layer before generating segmentation maps [7,8]. Such weak interaction at a single location was sufficient for their application because they could use a pretrained model, which already provides reasonably good features.

As we do not have a pretrained network, we propose establishing a strong interaction by incorporating the sSE blocks at multiple locations. Such interactions facilitate training the model from scratch.

10.3.2.1 Conditioner arm

The task of the conditioner arm is to process the support set by fusing the visual information of the support image I_s with the annotation L_s, and generate task-specific feature maps, capable of capturing what should be segmented in the query image I_q. We refer to the intermediate feature maps of the conditioner as *task representation*. We provide a 2-channel input to the conditioner arm by stacking I_s and binary map $L_s(\alpha)$. This is in contrast to [7], where they multiplied I_s and $L_s(\alpha)$ to generate the input. Their motivation was to suppress the background pixels so that the conditioner could focus on the patterns within the object (like eyes or nose patterns within a cat class). This does not hold for our scans due to the limited texture patterns within an organ class. For example, voxel intensities within the liver are homogeneous with limited edges. Thus, we feed both parts of the support set to the network and let it learn the optimal fusion that provides the best possible segmentation of the query image.

The conditioner arm has an encoder-decoder based architecture consisting of four encoder blocks, four decoder blocks, separated by a bottleneck layer, see Fig. 10.2. Both encoder and decoder blocks consist of a generic block constituting a convolutional layer with a kernel size of 5×5, stride of 1, and 16 output feature maps, followed by a parametric ReLU activation function [23] and a batch normalization layer. In the encoder block, the generic block is followed by a max-pooling layer of 2×2 and stride 2, which reduces the spatial dimension by half. In the decoder block, the generic block is preceded by an unpooling layer [4]. The pooling indices during the max-pool operations are stored and used in the corresponding unpooling stage of the decoder block for upsampling the feature map. Not only is the unpooling operation parameter-free, which reduces the model complexity, but it also aids in preserving the spatial consistency for fine-grained segmentation. Furthermore, it must be noted that *no skip connections* are used between the encoder and decoder blocks, unlike the standard U-net architecture [5]. The reason for this important design choice is discussed in Sec. 10.5.2.

10.3.2.2 Interaction block using 'squeeze & excitation' modules

The interaction blocks play a vital role in the few-shot segmentation framework. These blocks take the *task representation* of the conditioner as input and convey them to the segmenter to steer segmentation of the query image. Ideally, these blocks should: (i) be lightweight to only marginally increase the model complexity and computation time, and (ii) ease network training by improving gradient flow.

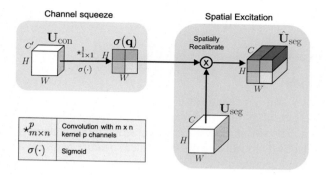

FIGURE 10.3

Illustration of the architecture of the 'channel squeeze & spatial excitation' (sSE) module, which is used as the interaction block within the few-shot segmenter. The block takes a conditioner feature map $\mathbf{U}_{con}$ and a segmenter feature map $\mathbf{U}_{seg}$ as inputs. 'Channel squeeze' is performed on $\mathbf{U}_{con}$ to generate a spatial map $\sigma(\mathbf{q})$, which is used for 'spatial excitation' of $\mathbf{U}_{seg}$, which promotes the interaction.

We use the recently introduced 'Squeeze & Excitation' (SE) modules for this purpose. SE modules are computational units to achieve adaptive recalibration of feature maps within any CNN [24]. SE blocks can boost the performance of CNNs while increasing model complexity only marginally. For classification [24], the feature maps are spatially squeezed to learn a channel descriptor, which is used to excite (or recalibrate) the feature map, emphasizing specific important channels. We refer to it as spatial squeeze and channel excitation block (cSE). In our recent work, we extended the idea to segmentation, where recalibration was performed by squeezing channel-wise and exciting spatially (sSE), emphasizing relevant spatial locations [12,13]. SE blocks are used for self-recalibration in both cases, i.e., the same feature map is used as input for squeezing and excitation operations. However, here we propose to use SE blocks for the interaction between the conditioner and the segmenter. The conditioner feature maps are taken as input for the squeezing operation, and its outputs are used to excite the segmentation feature maps as detailed below.

10.3.2.2.1 Channel squeeze & spatial excitation (sSE)

The sSE block squeezes a conditioner feature map $\mathbf{U}_{con} \in \mathbb{R}^{H \times W \times C'}$ along the channels and excites the corresponding segmenter feature map $\mathbf{U}_{seg} \in \mathbb{R}^{H \times W \times C}$ spatially, conveying the information from the support set to aid the segmentation of the query image. H, W are the height and width of feature maps, C' and C are the number of channels for the conditioner and the segmenter feature maps, respectively. Here, we consider a particular slicing strategy to represent the input tensor $\mathbf{U}_{con} = [\mathbf{u}_{con}^{1,1}, \mathbf{u}_{con}^{1,2} \dots, \mathbf{u}_{con}^{j,\iota}, \dots, \mathbf{u}_{con}^{H,W}]$, where $\mathbf{u}_{con}^{j,\iota} \in \mathbb{R}^{1 \times 1 \times C'}$ with $j \in \{1, 2, \dots, H\}$ and $\iota \in \{1, 2, \dots, W\}$. Similarly for segmenter feature map $\mathbf{U}_{seg} = [\mathbf{u}_{seg}^{1,1}, \mathbf{u}_{seg}^{1,2} \dots, \mathbf{u}_{seg}^{j,\iota}, \dots, \mathbf{u}_{seg}^{H,W}]$. The spatial squeeze operation is performed using a convolution $\mathbf{q} = \mathbf{W}_{sq} \star \mathbf{U}_{con}$ with $\mathbf{W}_{sq} \in \mathbb{R}^{1 \times 1 \times C'}$, generating a projection tensor $\mathbf{q} \in \mathbb{R}^{H \times W}$. This projection $\mathbf{q}$ is passed through a sigmoid gating layer $\sigma(\cdot)$ to rescale activations to [0, 1], which is used to re-calibrate or excite $\mathbf{U}_{seg}$ spatially to generate

$$\hat{\mathbf{U}}_{\text{seg}} = [\sigma(q_{1,1})\mathbf{u}_{\text{seg}}^{1,1}, \ldots, \sigma(q_{j,\iota})\mathbf{u}_{\text{seg}}^{j,\iota}, \ldots, \sigma(q_{H,W})\mathbf{u}_{\text{seg}}^{H,W}]. \tag{10.1}$$

The architectural details of this module are presented in Fig. 10.3.

10.3.2.3 Segmenter arm

The goal of the segmenter arm is to segment a given query image I_q for a new, unknown class α, by using the information passed by the conditioner, which captures high-level information about the previously unseen class α. The sSE modules in the interaction block compress the *task representation* of the conditioner and adaptively recalibrate the segmenter's feature maps by spatial excitation.

The encoder-decoder architecture of the segmenter is similar to the conditioner, with a few differences. Firstly, the convolutional layers of both the encoder and decoder blocks in the segmenter have 64 output feature maps, in contrast to 16 in the conditioner. This provides the segmenter arm with a higher model complexity than the conditioner arm. We will justify this choice in Sec. 10.5.3. Secondly, unlike the conditioner arm, the segmenter arm provides a segmentation map as output, see Fig. 10.2. Thus a classifier block is added, consisting of a 1×1 convolutional layer with 2 output feature maps (foreground, background), followed by a soft-max function for inferring the segmentation. Thirdly, after every encoder, decoder, and bottleneck block in the segmenter, the interaction block recalibrates the feature maps, which is not the case in the conditioner arm.

10.3.3 Training strategy

We use a similar training strategy to [7]. We simulate the one-shot segmentation task with the training dataset $\mathcal{D}_{\text{Train}}$ as described below. It consists of two stages (i) Select a mini-batch using the *Batch Sampler* and (ii) Training the network using the selected mini-batch.

10.3.3.0.1 Batch sampler

To simulate the one-shot segmentation task during training, we require a specific strategy for selecting samples in a mini-batch that differs from traditional supervised training. For each iteration, we follow the steps below to generate batch samples:

1. We first randomly sample a label $\alpha \in \mathcal{L}_{\text{Train}}$.
2. Next, we randomly select 2 image slices and their corresponding label maps, containing the semantic label α, from training data $\mathcal{D}_{\text{Train}}$.
3. The label maps are binarized, representing semantic class α as foreground and the rest as background.
4. One pair constitutes the support set $(I_s, L_s(\alpha))$ and the other pair the query set $(I_q, L_q(\alpha))$, where $L_q(\alpha)$ serves as ground truth segmentation for computing the loss.

10.3.3.0.2 Training

The network receives the support pair $(I_s, L_s(\alpha))$ and the query pair $(I_q, L_q(\alpha))$ as a batch for training purpose. The support pair $(I_s, L_s(\alpha))$ is concatenated and provided as 2-channeled input to the conditioner arm. The query image I_q is provided as input to the segmentation arm. With these inputs to the two arms, one feed-forward pass is performed to predict the segmentation $M_q(\alpha)$ for the query image I_q for label α. We use the Dice loss [6] as the cost function, which is computed between the prediction

$M_q(\alpha)$ and the ground truth $L_q(\alpha)$ as

$$\mathcal{L}_{\text{Dice}} = 1 - \frac{2\sum_{\mathbf{x}} M_q(\mathbf{x}) L_q(\mathbf{x})}{\sum_{\mathbf{x}} M_q(\mathbf{x}) + \sum_{\mathbf{x}} L_q(\mathbf{x})} \tag{10.2}$$

where $\mathbf{x}$ corresponds to the pixels of the prediction map. The learnable weight parameters of the network are optimized using stochastic gradient descent (SGD) with momentum to minimize $\mathcal{L}_{\text{Dice}}$. At every iteration, the batch sampler provides different samples corresponding to different α and the loss is computed for that specific α, and weights are updated accordingly. With the target class α changing at every iteration, the network converges. Thus, we can say that the prediction becomes agnostic to the chosen α after convergence. For a new α, the network should be able to perform segmentation, which is what we expect during inference of a one-shot segmentation framework.

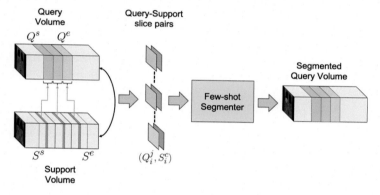

FIGURE 10.4

Illustration of the few-shot volumetric segmentation strategy for $k = 3$. We divide both the query volume and support volume into k group of slices. The annotated center slice of the ith group in the support volume is paired with all the slices of ith group of query volume to infer their segmentation. This is done for $i \in \{1, 2, 3\}$ and is passed to the few-shot segmenter for segmenting the whole volume.

10.3.4 Volumetric segmentation strategy

As mentioned in the previous section, the network is trained with 2D images as support set and query. However, a 3D query volume needs to be segmented during the testing phase. Therefore, we need to select a sparse set of annotated slices from the support volume that forms the support set. A straight-forward extension for segmenting the query volume is challenging as there is no established strategy to pair the above-selected support slices to all of the slices of the query volume, which would yield the best possible segmentation. In this section, we propose a strategy to tackle this problem.

Assume we have a budget of annotating only k slices in the support volume; a query volume is segmented following procedure:

1. Given a semantic class, we first indicate the range of slices (along a fixed orientation) where the organ lies for both support and query volume. Let us assume the ranges are $[S^s, S^e]$ for the support and $[Q^s, Q^e]$ for the query volume. Here the superscript indicates the start s and end e slice indices.

2. Based on the budget k, both ranges $[S^s, S^e]$ and $[Q^s, Q^e]$ are divided into k equi-spaced groups of slices. Let us indicate the groups by $[\{S_1^i\}, \ldots, \{S_k^i\}]$ and $[\{Q_1^i\}, \ldots, \{Q_k^i\}]$ respectively. Here the subscript indicates the group number.

3. In each of the k support volume groups, center slices $[S_1^c, \ldots, S_k^c]$ are annotated to serve as the support set.

4. We pair the annotated center slice S_j^c with all the slices of the group $\{Q_j^i\}$ for all $i \in \{1, \ldots, k\}$. This forms the input for the segmenter and the conditioner to generate the final volume segmentation.

The overall process of volumetric evaluation is illustrated in Fig. 10.4. Our experiments showed that if the support slice and query slice are similar, segmentation performance is better than very dissimilar support and query slices. Therefore, it is beneficial if the overall contrast of the scans (i.e., the intensity values or mutual information) is similar. This can intuitively show us that the quality of the support slice has a significant impact on the segmenter's performance. In our evaluation strategy, for a fixed budget k, we made sure that the dissimilarity between the support slice and the corresponding query slice is minimal. It must be noted that in the evaluation strategy, $[Q^s, Q^e]$ must be provided for the query volume. In our experiments, we precomputed them using the label mask of the target organ. In practice, this could be done manually by quickly scanning the slices or using a simple automated tool trained for this purpose.

10.4 Dataset and experimental setup

10.4.1 Dataset description

We choose the challenging task of organ segmentation from contrast-enhanced CT (ceCT) scans for evaluating our few-shot volumetric segmentation framework. We use the Visceral dataset [25], which consists of two parts (i) silver corpus (with 65 scans) and (ii) gold corpus (20 scans). All the scans were resampled to a voxel resolution of 2 mm^3.

10.4.2 Problem formulation

As there is no existing benchmark for few-shot image segmentation on volumetric medical images, we formulate our own experimental setup for the evaluation. We use the silver corpus scans for training ($\mathcal{D}_{\text{Train}}$). For testing, we use the gold corpus dataset. One volume is used to create the support set (Volume ID: `10000132_1_CTce_ThAb`), 14 volumes were used as the validation set, and 5 volumes as the test set. The IDs of the respective volumes are reported at the end of the manuscript. In the experiments presented in Sec. 10.5.1 to Sec. 10.5.4, we use the validation set as we use these results to determine the architectural configuration and number of support slices. Finally, we use these results and compare them against existing approaches on the test set in Sec. 10.5.5.

We consider the following six organs as semantic classes in our experiments:

1. Liver
2. Spleen
3. Right Kidney
4. Left Kidney

Table 10.1 Semantic labels used for training and testing in all the experimental folds. Left and Right are abbreviated as L., and R. Psoas Muscle is abbreviated as P.M.

	Fold 1	Fold 2	Fold 3	Fold 4
Liver	*Test*	Train	Train	Train
Spleen	Train	*Test*	Train	Train
L./R. Kidney	Train	Train	*Test*	Train
L./R. P. M.	Train	Train	Train	*Test*

Table 10.2 List of hyperparameters used for training the few-shot segmenter.

Hyperparameter	Value
Learning Rate	0.01
Weight decay constant	10^{-4}
Momentum	0.99
No. of epochs	10
Iterations per epoch	500

5. Right Psoas Muscle
6. Left Psoas Muscle

We perform experiments with 4 Folds, such that each organ is considered an unknown semantic class once per-fold. The training and testing labels for each of the folds are reported in Table 10.1.

10.4.3 Hyperparameters for training the network

Due to the lack of pretrained models, we could not use the setup from [7] for training.

Thus, we needed to define our own hyperparameter settings, listed in Table 10.2. Please note that the hyperparameters were estimated by manually trying out different combinations rather than employing a hyperparameter optimization framework, which could lead to better results but at the same time is time-consuming.

10.5 Experimental results and discussion

10.5.1 'Squeeze & excitation' based interaction

In this section, we investigate the optimal positions of the SE blocks for facilitating interaction and compare the performance of cSE and sSE blocks. Here, we set the number of convolution kernels of the conditioner arm to 16 and the segmenter arm to 64. We use $k = 12$ support slices from the support volume. Since this experiment aims to evaluate the position and type of SE blocks, we keep the above parameters fixed but evaluate them later. With four different possibilities of placing the SE blocks and

Table 10.3 The performance of our few-shot segmenter (per-fold and mean Dice score) by using either sSE or cSE module, at different locations (encoder, bottleneck and decoder) of the network. Left and Right are abbreviated as L. and R. Psoas Muscle is abbreviated as P.M.

	Position of SE			Type of SE		Dice Score on Validation set				
	Encoder	Bottleneck	Decoder	Spatial	Channel	Liver	Spleen	L/R kidney	L/R P.M.	Mean
BL-1	✓	✗	✗	✓	✗	0.667	0.599	0.385	0.339	0.497
BL-2	✓	✗	✗	✗	✓	0.086	0.032	0.087	0.017	0.056
BL-3	✗	✓	✗	✓	✗	0.680	0.398	0.335	0.252	0.416
BL-4	✗	✓	✗	✗	✓	0.060	0.018	0.090	0.032	0.050
BL-5	✗	✗	✓	✓	✗	0.683	0.534	0.278	0.159	0.414
BL-6	✗	✗	✓	✗	✓	0.051	0.014	0.010	0.003	0.020
BL-7	✓	✓	✓	✓	✗	0.700	0.607	0.464	0.499	**0.567**
BL-8	✓	✓	✓	✗	✓	0.026	0.003	0.001	0.001	0.008

two types, cSE or sSE, we have a total of 8 different baseline configurations. The configuration of each of these baselines and their corresponding segmentation performance per fold is reported in Table 10.3.

Firstly, one observes that BL-1, 3, 5, 7 with sSE have a decent performance (more than 0.4 Dice score), whereas BL-2, 4, 6, 8 have inferior performance (less than 0.1 Dice score). This demonstrates that sSE interaction modules are far superior to cSE modules in this application of few-shot segmentation. It is challenging to understand the network dynamics to say why such a behavior is observed. Our intuition is that channel SE blocks' underperformance is associated with the global average pooling layer it uses, which averages the spatial response to a scalar value. In our application (or medical scans in general), the target semantic class covers a small proportion of the support slice (around 5-10%). When averaged over all the pixels, the background activations highly influence the final value. The role of the interaction blocks is to convey the target class's semantic information from conditioner to segmenter. By using channel SE as global average pooling, the class information is mainly lost; thus, it can not convey the relevant information to the segmenter.

The second conclusion from Table 10.3 is that out of all the possible positions of the interaction block, BL-7, i.e., sSE blocks between all encoder, bottleneck, and decoder blocks, achieved the highest Dice score of 0.567. This result is consistent across all folds.

BL-7 outperformed the remaining baselines for Fold-1 (liver), Fold-2 (spleen), Fold-3 (L/R kidney), and Fold-4 (L/R psoas muscle) by a margin of 0.1 to 0.8 Dice points. This might be related to the relative difficulty associated with each organ. Due to the contrast and size, the liver is relatively easy to segment compared to the spleen, kidney, and psoas muscles. Also, BL-1, 3, and 5 performed poorly compared to BL-7. This indicates that more interactions aids in better training. Comparing BL-1, BL-3, and Bl-5, we observe that BL-1 provides better performance. This indicates that encoder interactions are much powerful than bottleneck or decoder interactions. However, as BL-7 has a much higher performance than BL-1, BL-3, and BL-5, we believe that encoder, bottleneck, and decoder interactions provide complementary information to the segmenter for more accurate query segmentation. From these results, we conclude that interaction blocks based on sSE are most effective, and we use sSE-based interactions between all encoder, bottleneck, and decoder blocks in subsequent experiments.

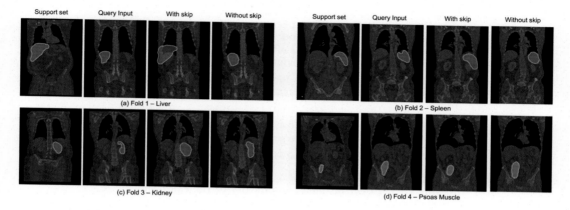

FIGURE 10.5

Qualitative results of few-shot segmenter with and without skip connections to demonstrate the *copy over effect*. The subfigures (a-d) refer to the examples from each of the folds, namely liver, spleen, left kidney, and right psoas muscles, respectively. For each subfigure, the first column indicates the support image with the manual outline of the organ, the second column indicates the query image with manual annotation, the third column indicates the prediction of the query image with skip connection, and the fourth column indicates the prediction of the query image without skip connections (proposed approach). All annotations are shown in green. A clear *copy over effect* can be observed for all the folds when analyzing the mask of the support annotation and the prediction with skip connections.

10.5.2 Effect of skip connections in the architecture

Due to the success of the U-net architecture [5], using skip connections in F-CNN models has become a prevalent design choice. With skip connections, the output feature map of an encoder block is concatenated with the input of the decoder block with an identical spatial resolution. In general, this connectivity aids in achieving a superior segmentation performance as it provides high contextual information in the decoding stage and facilitates gradient flow. In our experiments, we intuitively started off with having skip connections in both the conditioner arm and the segmenter arm, but observed an unexpected behavior in the predicted query segmentation masks. By including skip connections, the network mostly copies the binary mask of the support set to the output. This is observed for all the folds both in train and test set. We refer to this phenomenon as the *copy over effect*. Qualitative examples are illustrated for each fold in Fig. 10.5, where we see that, despite the support and the query images having different shapes, the prediction on the query image is almost identical to the support binary mask. We also performed a quantitative analysis to observe the effect on Dice scores due to this *copy over effect*. Table 10.4 reports the performance with and without skip connections, where we observe a 3% decrease in Dice points due to the addition of skip connections. We also performed experiments by adding the skip connections in the conditioner and the segmenter arm separately. We observe that the inclusion of skip connections only in the conditioner arm reduced the performance by 6% Dice points, whereas adding them only in the segmenter arm made the training unstable. For this evaluation, the number of convolution kernels for conditioner and segmenter was fixed at 16 and 64, respectively, and the evaluation was conducted with $k = 12$ support slices.

Table 10.4 The segmentation performance (per-fold and mean Dice score) on test scans, with and without using skip connections within our few-shot segmenter. Left and Right are abbreviated as L. and R. Psoas Muscle is abbreviated as P.M.

Skip Connections		Dice Score on Validation set				
Conditioner	Segmenter	Liver	Spleen	L/R kidney	L/R P.M.	Mean
×	×	0.700	0.607	0.464	0.499	**0.567**
✓	×	0.561	0.495	0.457	0.447	0.505
×	✓	0.096	0.026	0.025	0.019	0.042
✓	✓	0.561	0.549	0.543	0.501	0.538

Table 10.5 Effect of model complexity of the conditioner arm (Number of convolution kernels) on segmentation performance, provided a fixed model complexity (Number of convolution kernels fixed to 64) of the segmenter arm. Left and Right are abbreviated as L. and R. Psoas Muscle is abbreviated as P.M.

Channels in	Dice Score on Validation set				
Conditioner Arm	Liver	Spleen	L/R kidney	L/R P.M.	Mean
8	0.628	0.275	0.429	0.276	0.402
16	0.700	0.607	0.464	0.499	**0.567**
32	0.621	0.551	0.378	0.280	0.457
64	0.659	0.417	0.421	0.247	0.436

10.5.3 Model complexity of the conditioner arm

One important design choice is to decide the relative model complexity of the conditioner arm compared to the segmenter arm. As mentioned in Sec. 10.1.1, the conditioner takes in the support example and learns to generate *task representations*, which are passed to the segmenter arm through interaction blocks. This is utilized by the segmenter to segment the query image. We fix the number of kernels of the convolutional layers (for every encoder, bottleneck, and decoder) for the segmenter arm to 64. We use this setting as this has proven to work well in our prior segmentation works across different datasets [12,26]. Next, we vary the number of kernels of the conditioner arm to {8, 16, 32, 64}. The number of support slices remains fixed to $k = 12$. We report the segmentation results of these settings in Table 10.5. The best performance was observed for the conditioner with 16 convolution kernels. One possible explanation of this could be that too low conditioner complexity (like 8) leads to a very weak *task representation*, thereby failing to support the segmenter arm reliably. Whereas higher conditioner arm complexity, 32 and 64 kernels (same as segmenter complexity), might lead to improper training due to increased complexity under limited training data and interaction. We fix the number of conditioner convolution kernels to 16 in our following experiments.

10.5.4 Effect of the number of support slice budget

This section investigates the performance when changing the budget for the number of support slices k selected from the support volume for segmenting all the query volumes. Here, k can be considered the 'number of shots' for volumetric segmentation. In all the previous experiments, we fix $k = 12$. Here, we vary k between $\{1, 3, 5, 7, 10, 12, 15, 17, 20\}$ and report the per-fold and overall mean segmentation performance on validation set in Table 10.7. The per-fold performance analysis reveals that the minimum number of slices needed for a decent accuracy varies with the size of the target organ to be segmented.

For Fold-1 (liver), one-shot volume segmentation ($k = 1$) yielded a Dice score of 0.678, which increased to 0.701 with $k = 20$. We observed saturation in performance (Dice score of 0.70) with only 12 slices.

The segmentation performance only marginally increased with higher values of k. For Fold-2 (spleen), the segmentation performance initially increases with the increase in the value of k; then, the performance saturates with $k \geq 10$ at a Dice score of 0.60. The spleen is more difficult to segment than the liver, thus requiring more support. For Fold-3 (right/left kidney), we observe behavior similar to Fold-2. The segmentation performance increases initially with an increase in the value of k and then saturates at a Dice score of 0.46 (this is the mean between the two classes, left and the right kidney) at $k \geq 10$. Also for Fold-4 (right/left psoas muscle), we see the Dice score saturates at 0.50 for $k = 10$. The overall mean Dice score across all the folds also saturates at 0.56 with $k = 10$.

We conclude that $k = 10$ is the maximum number of support slices required for our application based on these results. Thus, we use this configuration in the subsequent experiments.

We also report in Table 10.6 the mean number of slices in the testing volumes for each organ to indicate how sparse the slices were selected for volumetric evaluation.

Table 10.6 Extent of slices (for coronal axis) for different target organs in the Visceral dataset.

Organs	Extent of Slices
Liver	106 ± 12
Spleen	50 ± 8
R. Kidney	34 ± 4
L. Kidney	36 ± 5
R. P.M.	31 ± 5
L. P.M	31 ± 3

10.5.5 Comparison with existing approaches

This section compares our proposed framework against the other existing few-shot segmentation approaches. It must be noted that all of the existing methods were proposed for computer vision applications and thus cannot directly be compared against our approach as explained in Sec. 10.1.2. Hence, we modified each of the existing approaches to suit our application. The results are summarized in Table 10.8. Also, we evaluate the results on the 5 test query volumes.

First, we try to compare against [7]. Their main contribution was that the conditioner arm regresses the convolutional weights used by the classifier block of the segmenter to infer the segmentation of the query image. As we do not have any pretrained models for our application, unlike [7], we use the same architecture as our proposed method for the segmenter and conditioner arms. No intermediate interac-

Table 10.7 The segmentation performance (per-fold and mean Dice score) on validation scans, by varying the number of the annotated slice (k) as support in the support volume. Left and Right are abbreviated as L., and R. Psoas Muscle is abbreviated as P.M.

No. of support slices (k)	Dice Score on Validation set				
	Liver	Spleen	L/R kidney	L/R P.M.	Mean
1	0.678	0.503	0.385	0.398	0.491
3	0.692	0.490	0.422	0.437	0.510
5	0.685	0.557	0.445	0.496	0.546
7	0.694	0.577	0.457	0.507	0.559
10	0.688	0.600	0.466	0.505	0.565
12	0.700	0.607	0.464	0.499	0.567
15	0.700	0.607	0.464	0.496	0.567
17	0.700	0.609	0.465	0.497	0.567
20	0.701	0.606	0.468	0.496	0.568

Table 10.8 Comparison of our proposed few-shot segmenter against the existing methods. For each method, per-fold and mean Dice score and average surface distance (in mm) are reported for the test set. Left and Right are abbreviated as L. and R. Psoas Muscle is abbreviated as P.M. *Classifier Regression [7] training resulted in mode-collapse, hence no Dice score is reported. Feature Fusion is abbreviated to F.F. and Classifier Regression to C.R.

Method	Dice Score on Test set				
	Liver	Spleen	L/R kidney	L/R P.M.	Mean
Proposed	0.680	0.475	0.338	0.450	**0.485**
C.R.* (Adapted from [7])	–	–	–	–	–
F.F. (Adapted from [8])	0.247	0.267	0.307	0.258	0.270
F.F. + C.R.	0.224	0.197	0.348	0.411	0.295
Fine-Tuning [20]	0.307	0.016	0.003	0.043	0.092
Method	**Average Surface Distance on Test set in mm**				
	Liver	Spleen	L/R kidney	L/R P.M.	Mean
Proposed	14.98	10.71	7.12	9.13	**10.48**
C.R.* (Adapted from [7])	–	–	–	–	–
F.F. (Adapted from [8])	32.25	18.24	17.16	12.35	20.00
F.F. + C.R.	38.71	17.60	12.64	10.60	19.88
Fine-Tuning [20]	26.35	–	–	–	–

tions were used other than the final classifier weight regression. We attempted to train the network on our dataset with a wide range of hyperparameters, but all the settings led to instability while training. It must be noted that one possible source of instability might be that we do not use a pretrained model, unlike the original method. Thus, we could not compare our proposed method with this approach.

Next, we compare our approach to [8]. Again, this approach is not directly comparable to our approach due to the lack of a pretrained model. One of the main contributions of their approach was the interaction strategy between the segmenter and the conditioner using a technique called *feature fusion*. They tiled the feature maps of the conditioner and concatenated them with the segmenter feature maps. Their implementation introduced the interaction only at a single location (bottleneck). We tried the same configuration, but the network did not converge. Thus, we modified the model by introducing the concatenation-based feature fusion (instead of our sSE modules) at multiple locations between the conditioner and segmenter arms. As we have a symmetric architecture, no tiling was needed. Similar to our proposed approach, we introduced this feature fusion-based interaction at every encoder, bottleneck, and decoder block. In this experiment, we compare our spatial SE-based interaction approach to the concatenation-based feature fusion approach. The results are reported in Table 10.8. We observe 21% higher Dice points and 10 mm lower average surface distance for our approach.

Next, we attempted to create hybrid baselines by combining the above adapted feature fusion approach [8] with classifier weight regression approach [7]. We observe that the performance increased by 3% Dice points by doing so. Still, it had a much lower Dice score (18% Dice points) in comparison to our proposed approach.

As a final baseline, we compare our proposed framework against the fine-tuning strategy similar to [20]. For a fair comparison, we only use the silver corpus scans ($\mathcal{D}_{\text{Train}}$) and 10 annotated slices from the support volume (`10000132_1_CTce_ThAb`) for training. We use our segmenter arm without the SE blocks as an architectural choice. We pretrain the model using $\mathcal{D}_{\text{Train}}$ to segment the classes of $\mathcal{L}_{\text{Train}}$. After pretraining, we use the learned weights of this model for the initialization of all the layers, except for the classifier block. Then, we fine-tune it using the 10 annotated slices of the support volume having a new class from $\mathcal{L}_{\text{Test}}$. We present the segmentation performance in Table 10.8. Fine-tuning was carefully performed with a low learning rate of 10^{-3} for 10 epochs. The 10 selected slices were augmented during the training process using translation (left, right, top, bottom) and rotation (-15, +15 degrees). Except for fold-1 (liver, Dice score 0.30) all the other folds had a Dice score < 0.01. Overall, this experiment substantiated the fact that fine-tuning under such a low-data regime is ineffective, whereas our few-shot segmentation technique is much more effective.

10.5.6 Comparison with upper bound model

In this section, we investigate the performance of our few-shot segmentation framework to the fully supervised upper bound model. For training this upper bound model, we used all the scans of the Silver Corpus (with annotations of all target organs) and deployed the trained model on the Gold Corpus. We use the standard U-Net [5] architecture for segmentation. Segmentation results are shown in Table 10.9.

We observe that this upper bound model has 20-40% higher Dice points and 1-7 mm lower average surface distance compared to our few-shot segmentation framework. It must be noted that this kind of difference in performance can be expected as all slices from 65 fully annotated scans were used for training. In contrast, only ten annotated slices from a single volume were used in our approach. If access to many fully annotated volumes is provided, it is always recommended to use fully supervised training. Whenever a new class needs to be learned from only a few slices, our few-shot segmentation framework excels. It is also worth mentioning that this drop in performance can also be observed in the

PASCAL VOC benchmark from computer vision, where the fully supervised upper bound has an IoU of 0.89 using the DeepLabv3 architecture, whereas few-shot segmentation has an IoU of 0.4 [7].

Table 10.9 Performance of upper bound model on the Test Set.

Organ	Mean Dice score	Avg. Surface Distance (mm)
Liver	0.900	13.15
Spleen	0.824	3.27
R. Kidney	0.845	3.45
L. Kidney	0.868	3.03
R. P.M.	0.685	8.31
L. P.M	0.680	7.19

10.5.7 Qualitative results

We present a set of qualitative segmentation results in Fig. 10.6(a-d) for folds 1-4, respectively. In Fig. 10.6(a), we show the segmentation of liver. From left to right, we present the support set with manual annotation, query input with its manual annotation, and prediction of the query input. We observe a proper segmentation despite the differences in the shape and size of the liver in the support and the query slices. Note that the only information the network has about the organ is from a single support slice. In Fig. 10.6(b), we show a similar result for spleen. This is a challenging case where the shape of the spleen is very different in the support and query slices. Also, there is a difference in image contrast between the support and query slices. There is a slight undersegmentation of the spleen, but, considering the weak support, the segmentation is surprisingly good. In Fig. 10.6(c), we present the results of the left kidney. Here, we again observe a huge difference in the size of the kidney in support and query slices. The kidney appears as a small dot in the support, making it a very difficult case. In Fig. 10.6(d), we show the segmentation for right psoas muscle. In this case, the support and query slices are visually similar to each other. The prediction from our framework shows a bit of overinclusion in the psoas muscle boundary but a proper localization and shape. Overall, the qualitative results visually present the effectiveness of our framework both under simple and very challenging conditions.

10.5.8 Dependence on support set

In all our previous experiments, one volume (`10000132_1_CTce_ThAb`) was used as a support volume, and the remaining 19 as query volumes for evaluation purposes. In this section, we investigate the sensitivity of segmentation performance on the selection of the support volume. In this experiment, we randomly choose 5 volumes as a support set from the validation set. We select one at a time and evaluate on the remaining 15 volumes (rest of the validation set and test set combined) and report the per-fold and global Dice scores in Table 10.10.

We observe that changing the support volume does affect the segmentation performance. In Fold-1 (liver), the performance varies by 6% Dice points across all the 5 selected support volume. This change is 5%, 8% and 5% Dice points for Fold-2 (spleen), Fold-3 (R/L kidney), Fold-4 (R/L psoas

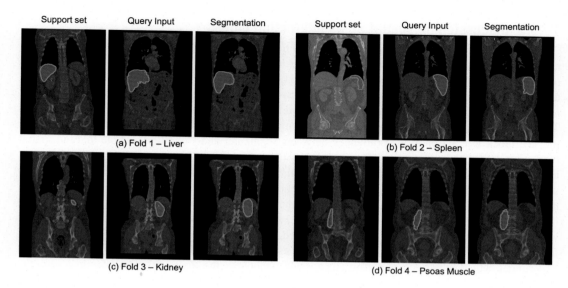

FIGURE 10.6

Qualitative results of our few-shot segmenter. The subfigures (a-d) refer to examples from each of the folds with liver, spleen, left kidney, and right psoas muscles, respectively. For each subfigure, the first column indicates the support image with the manual outline of the organ, the second column indicates the query image with manual annotation, and the third column indicates the predicted segmentation for the query image. All the annotations are shown in green.

Table 10.10 The segmentation performance (per-fold and mean Dice score) on silver corpus (validation set and test set combined), by using different volumes (Volume ID indicated in the first column) as the support volume. Left and Right are abbreviated as L. and R. Psoas Muscle is abbreviated as P.M.

Support Volume ID	Dice Score on rest of 15 volumes of the Dataset				
	Liver	Spleen	L/R kidney	L/R P.M.	Mean
10000100_1_CTce_ThAb	0.748	0.550	0.445	0.454	0.550
10000106_1_CTce_ThAb	0.690	0.514	0.444	0.464	0.528
10000108_1_CTce_ThAb	0.718	0.560	0.406	0.465	0.537
10000113_1_CTce_ThAb	0.689	0.505	0.392	0.453	0.510
10000132_1_CTce_ThAb	0.694	0.533	0.369	0.501	0.524

muscle), respectively. The overall mean Dice scores vary by 4% points. We conclude that it is essential to select an appropriate support volume representing the whole query set. Yet, a good strategy for making the selection remains as future work. Nevertheless, our framework shows some robustness to the selection.

10.5.9 Discussion on spatial SE as interaction blocks

One concern regarding the use of spatial SE blocks for interaction might be the spatial alignment of the target class between the support and query images. Although in our application, there exists some partial overlap of the target organ between the support and query slice, we believe the sSE based interaction is also capable of handling cases where there is no such overlap. We acknowledge that similarity in spatial location does help in our application. However, that is not the only factor driving the segmentation. In Table 10.3, we present experiments for a configuration denoted as BL-3. In this design, we only keep the sSE block interaction at the bottleneck between Segmenter and Conditioner. Note that the spatial resolution in the bottleneck feature map is very low (size: 16×32 for our case). This configuration can be considered as a spatially invariant fusion. In this scenario, we also achieve a decent segmentation score. This is further boosted by adding sSE at all encoder and decoder blocks. One important aspect of the sSE is that it has a sigmoidal gating function at the end before excitation. That means at any location, it has the capacity to saturate all the neurons (i.e., all the output feature map activations become 1), which keeps the segmenter feature maps unchanged. Consider such a case where the encoder/decoder feature maps are unchanged, and only the bottleneck is calibrated. This would be similar to the BL-3 experiment, which shows decent performance. Thus, we believe the sigmoidal gating would control the sSE blocks only to recalibrate the feature maps at scales it is necessary.

10.6 Conclusion

This chapter introduced a few-shot segmentation framework for volumetric medical scans. The main challenges were the absence of pretrained models and the volumetric nature of the scans. We proposed to use 'channel squeeze and spatial excitation' blocks for aiding the proper training of our framework from scratch. In addition, we proposed a volumetric segmentation strategy for segmenting a query volume scan with a support volume scan by pairing 2D slices appropriately. We evaluated our proposed framework, and several baselines on contrast-enhanced CT scans from the Visceral dataset. We compared our sSE based model to the existing approaches based on feature fusion [8], classifier regression [7] and their combination. Our framework outperformed all previous approaches by a large margin.

Besides comparing to existing methods, we also provided detailed experiments for architectural choices regarding the SE blocks, model complexity, and skip connections. We also investigated the effect on the performance of our few-shot segmentation by changing the support volume and the number of budget slices from a support volume.

Our proposed few-shot segmentation has the following limitations. Firstly, the start and end slices need to be indicated for a target organ to be segmented for a new query volume. This might require manual interaction. Secondly, a very precise segmentation cannot be achieved using few-shot segmentation due to minimal supervision and the level of difficulty of this task. If the application demands highly accurate segmentation, we recommend going the traditional supervised learning way by acquiring more annotations for training.

Despite the limitations, the exposition of our proposed approach is very generic and can easily be extended to other few-shot segmentation applications. Our approach is independent of the pretrained model, making it very useful for noncomputer vision applications.

List of IDs in the visceral dataset

The list of IDs in the dataset used for support set, validation query set, and testing query set are reported below.

Support set

1. 10000132_1_CTce_ThAb

Validation query set

1. 10000100_1_CTce_ThAb
2. 10000104_1_CTce_ThAb
3. 10000105_1_CTce_ThAb
4. 10000106_1_CTce_ThAb
5. 10000108_1_CTce_ThAb
6. 10000109_1_CTce_ThAb
7. 10000110_1_CTce_ThAb
8. 10000111_1_CTce_ThAb
9. 10000112_1_CTce_ThAb
10. 10000113_1_CTce_ThAb
11. 10000127_1_CTce_ThAb
12. 10000128_1_CTce_ThAb
13. 10000129_1_CTce_ThAb
14. 10000130_1_CTce_ThAb

Test query set

1. 10000131_1_CTce_ThAb
2. 10000133_1_CTce_ThAb
3. 10000134_1_CTce_ThAb
4. 10000135_1_CTce_ThAb
5. 10000136_1_CTce_ThAb

Acknowledgment

We thank SAP SE and the Bavarian State Ministry of Education, Science and the Arts in the framework of the Centre Digitisation. Bavaria (ZD.B) for funding and the NVIDIA corporation for GPU donation.

References

[1] S. Jégou, M. Drozdzal, D. Vazquez, A. Romero, Y. Bengio, The one hundred layers tiramisu: fully convolutional densenets for semantic segmentation, in: Computer Vision and Pattern Recognition Workshops

(CVPRW), 2017 IEEE Conference on, IEEE, 2017, pp. 1175–1183.

[2] H. Zhao, J. Shi, X. Qi, X. Wang, J. Jia, Pyramid scene parsing network, in: IEEE Conf. on Computer Vision and Pattern Recognition (CVPR), 2017, pp. 2881–2890.

[3] J. Long, E. Shelhamer, T. Darrell, Fully convolutional networks for semantic segmentation, in: Proceedings of the IEEE Conference on Computer Vision and Pattern Recognition, 2015, pp. 3431–3440.

[4] H. Noh, S. Hong, B. Han, Learning deconvolution network for semantic segmentation, in: Proceedings of the IEEE International Conference on Computer Vision, 2015, pp. 1520–1528.

[5] O. Ronneberger, P. Fischer, T. Brox, U-net: convolutional networks for biomedical image segmentation, in: International Conference on Medical Image Computing and Computer-Assisted Intervention 2015, Springer, 2015, pp. 234–241.

[6] F. Milletari, N. Navab, S.-A. Ahmadi, V-net: fully convolutional neural networks for volumetric medical image segmentation, in: 3D Vision (3DV), 2016 Fourth International Conference on, IEEE, 2016, pp. 565–571.

[7] A. Shaban, S. Bansal, Z. Liu, I. Essa, B. Boots, One-shot learning for semantic segmentation, arXiv preprint, arXiv:1709.03410, 2017.

[8] K. Rakelly, E. Shelhamer, T. Darrell, A.A. Efros, S. Levine, Few-shot segmentation propagation with guided networks, arXiv preprint, arXiv:1806.07373, 2018.

[9] L. Fei-Fei, R. Fergus, P. Perona, One-shot learning of object categories, IEEE Transactions on Pattern Analysis and Machine Intelligence 28 (4) (2006) 594–611.

[10] E.G. Miller, N.E. Matsakis, P.A. Viola, Learning from one example through shared densities on transforms, in: Computer Vision and Pattern Recognition, 2000. Proceedings. IEEE Conference on, vol. 1, IEEE, 2000, pp. 464–471.

[11] L. Fei-Fei, Knowledge transfer in learning to recognize visual objects classes, in: Proceedings of the International Conference on Development and Learning (ICDL), 2006, p. 11.

[12] A.G. Roy, N. Navab, C. Wachinger, Recalibrating fully convolutional networks with spatial and channel 'squeeze & excitation' blocks, IEEE Transactions on Medical Imaging (2018).

[13] A.G. Roy, N. Navab, C. Wachinger, Concurrent spatial and channel squeeze & excitation in fully convolutional networks, arXiv preprint, arXiv:1803.02579, 2018.

[14] E. Bart, S. Ullman, Cross-generalization: learning novel classes from a single example by feature replacement, in: Computer Vision and Pattern Recognition, 2005. CVPR 2005. IEEE Computer Society Conference on, vol. 1, IEEE, 2005, pp. 672–679.

[15] B. Hariharan, R. Girshick, Low-shot visual recognition by shrinking and hallucinating features, in: Proc. of IEEE Int. Conf. on Computer Vision (ICCV), Venice, Italy, 2017.

[16] L. Bertinetto, J.F. Henriques, J. Valmadre, P. Torr, A. Vedaldi, Learning feed-forward one-shot learners, in: Advances in Neural Information Processing Systems, 2016, pp. 523–531.

[17] Y.-X. Wang, M. Hebert, Learning to learn: model regression networks for easy small sample learning, in: European Conference on Computer Vision, Springer, 2016, pp. 616–634.

[18] G. Koch, R. Zemel, R. Salakhutdinov, Siamese neural networks for one-shot image recognition, in: ICML Deep Learning Workshop, vol. 2, 2015.

[19] O. Vinyals, C. Blundell, T. Lillicrap, D. Wierstra, et al., Matching networks for one shot learning, in: Advances in Neural Information Processing Systems, 2016, pp. 3630–3638.

[20] S. Caelles, K.-K. Maninis, J. Pont-Tuset, L. Leal-Taixé, D. Cremers, L. Van Gool, One-shot video object segmentation, in: CVPR 2017, IEEE, 2017.

[21] N. Dong, E.P. Xing, Few-shot semantic segmentation with prototype learning, in: BMVC, vol. 3, 2018, p. 4.

[22] A. Zhao, G. Balakrishnan, F. Durand, J.V. Guttag, A.V. Dalca, Data augmentation using learned transformations for one-shot medical image segmentation, in: Proceedings of the IEEE Conference on Computer Vision and Pattern Recognition, 2019, pp. 8543–8553.

[23] K. He, X. Zhang, S. Ren, J. Sun, Delving deep into rectifiers: surpassing human-level performance on imagenet classification, in: Proceedings of the IEEE International Conference on Computer Vision, 2015, pp. 1026–1034.

[24] J. Hu, L. Shen, G. Sun, Squeeze-and-excitation networks, in: Proceedings of the IEEE Conference on Computer Vision and Pattern Recognition, 2018, pp. 7132–7141.

[25] O. Jimenez-del Toro, H. Müller, M. Krenn, K. Gruenberg, A.A. Taha, M. Winterstein, I. Eggel, A. Foncubierta-Rodríguez, O. Goksel, A. Jakab, et al., Cloud-based evaluation of anatomical structure segmentation and landmark detection algorithms: visceral anatomy benchmarks, IEEE Transactions on Medical Imaging 35 (11) (2016) 2459–2475.

[26] A.G. Roy, S. Conjeti, N. Navab, C. Wachinger, Quicknat: a fully convolutional network for quick and accurate segmentation of neuroanatomy, NeuroImage 186 (2019) 713–727.

Smart task design for meta learning medical image analysis systems

Unsupervised, weakly-supervised, and cross-domain design of meta learning tasks

Cuong C. Nguyen[a], Youssef Dawoud[b], Thanh-Toan Do[c], Jacinto C. Nascimento[d],
Vasileios Belagiannis[b], and Gustavo Carneiro[a]

[a]*Australian Institute for Machine Learning, University of Adelaide, Adelaide, SA, Australia*
[b]*Universität Ulm, Ulm, Germany*
[c]*Department of Data Science and AI, Monash University, Clayton, VIC, Australia*
[d]*Institute for Systems and Robotics, Instituto Superior Técnico, Lisbon, Portugal*

11.1 Introduction

Modern medical image analysis systems are often trained following the single-task configuration, where training and testing images are sampled from the same distribution (e.g. classification of breast cancer from a particular population, or segmentation of a particular type of cell) [34]. Such conditions limit the capability of the systems to generalize to new testing tasks or testing images that are out of training distribution. The issue is even more severe when such testing tasks contain a small number of training images. To allow the translation of the systems to new distributions of images and tasks, the field has introduced many transfer-learning methods [9]. A particularly interesting transfer-learning approach is meta learning [27] that explicitly trains a model to perform well on new testing tasks and new testing image distributions. Such models can quickly adapt to new tasks, even if only a few training examples of those tasks are available, without sacrificing too much performance.

This chapter presents recently developed meta learning methods designed to adapt to new tasks and image distributions. To solve this problem, popular transfer-learning approaches often rely on pre-training on a source distribution of tasks, which is different from target distributions [9]. For example, models can be pretrained with (unrelated) supervised computer vision classification problems [4], or unsupervised classification problems using pseudo-labels estimated from clustering techniques [8], or self-supervised using pretext classification problems [3], or image reconstruction [15]. In general, the more correlated the pretraining source tasks and image distributions are to the target tasks and image distributions, the better the transfer-learning process. Unfortunately, the pretraining methods above either rely on nonmedical image datasets or unrelated tasks that may not be helpful for pretraining [47].

In the next sections of this chapter, we present details of our recently proposed meta learning algorithms:

Meta Learning With Medical Imaging and Health Informatics Applications. https://doi.org/10.1016/B978-0-32-399851-2.00019-3

1. the *weakly-supervised meta learning* that "augments" tasks with finer or coarser classification on the same image distribution and strategically samples those tasks [38] in Section 11.4,
2. the *unsupervised meta learning* that trains a meta learning model using tasks formed solely from unlabeled data [40] in Section 11.5, and
3. the *cross-domain few-shot meta learning* method robust to new image distributions and new segmentation tasks [13] in Section 11.6.

In particular, the weakly-supervised [38] and unsupervised [40] meta learning methods extend the popular meta learning algorithm model agnostic meta learning (MAML) [19], by designing several binary classification tasks, and employing a curriculum-learning [41] to sample these tasks for improving training efficiency. The dataset used for these weakly-supervised and unsupervised few-shot meta learning methods contains breast screening dynamic contrast-enhanced magnetic resonance imaging (DCE-MRI) images to evaluate the trained model on classifying images when *malignant lesions* are present or absent (see Fig. 11.1a). Forming tasks in the weakly-supervised method is based on the following image-level classes: *no findings*, *benign lesions* and *malignant lesions*, while the formation in the unsupervised method relies on pseudo-labels obtained from a clustering method [8]. The evaluation for breast screening classification using models trained with the weakly-supervised approach reaches 0.90 area under the ROC curve (AUC), while the unsupervised approach achieves 0.89 AUC. Both approaches outperform baselines such as DenseNet [29] with 0.83 AUC, multiple-instance learning [58] with 0.85 AUC, multitask learning [57] with 0.85 AUC, variational auto-encoder [31] with 0.84 AUC, and deep clustering [8] with 0.80 AUC.

The cross-domain few-shot meta learning approach addresses the few-shot learning problem on new image distributions and new segmentation tasks [13]. The dataset used consists of microscopy segmented images for different types of cell. This forms a realistic scenario where different types of microscopy images and segmentation tasks are leveraged to learn a metamodel that can be adapted to new types of cell segmentation problems using a handful of annotated training images (see Fig. 11.1b). In such setup, the cross-domain few-shot meta learning approach extends the objective in meta learning [16,19,46] by introducing additional terms that regularize the trained model to learn generic and domain-invariant representation. This model is then evaluated on the few annotated images (not more than 10 images) of a hold-out distribution. Empirically, the proposed approach shows promising results despite the small number of annotated training images available across different image distributions.

11.2 Literature review

This section presents a review on relevant meta learning methods, following by automated breast screening from DCE-MRI and microscopy image segmentation approaches.

11.2.1 Meta learning

Traditional machine learning models are trained to optimize a single objective function that addresses a particular task (e.g., classification cross-entropy loss) using a training set sampled from a single image distribution [21]. The transferring of these learnt models to new tasks or new image distributions usually

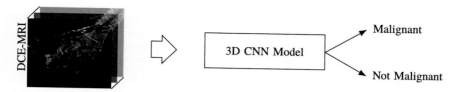

(a) Automated breast screening from breast DCE-MRI

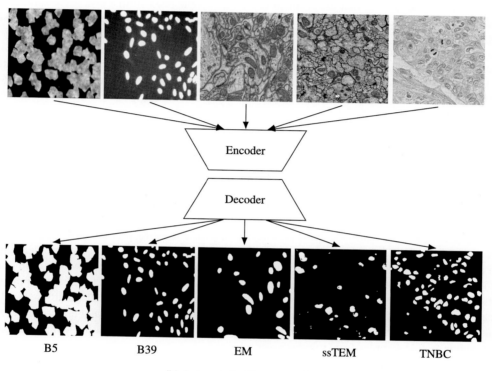

(b) Automated cell segmentation

FIGURE 11.1

The meta learning approaches proposed in this chapter are applied to (a) classify breast screening DCE-MRI volumes, and (b) to segment microscopy cell images. The tasks to metatrain the classification model in (a) are designed based either on manual annotations (no finding, benign findings, and malignant findings) or on pseudo labels from deep clustering methods [8]. The captions (B5, B39, EM, ssTEM, TNBC) in image (b) indicate the different segmentation tasks, where mutually exclusive subsets are used for metatraining and metatesting to demonstrate the ability of the algorithm to transfer to new image and task distributions.

demands a significant amount of re-training [9], depending on how closely related the new tasks and image distributions are to the ones used during training. Alternatively, this transfer-learning problem can be explicitly solved by meta learning methods with an optimization process that improves the ability of a metatrained model to be transferred to new tasks or image distributions [27].

Meta learning is designed to improve a learning algorithm through episodes sampled from a task set and consists of two iterative steps: 1) task adaptation that involves a learning objective to solve a particular task; and 2) meta learning represented by an outer algorithm that updates the inner learning algorithm to improve a metaobjective [27]. The metaobjective can be defined in many ways, such as by a quick adaptation to new distributions, or a few-shot learning in new tasks. An interesting point in the meta learning literature is that the problem of how to sample tasks from a task set to form training episodes is rarely studied, even though we see positive results from the related problem of how to select samples from a training set in supervised learning. For instance, better convergence and better generalization can be achieved by formulating the selection of training samples (i.e., not training tasks) as a multiarmed bandit problem [25]. Furthermore, curriculum-learning [6] has also been used by Matiisen et al. [41] to select training samples (again, not training tasks) based on accuracy improvement. Motivated by these results, we proposed the first approach in the field to apply curriculum-learning for task selection in meta learning [38].

Another interesting issue in meta learning algorithms is on the design of meta learning tasks. For instance, in computer vision problems, tasks can be formed by the classification of a fixed number of classes, sampled from a large pool of training classes [19,52]. A similar strategy can be applied in medical image analysis [38], but the small number of classes available limits the ability of meta learning algorithms to produce an effective metamodel. Therefore, many studies have been carried out to automatically design new classification tasks in an unsupervised way, using classes produced by clustering methods [28,40]. A key aspect behind this design lies on the number of possible classification tasks, where the larger this number, the more effective the meta learning process [40].

Few-shot adaptation to new image distributions and segmentation tasks is another problem investigated in this chapter [13]. This is challenging due to the limited training samples within each domain and the shift of data distributions between domains. To address this issue, a meta learning approach is proposed to train a generic and domain-invariant model using various datasets that are different in terms of image appearance and cell segmentation. The resulting model can quickly and effectively adapt to a new image distribution and segmentation task using a handful of labeled training samples to predict the remaining testing samples from the same test set.

11.2.2 Breast screening from DCE-MRI

Breast cancer screening for women at high risk is usually performed with DCE-MRI images [50]. However, analyzing DCE-MRI images is laborious with relatively high variability in the diagnosis outcome [53]. That motivates the need for an automated analysis that is efficient and consistent. For example, the automatic system is expected to work as an efficient second reader with the goals of decreasing the variability between radiologists' readings [23], increasing their sensitivity [53] and specificity [43]. Current automated breast cancer screening from DCE-MRI is done by models trained with large-scale strongly labeled training sets (where lesions are delineated and associated with class labels) [1,12,24,30,39]. This is, however, unsustainable due to the huge amount of annotation effort. Researchers have designed weakly-supervised training processes [58], where image samples contain only global classification, but no lesion delineation. Although weakly-supervised annotation reduces the amount of annotation effort, training the models for DCE-MRI still requires large-scale training sets, even when the model has been pretrained [4]. Our proposed methods [38,40] target the training of effective breast screening models from DCE-MRI that work not only with weakly-supervised but also with small training sets.

11.2.3 Microscopy image cell segmentation

Early approaches to address the cell segmentation from microscopy images [56] were based on image processing and computer vision techniques [18,36,54]. Fully convolutional neural networks (FCNs) [35] produce significantly more accurate cell segmentation results than these early approaches [10,11,44], with U-Nets [48] and fully convolutional regression network (FCRN) [55] representing influential models. Our cross-domain few-shot metatraining algorithm [13] can be used to train U-Net and FCRN models, where the main advantage lies in its ability to enable few-shot learning on new image distributions and new segmentation tasks. Our approach achieves promising segmentation performance regardless of the small target segmentation datasets.

11.3 Background

In this section, we first introduce the concept of a task, and then we present the meta learning problem formulation.

11.3.1 Task

Following the nomenclature presented in [27], a task is defined as a tuple $\mathcal{T}_i = (\mathcal{D}_i, \ell_i)$, comprising a dataset $\mathcal{D}_i$ and a loss function ℓ_i. The dataset associated with a task $\mathcal{T}_i$ is denoted as $\mathcal{D}_i = \{\mathbf{x}_{ij}, \mathbf{y}_{ij}\}_{j=1}^{m}$ where $\mathbf{x}_{ij} \in \mathcal{X} \subseteq \mathbb{R}^{H \times W \times R}$ is an image with a size of H-by-W and R channels, and $\mathbf{y}_{ij} \in \mathcal{Y}$ is the corresponding label of that image. In classification problems, $\mathcal{Y} \subseteq \{0, 1\}^C$, and in segmentation problems, $\mathcal{Y} \subseteq \{0, 1\}^{H \times W \times C}$, with C denoting the number of classes. Solving a task $\mathcal{T}_i$ requires to find a model parameter $\theta_i \in \Theta \subseteq \mathbb{R}^D$ such that:

$$\theta_i^* = \arg\min_{\theta_i} \mathbb{E}_{(\mathbf{x}_{ij}, \mathbf{y}_{ij}) \sim \mathcal{D}_i} \left[\ell\left(\mathbf{x}_{ij}, \mathbf{y}_{ij}; \theta_i\right) \right], \tag{11.1}$$

where $\ell_i : \mathcal{X} \times \mathcal{Y} \times \Theta \to \mathbb{R}$ is the loss function of task $\mathcal{T}_i$, and $\mathbb{E}$ denotes the expectation w.r.t. the distribution specified in its subscript.

11.3.2 Meta learning

Instead of separately solving each task in the training set $\{\mathcal{T}_m\}_{m=1}^{M}$, it is more beneficial to "jointly" learn from many available training tasks. One learning strategy that allows such joint learning is meta learning that introduces a metaparameter, $\omega \in \Omega$, to model the knowledge shared across all tasks. Such modeling allows meta learning to solve an unseen task more quickly and accurately, even if each task has a limited number of training examples.

In general, meta learning can be considered as an extension of cross-validation used to optimize hyperparameters when solving a single task. For simplicity, the loss function is assumed to be the same across different tasks and denoted as ℓ, so a task $\mathcal{T}_i$ is represented only by its dataset $\mathcal{D}_i$. The objective of meta learning can be defined as the following bi-level optimization:

$$\omega^* = \arg\min_{\omega} \mathbb{E}_{\mathcal{D}_i \sim p(\mathcal{T}^{\mathrm{src}})} \mathbb{E}_{\left(\mathbf{x}_{ij}^{(v)}, \mathbf{y}_{ij}^{(v)}\right) \sim \mathcal{D}_i^{(v)}} \left[\ell\left(\mathbf{x}_{ij}^{(v)}, \mathbf{y}_{ij}^{(v)}; \theta_i^*(\omega)\right) \right]$$

$$\text{subject to: } \theta_i^*(\omega) = \arg\min_{\theta_i} \mathbb{E}_{\left(\mathbf{x}_{ij}^{(t)}, \mathbf{y}_{ij}^{(t)}\right) \sim \mathcal{D}_i^{(t)}} \left[\ell\left(\mathbf{x}_{ij}^{(t)}, \mathbf{y}_{ij}^{(t)}; \theta_i\right) \right], \qquad (11.2)$$

where $\mathcal{D}_i^{(t)}$ and $\mathcal{D}_i^{(v)}$ respectively denote the training and validation subsets of task $\mathcal{T}_i$ with $\mathcal{D}_i^{(t)} \bigcup \mathcal{D}_i^{(v)} = \mathcal{D}_i$ and $\mathcal{D}_i^{(t)} \bigcap \mathcal{D}_i^{(v)} = \varnothing$, and i is the index of M tasks sampled from the training task distribution $p(\mathcal{T}^{\mathrm{src}})$, with $\mathcal{T}^{\mathrm{src}} = \{\mathcal{T}_m\}_{m=1}^M$.

The lower-level in (11.2) represents the adaptation for task $\mathcal{T}_i$, which coincides with the objective for solving single task in (11.1), while the upper-level denotes the learning of the metaparameter. Depending on the objective defined for a task family, different loss functions ℓ can be used. For example, ℓ is often considered as class-wise cross-entropy in classification [21], and pixel-wise cross-entropy in segmentation [35].

Once the metaparameter ω^* is obtained from the bi-level optimization in (11.2), the prediction on a novel task $\mathcal{T}_{M+1}$ can be done in two steps. The first step is to employ the training data subset $\mathcal{D}_{M+1}^{(t)}$ to produce a parameter specific for task $\mathcal{T}_{M+1}$:

$$\theta_{M+1}^*(\omega^*) = \arg\min_{\theta} \mathbb{E}_{\left(\mathbf{x}_{(M+1)j}^{(t)}, \mathbf{y}_{(M+1)j}^{(t)}\right) \sim \mathcal{D}_{M+1}^{(t)}} \left[\ell\left(\mathbf{x}_{(M+1)j}^{(t)}, \mathbf{y}_{(M+1)j}^{(t)}; \theta(\omega^*)\right) \right]. \qquad (11.3)$$

The second step is to evaluate the parameter $\theta_{M+1}^*(\omega^*)$ learned in (11.3) using the data in the validation subset $\mathcal{D}_{M+1}^{(v)}$.

Although the metaparameter ω can model different types of learning parameters shared across all tasks, such as feature extractor [51,52] or optimizer [2,33], all the algorithms in this chapter consider ω as the initialization of the model parameter used to solve each task [19]. Such modeling assumption indicates that $\Theta = \Omega$, and the learnt initialization ω^* can be used in (11.3) to quickly estimate a new parameter $\theta^*(\omega^*)$ for the target task $\mathcal{T}_{M+1}$, even if only a few training examples are available.

When optimizing (11.2) w.r.t. ω using gradient descent, the task-specific parameter in the lower-level can be obtained as:

$$\theta_i^*(\omega) = \omega - \gamma \mathbb{E}_{\mathcal{D}_i^{(t)}} \nabla_\omega \left[\ell\left(\mathbf{x}_{ij}^{(t)}, \mathbf{y}_{ij}^{(t)}; \omega\right) \right], \qquad (11.4)$$

where γ is a hyperparameter, and only one gradient descent update step is carried out to simplify the analysis.

The optimization of the upper-level w.r.t. the metaparameter ω requires the calculation of the corresponding gradient, which can be expressed as:

$$\mathbb{E}_{p(\mathcal{T}^{\mathrm{src}})}\mathbb{E}_{\mathcal{D}_i^{(v)}}\nabla_\omega\left[\ell\left(\mathbf{x}_{ij}^{(v)},\mathbf{y}_{ij}^{(v)};\theta_i^*(\omega)\right)\right]$$

$$=\mathbb{E}_{p(\mathcal{T}^{\mathrm{src}})}\mathbb{E}_{\mathcal{D}_i^{(v)}}\nabla_\omega^\top\left[\theta_i^*(\omega)\right]\times\nabla_{\theta_i^*(\omega)}\left[\ell\left(\mathbf{x}_{ij}^{(v)},\mathbf{y}_{ij}^{(v)};\theta_i^*(\omega)\right)\right]$$

$$=\mathbb{E}_{p(\mathcal{T}^{\mathrm{src}})}\left\{\mathbf{I}-\gamma\mathbb{E}_{\mathcal{D}_i^{(t)}}\nabla_\omega^2\left[\ell\left(\mathbf{x}_{ij}^{(t)},\mathbf{y}_{ij}^{(t)};\omega\right)\right]\right\}$$

$$\times\mathbb{E}_{\mathcal{D}_i^{(v)}}\nabla_{\theta_i^*(\omega)}\left[\ell\left(\mathbf{x}_{ij}^{(v)},\mathbf{y}_{ij}^{(v)};\theta_i^*(\omega)\right)\right], \tag{11.5}$$

where the factorization follows the chain rule and the result in (11.4), and $\mathbf{I}$ is the identity matrix.

Given the gradient obtained in (11.5), the metaparameter ω can be learnt using gradient descent as the following:

$$\omega\leftarrow\omega-\alpha\mathbb{E}_{p(\mathcal{T}^{\mathrm{src}})}\mathbb{E}_{\mathcal{D}_i^{(v)}}\nabla_\omega\left[\ell\left(\mathbf{x}_{ij}^{(v)},\mathbf{y}_{ij}^{(v)};\theta_i^*(\omega)\right)\right], \tag{11.6}$$

where α is the learning rate for ω.

Such learning requires to calculate the Hessian matrix $\nabla_\omega^2\left[\ell\left(\mathbf{x}_{ij}^{(t)},\mathbf{y}_{ij}^{(t)};\omega\right)\right]$, resulting in "second-order" meta learning methods, such as model-agnostic meta learning (MAML) [19]. "First-order" methods are proposed to omit the Hessian matrix to reduce the computation cost when updating ω. REPTILE [46] – a type of first-order method – additionally approximates the gradient of the loss on the validation subset, $\nabla_{\theta_i^*(\omega)}\left[\ell\left(\mathbf{x}_{ij}^{(v)},\mathbf{y}_{ij}^{(v)};\theta_i^*(\omega)\right)\right]$, by $\omega-\theta_i^*(\omega)$ to obtain a much simpler update:

$$\omega\leftarrow\omega+\frac{\gamma}{M}\sum_{i=1}^M\left(\theta_i^*(\omega)-\omega\right). \tag{11.7}$$

Although meta learning has demonstrated remarkable results in several few-shot learning benchmarks, its downside is the need of a large number of training tasks formed by hundreds of classes. This is, however, infeasible in the context of medical image analysis due to the limited number of classes and relatively small number of samples per class. The following subsections tackle such problems via (i) *weakly-supervised meta learning* that "augments" tasks with finer or coarser classification on the same data and strategically samples those tasks, (ii) *unsupervised meta learning* that trains a meta learning model using tasks formed solely from unlabeled data, or (iii) *cross-domain few-shot meta learning* that utilizes tasks from multiple sources where each task has at most 10 images.

11.4 Task-augmentation weakly-supervised meta learning

The *weakly-supervised meta learning that augments tasks* [38] is designed for the situation, where we have a limited number of training tasks and each task has a small number of training examples. By employing a medical semantics, the weakly-supervised meta learning augments more classes from the given classes to form more training tasks. Such training tasks are then sampled following the *teacher-student curriculum learning* [41] to train a model using MAML algorithm [19].

Breast screening exams are used through this subsection to demonstrate the weakly-supervised meta learning approach on such constrained situations. The **dataset** $\mathcal{D}=\{(\mathbf{x}_i,\mathbf{t}_i,b_i,d_i,\mathbf{y}_i)\}_{i=1}^{|\mathcal{D}|}$ consists of:

Algorithm 11.1 Weakly-supervised meta learning - training procedure.

1: **procedure** TRAINING(dataset $\mathcal{D}$, learning rates γ and α)
2:    Initialize metaparameter ω
3:    Form training task set $\mathcal{T}^{\text{src}} = \{\mathcal{T}_m\}_{m=1}^M$
4:    **while** ω not converged **do**
5:        Sample a mini-batch of tasks, $\mathcal{K} \subseteq \mathcal{T}^{\text{src}}$ using $p(\mathcal{T}^{\text{src}})$
6:        **for** each task $\mathcal{T}_i \in \mathcal{K}$ **do**
7:            Split the associated dataset $\mathcal{D}_i$ into $\mathcal{D}_i^{(t)}$ and $\mathcal{D}_i^{(v)}$
8:            Adapt metaparameter to task $\mathcal{T}_i$:   ▷ Eq. (11.4)

$$\theta_i^*(\omega) = \omega - \frac{\gamma}{|\mathcal{D}_i^{(t)}|} \sum_{j=1}^{|\mathcal{D}_i^{(t)}|} \nabla_\omega \left[\ell\left(\mathbf{x}_{ij}^{(t)}, \mathbf{y}_{ij}^{(t)}; \omega\right) \right]$$

9:        Update metaparameter: ▷ Eq. (11.6)

$$\omega \leftarrow \omega - \frac{\alpha}{|\mathcal{K}|} \sum_{i=1}^{|\mathcal{K}|} \frac{1}{|\mathcal{D}_i^{(v)}|} \sum_{j=1}^{|\mathcal{D}_i^{(v)}|} \nabla_\omega \left[\ell\left(\mathbf{x}_{ij}^{(v)}, \mathbf{y}_{ij}^{(v)}; \theta_i^*(\omega)\right) \right]$$

10:    **return** ω

- $\mathbf{x}_i \in \mathcal{X}$ denoting the first subtraction DCE-MRI volume,
- $\mathbf{t}_i \in \mathcal{X}$ denoting the T1-weighted volume,
- $b \in \{\text{left, right}\}$ indicating patient's left or right breast,
- $d_i \in \mathbb{N}$ denoting patient number (patients have been anonymized, and this number is used to split $\mathcal{D}$ into training and testing), and
- $\mathbf{y} \in \mathcal{Y}$ representing the volume weak (*i.e.*, global) label ($\mathbf{y} \in \{0, 1\}^3$, where $\mathbf{y} = [1, 0, 0]$ denotes no findings, $\mathbf{y} = [0, 1, 0]$ represents at least one benign and no malignant findings, and $\mathbf{y} = [0, 0, 1]$ represents at least one malignant finding).

This dataset is split into mutually exclusive training, validation, and testing sets, using the patient number.

Given three provided class labels, only $\binom{3}{2} = 3$ binary classification tasks can be formed per one image distribution. During training, additional two binary classification tasks are formed, resulting in a total of five tasks per image distribution. Such binary classification tasks can be described as follows (see Fig. 11.2a, left-hand side):

1. no findings ($\mathbf{y} = [1, 0, 0]$) versus malignant findings ($\mathbf{y} = [0, 0, 1]$),
2. no findings ($\mathbf{y} = [1, 0, 0]$) versus benign findings ($\mathbf{y} = [0, 1, 0]$),
3. benign findings ($\mathbf{y} = [0, 1, 0]$) versus malignant findings ($\mathbf{y} = [0, 0, 1]$),
4. no findings ($\mathbf{y} = [1, 0, 0]$) versus any (benign or malignant) findings ($\mathbf{y} \in \{[0, 1, 0], [0, 0, 1]\}$), and
5. malignant findings ($\mathbf{y} = [0, 0, 1]$) versus nonmalignant (no findings or benign) findings ($\mathbf{y} \in \{[1, 0, 0], [0, 1, 0]\}$).

The metaparameter ω is then learnt through several tasks where the number of training examples, $|\mathcal{D}_i^{(t)}|$, in each task is small. See Fig. 11.2b and Algorithm 11.1, for an overview of the methodology. Note that the loss function ℓ in Algorithm 11.1 is the binary cross-entropy loss.

In general, the mini-batch $\mathcal{K}$ is often selected by randomly sampling $|\mathcal{K}|$ tasks from $\{\mathcal{T}_m\}_{m=1}^M$, using the training task distribution $\{p(\mathcal{T}_m)\}_{m=1}^M$. Such random sampling assumes that all tasks are equally

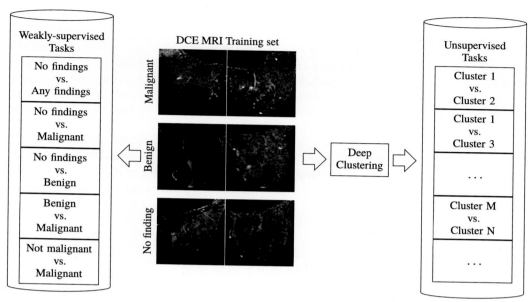

(a) Weakly-supervised and unsupervised task design.

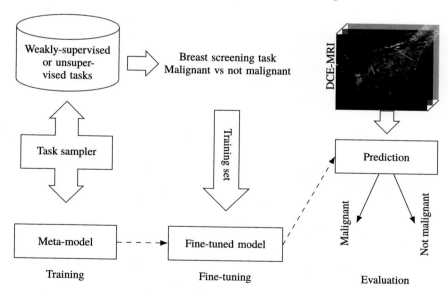

(b) Task augmentation weakly supervised and unsupervised meta learning

FIGURE 11.2

Depiction of (a) the weakly-supervised and unsupervised task design, and (b) the weakly-supervised and unsupervised few-shot meta learning model.

distributed (i.e., $p(\mathcal{T}_m) = 1/M$ for all $m \in \{1, ..., M\}$), and consequently, slowing down the learning progress due to wasting time on "easy" tasks that are familiar, while not properly learning "difficult" tasks that show poor performance. This issue motivates the integration of the teacher-student curriculum learning (CL) [41] into step 5 of Algorithm 11.1 when sampling a mini-batch of tasks. The introduced curriculum is designed to select tasks that achieve the largest changes of the metric used (AUC in this case) after each step that updates the metaparameter. Intuitively, tasks showing large AUC changes (either increasing or decreasing AUC changes) are unstable, and therefore need to be better learned before the tasks that show consistently low or high AUC values.

The evaluation on a testing task $\mathcal{T}_{M+1}$ is also similar to the general meta learning presented in Subsection 11.3.2 that is taken in two steps. In the first step, the learnt metaparameter ω^* is used to fine-tune on the training subset $\mathcal{D}_{M+1}^{(t)}$ to produce the task-specific parameter θ_{M+1}^*, which is similar to step 8 in Algorithm 11.1. The second step is then carried out by evaluating θ_{M+1}^* on the validation subset $\mathcal{D}_{M+1}^{(v)}$.

11.5 Unsupervised task formation meta learning

One issue with the task-augmentation weakly-supervised metatraining presented in Section 11.4 is the requirement of manually annotated classes to augment the classification tasks. For instance, the classes available from the dataset $\mathcal{D}$ are used to build five different training tasks as presented in Section 11.4. We relax this requirement by assuming that annotations are only available at evaluation phase, so the task formation needs to rely on unlabeled data. Using the same dataset as the one in Section 11.4, and the same training described in Algorithm 11.1, this section describes how to design classification tasks with an unsupervised learning method based on clustering techniques [40].

The main idea is to employ the "pseudo" labels of images obtained from the deep clustering method [8] to build classification tasks in an unsupervised fashion. The deep clustering model consists of a feature extractor $v : \mathcal{X} \times \Omega_v \to \mathcal{Z}$ (with $\mathcal{Z} \subset \mathbb{R}^Z$ denoting a feature space and $\omega_v \in \Omega_v$ representing the model parameter), and a linear classifier $g : \mathcal{Z} \times \Omega_g \to \mathcal{R}$ (with $\mathcal{R} \subset [0, 1]^R$, and $\omega_g \in \Omega_g$ denoting the classifier parameter) that outputs a probability vector for classifying one of the R clusters.

Fig. 11.3 illustrates the mechanism of the deep clustering, where the pseudo-labels obtained from a clustering method, such as K-means, are used to supervise the training of the whole model $g \circ v$. The objective function of the deep clustering model is a tri-level optimization expressed as:

$$\min_{\omega_v, \omega_g} \frac{1}{|\mathcal{D}|} \sum_{i=1}^{|\mathcal{D}|} \ell\left(g\left(v(\mathbf{x}; \omega_v); \omega_g\right), \mathbf{r}_i^*\right) \qquad \text{(learn model)}$$

$$\text{subject to: } \min_{\mathbf{M}} \frac{1}{|\mathcal{D}|} \sum_{i=1}^{|\mathcal{D}|} \left\| v(\mathbf{x}_i; \omega_v) - \mathbf{M}\mathbf{r}_i^* \right\|_2^2 \qquad \text{(learn centroids)}$$

$$\text{subject to: } \mathbf{r}_i^* = \arg\min_{\mathbf{r}_i} \left\| v(\mathbf{x}_i; \omega_v) - \mathbf{M}\mathbf{r}_i \right\|_2^2, \qquad \text{(assign cluster)} \qquad (11.8)$$

where $\mathbf{M} \in \mathbb{R}^{Z \times R}$ denotes a matrix containing R cluster centroids in the feature space $\mathcal{Z}$, and $\mathbf{r}_i \in \{0, 1\}^R$ denotes the one-hot pseudo-label obtained from the unsupervised clustering method.

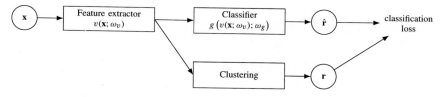

FIGURE 11.3

A process flow diagram illustrates the training of deep clustering method [8].

The optimization of (11.8) will iteratively update the values of the model parameters ω_v, ω_g, centroids $\mathbf{M}$ and pseudo-labels $\{\mathbf{r}_i\}_{i=1}^R$. Note that the solution of (11.8) varies when varying the number of clusters R. One way to obtain a local-optimal R is to maximize the clustering quality measured via the silhouette coefficient [49]:

$$R^* = \arg\max_R \frac{1}{|\mathcal{D}|} \sum_{i=1}^{|\mathcal{D}|} \frac{b(i) - a(i)}{\max\left(a(i), b(i)\right)}, \tag{11.9}$$

where:

$$a(i) = \mathbb{E}_{\substack{\mathbf{x}_j \sim \mathcal{D} \\ i \neq j \\ \mathbf{r}_i = \mathbf{r}_j}} \left\| v(\mathbf{x}_i; \omega_v) - v(\mathbf{x}_j; \omega_v) \right\|_2, \tag{11.10}$$

$$b(i) = \min_k \mathbb{E}_{\substack{\mathbf{x}_j \sim \mathcal{D} \\ \mathbf{r}_i \neq \mathbf{r}_j \\ \mathbf{r}_{ik} = 1}} \left\| v(\mathbf{x}_i; \omega_v) - v(\mathbf{x}_j; \omega_v) \right\|_2. \tag{11.11}$$

Once the deep cluster model is learnt with R clusters, one can form binary classification tasks by randomly selecting two subsets of nonempty and disjoint clusters and labeling their respective samples with pseudo-classes 0 and 1. Note that each one of these pseudo-classes can contain multiple clusters. The number of resulting binary classification tasks is, therefore, calculated as:

$$M = \sum_{i=1}^{K-1} \sum_{k=1}^{\min(i, K-i)} \frac{\binom{K}{i} \times \binom{K-i}{k}}{1 + \delta(i - k)}, \tag{11.12}$$

where $\binom{A}{B}$ denotes the binomial coefficient, and $\delta(.)$ represents the Dirac delta function. Hence, the metatraining with the unsupervised classification tasks uses Algorithm 11.1 with a set of M classification tasks.

11.6 Cross-domain few-shot meta learning

The cross-domain few-shot meta learning approach [13] assumes that there is a collection of five tasks, each defining a different segmentation problem on a distinct dataset, as follows:

1. BBBC005 cell segmentation task from the Broad Bioimage Benchmark Collection (BBBC) [32],

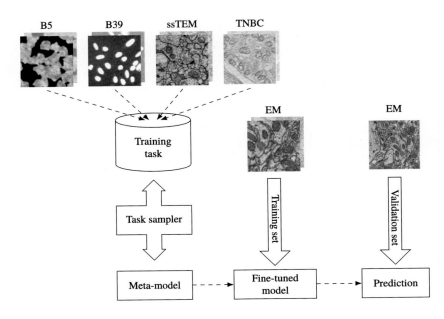

FIGURE 11.4

Cross-domain few-shot meta learning model for cell segmentation, with training tasks from datasets B5, B39, ssTEM, TNBC, and a testing task from EM. Note that not only EM, but all other datasets are used for testing.

2. BBBC039 cell segmentation task also from BBBC,
3. mitochondria segmentation task in neural tissues from the Serial Section Transmission Electron Microscopy (ssTEM) [20],
4. mitochondria and synapses cell segmentation task from the Electron Microscopy (EM) dataset [37], and
5. histology image segmentation task from the Triple Negative Breast Cancer (TNBC) database [45].

The given set of tasks is then split into four tasks for training (i.e., source tasks) and the remaining task for testing (i.e., target task). The dataset associated with each task $\mathcal{T}_i$ is denoted by $\mathcal{D}_i = \{(\mathbf{x}_{ij}, \mathbf{y}_{ij})\}_{j=1}^{|\mathcal{D}_i|}$ and consists of a microscopy image $\mathbf{x}_{ij} \in \mathcal{X} \subset \mathbb{R}^{H \times W}$, and the corresponding binary segmentation ground truth $\mathbf{y}_{ij} \in \{0, 1\}^{H \times W}$. The number of training images in the target task is assumed to be at most 10. The meta learning model is denoted as $f : \mathcal{X} \times \Omega \to [0, 1]^{H \times W}$.

The cross-domain few-shot meta learning (see Fig. 11.4) is developed based on REPTILE with a modification on the loss function in the task adaptation step from (11.4). Instead of relying solely on the pixel-wise binary cross-entropy (BCE) loss for segmentation, two additional losses – entropy regularization (ER) and distillation – are introduced to regularize and force the metamodel to learn an invariant representation shared across all tasks. Such additional losses require that in each training episode, we sample two additional tasks, $\mathcal{T}_e$ and $\mathcal{T}_d$ with $e \neq d \neq i$, to form the final loss to adapt the

---

Algorithm 11.2 Cross-domain few-shot meta learning - training procedure.

1: **procedure** TRAINING(set of M training tasks)
2:     Initialize model parameter ω
3:     **while** ω is not converged **do**
4:         **for** $i = 1, \ldots, M$ **do**
5:             Randomly sample 2 tasks $\mathcal{T}_e$ and $\mathcal{T}_d$ with $e \neq d \neq i$
6:             Adapt metaparameter to task $\mathcal{T}_i$:
$$\theta_i^* = \omega - \gamma \nabla_\omega \left[\mathsf{L} \left(\mathcal{T}_i, \mathcal{T}_e, \mathcal{T}_d; \omega \right) \right]$$
7:         Update metaparameter
$$\omega \leftarrow \omega + \frac{\gamma}{M} \sum_{i=1}^{M} \left(\theta_i^* - \omega \right)$$
8:     **return** ω

---

metaparameter ω to the current training task $\mathcal{T}_i$. Formally, the loss function can be expressed as:

$$\mathsf{L} \left(\mathcal{T}_i, \mathcal{T}_e, \mathcal{T}_d; \omega \right) = \mathsf{L}_{\text{BCE}} \left(\mathcal{T}_i; \omega \right) + \rho \mathsf{L}_{\text{ER}} \left(\mathcal{T}_e; \omega \right) + \nu \mathsf{L}_{\text{D}} \left(\mathcal{T}_i, \mathcal{T}_d; \omega \right), \qquad (11.13)$$

where $\rho, \nu \in (0, 1)$ are hyperparameters.

The pixel-wise binary segmentation cross-entropy loss is the main objective to predict the ground-truth mask, and can be expressed as:

$$\mathsf{L}_{\text{BCE}} \left(\mathcal{T}_i; \omega \right) = \mathbb{E}_{(\mathbf{x}_{ij}, \mathbf{y}_{ij}) \sim \mathcal{D}_i} \left[\ell_{\text{BCE}} \left(f \left(\mathbf{x}_{ij}; \omega \right), \mathbf{y}_{ij} \right) \right], \qquad (11.14)$$

where ℓ_{BCE} is the pixel-wise binary cross-entropy function with class 0 indicating background, and 1 indicating foreground.

The introduced entropy-based regularizer, L_{ER}, is motivated by works done in semisupervised learning [22] and few-shot classification [14], which can be written as:

$$\mathsf{L}_{\text{ER}} \left(\mathcal{T}_e; \omega \right) = \mathbb{E}_{\mathbf{x}_{ej} \sim \mathcal{D}_e} \left[\ell_{\text{PE}} \left(f \left(\mathbf{x}_{ej}; \omega \right) \right) \right], \qquad (11.15)$$

where ℓ_{PE} is the pixel-wise Shannon entropy.

The distillation loss is used to purposely learn a common representation between different source data sets [5,17,26]. Such domain-invariant representation can be obtained by minimizing the Euclidean distance between image representations sampled from two tasks $\mathcal{T}_i$ and $\mathcal{T}_d$ with $i \neq d$, and can be presented as:

$$\mathsf{L}_{\text{D}} \left(\mathcal{T}_i, \mathcal{T}_d; \omega \right) = \mathbb{E}_{\mathbf{x}_{ij} \sim \mathcal{D}_i} \mathbb{E}_{\mathbf{x}_{de} \sim \mathcal{D}_d} \left[\left\| f^{<l>} \left(\mathbf{x}_{ij}; \omega \right) - f^{<l>} \left(\mathbf{x}_{de}; \omega \right) \right\|_2^2 \right], \qquad (11.16)$$

where $f^{<l>} \left(\mathbf{x}; \omega \right)$ is the activation map at the l-th layer of the model.

The details of the training procedure for the cross-domain few-shot meta learning are shown in Algorithm 11.2, which returns the metatrained parameter ω^*.

In evaluation, the trained metamodel $f(.; \omega^*)$ is fine-tuned (i.e., metatested) with the training data of the target task $\mathcal{T}_{\text{target}}$ to produce the task-specific parameter $\theta^*(\omega^*)$. This is similar to step 6 in Algorithm 11.2, but only the pixel-wise BCE loss is used. The task-specific model $f_{\theta^*(\omega^*)}(.)$ is then

Table 11.1 Details of the five microscopy image datasets used to evaluate the cross-domain few-shot meta learning presented in Section 11.6 with examples of each task are shown in Fig. 11.1b.

Data set	B5	B39	ssTEM	EM	TNBC
Cell Type	synthetic stain	nuclei	mitochondria	mitochondria	nuclei
Resolution	696×520	696×520	1024×1024	768×1024	512×512
# of Samples	1200	200	20	165	50

evaluated by segmenting images in the testing subset of the target task $\mathcal{T}_{target}$. Note that the training subset of the target task has at most 10 images.

11.7 Experiments

11.7.1 Datasets

The **dataset** used in the evaluation of the **task-augmentation weakly-supervised and unsupervised task-formation meta learning** methods proposed in Sections 11.4 and 11.5 is the breast DCE-MRI dataset [38,40,42]. This dataset is split into training, validation, and testing sets in a patient-wise manner to contain 45, 13, and 59 patients, respectively. The T1-weighted MRI is used to separate the left and right breasts [38]. Each breast region is resized into a volume of $100 \times 100 \times 50$ voxels [38]. The breast screening problem is formulated as a binary classification, where breasts containing at least one malignant finding are labeled as positive, and breasts with only benign findings or no findings are labeled as negative. Three classes, namely, no findings, benign, and malignant, as explained in Section 11.4 are used for training. The dataset split contains 30, 9, and 38 positive and 60, 17, and 80 negative breasts in the training, validation and testing sets, respectively.

The **dataset** for the **cross-domain few-shot meta learning** is composed of five sets of different cell domains, as detailed in Section 11.6. Two of the datasets, BBBC005 and BBBC039, are from the Broad Bio-image Benchmark Collection (BBBC), which is a set microscopy cell image datasets [32]. BBBC005 (B5) has 1200 fluorescent synthetic stain cells, and BBBC039 (B39) contains 200 fluorescent nuclei cells. The third dataset is from the Serial Section Transmission Electron Microscopy (ssTEM) [20] database that contains 165 mitochondria cell images in neural tissues. The fourth dataset is from the Electron Microscopy (EM) database [37] which has 165 electron microscopy images of mitochondria and synapses cells. The fifth dataset is from the Triple Negative Breast Cancer (TNBC) database [45] that contains 50 histology images of breast biopsy. Table 11.1 provides a summary of these datasets. All training images are cropped to 256×256 pixels and testing images are used in full resolution.

11.7.2 Implementation details

The model used in the **task-augmentation weakly-supervised meta learning methods (TAWSML)** is based on the DenseNet [29], where hyperparameters are selected based on the highest AUC evaluated on the validation set. The model consists of five dense blocks, each containing two dense layers. In Algorithm 11.1, the number of steps to update the metaparameter is 3000, the learning rate for the upper-level metatraining in (11.2) is $\alpha = 0.001$, the number of training and validation volumes selected for task $\mathcal{T}_i$ is $|\mathcal{D}_i^{(t)}| = |\mathcal{D}_i^{(v)}| = 4$, the number of gradient descent steps to optimize for θ_i^* is 5, and the learning rate for the task adaptation in (11.4) is $\gamma = 0.1$. The mini-batch size $|\mathcal{K}| = 3$ is used with tasks being sampled according to a random or a curriculum learning strategy [38], as explained in Section 11.4. The TAWSML is trained and evaluated on two settings: one using all five tasks, as presented in Subsection 11.4, denoted as TAWSML, and one without using task 5: malignant versus nonmalignant findings, denoted as TAWSML-NS.

For **the unsupervised task-formation meta learning (UTFML)**, the model used is also based on DenseNet [29] with five dense blocks, each containing two dense layers, where the feature extractor $v_{\omega_v}(.)$ is represented by the whole model excluding the last classification layer, and the classifier $g_{\omega_g}(.)$ is that last classification layer. The lower-level optimization of (11.2) uses a learning rate $\gamma = 0.001$. Three mini-batch sizes, $|\mathcal{K}| \in \{3, 4, 5\}$, are used with tasks being sampled according to a random or a curriculum learning, as explained in Section 11.4.

Once the metamodel is trained according to TAWSML, TAWSML-NS, and UTFML, the evaluation is then carried out on a hold-out breast screening task that classifies malignant versus nonmalignant findings. The test results consist of the area under the ROC curve (AUC) computed on the validation subset $\mathcal{D}_{M+1}^{(v)}$ of the testing task $\mathcal{T}_{M+1}$.

In addition to AUC, standard errors with a Wilcoxon test estimation [7] based on confidence intervals computed from the testing set are reported for comparison. The influence of the number of tasks $|\mathcal{K}|$ to use in each metatraining episode is also studied for UTFML. The results obtained from the proposed algorithms are compared to:

1. DenseNet trained from scratch [29],
2. DenseNet from fine-tuned with multiple instance learning (MIL) [58],
3. DenseNet trained with multitasking (using the "augmented" five tasks in Section 11.4) [57],
4. DenseNet pretrained with a variational autoencoder (VAE) [31] and fine-tuned for breast screening, and
5. DenseNet pretrained with deep clustering (DC) [8] and fine-tuned for breast screening.

The results are compared with models 4. and 5. to assess other unsupervised pretraining methods based on image reconstruction or clustering. All DenseNet models above rely on the same architecture as our proposed TAWSML, TAWSML-NS, and UTFML.

The **cross-domain few-shot meta learning** is evaluated on two different encoder-decoder network architectures: the fully convolutional regression network (FCRN) [55] and the U-Net [48], with slight modifications. In FCRN, bi-linear upsampling operators are replaced by transposed convolutions, and heat-map predictions are changed to sigmoid activations. In U-Net, a lightweight variant that reduces the number of layers from 23 to 12 is employed for the experiments. These modifications showed better performance. The proposed cross-domain few-shot meta learning is optimized with Adam optimizer with learning rate $\gamma = 1$ (see Algorithm 11.2). Both FCRN and U-Net have batch-normalization. For the lower-level optimization corresponding to step 6, Adam optimizer with learning rate 0.0001, and weight decay 0.0005 is used to calculate θ_i^*. The same parameters are used for the baseline transfer learning methods, shown in the results. The quantitative results are based on the mean intersection over union (IoU) [16,35]. The results are computed with a leave-one-dataset-out cross-validation [17] to verify if the proposed metatraining enables generalization to new image distributions and new segmentation

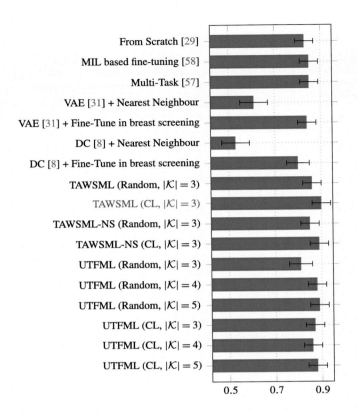

FIGURE 11.5

The AUC results (mean ± standard error) for breast screening between baselines and the proposed methods TAWSML, TAWSML-NS and UTFML as a function of the number of tasks $|\mathcal{K}|$ per training episode, and the task sampling method (random and CL). All models are relied on DenseNet [29] and the best result in terms of mean AUC is highlighted.

tasks. More specifically, four microscopy image datasets are used for training and the remaining unseen dataset is used for testing. For the evaluation in the remaining dataset, the number of samples K is randomly selected from $\{1, 3, 5, 7, 10\}$ and repeated 10 times to report mean and standard deviation results. The transfer-learning baseline approach is also evaluated in the same manner.

11.7.3 Results

The mean and standard error of the AUC results from the baselines (listed in Section 11.7.2) and the proposed methods **TAWSML**, **TAWSML-NS**, and **UTFML** are shown in Fig. 11.5. The results of the proposed methods are reported as a function of number of tasks $|\mathcal{K}| \in \{3, 4, 5\}$, using random and curriculum-learning (CL) task sampling methods. The statistical significance of the AUC results produced by the best performing models trained by the proposed algorithms (i.e. TAWSML (CL and

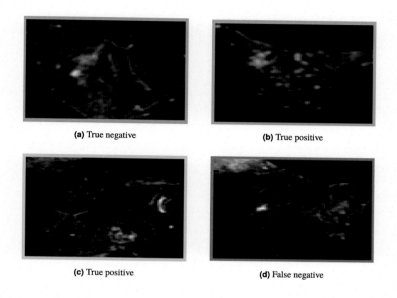

(a) True negative

(b) True positive

(c) True positive

(d) False negative

FIGURE 11.6

Examples of breast screening diagnosis produced by the TAWSML: (a) shows a true negative case of a breast containing a benign lesion; (b) and (c) display true positive diagnosis of breasts containing malignant lesions; and (d) shows a false negative diagnosis of a volume containing a small malignant lesion.

$|\mathcal{K}| = 3$), TAWSML-NS (CL and $|\mathcal{K}| = 3$), UTFML (Random and $|\mathcal{K}| = 5$), and UTFML (CL and $|\mathcal{K}| = 5$)) are calculated to compare with all baseline methods, and the resulting p-value $p \leq 0.001$ for all cases (unpaired two-tailed t-test). The statistical significance of the AUC results between all the best performing models trained by the proposed approaches (listed above) show p-value $p > 0.05$. A few examples of breast screening classification results by TAWSML and UTFML are shown in Fig. 11.6 and Fig. 11.7, respectively.

For the proposed **cross-domain few-shot meta learning**, the impact of each loss term in (11.13) is analyzed through the mean IoU results on all datasets evaluated on FCRN and U-Net models. The analysis is carried out with $k - \text{shot} \in \{1, 3, 5, 7, 10\}$, where k-shot is the number of training images in the metatesting optimization and shown in Fig. 11.8. Note that when all loss terms are used, the entropy-regularization loss L_{ER} is weighted by a factor $\rho = 0.01$, while the distillation loss L_D is weighted by $\nu = 0.01$. For the loss composed of L_{ER} and L_{BCE}, $\rho = 0.1$, and for the loss containing L_D and L_{BCE}, $\nu = 0.01$. These values are found with grid search on the validation set. The mean IoU results in Fig. 11.8 show that the loss with all terms produce either competitive or the best results, compared with the other losses for the majority of k-shot values. A qualitative comparison of the segmentation results using different combination of the loss functions is provided in Fig. 11.9. A visual comparison between the proposed method and transfer-learning using U-Net on all five datasets is shown in Fig. 11.11. The detailed results on each of the five datasets are shown in Fig. 11.10.

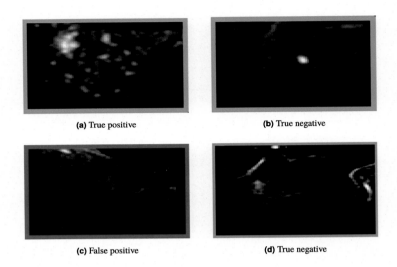

(a) True positive

(b) True negative

(c) False positive

(d) True negative

FIGURE 11.7

Examples of breast screening diagnosis produced by the UTFML: (a) shows a true positive case of a breast containing a malignant tumor; (b) displays a true negative diagnosis of a breast with a benign tumor; (c) shows a false positive classification of a breast containing no tumors; and (d) shows a true negative diagnosis of a breast with a benign tumor.

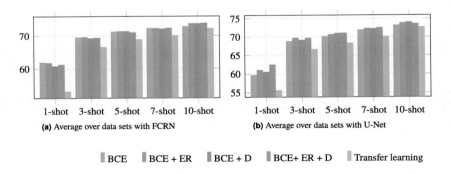

(a) Average over data sets with FCRN

(b) Average over data sets with U-Net

▌BCE   ▌BCE + ER   ▌BCE + D   ▌BCE+ ER + D   ▌Transfer learning

FIGURE 11.8

Mean intersection over union (IoU) comparison for all datasets using different combinations of the loss terms in (11.13) for: (a) FCRN and (b) U-Net using our cross-domain k-shot $\in \{1, 3, 5, 7, 10\}$ meta learning.

11.7.4 Discussion

Given the promising experimental results shown in Subsection 11.7.3, meta learning can be considered as an important method to mitigate the need for large-scale annotated datasets.

The proposed task-augmentation weakly-supervised and task-formation unsupervised meta learning methods, TAWSML and UTFML respectively, show competitive results for the breast screening

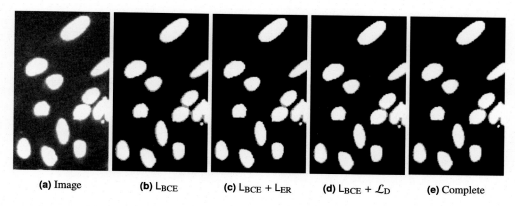

(a) Image   (b) L_{BCE} (c) $L_{BCE} + L_{ER}$ (d) $L_{BCE} + \mathcal{L}_D$ (e) Complete

FIGURE 11.9

Visual comparison of the results obtained from different combinations of loss terms in (11.13) on a test image of the task B39, where the complete image (e) refers to metatraining with all loss terms, namely $L_{BCE} + L_{ER} + L_D$. The green color corresponds to false negative, the white color to true positive and black to the true negative.

problem from DCE-MRI volume in Fig. 11.5. In both TAWSML and UTFML, the model of interest is trained using binary classification tasks generated from small training sets, and is evaluated by adapting to the breast-screening problem using a small number of training examples. The results from both models achieve better results than all baselines, consisting of traditional pretraining methods based on VAE, deep clustering, MIL, and multitask learning (see Fig. 11.5). An interesting observation is that the task sampling algorithm enables large differences for TAWSML, with CL showing better results than random, and for UTFML, random showing slightly better results than CL. Since CL focuses on sampling tasks with a larger margin for improvement, it might benefit TAWSML more because all manually designed tasks are important for breast-screening. Another interesting observation is that UTFML (random, $|\mathcal{K}| = 5$) has the same performance as TAWSML-NS (CL, $|\mathcal{K}| = 3$), showing that the use of unsupervised task design is at least as effective as the manually defined tasks, even when the task of interest (breast screening) is not present in the set of metatraining tasks. This is relevant given that many medical image analysis problems will not have annotations beyond the annotation of interest, so the use of our meta learning methods will allow the use of unsupervised tasks, which produces competitive the results.

In the cross-domain few-shot meta learning results in Figs. 11.8, 11.9, 11.11, 11.10, transfer-learning is assumed to be the main baseline result. The use of the meta learning in Algorithm 11.2 with the BCE loss L_{BCE} shows the worse quantitative and qualitative performances. Adding the entropy regularization loss L_{ER} improves the results. Furthermore, combining the distillation and BCE losses also improves the results, particularly for U-Net. The use of all loss terms from (11.8) produces the best mean IoU results for most of the k-shot cases. U-Net delivers slightly better results than FCRN when all loss terms are used, but both perform similarly when varying the combination of loss terms used and the number of k-shots. Fig. 11.10 shows that transfer learning is comparable to the proposed cross-domain few-shot meta learning for 10-shot learning in some cases, such as Figs. 11.10i and 11.10j. We

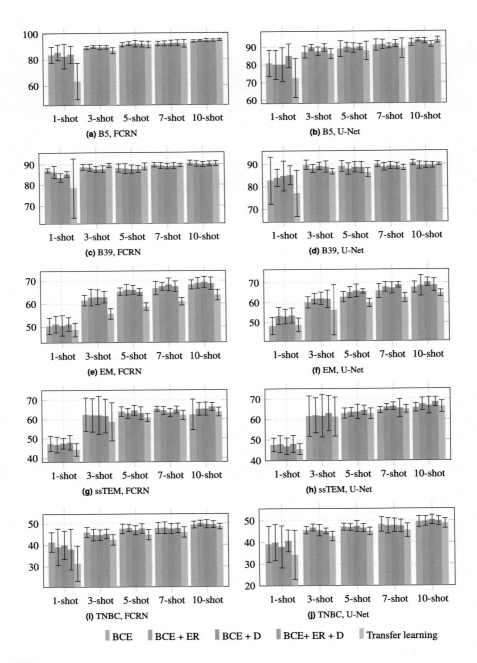

FIGURE 11.10

Intersection over union (mean and standard deviation) for FCRN (left column) and U-Net (right column) using transfer learning and meta learning (ML) with different combinations of the loss terms in (11.13).

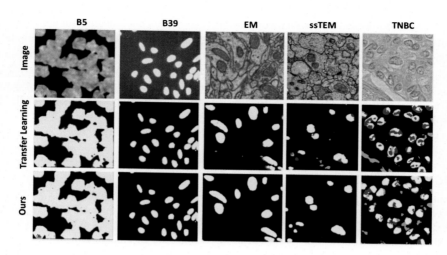

FIGURE 11.11

Comparison of the visual results between our cross-domain few-shot meta learning method and transfer learning using the U-Net architecture on all five microscopy cell segmentation datasets. These results are obtained using all loss terms in (11.13). The red pixels correspond to false positive, the green pixels to false negative, the black pixels to true negative, and the white pixels to true positive.

speculate that transfer-learning will improve performance as the number of k-shots starts to increase and for large number of k-shots, transfer-learning and meta learning will have similar performance. Nevertheless, the proposed meta learning algorithm is observed to converge faster – in the reported experiments, the proposed meta learning converged 40x faster for FCRN and around 60x faster for U-Net. One disadvantage of the proposed meta learning algorithm is the need to carefully select the optimizer, and the hyperparameters ρ and ν in (11.13), while transfer-learning only needs to address the selection of the optimizer.

11.8 Conclusions

We have presented new methods to design and sample classification tasks for the meta learning of medical image classifiers. The results show that our data-augmentation weakly-supervised and data-formation unsupervised methods perform comparably to each other, but they significantly outperform pretraining methods based on VAE, deep clustering, MIL, and multitask learning (see Fig. 11.5). The results from the UTFML confirm our hypothesis that it is important to automatically build a large number of meta learning tasks for medical image classification problems, where image labels that allow a large number of tasks are costly to obtain. We also note that for TAWSML, curriculum learning improves classification accuracy compared to random task sampling, confirming our hypothesis that CL helps the metatraining to generalize better to new tasks.

Regarding the cross-domain few-shot meta learning results, we conclude that our approach produces better results than transfer-learning for most of the datasets and k-shots. We also conclude that the combination of the three loss functions in (11.13) is important to yield the best performance in general. The different results shown by different datasets, such as a mean IoU of around 50% on TNBC, and of around 70% on EM can be explained by the fact that the source domains used for meta learning are more correlated to the fine-tuning task. Finally, our approach produces promising results for meta learning problems with fairly few samples (e.g. k-shots ≤ 5).

References

[1] G. Amit, O. Hadad, S. Alpert, T. Tlusty, Y. Gur, R. Ben-Ari, S. Hashoul, Hybrid mass detection in breast MRI combining unsupervised saliency analysis and deep learning, in: International Conference on Medical Image Computing and Computer-Assisted Intervention, Springer, 2017, pp. 594–602.

[2] M. Andrychowicz, M. Denil, S.G. Colmenarejo, M.W. Hoffman, D. Pfau, T. Schaul, B. Shillingford, N. de Freitas, Learning to learn by gradient descent by gradient descent, in: Advances in Neural Information Processing Systems, 2016, pp. 3988–3996.

[3] S. Azizi, B. Mustafa, F. Ryan, Z. Beaver, J. Freyberg, J. Deaton, A. Loh, A. Karthikesalingam, S. Kornblith, T. Chen, et al., Big self-supervised models advance medical image classification, arXiv preprint, arXiv:2101.05224, 2021.

[4] Y. Bar, I. Diamant, L. Wolf, S. Lieberman, E. Konen, H. Greenspan, Chest pathology detection using deep learning with non-medical training, in: International Symposium on Biomedical Imaging (ISBI), IEEE, 2015, pp. 294–297.

[5] V. Belagiannis, A. Farshad, F. Galasso, Adversarial network compression, in: European Conference on Computer Vision (ECCV) Workshops, 2018.

[6] Y. Bengio, J. Louradour, R. Collobert, J. Weston, Curriculum learning, in: International Conference on Machine Learning, 2009, pp. 41–48.

[7] A.P. Bradley, The use of the area under the ROC curve in the evaluation of machine learning algorithms, Pattern Recognition (1997).

[8] M. Caron, P. Bojanowski, et al., Deep clustering for unsupervised learning of visual features, in: European Conference on Computer Vision (ECCV), 2018.

[9] V. Cheplygina, M. de Bruijne, J.P. Pluim, Not-so-supervised: a survey of semi-supervised, multi-instance, and transfer learning in medical image analysis, International Conference on Machine Learning 54 (2019) 280–296.

[10] D. Cireşan, A. Giusti, L. Gambardella, J. Schmidhuber, Deep neural networks segment neuronal membranes in electron microscopy images, Advances in Neural Information Processing Systems 25 (2012) 2843–2851.

[11] D.C. Cireşan, A. Giusti, L.M. Gambardella, J. Schmidhuber, Mitosis detection in breast cancer histology images with deep neural networks, in: International Conference on Medical Image Computing and Computer-Assisted Intervention, Springer, 2013, pp. 411–418.

[12] M.U. Dalmış, S. Vreemann, et al., Fully automated detection of breast cancer in screening MRI using convolutional neural networks, Journal of Medical Imaging (2017).

[13] Y. Dawoud, J. Hornauer, G. Carneiro, V. Belagiannis, Few-shot microscopy image cell segmentation, in: Machine Learning and Knowledge Discovery in Databases. Applied Data Science and Demo Track, Springer International Publishing, 2021.

[14] G.S. Dhillon, P. Chaudhari, A. Ravichandran, S. Soatto, A baseline for few-shot image classification, in: International Conference on Learning Representation, 2019.

[15] L.F. Dong, Y.Z. Gan, et al., Learning deep representations using convolutional auto-encoders with symmetric skip connections, in: IEEE International Conference on Acoustics, Speech, and Signal Processing, 2018.

[16] N. Dong, E.P. Xing, Few-shot semantic segmentation with prototype learning, in: The British Machine Vision Conference, 2018.

[17] Q. Dou, D. Coelho de Castro, K. Kamnitsas, B. Glocker, Domain generalization via model-agnostic learning of semantic features, in: Advances in Neural Information Processing Systems, 2019, pp. 6450–6461.

[18] G.M. Faustino, M. Gattass, S. Rehen, C.J. de Lucena, Automatic embryonic stem cells detection and counting method in fluorescence microscopy images, in: International Symposium on Biomedical Imaging: From Nano to Macro, IEEE, 2009, pp. 799–802.

[19] C. Finn, P. Abbeel, S. Levine, Model-agnostic meta-learning for fast adaptation of deep networks, in: International Conference on Machine Learning, 2017.

[20] S. Gerhard, J. Funke, J. Martel, A. Cardona, R. Fetter, Segmented anisotropic ssTEM dataset of neural tissue, figshare. Dataset (2013), https://doi.org/10.6084/m9.figshare.856713.v1.

[21] I. Goodfellow, Y. Bengio, A. Courville, Deep Learning, MIT Press, 2016.

[22] Y. Grandvalet, Y. Bengio, Semi-supervised learning by entropy minimization, in: Advances in Neural Information Processing Systems, 2004, pp. 529–536.

[23] L.J. Grimm, A.L. Anderson, et al., Interobserver variability between breast imagers using the fifth edition of the BI-RADS MRI lexicon, American Journal of Roentgenology (2015).

[24] A. Gubern-Mérida, R. Martí, J. Melendez, et al., Automated localization of breast cancer in DCE-MRI, International Conference on Machine Learning 20 (2015) 265–274.

[25] B. Gutiérrez, L. Peter, T. Klein, C. Wachinger, A multi-armed bandit to smartly select a training set from big medical data, in: International Conference on Medical Image Computing and Computer-Assisted Intervention, Springer, 2017, pp. 38–45.

[26] G. Hinton, O. Vinyals, J. Dean, Distilling the knowledge in a neural network, in: NIPS 2014 Deep Learning and Representation Learning Workshop, 2014.

[27] T.M. Hospedales, A. Antoniou, P. Micaelli, A.J. Storkey, Meta-learning in neural networks: a survey, IEEE Transactions on Pattern Analysis and Machine Intelligence (2021), https://doi.org/10.1109/TPAMI.2021.3079209.

[28] K. Hsu, S. Levine, C. Finn, Unsupervised learning via meta-learning, in: International Conference on Learning Representation, 2019.

[29] G. Huang, Z. Liu, Densely connected convolutional networks, in: The Conference on Computer Vision and Pattern Recognition, 2017.

[30] P.F. Jäger, S. Bickelhaupt, F.B. Laun, W. Lederer, D. Heidi, T.A. Kuder, D. Paech, D. Bonekamp, A. Radbruch, S. Delorme, et al., Revealing hidden potentials of the q-space signal in breast cancer, in: International Conference on Medical Image Computing and Computer-Assisted Intervention, Springer, 2017, pp. 664–671.

[31] D.P. Kingma, M. Welling, Auto-encoding variational Bayes, in: International Conference on Learning Representations, 2014.

[32] A. Lehmussola, P. Ruusuvuori, J. Selinummi, H. Huttunen, O. Yli-Harja, Computational framework for simulating fluorescence microscope images with cell populations, IEEE Transactions on Medical Imaging 26 (2007) 1010–1016.

[33] K. Li, J. Malik, Learning to optimize, in: International Conference on Learning Representation, 2017.

[34] G. Litjens, T. Kooi, B.E. Bejnordi, A.A.A. Setio, F. Ciompi, M. Ghafoorian, J.A. Van Der Laak, B. Van Ginneken, C.I. Sánchez, A survey on deep learning in medical image analysis, International Conference on Machine Learning 42 (2017) 60–88.

[35] J. Long, E. Shelhamer, T. Darrell, Fully convolutional networks for semantic segmentation, in: The Conference on Computer Vision and Pattern Recognition, 2015, pp. 3431–3440.

[36] Z. Lu, G. Carneiro, A.P. Bradley, An improved joint optimization of multiple level set functions for the segmentation of overlapping cervical cells, IEEE Transactions on Image Processing 24 (2015) 1261–1272.

[37] A. Lucchi, Y. Li, P. Fua, Learning for structured prediction using approximate subgradient descent with working sets, in: IEEE Conference on Computer Vision and Pattern Recognition, 2013, pp. 1987–1994.

[38] G. Maicas, A.P. Bradley, J.C. Nascimento, I. Reid, G. Carneiro, Training medical image analysis systems like radiologists, in: International Conference on Medical Image Computing and Computer-Assisted Intervention, Springer, 2018, pp. 546–554.

[39] G. Maicas, G. Carneiro, A.P. Bradley, J.C. Nascimento, I. Reid, Deep reinforcement learning for active breast lesion detection from DCE-MRI, in: International Conference on Medical Image Computing and Computer-Assisted Intervention, Springer, 2017, pp. 665–673.

[40] G. Maicas, C. Nguyen, F. Motlagh, J.C. Nascimento, G. Carneiro, Unsupervised task design to meta-train medical image classifiers, in: International Symposium on Biomedical Imaging (ISBI), IEEE, 2020, pp. 1339–1342.

[41] T. Matiisen, A. Oliver, T. Cohen, J. Schulman, Teacher–student curriculum learning, IEEE Transactions on Neural Networks and Learning Systems 31 (2019) 3732–3740.

[42] D. McClymont, A. Mehnert, et al., Fully automatic lesion segmentation in breast MRI using mean-shift and graph-cuts on a region adjacency graph, Journal of Magnetic Resonance Imaging (2014).

[43] L.A. Meinel, A.H. Stolpen, et al., Breast MRI lesion classification: improved performance of human readers with a backpropagation neural network computer-aided diagnosis (CAD) system, Journal of Magnetic Resonance Imaging (2007).

[44] P. Naylor, M. Laé, F. Reyal, T. Walter, Nuclei segmentation in histopathology images using deep neural networks, in: International Symposium on Biomedical Imaging (ISBI 2017), IEEE, 2017, pp. 933–936.

[45] P. Naylor, M. Laé, F. Reyal, T. Walter, Segmentation of nuclei in histopathology images by deep regression of the distance map, IEEE Transactions on Medical Imaging 38 (2018) 448–459.

[46] A. Nichol, J. Achiam, J. Schulman, On first-order meta-learning algorithms, arXiv preprint, arXiv:1803.02999, 2018.

[47] M. Raghu, C. Zhang, J. Kleinberg, S. Bengio, Transfusion: understanding transfer learning for medical imaging, in: Advances in Neural Information Processing Systems, 2019.

[48] O. Ronneberger, P. Fischer, T. Brox, U-net: convolutional networks for biomedical image segmentation, in: International Conference on Medical Image Computing and Computer-Assisted Intervention, Springer, 2015, pp. 234–241.

[49] P.J. Rousseeuw, Silhouettes: a graphical aid to the interpretation and validation of cluster analysis, Journal of Computational and Applied Mathematics (1987).

[50] R.A. Smith, K.S. Andrews, D. Brooks, S.A. Fedewa, D. Manassaram-Baptiste, D. Saslow, O.W. Brawley, R.C. Wender, Cancer screening in the United States, 2017: a review of current American cancer society guidelines and current issues in cancer screening, CA: A Cancer Journal for Clinicians 67 (2017) 100–121.

[51] J. Snell, K. Swersky, R. Zemel, Prototypical networks for few-shot learning, in: Advances in Neural Information Processing Systems, 2017, pp. 4077–4087.

[52] O. Vinyals, C. Blundell, T. Lillicrap, D. Wierstra, et al., Matching networks for one shot learning, in: Advances in Neural Information Processing Systems, 2016, pp. 3630–3638.

[53] S. Vreemann, A. Gubern-Merida, et al., The frequency of missed breast cancers in women participating in a high-risk MRI screening program, Breast Cancer Research and Treatment (2018).

[54] C. Wählby, I.M. Sintorn, F. Erlandsson, G. Borgefors, E. Bengtsson, Combining intensity, edge and shape information for 2D and 3D segmentation of cell nuclei in tissue sections, Journal of Microscopy 215 (2004) 67–76.

[55] W. Xie, J.A. Noble, A. Zisserman, Microscopy cell counting and detection with fully convolutional regression networks, Computer Methods in Biomechanics and Biomedical Engineering: Imaging & Visualization 6 (2018) 283–292.

[56] F. Xing, L. Yang, Robust nucleus/cell detection and segmentation in digital pathology and microscopy images: a comprehensive review, IEEE Reviews in Biomedical Engineering 9 (2016) 234–263.

[57] W. Xue, G. Brahm, S. Pandey, S. Leung, S. Li, Full left ventricle quantification via deep multitask relationships learning, International Conference on Machine Learning 43 (2018) 54–65.

[58] W. Zhu, Q. Lou, et al., Deep multi-instance networks with sparse label assignment for whole mammogram classification, in: International Conference on Medical Image Computing and Computer Assisted Interventions, 2017.

Meta learning for biomedical and health informatics

AGILE - a meta learning framework for few-shot brain cell classification

12

Pengyu Yuan and Hien Van Nguyen

Department of Engineering & Computer Engineering, University of Houston, Houston, TX, United States

12.1 Introduction

The ability of Deep Neural Networks (or DNNs) to generalize to a given target concept is dependent on the amount of training data used to generate the model. This is a significant limitation, as many real-world classification tasks depend on a limited number of training samples for accurate classification. Various research groups have developed techniques that utilize different underlying principles to address this issue. These techniques include data augmentation [1] and generative models [2,3,4], which try to directly increase the number of training samples. The concern of this type of approach is that the generated data always requires validation to avoid out-of-distribution samples that may negatively affect the performance of the model. Active learning is another technique that aims to select the most valuable samples to include in the training set [5,6], so that the "Return On Investment" can be maximized. The drawback of this is that it requires the involvement of the expert labeling and the amount of labeling effort to be invested varies from different applications. Finally, transfer learning allows the model to adapt to new and unseen tasks by using its own previous knowledge, often reducing the amount of data needed for generalization [7,8,9] by a simple fine-tuning process.

However, transferring knowledge always requires at least two tasks/datasets, which inevitably introduces the covariate shift or dataset bias problem [10], caused by the difference in the conditions, or domains, under which the systems were developed and those in which we use the systems. Medical data is characterized by significant distribution shifts and small samples sets that negatively affect the quality of the generated model. In the cell classification task [11], there are several contributing factors for poor generalization; different biomarkers, unique cell morphologies, variations in stain intensity, and image quality all contribute to the variability of the data. Each of these factors could be considered a unique parameter with which to create unique classification tasks. Traditional transfer learning methods pretrained on various source tasks may not perform well; poor model initialization parameters coupled with unadjusted hyperparameters may cause the model to fall into a bad local minimum. Mainstream transfer learning methods also require a time-consuming model retraining process [12].

In recent years, a more advanced model architecture called meta learning has been developed to address these adaptability issues [13]. Meta learning approaches try to generate a more robust model that can learn to quickly adapt to new tasks with minimal labeled samples. Meta learning aims to study how meta learning algorithms can acquire fast adaptation capability over multiple learning episodes - often from a collection of related tasks - and uses it to improve its future learning performance [14].

Meta Learning With Medical Imaging and Health Informatics Applications. https://doi.org/10.1016/B978-0-32-399851-2.00021-1

213

Meta learning is trying to align with human learning, where the human can learn from many tasks and keeps updating its learning strategy, so it is also called "learning to learn". It can be applied to both multitask scenarios where task-agnostic knowledge is extracted from a task distribution and used to improve the learning of new tasks from that family [15]; and single-task scenarios where a single problem is solved repeatedly and improved over multiple episodes [16,17]. Meta learning can not only reduce the dependency of deep learning systems on data but also largely reduce the learning time when it is adapted to the new task. It in general has better generalization ability than other transfer models which can perform well on new unseen data. Meta learning has achieved success in a variety of problems such as few-shot image classification [15,18], unsupervised learning with task generation [19], metareinforcement learning (RL) [20], hyperparameter optimization [16], and neural architecture search [21].

Although meta learning does not require many labeled samples for each task, it requires many different tasks to effectively learn how to adapt; this may be a problem when the number of tasks is limited. We tackled this problem by introducing the task augmentation step for each of the batch during the metatraining, and showed that this process can substantially enrich task diversity and help to improve the effectiveness of the pretrained metaparameters. Another limitation of the standard meta learning approach is that it selects training samples randomly for each new task, which may negatively impact the strength of the model if it is trained on easier samples. We solve it by first making the network Bayesian, so that it can give an uncertainty estimation together with the prediction result for each sample. Then incorporating a simple active learning approach to select the most uncertain samples for adapting the metaparameters on the new data. In this chapter, we utilize various strategies to create an adaptive framework called tAsk-auGmented actIve meta LEarning (or AGILE) which allows the classifier to achieve high performance with few training samples and gradient updates for each new task. The experiments we perform on two brain cell type classification datasets show that the AGILE classifier can quickly adapt to new cell types by utilizing very few labeled training samples. The authors are expected to learn the following items from this chapter:

1. Formulate the imbalanced brain cell classification task as a meta learning problem.
2. Task augmentation for boosting the metatraining process.
3. Active learning approach to select the most informative samples.
4. Fast and efficient model adaptation in the AGILE framework on two brain cell classification datasets.

12.2 Related works

12.2.1 Brain cell type classification

The brain is a highly complex organ made up of myriad different cell types, each with their own unique properties [22]. The human cortex has a complex architecture that includes many different types of neurons, glia, and other cells such as microglia, peripheral immune cells, and endothelial cells from cortical capillaries. Gene expression experiments have highlighted cell type composition based on the expression value of markers for five major cell types: neurons, astrocytes, oligodendrocytes, microglia, and endothelial cells [23,24]. Besides that, there are around 50-250 neuronal subcell types purported to exist [25]. Different cell types may express different biomarkers or unique combinations of biomarkers, with some of them shared with other cell types. Correctly identifying the cell type using these biomarkers is essential for many medical researches such as schizophrenia [26], brain cell type specific gene expression [24], and study of the methylation state of the brain's DNA in relation to Alzheimer's disease [23].

In the real application, there are plenty of annotated samples available for certain of the cell types (e.g. neurons). But for some other cell types, there are limited number of samples in the datasets. It could be that the cell density is low in certain regions [27] (e.g. interneuron subtypes), or data annotation is so costly that only a few positive samples are provided. DNNs normally perform well on identifying cell types with large sample quantities but suffer from the cell types with few annotated samples. Training a multiclass brain cell classifier is a standard way to consider this problem. But the natural data imbalanced situation is going to introduce a huge bias towards classifying the cell types with larger sample size. Other than that, whenever there is a new cell type added as the interested class, the whole classifier needs to be retrained. This is not conducive to the model scale up considering there are more than 100 subcell types. Instead of training a multiclass classifier, we formulate this problem as multiple binary classification tasks. Each task is aimed purely at differentiating the positive samples for a certain cell type against the rest. The model is first metatrained on the metadatasets where sufficient annotated samples are provided, then adapted to identifying the cell type with less annotated samples. Our meta learning framework provides an adaptive model that can rapidly adjust itself to new classification tasks.

12.2.2 Few-shot classification (FSC)

The few-shot classification problem is one of the first instances of the few-shot learning problem to be studied, where only a few annotated samples are provided for training a task-specific model. A standard few-shot classification problem always contains many N-way-K-shot classification tasks, where N is the number of classes in one task and K is the number of annotated samples for training this task-specific model. K is usually a small number to make the problem more challenging. Dataset used in the FSC often contains many classes and can be divided into base classes and novel classes. For base classes, there are many annotated samples. But only K annotated samples are provided for the novel classes. Tasks consist of base classes are called metatasks and those consist of novel classes are called real tasks in our definition. One method of solving the FSC problem is by fine-tuning a pretrained embedding network which is trained on metatasks [28,29]. However, the model is likely to overfit on real tasks without a complicated regularization design. Another branch of solving FSC is through the meta learning approach.

Meta learning aims to study how meta learning algorithms can acquire fast adaptation capability from a collection of tasks [30,31,13,32]. Meta learning often consists of a metalearner and a learner that learn at two levels of different time scales [33,34]. Santoro et al. Koch et al. [35], Vinyals et al. [36], and Snell et al. [18] proposed to learn a robust kernel function of feature embeddings to illustrate the similarities between different samples. Another popular approach is to directly optimize the metalearner through the gradient descent [37,17,38,15]. Model agnostic meta learning (MAML) [15] is proven to be one of the state-of-the-art approaches in the meta learning field. Triantafillou et al. [39] showed that prototypical networks and MAML could be combined by leveraging prototypes for the initialization of the output weights value in the inner loop. These methods demonstrated human-level accuracy on many classification tasks. However most of them require a lot of tasks to train the metalearner. All public datasets used to validate the meta learning algorithm for few-shot image classification task have many classes (e.g. Omniglot [40] has 1623 classes, miniImageNet [36] has 100 classes, CUB-200-2011

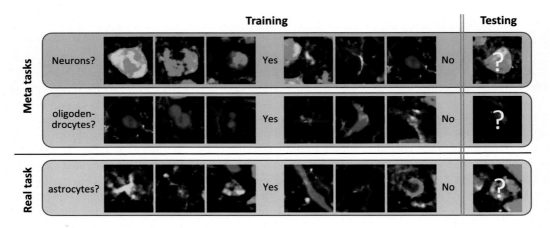

FIGURE 12.1

Multitask brain cell classification. Each task is a binary classification problem for a specific brain cell type. The cell to be classified is located in the center of the image. The model needs to be adapted to the unseen real task with few training samples. (Cell color is synthesized based on all biomarker channels.)

[41] has 200 classes), where many different tasks can be generated for metatraining. For the brain cell dataset, there are only 5 main cell types as shown in Fig. 12.1, which means only 5 binary classification tasks are available. We showed that task augmentation can be very useful to train an adaptive classifier. Another limitation of the current meta learning approaches is that they can not actively select training samples which might not be the optimal case in practice.

12.2.3 Active learning

Active learning has been used to interactively and efficiently query information to achieve optimal performance for the task of interest. These methods select training samples based on information theory [42], ensemble approaches [43], and uncertainty measurements [44,45]. However, these methods may not be effective for deep networks. Deep neural networks are not good at probability prediction. The output from the final softmax layer tends to be overconfident. Gal et al. [46,47], Sener et al. [6], and Fang et al. [48] did a lot of studies in finding heuristics of annotating new samples for deep networks. However, few of them have been applied to domain adaptation or meta learning problems. Woodward et al. [49] added an active part in one-shot learning but did not utilize the best meta learning structure. In this chapter, we combine the advantages of both meta learning and active learning to get a fast adaptive model which can use the fewest data to achieve a good performance.

12.3 Methodology

Consider a dataset consisting Q samples: $\mathcal{D} = \left\{ (\mathbf{x}_q, \mathbf{y}_q) \right\}_{q=1}^{Q}$, where $(\mathbf{x}_q, \mathbf{y}_q)$ is an input-output pair sampled from the joint distribution $P(\mathcal{X}, \mathcal{Y})$. A task can be specifically defined by learning a model

$f_\phi(\mathbf{x}) : \mathcal{X} \to \mathcal{Y}$ which is parameterized by ϕ to maximize the conditional probability $P_\phi(\mathcal{Y}|\mathcal{X})$. Thus whenever there is a change in the conditional distribution which is mainly caused by distribution shifts in $\mathcal{X}$ or $\mathcal{Y}$, it can be viewed as a new task. When dealing with multiple tasks drawn from $P(\mathcal{T})$, each task $\mathcal{T}_i$ is associated with a unique dataset $\mathcal{D}_i$. We split these tasks into two parts: metatasks $\mathcal{T}_{\text{meta}}$ and real tasks $\mathcal{T}_{\text{real}}$. Real tasks are the tasks we used to evaluate the model performance and Metatasks are what we used to pretrain the model. If there is no model adaptation such as vanilla classification approach, then the metatasks are not needed. For each task $\mathcal{T}_i$, we have a train/test split $\mathcal{D}_i^{\text{train}}/\mathcal{D}_i^{\text{test}} \subset \mathcal{D}_i$. The goal for task $\mathcal{T}_i$ is to learn a set of parameters ϕ_i from the $\mathcal{D}_i^{\text{train}}$ to get the minimal loss on the test data, i.e. $\mathcal{L}(\phi_i, \mathcal{D}_i^{test})$. It is important that the labels are not revealed for the test subset of the real tasks, but are always available in the metatasks.

In this section, we proposed a fast adaptive framework to train a dynamic model which is sensitive to the changes in the task by using $\mathcal{T}_{\text{meta}}$ and an efficient way to apply the adaptive model on $\mathcal{T}_{\text{real}}$. The fast adaptive framework consists of two parts. The first part is to obtain a model with task-augmented meta learning which can update efficiently with any number of training samples and is not restricted by the limited number of metatasks. The second part is to apply this model in an active way with Bayesian dropout uncertainties on the new task, so that only informative samples are used to update the model. The active setting is meaningful because it reduces the amount of human annotation which is expensive and time-consuming for biomedical data.

12.3.1 Task-augmented meta learning

The phase I of our AGILE framework is the task-augmented meta learning module. For the meta learning setting, we have a learner which operates at a fast time-scale and parameterized by $\phi \in \Phi$, and a metalearner at a slower time-scale parameterized by $\theta \in \Theta$. The goal of meta learning is to learn meta-parameters θ that can produce good task-specific parameters ϕ for all M tasks after the fast adaptation:

$$\theta^* = \underset{\theta \in \Theta}{\arg\min} \frac{1}{M} \sum_{i=1}^{M} \mathcal{L}\left(Adapt(\theta, \mathcal{D}_i^{\text{train}}), \mathcal{D}_i^{\text{test}}\right) \tag{12.1}$$

where $Adapt()$ function is an adaptation step completed by the learner. We employ model agnostic meta learning (MAML) [15] which initializes the model at θ then updates it using training data for each task $\mathcal{D}_i^{\text{train}}$ as follows:

$$\phi_i \equiv Adapt(\theta, \mathcal{D}_i^{\text{train}}) = \theta \overset{Z}{-} \alpha \nabla_\theta \mathcal{L}(\theta, \{(\mathbf{x}_k, \mathbf{y}_k)\}_{k=1}^{K})), \quad (\mathbf{x}, \mathbf{y}) \sim \mathcal{D}_i^{\text{train}} \tag{12.2}$$

where $\mathcal{L}$ is the loss function, α the learning rate for the learner, and $\overset{Z}{-}$ a short-hand notation for running a Z-step gradient descent which is relatively fast. A fixed number of K class-balanced samples $\{(\mathbf{x}_k, \mathbf{y}_k)\}_{k=1}^{K}$ randomly sampled from $\mathcal{D}_i^{\text{train}}$ are used to update the learner for every iteration.

12.3.1.1 Task augmentation

Metalearner is trained on the metatasks. Our experiments show that when the number of metatasks is not big enough, it can not obtain the general fast adaptation ability on $\mathcal{T}_{\text{real}} \sim P(\mathcal{T})$. One task is considered as one data sample in the meta learning training paradigm, like an image to the normal classification task. Similar as data augmentation in normal learning task, we applied a set of task-augmentation functions $\{\mathcal{G}_l\}_{l=1}^{L} : \mathcal{T} \to \mathcal{T}'$ on existing tasks to create new tasks. Because the task is specifically determined by the conditional probability $P(\mathcal{Y}|\mathcal{X})$, either change $\mathcal{X}$ or $\mathcal{Y}$ will lead to a new task. Same task-augmentation transformation must be applied to all training and test data in one dataset during the metatraining to keep the data consistency:

$$\{\mathcal{D}_i^{\text{train}}, \mathcal{D}_i^{\text{test}}\}^{(l)} = \{\mathcal{G}_l(\mathcal{D}_i^{\text{train}}), \mathcal{G}_l(\mathcal{D}_i^{\text{test}})\}, \quad \mathcal{T}_i \in \mathcal{T}_{\text{meta}} \tag{12.3}$$

We now describe three different ways we designed for task augmentation:

- **Flipping the label:** Binary classification task has only two labels. Before the task transformation, 1 means positive samples from certain cell type and 0 means negative samples. Considering the binary label $y \in \mathbb{R}$, flipping the label would switch the label of positive and negative samples:

$$y' = z(1 - y) + (1 - z)y, \quad \text{where } z \sim \text{Bernoulli}(p_l), \tag{12.4}$$

where p_f is the probability of flipping the label. The idea behind the flipping label is to reduce the change of learning a fixed mapping between the image to the label. The classifier trained on transformed labels is forced to learn the dependency between the labels in the training subset and the test subset.

- **Shuffling input channels:** Considering the input image with c biomarkers $\mathbf{x} \in \mathbb{R}^{w \times h \times c}$, the order of the biomarker channel is not a determiner for the cell type classification task. For example, the first channel can be DAPI or NeuN or any other biomarkers, as long as the channel order is consistent between training and test samples in the same task. By constructing c different one-by-one kernels $\{\mathbf{s}_{ij}\}_{i=1}^{c} \in \mathbb{R}^{1 \times 1 \times c}$ where $\mathbf{s}_{ij} = 1$ only if the jth bio-marker is placed at i^{th} channel after the random shuffling, the shuffled images are obtained by the convolution:

$$\mathbf{x}' = \mathbf{x} * \mathbf{s}_{ij}, \quad i, j = 1, 2, 3 \ldots c. \tag{12.5}$$

Shuffling the input channels is selected with a probability of p_s. Similar to flipping the label transformation, shuffling input channel forces the classifier to be channel-order invariant and focus on the content information alone.

- **Image augmentation:** In general, all image augmentation techniques such as image flipping, rotation, blurring, translation, contrast changing can be applied here to augment the tasks as the distribution of $\mathcal{X}$ is slightly changed. However, for the cell type classification case, as each cell to be classified is centered in each image and the intensity of each channel has the physical meaning of the gene expression, we avoided image translation, blurring, and contrast changing. In the end, all channels are rotated for $90°$, $180°$ or $270°$ with the probability of p_r or flipped left and right or up and down with the probability of p_f.

In the experiment, we set $p_l = p_s = p_r = p_f$. By increasing the diversity of the metatasks, the metalearner can be well trained to extract useful features after adapting to training data in any task. The comparison between task augmented meta learning and plain transfer learning is illustrated in Fig. 12.2. Blue and red dots represent the optimal model parameters of the metatasks and the real task respectively. The solid line shows the pretraining process on the metadatasets while the dashed line shows the adaptation process. After pretraining on very few metatasks, the model is pulled closer to

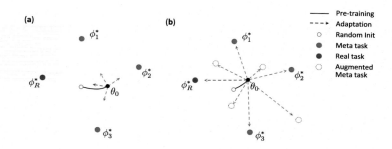

FIGURE 12.2

Comparison of (**a**) transfer learning and (**b**) task-augmented meta learning. (**a**) After pretraining on very few number of metatasks, the model is pulled closer to the metatasks and may be far from the real task. (**b**) By creating pseudo metatasks to pretrain the meta learning model, it gains the ability of adapting to the new tasks with only one gradient step updating.

the metatasks and may be far from the real task. If the model is not metatrained, the model is learned to be an average of different metatask, and requires many training data and steps to reach the optimal points for all tasks. If the model is metatrained without task augmentation, the metamodel would be able to quickly adapt to the metatasks but the generalization ability to the real task is poor. When the model is trained with augmented tasks, its learning ability is improved and can perform well on the real task.

12.3.2 Active learning with Bayesian uncertainty

The phase II of AGILE is to apply the pretrained model with active learning. Previous meta learning methods consider training and testing the meta learning algorithm in the exact same manner, which might not be practical. They fixed the number of training samples for each task, which means if there are five annotated samples per class in the real tasks, then the meta learning model needs to be trained on 5 shots as well. If the annotation samples are increased to ten samples per class, the model needs to be retrained on the same 10 shots setting. Meta learning model trained in this way is not very adaptive as it depends on the number K. In reality, K in the real task $\mathcal{T}_{real}$ may vary, especially when users want to annotate some new samples to improve the performance of the model. When the number of training samples is extremely small, how to unsupervised select the most informative samples to annotate is an important question. Thus, we make the adaptive learner be K-invariant and adopt active learning to select the best training samples.

12.3.2.1 Dynamic training size

The most straight-forward way to make the model to be K-independent is to update the learner during the meta learning training process, so that the model is forced to learn with a different training size. Suppose the maximum number of annotated samples per class allowed by the label budget for the real task is K_{max}, then the adaptation function in (12.2) can be changed to:

$$\phi_i = \theta - \alpha \nabla_\theta \mathcal{L}(\theta, \{(\mathbf{x}_k, \mathbf{y}_k)\}_{k=1}^{\widetilde{K}})), \quad (\mathbf{x}, \mathbf{y}) \sim \mathcal{D}_i^{train} \tag{12.6}$$

where $1 \leqslant \widetilde{K} \leqslant K_{max} \ll Q$ and Q is the number of samples for base classes. Average cross-entropy loss is used in this classification task to eliminate the scale difference introduced by $\widetilde{K}$:

$$\mathcal{L}(\theta, \{(\mathbf{x}_k, \mathbf{y}_k)\}_{k=1}^{\widetilde{K}})) = -\frac{1}{\widetilde{K}} \sum_{k=1}^{\widetilde{K}} \sum_{c=1}^{C} \mathbf{1}(y_k = c) \log p(y_k = c | \mathbf{x}_k, \theta), \qquad (12.7)$$

where $\mathbf{1}(\cdot)$ is the indicator function, C is the total number of classes, and $p(y_k = c | \mathbf{x}_k, \theta)$ is the softmax probability of sample $\mathbf{x}_k$ for class c parametrized by θ.

12.3.2.2 Bayesian neural networks (BNNs)

To perform active learning, we need to rank unlabeled images for annotation. A common way to rank them is by sampling uncertainty. The standard neural network is a point estimate approach and tends to be overconfident when making predictions on the out-of-distribution data points. From a probabilistic perspective, the optimal weights are obtained by maximum likelihood estimation (MLE) which ignores the uncertainty information existing in the weights. Bayesian neural network, on the other hand, places a prior distribution over the network weights and then using Bayesian inference to make the prediction and obtain the uncertainty.

Suppose the weights of an L-layer BNN have a prior distribution:

$$\phi \sim p(\phi), \quad \phi = \{\Phi_i\}_{i=1}^{L}. \qquad (12.8)$$

Given a training dataset $\mathcal{D}^{\text{train}} = (X^{\text{tr}}, Y^{\text{tr}})$, the posterior of the weights can be calculated from the Bayes theorem:

$$p(\phi | \mathcal{D}^{\text{train}}) = \frac{p(\phi, Y^{\text{tr}} | X^{\text{tr}})}{p(Y^{\text{tr}} | X^{\text{tr}})} = \frac{p(Y^{\text{tr}} | X^{\text{tr}}, \phi) p(\phi)}{\int p(Y^{\text{tr}} | X^{\text{tr}}, \phi) p(\phi) d\phi}. \qquad (12.9)$$

Then for an unlabeled input image $\mathbf{x}^{\text{te}}$, the predictive distribution of the label $\mathbf{y}^{\text{te}}$ is given by marginalized over the posterior:

$$p(\mathbf{y}^{\text{te}} | \mathbf{x}^{\text{te}}, \mathcal{D}^{\text{train}}) = \int p(\mathbf{y}^{\text{te}} | \mathbf{x}^{\text{te}}, \phi) p(\phi | \mathcal{D}^{\text{train}}) d\phi. \qquad (12.10)$$

However, both the integration in Eq. (12.9) and (12.10) are computationally intractable for the neural networks as we cannot integrate over all possible parameters. Using variational inference to approximate the true posterior distribution (Eq. (12.9)) and Monte Carlo approximation for the Bayesian prediction (Eq. (12.10)) is a common approach to solve it. The idea of variational inference is that we can use a variational distribution $q_\gamma(\phi)$ to approximate the true posterior by minimizing the Kullback-Leibler (KL) divergence between these two. This is equivalent to maximize the evidence lower bound (ELBO):

$$\gamma^* = \underset{\gamma}{\text{argmin}} \ \text{KL}(q_\gamma(\phi) || p(\phi | \mathcal{D}^{\text{train}}))$$

$$= \underset{\gamma}{\text{argmax}} \int q_\gamma(\phi) \log p(Y^{\text{tr}} | X^{\text{tr}}, \phi) d\phi - \text{KL}(q_\gamma(\phi) || p(\phi)), \qquad (12.11)$$

where γ is the variational parameters. The first term encourages the weights sampled from $q_\gamma(\phi)$ to perform well on the training data while the second term is a regularization term that minimize the difference between the variational distribution and the prior distribution. Gal, et al. [46] proved that Dropout can be interpreted as a variational Bayesian approximation, where the approximating distribution is a mixture of two Gaussians. More specifically, it means the variational distribution $q_\gamma(\phi)$ can be obtained by training a model with dropout for every weight layer (including the convolutional layer). Finally, the Bayesian prediction using Monte Carlo integration is given by:

$$
\begin{aligned}
p(\mathbf{y}^{\text{te}}|\mathbf{x}^{\text{te}}, \mathcal{D}^{\text{train}}) &\approx \int p(\mathbf{y}^{\text{te}}|\mathbf{x}^{\text{te}}, \phi) q_\gamma(\phi) d\phi \\
&\approx \frac{1}{T} \sum_{t=1}^{T} p_{\phi'}\left(\mathbf{y}^{\text{te}}|\mathbf{x}^{\text{te}}, \phi'\right), \quad \phi' \sim q_\gamma(\phi),
\end{aligned}
\tag{12.12}
$$

where T is the number of Monte-Carlo experiments.

12.3.2.3 Bayesian meta learning

When apply the BNN into the meta learning framework, the posterior distribution now is dependent on the metaparameters, so the Bayesian predictive distribution becomes:

$$
p(\mathbf{y}^{\text{te}}|\mathbf{x}^{\text{te}}, \mathcal{D}^{\text{train}}, \theta) = \int p(\mathbf{y}^{\text{te}}|\mathbf{x}^{\text{te}}, \phi) p(\phi|\mathcal{D}^{\text{train}}, \theta) d\phi.
\tag{12.13}
$$

Compared with Eq. (12.10), we now need to inference the conditional posterior distribution $p(\phi|\mathcal{D}^{\text{train}}, \theta)$. From the adapt function Eq. (12.2) and (12.6), there is a connection between parameters ϕ and θ, so the conditional posterior distribution can be inferred from $q_\gamma(\phi|\mathcal{D}^{\text{train}}, \theta)$ by:

$$
\begin{aligned}
\gamma^* &= \underset{\gamma}{\text{argmin}}\ \text{KL}(q_\gamma(\phi|\mathcal{D}^{\text{train}}, \theta) || p(\phi|\mathcal{D}^{\text{train}}, \theta)) \\
&= \underset{\gamma}{\text{argmax}} \int q_\gamma(\phi|\mathcal{D}^{\text{train}}, \theta) \log p(Y^{\text{tr}}|X^{\text{tr}}, \phi) d\phi \\
&\quad - \text{KL}(q_\gamma(\phi|\mathcal{D}^{\text{train}}, \theta) || p(\phi|\theta)),
\end{aligned}
\tag{12.14}
$$

where variational distribution of ϕ is obtained by initializing a model with θ, then adapt on $\mathcal{D}^{\text{train}}$ with dropout:

$$
q_\gamma(\phi|\mathcal{D}^{\text{train}}, \theta) = q(\phi; \mathcal{A}dapt(\theta, \mathcal{D}^{\text{train}}, p_{\text{drop}})),
\tag{12.15}
$$

where $\mathcal{A}dapt$ is extended with dropout and p_{drop} is the dropout rate for all layers. The final question is how to get the optimal metaparameter θ^* from the metatraining process using datasets from metatasks $\mathcal{T}_{\text{meta}}$? From the probability perspective, Eq. (12.1) can be replaced with:

$$\theta^* = \underset{\theta \in \Theta}{\operatorname{argmax}} \prod_{i=1}^{M} p(\mathcal{D}_i^{\text{test}} | \mathcal{D}_i^{\text{train}}, \theta)$$

$$= \underset{\theta \in \Theta}{\operatorname{argmax}} \prod_{i=1}^{M} \left(\int p(\mathcal{D}_i^{\text{test}} | \phi_i) p(\phi_i | \mathcal{D}_i^{\text{train}}, \theta) d\phi_i \right) \qquad (12.16)$$

$$\approx \underset{\theta \in \Theta}{\operatorname{argmax}} \prod_{i=1}^{M} \left(\frac{1}{T} \sum_{t=1}^{t} p(Y_i^{\text{te}} | X_i^{\text{te}}, \phi_i^t) \right), \quad \text{where } \phi_i^t \sim q_\gamma(\phi | \mathcal{D}_i^{\text{train}}, \theta).$$

Note that dropout is only applied on X^{tr} and not on X^{te}.

12.3.2.4 Active learning with Bayesian meta learning

To apply the active learning, first we need to obtain the predictive distribution for every unlabeled sample in each task using the BNN model (use Eq. (12.13)). Then we need to define the uncertainty so that we can rank them based on their uncertainties and choose the samples with high uncertainty values to be included in the training set for the real tasks. There are two types of uncertainty in Bayesian modeling [50]. One is Epistemic uncertainty as a reason for lack of training data, another is Aleatoric uncertainty as a result of system noise. For the classification method, there are several ways to measure the uncertainty. The most straightforward way is to calculated predictive variance from the Monte-Carlo outputs for each class and then take the average over all classes [51]. But the simple average may not be ideal for aggregating the uncertainty from different classes:

$$\sigma^2 = \frac{1}{|\mathcal{Y}|} \sum_{\mathbf{y}^{\text{te}} \in \mathcal{Y}} \left[\mathbb{E}_{q_\gamma(\phi)} \left[p(\mathbf{y}^{\text{te}} | \mathbf{x}^{\text{te}}, \phi)^2 \right] - \mathbb{E}_{q_\gamma(\phi)} [p(\mathbf{y}^{\text{te}} | \mathbf{x}^{\text{te}}, \phi)]^2 \right] \qquad (12.17)$$

where $|\mathcal{Y}|$ is the total number of classes ($|\mathcal{Y}| = 2$ for our cases). Another common approach is using predictive entropy [52], which captures both Epistemic and Aleatoric uncertainty. The higher the entropy is, the less confident the model is about the prediction:

$$H\left(\mathbf{y}^{\text{te}} | \mathbf{x}^{\text{te}}, \mathcal{D}^{\text{train}} \right) = - \sum_{\mathbf{y}^{\text{te}} \in \mathcal{Y}} p(\mathbf{y}^{\text{te}} | \mathbf{x}^{\text{te}}, \mathcal{D}^{\text{train}}) \log p(\mathbf{y}^{\text{te}} | \mathbf{x}^{\text{te}}, \mathcal{D}^{\text{train}}) \qquad (12.18)$$

The last approach is using the mutual information between the label and the model parameters, which describe how much information can be gained for the model parameters if the label is presented:

$$I\left[\phi; \mathbf{y}^{\text{te}} | \mathbf{x}^{\text{te}}, \mathcal{D}^{\text{train}} \right] = H\left(\mathbf{y}^{\text{te}} | \mathbf{x}^{\text{te}}, \mathcal{D}^{\text{train}} \right) - \mathbb{E}_{p(\phi | \mathcal{D}^{\text{train}})} [H\left(\mathbf{y}^{\text{te}} | \mathbf{x}^{\text{te}}, \phi \right)], \qquad (12.19)$$

where $p(\phi | \mathcal{D}^{\text{train}})$ is approximated by $q_\gamma(\phi)$. We tested all approaches, and found out that the predictive entropy and mutual information gave similar uncertainty rank for the unlabeled samples, which is better than using the predictive variance. We then used predictive entropy as the measurement for our AGILE framework.

12.3.3 Binary cell type classifier

The cell type classification task is a multiclass classification task. The conventional way to solve it is to train a network that has the same number of outputs as the number of classes. However, we have the data-imbalanced problem. We have limited samples for certain cell types (positive samples in the real task). If we simply train a multiclass classifier, samples from the metadata (positive samples in the metatasks) would domain the training of the network as they share the same network up to the last layer. Replacing the original n-class classification problem with n binary classification problem helps to reduce the influence of the sample imbalance. All n binary classifiers share the same network structure but use different weights and biases.

A binary cell type classifier is a simple network with 4 convolution blocks. Each block consists of a convolutional layer with 32 filters of size 3*3, a batch normalization layer, and a max-pooling layer. Relu activation is used after each convolutional layer. After the last convolution block, a dense layer is added to project the 32 feature maps to only two classes. The learning rate is set to be $\alpha = 0.01$ after the hyperparameter search.

12.4 Experiments and results

12.4.1 Datasets

12.4.1.1 Rat brain cell

For the first dataset, we collected 4000 cells from 5 major cell types imaged from rat brain tissue sections: neurons, astrocytes, oligodendrocytes, microglia, and endothelial cells. There are 800 cells for each cell type. 7 biomarkers are used as the feature channels: DAPI, Histones, NeuN, S100, Olig 2, Iba1, and RECA1. DAPI and Histones are used to indicate the location of the cells while others are biomarkers for the classification of specific cell types. More specifically, we would observe strong protein expression in the NeuN channel for neurons, Iba1 channel for microglia, S100 for astrocytes, Olig2 for oligodendrocytes, and RECA1 for endothelial cells as shown in Fig. 12.3. Each cell to be classified is located in the center of a patch with a size of 100×100 pixels. No cell detection preprocessing has been applied to these patches, thus some patches may contain more than one cell, but only the central cell is what we are interested and all other cells are in general considered as the background for the cell type classification task.

12.4.1.2 Human brain cell

We collect another brain cell dataset from Alzheimer's patients. There are the same five main cell types: neurons, astrocytes, oligodendrocytes, microglia, and endothelial cells, but the channels for each cell sample are different, namely: DAPI, CD31, Iba1, NeuN, Olig2, and S100. 1000 cells are collected from each of the cell types, making it a dataset with 5000 cells in total. Different from the rat brain cell dataset, there is only one cell sample in the image (i.e. each cell is tightly cropped based on the cell detection results). The size of the cell varies from 12 to 48 pixels, and the shape distribution is illustrated in Fig. 12.5. As each cell is nicely detected, we add an additional channel of cell profile as an indicator of the cell size and the location. The human brain cell samples can be found in Fig. 12.4, all images are padded to be 48×48.

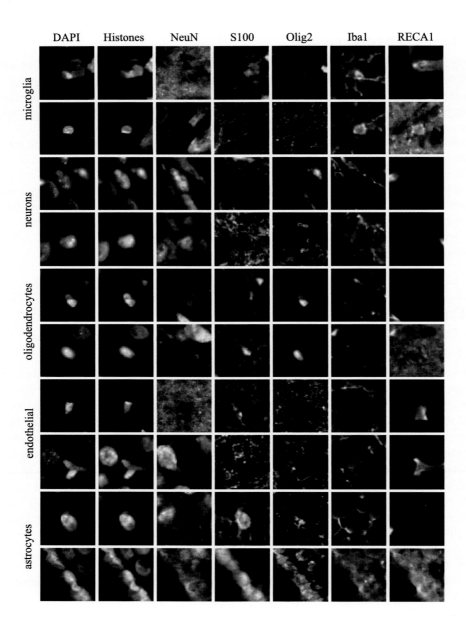

FIGURE 12.3

Rat brain cell samples. There are five cell types: neurons, astrocytes, oligodendrocytes, microglia, and endothelial cells and seven biomarkers: DAPI, Histones, NeuN, S100, Olig 2, Iba1, and RECA1. 2 samples are shown here for each of the cell type. DAPI and Histones are used to indicate the location of the cells while others are biomarkers for classification of specific cell types. High correlation can be found between NeuN and neurons, Iba1 and microglia, S100 and astrocytes, Olig2 and oligodendrocytes, RECA1 and endothelial cells.

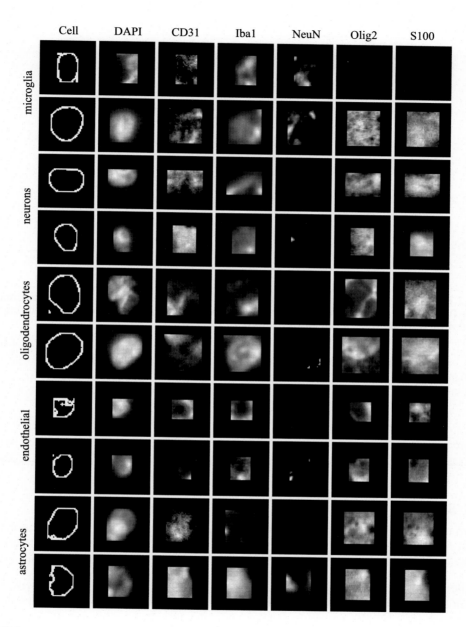

FIGURE 12.4

Human brain cell samples (zero padded). Same five cell types: neurons, astrocytes, oligodendrocytes, microglia, and endothelial cells, 1 detection channel: cell outline, and 6 biomarkers: DAPI, CD31, Iba1, NeuN, Olig2, and S100. 2 samples are shown here for each of the cell types. Cell and DAPI and Histones are used to indicate the location of the cells while others are biomarkers for the classification of specific cell types.

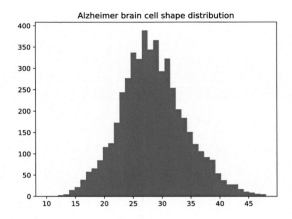

FIGURE 12.5

Distribution of the human brain cells size.

Table 12.1 Methods configuration comparison which differ mainly in the data they use and the training framework. Meta learning methods are supposed to perform well with few training samples and little training time. (# means the number of).

Methods	Use data			in Real-train		# Metatasks
	Metatrain	**Metatest**	**Real-train**	**# samples**	**# gradient updates**	
Vanilla_limit	-	-	✓	16/20 (1%)	200	0
Vanilla_full	-	-	✓	960/1000 (60%)	200	0
Transfer	✓	-	✓	16/20 (1%)	200	3
MAML	✓	✓	✓	16/20 (1%)	1 - 10	3
AGILE (phase I)	✓	✓	✓	16/20 (1%)	1 - 10	many
AGILE (phase II)	✓	✓	✓	16/20 (1%)	1 - 10	many

12.4.2 Baselines and metrics

As shown in Table 12.1, we used three methods and constructed four baselines for comparison: a state-of-the-art method (MAML), the upper bound (fully supervised training, Vanilla_full), lower bound (supervised training with a small dataset, Vanilla_limit), and a pretrained model (transfer learning).

- **Vanilla:** This is the most straightforward baseline. The vanilla approach is to train a network from scratch on real tasks without any adaptation. As we have a task split ($\mathcal{T}_{meta}/\mathcal{T}_{real}$) and a data split in each task ($\mathcal{D}^{train}/\mathcal{D}^{test}$), we can have 4 subsets of the data. The vanilla method only uses $\mathcal{D}_{real}^{train}$ for learning the real task model parameters. We further constructed the lower bound and the upper bound by selecting the different sizes of the training set from the real tasks. Vanilla_limit uses only 1% of data to train the classifier, which includes 16 cells in rat brain cell experiment and 20 cells in human brain cell experiment. Vanilla_full means fully supervised training which uses 60% data to train as the rest 40% data are fixed as the test set across all different approaches. We ran 500 repeated experiments for Vanilla_limit and 10 experiments for Vanilla_high to create different train-test splits. 200 gradient updates are applied to guarantee the convergence of the training process.

- **Transfer learning:** This is also a commonly used baseline for comparison. Compared with the vanilla method, transfer learning utilized the $\mathcal{D}_{meta}^{train}$ dataset to get a pretrained model, then it will be adapted on the real tasks with $\mathcal{D}_{real}^{train}$. In fact, this method uses all training samples in metatasks as the meta learning based method because of the sampling strategy. But according to the training strategy, metatest data is not used in the model updates. Only 1% of labeled data is used inf fine-tuning stage for 2 real tasks. 200 gradient updates are applied in both pretraining and fine-tuning. 500 repeated experiments are executed to capture the statistical results.

- **MAML:** The last baseline is the MAML approach [15]. Training data is small for two real tasks but efficient for the metatasks. MAML uses all data available from the metatasks and the real tasks, but there is no task augmentation applied here. It is supposed to learn fast, so at most 10 gradient updates are allowed for this approach. Same 500 repeated experiments are run on the real tasks for different train test splits.

All methods including the proposed AGILE method share the same neural network structure. And all methods are tuned for the hyperparameters individually. The learning rate is 0.01 for all classifiers and 0.001 for the metalearner if applied. SGD is used for classifier (learner) updates while the Adam optimizer is used for metalearner updates. Training iterations are set as 12,000 for all methods. 12 replaced tasks are used in one iteration during the training on metatasks.

The metrics we used to evaluate the performance of each method are precision, recall, F1-score, accuracy, and confidence interval.

12.4.3 Rat brain cell FSC

12.4.3.1 FSC experiments

For rat brain cells, there are five cell types: neurons, astrocytes, oligodendrocytes, microglia, and endothelial cells. We considered two task splits to show the generalization of the proposed methods. In the first task split, binary classification for neurons, oligodendrocytes, and microglia is considered as the metatasks, while detecting astrocytes and endothelial cells are considered as real tasks. In the second task split, detecting neurons, astrocytes and endothelial cells is metatasks, and the real tasks are to identify the remaining two cell types.

The quantitative results on the real tasks for the first task split are summarized in Table 12.2. The upper bound we can get by using all training data is 95% of classification accuracy while the lower bound is 63.7%. The transfer learning method has worse performance than the lower bound. The reason is that it does not learn a good initialization from the pretraining on this multitask classification problem. These three metatasks are too different from the real tasks so that transfer learning actually harms the real tasks. The MAML approach also performs worse than the baseline because of the metaoverfitting problem. When we have only 3 samples (tasks) in the metatraining space, the model can do well on these tasks but will lose the generalization ability on the new real tasks. Our proposed task-augmented meta learning can solve this issue. It is able to quickly adapt with few training samples and gradient updates. With only 16 training samples (1%), the AGILE method can reach 90% accuracy. With 160 training samples (10%), AGILE reaches the upper bound. The 95% confidence interval is presented in Table 12.2.

Table 12.2 Quantitative results of different methods in rat brain cell classification experiments with first task split. Vanilla method uses all available training data (60%) and act as the upper bound while AGILE method gets the highest accuracy using very few training data (1%).

Methods (Size %)	Precision	Recall	F1-score	Accuracy($\pm$ Std)	CI$_{95}$
Vanilla_limit (1%)	0.642	0.622	0.632	0.637($\pm$0.062)	0.632 - 0.642
Vanilla_full (60%)	0.937	**0.965**	**0.951**	**0.950**($\pm$0.021)	0.948 - 0.952
Transfer (1%)	0.447	0.433	0.440	0.449($\pm$0.085)	0.449 - 0.456
MAML (1%)	0.408	0.402	0.405	0.409($\pm$0.030)	0.406 - 0.412
AGILE (phase I) (1%)	0.791	0.790	0.791	0.791($\pm$0.054)	0.786 - 0.796
AGILE (phase II) (1%)	0.883	0.926	0.904	0.902($\pm$0.048)	0.898 - 0.906
AGILE (phase II) (10%)	**0.950**	0.951	**0.951**	**0.950**($\pm$0.044)	0.946 - 0.954

Table 12.3 Quantitative results of different methods in rat brain cell classification experiments with second task split.

Methods (Size %)	Precision	Recall	F1-score	Accuracy($\pm$ Std)	CI$_{95}$
Vanilla_limit (1%)	0.745	0.711	0.728	0.738($\pm$0.084)	0.715 - 0.761
Vanilla_full (60%)	**0.948**	0.958	**0.952**	**0.952**($\pm$0.011)	0.946 - 0.960
Transfer (1%)	0.713	0.710	0.712	0.708($\pm$0.089)	0.700 - 0.716
MAML (1%)	0.669	0.678	0.674	0.675($\pm$0.108)	0.666 - 0.684
AGILE (phase I) (1%)	0.929	0.892	0.910	0.913($\pm$0.055)	0.908 - 0.918
AGILE (phase II) (1%)	0.896	0.874	0.885	0.888($\pm$0.088)	0.861 - 0.915
AGILE (phase II) (4%)	0.939	**0.965**	**0.952**	**0.952**($\pm$0.053)	0.936 - 0.968

Similar results can be found for the second task split as summarized in Table 12.3. The upper bound of the accuracy is 95.2% in this case while the lower bound is 73.8%. Compared with the results in the first task split, it probably means the oligodendrocytes and microglia cells are easier to be identified than the astrocytes and endothelial cells. The transfer learning approach and MAML do not perform well in experiments either because of the local minimum problem. By using AGILE (phase I) which has the task augmentation, the performance significantly increases to 91.3% for training with 16 labeled cells. When we included active learning in the AGILE phase II, the performance drops a little bit. The reason is that for the phase II model, 16 labeled cells are selected using uncertainties from the Bayesian neural networks. It is not guaranteed that these training samples are class-balanced. But for the phase I model in this experiment, the training samples are preselected with a balanced class. In other words, the phase I model has more information provided that the phase II model. We can see the effectiveness of the active framework in the active learning experiments when we gradually increasing the training size as in Fig. 12.8 (**b**).

The adaptation processes when using only 1% of training samples are shown in Fig. 12.6 (**a**) for the first task split and in Fig. 12.7 for the second task split (**a**). The solid line is the mean value and the shaded area shows the variance. Without any prior knowledge, the vanilla model starts with a classification accuracy of around 50%. Transferring an existing model has the lowest starting point because

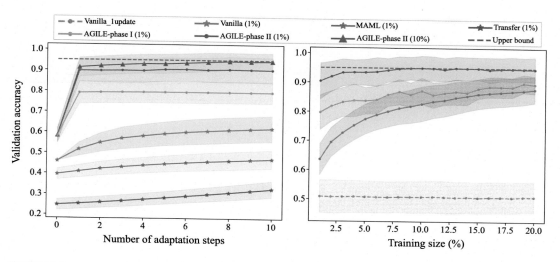

FIGURE 12.6

(**a**) Comparison of different methods when adapting to new real task with only 1% labeled training data under the first task split, AGILE method shows its fast adapting ability. Upper bound is obtained by training on all 60% training data with Vanilla method. (**b**) The impact of the training size on the AGILE method and the vanilla method.

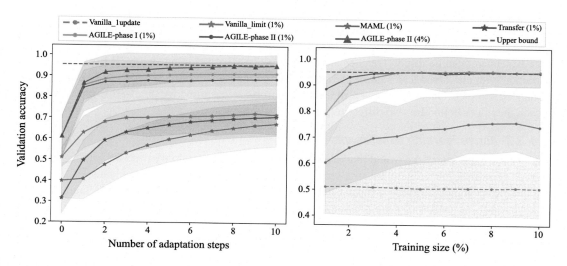

FIGURE 12.7

(**a**) Comparison of different methods when adapting to new real task with only 1% labeled training data under the second task split. (**b**) The impact of the training size on the AGILE method and the vanilla method.

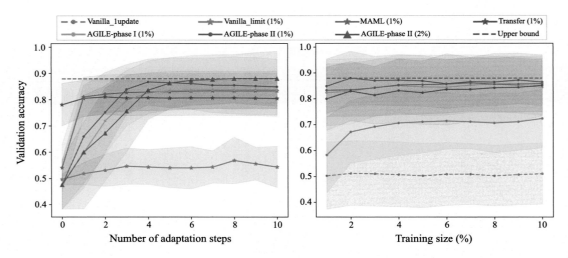

FIGURE 12.8

(**a**) Comparison of different methods when adapting to new real task with only 1% labeled training data for human Alzheimer data. (**b**) The impact of the training size on the AGILE method and other baselines.

images labeled as "1" in one task should be labeled as "0" in other tasks. The original MAML method also does not help for this brain cell type binary classification problem. Our results show that MAML is unable to adapt effectively due to the small number of training tasks. In contrast, the AGILE model has a sharp increase in accuracy after 1 gradient update. Note that although the AGILE model is trained for maximal performance after one gradient step, it continues to improve with additional gradient steps. Three baselines (Vanilla_limit, Transfer learning, and MAML) including the AGILE phase I model are trained with class-balanced samples while the AGILE-phase II models are trained with potentially unbalanced samples. Only 10% and 4% of training samples are required for the AGILE-phase II model to reach the upper bound for two different task split respectively.

12.4.3.2 Active learning experiments

In the second experiment, we would like to find out how many samples do we need for solving the brain cell type classification problem because some features might only exist in certain samples. Different from the common meta learning setting, where all the training set is class-balanced by default, no pres-elected class-balanced samples are provided when fine-tuning/adapting an existing model or training a new vanilla model in this experiment. As the pretrained models from transfer learning and MAML are even worse than the vanilla baselines as shown in the first experiment, we did not include them in this active learning experiment.

For the first task split, Fig. 12.6 (**b**) illustrates the relationship between the training size and the performances of the AGILE method and the baseline methods. AGILE performs extremely well when the training size is small. AGILE method reaches validation accuracy of 95% with 10% of data (about 160 samples). Active learning with Bayesian meta learning is effective as the blue line is constantly

Table 12.4 Quantitative results of different methods in human Alzheimer brain cell classification experiments.

Methods (Size %)	Precision	Recall	F1-score	Accuracy(± Std)	CI₉₅
Vanilla_limit (1%)	0.571	0.600	0.585	0.584(±0.079)	0.535 - 0.633
Vanilla_full (60%)	0.875	**0.850**	0.862	0.879(±0.003)	0.860 - 0.898
Transfer (1%)	0.816	0.789	0.802	0.804(±0.067)	0.798 - 0.810
MAML (1%)	0.835	0.832	0.833	0.833(±0.068)	0.827 - 0.839
AGILE (phase I) (1%)	0.851	0.816	0.833	0.837(±0.071)	0.831 - 0.843
AGILE (phase II) (1%)	0.864	0.810	836	0.848(±0.105)	0.815 - 0.881
AGILE (phase II) (2%)	**0.899**	0.843	**0.870**	**0.880**(±0.104)	0.848 - 0.912

above the orange line. Meantime, the vanilla model with 200 gradient updates gets an accuracy of around 84% and the vanilla model with only 1 update basically cannot learn anything.

For the second task split, AGILE equipped with active learning is still the winner of this active learning experiment, especially when the training size is really small. By only including the task augmentation technique, the AGILE-phase I model can get 90% accuracy with 2% of training samples. It is higher than the same model performed in the first task split, which shows the difficulty varies from the task. The AGILE method can reach the upper bound with 4% of training samples (64 samples), while the accuracy for the vanilla approach is around 70%.

12.4.4 Human brain cell FSC

12.4.4.1 FSC experiments

For human brain cells, there are the same five cell types: neurons, astrocytes, oligodendrocytes, microglia, and endothelial cells. We randomly selected detecting neurons, astrocytes, and microglia as the metatasks, and the rest two cell types are the real tasks. We first compare different methods on this dataset, then we tried to test the model pretrained on rat brain cells to see if there is some generalization ability of the proposed model.

The quantitative results on the real tasks are summarized in Table 12.4. The upper bound we can get by using all training data is 87.9% of classification accuracy while the lower bound with only 1% of training samples is 58.4%. For this dataset, both the transfer learning approach and MAML approach can get decent results, with an accuracy of 80.4% and 83.3% respectively. Our AGILE framework can get 83.7% accuracy with task augmentation and 84.8% with additional active selected training samples. With about 2% of training samples (40 cells), it can reach the upper bound.

The adaptation processes when using only 1% of training samples are shown in Fig. 12.6 (**a**). The original model starts with the classification accuracy of around 50%, and transferring an existing model has the highest starting point which also proves that cell types classification tasks are very similar. The results suggest that all methods utilizing the metadatasets can perform very well after adapting to real tasks. The AGILE method is still the best method in this experiment according to the accuracy. MAML has a sharp increase in accuracy after 1 gradient update, while the AGILE methods require 4 to 5 steps to reach the highest accuracy. Only 2% of training samples are required for the AGILE-phase II model to reach the upper bound.

12.4.4.2 Active learning experiments

Like the previous experiments in the rat brain cell active learning experiment, we plotted the figure of the accuracy versus the number of training samples for different approaches. There are almost no improvements from the augmented tasks when we compare the AGILE-phase I model with the MAML approach, as the metatasks are very similar to the real tasks, which also means that the pretrained model can work relatively well. However, we can still observe a little improvement from the AGILE-phase II for training with more informative samples.

12.5 Conclusion

In this chapter, we proposed a fast adaptation framework AGILE combining data augmentation, meta learning, and active learning to deliver a model which is sensitive to the data distribution/task changes and able to adjust itself with few training samples and few updating steps. The results show that only 2 - 10% of training data and few gradient updates are enough to get the best performance on identifying unseen brain cell types for both rats or humans. AGILE can be used in many diagnosis systems or detection algorithms which have to deal with various input data.

References

[1] C. Shorten, T.M. Khoshgoftaar, A survey on image data augmentation for deep learning, Journal of Big Data 6 (1) (2019) 60.

[2] X. Zhu, A.B. Goldberg, Introduction to semi-supervised learning, Synthesis Lectures on Artificial Intelligence and Machine Learning 3 (1) (2009) 1–130.

[3] D.P. Kingma, S. Mohamed, D.J. Rezende, M. Welling, Semi-supervised learning with deep generative models, in: Advances in Neural Information Processing Systems, 2014, pp. 3581–3589.

[4] I. Goodfellow, J. Pouget-Abadie, M. Mirza, B. Xu, D. Warde-Farley, S. Ozair, A. Courville, Y. Bengio, Generative adversarial nets, in: Advances in Neural Information Processing Systems, 2014, pp. 2672–2680.

[5] B. Settles, Active learning literature survey, Tech. rep., University of Wisconsin-Madison Department of Computer Sciences, 2009.

[6] O. Sener, S. Savarese, Active learning for convolutional neural networks: a core-set approach, arXiv preprint, arXiv:1708.00489, 2017.

[7] Y. Bengio, Deep learning of representations for unsupervised and transfer learning, in: Proceedings of ICML Workshop on Unsupervised and Transfer Learning, 2012, pp. 17–36.

[8] R. Gopalan, R. Li, R. Chellappa, Domain adaptation for object recognition: an unsupervised approach, in: 2011 International Conference on Computer Vision, IEEE, 2011, pp. 999–1006.

[9] K. Saenko, B. Kulis, M. Fritz, T. Darrell, Adapting visual category models to new domains, in: European Conference on Computer Vision, Springer, 2010, pp. 213–226.

[10] A. Torralba, A.A. Efros, Unbiased look at dataset bias, in: CVPR 2011, IEEE, 2011, pp. 1521–1528.

[11] H. Zeng, J.R. Sanes, Neuronal cell-type classification: challenges, opportunities and the path forward, Nature Reviews Neuroscience 18 (9) (2017) 530.

[12] S.J. Pan, Q. Yang, A survey on transfer learning, IEEE Transactions on Knowledge and Data Engineering 22 (10) (2009) 1345–1359.

[13] R. Vilalta, Y. Drissi, A perspective view and survey of meta-learning, Artificial Intelligence Review 18 (2) (2002) 77–95.

[14] T. Hospedales, A. Antoniou, P. Micaelli, A. Storkey, Meta-learning in neural networks: a survey, arXiv preprint, arXiv:2004.05439, 2020.

[15] C. Finn, P. Abbeel, S. Levine, Model-agnostic meta-learning for fast adaptation of deep networks, in: Proceedings of the 34th International Conference on Machine Learning-Volume 70, JMLR. org, 2017, pp. 1126–1135.

[16] L. Franceschi, P. Frasconi, S. Salzo, R. Grazzi, M. Pontil, Bilevel programming for hyperparameter optimization and meta-learning, in: International Conference on Machine Learning, PMLR, 2018, pp. 1568–1577.

[17] M. Andrychowicz, M. Denil, S. Gomez, M.W. Hoffman, D. Pfau, T. Schaul, B. Shillingford, N. De Freitas, Learning to learn by gradient descent by gradient descent, in: Advances in Neural Information Processing Systems, 2016, pp. 3981–3989.

[18] J. Snell, K. Swersky, R. Zemel, Prototypical networks for few-shot learning, in: Advances in Neural Information Processing Systems, 2017, pp. 4077–4087.

[19] K. Hsu, S. Levine, C. Finn, Unsupervised learning via meta-learning, arXiv preprint, arXiv:1810.02334, 2018.

[20] A. Nagabandi, I. Clavera, S. Liu, R.S. Fearing, P. Abbeel, S. Levine, C. Finn, Learning to adapt in dynamic, real-world environments through meta-reinforcement learning, arXiv preprint, arXiv:1803.11347, 2018.

[21] E. Real, A. Aggarwal, Y. Huang, Q.V. Le, Regularized evolution for image classifier architecture search, in: Proceedings of the Aaai Conference on Artificial Intelligence, vol. 33, 2019, pp. 4780–4789.

[22] H.H.D. Elizabeth A. Weaver II, Cells of the brain, https://www.dana.org/article/cells-of-the-brain/, August 2019.

[23] P.L. De Jager, G. Srivastava, K. Lunnon, J. Burgess, L.C. Schalkwyk, L. Yu, M.L. Eaton, B.T. Keenan, J. Ernst, C. McCabe, et al., Alzheimer's disease: early alterations in brain dna methylation at ank1, bin1, rhbdf2 and other loci, Nature Neuroscience 17 (9) (2014) 1156–1163.

[24] A.T. McKenzie, M. Wang, M.E. Hauberg, J.F. Fullard, A. Kozlenkov, A. Keenan, Y.L. Hurd, S. Dracheva, P. Casaccia, P. Roussos, et al., Brain cell type specific gene expression and co-expression network architectures, Scientific Reports 8 (1) (2018) 1–19.

[25] G.A. Ascoli, D.E. Donohue, M. Halavi, Neuromorpho. org: a central resource for neuronal morphologies, Journal of Neuroscience 27 (35) (2007) 9247–9251.

[26] N.G. Skene, J. Bryois, T.E. Bakken, G. Breen, J.J. Crowley, H.A. Gaspar, P. Giusti-Rodriguez, R.D. Hodge, J.A. Miller, A.B. Muñoz-Manchado, et al., Genetic identification of brain cell types underlying schizophrenia, Nature Genetics 50 (6) (2018) 825–833.

[27] D. Keller, C. Erö, H. Markram, Cell densities in the mouse brain: a systematic review, Frontiers in Neuroanatomy 12 (2018) 83.

[28] G.S. Dhillon, P. Chaudhari, A. Ravichandran, S. Soatto, A baseline for few-shot image classification, in: International Conference on Learning Representations, 2019.

[29] Y. Wang, W.-L. Chao, K.Q. Weinberger, L. van der Maaten, Simpleshot: revisiting nearest-neighbor classification for few-shot learning, arXiv preprint, arXiv:1911.04623, 2019.

[30] Y. Bengio, S. Bengio, J. Cloutier, Learning a Synaptic Learning Rule, Université de Montréal, Département d'informatique et de recherche …, 1990.

[31] S. Bengio, Y. Bengio, J. Cloutier, J. Gecsei, On the optimization of a synaptic learning rule, in: Preprints Conf. Optimality in Artificial and Biological Neural Networks, vol. 2, Univ. of Texas, 1992.

[32] A. Santoro, S. Bartunov, M. Botvinick, D. Wierstra, T. Lillicrap, One-shot learning with memory-augmented neural networks, arXiv preprint, arXiv:1605.06065, 2016.

[33] S. Hochreiter, J. Schmidhuber, Long short-term memory, Neural Computation 9 (8) (1997) 1735–1780.

[34] N. Schweighofer, K. Doya, Meta-learning in reinforcement learning, Neural Networks 16 (1) (2003) 5–9.

[35] G. Koch, R. Zemel, R. Salakhutdinov, Siamese neural networks for one-shot image recognition, in: ICML Deep Learning Workshop, vol. 2, Lille, 2015.

[36] O. Vinyals, C. Blundell, T. Lillicrap, D. Wierstra, et al., Matching networks for one shot learning, Advances in Neural Information Processing Systems 29 (2016) 3630–3638.

[37] S. Hochreiter, A.S. Younger, P.R. Conwell, Learning to learn using gradient descent, in: International Conference on Artificial Neural Networks, Springer, 2001, pp. 87–94.

[38] S. Ravi, H. Larochelle, Optimization as a model for few-shot learning, 2016.

[39] E. Triantafillou, T. Zhu, V. Dumoulin, P. Lamblin, U. Evci, K. Xu, R. Goroshin, C. Gelada, K. Swersky, P.-A. Manzagol, et al., Meta-dataset: a dataset of datasets for learning to learn from few examples, arXiv preprint, arXiv:1903.03096, 2019.

[40] B.M. Lake, R. Salakhutdinov, J.B. Tenenbaum, Human-level concept learning through probabilistic program induction, Science 350 (6266) (2015) 1332–1338.

[41] C. Wah, S. Branson, P. Welinder, P. Perona, S. Belongie, The caltech-ucsd birds-200-2011 dataset, 2011.

[42] D.J. MacKay, Information-based objective functions for active data selection, Neural Computation 4 (4) (1992) 590–604.

[43] A.K. McCallumzy, K. Nigamy, Employing em and pool-based active learning for text classification, in: Proc. International Conference on Machine Learning (ICML), Citeseer, 1998, pp. 359–367.

[44] A.J. Joshi, F. Porikli, N. Papanikolopoulos, Multi-class active learning for image classification, in: 2009 IEEE Conference on Computer Vision and Pattern Recognition, IEEE, 2009, pp. 2372–2379.

[45] X. Li, Y. Guo, Adaptive active learning for image classification, in: Proceedings of the IEEE Conference on Computer Vision and Pattern Recognition, 2013, pp. 859–866.

[46] Y. Gal, Z. Ghahramani, Dropout as a Bayesian approximation: representing model uncertainty in deep learning, in: International Conference on Machine Learning, 2016, pp. 1050–1059.

[47] Y. Gal, R. Islam, Z. Ghahramani, Deep Bayesian active learning with image data, in: Proceedings of the 34th International Conference on Machine Learning-Volume 70, JMLR. org, 2017, pp. 1183–1192.

[48] M. Fang, Y. Li, T. Cohn, Learning how to active learn: a deep reinforcement learning approach, arXiv preprint, arXiv:1708.02383, 2017.

[49] M. Woodward, C. Finn, Active one-shot learning, arXiv preprint, arXiv:1702.06559, 2017.

[50] A. Der Kiureghian, O. Ditlevsen, Aleatory or epistemic? Does it matter?, Structural Safety 31 (2) (2009) 105–112.

[51] A. Kendall, V. Badrinarayanan, R. Cipolla, Bayesian segnet: model uncertainty in deep convolutional encoder-decoder architectures for scene understanding, arXiv preprint, arXiv:1511.02680, 2015.

[52] C.E. Shannon, A mathematical theory of communication, ACM SIGMOBILE Mobile Computing and Communications Review 5 (1) (2001) 3–55.

Few-shot learning for dermatological disease diagnosis[☆]

13

Viraj Prabhu[a], **Anitha Kannan**[b], **Murali Ravuri**[b], **Manish Chablani**[b], **David Sontag**[c], **and Xavier Amatriain**[b]

[a]*Georgia Tech, Atlanta, GA, United States*
[b]*Curai, Palo Alto, CA, United States*
[c]*MIT, Cambridge, MA, United States*

13.1 Introduction

Globally, skin disease is one of the most common human illnesses that affects 30% to 70% of individuals, with even higher rates in at-risk subpopulations where access to care is scarce [19,3,14,12,2]. Untreated or mistreated skin conditions often lead to detrimental effects including physical disability and death [2]. A large fraction of skin conditions are diagnosed and treated at the first point of contact, *i.e.* by primary care practitioners (PCPs), either in a clinical setting or in a telemedicine scenario. While this makes access to care faster, recent studies indicate that general physicians, especially those with limited experience, may not be well-trained for diagnosing many skin conditions [6,10]. Effective solutions to *aid* scale doctors in accurate diagnosis motivate this work.

What makes diagnosis of skin conditions challenging? One important factor is the sheer number of dermatological conditions. The International Classification for human Diseases [1] enumerates more than 1000 skin or skin-related illnesses. However, most PCPs are trained on a few tens of common skin ailments [32]. To make an accurate diagnosis, the knowledge of all possible diseases is important, especially to workup and eliminate potentially life-threatening conditions. The difficulty of diagnosis is further compounded by large intra-class variability (*e.g.* acne may occur on the face, hand, scalp, etc.). To motivate the scale of this problem, see Fig. 13.1, where we show the class distribution of the Dermnet Skin Disease Atlas,[1] a publicly available large-scale dataset of dermatological conditions.

These issues create an opportunity for incorporating machine learning systems into the doctor's workflow, aiding them in sieving through possible skin conditions. AI systems have shown promising results in the healthcare domain, with early applications on automated detection of skin lesions from images (*c.f.* [5]), and diagnosis based on radiology data (*c.f.* [17]).

[☆] Adapted from "Few-shot Learning for Dermatological Disease Diagnosis, Proceedings of the Machine Learning for Healthcare Conference, 2019."

[1] http://www.dermnet.com/.

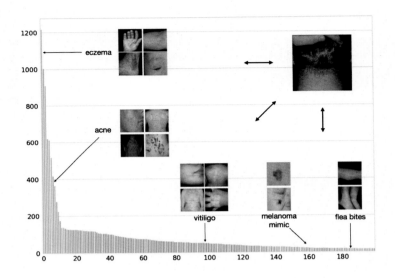

FIGURE 13.1

Long-tailed class distribution of Dermnet (shown here for the top-200 classes). Also shown are nearest neighbors to four of the many prototypes learned for select classes using the proposed Prototypical Clustering Network approach. This is illustrative of the huge intra-class variability in the data. For a novel test image, shown at the upper right corner, the model predicts the correct class by measuring weighted similarity to per-class clusters in the embedding space learned through a deep convolutional neural network.

Inspired by these successes, this paper tackles the problem of fine-grained skin disease classification. We conjecture that a high-fidelity AI system can serve as a diagnostic decision support system to general physicians. By suggesting candidate diagnoses, it can greatly reduce effort and compensate for the possible lack of experience or time at the point of care. In the context of teledermatology with a store-and-forward approach that involves asynchronous evaluation by dermatologists, such a system can aid in triaging the right doctor resource in a timely manner, especially when acute conditions need immediate care [10]. Our primary goal is to design a dermatological diagnosis model amenable to deployment in a primary care setting, that can aid doctors by providing a list of candidate diagnoses. Additionally, we seek to expand the scope of diagnosis to data-poor diseases, as well as diseases exhibiting significant variability in manifestation, in an attempt to improve the coverage, applicability, and cost-effectiveness of such services.

Motivated by the long-tailed and diverse characteristics of dermatological data, we formulate dermatological diagnosis as a *few-shot learning* problem and propose models that can both effectively learn from such data and easily be extended to diagnose new conditions given very few labeled examples. Specifically, our task is to learn a base diagnosis model that, once deployed, can be easily extended to new classes from a few labeled examples (potentially labeled by a physician). To our knowledge, ours is the first work to study the applicability of few-shot learning in assistive diagnosis. Our approach pursues the following objectives:

- **Modeling intra-class variability:** Several conditions contain significant intra-class variability, *e.g.* a condition like acne may occur on the face, back, scalp, etc.
- **Modeling the long-tail.** The data distribution is invariably long tailed. Some conditions are rare and may not have many recorded examples (Fig. 13.1, "melanoma mimic"), while others may be common but easy to diagnose and so not frequently recorded (Fig. 13.1, "flea bites").
- **Learning without forgetting:** The ability to diagnose novel conditions must not compromise the performance on base classes.
- **Privacy preservation:** As access to most dermatological data (usually part of Electronic Health Records) is strictly controlled, the model should not require access to the original (potentially, proprietary) training data when being extended.

Our proposed model, that we call Prototypical Clustering Networks (PCN) [20], extends prior few-shot learning work on Prototypical Networks [26], which have been shown to be a simple and highly effective metric learning formulation to learn from limited data. Specifically, to model the diversity of dermatological data, we represent each class as a mixture of learned representative "prototypes", instead of a single prototype. Training this classifier involves learning an embedding space while simultaneously learning to represent each class by a set of prototypes. Prototypes are initialized for each class via clustering and refined via an online update scheme. Classification is performed by measuring similarity to a weighted combination of prototypes within a class, where the weights are the inferred cluster responsibilities. The examples shown in Fig. 13.1 are, in fact, nearest neighbors to prototypes of the classes learned using the proposed approach. Quantitative results demonstrate the strengths of our approach for dermatological disease diagnosis against strong baselines, and we further provide detailed analyses of the learned representations.

13.2 Related work

Talk about recent derm papers.

Dermatological Classification. A few prior works address the problem of dermatological classification. In [5], authors focus specifically on diagnosing skin cancer, and establish a benchmark on a large closed-source dataset of skin lesions by finetuning a pretrained deep convolutional neural network (CNN). In [18], authors study the problem of skin disease diagnosis on the Dermnet dataset but focus on coarse 23-way classification using its top-level hierarchy. In [27], the authors propose a benchmark dataset for skin disease diagnosis containing 6584 clinical images. In follow up work, [33] propose an approach to learn representations inspired by diagnostic criteria employed by dermatologists on this dataset. In this work, we study fine-grained recognition of skin conditions on the Dermnet dataset which is a significantly larger dermatological resource containing over 23,000 images. Further, we formulate this as a few-shot learning setup, and propose a method to model diverse classes and generalize effectively to previously unseen novel classes with very little labeled data.

Class-imbalanced datasets. Real-world visual datasets frequently possess long tails [29,31,35], and learning robust representations from such data is a topic of active research. Conventional training methods typically lead to poor generalization on tail classes as class-prior statistics are skewed towards the head of the distribution. Simple techniques such as random oversampling (or undersampling) by repeating (or removing) tail instances are found to help mitigate this issue to a degree [4]. Alternative approaches perform meta learning to transfer knowledge from data-rich head classes to the tail [31]. In this work, we propose a few-shot learning approach on a real-world imbalanced dataset of dermatological conditions, and demonstrate strong few-shot generalization capabilities.

Few-shot learning. Few-shot learning aims to learn good class representations given very few training examples [16,25,30,26]. Main paradigms of approaches include simulating data starved environments at training time, and including nonparametric structures in the model as regularizers. Matching networks [30] learn an attention mechanism over support set labels to predict query set labels for novel classes. Prototypical networks [26] jointly learn an embedding and centroid representations (as class *prototypes*), that are used to classify novel examples based on Euclidean distance. In both [30] and [26], embeddings are learned end-to-end and training employs episodic sampling. Some recent approaches learn to directly predict weights for new layers from embedding layer activations of support examples [21,22]. In [9], the motivation is to perform few shot learning 'without forgetting', i.e. extending to novel classes without catastrophic forgetting (also studied as generalized few-shot learning). In [11], authors study few-shot learning by creating an imbalanced few-shot benchmark from ImageNet [24], and propose a method to "hallucinate" additional samples for such data-starved classes. In this work, we focus on a similar setup on the real-world long-tailed Dermnet dataset.

Prototypical Networks. Prior extensions to Prototypical Networks exist in the literature, and here we distinguish our contributions [28,7]. In [28], authors propose extending Prototypical Networks to a semisupervised setting by using unlabeled examples while producing prototypes. In [7], authors propose additionally predicting a covariance estimate for each embedding and using a direction and class dependent distance metric instead of Euclidean distance. In this work, we extend prototypical networks to model multimodal classes in an automated diagnostic setting by learning multiple prototypes per class, that are initialized via clustering and refined via an online update scheme.

13.3 Approach

We formulate dermatological image classification as a low-shot learning problem. During training time, we have access to a labeled dataset of images $S = \{(\mathbf{x}_1, y_1), ..., (\mathbf{x}_N, y_N)\}$ where each x_i is an observation and $y_i \in \{1, ..., K_{base}\}$ is the label mapping to one of the *base* classes known at training time. At test time, we are also provided with a small labeled dataset corresponding to K_{novel} novel classes, and must learn to perform $K_{base+novel}$ way classification.

13.3.1 Model

Prototypical Clustering Networks (PCN) build upon recent work in Prototypical Networks [26]. PCN represents each class using a set of prototypical representations learned from the data. Let $\{\mu_{z,k}\}_{z=1}^{M_k}$ be the collection of M_k prototypes for class k. Then, at test time, we measure similarity to these representations to derive its corresponding class label. In particular,

$$p(y = k|\mathbf{x}) = \frac{\exp(-\sum_z q(z|k, x)d(f_\phi(x), \mu_{z,k}))}{\sum_{k'} \exp(-\sum_z q(z|k, x)d(f_\phi(x), \mu_{z,k'}))} \qquad (13.1)$$

where $f_\phi(x)$ is the embedding function with learnable parameters ϕ that maps input x to a learned representation space, d is a distance function and $q(z|k, x)$ (Eq. (13.2)) is a soft assignment of examples to clusters from the class. When $M_k = 1$ for all classes, we revert to prototypical networks.

13.3.1.1 Model training

Our goal is to learn a model with parameters ϕ so as to maximize the probability of the correct class such that

$\phi^* = \arg\max_\phi \sum_{(\mathbf{x}, y)} \log p(y|\mathbf{x}; \phi) = \arg\min_\phi L_\phi$, where L_ϕ is the corresponding loss function.

We use episodic training [26,30,23] to learn the embedding function by optimizing the loss and updating the cluster prototypes for each class. In particular, a training epoch consists of E episodes. Algorithm 13.1 provides the details of computing the loss for one episode that is used in learning the function.

Class-specific cluster responsibilities: The assignment of an example within a class is given by:

$$q(z|k, x) = \frac{\exp(-d(f_\phi(x), \mu_{z,k})/\tau)}{\sum_{z'} \exp(-d(f_\phi(x), \mu_{z',k})/\tau)}, \tag{13.2}$$

where τ is temperature parameter that controls the variance of the distribution. As we decrease the temperature, the distribution becomes more peaky, and becomes flatter as we increase it.

The importance of τ can be understood by studying the loss function L_ϕ in line 15 of Algorithm 13.1. During training, if clusters are well-separated, $q(z|k, x)$ will be peaky so that each example effectively contributes to the update of a single cluster in a class, whereas if clusters overlap, $q(z|k, x)$ will be diffuse and the corresponding example will contribute to multiple prototypes. Therefore, during training, we typically set τ to favor peaky distributions so that learned clusters focus on different regions of the input space.

Class-specific cluster prototypes: In episodic training, an epoch corresponds to a fixed number of episodes and within each episode, classes are sampled uniformly. In our setting with huge class imbalance, this translates to oversampling examples from the tail and undersampling examples from the head, which can adversely affect model training. To mitigate this, at the start of an epoch, we initialize cluster prototypes for each class using k-means[2] on the learned embedding representation of examples from the entire training set of that class. We rerun this clustering step at the start of each epoch to prevent collapse to using only a single cluster per class.

Subsequently, in each episode, we use an *online* update scheme that balances between the local estimate of the prototype computed from embeddings of the current support set (to account for the evolving embedding space), and the prototypes learned so far:

$$\mu_{z,k}^{new} \leftarrow \alpha \mu_{z,k}^{old} + (1 - \alpha) \frac{\sum_{(x,y) \in S_k} q(z|k, x) f_\phi(x)}{\sum_{(x,y) \in S_k} q(z|k, x)}, \tag{13.3}$$

where α trades off memory from previous episodes and its current estimate.

---

[2] We empirically found using a fixed number of clusters per class to work best. Choosing an optimal number of clusters per class is challenging, largely due to differences in the amount of intra-class variability across classes. In an attempt to bypass this challenge, we experimented with using affinity propagation [8], but found it to be highly unstable as a) the similarity function

---

Algorithm 13.1 Training episode loss computation for Prototypical Clustering Networks. N is the number of examples in the training set, K_{base} is the number of base classes for training, M_k is the number of clusters for class k, $N_C \leq K_{base}$ is the number of classes per episode, N_S is the number of support examples per class, N_Q is the number of query examples per class. RANDOMSAMPLE(S, N) denotes a set of N elements chosen uniformly at random from set S, without replacement. *Differences from Algorithm 1 in [26] in blue (black in print version).*

1: **Input**: Training set $\mathcal{D} = \{(x_1, y_1), \cdots, (x_N, y_N)\}$, where each $y_i \in \{1, \cdots, K\}$. $\mathcal{D}_k$ denotes the sub-set of $\mathcal{D}$ containing all class prototypes, i.e. elements $(x_i, y_i) = \{\mu_{z,k}\}_{z=1}^{M_k} \forall k \in \{1, \cdots, K\}$

2: **Output**: The loss L_ϕ for a randomly generated training episode

3: $V \leftarrow$ RANDOMSAMPLE($\{1, \cdots, K\}, N_C$)   // Select class indices for episode

4: **for** $k \in \{1, \cdots, N_C\}$ **do**

5:     $S_k \leftarrow$ RANDOMSAMPLE($\mathcal{D}_{v_k}, N_S$)   // Select support examples

6:     $Q_k \leftarrow$ RANDOMSAMPLE($\mathcal{D}_{v_k \setminus S_k}, N_Q$)   // Select query examples

7:     // Compute probabilistic assignment of x to y's clusters

8:     **for** $z \in \{1, \cdots, M_k\}$ **do**

9:         **for** $(x, y) \in S_k$ **do**

10:            $q(z|k, x) = \frac{\exp(-d(f_\phi(x), \mu_{z,k})/\tau)}{\sum_{z'} \exp(-d(f_\phi(x), \mu_{z',k})/\tau)}$

11:        **end for**

12:        $\mu_{z,k}^{new} \leftarrow \alpha \mu_{z,k}^{old} + (1 - \alpha) \frac{\sum_{(x,y) \in S_k} q(z|k,x) f_\phi(x)}{\sum_{(x,y) \in S_k} q(z|k,x)}$

13:    **end for**

14: **end for**

15: $L_\phi \leftarrow 0$

16: **for** $k \in \{1, \cdots, N_C\}$ **do**

17:    **for** $(x, y) \in Q_k$ **do**

18:

$$r_{x,y} \leftarrow \sum_z q(z|k, x) d(f_\phi(x), \mu_{z,k})$$
$$+ \log \sum_{k'} \exp(-\sum_{z'} q(z'|k', x) d(f_\phi(x), \mu_{z',k'})) \qquad (13.4)$$

19:        $L_\phi \leftarrow L_\phi + \frac{r_{x,y}}{N_C N_Q}$

20:    **end for**

21: **end for**

13.3.2 Understanding the role of multiple clusters

We can derive insights about the role of multiple clusters by interpreting PCN as a nonlinear generalization of PN [26]. Using squared Euclidean distance in Eq. (13.1), we expand the term in the exponent

---

(needed for clustering) is based on the embedding representation that is optimized concurrently, and b) there is no straightforward online update rule (equivalent to Eq. (13.3)) to subsequently update within an episode.

so that:

$$-\sum_z q(z|k,x)||f_\phi(x) - \mu_{z,k}||^2 = \text{const. for k} + 2\sum_z q(z|k,x)f_\phi(x)^T\mu_{z,k}$$

$$-\sum_z q(z|k,x)\mu_{z,k}^T\mu_{z,k} \tag{13.5}$$

$$= \text{const. for k} + 2w_{k,x}^T f_\phi(x) - b_{k,x}$$

where

$$w_{k,x} = \sum_z q(z|k,x)\mu_{z,k}$$

$$b_{k,x} = \sum_z q(z|k,x)\mu_{z,k}^T\mu_{z,k} \tag{13.6}$$

The last two terms in Eq. (13.5) are nonlinear functions of the data, where the nonlinearity is captured through both the embedding and the mixing variables. The functional forms of the factors, namely $w_{k,x}$ and $b_{k,x}$, also shed light on the advantage of using multiple clusters per class. In particular, unlike in prototypical networks, $w_{k,x}$ is an *example-specific* "prototypical" representation for class k, obtained by using a convex combination of prototypes for the class, weighted by posterior probability over within-class cluster assignments. When $q(z|k,x)$ is confident with a peaky posterior, the model behaves like a regular prototypical network. In contrast, when the posterior has uncertainty, PCN interpolates between the prototypes by modulating $q(z|k,x)$.

13.4 Results
13.4.1 Experimental setup

Dataset: We construct our dataset from the Dermnet Skin Disease Atlas, one of the largest public photo dermatology sources containing over 23,000 images of dermatological conditions. These images are clinical images collected through various sources, including mobile phones, digital cameras, etc. and so vary in pose, lighting, and resolution. Images are annotated at a two level hierarchy – a coarse top-level containing parent 23 categories, and a fine-grained bottom-level containing more than 600 skin conditions. We focus on the more challenging bottom-level hierarchy for our experiments. First, we remove duplicates from the dataset based on name, and also based on collisions found using perceptual image hashing [34].

Fig. 13.1 presents a histogram of the resulting class distribution, filtered to the top-200 classes. We can see that the dataset has a long tail with only the 100 largest classes having more than 50 images; beyond 200 classes, the number of images per class reduces to double digits, and with 300 classes to single digits. Unless otherwise stated, for experimental comparisons, we focus on the top-200 classes so that $K_{base+novel} = 200$, which contains 15,507 images. Similar to [11], we treat the largest 150 classes as base classes ($K_{base} = 150$) and the remaining 50 classes as novel ($K_{novel} = 50$). This helps in ensuring reasonably sized splits for training, validation, and testing. In particular, we sample $max(5, 20\%)$ without replacement for each base class to get validation and test splits (3163 images each). The remaining is used for training (9181 images). For the low-shot learning phase, following the procedure used in [11], we sample 5 examples each for training and testing, respectively. We report mean and standard deviation of metrics over 10 cross validation runs.

Metrics: As our dataset is imbalanced, we report mean of per-class accuracy (mca) as our metric, treating each class as equally important. For a dataset consisting of C classes, with T_c examples in each class, mean accuracy is the average of per-class accuracies: $\text{mca} = \frac{1}{C} \sum_c \frac{\sum_{t=1}^{T_c} I[\hat{y}^{(t)}[0]=y^{(t)}]}{T_k}$, where, for t^{th} example, $\hat{y}^{(t)}[j]$ is the jth top class predicted from a model and $y^{(t)}$ is its corresponding ground truth label, where I denotes the indicator function.

We use $\text{mca}_{base+novel}$ to report combined mca performance of examples from all classes. mca_{base} corresponds to similar $K_{base+novel}$-way evaluation but restricted to test examples from base classes, and mca_{novel} corresponds to evaluation on test examples belonging to novel classes alone.

We also report recall@k ($k \in \{5, 10\}$). Over a test set of size T:

$$\text{recall@k} = \frac{\sum_{t=1}^{T} \sum_{j=1}^{j=K} [\hat{y}^{(t)}[j] = y^{(t)}]}{T}. \tag{13.7}$$

This metric (also called *sensitivity*) is valuable in deployment contexts that involve aiding doctors in diagnosis, as it ensures that the relevant condition is considered within a small range of false positives. However, since our test set is imbalanced, recall@k metrics unfairly reward strong performance on the head classes, and so to provide a fairer comparison, we report *balanced* (or macro) recall@k metrics, wherein we compute recall@k for each class and average, treating each as equally important.

Model: We initialize a 50-layer ResNet-v2 [13], a state-of-the-art convolutional neural network architecture for image classification, with ImageNet pretraining,[3] and train a Prototypical Clustering Network as described in Sec. 13.3 on K_{base} classes. We use 10 and 4 clusters per class for base and novel classes respectively, and a temperature of 1.0 (all picked via grid search).

Baselines

- Prototypical Network (PN): We train an ImageNet-pretrained ResNet-V2 CNN as a Prototypical Network [26] on K_{base} classes.
- Finetuned Resnet with nearest neighbor (FT_K-*NN): Here, we finetune an ImageNet-pretrained ResNet-v2 convolutional neural network with 50 layers [13] on training data from K classes. We report numbers for $K \in \{K_{base}, K_{base+novel}\}$. The model is trained as a softmax classifier with a standard cross entropy objective. Then, we obtain embeddings for the entire training set consisting of $K_{base+novel}$ classes, followed by *-nearest neighbor classification on the test set belonging to $K_{base+novel}$ classes.
- Finetuned ResNet (FT_K-CE): We use the same ResNet model as above, with $K = K_{base+novel}$, i.e. trained for $K_{base+novel}$ way classification using training data from both base and novel classes, and validated using the corresponding validation set on the base classes alone (due to lack of data in novel classes). We train the model with class balancing. This is a strong baseline as we use all $K_{base+novel}$ during training, and also due to class balancing, which has been shown to be an effective strategy for training CNN models in the presence of class imbalance [4].

---

[3] We also experimented with training from scratch, and found it to perform significantly worse.

Table 13.1 Mean per-class accuracy (MCA) on top 200 classes. We focus on the low-shot setting, using all training data for the base classes (the largest 150) and $n = 5$ or 10 examples for the remaining 50 classes (denoted as "novel"). Note that FT_{200}-CE and FT_{200}-*NN use training data for all 200 classes, whereas others use only the base classes for representation learning, using support sets from novel classes after training to directly derive prototypes.

Approach	$n = 5$			$n = 10$		
	$mca_{base+novel}$	mca_{base}	mca_{novel}	$mca_{base+novel}$	mca_{base}	mca_{novel}
FT_{150}-1NN	46.2 ± 0.8	55.3 ± 0.3	18.8 ± 3.3	49.5 ± 0.3	54.9 ± 0.5	33.4 ± 1.4
FT_{150}-3NN	44.3 ± 0.3	54.8 ± 0.5	12.8 ± 1.5	47.0 ± 0.6	54.1 ± 0.4	25.6 ± 1.5
FT_{200}-1NN	46.5 ± 0.4	54.2 ± 0.3	22.5 ± 0.8	49.9 ± 0.5	53.8 ± 0.4	38.3 ± 1.3
FT_{200}-3NN	44.7 ± 0.4	52.6 ± 0.2	20.9 ± 2.0	48.0 ± 0.1	52.5 ± 0.1	34.3 ± 0.2
FT_{200}-CE	$\mathbf{47.8 \pm 0.5}$	$\mathbf{55.8 \pm 0.7}$	24.0 ± 3.2	$\mathbf{51.5 \pm 0.4}$	$\mathbf{55.2 \pm 0.3}$	40.4 ± 2.4
PN	43.9 ± 0.4	48.7 ± 0.4	29.6 ± 2.4	44.9 ± 0.8	47.6 ± 0.4	37.1 ± 3.4
PCN (ours)	$\mathbf{47.8 \pm 0.7}$	53.7 ± 0.2	$\mathbf{30.0 \pm 2.8}$	50.9 ± 0.6	51.4 ± 0.3	$\mathbf{49.6 \pm 2.8}$

Hyperparameters: For PN and PCN, we use episodic batching with 10-way 10-shot classification (at train), and 200 episodes per epoch. At test, we compute per-class prototypes using the training set for all $K_{base+novel}$ classes, and perform $K_{base+novel}$ way classification. The embedding function for PCN and PN produces 256-dimensional embeddings, and uses the same architecture as in FT_K-CE (with one less fully connected layer). Models are trained with early stopping using Adam [15], a learning rate of 10^{-4}, and L2 weight decay of 10^{-5}.

13.4.2 Main results

Table 13.1 highlights our main MCA results. The table shows test set MCA over the 200 classes available during test time for two different low shot settings: train shots of 5 and 10 with test shot of 5. In both low shot settings, we observe the following trends:

▷ FT_K-CE and PCN share similar performance on combined MCA. However, their performance on base and novel classes is quite distinct. Much of the performance gains for FT_K-CE come from the base classes that have a lot more training examples than novel classes. In contrast, PCN, through episodic training aims at learning discriminative feature representations that are generalizable to novel classes with highly constrained numbers of examples; this is evident by its significantly better performance (9% absolute gains) in generalizing to novel classes. At the same time, PCN ensures that performance on novel classes does not come at the cost of lower accuracy on base classes. Also note that the FT_K-CE model requires re-training for adding novel classes while PCN only requires a single forward pass to learn prototypes for novel classes.

▷ FT_K-*NN models learn robust representations for base classes, but are unable to generalize to novel classes, outperforming a regular PN model on top-200 MCA but underperforming against PCN. Interestingly, we find that increasing the number of nearest neighbors leads to poor performance, especially on novel classes. This could be due to sparsity of training data.

▷ PCN outperforms PN on combined base and novel classes by a large margin. This demonstrates that representing classes with multiple prototypes leads to better generalization on both base and novel classes. In Fig. 13.2, we show the nearest neighbor to class prototype for PN and to four of the PCN

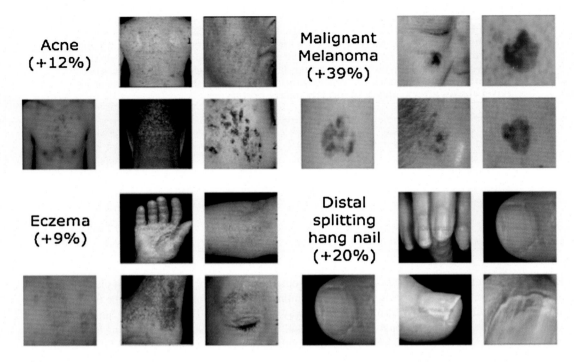

FIGURE 13.2

Learned prototypes shown using their nearest neighbors in the training set. Each condition is displayed in a 2 × 3 grid; The image below the name of the condition corresponds to PN, while the 2 × 2 grid to its right corresponds to nearest neighbors of four (randomly selected) cluster prototypes. +X% below the name denotes $mca_{base+novel}$ improvement of PCN over PN for that class. Note that novel classes such as 'Distal splitting hang nail' can also be diverse, as shown by clusters identified with PCN.

prototypes, for select classes. We can see that PCN has learned to model intra-class variability much more effectively. As an example, for eczema and acne classes we can see that PCN learns clusters corresponding to these skin conditions in different anatomical regions. We provide a more in-depth comparison in the next section.

In Table 13.2 we report balanced recall@k (br@k) performance. Here we clearly find PCN to outperform all baselines owing to strong performance across the board on base and novel classes.

13.4.3 Comparison between PCN and PN

PCN or PN with posthoc clustering? To understand the effectiveness of PCN, we compare it to a PN model with which we perform "posthoc" clustering: (a) cluster novel class representations using the PN model's learned embeddings (with cluster size of 4) (b) cluster both base and novel class representations (with cluster size of 10 and 4, as in PCN). Rows 1-3 in Table 13.3 compare the performance between different posthoc clustering variants of PN against PCN. We see that PCN leads in all metrics across

Table 13.2 Balanced Recall@k on top 200 classes.

	Approach	$br@5_{base+novel}$	$br@5_{base}$	$br@5_{novel}$	$br@10_{base+novel}$	$br@10_{base}$	$br@10_{novel}$
n=5	FT_{200}-CE	65.4 ± 0.7	74.6 ± 0.2	38.0 ± 2.1	73.1 ± 0.5	82.3 ± 0.2	45.3 ± 1.5
	PN	66.5 ± 0.6	67.6 ± 0.2	$\mathbf{63.2 \pm 2.3}$	75.3 ± 0.5	74.9 ± 0.1	$\mathbf{76.3 \pm 2.1}$
	PCN (ours)	$\mathbf{70.7 \pm 0.6}$	$\mathbf{74.5 \pm 0.2}$	59.2 ± 2.6	$\mathbf{79.1 \pm 1.0}$	$\mathbf{81.4 \pm 0.3}$	72.2 ± 3.6
n=10	FT_{200}-CE	69.9 ± 0.5	$\mathbf{73.8 \pm 0.6}$	58.0 ± 3.2	77.9 ± 0.6	81.9 ± 0.2	65.9 ± 2.6
	PN	67.5 ± 0.4	66.0 ± 0.3	72.2 ± 1.7	75.9 ± 0.6	72.9 ± 0.3	$\mathbf{84.7 \pm 2.2}$
	PCN (ours)	$\mathbf{71.4 \pm 0.7}$	70.4 ± 0.2	$\mathbf{74.5 \pm 2.6}$	$\mathbf{79.9 \pm 0.5}$	78.2 ± 0.2	$\mathbf{85.0 \pm 2.0}$

Table 13.3 Does posthoc clustering on PN help?

Model	Eval CPC (base / novel)	$mca_{base+novel}$	mca_{base}	mca_{novel}	recall@5	recall@10
PN	1 / 1	43.9 ± 0.4	48.7 ± 0.4	29.6 ± 2.4	70.9 ± 0.4	80.2 ± 0.3
PN	1 / 4	44.4 ± 0.5	50.4 ± 0.4	26.4 ± 2.3	74.2 ± 0.2	83.5 ± 0.3
PN	10 / 4	43.8 ± 0.8	50.3 ± 0.2	24.2 ± 3.0	75.6 ± 0.2	84.0 ± 0.2
PCN (ours)	10 / 4	$\mathbf{47.8 \pm 0.7}$	$\mathbf{53.7 \pm 0.2}$	$\mathbf{30.0 \pm 2.8}$	$\mathbf{77.8 \pm 0.2}$	$\mathbf{86.0 \pm 0.4}$

the board; thus such posthoc clustering does not lead to improved performance. A reason for this is that the PN model is optimized to learn representations assuming a projection to a single cluster for each class, and hence clustering on such learned representation does not improve performance. This further validates the importance of training with multiple clusters.

Varying test shot: Table 13.4 highlights the effect of number of support examples (shot). As we increase the shot, the performance improves on both methods, but that improvement is larger for PCN than for PN. Because of this, the performance gap between the two methods drastically increases. PCN is better at utilizing the availability of more data by partitioning the space with clusters.

Extending the tail: We now vary the number of novel classes at test time from 50 to 150, bringing the total number of classes up from 200 to 300. Table 13.4 reports results. We use a train and test shot of 2 and 5 respectively, as tail classes are extremely sparse. Results are reported with 10-fold cross validation. While there is a drop in performance for both models due to small shot sizes, we can see that the performance gap between PCN and PN continues to hold.

Table 13.4 Extending Shot, Tail.

		PN	PCN
Shot	2	42.26	45.36
	5	44.35	47.79
	10	44.93	50.92
K	200	42.26	45.58
	250	37.08	40.37
	300	34.70	37.67

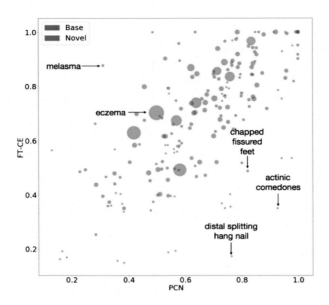

FIGURE 13.3

Comparison between FT_{200}-CE and PCN: Per-class accuracy. Each class is denoted by a dot and the area of dot is proportional to the number of training examples for the class.

13.5 Per-class accuracy

In Fig. 13.3 we provide a class-wise performance comparison on the Dermnet dataset between the PCN and FT_{200}-CE models as a scatter plot (shown here for the best performing PCN model evaluated with a train shot of 10 with mca$_{base+novel}$ = 50.92).

We make the following observations: Overall metrics indicate that FT_{200}-CE demonstrates slightly stronger average performance on base classes. For a large fraction of the base classes, both methods have similar performance. For the ones in which PCN performance is lower, there is usually a reasonable lower bound on the classification accuracy. In contrast, for novel classes, PCN performs better on average. Importantly, when FT_{200}-CE performance is lower than PCN, it is usually significantly lower. As an example is the novel class 'distal splitting hang nail' for which PCN performs significantly better.

13.6 Role of hyperparameters

Importance of Temperature: Table 13.5b reports performance by varying $\Delta_\tau = \tau_{test} - \tau_{train}$, the difference in temperature used in test versus train time. We can see that while performance is agnostic for base classes, higher interpolation through an increased temperature leading to $\Delta_\tau > 0$ leads to

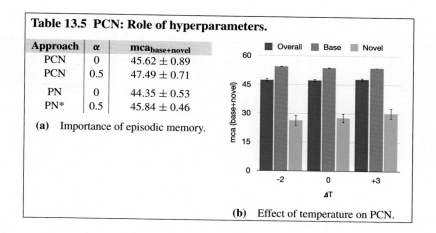

Table 13.5 PCN: Role of hyperparameters.

Approach	α	$mca_{base+novel}$
PCN	0	45.62 ± 0.89
PCN	0.5	47.49 ± 0.71
PN	0	44.35 ± 0.53
PN*	0.5	45.84 ± 0.46

(a)   Importance of episodic memory.

(b)   Effect of temperature on PCN.

improved performance on novel classes. Conversely, when $\Delta_\tau < 0$, performance drops. This suggests that at inference time, the model requires interpolating between the cluster prototypes to effectively predict a class label.

Does episodic memory help? Table 13.5a shows that we can get improvements even with a simple online update rule that blends prototypes computed using the support set in the current episode with the past, using $\alpha = 0.5$. This trend is also seen for prototypical networks (denoted by PN*). We leave as future work the task of modeling adaptive α.

13.6.1 Qualitative results

Fig. 13.4 provides qualitative examples comparing the three methods. Consider column 1. Acne is one of the largest classes in the base classes with large intra-class variability. Both FT_{200}-CE and PCN can diagnose this example correctly. However, PN due to its limited capacity to represent the huge variability in the class is confused with another large class, eczema. PCN, due to having access to multiple clusters can learn a better representation and correctly diagnose acne. The last two columns correspond to novel classes.

Effectiveness of multiple clusters. In Sec. 13.3, we show how PCN can interpolate between the learned prototypes by modulating $q(z|c, x)$. In Fig. 13.6 we show some qualitative examples to illustrate this. We show query images from the test set for various classes, with a mix of correct and incorrectly classified examples. Below the class label, we show the nearest neighbor image from the training set to each of the learned prototypes for the class *predicted* by PCN, and below each query image, cluster responsibilities placed by the model on each of these prototypes. As an example, consider Fig. 13.6(a). This example (acne) is correctly classified by PCN. Interestingly, Fig. 13.6(a), the model appears to interpolate between two prototypes that are similar to the query image in pose and skin texture respectively to make its prediction. We can see that the $q(z|c, x)$ distribution varies quite a bit across examples, being a lot more diffuse in some cases than others. It can also be seen that the model learns to accurate place probability mass on similar prototypes.

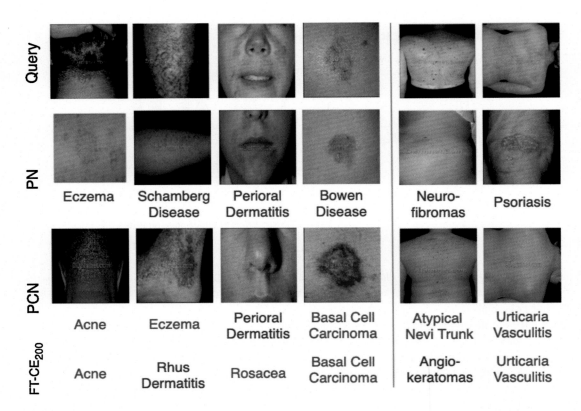

FIGURE 13.4

We compare PCN with PN and FT_{200}-CE on query images from the test set. For each image, we color code correct predictions in green and incorrect predictions in red. For PN, we show the nearest neighbor to the prototype of the predicted class. Similarly, for PCN, we show the nearest neighbor of the *top cluster* according to $q(z|c, x)$ of the predicted class. The last two columns correspond to examples from novel classes.

Fig. 13.6(c), (d)(bottom) shows incorrectly predicted examples; Even for these examples, the model seems to interpolate, albeit incorrectly, to make predictions. Note that Fig. 13.6(d) corresponds to examples from novel classes. Such visualizations lend a degree of interpretability to the model's decision process.

In Fig. 13.5, we provide additional qualitative examples of how PCN can interpolate between the learned prototypes by modulating $q(z|c, x)$. We can see that the $q(z|c, x)$ distribution varies quite a bit across examples, being a lot more diffuse in some cases than others. For instance, while classes in the first row see relatively diffuse responsibility distributions, the distribution is far more peaked for the varicella class in (d). Overall, it can be seen that the model learns to accurately place probability mass on similar prototypes. Fig. 13.5(c) shows an incorrectly predicted example. In Fig. 13.5(e), we show similar examples for novel classes.

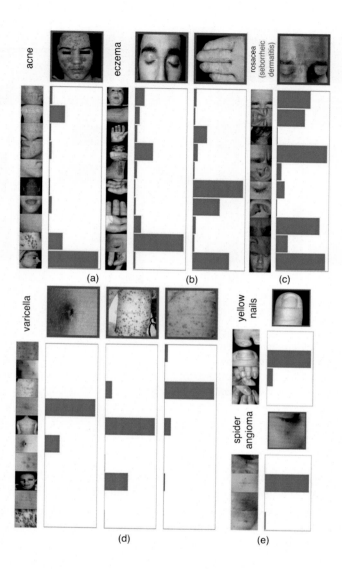

FIGURE 13.5

Effectiveness of using multiple clusters. Shown for base and novel classes. (a), (b), (d), (e): Examples from test set that are correctly classified by PCN. For each class, we show the nearest neighbor to the learned prototypes. We also present examples (columns) whose labels are correctly predicted and the inferred cluster responsibilities $q(z|c, x)$ conditioned on the correct class. (c): Test set example that is misclassified by PCN. Correct label is shown in black, while the incorrect prediction is shown in red. We show the nearest neighbors to the learned cluster prototypes of the *predicted* (incorrect) class, and the corresponding cluster responsibilities. Note that green outlines around query images denote correct classification while red denotes incorrect classification. (e) corresponds to novel classes.

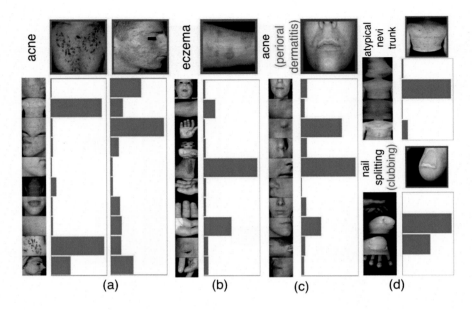

FIGURE 13.6

Effectiveness of using multiple clusters (continued). Shown for base and novel classes. For each class, we show the nearest neighbor to the learned prototypes of the class *predicted* by PCN, as well as inferred cluster responsibilities $q(z|c, x)$ conditioned on the prediction. (a)-(b): Correctly classified test examples. (c): "Acne" test example misclassified as "perioral dermatitis" (d): Test examples corresponding to novel classes.

13.7 Conclusion

We propose Prototypical Clustering Networks, a few shot learning approach to dermatological image classification. This method is scalable to novel classes, and can effectively capture intra-class variability. We observe that our approach outperforms strong baselines on this task, especially on the long tail of the data distribution. Such a machine learning system can be a valuable aid to medical providers, and improve access, equity, quality, and cost-effectiveness of healthcare.

There exist a number of future directions worth pursuing. The true utility of our system is in aiding the physician, and this requires studies that include such a deployment. Other extensions include determining the absence of any condition (adding *i.e.* a 'normal' class), and controlling for demographic variables when appropriate. Another interesting direction would be to incorporate additional modalities of data for more robust diagnosis. Further, while our approach learns features end to end, a natural alternative would be to fuse such learned representations with features designed using domain expertise, such as diagnostic markers and patient symptoms that are typically tracked by dermatologists. Incorporating such medical symptoms into the classification task will be another interesting direction of future work.

References

[1] World health organization, Diseases of the skin and subcutaneous tissue, in: International Statistical Classification of Diseases and Related Health Problems, 2004, Chapter xii.

[2] M. Basra, M. Shahrukh, Burden of skin diseases, Expert Review Pharmacoeconomics Outcomes Research (2009).

[3] D. Bickers, H. Lim, D. Margolis, The burden of skin diseases: 2004 a joint project of the American academy of dermatology association and the society for investigative dermatology, Journal of American Academy Dermatology (2006).

[4] M. Buda, A. Maki, M.A. Mazurowski, A systematic study of the class imbalance problem in convolutional neural networks, Neural Networks 106 (2018) 249–259.

[5] A. Esteva, B. Kuprel, R.A. Novoa, J. Ko, S.M. Swetter, H.M. Blau, S. Thrun, Dermatologist-level classification of skin cancer with deep neural networks, Nature 542 (7639) (2017) 115.

[6] D. Federman, J. Concato, R. Kirsner, Comparison of dermatologic diagnoses by primary care practitioners and dermatologists. A review of the literature, Archives of Family Medicine 8 (2) (1999).

[7] S. Fort, Gaussian prototypical networks for few-shot learning on omniglot, arXiv preprint, arXiv:1708.02735, 2017.

[8] B.J. Frey, D. Dueck, Clustering by passing messages between data points, Science 315 (2007) 2007.

[9] S. Gidaris, N. Komodakis, Dynamic few-shot visual learning without forgetting, in: Proceedings of the IEEE Conference on Computer Vision and Pattern Recognition, 2018, pp. 4367–4375.

[10] E.E. Goldman, Skin diseases get misdiagnosed in primary care, Family Practice News (2007).

[11] B. Hariharan, R.B. Girshick, Low-shot visual recognition by shrinking and hallucinating features, in: ICCV, 2017, pp. 3037–3046.

[12] R. Hay, L. Fuller, The assessment of dermatological needs in resource-poor regions, International Journal of Dermatology (2012).

[13] K. He, X. Zhang, S. Ren, J. Sun, Deep residual learning for image recognition, in: Proceedings of the IEEE Conference on Computer Vision and Pattern Recognition, 2016, pp. 770–778.

[14] J.K. Scholfield, D. Grindlay, H. Williams, Skin Conditions in the UK: A Health Needs Assessment, University of Nottingham, Centre of Evidence Based Dermatology UK, Nottingham, UK, 2009.

[15] D.P. Kingma, J. Ba, Adam: a method for stochastic optimization, arXiv preprint, arXiv:1412.6980, 2014.

[16] G. Koch, R. Zemel, R. Salakhutdinov, Siamese neural networks for one-shot image recognition, in: ICML Deep Learning Workshop, vol. 2, 2015.

[17] Z. Li, C. Wang, M. Han, Y. Xue, W. Wei, L. Li, F. Li, Thoracic disease identification and localization with limited supervision, in: IEEE Computer Vision and Pattern Recognition, 2018.

[18] H. Liao, A Deep Learning Approach to Universal Skin Disease Classification, University of Rochester Department of Computer Science, CSC, 2016.

[19] NHANES, Skin Conditions and Related Need for Medical Care Among Persons 1–74 Years, NHANES, United States, 1978.

[20] V. Prabhu, A. Kannan, M. Ravuri, M. Chaplain, D. Sontag, X. Amatriain, Few-shot learning for dermatological disease diagnosis, in: Machine Learning for Healthcare Conference, PMLR, 2019, pp. 532–552.

[21] H. Qi, M. Brown, D.G. Lowe, Low-shot learning with imprinted weights, in: Proceedings of the IEEE Conference on Computer Vision and Pattern Recognition, 2018, pp. 5822–5830.

[22] S. Qiao, C. Liu, W. Shen, A. Yuille, Few-shot image recognition by predicting parameters from activations, arXiv preprint, arXiv:1706.03466, 2017, 2.

[23] S. Ravi, H. Larochelle, Optimization as a model for few-shot learning, 2016.

[24] O. Russakovsky, J. Deng, H. Su, J. Krause, S. Satheesh, S. Ma, Z. Huang, A. Karpathy, A. Khosla, M. Bernstein, et al., Imagenet large scale visual recognition challenge, International Journal of Computer Vision 115 (3) (2015) 211–252.

[25] A. Santoro, S. Bartunov, M. Botvinick, D. Wierstra, T. Lillicrap, One-shot learning with memory-augmented neural networks, arXiv preprint, arXiv:1605.06065, 2016.

[26] J. Snell, K. Swersky, R. Zemel, Prototypical networks for few-shot learning, in: Advances in Neural Information Processing Systems, 2017, pp. 4077–4087.

[27] X. Sun, J. Yang, M. Sun, K. Wang, A benchmark for automatic visual classification of clinical skin disease images, in: European Conference on Computer Vision, Springer, 2016, pp. 206–222.

[28] E. Triantafillou, H. Larochelle, J. Snell, J. Tenenbaum, K.J. Swersky, M. Ren, R. Zemel, S. Ravi, Meta-learning for semi-supervised few-shot classification, 2018.

[29] G. Van Horn, P. Perona, The devil is in the tails: fine-grained classification in the wild, arXiv preprint, arXiv: 1709.01450, 2017.

[30] O. Vinyals, C. Blundell, T. Lillicrap, D. Wierstra, et al., Matching networks for one shot learning, in: Advances in Neural Information Processing Systems, 2016, pp. 3630–3638.

[31] Y.-X. Wang, D. Ramanan, M. Hebert, Learning to model the tail, in: Advances in Neural Information Processing Systems, 2017, pp. 7029–7039.

[32] E. Wilmer, C. Gustafson, C. Ahn, S. Davis, S. Feldman, W. Huang, Most common dermatologic conditions encountered by dermatologists and nondermatologists, Cutis 94 (6) (2014).

[33] J. Yang, X. Sun, J. Liang, P.L. Rosin, Clinical skin lesion diagnosis using representations inspired by dermatologist criteria, in: Proceedings of the IEEE Conference on Computer Vision and Pattern Recognition, 2018, pp. 1258–1266.

[34] C. Zauner, Implementation and benchmarking of perceptual image hash functions, 2010.

[35] X. Zhu, D. Anguelov, D. Ramanan, Capturing long-tail distributions of object subcategories, in: Proceedings of the IEEE Conference on Computer Vision and Pattern Recognition, 2014, pp. 915–922.

Knowledge-guided meta learning for disease prediction

14

Qiuling Suo, Hyun Jae Cho, Jingyuan Chou, Stefan Bekiranov, Chongzhi Zang, and Aidong Zhang

University of Virginia, Charlottesville, VA, United States

14.1 Introduction

In many biomedical application scenarios, labeling data can be very expensive and time consuming, making the number of training data points extremely limited. For example, in the task of disease prediction, as shown in Fig. 14.1, the prevalence of many diseases in the population can be very low. We need to learn predictive information from small datasets, and predict which type of diseases the incoming patients may suffer from, in order to improve the chance of curing them. The data scarcity issue in various fields, especially the healthcare area, brings a critical challenge in the development of machine learning algorithms.

Few-shot learning [2], which learns new concepts and recognizes new categories with limited annotations, has attracted great interest of the community in recent years. Meta learning [3], which is to acquire task-shared knowledge across multiple tasks, has emerged as a major direction to deal with the few-shot learning problem. Meta learning learns transferable knowledge from multiple training tasks, and rapidly adapts to a new condition with a few examples. In contrast, traditional learning, which focuses on one particular task, for example, breast cancer diagnosis, every instance will be composed of features which describe one patient in a way that facilitates a machine learning algorithm to classify whether someone has breast cancer or not. Meta learning occurs over multiple tasks, so the questions shift from predicting if a new patient has cancer or not to what is the best algorithm to predict if a patient has cancer or not (algorithm selection); or how to optimize the performance of a parameterized algorithm of cancer detection.

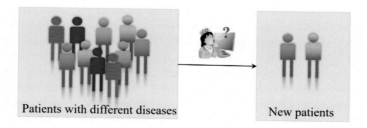

Patients with different diseases New patients

FIGURE 14.1

Disease classification. Limited diagnosed patients are available.

Meta Learning With Medical Imaging and Health Informatics Applications. https://doi.org/10.1016/B978-0-32-399851-2.00023-5

Compared to regular transfer learning [4,5,6,7,8,9,10,11,12] which minimizes loss of training tasks and further optimizes the learned model on testing tasks, meta learning focuses on enabling the model to have the potential/ability to be generalized well on target tasks. Intuitively, transfer learning can well optimize training tasks, but lacks the ability to generalize well on testing tasks with a few data available. Domain adaptation [13] enables knowledge transfer by minimizing the discrepancy between source and target data distributions. Although unsupervised domain adaptation does not require label information in the target domain, it still requires a number of target data examples to learn the distribution of the target domain, and, thus, has limited performance when only a few target examples are available. Therefore, meta learning is considered a promising solution to handle limited data in real-world applications.

With the prevalence of meta learning, promising results of meta learning based approaches have been reported in various fields, such as natural language processing [14], computer vision [15], recommendation systems [16,17] and spatial-temporal prediction [18]. In the healthcare domain, several papers [19] have applied meta learning to predict the risk of target diseases with limited data samples from patient health records and have shown promising results of meta learning in healthcare compared with training on limited samples directly. However, there are still some important fields in healthcare where few-shot learning is needed but under-explored, such as cancer prediction. The collection of TCGA pan-cancer benchmark dataset [1] provides a data resource for meta learning techniques to test their capability to make use of the interrelated clinical tasks of gene-expression data to learn effective classification models despite the small sample size of each individual task.

In general, the meta learning methods learn global initialization, metric or optimizers, and implicitly assume that the globally shared information can be transferred across all tasks. However, task distributions can be diverse, and it is difficult to find a global condition that is the desired metric space or can be quickly adapted to the desired parameters for all tasks. If the underlying data distributions are significantly different among tasks, globally shared knowledge may not make positive contributions. This problem is known as task heterogeneity. Many recent advances in meta learning to handle the task heterogeneity problem are about learning task embeddings by aggregating data examples within a task [20,21,22] or using handcrafted relationship structure, such as clustering algorithms [23]. The key idea of these methods is to customize the global parameters with task-specific conditioning. However, these methods rely purely on data itself to learn task relations. When there are only a few, highly heterogeneous, data examples of each task which overlap across tasks, it can be difficult to learn accurate task relationships. Therefore, our proposed solution is to use external knowledge to effectively capture and utilize task relationships in meta learning.

In this chapter, we explore and propose meta learning solutions for healthcare problems. In particular, we first explore the effectiveness of the popular meta learning method MAML [24] on TCGA pan-cancer dataset, including genomic, proteomic and clinical data. Our experiments show that MAML with the modified base learner outperforms traditional machine learning algorithms in the few-shot learning setting, paving the way to build models that can classify rare cancer subtypes with high accuracy. We will also experimentally demonstrate that meta learning outperforms the conventional transfer learning in prediction problems. Furthermore, we propose a task-adaptive meta learning framework that incorporates a domain-knowledge graph and promotes metaknowledge customization for heterogeneous tasks. The data representations are enriched by aggregating the information from their neighboring classes, and task relationships are captured by message passing the graph. Our experiments show the effectiveness of the proposed method over various meta learning approaches. We also show that our method can be effectively applied to a disease classification problem by incorporating domain knowledge, specifically, disease ontology.

14.2 **Related work**

Meta learning approaches for the few-shot learning problem mainly include optimization-based methods [24,25,26,27,28] and metric-based methods [29,20,30,31]. Metric-based approaches focus on learning a single generalizable embedding function shared by all tasks to directly measure data distances of all tasks in a common metric space. For example, Matching Network [31] integrates metric learning with meta learning for the first time by training a learnable nearest neighbor classifier with deep neural networks. Prototypical Network [29] utilizes class prototype representations to assign labels for query points and formulates the final loss function with Euclidean distance directly. Relation Network [32] trains an auxiliary network to compute the similarity score between each query and the support set, which is equivalent to further learn a nonlinear metric. These approaches assume all samples are embedded into a task-agnostic metric space.

While metric-based meta learning aims to directly measure data distances of all tasks in a common metric space, optimization-based meta learning mainly uses a gradient-based method which employs a bilevel learning framework where metaknowledge is used for within-task parameter adaptions. For example, MAML [24], tries to learn a good model parameter initialization strategy that generalizes better to similar tasks. Similarly, Reptile [25] is an approximation of MAML that executes stochastic gradient descent with a first-order form. MetaSGD goes further in meta learning by arguing to learn the weights' initialization, gradient update direction and learning rate within a single step.

To generalize the meta learning scheme over tasks, recent works leverage task-specific information to tailor the shared knowledge for each task. These approaches have shown the benefits of encoding task information to customize the initial parameters or metric space. For example, [20] learns a task-dependent metric space by scaling and shifting the feature extractors conditioned on the task sample set. [22] generates functional weights for the target prediction network of each task. [33] linearly projects sample embeddings to a task adaptive space, and calculates the distance metric in the projection space. [26] enables a metalearner to learn on each layer's activation space, so that task-specific learners perform gradient descent on their corresponding subspaces. [21] modulates the metalearned prior parameters according to the mode of each task sampled from a multimodal task distribution. These approaches have shown the benefits of customizing task-specific representations compared to the globally shared parameters. However, they ignore the relationships between tasks, which may limit the model expressiveness. Considering task-relatedness, [23] proposes to cluster tasks into several states through hierarchical clustering, and trigger the initialization of each task through a cluster-specific parameter gate; and [34] constructs a metaknowledge graph to extract cross-task relations. The two methods learn task relationship from the training data but ignore the inherent relationship expressed by external knowledge.

Most recent meta learning studies in the biomedical field lie in image classification and drug discovery. Progresses in the medical domain are especially relevant given the global shortage of pathologists. In [35], MAML is adapted to weakly-supervised breast cancer detection tasks, and the order of tasks is selected according to a curriculum rather than randomly. MAML has also been combined with denoising autoencoders to do medical visual question answering [36], while learning to weigh support samples is adapted to pixel-wise weighting in order to tackle skin lesion segmentation tasks that have noisy labels [37]. Considering pan-cancer prediction, [38] provides an initiative to develop meta learning techniques that make use of interrelated clinical tasks using genomic data to learn effective classification models. Continuing the effort of few-shot learning, we apply MAML with specific base learner modified for each training task, and randomly generate a series of tasks with limited samples to simulate the few-shot setting, in order to investigate the effectiveness of meta learning on cancer prediction.

14.3 Analysis of meta learning on TCGA data

In this section, we describe a MAML-based approach with a modified base learner and make a comparison between traditional machine learning methods and meta learning family methods for TCGA pan-cancer prediction. More details can be found in our paper [39].

14.3.1 Modified MAML for pan-cancer prediction

In the meta learning setting, there are a series of training tasks $\{\mathcal{T}_1, \mathcal{T}_2, \mathcal{T}_3, ...\}$ sampled from the task distribution $p(\mathcal{T})$. In each task $\mathcal{T}_i \sim p(\mathcal{T})$, it contains a set of support examples $\mathcal{D}_i^{tr}$ and query examples $\mathcal{D}_i^{te}$. The support set contains N classes randomly selected from the metadataset and K examples of each class (the so called N-way K-shot setting). In the training phase, the query set contains unseen examples from the same classes in the support set, and the labels are to be learned. The parameters θ of the base-learner, which is the backbone prediction model, will be adapted on the support set of a training task within a fixed number of steps and updated on the corresponding query set, then passed to the next task of a batch of training tasks until the iteration ends. Through the above metatraining phase, the initialization θ is obtained and will be fine-tuned using a few examples from testing tasks. A testing task $\mathcal{T}_{test}$ also contains a support set and a query set, with novel classes that are different from the training phase. It is expected that the θ can reach an optimum through training a few support examples from the testing task. In cancer prediction, we aim to train a predictive model that can quickly adapt to a new task that contains unseen cancer types with a few patient examples and can make predictions for undiagnosed patients. To achieve this goal, we explore the effectiveness of a popular meta learning framework named MAML [24] on the TCGA dataset, since MAML can relax the requirements on the specific base model architecture and thus is applicable to different choices of the base model.

The overall procedure is illustrated in Fig. 14.2. Suppose that each task is to identify whether the patients have a specific cancer or not. In Fig. 14.2, the training tasks $\mathcal{T}_1$, $\mathcal{T}_2$, and $\mathcal{T}_3$ are to diagnose BRCA (Breast cancer), LUAD (Lung Adenocarcinoma), and GBM (Glioblastoma Multiforme) respectively. After meta learning, the optimized parameters θ are adapted to new tasks in the testing set, including diagnosis of KIRC (Kidney Renal Clear Cell Carcinoma) and HNSC (Head and Neck Squamous Cell Carcinoma). Details of the meta learning process are as below.

Consider a base learner model f_θ parameterized by θ. For a training task $\mathcal{T}_i$, its support set $\mathcal{D}_i^{tr}$ is used to adapt θ to θ_i' through a few gradient descent steps, and its query set $\mathcal{D}_i^{te}$ is used to evaluate the generalization performance of the adapted parameters θ_i' and to update the initial parameters θ. We use $\mathcal{L}_{\mathcal{T}_i}$ to denote the prediction loss of task $\mathcal{T}_i$. For each task, the model parameters θ are adapted via one

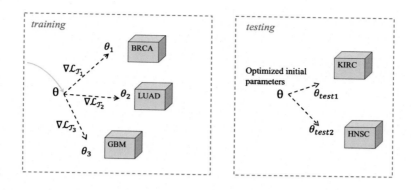

FIGURE 14.2

Illustration of MAML for pan-cancer prediction. Cubes represent the tasks sampled from different cancer data (BRCA – Breast cancer; LUAD – Lung Adenocarcinoma; GBM – Glioblastoma Multiforme; KIRC – Kidney Renal Clear Cell Carcinoma; HNSC – Head and Neck Squamous Cell Carcinoma). During the training process, we adapt the initial parameters θ to different cancer prediction tasks through gradient descent, evaluate the loss using the adapted parameters, and update θ accordingly. In the testing phase, the optimized initial parameters θ are adapted to new cancer types to fit the prediction task.

or multiple gradient steps. Taking one gradient update as an example, we have

$$\theta_i' = \theta - \alpha \nabla_\theta \mathcal{L}_{\mathcal{T}_i}(f_\theta), \tag{14.1}$$

where α is the step size. The metatraining process involves a series of tasks, which update the parameters θ through the series. The goal is to minimize the loss of tasks of the whole series. With all the sampled training tasks, the optimization function is,

$$\min_\theta \sum_{\mathcal{T}_i \sim p(\mathcal{T})} \mathcal{L}_{\mathcal{T}_i}(f_{\theta_i'}) = \sum_{\mathcal{T}_i \sim p(\mathcal{T})} \mathcal{L}_{\mathcal{T}_i}(f_{\theta - \alpha \nabla_\theta \mathcal{L}_{\mathcal{T}_i}(f_\theta)}), \tag{14.2}$$

where $f_{\theta_i'}$ stands for an optimized f_θ with respect to θ across tasks sampled from $P(\mathcal{T})$. By solving Eq. (14.2) using training tasks, we obtain the optimized parameters θ^*. When applied on an unseen testing task $\mathcal{T}_{test}$, the parameters θ^* are adapted to θ_{test} on the support data of $\mathcal{T}_{test}$, which can be computed by one or multiple gradient steps as,

$$\theta_{test}' = \theta^* - \alpha \nabla_{\theta^*} \mathcal{L}_{\mathcal{T}_i}(f_{\theta^*}). \tag{14.3}$$

The main difference in our method from the original MAML [24] is the specific base learner designed for each task. In the original MAML framework, the specific model designed for the classification task is a convolutional neural network (CNN) with four hidden layers, which is designed for image classification. In this work, the goal is to classify cancers using genomic, proteomic, and clinical data for patients with the data in matrix form, as opposed to a general 3D tensor. Thus, we degrade the CNN to a multilayer perceptron (MLP) with residual connections, but still follow the basic meta learning process. In general, each task will go through a four layer neural network with residual connections and the ReLU activation function.

14.3.2 Pan-cancer prediction

14.3.2.1 Dataset preprocessing

The Cancer Genome Atlas (TCGA) [1] is a landmark cancer genomics program in the United States. It characterizes the molecular profiles of over 20,000 primary cancer and normal samples spanning 33 cancer types. There are over 11,000 patients monitored over a 12 year period in each of the studies across 33 cancers. The number of patients for each cancer type varies from 51 (cholangiocarcinoma) to 1098 (breast cancer). Each group collects multimodal patient data, including clinical information, molecular analyte metadata, and molecular profiling data. We select 31 from the 33 available cancer types from TCGA. Two cancer types (cholangiocarcinoma and uterine carcinosarcoma) are excluded because they have less than 60 samples to fit the meta learning model. We extract all representative features using Firebrowse[1] and TCPA [40] tools. The extracted features include clinical variables, genes with somatic mutations, mRNA expression, significant DNA copy number alternation, marker genes in mRNA-seq clustering subtypes, and functional protein expression data. In total, there are 7504 patients from 31 cancer types available for the experiments, and more than 20,000 aggregated features of patients are available, including both continuous and categorical features. The available cancer types are randomly split into three different sets of classes. 21 cancers form the set of training classes, and 5 cancers form the set of validation classes, and the remaining 5 cancers serve as the target classes in the testing set.

14.3.2.2 Experimental results

To compare between traditional machine learning and meta learning family methods under the few-shot setting, we select K-nearest neighbor (KNN) [41] and random forest (RF) [42] as the baseline machine learning methods. We also adopt matching network [31], prototypical network [29], and MAML with modified base learner in this work as the meta learning family methods.

We selected a set of samples from each cancer to follow the N-way K-shot setting (e.g., 3-way 1-shot means that there are three disease classes in a task and there is only one training sample in each class) to form a series of few-shot learning tasks. More specifically, we design two settings for the experiments: 3-way and 5-way. Specifically, we take 3-way-1-shot, 3-way-3-shots, 5-way-1-shot and 5-way-5-shots experiments using all the methods that we mention above. For the meta learning methods, both metatraining and metatesting require a series of tasks $\{\mathcal{T}_i\}_{i=1}^{N}$ for all sets of classes, where N is the number of tasks in an episode E. In more detail, we highlight the 3-way-3-shots setting as an example. Randomly selected training tasks contain 9 samples (3 classes × 3 examples) for the support set. In this work, we set the size of the query set, in both the training task and testing task, to be 5, for both the 3-way and 5-way settings. We also design the corresponding setups for the traditional machine learning algorithms: For KNN, we set $K = 3$ for the 3-way setting, and $K = 5$ for the 5-way setting. Because there is no training for KNN, we directly apply KNN on the testing dataset. For RF, we apply the default

---

[1] http://firebrowse.org/.

setting of the *Python scikit − learn*[2] package, set the number of trees to 100 and directly apply it to the query sets of testing tasks as well.

To investigate the performance of the meta learning family methods under different scenarios of data availability, we experimented under three sets of selected variables, including proteomics features alone, adding clinical features and RNA expressions, and all available features.

Table 14.1 Performance comparison using proteomics features alone.

Methods	3-way 1-shot	3-way 3-shot	5-way 1-shot	5-way 5-shot
KNN	33.3%	84.5%	33.2%	93.5%
RF	56.2%	80.2%	51.1%	92.0%
Matching Network	86.2%	87.6%	81.3%	95.2%
Prototypical Network	86.6%	87.8%	83.2%	97.1%
Modified MAML	**92.5%**	**94.3%**	**89.6%**	**97.4%**

The first set of variables only include proteomics variables from the TCPA [40] portal. There are 216 functional proteomics features for 7693 patients across 31 cancers. The missing values are imputed by the mean value of all patients in each cancer type respectively. As Table 14.1 shows, in the 3-way-1-shot setting, matching network and prototypical network perform similarly, which is consistent with the claim by [43] that they are identical under the 1-shot setting. RF performs better than KNN, which can be explained by the claim in [44] that KNN and RF can have large performance differences when the sample size is small. Importantly, it shows that MAML performs far better than other methods: MAML achieves the best accuracy, even under 3-way-1-shot setting, and the performance of MAML is significantly higher than that of two few-shot learning methods, matching network and prototypical network, with $p < 0.05$ via a one-tailed t-test.

As the sample size increases to 3-way-3-shots, all the methods improve compared to their performance on 3-way-1-shot, which is expected. The performance of the matching network and prototypical network is still similar, with matching network performing slightly better. The performance of traditional methods improves drastically: KNN and RF both reach a relatively higher level, but are still inferior to the few-shot learning methods. As expected, MAML also improves as the number of shots increases, and the performance of MAML is still significantly higher than that of the other methods, with $p < 0.05$ via a one-tailed t-test. The results of the 5-way setting are similar to that of the 3-way setting. Under the 5-way-1-shot scenario, the performance of MAML slightly decreases compared to 3-way-1-shot, but largely increases as more shots are made available, even better than the 3-way-3-shot, which is also expected. Here, our experimental results demonstrate that MAML performs better than baseline methods in predicting cancer types from proteomics data under the same few-shots setting.

To further assess the performance comparison, we not only include the proteomics data, but also include clinical features as well as a subset of frequently occurring features from RNA expression data. The generated cohort for the experiment includes 7581 patients and 962 features. Table 14.2 shows the performance of all methods on the enriched set of features. As shown in the table, under the 3-way-1-shot setting, MAML still performs the best among all the methods, and the performance is still

---

2 https://scikit-learn.org/stable/modules/generated/sklearn.ensemble.RandomForestClassifier.html.

Table 14.2 Performance on the proteomics and selected clinical and RNA expression features.

Methods	3-way 1-shot	3-way 3-shot	5-way 1-shot	5-way 5-shot
KNN	33.3%	83.1%	33.9%	91.2%
RF	63.5%	81.9%	53.2%	90.6%
Matching Network	87.3%	87.1%	85.2%	96.1%
Prototypical Network	88.3%	87.5%	89.6%	97.8%
Modified MAML	**94.2%**	**94.7%**	**91.65%**	**98.9%**

significantly higher than both matching network and prototypical network, with $p < 0.05$ via a one-tailed t-test. RF also becomes better compared to the proteomics only experiment when more features are included. Overall, for the 3-way-1-shot setting, the performance of all methods improves with more data included, which is expected as the enriched dataset can help improve the accuracy of algorithms.

Table 14.3 Performance on the overall dataset.

Methods	3-way 1-shot	3-way 3-shot	5-way 1-shot	5-way 5-shot
KNN	33.3%	84.5%	33.2%	93.5%
RF	55.6%	80.2%	51.1%	92.0%
Matching Network	86.2%	88.6%	81.3%	95.2%
Prototypical Network	86.6%	87.8%	83.2%	97.1%
Modified MAML	**92.5%**	**95.3%**	**89.6%**	**97.4%**

Finally, we performed experiments using all the available features. Table 14.3 summarizes the performance for all methods trained with all the available features. MAML still performs the best among all methods for both the 3-way and 5-way settings. However, compared to the results in Table 14.2, we observe that the performance of MAML decreases in three of the four specific settings, except for the 3-way-3-shots scenario, which differs from our expectation. The problems may lie in the training strategy of MAML. As we employ a first-order approximation to speed up the training process, we ignore the second-order derivative computation (gradient through gradient), which can cause a problem given that directly using the first-order approximation has been shown to have a negative impact on generalization error [45]. Authors in [25] also attempt to apply SGD on a base model and then take a leap from their initialization parameters towards the parameters of the base-model after N steps, but the results from their experiments vary, in some cases yielding inferior results and in others yielding superior results. [25] and [45] show that the training of MAML is not stable enough to generate efficient and effective results for all types of data. Further possible explanations to the varied performance in increasing the dimension of features include the fact that there may exist more redundant features or noise with more features included or there might be greater opportunity for gradients in the source domain to lead the model to suboptimal parameters in the target domain.

14.4 Transfer learning vs. meta learning

In Section 14.3, we have shown the advantage of meta learning over some conventional classification methods in performing few-shot learning applications. In this section, we will conduct detailed analysis to show the different performance between transfer learning and meta learning. As we have mentioned in the introduction, labeled data can be expensive in general or simply unavailable to the public in healthcare due to privacy. Both transfer learning and meta learning have been successfully applied for handling small datasets.

One area where transfer learning is commonly used is computer vision. Prior to training directly to the target image dataset, it is common to pretrain the learning model on a similar yet larger datasets, such as ImageNet, which consists of 1000 object classes and well over one million images in total [46, 47]. Pretraining a deep neural network on a large dataset like ImageNet has multiple advantages. First, the learned model parameters become a good initialization for training the model on the target dataset. This will enable the model to train more quickly than random parameter initialization. This technique is sometimes referred to as knowledge transfer. Second, since the model was pretrained on a diverse dataset with a large scale, the parameters can reduce the risk of overfitting. Such reasons made transfer learning one of the go-to methods for training small datasets. As shown in the objective function in Eq. (14.4), transfer learning tries to find the parameters that minimize the loss of a particular target dataset,

$$\min_{\theta} \mathbb{E}_{(x,y) \in D}[l_\theta(x, y)], \tag{14.4}$$

where x and y represent data samples and labels in dataset D, $l_\theta(\cdot)$ represents the loss function parameterized by the set of model parameters θ.

However, despite such advantages, there are cases where transfer learning comes short, and meta learning becomes a more reasonable solution [24,31,43]. For example, let us assume that we want to train a model that predicts patient survival given a cancer type dataset, such as breast cancer, in TCGA [1]. Applying transfer learning in this scenario would imply that we would first train our model on another cancer type, such ovarian cancer or lung cancer. However, the relationships among different cancer types are not clear, and using a dataset that is not clearly related to the task at hand may in fact impair or have no effect on the performance instead of improving it.

To make the situation even harder, let's say that we need to predict patient survival in multiple cancer types. Instead of having a pretrained model on some arbitrarily related datasets that are similar in size with the target dataset, it would be more beneficial to have a model that is trained to learn quickly on similar datasets, which is what meta learning does.

Human beings are extremely efficient in identifying objects that we have seen only a few samples of. This is because we are often very good at recognizing the general structures of objects, instead of particular or specific structures. The meta learning way of learning tries to train the model to do just that. Transfer learning assumes that the learned representation is directly transferable to the target task, which may not be true especially when the target task is from a different domain. In contrast, through meta learning, transferable knowledge across tasks can be efficiently acquired, resulting in improved generalization performance on unseen tasks. As shown in the objective function in Eq. (14.5), meta learning finds a set of parameters such that the loss on a distribution of datasets is minimized,

$$\min_{\theta} \mathbb{E}_{D \in p(D)}[l_\theta(D)], \tag{14.5}$$

where $p(D)$ represents a distribution of datasets.

14.4.1 Experimental results

In Tables 14.4 and 14.5, we show the performance of running transfer learning and MAML on predicting patient survival on the TCGA RNA-seq and proteomics datasets respectively. Note that there is an approximate 3:1 ratio of survived and dead patients in the entire dataset, indicating a data imbalance. We trained both models on 12 cancer types and tested on other 4 cancer types. Please note that we use precision, recall, and F-score to demonstrate the models' abilities to handle data imbalance, but Cox proportional hazard models are often used in real-world survival analysis [48,49,50].

Table 14.4 Performance of transfer learning and MAML on survival analysis using TCGA RNA-seq data. The models were pretrained on 12 other cancer types and fine-tuned and tested on pancreatic adenocarcinoma (PAAD), rectum adenocarcinoma (READ), stomach adenocarcinoma (STAD), and thyroid carcinoma (THCA). The test set for each cancer type consists of 43/46, 70/10, 131/78, 248/4 survived/dead patients respectively.

Cancer Types	Method	Transfer Learning		MAML	
		Survival	Death	Survival	Death
PAAD	precision	41.51%	52.78%	**79.72%**	**81.83%**
	recall	56.41%	38.00%	**80.38%**	**81.21%**
	F-score	47.83%	44.19%	**80.05%**	**81.52%**
READ	precision	82.82%	42.86%	**91.71%**	**55.04%**
	recall	**93.65%**	17.65%	91.77%	**54.84%**
	F-score	86.76%	25.00%	**91.74%**	**54.94%**
STAD	precision	59.83%	40.22%	**74.72%**	**70.05%**
	recall	56.00%	44.05%	**86.76%**	**51.33%**
	F-score	57.85%	42.05%	**80.29%**	**59.24%**
THCA	precision	96.43%	0.00%	**99.62%**	**42.36%**
	recall	**100.00%**	0.00%	96.05%	**88.79%**
	F-score	**98.18%**	0.00%	97.80%	**57.35%**

We can make several observations through these results. First, MAML's performance is generally higher than transfer learning. Second, even for the instances where transfer learning performs better than MAML, the difference is often marginal, or occurs when the performances of the two models are close to 1. Finally, MAML is significantly better than transfer learning for predicting death. Since there is a 3:1 ratio of survival and death, transfer learning is prone to make many false negative predictions (predict survival most of the time). This suggests that it is safe to conclude that the MAML model is more robust to data imbalance.

Generally speaking, meta learning is designed to explicitly learn how to adapt to a specific task by introducing two loops of optimization, i.e., the inner loop and the outer loop. The inner loop is responsible for adapting to a given task, while the outer loop evaluates the adapted model and updates

Table 14.5 Performance of transfer learning and MAML on the TCGA Proteomics dataset.

Cancer Types	Method	Transfer Learning		MAML	
		Survival	Death	Survival	Death
PAAD	precision	47.62%	57.14%	**80.29%**	**81.87%**
	recall	45.45%	59.26%	**80.55%**	**81.62%**
	F-score	46.51%	58.18%	**80.43%**	**81.75%**
READ	precision	85.11%	21.43%	**91.46%**	**55.31%**
	recall	78.43%	30.00%	**91.96%**	**53.67%**
	F-score	81.63%	25.00%	**91.71%**	**54.48%**
STAD	precision	63.08%	52.50%	**74.25%**	**71.11%**
	recall	81.19%	30.43%	**86.83%**	**51.84%**
	F-score	71.00%	38.53%	**80.04%**	**59.96%**
THCA	precision	94.57%	0.00%	**99.61%**	**42.81%**
	recall	**99.43%**	0.00%	96.06%	**88.79%**
	F-score	96.94%	0.00%	**97.81%**	**57.76%**

it accordingly. Through meta learning, transferable knowledge across tasks can be efficiently acquired, resulting in improved generalization performance on unseen tasks [24]. On the other hand, transfer learning [4] aims to learn a transferable feature representation by pretraining a model on a single task, and fine tunes part of the model on the target task. It assumes that the learned representation is directly transferable to the target task, which may not be true especially when the target task is from a different domain. Moreover, transfer learning generally requires more samples in fine-tuning the model than meta learning, since the latter learns how to adapt, while the former doesn't and requires many samples for training. We have shown that meta learning can perform better in few-shot learning problems than transfer learning.

14.5 Knowledge-guided meta learning for healthcare

In this section, we explore a potential way to improve the performance of meta learning with external knowledge. In paper [51], we proposed a task-adaptive network (TAdaNet) that makes use of a domain-knowledge graph to enrich data representations and capture task relationships, in order to boost few-shot learning. This is achieved by incorporating domain-knowledge to adjust class representations, message passing across the external graph and producing task-aware parameter adjustment for each task. The overall learning framework is shown in Fig. 14.3. The proposed framework contains three key modules: graph-enriched prototypes, task context embedding and customized target prediction. We first learn prototypes which can be considered as class representations by aggregating information from neighbor nodes in the graph through graph attention mechanism. After that, we learn task embeddings regularized by the graph-enriched prototypes and retrieve information from task memory network. Finally, we learn a set of task-adaptive parameter gates to customize model parameters and perform prediction.

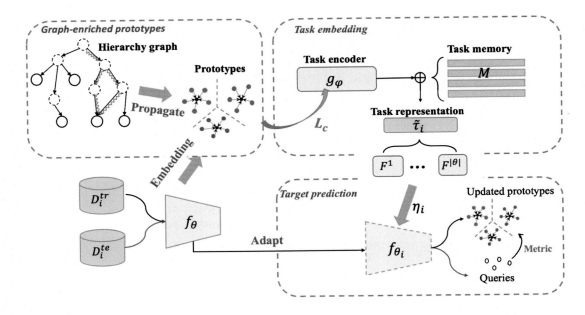

FIGURE 14.3

Illustration of the overall framework. For a task $\mathcal{T}_i$, the support $\mathcal{D}_i^{tr}$ and query $\mathcal{D}_i^{te}$ samples are first embedded into a metric space through a feature extraction network $f_\theta(\cdot)$. Prototypes are updated via message propagation across the knowledge graph. The task encoder $g_\varphi(\cdot)$ extracts task representation which is enhanced through a memory network. The obtained task representation incorporates task relationships from the knowledge graph. After that, a set of modulation networks $F_c(\cdot)$ generate a gate η for each parameter θ conditioned on the enhanced task representations $\tilde{\tau}_i$. The customized parameter θ_i is used to obtain the prototype embeddings for input classes and to perform classification for query examples. The learning process is facilitated by leveraging the information on hierarchical graph and transferable knowledge from related tasks.

14.5.1 Methodology

14.5.1.1 External knowledge

In this work, we seek to utilize external knowledge to enhance the learning of the data representations and task relationships in the meta learning process. In many applications, domain knowledge is often represented in the form of graphs, which can be useful to learn data representations and to characterize internal relationships. For example, ImageNet is organized according to WordNet hierarchy,[3] where each node represents a semantic category of images, as shown in Fig. 14.4a. In the healthcare domain, there are well organized disease ontologies, such as the International Classification of Diseases[4] (ICD) and Clinical Classifications Software[5] (CCS), where each node represents a disease and the edges

---

[3] https://wordnet.princeton.edu.
[4] http://www.icd9data.com.
[5] https://www.hcup-us.ahrq.gov/toolssoftware/ccs/ccs.jsp.

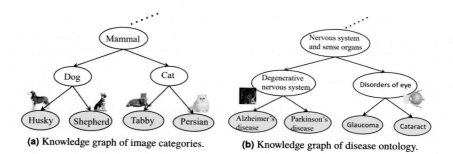

(a) Knowledge graph of image categories.   **(b)** Knowledge graph of disease ontology.

FIGURE 14.4

External knowledge represented in hierarchical graphs for images and diseases respectively. In the graph, nodes represent image/disease categories, and edges connect parent and child nodes, reflecting semantic relationships between the nodes.

provide connections among diseases. In Fig. 14.4b, we can see that Alzheimer's disease and Parkinson's disease both belong to degenerative nervous system diseases. If an intelligent system learns how to detect Alzheimer's disease, one can imagine that it could be easily modulated to detect Parkinson's disease than other less related diseases such as heart failure.

This kind of external knowledge graphs is often known in advance or can be extracted from a knowledge base. Nodes (e.g., diseases or words) sharing the same parent nodes are likely to be associated with similar data examples (e.g., patients or images), allowing knowledge transfer between them. The graph-enriched information helps representation learning, especially when the data is limited in the setting of few-shot learning. Since a task contains several classes that are represented as nodes in the graph, each task can be regarded as a subset of nodes. Thus tasks are related through the paths that link their nodes. In our problem, a graph $\mathcal{G}(\mathcal{Y}, \mathcal{E})$ indicates the relationship between classes, where $\mathcal{Y}$ is a set of nodes (i.e., classes), and $\mathcal{E}$ is the edge set. In the graph, each node $y \in \mathcal{Y}$ denotes a specific data class and each edge $y_i \rightarrow y_j \in \mathcal{E}$ connects a parent class y_i to its child class y_j on the graph. We assume that there are two types of nodes in $\mathcal{G}$: the leaf nodes $\mathcal{Y}^t$ are the target fine-grained classes; the ancestor nodes $\mathcal{Y}^c$ form the coarse classes. The fine-grained classes are the target classes which we are interested in for classification, and the coarse classes are expected to provide additional information that can help the few-shot learning process. For example, in the graph of disease ontology, "Parkinson's disease" has two children "Paralysis agitans" and "Secondary parkinsonism", while its ancestor classes are "Hereditary and degenerative nervous system conditions" and "Diseases of nervous system and sense organs". Following the settings of few-shot learning, we draw a task $\mathcal{T}_i \sim p(\mathcal{T})$ which contains classes in the leaf nodes as the target classes and extract the ancestors for the target classes, which forms a subset of nodes in $\mathcal{G}$.

We make two assumptions: 1) A task is considered more similar to another task sharing nodes in the graph, than the one that has disjoint classes with it; and 2) Similar tasks should share more information and have similar model parameters. Based on these assumptions, it is likely that the information in the domain-knowledge graph can assist in learning data representations for related tasks. In the following subsections, we introduce details of the proposed method.

14.5.1.2 Graph-based prototype learning

Typically, a prototype is calculated as the mean vector of the embedded support examples belonging to a certain class. The initial prototype for a class k can be calculated as the mean of example embeddings within it. Following [29], we obtain the initial prototype $\mathbf{c}_i^{k,0}$ of class k in task $\mathcal{T}_i$ by calculating the mean vector of sample embeddings in the class:

$$\mathbf{c}_i^{k,0} = \frac{1}{n_i^{tr,k}} \sum_{(\mathbf{x}_{i,j}, y_{i,j}) \in \mathcal{D}_i^{tr,k}} f_\theta(\mathbf{x}_{i,j}), \tag{14.6}$$

where $\mathcal{D}_i^{tr,k}$ is the support example set of the k-th class in task $\mathcal{T}_i$, $n_i^{tr,k}$ is the number of examples in the set, $\mathbf{x}_{i,j}$ is the j-th example in $\mathcal{T}_i$, and $f_\theta(\cdot)$ is the feature extraction network with learnable parameters θ. Eq. (14.6) calculates the prototype using limited samples in a class, which may be inaccurate and sensitive to outliers due to data scarcity of each class.

Therefore, we utilize the given hierarchical graph to align related classes, in order to learn more informative class prototypes. In the graph, the target few-shot classes come from the leaf nodes, while the coarse nodes from the ancestors indicate the distance between two target classes. For example, if two few-shot classes share some ancestor nodes in the hierarchical graph $\mathcal{G}$, they are likely to have common characteristics, so that their prototypes should be similar. To incorporate the information of the class relatedness from graph $\mathcal{G}$, we update the prototypes through graph attention mechanism [52], and obtain $\mathbf{c}_i^{k,L}$ which is the graph-enriched prototype for class k, and L is the number of propagation iterations. The updated prototype of class k in task $\mathcal{T}_i$ is the weighted average of example mean $\mathbf{c}_i^{k,0}$ and graph-enriched embeddings $\mathbf{c}_i^{k,L}$ as,

$$\mathbf{c}_i^k = (1-\lambda)\mathbf{c}_i^{k,0} + \lambda\mathbf{c}_i^{k,L}, \tag{14.7}$$

where the weight $\lambda \in [0, 1]$ is a hyperparameter to adjust the weight between information from the examples in class k and its ancestor classes.

14.5.1.3 Task representation learning

Metric-based few-shot learning methods [31,29,32,53] typically learn a task-invariant metric for all the tasks. This may limit the model's expressive ability since the optimal metric may vary across different tasks. To improve the model expressiveness, we introduce parameter customization to make feature extractor behavior task-adaptive. The task-specific parameters are conditioned on task representations. Learning a task representation is expected to account for the following properties: enough distinctions between different tasks, sufficient similarities between related tasks, and insensitivity to the number and order of samples in a certain task.

We use an auxiliary network $g_\varphi(\cdot)$ to learn task representations. The task representation τ_i is obtained by aggregating the example embeddings in the task with a mean pooling operation, e.g., $g_\varphi(\mathbf{x}_{i,j})$ is the representation of the j-th example. We leverage the underlying knowledge obtained from historical tasks to enhance the task representation, in order to better characterize task relationships. To extract knowledge from a historical learning process, we construct a parameterized memory matrix $\mathcal{M} \in \mathbb{R}^{S \times d}$, where S denotes the predefined knowledge types and d is the dimension of prototype embeddings. We utilize the knowledge patterns of task relations stored in $\mathcal{M}$ via an attention mechanism [54]. We calculate the attention score between prototype $\mathbf{c}_i^k$ of task i and the stored memory patterns, and then aggregate the information passing from the memory to enhance prototype representations. Now the task representation $\tilde{\tau}_i$ is learned based on example embeddings within the task and historical tasks.

In this way, information from the hierarchical graph is incorporated into task representations, so that task representations can reflect class relatedness. If two tasks have similar class prototypes, they should have close task representations. With the learned task representation, we then perform task-specific customization for the prediction model of each task.

14.5.1.4 Task-specific prediction

Finally, we perform target class prediction for the query examples. Inspired by [23], we learn a series of task-specific parameter gates η_i^j using task representations $\tilde{\tau}_i$ by:

$$\eta_i^j = F^j(\tilde{\tau}_i), \forall j \in 1, ..., |\theta|, \tag{14.8}$$

to enforce the task-specific property on the embedding network, where F^j is the j-th fully-connected network, and $|\theta|$ is the number of parameters in θ. Note that $\eta_i = \{\eta_i^j\}_{j=1}^{|\theta|}$ has the same dimension as the feature embedding parameter θ, so that each element in η_i controls the weight of neurons to be adapted to each task. With the parameter gates, globally transferable knowledge is adapted to the task-specific embedding parameter $\theta_i = \theta \circ \eta_i$, where $\circ$ is the element-wise multiplication. Therefore, similar task embeddings will trigger similar parameter gates, resulting in similar model parameters and allowing more information to be shared, while dissimilar tasks are controlled to share less information.

With the task-adaptive feature extractor $f_{\theta_i}(\cdot)$, we embed the support and query examples in task $\mathcal{T}_i$ to obtain the data representations conditioned on the task. We can then obtain the task-adaptive prototype $\tilde{\mathbf{c}}_i^k$ for class k following the same procedure as Section 14.5.1.2 with θ substituted by θ_i: first calculating the prototype per class by calculating the mean of supports to obtain the initial value, and then aggregating the information propagated through the ancestor nodes in $\mathcal{G}$. The prototype $\tilde{\mathbf{c}}_i^k$ is used to assign the predicted class label for a query data point $\mathbf{x}_{i,j}'$ based on a softmax function over distances between prototypes and the query embedding:

$$p(y_{i,j}' = k|\mathbf{x}_{i,j}') = \frac{\exp(-d(f_{\theta_i}(\mathbf{x}_{i,j}'), \tilde{\mathbf{c}}_i^k))}{\sum_{k'} \exp(-d(f_{\theta_i}(\mathbf{x}_{i,j}'), \tilde{\mathbf{c}}_i^{k'}))}, \tag{14.9}$$

where the distance function $d(\cdot)$ is Euclidean distance. The classification process is to minimize the cross-entropy loss function as,

$$\mathcal{L}_p(\mathcal{T}_i) = -\sum_{k=1}^{K} \sum_{\mathbf{x}_{i,j}' \in \mathcal{D}_i^{te,k}} \log p(y_{i,j}' = k|\mathbf{x}_{i,j}'). \tag{14.10}$$

14.5.2 Experiments

14.5.2.1 Dataset description

Multiparameter Intelligent Monitoring in Intensive Care (MIMIC-III) is a large publicly available dataset for medical analysis. We select 446 diagnosis codes which serve as the labels for disease pre-

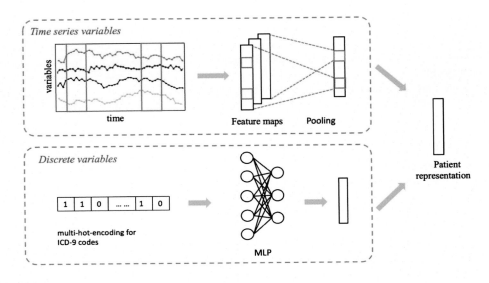

FIGURE 14.5

Backbone model structure for the MIMIC dataset. Features in MIMIC dataset include time series and discrete variables. We adopt the one-directional convolution operations to capture patterns across the temporal dimension, followed by max pooling and a fully connected layer. For discrete variables, we use a two-layer MLP to learn an embedding vector. Embeddings from the two parts are combined through a fully-connected layer, producing the patient embedding for meta learning.

diction, and ensure that different target disease cohorts have no overlapped patients. For each patient, we extract two types of features: time series variables and discrete variables. The time series are informative physiological variables suggested in [55,56] such as heart rate, systolic blood pressure, oxygen saturation, and respiratory rate. We use the records of 31 variables during the first 48 hours after patients' admission to the ICU. Therefore, the time series record of each patient can be viewed as a matrix, where the horizontal dimension corresponds to timestamps and the vertical dimension to physiological variables. The discrete variables include 3103 ICD-9 codes with the 446 selected disease codes being removed. The discrete variables are represented as a binary vector, where each element indicates the absence or occurrence of a variable. We use ICD ontology as the external graph which provides category relationship among diseases.

For the disease prediction task on MIMIC, we use a CNN-based sequence learning structure for time series and a multilayer perceptron (MLP) for discrete variables. For time series, we adopt the one-directional convolution operations to capture patterns across the temporal dimension. For all the baseline approaches and proposed method, we use a one-layer CNN network with 64 filters for time series and a two-layer MLP for discrete data, and combine the learned vector representations through a fully-connected layer to produce the prediction. The network architecture is shown in Fig. 14.5. This architecture is served as the backbone network (i.e., $f_\theta(\cdot)$ in Section 14.5.1) in meta learning.

14.5.2.2 Experimental results

We compare the proposed method with two types of baselines, including gradient-based meta learning methods and metric-based methods. For the gradient-based methods, we compare with MAML [24], MMAML [21] and HSML [23]. Among the methods, MAML learns globally shared initial parameters across tasks and then adapts the parameters to new tasks through a few gradient steps, while MMAML and HSML learn task-specific initialization to customize the learning process. The metric-based methods to be compared include MatchingNet [31], ProtoNet [29], RelationNet [32] and PPN [57]. These methods measure distances between query and support examples using a shared metric for all tasks. Briefly, MatchingNet produces a weighted nearest neighbor classifier; ProtoNet computes distances between a query point and prototypes; RelationNet learns a nonlinear comparison on top of metric space; and PPN learns the propagated prototypes by accumulating the level-wise classification loss on each level of classes sampled from the graph. Note that both PPN and TAdaNet adopt prototype update via graph propagation. However, different from PPN, we do not rely on level-wise training on subgraphs and buffered prototypes for update. Our model learns task-adaptive metric by considering the task relationships provided on the given graph.

Table 14.6 Comparison between the proposed and baseline approaches on MIMIC of disease classification problem. Accuracies ±95% confidence intervals are reported.

Methods	3-way 1-shot	3-way 5-shot	5-way 1-shot
MAML	46.20±0.97%	53.70±0.94%	31.97±0.74%
MMAML	45.91±0.98%	54.93±0.90%	32.25±0.78%
HSML	45.94±0.84%	53.14±0.41%	31.04±0.70%
MatchingNet	43.87±0.77%	50.92±0.92%	29.64±0.63%
ProtoNet	42.92±0.72%	54.08±1.00%	29.61±0.65%
RelationNet	43.85±0.89%	52.23±0.95%	28.67±0.61%
PPN	51.54±0.90%	58.16±0.93%	38.59±0.68%
TAdaNet	**54.06±0.94%**	**59.05±0.92%**	**40.31±0.72%**

In Table 14.6, we show the performance comparison of different methods on a MIMIC disease classification problem under 3-way 1-shot, 3-way 5-shot and 5-way 1-shot settings. In this problem, each task is comprised of sampling 3 or 5 diseases from the target nodes of the disease ontology, and each disease contains a few patient examples. Due to the sparsity and complexity of healthcare data, disease classification is a more difficult problem than image classification. Our method significantly outperforms baseline approaches, especially on 1-shot classification. This is due to the fact that 1-shot learning is more difficult than 5-shot learning for lack of training data, so that the information from ancestors of the graph can be more helpful to learn representations for the target classes. From the table, we observe that the PPN baseline method outperforms most of the baseline approaches, especially under 1-shot learning. PPN propagates the prototype of each class to its child classes on the graph and buffers the prototypes for further updates. This indicates the effectiveness of learning from external information in the graph. Besides message passing through graphs for prototype learning, the proposed method TAdaNet also learns task relationships and customizes model parameters for different tasks, so that it outperforms baseline approaches.

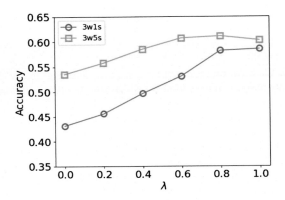

FIGURE 14.6

Accuracy with respect to λ on MIMIC dataset.

To investigate the properties of TAdaNet w.r.t. hyperparameters, we vary the value of λ and report the achieved accuracy values on the MIMIC dataset. λ is used in Eq. (14.7) for balancing the contribution of the initial prototype to the final updated one. The trends under 3-way 1-shot and 3-way 5-shot are depicted in Fig. 14.6. The x-axis shows different values of λ within [0, 1], and the y-axis is the prediction accuracy using TAdaNet. In Fig. 14.6, under the setting of 5-way 1-shot, the accuracy value improves with respect to λ, while it does not change much under 5-way 5-shot. This indicates that more information from the ancestors can help the learning process, especially for 1-shot learning. The parameter study on λ suggests that graph information can be more helpful when there are very limited data examples.

14.6 Conclusion

In this chapter, we have applied meta learning to TCGA data and have shown the advantage of meta learning over traditional classification in prediction problems. We have also experimentally demonstrated that meta learning outperforms conventional transfer learning in prediction problems. Furthermore, we described a knowledge-guided meta learning strategy which integrates biological knowledge with meta learning for improved classification performance on few-shot learning problems. As the conventional deep learning systems must be shown many examples before they can classify things accurately, meta learning has become a promising approach for biomedical applications that typically have few training samples.

References

[1] C. Hutter, J.C. Zenklusen, The cancer genome atlas: creating lasting value beyond its data, Cell 173 (2) (2018) 283–285.

[2] Y. Wang, Q. Yao, J.T. Kwok, L.M. Ni, Generalizing from a few examples: a survey on few-shot learning, ACM Computing Surveys (CSUR) 53 (3) (2020) 1–34.

[3] M. Huisman, J.N. van Rijn, A. Plaat, A survey of deep meta-learning, Artificial Intelligence Review (2021) 1–59.

[4] F. Zhuang, Z. Qi, K. Duan, D. Xi, Y. Zhu, H. Zhu, H. Xiong, Q. He, A comprehensive survey on transfer learning, Proceedings of the IEEE 109 (2021) 43–76.

[5] Y. li, L. Wang, J. Wang, J. Ye, C. Reddy, Transfer learning for survival analysis via efficient l2, 1-norm regularized Cox regression, in: 2016 IEEE 16th International Conference on Data Mining (ICDM), 12 2016, pp. 231–240.

[6] H. Chougrad, H. Zouaki, O. Alheyane, Multi-label transfer learning for the early diagnosis of breast cancer, Neurocomputing 392 (2020) 168–180 [online], available: http://www.sciencedirect.com/science/article/pii/S0925231219304710.

[7] R. Mehrotra, M. Ansari, R. Agrawal, R. Anand, A transfer learning approach for ai-based classification of brain tumors, Machine Learning with Applications 2 (2020) 100003 [online], available: http://www.sciencedirect.com/science/article/pii/S2666827020300037.

[8] S.H. Kassani, P.H. Kassani, M.J. Wesolowski, K.A. Schneider, R. Deters, Breast cancer diagnosis with transfer learning and global pooling, in: 2019 International Conference on Information and Communication Technology Convergence (ICTC), 2019, pp. 519–524.

[9] S.R. Dhruba, R. Rahman, K. Matlock, S. Ghosh, R. Pal, Application of transfer learning for cancer drug sensitivity prediction, BMC Bioinformatics 19 (12 2018).

[10] G. López-García, J.M. Jerez, L. Franco, F.J. Veredas, Transfer learning with convolutional neural networks for cancer survival prediction using gene-expression data, PLoS ONE 15 (3) (03 2020) 1–24, https://doi.org/10.1371/journal.pone.0230536.

[11] S. Kim, K. Kim, J. Choe, I. Lee, J. Kang, Improved survival analysis by learning shared genomic information from pan-cancer data, Bioinformatics 36 (07 2020) i389–i398.

[12] Y. Gao, Y. Cui, Deep transfer learning for reducing health care disparities arising from biomedical data inequality, Nature Communications 11 (12 2020).

[13] E. Tzeng, J. Hoffman, K. Saenko, T. Darrell, Adversarial discriminative domain adaptation, in: Proceedings of the IEEE Conference on Computer Vision and Pattern Recognition, 2017, pp. 7167–7176.

[14] J. Gu, Y. Wang, Y. Chen, K. Cho, V.O. Li, Meta-learning for low-resource neural machine translation, in: EMNLP, 2018.

[15] B. Kang, Z. Liu, X. Wang, F. Yu, J. Feng, T. Darrell, Few-shot object detection via feature reweighting, in: Proceedings of the IEEE International Conference on Computer Vision, 2019, pp. 8420–8429.

[16] Z. Du, X. Wang, H. Yang, J. Zhou, J. Tang, Sequential scenario-specific meta learner for online recommendation, in: Proceedings of the 25th ACM SIGKDD International Conference on Knowledge Discovery & Data Mining, 2019, pp. 2895–2904.

[17] H. Lee, J. Im, S. Jang, H. Cho, S. Chung, Melu: meta-learned user preference estimator for cold-start recommendation, in: Proceedings of the 25th ACM SIGKDD International Conference on Knowledge Discovery & Data Mining, 2019, pp. 1073–1082.

[18] H. Yao, Y. Liu, Y. Wei, X. Tang, Z. Li, Learning from multiple cities: a meta-learning approach for spatial-temporal prediction, in: The World Wide Web Conference, 2019, pp. 2181–2191.

[19] X.S. Zhang, F. Tang, H.H. Dodge, J. Zhou, F. Wang, Metapred: meta-learning for clinical risk prediction with limited patient electronic health records, in: Proceedings of the 25th ACM SIGKDD International Conference on Knowledge Discovery & Data Mining, 2019, pp. 2487–2495.

[20] B. Oreshkin, P.R. López, A. Lacoste, Tadam: task dependent adaptive metric for improved few-shot learning, in: Advances in Neural Information Processing Systems, 2018, pp. 721–731.

[21] R. Vuorio, S.-H. Sun, H. Hu, J.J. Lim, Multimodal model-agnostic meta-learning via task-aware modulation, in: Advances in Neural Information Processing Systems, 2019, pp. 1–12.

[22] H. Li, W. Dong, X. Mei, C. Ma, F. huang, B. Hu, Lgm-net: learning to generate matching networks for few-shot learning, in: ICML, 2019.

[23] H. Yao, Y. Wei, J. Huang, Z. Li, Hierarchically structured meta-learning, in: ICML, 2019.

[24] C. Finn, P. Abbeel, S. Levine, Model-agnostic meta-learning for fast adaptation of deep networks, in: Proceedings of the 34th International Conference on Machine Learning-Volume 70, JMLR, 2017, pp. 1126–1135.

[25] A. Nichol, J. Achiam, J. Schulman, On first-order meta-learning algorithms, arXiv preprint, arXiv:1803.02999, 2018.

[26] Y. Lee, S. Choi, Gradient-based meta-learning with learned layerwise metric and subspace, in: ICML, 2018.

[27] N. Mishra, M. Rohaninejad, X. Chen, P. Abbeel, A simple neural attentive meta-learner, in: ICLR, 2018.

[28] J. Yoon, T. Kim, O. Dia, S. Kim, Y. Bengio, S. Ahn, Bayesian model-agnostic meta-learning, in: Advances in Neural Information Processing Systems, 2018, pp. 7332–7342.

[29] J. Snell, K. Swersky, R. Zemel, Prototypical networks for few-shot learning, in: Advances in Neural Information Processing Systems, 2017, pp. 4077–4087.

[30] G. Koch, R. Zemel, R. Salakhutdinov, Siamese neural networks for one-shot image recognition, in: ICML Deep Learning Workshop, vol. 2, Lille, 2015.

[31] O. Vinyals, C. Blundell, T. Lillicrap, D. Wierstra, Matching networks for one shot learning, in: Advances in Neural Information Processing Systems, 2016, pp. 3630–3638.

[32] F. Sung, Y. Yang, L. Zhang, T. Xiang, P.H. Torr, T.M. Hospedales, Learning to compare: relation network for few-shot learning, in: Proceedings of the IEEE Conference on Computer Vision and Pattern Recognition, 2018, pp. 1199–1208.

[33] S.W. Yoon, J. Seo, J. Moon, Tapnet: neural network augmented with task-adaptive projection for few-shot learning, in: ICML, 2019.

[34] H. Yao, X. Wu, R. Li, Z. Tao, Y. Li, B. Ding, Z. Li, Automated relational meta-learning, in: ICLR, 2020.

[35] G. Maicas, A.P. Bradley, J.C. Nascimento, I. Reid, G. Carneiro, Training medical image analysis systems like radiologists, in: International Conference on Medical Image Computing and Computer-Assisted Intervention, Springer, 2018, pp. 546–554.

[36] B.D. Nguyen, T.-T. Do, B.X. Nguyen, T. Do, E. Tjiputra, Q.D. Tran, Overcoming data limitation in medical visual question answering, in: International Conference on Medical Image Computing and Computer-Assisted Intervention, Springer, 2019, pp. 522–530.

[37] Z. Mirikharaji, Y. Yan, G. Hamarneh, Learning to segment skin lesions from noisy annotations, in: Domain Adaptation and Representation Transfer and Medical Image Learning with Less Labels and Imperfect Data, Springer, 2019, pp. 207–215.

[38] M. Samiei, T. Würfl, T. Deleu, M. Weiss, F. Dutil, T. Fevens, G. Boucher, S. Lemieux, J.P. Cohen, The tcga meta-dataset clinical benchmark, CoRR, arXiv:1910.08636 [abs], 2019.

[39] J. Chou, S. Bekiranov, C. Zang, M. Huai, A. Zhang, Analysis of meta-learning approaches for tcga pan-cancer datasets, in: 2020 IEEE International Conference on Bioinformatics and Biomedicine (BIBM), IEEE, 2020, pp. 257–262.

[40] J. Li, Y. Lu, R. Akbani, Z. Ju, P.L. Roebuck, W. Liu, J.-Y. Yang, B.M. Broom, R.G. Verhaak, D.W. Kane, et al., Tcpa: a resource for cancer functional proteomics data, Nature Methods 10 (11) (2013) 1046–1047.

[41] J.M. Keller, M.R. Gray, J.A. Givens, A fuzzy k-nearest neighbor algorithm, IEEE Transactions on Systems, Man and Cybernetics 4 (1985) 580–585.

[42] G. Biau, E. Scornet, A random forest guided tour, Test 25 (2) (2016) 197–227.

[43] T. Hospedales, A. Antoniou, P. Micaelli, A. Storkey, Meta-learning in neural networks: a survey, arXiv preprint, arXiv:2004.05439, 2020.

[44] P. Thanh Noi, M. Kappas, Comparison of random forest, k-nearest neighbor, and support vector machine classifiers for land cover classification using sentinel-2 imagery, Sensors 18 (1) (2018) 18.

[45] A. Antoniou, H. Edwards, A. Storkey, How to train your maml, in: ICLR, 2019.

[46] K. He, X. Zhang, S. Ren, J. Sun, Deep residual learning for image recognition, CoRR, arXiv:1512.03385 [abs], 2015.

[47] J. Deng, W. Dong, R. Socher, L.-J. Li, K. Li, L. Fei-Fei, Imagenet: a large-scale hierarchical image database, in: 2009 IEEE Conference on Computer Vision and Pattern Recognition, IEEE, 2009, pp. 248–255.

[48] D.R. Cox, Regression models and life-tables, Journal of the Royal Statistical Society. Series B (Methodological) 34 (2) (1972) 187–220 [online], available: http://www.jstor.org/stable/2985181.

[49] N. Breslow, Covariance analysis of censored survival data, Biometrics 30 (1) (1974) 89–99 [online], available: http://www.jstor.org/stable/2529620.

[50] B. Efron, The efficiency of Cox's likelihood function for censored data, Journal of the American Statistical Association 72 (359) (1977) 557–565 [online], available: http://www.jstor.org/stable/2286217.

[51] Q. Suo, J. Chou, W. Zhong, A. Zhang, Tadanet: task-adaptive network for graph-enriched meta-learning, in: Proceedings of the 26th ACM SIGKDD International Conference on Knowledge Discovery & Data Mining, 2020, pp. 1789–1799.

[52] P. Veličković, G. Cucurull, A. Casanova, A. Romero, P. Lio, Y. Bengio, Graph attention networks, in: ICLR, 2018.

[53] V. Garcia, J. Bruna, Few-shot learning with graph neural networks, in: ICLR, 2018.

[54] M.-T. Luong, H. Pham, C.D. Manning, Effective approaches to attention-based neural machine translation, arXiv preprint, arXiv:1508.04025, 2015.

[55] H. Harutyunyan, H. Khachatrian, D.C. Kale, G.V. Steeg, A. Galstyan, Multitask learning and benchmarking with clinical time series data, arXiv preprint, arXiv:1703.07771, 2017.

[56] L. Wang, W. Zhang, X. He, H. Zha, Supervised reinforcement learning with recurrent neural network for dynamic treatment recommendation, in: Proceedings of the 24th ACM SIGKDD International Conference on Knowledge Discovery & Data Mining, 2018, pp. 2447–2456.

[57] L. Liu, T. Zhou, G. Long, J. Jiang, L. Yao, C. Zhang, Prototype propagation networks (ppn) for weakly-supervised few-shot learning on category graph, in: IJCAI, 2019.

Case study: few-shot pill recognition

15

How to train an AI model to recognize a new category of pill from only a few samples like humans?

Andreas Pastor[a], Suiyi Ling[a], Jieum Kim[b], and Patrick Le Callet[a]

[a]Nantes Université, Centrale Nantes, CNRS, LS2N, Nantes, France
[b]Hanyang University, Seoul, South Korea

15.1 Introduction

Human is capable to recognize novel object categories with very few samples of a target category. Nevertheless, the performances of most of the transitional AI based recognition models depend upon thousands of instances per category to obtain similar accuracy. Few-shot learning is one stake in the ground, whose goal is to enable models for recognition, detection, segmentation, *etc.* to utilize only a few training instances per category. In extreme cases, when only one or no instance is available, one-shot, zero-shot based learning models should still be able to accomplish the task like humans. In real-world cases, few-shot learning is valuable for a bountiful of tasks when 1) training examples are rare; 2) there are always novel categories; or 3) the cost of large-scale labeling is costly.

Few-shot learning is usually studied under a *N-way-K-shot* regime, where the goal of the task is to discriminate among N categories with only K samples of each. Typically in the literature, $N = 10$, $K = 5$. As there are limited samples per category, most of the modern classification algorithms need to rely on more complicated network architecture (with significantly more parameters) to achieve acceptable performance on a given dataset, which generally leads to poor generalization. As the samples size is insufficient to constrain the problem, one of the alternatives is to learn from other similar problems in the domain. To this end, in the community, most approaches characterize few-shot learning as a meta learning problem.

Accurately recognizing prescription pill images according to their visual appearance helps to ensure patients' safety and facilitates contemporary healthcare systems for patients/old people. Furthermore, it can be useful in avoiding errors across the pharmacological chain, such as prescription/transcription errors; it can also improve the care provided by experts on poison control [2], increase medication persistence [3], minimize the loss of medications and prescriptions in evacuation scenarios [4], and promote the development of remote/self-diagnosis technology and smart healthcare applications [5].

However, accurate pill recognition in daily life is usually hindered by the few-shot learning problem, where the number of samples per category is small. For instance, the NIH dataset [6] contains only 7 samples per pill category. Moreover, although there are various commercial products and web-based

FIGURE 15.1

Examples of *hard samples* in pill recognition from left to right: hard positive pill samples from *CURE* dataset; hard negative pill samples from *NIH* dataset; texture maps obtained using low-pass filtering of the hard negative samples.

services for pill image identification, no complete solution has been found to make the system sufficiently robust to different noisy imaging conditions in both professional and general public healthcare services.

In academic literature, most existing pill recognition models fail in the few-shot regime. This failure is more likely under less-controlled noisy imaging conditions, especially regarding the *hard samples*. There are mainly two types of **hard samples**:

1) **hard negatives**: different pill categories with similar visual appearance;
2) **hard positives**: pills under the same category but with significantly different visual characteristics due to the noisy imaging conditions.

For instance, in Fig. 15.1 (a), the same pill under different lighting conditions has different colors, while in Fig. 15.1 (b), the three different pills tend to be classified under the same pill category by existing pill recognizers because of the similarity in shape and color. The main characteristic that distinguishes the three different pills in Fig. 15.1 (b) is the imprinted texts, which are however difficult to identify even for human eyes. As noted in [7], imprinted text plays a key role in facilitating accurate pill recognition; thus approaches that make better use of the domain-related information, such as text information, could hold the key to more effective pill recognition with limited samples. According to our observations, more imprinted information can be gleaned from the pill's texture. For example, Fig. 15.1 (c) shows the texture map of (b). A comparison of the texture maps and the original RGB images shows that the imprinted texts on the pills are more visible in the texture maps.

Therefore, we propose a MultiStream (MS) deep learning model based on a novel two-stage training strategy. Where individual streams are first trained separately using the *Batch All* (BA) strategy that considers all the samples. Then in addition a late fusion process implements the *Batch Hard* (BH) strategy, which solely focuses on the hard samples that could not be processed by the individual streams in the preceding training stage. It is worthy to note that the *BH* proposed in this study is different from the one in [8], which selects only the hardest positive/negative samples from each batch using min/max function. The overall framework is depicted in Fig. 15.2.

More specifically, we proposed a W^2-net to extract the pills' regions from the background. Using the segmented pill regions, we trained three streams that process the RGB image, contour, and texture maps separately using the triplet loss with the BA strategy. Furthermore, we retrained the *Deep TextSpotter* (DTS) [9] that detects and recognizes imprinted texts on the texture maps of pill image as the fourth stream. Finally, we trained a fusion network to combine the four streams using triplet loss considering only the *hard samples* that violate the triplet constraint in the first stage, along with the imprinted text

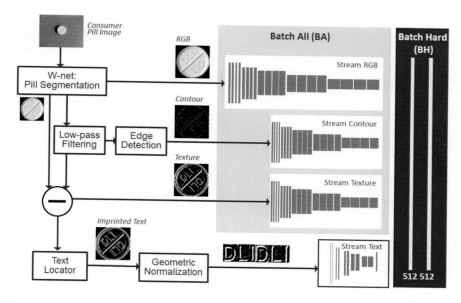

FIGURE 15.2

The framework of the proposed pill recognition model uses color, texture, contour, and imprinted text information. First, *Batch ALL* (BA) strategy extracts features in each separated stream, and then *Batch Hard* (BH) strategy combines and refines the prediction. ⊖ denotes the subtraction operation.

information provided by the retrained DTS. Specifically, this scheme facilitates the compensation of different features with the auxiliary information of the high-level imprinted text. For instance, the pill characteristics that could not be represented by RGB information would be emphasized in the second training stage and compensated by other information such as imprinted text information.

The rest of the chapter is structured as follows and closely matching the structure of original conference paper [1]. In Section 15.2 related work is reviewed. Details of the proposed model are described in Section 15.3. The new *CURE* pill dataset is introduced in Section 15.4. In Section 15.5, experimental results are summarized. Visuals from an application showcasing the use of the algorithm is provided in Section 15.6. Conclusions are given in Section 15.7.

15.2 Related work

Pill dataset: Recently, the U.S. National Library of Medicine (NLM) of the NIH released a pill image dataset and called in a challenge for submission of prescription pill images recognition models [6]. However, the images in the *NIH* dataset have limitations on lighting, background conditions, and equipment, among others. The summary of the *NIH* database is shown in Table 15.1.

Pill recognition model: In addition to designing invariant descriptors for identifying pills, Caban *et al.* [10] proposed a modified shape distribution technique for examining the shape, color, and imprinted text of pills. However, the imprint descriptors within the model are limited, and the images considered are not representative of the variability of practical situations. In [11], the structure-related features of pills were exploited by first localizing the pills within query images according to nonzero gradient magnitude. Nevertheless, this model may not be applicable under a less-controlled imaging condition. Similar features were considered in [12,13] to estimate the size of pills, and recognize them. Unfortunately, these methods disregard the fact that the sizes of pills can easily change under different zooming effects. Yu *et al.* [14] suggested exploiting the shape and other features of pills to represent the imprinted symbols on pills; however, this method fails in some cases, where the imprints of the captured pill images are obscure or invisible to humans.

Table 15.1 Comparison of the CURE and the NIH dataset.

	NIH NLM	CURE
Number of pill images	7000	8973
Number of pill categories	1000	196
Instance per category	7	40-50
Illumination conditions	1	3
Backgrounds	1	6
Imprinted text labels	No	yes
Segmentation labels	No	partially labeled

Apart from the approaches that exploit the traditional handcrafted features of pills, recently, with the breakthrough of deep learning in computer vision and image processing, four deep-features-based methods [6] have been proposed, and have yielded reasonable results on the NLM NIH pill image recognition challenge. Among them, *MobileDeepPill* (MDP) [15], one of the state-of-the-art proposals, won the first prize in the challenge. First, three convolutional neural networks (CNN) that take RGB image, gray-level image, and edge maps as input correspondingly are trained; then, the dissimilarity values calculated using each single CNN model for pill recognition are linearly summed.

Although some of the aforementioned models consider the imprinted text on pills, they solely use structural descriptors and do not attempt to recognize the symbols on the pills. Furthermore, most of them fail to cater for the *hard samples* described in the previous section under noisy conditions as they simply extract different features, and proceed straightaway to train the classifiers without considering the complementary relations between different features using a well-designed learning strategy.

Few-shot learning algorithms have been developed and proven to be a promising tool in small data scenarios. They could be categorized as

1) metric learning based approaches [16,17,18,19] whereby a similarity metric/space is learned;
2) memory network approaches [20,21,22,23] whereby the model is trained to store 'experience';
3) gradient-descent-based approaches [24,23], where a metalearner is trained to adapt a base-learner through different tasks.

Since most of these models use shallow networks to avoid the overfitting problem with limited samples, their performances are limited. To tackle this limitation, metatransfer learning *MTL* [25] was proposed to utilize a deep network for few-shot cases based on the hard task metabatch strategy. In [26], a category traversal module *CTM* was proposed to handle few-shot problems by selecting the most relevant feature dimensions after traversing both across and within categories. Nevertheless, none of these models are designed for pill recognition. Therefore, they do not sufficiently exploit the domain-related information in small data scenarios to deal with the *hard samples*.

15.3 The proposed model
15.3.1 Pill segmentation and localization

Backgrounds of pill images provide little useful information and could even deteriorate the training process of a pill recognizer as a source of noise. Dealing with different noisy backgrounds, challenging lighting, and zoom in/out conditions necessitates a model that yields more precise segmentation results. Thus, we propose a W^2-net to delimitate the pill regions from the backgrounds so that a pill recognizer can be trained on localized pill images, and ignore the perturbations from noisy and superfluous backgrounds.

It has been demonstrated in [27] that repeated bottom-up, top-down processing used in conjunction with intermediate supervision is critical for improving the performance of a network. Inspired by this idea and the concept of *Knowledge Distilling* [28], the proposed W^2-net was constructed using four simplified U-Net [29]: the input of each intermediate U-net is the concatenation of

1) the segmentation output from previous U-net,
2) the output of the second last layer from the previous U-net
3) the input image.

It is worth noting that, W^2 is 17.5 times smaller than U-Net, *i.e.*, 2 million versus 35 million parameters. This was achieved through:

1) Using 1.4% of the parameters of the original U-net for each simplified U-net;
2) Feeding the intermediate output from the previous simplified U-Net into the next one.

This simplification of the number of parameters has a direct influence on the size of the network to store on the targeted device/application. Moreover, the computation needed to perform the segmentation is reduced and helps achieve closer to real-time inference.

The detailed network architecture W^2-Net is shown in Fig. 15.3. As there are only two semantic categories in our study, *i.e.*, background and pill regions, we employ the pixel-wise binary cross-entropy loss for the i_{th} simplified U-net:

$$\mathcal{L}_{U_i} = \sum_{p \in P_I} -(l(p) \cdot log(s(p)) + (1 - l(p)) \cdot log(1 - s(p))), \qquad (15.1)$$

where $l(\cdot)$ is the true label of each pixel $p \in P_I$ and $s(\cdot)$ is the score predicted by the i_{th} U-net with sigmoid function as activation function. The loss function of the proposed W^2-net is then defined as:

$$\mathcal{L}_{W^2} = \sum_{i=1}^{4} \lambda_{U_i} \mathcal{L}_{U_i}, \qquad (15.2)$$

where λ_{U_i} are the parameters balancing the losses of the corresponding simplified U-nets and are

Table 15.2 Notation of variables and function used in the chapter.

Notation	Description
$l(\cdot)$	the true label of each pixel within image
p	the p_{th} pixel within an image
P_I	the entire pixel set for a certain image
λ_{U_i}	the i_{th} parameter for the i_{th} U-net within the proposed W^2-net, $i = 1, 2, 3, 4$
$\mathcal{L}_{U_i}$	the cross-entropy loss for the i_{th} U-net within the proposed W^2-net, $i = 1, 2, 3, 4$
$\mathcal{L}_{W^2}$	the cross-entropy loss for the proposed W^2-net
I_a	the anchor image within one triplet
I_p	the positive image within one triplet that belongs to the same pill class as I_a
I_n	the negative image within one triplet that belongs to a different pill class as I_a
m	the margin in the triplet loss function
θ	the parameter of a certain function
$\mathbb{R}^F$	data feature manifold
$\mathbb{R}^B$	embedding feature space after metric embedding learning
f_θ	the function that maps images from the feature manifold $\mathbb{R}^F$ to the embedding space $\mathbb{R}^E$
$D(\cdot)$	the metric function that measure the distance between two images
$\mathcal{L}_{tri}$	the triplet loss
y_i	the pill category label of the i_{th} image
I_{RGB}	the RGB image after pill segmentation
I_{gray}	the gray-level image of I_{RGB}
I_{res}	the response of low-pass filter of I_{RGB}
I_t	the residual obtained by subtracting the low-pass filtering response I_{res} from I_{RGB}
I_c	the contour map obtained using *Canny* edge detector on I_{res}
X	the training data set of each batch
P	the numbers of pills category in one batch
K	the numbers of instances for each pill category in P in one batch
r	the detected text regions with pill images
w	the width of r
h	the height of r
C	the color channels of r
H'	the predefined fix-height of text region
$\tau(\cdot)$	the point-wise transformation function for normalization of text regions
r_n	the normalized text region
$\overline{W}$	the normalized width of one text region r, $\overline{W} = \frac{wH'}{h}$
$\mathcal{A}$	the alphabet of text recognizer, *i.e.*, the dictionary for all the possible letters/symbols
$|\mathcal{A}|$	the size of $\mathcal{A}$, *i.e.*, numbers of letters/symbols within the alphabet
$\mathcal{L}_{BA}$	the triplet loss function based on *Batch All* strategy
$\mathcal{L}_{BH}$	the triplet loss function based on *Batch Hard* strategy
v	the matrix of size $\frac{\overline{W}}{4} \times |\mathcal{A}|$ returned by the text recognizer give a normalized region r_n
v_j^i	the vector indicates the likelihood of the j_{th} label of the alphabet exists at position i in r_n
s	the initial sequence of labels within a detected region r_n
$\mathcal{M}_\mathcal{A}(\cdot)$	the many-to-one mapping function to remove the blanks or repeated labels in s
s_f	the final sequence of letters/symbols after many-to-one mapping with s as input
$f_{text}(\cdot)$	the retrained text recognizer taking I_t as input
$f_{text}^{avg}(\cdot)$	the function that sums over matrix M_t along the position dimension, *i.e.*, the width of the tailed text region
v_t	the final text probability vector in size of $(1, |\mathcal{A}|)$, where each dimension of the vector corresponds to one item in $\mathcal{A}$ showing the averaged probability value of how likely this corresponding symbol appears in the pill image
H_{str}	the sets of hard samples obtained during the first training stage for the str_{th} stream

set equally to 1/4 in this study. In the following sections, only the segmented/located pill images are considered.

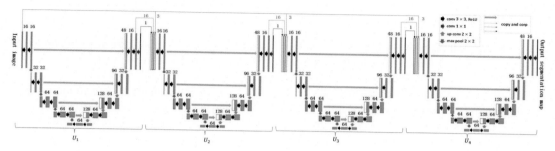

FIGURE 15.3

The W^2-net architecture.

15.3.2 Multistream CNN for pill recognition

15.3.2.1 Metric embedding learning using triplet loss

Pill recognition is a typical few-shot learning problem, where insufficient data is available for each pill class. Recently, effective few-shot methodologies adapted a metric-learning scheme to learn a similarity metric to compare the difference between a test/query example and the few ones used in training [26, 16]. In this study, to better handle the positive/negative hard samples described in Section 15.1, the triplet loss was employed to optimize the similarity metric (embedding space) such that images of the same pill are closer to each other and inversely for the images from different pills.

Theoretically speaking, given a set of triplets (I_a, I_p, I_n) (I_a is considered as an anchor image, I_p is the positive sample that is of the same category with I_a, while I_n is the negative sample that is of a different category), the goal of metric embedding learning is to learn a function $f_\theta(I) : \mathbb{R}^F \to \mathbb{R}^E$ parametrized by θ to map similar or different pill images, i.e., (I_a, I_p) for same pills or (I_a, I_n) for different pills, from the feature manifold $\mathbb{R}^F$ onto metrically close/far points in an embedding space $\mathbb{R}^E$ with the objective function defined as [30]:

$$\mathcal{L}_{tri}(\theta) = \sum_{\substack{a,p,n \\ y_a = y_p \neq y_n}} [m + D(f_\theta(I_a), f_\theta(I_p)) - D(f_\theta(I_a), f_\theta(I_n))]_+ \qquad (15.3)$$

where m is a margin that is enforced between positive and negative pairs [30], $[x]_+ = max\{0, x\}$, (y_a, y_p, y_n) are the pill category labels for the samples used in a valid triplet, $D(f_\theta(I_i), f_\theta(I_j)) : \mathbb{R}^E \times \mathbb{R}^E \to \mathbb{R}$ denotes the metric function that measures the distances between two images I_i, I_j in the embedding space. Throughout this study, *Euclidean* distance was used as the distance measure, *i.e.*, $D(\cdot)$, as in [8]. Nevertheless, a pill recognition model that processes different features separately, *e.g.*, MDP [15], cannot effectively handle the *hard samples*. Thus, it is important to devise a proper strategy for training considering the fact that

1) If using all the possible triplets, the number of triplets will increase cubically with the growth of data numbers, rendering the training inefficient;

2) If only the *hardest triplets* are considered, the model would select the outliers in the dataset, resulting in the failure of f_θ in learning the 'normal' associations [8];

3) Training separate networks using different features as done in [15] neglects the complementary relationships between different features.

To this end, we propose an MS CNN that is composed of four individual streams (*stream RGB, Texture, Contour*, and *Imprinted Text*) that are consecutively combined with a late fusion network. The proposed MS CNN was trained in a stage-wise manner, similarly to [31]. In the first training stage, we used the *BA* strategy to train the stream *RGB, Texture*, and *Contour* individually, where all the samples are considered. In this stage, the hard samples that could not be tackled using each stream alone were selected for the second stage. For example, for stream *RGB*, the hard samples could be the same pill but under different illumination conditions as shown in Fig. 15.1 (a); for stream *Texture*, hard samples could be different pills with the same texture, shape, imprinted text but different color; for stream *Contour*, hard samples could be different pills with the same shape but different texture or imprinted text, when imprinted texts are visually unclear. In the second training stage, we propose a new *BH* strategy to train the fusion net to combine the three individual streams along with a retrained imprinted text stream, based on text-regions detection and recognition.

During the second training stage, the four streams were fixed and the fusion network was trained using only the hard samples mined in the first stage. The rationale behind this two-stage training strategy is to build a bridge between different feature spaces so that they could compensate each other by concentrating on the *hard samples* excavated in the first training stage. Details are given in the following subsections aligned with the two-stage learning procedure, which is summarized in Algorithm 15.1.

15.3.2.2 RGB, texture, and contour streams

Among the hand-crafted features based pill recognition models [10,11,12,13,14], color, contour, and texture related descriptors were commonly considered and proven to be effective in the task. Therefore, we selected color, contour and texture channel (task-related channels) as the input of the substreams $f_{rgb}(\cdot)$, $f_{texture}(\cdot)$, and $f_{contour}(\cdot)$ empirically. The first training stage is summarized in Algorithm 15.1 (line: 3-16). Details are described below.

Firstly, based on the perceptual study conducted in [32], a low-pass-based model is proposed in [33] to separate structural information from the textural one. It is adapted in this paper to obtain clearer contour and texture maps. More specifically, as depicted in Fig. 15.2, given the gray-level image I_{gray} of a segmented pill image I_{RGB}, the contour map I_c is obtained by employing *Canny* edge detector on the response I_{res} of using *Gaussian* filter on I_{gray}. Then, the residual that maintains the high-frequency components, where texture information is emphasized, is obtained by subtracting the I_{res} from I_{gray}. Here, it is named as the texture map and denoted as I_t. Afterwards, the three individual streams taking RGB image I_{RGB}, contour map I_c and texture map I_t as input separately using the *BA* strategy [8]:

$$\mathcal{L}_{BA}(\theta, X_b) = \overbrace{\sum_{i=1}^{P}\sum_{a=1}^{K}}^{all\ anchors} \overbrace{\sum_{\substack{i=1\\p\neq a}}^{K}}^{all\ pos.} \overbrace{\sum_{\substack{j=1\\j\neq i}}^{P}\sum_{n=1}^{K}}^{all\ neg.} \left[m + d_{j,a,n}^{i,a,p}\right]_+ , \tag{15.4}$$

$$d_{j,a,n}^{i,a,p} = D(f_\theta(I_a^i), f_\theta(I_p^i)) - D(f_\theta(I_a^i), f_\theta(I_n^j)),$$

Algorithm 15.1 Two stage BA-BH learning strategy.

1: **Input:** Data set X. Triplet generator $\tau_g(\cdot)$.
2: **Output:** MultiStream pill recognizer $f_{MS}(\cdot)$.
3: **Stage 1** Task-related streams training (Section 15.3.2.2):
4: Randomly initialize three individual streams $f_{rgb}(\cdot)$, $f_{texture}(\cdot)$, and $f_{contour}(\cdot)$.
5: Initialize Hard triplet set: $H_{str} \leftarrow \emptyset$, where $str = \{rgb, contour, texture\}$
6: **for** batch X_b in X **do**
7:     $T_a = \tau_g(X_b)$, T_a is the set contains all the possible triplets from batch X_b.
8:     Evaluate $\mathcal{L}_{BA}(f_{rgb}(\cdot), T_a)$, $\mathcal{L}_{BA}(f_{texture}(\cdot), T_a)$, and $\mathcal{L}_{BA}(f_{contour}(\cdot), T_a)$ by Eq. (15.4).
9:     Optimize $f_{rgb}(\cdot)$, $f_{texture}(\cdot)$, and $f_{contour}(\cdot)$ by Adam optimizer.
10: **end for**
11: Freeze $f_{rgb}(\cdot)$, $f_{texture}(\cdot)$, and $f_{contour}(\cdot)$.
12: **for** any triplet $(I_a^i, I_p^i, I_n^j) \in T_g(X)$ **do**
13:     **if** $D(f_{str}(I_a^i), f_{str}(I_p^i)) - D(f_{str}(I_a^i) f_{str}(I_n^j)) < m$, where $str = \{rgb, contour, texture\}$ **then**
14:         $H_{str} \leftarrow (I_a^i, I_p^i, I_n^j)$
15:     **end if**
16: **end for**
17: Retrain DTS, and obtain $f_{text}^{avg}(\cdot)$ (Section 15.3.2.3).
18: Randomly initialize fusion network $f_{fusion}(\cdot)$.
19: **Stage 2** Fusion Network training, focuses on hard triplets (Section 15.3.2.4):
20: **for** batch X_b in $\{H_{rgb} \cup H_{contour} \cup H_{texture}\}$ **do**
21:     $T_h = \tau_g(X_b)$, T_h is the triplet set contains hard triplets within batch X_b minded in the first stage.

22:     Obtain $f_{MS}(\cdot)$ by plugging $f_{text}^{avg}(\cdot)$, $f_{rgb}(\cdot)$, $f_{texture}(\cdot)$, and $f_{contour}(\cdot)$ with $f_{fusion}(\cdot)$ as shown in Fig. 15.2.
23:     Evaluate $\mathcal{L}_{BH}(f_{MS}(\cdot), T_h)$ by Eq. (15.8).
24:     Optimize $f_{fusion}(\cdot)$ by Adam optimizer.
25: **end for**

---

where I_j^i denotes the data points of the j_{th} instance for the i_{th} pill category in the current mini-batch X_b. P and K are the numbers of randomly sampled pills categories and the corresponding pill images in each batch. For each batch, all possible $PK(PK - K)(K - 1)$ combinations of triplets were considered. During the first training stage, the hard samples that violated the constraint $d_{j,a,n}^{i,a,p} < m$ were forwarded to the second training stage.

The usage of a pretrained network could lead to a design lock-in [8]. Therefore, in this study, we designed the three individual streams from scratch.

The architecture of RGB stream is presented in Table 15.3, when the ones of Contour and Texture streams are summarized in Table 15.4. The *Texture* and *Contour* streams share the same smaller architecture compared to the RGB stream. The only difference between their architecture and the one of the RGB stream is the number of channels (*i.e.*, the network of the RGB stream has twice the numbers of channels) at each layer. The number of parameters of *RGB*, *Contour*, *Texture* streams are 9 M, 2.2 M and 2.2 M respectively. We trained with more complex architectures with a larger number of parame-

Table 15.3 The CNN architecture of the *RGB* stream.

Type	nb channels	output size	stride	kernel
Input	3	128×128	-	-
conv1	64	64×64	2	7×7
conv2	64	64×64	1	3×3
conv3	64	64×64	1	3×3
pool1	64	32×32	-	4×4
conv4	96	32×32	1	3×3
conv5	96	32×32	1	3×3
conv6	96	32×32	1	3×3
pool2	96	16×16	-	4×4
conv7	128	16×16	1	3×3
conv8	128	16×16	1	3×3
conv9	128	16×16	1	3×3
pool3	128	8×8	-	4×4
conv10	256	8×8	1	3×3
conv11	256	8×8	1	3×3
conv12	256	8×8	1	3×3
pool4	256	4×4	-	4×4
conv13	384	4×4	1	3×3
conv14	384	4×4	1	3×3
conv15	384	4×4	1	3×3
fc	-	512	-	-
reg	-	256	-	-

ters for the three streams, however, performances drop. Please refer to Section 15.11 in this chapter for more details about learning from single streams and networks with larger capacities.

15.3.2.3 Imprinted text stream

In the proposed model, imprinted text information on pills was captured by first detecting possible text regions and then recognizing the texts/symbols within them by retraining the DTS model [9] as depicted in the lower part of Fig. 15.2. To reshape detected text regions into canonical tensors with consistent dimension, adapted bilinear sampling proposed in [9] was first employed. For a detected text region $r \in \mathbb{R}^{w \times h \times C}$, it is normalized into a tensor with a fixed-height $r_n \in \mathbb{R}^{\frac{wH'}{h} \times H' \times C}$ using:

$$r_n = \sum_{x=1}^{w}\sum_{y=1}^{h} max(0, 1 - |x - \tau_x(x')|) \cdot max(0, 1 - |y - \tau_y(y')|)), \qquad (15.5)$$

where τ is a point-wise coordinate transformation and H' is the fixed-height that was set as 32 in [9]. We adapted the text recognizer proposed in [9] using the texture image I_t obtained after low-pass filtering as input. For each normalized r_n, it was converted into a conditional probability distribution using *Connectionist Temporal Classification* [34], so that the most probable series of symbols could

Table 15.4 The CNN architecture of the *Texture* and *Contour* streams.

Type	nb channels	output size	stride	kernel
Input	1	128×128	-	-
conv1	32	64×64	2	7×7
conv2	32	64×64	1	3×3
conv3	32	64×64	1	3×3
pool1	32	32×32	-	4×4
conv4	48	32×32	1	3×3
conv5	48	32×32	1	3×3
conv6	48	32×32	1	3×3
pool2	48	16×16	-	4×4
conv7	64	16×16	1	3×3
conv8	64	16×16	1	3×3
conv9	64	16×16	1	3×3
pool3	64	8×8	-	4×4
conv10	128	8×8	1	3×3
conv11	128	8×8	1	3×3
conv12	128	8×8	1	3×3
pool4	128	4×4	-	4×4
conv13	192	4×4	1	3×3
conv14	192	4×4	1	3×3
conv15	192	4×4	1	3×3
fc	-	256	-	-
reg	-	128	-	-

be chosen for the text regions. More specifically, the text recognizer in DTS was trained with an alphabet $\mathcal{A}$ to return a matrix $\mathbf{M_t}$ of size $\frac{\overline{W}}{4} \times |\mathcal{A}|$ for an input r_n of size $\overline{W} \times H'$, where $\overline{W} = \frac{wH'}{h}$ and $|\mathcal{A}|$ is the length of the alphabet. Here, each column at a position i of the matrix is a vector $\mathbf{v}^i = (v_1^i, \ldots, v_j^i, \ldots, v_{|\mathcal{A}|}^i)$, where each v_j^i indicates the likelihood of the j_{th} label within the alphabet, *e.g.* letter 'a', exists at the i_{th} position, and $\sum_{j=1}^{\mathcal{A}} v_j^i = 1$. Then, the probability of a sequence of labels s within a detected region r_n is defined as

$$p(s|\mathbf{v}) = \prod_{i=1}^{\overline{W}/4} v_{s_i}^i, \ s \in \mathcal{A}^{\overline{W}/4}, \tag{15.6}$$

where $v_{s_i}^i$ denotes the output probability of the network predicting the label s_i at the position i.

To remove the blanks or repeated labels, the many-to-one mapping $\mathcal{M}_\mathcal{A}: \mathcal{A}^{\overline{W}/4} \mapsto \mathcal{A}^{\leq \overline{W}/4}$, was employed to get the conditional probability of the final sequence s_f. The objective function used for training the text recognition network could be then defined as in [9,34]:

$$\underset{s_f \in \mathcal{A}^{\leq \overline{W}/4}}{\arg\max} \sum_{s:\mathcal{M}_\mathcal{A}(\mathbf{v})=s_f} p(s|\mathbf{v}). \tag{15.7}$$

After retraining the network $f_{text}(\cdot)$, for an input I_{RGB}, the texture map I_t was first generated. Then I_t was fed to the text detection network to generate all the possible text regions, the two highest ranked text proposals were normalized, tailed as one r_n and then fed to the text recognition network to obtain the matrix $\mathbf{M_t} = f_{text}(r_n)$ in size of $\frac{\overline{W}}{4} \times |\mathcal{A}|$. Afterwards, it was averaged over the position dimension, *i.e.*, the width of the tailed text region, to obtain a final text probability vector $\mathbf{v_t}$ with a size of $(1, |\mathcal{A}|)$, where each dimension of the vector $\mathbf{v_{t_j}} = \frac{\sum_{i=1}^{\overline{W}/4} v_j^i}{\overline{W}/4}$ corresponds to one item in the alphabet $\mathcal{A}$ showing the average probability value of the likelihood of this corresponding symbol appears in the pill image over the entire tailed text regions. The procedure of taking one I_t as input to obtain the average text vector $\mathbf{v_t}$ is denoted as $f_{text}^{avg}(\mathbf{M_t}) = \mathbf{v_t}$. The retrained DTS is fixed and will be then combined by the later fusion net with other streams in the fusion stage. Intuitively, $\mathbf{v_t}$ provides information of the existence of imprinted symbols on the pills, and was subsequently utilized to compensate the other three streams.

15.3.2.4 Multistream fusion network

The second training stage is summarized in Algorithm 15.1 (line: 11-24). After training the *RGB*, *Texture*, and *Contour* streams separately using the *BA* strategy in the first training stage, where the hard samples were selected, they were then fixed. Afterward, in the second training stage, they were combined with the *Imprinted Text* stream (it was fixed after retraining with texture maps, and was used as extra information) to train the fusion network $f_{fusion}(\cdot)$ using *BH* strategy that focuses only on the hard samples. More specifically, they were concatenated with two fully connected layers (white color layers in Fig. 15.2). The remaining fusion network was trained with an emphasis on the *hard samples* collected during the first training stage (*i.e.*, pretraining of individual streams) with the following objective function:

$$\mathcal{L}_{BH}(\theta, X_b) = \sum_{str=1}^{3} \sum_{\substack{(I_a^i, I_p^i, I_n^j) \in H_{str} \\ (I_a^i, I_p^i, I_n^j) \in X_b}}^{N_{str}} [m + \overbrace{D(f_\theta(I_a^i), f_\theta(I_p^i))}^{str_{th}\ hard\ pos.} - \underbrace{D(f_\theta(I_a^i), f_\theta(I_n^j))}_{str_{th}\ hard\ neg.}]_+, \tag{15.8}$$

where H_{str} is the set of hard samples obtained during the first training stage, $str = \{rgb, texture, contour\}$ corresponds to the *RGB*, *Texture* and *Contour* streams respectively. N_{str} is the number of hard samples from the stream of str in the batch. It must be emphasized that only the *RGB*, *Texture*, and *Contour* streams were trained firstly using the triplet loss with the *BA* strategy to mine the hard samples that could not be settled by the corresponding feature. The *Imprinted Text* stream was combined directly with the other streams as auxiliary information, where the fusion net was trained using the *BH* strategy in the second stage for the following reasons:

1) the bottom-side of a great number of pills do not contain any imprinted text;
2) imprinted texts could be occluded;
3) pills with different characteristics but from the same manufacturer could have the same imprinted text.

Thus, most of the samples that could be easily represented by other information, *e.g.*, shape, would become hard samples for stream *Imprinted Text*, and hence weaken the advantage of using the proposed two-stage strategy.

15.3.2.5 Pill retrieval/recognition

With the embedded metric learned using the proposed multistream model f_{MS}, the category of any query consumer image I_{con} could then be predicted by measuring the similarity between I_{con} and all the reference images I_{ref} in the learned embedded space. In this study, the similarity score was computed directly using $D(f_{MS}(I_{con}), f_{MS}(I_{ref}))$ instead of firstly summing the similarity scores computed by different networks based on different features as done in [15].

15.4 Proposed CURE pill database

In this section, the novel *CURE* pill dataset is introduced. This dataset summarized in Table 15.1, contains 8973 images of 196 categories, and approximately 40 to 50 samples were obtained for each pill category.

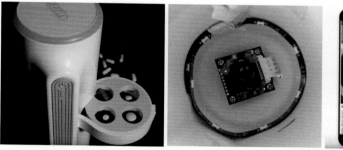

FIGURE 15.4

(a) *MPI* device; (b) embedded camera in the device; (c) smartphone software connected to the device.

Equipment: The pill images within this database were taken using three phones (*i.e.*, *Samsung SM-J320FN*, *Samsung SM-N920S*, and *LG F500L*) and one *MultiPill Identifier* (MPI) device equipped with a Raspberry Pi Camera Module. The MPI device provides healthcare personnel and the general public with descriptions for unknown pills. Furthermore, information obtained using this device could be used for purposes such as checking the compatibility between different pills, detecting expired medicines, and toxicity of molecules during the recycling phase. The device is shown in Fig. 15.4 (a), where a camera was mounted on a *Raspberry Pi 3*, as shown in Fig. 15.4 (b) is set above the pill holder. The image resolution is 2448 × 2448 or 2976 × 2976, for those taken using the mobile phone, and 640 × 640 for those taken using the MPI device.

Consumer Images: are pictures not taken under professionally controlled conditions [6]. In real cases, consumer images are likely to be taken with varying devices, backgrounds, illuminations, focus, and orientations. To make the database more diverse, when collecting the consumer images, backgrounds of different levels of texture granularity, illumination, and dynamic zooming in/out conditions

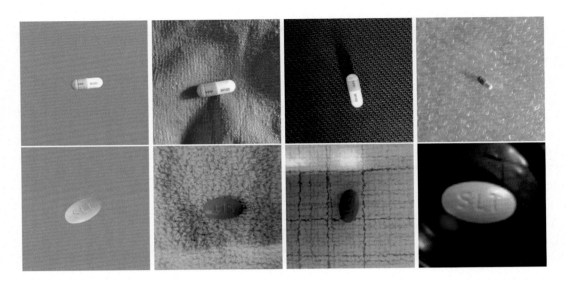

FIGURE 15.5

Examples of images in CURE. Row: each row corresponds to one category of the pill. Column: (1) 1st column: reference images; (2) other columns: consumer images.

are considered. The illumination conditions include 1) indoor light, 2) weak outdoor light, and 3) strong outdoor light.

Reference Images: For each pill category, the reference image was generated using the best-quality consumer images. More specifically, the pixel-level pill regions in the selected pill images with the better-controlled conditions are first manually labeled. Then, the backgrounds of the selected images are replaced with clean gray backgrounds. Examples of the reference images in the dataset are shown in the first column of Fig. 15.5. We believe that generating reference images using consumer images is more practical, for the following reasons:

1) In cases where reference images are uploaded by the pill manufacturers, high-quality cameras could be too expensive, and collecting professional images under professionally controlled conditions is more time consuming;
2) In cases where reference images are uploaded by consumers, the developed pill recognition models should achieve acceptable performances even with lower quality reference images.

All of these reference images are labeled with pixel-wise pill location and imprinted text/symbols.

As summarized in Table 15.1, this dataset considers more challenging real-world conditions (*i.e.*, with more diverse backgrounds, light, and zooming conditions); thus, it reflects practical cases better, compared to the *NIH* dataset [6]. Examples of images in the dataset are shown in Fig. 15.5, as observed, 1) images in the last row were taken under different light conditions, which could result in significant changes to the pill color (especially for (h), where the color of the images taken under different lighting conditions with the MPI equipment vary significantly); 2) (c) and (d) are taken under different zooming conditions; 3) the backgrounds considered in this dataset are diverse.

More examples from the proposed CURE pill image dataset are presented in Fig. 15.6. It could be observed that diverse lighting, zooming, backgrounds conditions are considered.

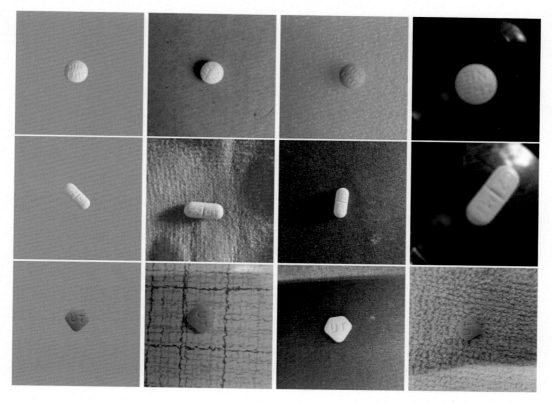

FIGURE 15.6

Examples of images in CURE. Row: each row corresponds to one category of the pill. Column: (1) 1st column: reference images; (2) other columns: consumer images.

15.5 Experimental results
15.5.1 Pill segmentation

The W^2-net was trained using our *CURE* dataset. Reference images were utilized via data augmentation to train the network and the performance was tested on 20% of the consumer images with pixel-wise labels. To augment the training set, we synthesized around 10^5 customer images by:

1) replacing the background using the texture images from the *Describable Textures Dataset* [35] or background patches manually extracted from the *CURE* dataset;
2) rotating the labeled pill region in the range of $(-180°, 180°)$;

3) changing foreground-background contrast calculated in terms of the ratio of foreground-background illuminance;
4) randomly changing the ratio of the height/width of the maximum circumscribed rectangle of foreground pill area versus the height/width of the image to mimic different zoom in/out conditions. As thus, the network is robust to the variance of pill sizes;
5) randomly switching the pill location.

The W^2-net was trained for 5 epochs using *Adam* optimizer with a learning rate started from 10^{-4} (divided by 10 every 2 epochs). Intersection Over Union (IOU) [29] was applied to demonstrate the performance of the proposed model.

- **Intersection Over Union (IOU):**

$$IOU = \frac{Px_{prediction} \times Px_{label}}{Px_{label} + ((1 - Px_{label}) \times Px_{prediction})}, \tag{15.9}$$

where $Px_{prediction}$ are the binary predictions made for each pixel by the model and Px_{label} the binary labels of the segmentation mask.

Table 15.5 Performances of pill segmentation.

	U-net (35 M)	Espnetv2 (0.3 M)	W²-net (2 M)
IOU	0.90	0.78	**0.94**

To check the superiority of W^2-net, it was compared to the original U-net proposed in [29], and the state-of-the-art light-weight *Espnetv2* [36]. The performances are summarized in Table 15.5. As observed, the proposed network achieves superior performance even compared with the original U-net (35 M). Examples of segmentation results on both the *CURE* dataset are shown in Fig. 15.7. As shown, 1) the first row that W^2-net is more robust to complicated backgrounds; 2) the second row that W^2-net is better in dealing with the regions of pills' shadows.

15.5.2 Imprinted text detection & recognition

The DTS [9] that detects and recognizes imprinted text in pill images was retrained on our novel *CURE* dataset.

We first used their text regions proposal model to generate possible text regions and manually selected the correct text regions as ground-truth text regions. Since imprinted texts are challenging to be detected and recognized by their model, for images where no text region candidate was returned, we manually labeled the bounding boxes for all the text regions. For those pill images that contain no text, the largest inscribed rectangular of the pill mask obtained after pill segmentation was taken as the ground-truth regions, and labeled with a blank symbol '-'. As the imprinted text/symbol regions were labeled, we augmented the data by:

1) blurring the text regions using *Gaussian* filtering;
2) rotating the text boxes in the range of $(-180°, 180°)$ with a constraint that the rotated bounding boxes should still locate within the pill.

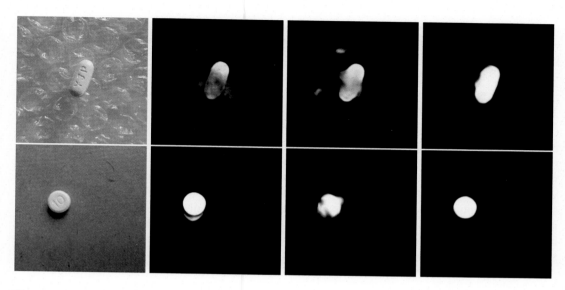

FIGURE 15.7

Columns: from left to right are the pill image, the segmented results using (1) *U*-net; (2) *ESPNetv2*; (3) W^2-net.

We directly retrained both the text detection and recognition network of the DTS simultaneously for 6 epochs using mini-batch Stochastic Gradient Descent (SGD) with a momentum of 0.9 and a learning rate of 10^{-3}, divided by 10 every two epochs.

The performance of the imprinted text recognition model was evaluated by the *f-measure*. As done in [9], when the IOU of a predicted text region is higher than 0.5 and the transcription is identical (using case-insensitive comparison [38]), it is considered as correctly recognized. Performance is then evaluated with *f-measure*.

- F_1 **score:**

$$F_1 = \frac{2 \times precision \times recall}{precision + recall},\qquad(15.10)$$

where $precision = \frac{t_p}{t_p + f_p}$, and $recall = \frac{t_p}{t_p + f_n}$. t_p, f_p, and f_n indicates the true positives, the false positives and the false negatives correspondingly.

Table 15.6 Performances of imprinted text recognition.			
	MTS-RGB [37]	*DTS-RGB* [9]	*DTS-Texture*
f-measure	0.446	0.47	**0.56**

To confirm our hypothesis that imprinted texts on pills could be more easily recognized using the texture map compared to the RGB image, we conducted our experiment using the DTS model on both texture maps and RGB images. Results shown in Table 15.6 demonstrate that the model trained with texture maps yields superior performance. Except for DTS, we have also tested the state-of-the-art end-to-end Mask TextSpotter (MTS) [37] using RGB images. However, its performance is lower compared to using DTS on RGB images.

15.5.3 Pill recognition

Our MS model was tested on both the *NIH* and *CURE* datasets. In the first training stage, for the three individual streams, dropout (with $p_d = 0.9, 0.8, 0.8$ for the *RGB, Texture*, and *Contour* streams respectively, where p_d is the probability of retaining the hidden unit) and l_2 norm regularization (λ_{l_2} was set as 0.1, 0.06, 0.06 for the three streams respectively, where λ_{l_2} is the regularization parameter) were used on each of the fully connected (dense) layers before the output. The mini-batch Adam was selected as the optimizer, with learning rate l_r equal to 3×10^{-4} and divided by 3 after every 5 iterations until 20 iterations are complete. During the second training stage, $p_d = 0.5$, $\lambda_{l_2} = 10^{-3}$, and the mini-batch Adam is employed with $l_r = 10^{-4}$, which is divided by 3 for every 2 epochs. For both training stages, margin m was set to 0.5 and the mini-batch size was 64.

The performances of the pill recognition models were evaluated based on the Mean Average Precision (MAP), and Top-K accuracy [15,6].

- **Mean Average Precision (MAP):**

$$MAP = \frac{1}{N} \sum_{i=1}^{N} \left(\frac{1}{N_i} \sum_{j=1}^{N_i} \frac{j}{MT(i,j)} \right), \tag{15.11}$$

  where N denotes the number of consumer images, N_i represents the number of the reference images, j is the number of correctly matched images (*i.e.*, 1/2), and $MT(i,j)$ indicates the correct ranking of the reference images.
- **Top-K Accuracy:** the proportion of query images, whose correct pill category labels are within the top K retrieval results obtained by the model, to the number of all the query images.

The evaluation scheme of *one-side pill recognition* with 5-fold cross validation [15] was used. The performances of the proposed model compared to MDP [15], the state-of-the-art pill recognition model,[1] on the *NIH* and *CURE* datasets are listed in Table 15.7. As shown, the proposed MS model outperforms MDP on both of the datasets in terms of Top-1 and MAP values. It is noteworthy that, our network, including segmentation and recognition, is much lighter than the one of MDP with 15.6 M parameters against 39 M, and the inference time is shorter 57 ms versus 89.8 ms.

Solved hard samples: To showcase the advantage of using our proposed two-stage learning strategies, examples of hard triplets from the NIH/CURE dataset, which are mined in the first stage, violating the triplet constraint $d_{j,a,n}^{i,a,p} < m$, and solved (accurately recognized) in the second stage, are shown in Fig. 15.8. Images on the right, middle, and right of each triplet are the positive samples, the anchor images, and the negative samples respectively. Samples (negative/positive) within the hard triplets are hard

---

[1] Neither the descriptions of algorithms nor the source codes of other deep models summarized in [6] are published.

Table 15.7 Performance of pill recognition models (one-side).

Database	NIH		CURE	
	MAP	TOP-1	MAP	TOP-1
MDP [15]	0.582	53.1	0.704	63.7
MS (ours)	**0.722**	**65.9**	**0.749**	**68.3**

samples. For clear comparisons, only the hard-triplets, where both the positive and negative samples are reference images, were selected.

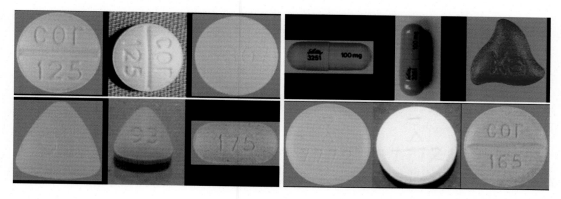

FIGURE 15.8

Examples of hard triplets that are minded in the first stage but are solved (accurately recognized) in the second stage.

Table 15.8   Performance comparison with few-shot learning models (5-way 1-shot Accuracy (%)).

Database	NIH	CURE
CTM [26]	61.2	50.4
MTL [25]	58.7	47.7
MS (ours)	**64.2**	**53.7**

Few-shot/meta learning regime: We also compared our model with state-of-the-art meta/few-shot learning models, *i.e.*, MTL [25] and CTM [26]. Similar to the experimental setup on MiniImagenet dataset in [24,16], we followed the protocol proposed in [16] and divided the NIH and our CURE dataset into 16%, 64%, and 20% as metavalidation (NIH:160, CURE:31 classes), metatrain (NIH:640, CURE:125 classes), and metatest (NIH:200, CURE:40 classes) sets according to the pills' categories. Categories in the test set are unseen during the training/validation process. During the metatraining phase, as done in [26], the entire metatrain set was employed to train the similarity metric/embedder with the proposed multistream network boosted by the two-stage learning strategy. During the metatesting phase, to set up an $N-$way $K-$shots recognition evaluation scheme, N unseen classes were selected, provide the model with K different instances of each of the N classes, and evaluate the model's ability to classify new instances within the N classes [16,24]. For a fair comparison, only the segmented images obtained using W^2-net are considered for the compared few-shot models. For the MTL model, the ResNet-12 architecture was adopted as in their paper and in [39,40]. For CTM, as their model achieved better performance by employing a deeper backbone for the feature extractors [26], we tested CTM with ResNet-18 in the experiment. Please refer to the supplementary material for more details on the experimental setup. The results are presented in Table 15.8. As shown, our model achieves the best few-shot classification performance.

Table 15.9 Performance of pill recognition models (two-side).

Database	NIH		CURE	
	MAP	**TOP-1**	**MAP**	**TOP-1**
MDP [15]	0.837	74.1	0.853	79.8
MS (ours)	**0.852**	**77.3**	**0.876**	**84.6**

Furthermore, we can see that models obtain higher performances on the *CURE* dataset compared to the one on NIH in Table 15.7, while totally opposite phenomenon is observed under few-shot setting in Table 15.8. It indicates that:

1) the sufficient number of instances per class in our *CURE* database enable the studies of nonfew-shot learning approaches
2) our *CURE* dataset (contains difficult *hard samples*) is more challenging for state-of-the-art few-shot learning models.

The performance comparison results in terms of two-side MAP, Top-1 are summarized in Table 15.9. As shown, in the two-side case, the proposed model is also superior to the state-of-the-art model MDP. Similar to [6], under two-side setting, if one pill recognizer is able to indicate the category of the query pill image no matter which side it is (top/bottom), then the image is considered as accurately recognized. However, under one-side setting, top and bottom side of one pill category are considered as different categories [15]. Therefore, the two-side setting is commonly easier than the one-side setting, and the pill recognizers could achieve higher performance under the two-side setting.

Ablation Study: Extensive comparisons with ablative models were performed, and the results are presented in Table 15.10. By comparing the performances of the ablative models to the one of the MS model shown in Table 15.7, it could be seen that:

1) Impact of each stream (row 3-8): the proposed MS model outperforms the individual models. By removing a certain stream, the performance drops. Domain-related information, *e.g.*, imprinted text, helps to improve the recognition performance;
2) Impact of segmentation models (row 9-10): by removing/replacing the proposed W^2-net, the performances drop;
3) Impact of learning batch strategy (row 10-12): the proposed two-stage BA-BH learning strategy is superior to the traditional BH and BA strategy.

Ablation Study on network sizes: With enough samples and network parameters, network with deeper and/or wider enough architecture, important domain-related information, such as texture, contour characteristics or imprinted text could be extracted and applicable for the task. But for this few-shot

Table 15.10 Recognition results for ablative models (one-side).

Database	Ablative models	NIH		CURE	
		MAP	TOP-1	MAP	TOP-1
Individual stream	Stream RGB	0.612	54.6	0.562	50.9
	Stream Texture	0.259	20.6	0.507	49.2
	Stream Contour	0.179	12.6	0.348	25.98
Impact of domain-related features	Without Text	0.612	54.4	0.594	52.2
	Without Contour	0.653	60.9	0.677	66.9
	Without Texture	0.633	56.9	0.604	54.5
Impact of segmentation	No segmentation	0.406	45.6	0.447	48.7
	With U-net (35 M)	0.577	54.1	0.641	60.4
Impact of strategy	With BA	0.664	60.2	0.682	65.1
	With BH	0.651	58.7	0.677	64.5

learning task, we found it much more efficient to take advantage of hand-crafted features as domain knowledge at the first stage with simpler networks, and then boost at the second stage.

Table 15.11 Extra ablation study on the *CURE* and NIH database.

Database Model	NIH		CURE	
	MAP	TOP-1	MAP	TOP-1
Stream RGB (18.1 M)	0.573	42.0	0.482	48.0
Stream Contour (9 M)	0.172	8.8	0.281	14.9
Stream Texture (9 M)	0.577	43.8	0.241	19.5

For comparisons, we have added extra experiments on the CURE dataset:

1) single complicated stream RGB 50% more parameters (see row 1 in Table 15.11);
2) same architecture, as the one proposed for the RGB stream, for stream *Contour* and *Texture* (9 M) are checked: see row 2&3 in Table 15.11.

It could be observed that using more complicated networks in a few-shot regime does not guarantee performance gains. For all of these ablations studies, we performed at least a small search of hyperparameters to avoid overfitting during the training.

15.6 Demonstration for few-shot pill recognition: the 'Pill Finder' application

The 'Pill Finder' application is an android mobile application developed for demonstrating our few-shot pill recognition AI engine. It is connected to a database of pill images, where reference images of each pill category are stored. The goal of the app is to facilitate pill matching, pill information gathering and later provide users with pill information in real-life scenarios. Users are allowed to take an image of

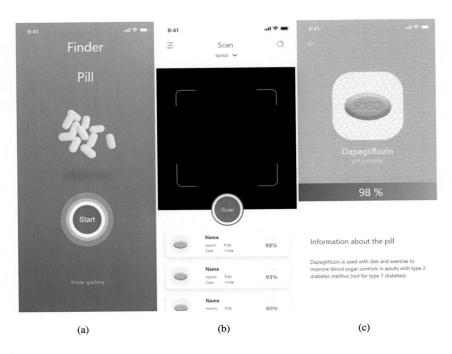

FIGURE 15.9

UIs of the 'Pill Finder' application: (a) the landing page (b) recognition performed through phone camera and display of top matching candidates (c) a pill description page.

pills, upload them to the app and then the pill category is suggested by our model with its corresponding information.

The User Interface (UI) of the 'Pill Founder' is depicted in Fig. 15.9. The app starts with a simple and user-experience-optimized landing page, as shown in Fig. 15.9 (a). Users could start the pill recognition by 1) either taking a photo with their smartphone camera via clicking the 'start' button 2) or by selecting a picture from their smartphone gallery via clicking 'From gallery'.

Afterwards, in either way, the top candidates that match the input pill image are presented in a list ranked based on their similarities to the input pill picture.

Moreover, as shown in Fig. 15.9 (c), descriptions of the pills are available to the users. This page contains all the information about a pill, how to take it, dispose of it, its molecules, and the relevant contraindications.

15.7 Conclusion

In this chapter, via pill recognition, we demonstrate how few-shot learning/meta learning could be applied for medical imaging. Concretely, we present a new pill images dataset *CURE*, which provides more instances per class. To better tackle the few-shot pill recognition problem, a W^2-net is first proposed for pill segmentation/localization. Then, a multistream deep architecture along with a two-stage learning strategy is proposed to better exploit the domain-related information in small data scenarios. It deploys first the *BA* strategy for the *RGB, Texture, Contour* streams to mine the *hard samples*, and second a novel *BH* strategy to train a fusion-net that combines the three individual streams with a stream of imprinted text as auxiliary information. Experimental results show that 1) W^2-net is superior to both *U*-net and *ESPNetv2* segmentation networks; 2) using high-frequency components with emphasized texture helps to solve the formidable problem of recognizing imprinted text on pills; 3) The proposed model achieves top performance by its more accurate recognition of the *hard samples* that cannot be handled by individual features streams.

References

[1] S. Ling, A. Pastor, J. Li, Z. Che, J. Wang, J. Kim, et al., Few-shot pill recognition, in: Proceedings of the IEEE/CVF Conference on Computer Vision and Pattern Recognition, 2020, pp. 9789–9798.

[2] H.A. Spiller, J.R. Griffith, Increasing burden of pill identification requests to US Poison Centers, Clinical Toxicology 47 (3) (2009) 253–255.

[3] J.A. Cramer, A. Roy, A. Burrell, C.J. Fairchild, M.J. Fuldeore, D.A. Ollendorf, et al., Medication compliance and persistence: terminology and definitions, Value in Health 11 (1) (2008) 44–47.

[4] S. Ochi, S. Hodgson, O. Landeg, L. Mayner, V. Murray, Disaster-driven evacuation and medication loss: a systematic literature review, PLoS Currents (2014) 6.

[5] D. West, et al., How mobile devices are transforming healthcare, Issues in Technology Innovation 18 (1) (2012) 1–11.

[6] Z. Yaniv, J. Faruque, S. Howe, K. Dunn, D. Sharlip, A. Bond, et al., The national library of medicine pill image recognition challenge: an initial report, in: 2016 IEEE Applied Imagery Pattern Recognition Workshop (AIPR), IEEE, 2016, pp. 1–9.

[7] I. Lütkebohle, NIH NLM pill image recognition challenge, https://pir.nlm.nih.gov/challenge/, 2016.

[8] A. Hermans, L. Beyer, B. Leibe, In defense of the triplet loss for person re-identification, arXiv preprint, arXiv:1703.07737, 2017.

[9] M. Busta, L. Neumann, J. Matas, Deep textspotter: an end-to-end trainable scene text localization and recognition framework, in: Proceedings of the IEEE International Conference on Computer Vision, 2017, pp. 2204–2212.

[10] J.J. Caban, A. Rosebrock, T.S. Yoo, Automatic identification of prescription drugs using shape distribution models, in: 2012 19th IEEE International Conference on Image Processing, IEEE, 2012, pp. 1005–1008.

[11] Y.B. Lee, U. Park, A.K. Jain, S.W. Lee, Pill-ID: matching and retrieval of drug pill images, Pattern Recognition Letters 33 (7) (2012) 904–910.

[12] R.C. Chen, Y.K. Chan, Y.H. Chen, C.T. Bau, An automatic drug image identification system based on multiple image features and dynamic weights, International Journal of Innovative Computing, Information and Control 8 (5) (2012) 2995–3013.

[13] A. Cunha, T. Adão, P. Trigueiros, Helpmepills: a mobile pill recognition tool for elderly persons, Procedia Technology 16 (2014) 1523–1532.

[14] J. Yu, Z. Chen, Si Kamata, J. Yang, Accurate system for automatic pill recognition using imprint information, IET Image Processing 9 (12) (2015) 1039–1047.

[15] X. Zeng, K. Cao, M. Zhang, MobileDeepPill: a small-footprint mobile deep learning system for recognizing unconstrained pill images, in: Proceedings of the 15th Annual International Conference on Mobile Systems, Applications, and Services, ACM, 2017, pp. 56–67.

[16] O. Vinyals, C. Blundell, T. Lillicrap, D. Wierstra, et al., Matching networks for one shot learning, in: Advances in Neural Information Processing Systems, 2016, pp. 3630–3638.

[17] J. Snell, K. Swersky, R. Zemel, Prototypical networks for few-shot learning, in: Advances in Neural Information Processing Systems, 2017, pp. 4077–4087.

[18] F. Sung, Y. Yang, L. Zhang, T. Xiang, P.H. Torr, T.M. Hospedales, Learning to compare: relation network for few-shot learning, in: Proceedings of the IEEE Conference on Computer Vision and Pattern Recognition, 2018, pp. 1199–1208.

[19] W. Wang, Y. Pu, V.K. Verma, K. Fan, Y. Zhang, C. Chen, et al., Zero-shot learning via class-conditioned deep generative models, in: Thirty-Second AAAI Conference on Artificial Intelligence, 2018.

[20] T. Munkhdalai, H. Yu, Meta networks, in: Proceedings of the 34th International Conference on Machine Learning-Volume 70, JMLR. org, 2017, pp. 2554–2563.

[21] A. Santoro, S. Bartunov, M. Botvinick, D. Wierstra, T. Lillicrap, Meta-learning with memory-augmented neural networks, in: International Conference on Machine Learning, 2016, pp. 1842–1850.

[22] B. Oreshkin, P.R. López, A. Lacoste, Tadam: task dependent adaptive metric for improved few-shot learning, in: Advances in Neural Information Processing Systems, 2018, pp. 721–731.

[23] E. Grant, C. Finn, S. Levine, T. Darrell, T. Griffiths, Recasting gradient-based meta-learning as hierarchical Bayes, arXiv preprint, arXiv:1801.08930, 2018.

[24] C. Finn, P. Abbeel, S. Levine, Model-agnostic meta-learning for fast adaptation of deep networks, in: Proceedings of the 34th International Conference on Machine Learning-Volume 70, JMLR. org, 2017, pp. 1126–1135.

[25] Q. Sun, Y. Liu, T.S. Chua, B. Schiele, Meta-transfer learning for few-shot learning, in: Proceedings of the IEEE Conference on Computer Vision and Pattern Recognition, 2019, pp. 403–412.

[26] H. Li, D. Eigen, S. Dodge, M. Zeiler, X. Wang, Finding task-relevant features for few-shot learning by category traversal, in: Proceedings of the IEEE Conference on Computer Vision and Pattern Recognition, 2019, pp. 1–10.

[27] A. Newell, K. Yang, J. Deng, Stacked hourglass networks for human pose estimation, in: European Conference on Computer Vision, Springer, 2016, pp. 483–499.

[28] G. Hinton, O. Vinyals, J. Dean, Distilling the knowledge in a neural network, arXiv preprint, arXiv:1503.02531, 2015.

[29] O. Ronneberger, P. Fischer, T. Brox, U-net: convolutional networks for biomedical image segmentation, in: International Conference on Medical Image Computing and Computer-Assisted Intervention, Springer, 2015, pp. 234–241.

[30] F. Schroff, D. Kalenichenko, J. Philbin, Facenet: a unified embedding for face recognition and clustering, in: Proceedings of the IEEE Conference on Computer Vision and Pattern Recognition, 2015, pp. 815–823.

[31] A. Eitel, J.T. Springenberg, L. Spinello, M. Riedmiller, W. Burgard, Multimodal deep learning for robust RGB-D object recognition, in: 2015 IEEE/RSJ International Conference on Intelligent Robots and Systems (IROS), IEEE, 2015, pp. 681–687.

[32] L. Sharan, C. Liu, R. Rosenholtz, E.H. Adelson, Recognizing materials using perceptually inspired features, International Journal of Computer Vision 103 (3) (2013) 348–371.

[33] S. Ling, P.L. Callet, Z. Yu, The role of structure and textural information in image utility and quality assessment tasks, Electronic Imaging 2018 (14) (2018) 1–13.

[34] A. Graves, S. Fernández, F. Gomez, J. Schmidhuber, Connectionist temporal classification: labelling unsegmented sequence data with recurrent neural networks, in: Proceedings of the 23rd International Conference on Machine Learning, ACM, 2006, pp. 369–376.

[35] M. Cimpoi, S. Maji, I. Kokkinos, S. Mohamed, A. Vedaldi, Describing textures in the wild, in: Proceedings of the IEEE Conf. on Computer Vision and Pattern Recognition (CVPR), 2014.

[36] S. Mehta, M. Rastegari, L. Shapiro, H. Hajishirzi, Espnetv2: a light-weight, power efficient, and general purpose convolutional neural network, in: Proceedings of the IEEE Conference on Computer Vision and Pattern Recognition, 2019, pp. 9190–9200.

[37] P. Lyu, M. Liao, C. Yao, W. Wu, X. Bai, Mask textspotter: an end-to-end trainable neural network for spotting text with arbitrary shapes, in: Proceedings of the European Conference on Computer Vision (ECCV), 2018, pp. 67–83.

[38] D. Karatzas, L. Gomez-Bigorda, A. Nicolaou, S. Ghosh, A. Bagdanov, ICDAR 2015 competition on robust reading, in: 2015 13th International Conference on Document Analysis and Recognition (ICDAR), 2015, pp. 1156–1160.

[39] L. Franceschi, P. Frasconi, S. Salzo, R. Grazzi, M. Pontil, Bilevel programming for hyperparameter optimization and meta-learning, arXiv preprint, arXiv:1806.04910, 2018.

[40] T. Munkhdalai, X. Yuan, S. Mehri, A. Trischler, Rapid adaptation with conditionally shifted neurons, arXiv preprint, arXiv:1712.09926, 2017.

Meta learning for anomaly detection in fundus photographs

Sarah Matta[a,b], **Mathieu Lamard**[a,b], **Pierre-Henri Conze**[c], **Alexandre Le Guilcher**[d],
Vincent Ricquebourg[d], **Anas-Alexis Benyoussef**[f], **Pascale Massin**[e], **Jean-Bernard Rottier**[g],
Béatrice Cochener[f], **and Gwenolé Quellec**[b]

[a]*Univ Bretagne Occidentale, Brest, France*
[b]*Inserm, UMR 1101, Brest, France*
[c]*IMT Atlantique, Brest, France*
[d]*Evolucare, Le Pecq, France*
[e]*Ophthalmology Department, Lariboisiére Hospital, APHP, Paris, France*
[f]*Ophthalmology Department, CHRU Brest, Brest, France*
[g]*Centre Médico Chirurgical du Mans, Le Mans, France*

16.1 Introduction

According to the World Health Organization (WHO), at least 2.2 billion people suffer from visual impairment or blindness, with at least 1 billion of them having a vision impairment that might have been prevented or that has yet to be addressed [1,43]. Therefore, the early diagnosis and management of ocular conditions is crucial for preventing visual impairment. However, the growing shortage of ophthalmologists makes it hard to meet the rising need for screening [36]. To overcome this gap, AI solutions seem very relevant.

In the light of the above, over the past fifteen years, we have developed various AI solutions for screening diabetic retinopathy (DR), one of the most frequent sight-threatening ocular anomalies, based on fundus photography. These research works were done in collaboration with Paris Hospitals (AP-HP), Mines ParisTech, and the ADCIS and Evolucare companies. We were among the first research groups to tackle this subject. However, nowadays detecting DR in fundus photographs has become a very popular research field worldwide [47].

Initially, our goal was to automatically detect early signs of DR, in order to mimic the way clinicians grade DR severity. A dataset of 1200 images, the well-know Messidor public dataset [6], was collected for this purpose and clinicians provided us with lesion-level annotations. Efficient lesion detectors were designed [34], one of which won the Retinopathy Online Challenge [22], the first international competition in this domain.

Lesion-level annotations simplify the training process. However, collecting enough annotations for all lesion types is challenging. Therefore, we moved to directly classifying DR severity using image-level annotations only. For this purpose, more than 100,000 images, with image-level annotations, were extracted from the Parisian OPHDIAT screening network [5]. Initially, we solved this problem with multiple-instance learning [30] and data mining [33]. Next, we investigated deep learning [29] and

100,000 images proved to be suboptimal. Therefore, an even larger dataset (760,000 images) was extracted [35]. Recently, one of these algorithms, commercialized by ADCIS and Evolucare (OphtAI), was evaluated independently on more than 300,000 images from two US Veterans Affairs Hospitals [17]. According to that study, our algorithm is safe (as sensitive as an ophthalmologist) and it could save more than 15 USD per visit.

Besides DR, various pathologies are encountered in DR screening networks. Clinicians generally indicate their presence in screening reports. So, in subsequent studies, we also designed deep learning solutions for AMD and glaucoma, two frequent pathologies [16]. More generally, many deep learning algorithms have been proposed in the literature for recognizing frequent conditions such as DR [9,18,35,38], glaucoma [14,19,23,26], AMD [10,13,37,51] as well as other conditions like cataract [28] and degenerative myopia [7]. A few studies have also targeted multiple frequent pathology screening [4,14]. In screening datasets, including the OPHDIAT dataset, many rare pathologies are also annotated, but standard deep learning solutions may be suboptimal to detect them due to lack of training data. However, automated recognition of rare pathologies is important in real-life clinical scenarios: it ensures that no anomaly is missed and that automatic screening is safe. Ideally, we would enumerate all conditions (rare or frequent) in an image. However, it may be sufficient to indicate that the image contains at least one anomaly, without explicitly indicating which one.

In this chapter, we propose two meta learning based approaches for each of the aforementioned scenarios: 1) an anomaly characterization algorithm, to enumerate all rare visible ocular pathologies and 2) an anomaly detection algorithm, which optimally combines multiple pathology detectors to make a "normal vs anomalous" referral decision.

The anomaly characterization algorithm trains a conventional deep learning classifier for detecting frequent conditions and then extends it to detect rare conditions through simple probabilistic models. A key feature of this framework is the use of t-distributed stochastic neighbor embedding (t-SNE) in the development of an image feature space [48]. As proven in this chapter, this framework combines ideas from transfer learning and multitask learning, while outperforming each paradigm separately. It is presented in more details in [32].

The anomaly detection algorithm trains several specific anomaly detectors and optimally integrates joint learned features from the trained detectors to predict the final referral decision. In this chapter, we apply it in two different populations: the diabetic and the general populations. Initially, we investigate it on the diabetic population, using a large dataset of fundus photographs collected from OPHDIAT screening network. Next, we explore it on a smaller dataset collected from a general purpose screening network, OphtaMaine. This algorithm is shown to achieve good performances in both populations.

16.2 Related machine learning frameworks

Detecting rare anomalies in fundus photographs has not been tackled in the literature yet. In addition, no algorithm addresses the general problem of anomaly detection in fundus photographs: is a fundus photograph free of any anomaly? The closest works target multilabel classification of a predefined set of conditions (does a patient have DR? does he/she have glaucoma? etc.). For instance, Son et al. [42] developed a deep learning classification algorithm for detecting 12 major findings in fundus images. Their approach consisted of separately training 12 binary neural networks, each one of them specialized in identifying a unique finding. The independent classifiers were trained and evaluated using a dataset of 95,350 fundus images, collected in the health screening center and ophthalmology outpatient clinic at Seoul National University Bundang Hospital. Each image was labeled by 3 independent ophthalmologists and ground truth for each finding was defined by either the majority or the unanimity rule. The results of this study showed that the classifiers achieved good performance with AUC ranging from 96.2% to 99.9% for the 12 abnormal findings. In addition, the authors reported a comparable performance (AUC ranging from 96.2% to 99.9%) in two external DR-specific datasets (the Indian Diabetic Retinopathy image Database and e-ophtha). Despite encouraging results, the algorithm was not assessed for rare conditions and the performance of anomaly detection in general, for mass ocular screening was not investigated. One drawback of the aforementioned deep learning algorithms is that they do not identify all types of anomalies equally well, in part because some anomalies are inherently more difficult to detect, and in part because data scarcity prevents the training of reliable detectors. To deal with data scarcity, a popular technique, *transfer learning*, has been proposed [3]. In this technique, a model is firstly trained on a large dataset, e.g. ImageNet (1.2 million images),[1] to accomplish an unrelated classification problem. It is then fine-tuned on the targeted dataset, to perform the task of interest, e.g. to detect a specific condition.

A different approach to address this problem is *multitask learning* [2]. Instead of dealing with the tasks sequentially as in transfer learning, multiple tasks are addressed simultaneously. In this paradigm, auxiliary tasks are typically used because training labels are abundant or not needed, in contrast to the target task [21,53]. For instance, for the main goal of detecting rare conditions, the detection of frequent conditions can be considered as an auxiliary task. As such, a unique model can be trained for detecting both rare and frequent conditions simultaneously [11].

More recent work proposed the *one-shot learning* [8] or more broadly *few-shot learning* [50]. In this technique, a classifier must generalize to a new category not seen in training, given only one or a few samples of this category. Siamese networks [15,40], matching networks [49] or relation networks [44] are one of the most popular deep learning networks applied in *few-shot learning*. These networks take two images as inputs and should output whether or not these images belong to the same category. An alternative deep learning solution in few-shot learning is to develop a simple probabilistic model for the new category: this model works in an image feature space produced by the initial training [8]. This strategy was applied to local features [8], or to image feature space arising from matching networks [49].

16.3 Screening networks

The datasets used in this study come from two French screening networks:

- the OPHDIAT telemedical network, to develop and evaluate the anomaly characterization algorithm and the anomaly detection algorithm in a diabetic population,
- the OphtaMaine private screening network, to adapt and assess the anomaly detection algorithm in the general population.

---

[1] http://www.image-net.org.

16.3.1 The OPHDIAT screening network

The OPHDIAT network consists of 40 screening centers located in 22 diabetic wards of hospitals, 15 primary health-care centers and 3 prisons in the Ile-de-France area [20]. Each center is equipped with one of the following 45° digital nonmydriatic cameras: Canon CR-DGI or CR2 (Tokyo, Japan), Topcon TRC-NW6 or TR-NW400 (Rotterdam, The Netherlands). Two photographs were taken per eye, one centered on the posterior pole and the other on the optic disc. From 2004 to the end of 2017, a total of 164,660 screening procedures were performed and 763,848 images were collected. Each screening exam was analyzed by one of the seven certified ophthalmologists of the OPHDIAT Reading Center, in order to generate a structured report [20]. This structured report includes the grading of DR in each eye. It also indicates the presence or suspicion of presence of a few other pathologies in each eye. In addition to the structured report, the ophthalmologist also indicated his or her findings in free-form text.

16.3.2 The OphtaMaine screening network

OphtaMaine[2] is a private screening network targeting any eye pathology in the general population. The screening network consists of two screening centers located in Le Mans and Chateau-du-Loir, France. Fundus photographs are acquired by one of the six orthoptists using one of the following 45° digital nonmydriatic Canon® camera: CR-2AF, CR-2, and CR-AF. All fundus photographs are read by the same ophthalmologist (JBR). One fundus photograph, centered on the posterior pole, is acquired per eye. Each examination record is labeled as "normal", "suspicion of disease presence" or "poor quality". Additionally, a free-form commentary specifies, when appropriate, the detected anomalies.

16.4 Datasets
16.4.1 The OPHDIAT dataset

For the purpose of this study, a retina specialist analyzed the structured reports and identified a total of $N = 41$ conditions. For each eye, ground truth annotations were obtained by combining structured information and manually-extracted textual information. Our laterality identification algorithm was then used to assign these annotations to images [35]. The conditions $(c_n)_{n=1..N}$ are sorted by decreasing frequency order in the obtained image dataset.

Ophthalmologists may not have written all their findings. To ensure that "normal images" are indeed nonpathological, the retina specialist visually inspected normal images and discarded images containing anomalies: a total of 16,955 normal images, out of 18,000 inspected images, were included. Regarding DR, the most common condition, a different number of images was considered for each algorithm: a smaller subset of images was used for the anomaly detection algorithm, which requires a more balanced dataset, since we build a single model for all anomalies. Overall, the dataset $\mathcal{D}$ used for development and testing of the anomaly characterization algorithm comprised 115,159 images. The dataset $\mathcal{O}$ used for development and testing of the anomaly detection algorithm comprised 77,812 images.

Dataset $\mathcal{D}$ (respectively $\mathcal{O}$) was split into three mutually exclusive subsets: a learning (or training) subset $\mathcal{D}_L$ (respectively $\mathcal{O}_L$), used for deep learning, a validation subset $\mathcal{D}_V$ (respectively $\mathcal{O}_V$), and

---

[2] https://www.opthamaine.fr.

a test subset $\mathcal{D}_T$ (respectively $\mathcal{O}_T$). All fundus photographs from the same patient were assigned to the same subset (this applies to all datasets in this chapter). For the anomaly detection algorithm, $\mathcal{O}_L$ was assigned 80% of $\mathcal{O}$, $\mathcal{O}_V$, and $\mathcal{O}_T$ were assigned 10% of $\mathcal{O}$ each. In the proposed few-shot learning framework, learning/validation/testing split depends on the number M of conditions considered frequent: images with rare anomalies are not used for deep learning. Details are given in Table 16.1.

For the first step of the anomaly detection algorithm, we also define a DR-specific development dataset ($\mathcal{R}$), to compensate for the image removal in dataset $\mathcal{O}$. This dataset contains images having at least moderate nonproliferative DR (positive images) and images associated with the absence of DR (negative images). $\mathcal{R}$ was split into a training subset $\mathcal{R}_L$ (89% of $\mathcal{R}$) and a validation subset $\mathcal{R}_V$ (11% of $\mathcal{R}$). We ensured that $\mathcal{O}_L$ is a subset of $\mathcal{R}_L$, $\mathcal{O}_V$ is a subset of $\mathcal{R}_V$ and $\mathcal{O}_T$ does not intersect with $\mathcal{R}$. The dataset $\mathcal{R}$ contains 168,553 images including 25,445 images with DR signs.

16.4.2 The OphtaMaine dataset

All examination records performed in OphtaMaine from 2017 to 2019 were included in this study, with the exception of those labeled "poor quality". Similarly to OPHDIAT, the free-form comments were retrospectively analyzed to group examinations by types of anomalies (pathologies or pathological signs). The dataset ($\mathcal{A}$) was split as follows: a training subset $\mathcal{A}_L$ (40% of $\mathcal{A}$), a validation subset $\mathcal{A}_V$ (10% of $\mathcal{A}$), and a testing subset $\mathcal{A}_T$ (50% of $\mathcal{A}$). Patients were assigned to these subsets in such a way that the frequency of each anomaly is approximately the same in each subset. Besides this criterion, assignment to subsets was made randomly.

For comparing the performances of the automated algorithm and of ophthalmologists, a total of 2281 examinations (4763 images) were randomly selected from $\mathcal{A}_T$ (subset $\mathcal{H}$) and were read again by a second ophthalmologist from Brest University Hospital (AAB). Following OphtaMaine's labeling scheme, each examination record in $\mathcal{H}$ was labeled as "normal", "suspicion of disease presence" or "poor quality". The final comparison set, $\mathcal{C}$, comprised all examination records deemed of sufficient quality by both readers (AAB and JBR). It consisted of 2014 examinations (4220 images) of sufficient quality. The distribution of anomalies in the $\mathcal{A}_L$, $\mathcal{A}_V$, and $\mathcal{A}_T$ subsets is reported in Table 16.2.

16.5 From frequent to rare ocular anomaly detection

For the purpose of detecting rare ocular anomalies, an anomaly characterization algorithm is proposed. As illustrated in Fig. 16.1, first, a multitask detector for frequent conditions is trained. Next, a probabilistic detection model is defined for each rare condition. Then, predictions can be inferred for new images: predictions are computed for both frequent and rare conditions.

To allow device-independent analysis, all images are first preprocessed as described in [32]: they are resized to 299×299 pixels and their intensity is normalized. The following processing steps are thus performed on the resulting preprocessed images.

For simplicity, I denotes the preprocessed image in the following sections. Various spaces are defined hereafter to compute presence probabilities for rare conditions: those notations are summarized in Fig. 16.2.

Table 16.1 Frequency of each condition in the full datasets ($\mathcal{D}$ for the anomaly characterization algorithm and $\mathcal{O}$ for the anomaly detection algorithm) and in their learning (L), validation (V) and testing (T) subsets. For the anomaly characterization algorithm, $M = 17$ conditions are considered frequent in this table. DR: diabetic retinopathy; AMD: age-related macular degeneration; DME: diabetic macular edema; HR: hypertensive retinopathy; BRVO: branch retinal vein occlusion; RPE: retinal pigment epithelium; CRVO: central retinal vein occlusion; MIDD: maternally inherited diabetes and deafness; AION: anterior ischemic optic neuropathy.

condition (c_n)	$\mathcal{D}$	$\mathcal{D}_L$	$\mathcal{D}_V$	$\mathcal{D}_T$	$\mathcal{O}$	$\mathcal{O}_L$	$\mathcal{O}_V$	$\mathcal{O}_T$
normal images	16,955	3992	2890	10,073	16,940	13,626	1706	1608
referable DR	65,560	2406	12,819	50,335	28,366	22,618	2893	2855
glaucoma	10,624	1176	1992	7456	10,624	8537	1080	1007
cataract	3540	1253	546	1741	3540	2844	358	338
AMD	3173	1336	442	1395	3173	2570	316	287
drusen	3164	1179	511	1474	3164	2551	314	299
DME	3024	1168	463	1393	3024	2338	307	379
HR	3018	1184	453	1381	3018	2420	305	293
laser scars	1450	796	204	450	1450	1155	147	148
arteriosclerosis	1235	629	161	445	1235	998	123	114
tortuous vessels	1222	830	161	231	1222	978	127	117
degenerative myopia	1209	859	145	205	1209	967	122	120
BRVO	752	429	117	206	752	605	75	72
epiretinal membrane	674	447	78	149	674	539	68	67
nevi	628	466	55	107	628	501	64	63
retinal atrophy	546	340	67	139	546	442	47	57
myelinated nerve fibers	531	372	62	97	531	421	58	52
RPE alterations	508	370	50	88	508	409	53	46
optic disc pallor	455	0	91	364	455	361	46	48
synchisis	366	0	73	293	366	289	40	37
tilted optic disc	334	0	67	267	334	261	37	36
CRVO	297	0	59	238	297	239	30	28
chorioretinitis	294	0	59	235	294	233	31	30
dystrophy	217	0	43	174	217	171	25	21
retinis pigmentosa	183	0	37	146	183	146	17	20
chorioretinal atrophy	182	0	36	146	182	143	21	18
dilated veins	165	0	33	132	165	127	15	23
angioid streaks	145	0	29	116	145	117	16	12
papilledema	99	0	20	79	99	80	11	8
macular hole	78	0	16	62	78	62	8	8
embolus	74	0	15	59	74	59	9	6
MIDD	70	0	14	56	70	55	8	7
coloboma	52	0	11	41	52	40	5	7
shunt	51	0	10	41	51	35	9	7
AION	43	0	9	34	43	37	3	3
bear track dystrophy	42	0	8	34	42	31	7	4
pseudovitelliform dystrophy	29	0	6	23	29	25	2	2
pigmentary migration	28	0	6	22	28	22	2	4
prethrombosis	28	0	5	23	28	21	4	3
hyaloid remnant	16	0	4	12	16	12	2	2
asteroid hyalosis	15	0	3	12	15	12	2	1
telangiectasia	15	0	3	12	15	9	2	4

Table 16.2 Frequency of each category, represented as number of examinations (number of images), in the full dataset ($\mathcal{A}$) and in the training ($\mathcal{A}_L$), validation ($\mathcal{A}_V$), and testing ($\mathcal{A}_T$) subsets extracted from the OphtaMaine dataset.

Categories	$\mathcal{A}$	$\mathcal{A}_L$	$\mathcal{A}_V$	$\mathcal{A}_T$
Normal	7104 (14,785)	2856 (5935)	701 (1452)	3547 (7398)
Abnormal optic disc	393 (825)	158 (325)	39 (82)	196 (418)
Other	352 (840)	137 (328)	38 (90)	177 (422)
Nevi	67 (179)	27 (72)	6 (14)	34 (93)
Age-related maculopathy and drusen	49 (109)	20 (43)	4 (8)	25 (58)
Hemorrhage	29 (78)	12 (27)	3 (10)	14 (41)
Age-related macular degeneration	28 (50)	10 (18)	4 (5)	14 (27)
Epiretinal membrane & macular epiretinal membrane	23 (56)	9 (20)	2 (10)	12 (26)
Pigmentary	22 (45)	8 (19)	3 (6)	11 (20)
Depigmentation	18 (38)	7 (15)	2 (4)	9 (19)
Degenerative myopia	12 (24)	5 (10)	1 (2)	6 (12)
Atrophy	10 (28)	4 (13)	1 (2)	5 (13)
Choroidal myopia	7 (14)	2 (4)	1 (2)	4 (8)
Vitreous detachment	7 (14)	2 (4)	1 (2)	4 (8)
Tortuous vessels	6 (12)	2 (4)	1 (2)	3 (6)
Alteration	6 (17)	2 (8)	1 (3)	3 (6)
Macular pigment	6 (16)	1 (2)	1 (2)	4 (12)
Coloboma	6 (17)	2 (5)	1 (2)	3 (10)
Exudate & microaneurysm	6 (16)	2 (8)	1 (2)	3 (6)
Toxoplasmosis	3 (11)	0 (0)	1 (6)	2 (5)
Tilted optic disc	2 (4)	0 (0)	1 (2)	1 (2)
Cataract	2 (4)	0 (0)	1 (3)	1 (1)

16.5.1 Deep learning for frequent condition detection

The first step is to define a deep learning model for recognizing the $M \leq N$ most frequent conditions. A convolutional neural network (CNN) is thus trained to minimize the binary cross-entropy loss $\mathcal{L}$ between:

- the probabilities $p_{I,n} \in [0, 1]$, $n \leq M$, that an image I contains the conditions c_n, according to the CNN,
- and the labels $y_{I,n} \in \{0, 1\}$, $n \leq M$, indicating the presence ($y_{I,n} = 1$) or absence ($y_{I,n} = 0$) of each condition c_n in image I, according to experts.

The sigmoid function is used as final activation function since patients can have multiple conditions simultaneously, so probabilities $p_{I,n}, n \leq M$, should be independent. We note that training this initial classification model, defined for frequent conditions, is a multitask learning problem (see Section 16.2): the proposed framework extends multitask learning to rare conditions as described hereafter.

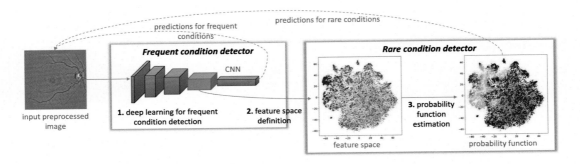

FIGURE 16.1

Proposed pipeline (learning and inference). To initiate the learning phase, a CNN is trained to detect frequent conditions in preprocessed images (**1.**). This CNN is then used to build detectors for rare conditions. In that purpose, a feature space is designed: features derive from the output of selected neurons of the CNN (**2.**). Next, a probabilistic model is trained for each rare condition in this feature space (**3.**). The inference phase is similar: preprocessed images are processed by the CNN, and a prediction is made for both frequent and rare conditions. Predictions for frequent conditions simply are the CNN outputs. Predictions for rare condition are further inferred by the probabilistic models.

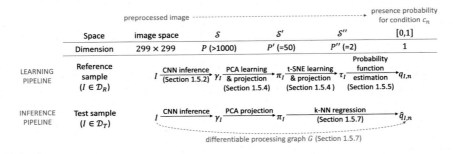

FIGURE 16.2

Detailed pipeline for rare condition detection. This figure summarizes the intermediate steps for detecting a rare condition in images, as well as the associated notations. Two different pipelines are presented. The first pipeline is applied to "reference images" for learning a presence probability function (learning pipeline). The second pipeline is applied to test images for inferring presence probabilities (inference pipeline). Section 16.6 explains how the value of each dimension was determined.

16.5.2 Feature space definition

Since a unique CNN is defined to detect the M most frequent conditions, the penultimate layer of this CNN is very general: it extracts all features required to detect M conditions. We use the output of this layer to define a feature space in which the remaining $N - M$ conditions will be detected. Let $\mathcal{S}$ denote this feature space, let P denote its dimension and let γ_I denote the projection of a given image I in this space (see Fig. 16.2). The number of neurons in the penultimate layer of a classification CNN is generally high: for instance, $P = 2049$ for Inception-v3 [46].

To address the curse of dimensionality, dimension reduction is performed afterwards. For this purpose, we propose the use of t-SNE, a nonlinear technique for embedding high-dimensional data in a low-dimensional space suited for visualization: typically a 2-D or 3-D space [48]. In t-SNE, dimension reduction is unsupervised, but it is data-driven: it relies on a set $\mathcal{D}_R$ of "reference images".

16.5.3 *t*-distributed stochastic neighbor embedding (t-SNE)

In t-SNE, some high-dimensional input vectors $(\pi_I)_{I \in \mathcal{D}_R}$ are mapped to low-dimensional output vectors $(\tau_I)_{I \in \mathcal{D}_R}$ in such a way that similar input vectors are mapped to nearby output vectors and dissimilar input vectors are mapped to distant output vectors. First, t-SNE defines the conditional probability $p_{J|I}$ that sample I picks sample J as a neighbor. It assumes that neighbors are picked in proportion to their probability density under a Gaussian centered at π_I:

$$p_{J|I} = \frac{\Gamma\left(\frac{\pi_I - \pi_J}{h_I}\right)}{\sum_{K \in \mathcal{D}_R \setminus \{I\}} \Gamma\left(\frac{\pi_I - \pi_K}{h_I}\right)} \ , \tag{16.1}$$

where Γ is a Gaussian kernel and h_I is a sample-specific bandwidth. Let $P_I = (p_{J|I})_{J \in \mathcal{D}_R}$ denote the conditional distribution thus defined. Bandwidths are set in such a way that the perplexity $\rho(P_I)$ of P_I, interpreted by van der Maaten and Hinton [48] as a smooth measure of the effective number of neighbors of π_I, equals a predefined perplexity $\bar{\rho}$:

$$\rho(P_I) = 2^{-\sum_{J \in \mathcal{D}_R} p_{J|I} \log_2 p_{J|I}} . \tag{16.2}$$

Similar conditional distributions $Q_I = (q_{J|I})_{J \in \mathcal{D}_R}$ are defined for output vectors $(\tau_I)_{I \in \mathcal{D}_R}$, using a constant bandwidth $h = 1/\sqrt{2}$. These output vectors can thus be found by minimizing the sum of Kullback-Leibler divergences between conditional distributions P_I and Q_I, $I \in \mathcal{D}_R$, using a gradient descent.

16.5.4 Feature space dimension reduction

In details, a two-step procedure, recommended by van der Maaten and Hinton [48], was adopted for dimension reduction (see Fig. 16.2):

- A first reduction step relies on principal component analysis (PCA), which transforms the initial feature space $\mathcal{S}$ into a new P'-dimensional feature space $\mathcal{S}'$. Let π_I denote the projection of image I into $\mathcal{S}'$: this will be the high-dimensional input vector of Section 16.5.3.
- In a second step, t-SNE itself transforms $\mathcal{S}'$ into a P''-dimensional feature space $\mathcal{S}''$. Let τ_I denote the projection of image I into $\mathcal{S}''$: this is the low-dimensional output vector of Section 16.5.3.

As explained by van der Maaten and Hinton [48], the use of PCA speeds up computation of pairwise distances between input vectors and it suppresses some noise without severely distorting the intersample distances.

16.5.5 Probability function estimation

As mentioned in the introduction, we observed that the t-SNE algorithm generates a feature space $\mathcal{S}''$ allowing very good separation of the various $(c_n)_{n=1..N}$ conditions, even though it is unsupervised. This observation is leveraged to define a probabilistic condition detection model in $\mathcal{S}''$ space. For that purpose, a density probability function F_n is first defined in $\mathcal{S}''$ for each condition c_n, $n \le N$. Probability density functions $\overline{F_n}$ are also defined for the absence of each condition. These estimations are performed in the $\mathcal{D}_R$ reference subset; training images are discarded in case the CNN has overfitted the training data. Density estimations rely on the Parzen-Rosenblatt method [24], using a Gaussian kernel Γ. For each location $\tau \in \mathcal{S}''$:

$$\begin{cases} F_n(\tau) & = & \dfrac{1}{\sum_{I \in \mathcal{D}_R} y_{I,n}} \displaystyle\sum_{I \in \mathcal{D}_R} \Gamma\left(\dfrac{\tau - \tau_I}{h_n}\right) \\[3mm] \overline{F_n}(\tau) & = & \dfrac{1}{\sum_{I \in \mathcal{D}_R} [1 - y_{I,n}]} \displaystyle\sum_{I \in \mathcal{D}_R} \Gamma\left(\dfrac{\tau - \tau_I}{\overline{h_n}}\right) \end{cases} . \tag{16.3}$$

For each density function, one parameter needs to be set: the h_n or $\overline{h_n}$ bandwidth, which controls the smoothness of the estimated function. It is set according to Scott's criterion [39]:

$$h_n = \left(\sum_{I \in \mathcal{D}_R} y_{I,n}\right)^{-\frac{1}{P''+4}} , \quad \overline{h_n} = \left(\sum_{I \in \mathcal{D}_R} [1 - y_{I,n}]\right)^{-\frac{1}{P''+4}} . \tag{16.4}$$

Finally, based on these two probability density functions, F_n and $\overline{F_n}$, the probability $q^M_{I,n}$ that image I contains condition c_n (simply noted $q_{I,n}$ in the absence of ambiguity) is defined as follows (see Fig. 16.2):

$$q_{I,n} = \frac{F_n(\tau_I)}{F_n(\tau_I) + \overline{F_n}(\tau_I)} . \tag{16.5}$$

Eq. (16.1) of t-SNE is similar to Eqs. (16.3) and (16.5) of probability function estimation: we essentially change the emphasis from sample-level in t-SNE to class-level in probability function estimation.

16.5.6 Detecting rare conditions in one image

One challenge arises once we need to process a new image: Eq. (16.5) is only defined for the development samples (i.e. $\forall I \in \mathcal{D}_R$). It does not allow projection of new samples from the $\mathcal{S}'$ to the $\mathcal{S}''$ feature space. To bypass this limitation, the following pipeline is proposed to determine the probability that condition c_n is present in a new image $I \in \mathcal{D}_T$ (see Fig. 16.2):

1. I is processed by the CNN and the output γ_I of the penultimate layer are computed (see Sections 16.5.1 and 16.5.2).
2. The PCA-based $\mathcal{S} \to \mathcal{S}'$ projection is applied to obtain π_I (see Section 16.5.4).
3. A K-nearest neighbor regression is performed to approximate $q_{I,n}$. The search for the K nearest neighbors $(V_k)_{k=1..K}$ is performed in $\mathcal{S}'$. The reference samples are the $(\langle \pi_J, q_{J,n} \rangle)_{J \in \mathcal{D}_R}$ couples,

where the $q_{J,n}$ values are computed exactly through Eq. (16.5). The approximate prediction $\hat{q}_{I,n}$ is given by:

$$\hat{q}_{I,n} = \frac{1}{\displaystyle\sum_{k=1}^{K} \frac{1}{\|\pi_I - \pi_{V_k}\|}} \sum_{k=1}^{K} \frac{q_{V_k,n}}{\|\pi_I - \pi_{V_k}\|} \; . \tag{16.6}$$

The $\hat{q}_{I,n}$ prediction is a weighted arithmetic mean of exact predictions $q_{V_k,n}$, computed for the neighbors V_k of I in $\mathcal{S}'$: the weight assigned to V_k is inversely proportional to the distance between I and V_k in $\mathcal{S}'$.

Note that the above pipeline for test images is differentiable, provided that the K nearest neighbors of I are considered constant. It can thus be implemented as a differentiable processing graph G (see Fig. 16.2), stacking the following operations:

1. the CNN up to the penultimate layer,
2. the PCA-based $\mathcal{S} \rightarrow \mathcal{S}'$ linear projection,
3. and the regression of Eq. (16.6).

This property allows heatmap generation (see Section 16.6.4) and may also allow fine-tuning of CNN weights.

In summary, the probability that a condition c_n is present in any image I can be estimated using Eq. (16.6). If $n \leq M$, two probabilities of presence can be used: either $\hat{q}_{I,n}^M$ or $p_{I,n}^M$ (see Section 16.5.1).

16.6 Experiments in the OPHDIAT dataset

We have presented a probabilistic framework for detecting rare conditions in images. This framework is now applied to DR screening in images from the OPHDIAT network.

16.6.1 Reference, validation, and testing

For validation and testing, performance is evaluated using the area under the ROC (Receiver-Operating Characteristic) curve, noted AUC. One ROC curve is built for each condition c_n.

The usual validation and testing strategy was followed for CNN-based frequent anomaly detectors. However, validating and testing the rare anomaly detectors is more challenging: ideally, we would need a fourth independent subset $\mathcal{D}_R$ of reference images. In order to maximize the size of the testing, validation, and reference subsets, which is particularly critical for rare conditions, a different solution was used instead. First, validation relied on a 10-fold cross-validation strategy: for each fold, probability functions were built using 90% of $\mathcal{D}_V$ as reference images ($\mathcal{D}_R$), and $\hat{q}_{I,n}$ predictions were computed for the remaining 10%. Similarly, a 10-fold cross-testing strategy was followed: for each fold, probability functions were built using $\mathcal{D}_V$ plus 90% of $\mathcal{D}_T$ as reference images, and $\hat{q}_{I,n}$ predictions were computed for the remaining 10% of $\mathcal{D}_T$. In both cross-validation and cross-testing, images from the same patient were all assigned to the same fold, to avoid evaluation biases. Finally, in both cross-validation and cross-testing, a single ROC curve was built for c_n by joining all the $\hat{q}_{I,n}$ predictions, computed in all ten folds, together with the associated $y_{I,n}$ target labels.

16.6.2 Parameter selection

The choice of M frequent conditions is arbitrary. In initial experiments, we set $M = M_0 = 11$: M_0 was chosen such that $f_n \geq 1000$, $\forall n \leq M_0$. The following CNN architectures were investigated: Inception-v3 [46], Inception-v4 [45], ResNet-50, ResNet-101 and ResNet-152 [12], and NASNet-A [54]. These CNNs were pretrained on the public ImageNet dataset and fine-tuned on the $\mathcal{D}_L$ learning subset. The combination of two CNNs was also investigated: in that case, their penultimate layers were concatenated to define the initial S feature space. An experiment involving the $M_0 = 11$ most frequent conditions was performed to select the most promising architectures. This experiment reveals that three architectures lead to particularly good classification performance: Inception-v3, Inception-v4 and "Inception-v3 + Inception-v4". We only considered those three architectures in subsequent experiments.

Two important parameters also had to be set:

- the dimension P'' of the reduced feature space generated by t-SNE (for visualization, P'' is generally set to 2 or 3, but higher values can be used),
- the number K of neighbors to approximate the $\hat{q}_{I,n}$ predictions in Eq. (16.6).

These parameters were chosen to maximize classification performance on the validation subset using $M = M_0$. The optimal parameter values were: $P'' = 2$ and $K = 3$. Other dimension reduction parameters were set to commonly used values: the number of dimensions after PCA was set to $P' = 50$ (see Section 16.5.4) and perplexity in t-SNE was set to $\bar{\rho} = 30$ (see Section 16.5.3).[3] As an illustration, the probability density functions obtained for Inception-v3, with the selected parameter values, are shown in Fig. 16.3.

In subsequent experiments, multiple values for M were investigated. We varied M from $M_0 = 11$ to $N = 41$ by steps of 6 conditions: $M \in \{11, 17, 23, 29, 35, 41\}$. A different value for M and a different CNN architecture were selected for each condition: the combinations maximizing the AUC on the $\mathcal{D}_V$ validation subset were selected.

16.6.3 Detection performance

Detection performance in the test subset, as a function of condition frequency, is illustrated in Fig. 16.4. In this figure, a different model is used for each condition: the one maximizing the AUC on the validation subset. We observe that detection performance is poorly correlated with the frequency of a condition.

Because a different model was trained for each condition, computation times can be an issue. Therefore, we studied how fast a test image can be processed. Computation times were measured on a desktop computer with one Intel Xeon E5-1650 v2 Hexa-core 3.50 GHz CPU and one Nvidia GeForce GTX 1070 GPU. On average, running the 41 models on a single image takes 5.3 seconds on GPU.

---

[3] https://scikit-learn.org/stable/modules/generated/sklearn.manifold.TSNE.html.

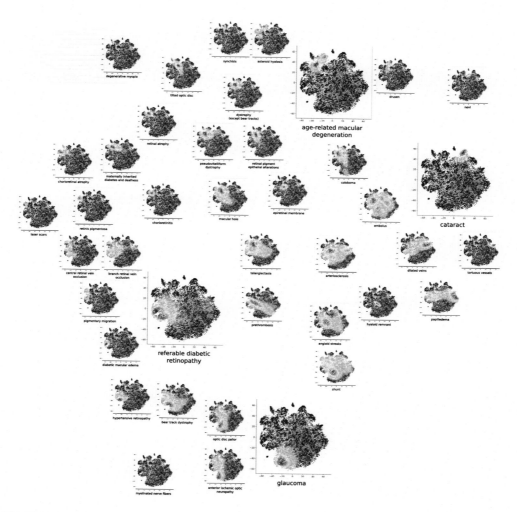

FIGURE 16.3

Probability density functions obtained using Inception-v3 when $M = 17$ conditions are considered frequent. One subfigure is obtained per condition: for each location in feature space, red (respectively blue) indicates a large (respectively low) probability density for that condition. Figures associated with the four most frequent conditions are emphasized. A widespread probability density function (e.g. 'embolus') indicates that images with or without the condition could not be separated well. Conversely, a narrow distribution (e.g. 'degenerative myopia') indicates good separation. Additionally, two overlapping distributions (e.g. 'synchisis' and 'asteroid hyalosis' — two types of vitreous opacities) indicate that the associated conditions could not be separated well; for convenience, subfigures are grouped by similarity of the probability density functions. It can be noted that 'drusen' and 'pseudovitelliform dystrophy' overlap with 'age-related macular degeneration (AMD)', which makes sense since these conditions are generally associated with AMD.

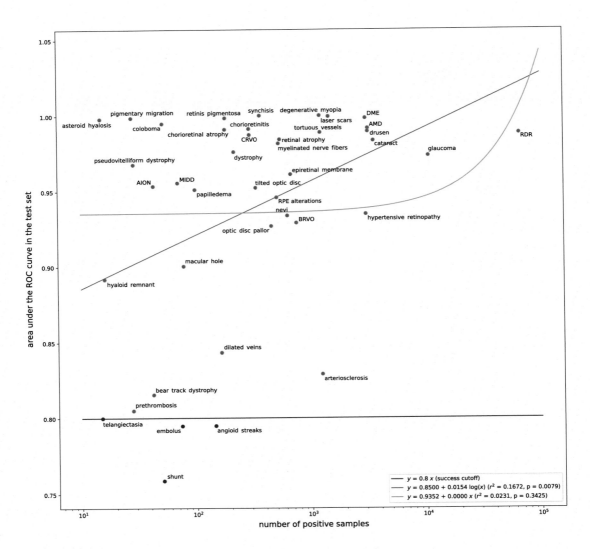

FIGURE 16.4

Detection performance of conditions c_n on the test subset as a function of frequency f_n. An area under the ROC curve less than 0.8 is considered a failure.

16.6.4 Heatmap generation

Sensitivity analysis [41] is used to measure how much each pixel I_{xy} contributes to the prediction: it computes the gradient of the model predictions with respect to each input pixel, using the back-propagation algorithm. When predictions rely on $\hat{q}_{I,n}^M$, the backpropagation algorithm is applied to the

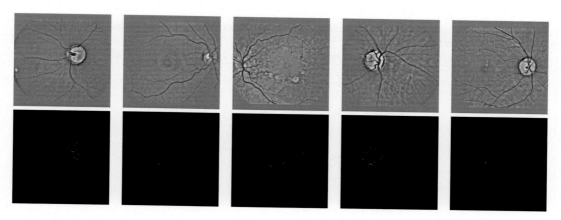

FIGURE 16.5

Heatmap generation. Examples of images are given in the first row. From left to right, these images present an anterior ischemic optic neuropathy, a macular hole, maternally inherited diabetes and deafness, optic disc pallor and retinal pigment epithelium alterations. Heatmaps are given in the second row for those conditions. Black means zero; positive values are in green. The CNN of Fig. 16.3 was used (Inception-v3 CNN — $M = 17$): with the exception of RPE alterations (last column), those conditions are thus unknown to this CNN.

differentiable processing graph G of Section 16.5.6. Heatmap examples for conditions unknown to the CNNs (i.e. for rare conditions) are given in Fig. 16.5.

16.6.5 Comparison with other machine learning frameworks

The proposed framework is now compared with competing machine learning (ML) frameworks, namely Siamese networks [15], a popular few-shot learning algorithm, transfer learning, and multitask learning. The same CNN architectures (Inception-v3, Inception-v4, and "Inception-v3 + Inception-v4") were considered in all experiments.

In the reference few-shot learning algorithm, the similarity between two images I and J was defined using Siamese networks [15]. For a fair comparison, the basis network inside the Siamese networks was replaced by one of the three selected CNN architectures. The outputs of the penultimate CNN layer, i.e. the γ_I and γ_J vectors, were used to compute the similarity between I and J. This similarity is defined as a logistic regression of the absolute difference between γ_I and γ_J [15]. For training the Siamese networks, I and J were considered to match if at least one condition was present in both images. To detect c_n in a test image, the average similarity to validation images containing condition c_n was used: it proved more efficient than considering the maximal similarity [15].

For transfer learning, CNNs were trained for the $M_0 = 11$ most frequent conditions. Then, these CNNs were fine-tuned to detect each of the remaining 30 conditions individually. For multitask learning, CNNs were trained to detect the 41 conditions altogether.

Results are reported in Table 16.3.

Table 16.3 Comparison between ML frameworks in terms of AUC on the test subset. The best AUC for each condition is in bold.

condition (c_n)	proposed	Siamese networks	transfer learning	multitask learning
referable DR	**0.9882**	0.7422	**0.9882**	0.9251
glaucoma	**0.9733**	0.7567	**0.9733**	0.9600
cataract	**0.9834**	0.7947	0.9780	0.9754
AMD	**0.9916**	0.7441	**0.9916**	0.9717
drusen	**0.9895**	0.8304	**0.9895**	0.9470
DME	**0.9982**	0.8709	0.9959	0.9973
HR	**0.9347**	0.8087	0.9299	0.8568
laser scars	**0.9993**	0.7647	**0.9993**	0.9971
arteriosclerosis	**0.8289**	0.8110	0.7998	0.8083
tortuous vessels	**0.9888**	0.7603	**0.9888**	0.9774
degenerative myopia	**0.9999**	0.8726	**0.9999**	0.9973
BRVO	**0.9289**	0.8285	0.8020	0.8613
epiretinal membrane	**0.9611**	0.8521	0.9162	0.9456
nevi	**0.9337**	0.8250	0.8035	0.6311
retinal atrophy	**0.9842**	0.7605	0.8293	0.9178
myelinated nerve fibers	**0.9815**	0.8255	0.9462	0.9059
RPE alterations	**0.9458**	0.8600	0.9177	0.8818
optic disc pallor	**0.9268**	0.8537	0.8794	0.8878
synchisis	**1,0000**	0.9091	0.9932	0.9991
tilted optic disc	**0.9522**	0.8568	0.9031	0.9258
CRVO	0.9873	0.8325	0.9028	**0.9879**
chorioretinitis	**0.9913**	0.7635	0.9555	0.9862
dystrophy	**0.9760**	0.9493	0.8303	0.9058
retinis pigmentosa	**0.9984**	0.9889	0.9740	0.9967
chorioretinal atrophy	**0.9909**	0.8435	0.8405	0.9714
dilated veins	0.8433	**0.8804**	0.8093	0.8063
angioid streaks	0.7947	**0.9314**	0.7594	0.8090
papilledema	**0.9510**	0.9403	0.9363	0.9192
macular hole	**0.9002**	0.8784	0.6734	0.7404
embolus	0.7946	**0.8565**	0.6690	0.6916
MIDD	**0.9555**	0.9132	0.9206	0.9270
coloboma	**0.9948**	0.7188	0.9346	0.6446
shunt	0.7586	**0.8380**	0.6818	0.6782
AION	**0.9534**	0.9330	0.9108	0.8330
bear track dystrophy	**0.8154**	0.6921	0.6245	0.5912
pseudovitelliform dystrophy	**0.9676**	0.9412	0.9176	0.9157
pigmentary migration	**0.9986**	0.7750	0.8714	0.9251
prethrombosis	**0.8050**	0.6688	0.5123	0.4325
hyaloid remnant	**0.8916**	0.7247	0.8000	0.6426
asteroid hyalosis	**0.9979**	0.7635	0.9327	0.8382
telangiectasia	**0.7999**	0.6423	0.3982	0.4236
average ($\forall n$)	**0.9380**	0.8245	0.8654	0.8545
average ($\forall n > 11$)	0.9260	0.8349	0.8282	0.8207

16.7 From specific to general ocular anomaly detection
16.7.1 The anomaly detection algorithm

For the purpose of classifying fundus photographs into "normal" or "anomalous", we propose an anomaly detection algorithm which comprises two stages:

- The first stage (i) consists of different anomaly-specific detectors (CNNs), i.e. one detector per anomaly.
- The second stage (ii) consists of building the final classifier "normal vs. anomalous" by combining the aforementioned detectors.

The combining strategy in the second stage, consists of two steps. Firstly, extracting the output of the penultimate layer of each detector named α_I, where I corresponds a training image. Then, training a customized network, called Combination Network (CN), on the concatenated α_I arising from the multiple detectors.

This CN is a multilayer perceptron network that maps features arising from the detectors to the final referral decision "normal vs. anomalous". Different configurations for designing the architecture of the combination network can be explored. For each studied architecture, the combination network is trained using a different number of input detectors (ensemble models). For instance, let $i = 1, ..., M$ be the number of the used detectors that are arranged in decreasing frequency order of anomaly. For a given architecture, M combination networks are trained on M distinct ensembles of detectors. Each ensemble of detectors is formed by incrementally adding the detectors.

16.7.2 Development of the anomaly detection algorithm using OPHDIAT dataset

To allow device-independent analysis, the preprocessing described in [32] was adopted: fundus photographs were normalized and resized to 448×448 pixels. The anomaly detection algorithm was developed according to the following two stages: (i) training different pathology-specific detectors and (ii) training a general pathology detector combining features arising from those pathology-specific detectors.

The first stage comprised 41 independent deep learning models (anomaly-specific detectors): each model was meant to detect a specific pathology or pathological sign in the OPHDIAT dataset. The DR detection model was trained and validated on $\mathcal{R}$. All other anomaly detectors were trained, validated and tested on $\mathcal{O}$. Positive images are those containing the targeted anomaly. Negative images are normal images. Two deep learning architectures were studied per pathology detector to optimize the detector performance: "Inception-v4" [45] and "ResNet-101" [12].

These CNNs were pretrained on the public ImageNet dataset. Finally, a detector for each pathology or pathological sign was chosen based on its performance on $\mathcal{O}_V$.

The second stage consisted of building the final "normal vs anomalous" classifier (the combination network) by merging different ensemble of the aforementioned detectors. Six different architectures were studied for the combination network. The tested architectures comprised a single neuron, two dense layers and three dense layers. Table 16.4 shows the number of neurons examined for each adopted CN architecture. The activation function was ReLU for the intermediate layers and sigmoid for the output layer. Each studied CN was trained and validated on features arising from the considered detectors using $\mathcal{O}_L$ and $\mathcal{O}_V$ subsets.

The combination network was trained using the binary cross entropy loss.

Table 16.4 The explored combination network architectures.

	Architecture	Nb of neurons in dense layers
CN1	1 neuron	–
CN2	2 dense layers	{1000, 1}
CN3	2 dense layers	{3000, 1}
CN4	2 dense layers	{5000, 1}
CN5	3 dense layers	{1000, 800, 1}
CN6	3 dense layers	{2000, 1000, 1}

16.7.3 Performance comparison with the baseline method

The performances of the anomaly detection algorithm for detecting anomalies in the diabetic population were compared with a baseline method that uses the predictions of multiple anomaly detectors. The following strategy was adopted to infer the referral decision for the baseline method. We used the 41 anomaly-specific detectors of the anomaly detection algorithm that were trained on OPHDIAT. For inference, an image was classified as "normal" when all the anomaly-specific detectors have a negative prediction and classified as "anomalous" when at least one of them has a positive prediction. Thus, a threshold per anomaly detector should be determined to predict the presence or absence of the anomaly for each image in O_T. Different methods were explored to determine the binary detection thresholds on O_V: the Youden's J statistic [27,52], the distance to corner [25], cutoff when specificity is set to higher or equal to 95% and cutoff when sensitivity is set to higher or equal to 95%.

16.7.4 Adaptation of the anomaly detection algorithm to the general population

To adapt the anomaly detection algorithm to a general population with anomaly characteristics that differ from diabetic pathological ones, $\mathcal{A}_L$ of the OphtaMaine dataset was used. Only the combination network, pretrained on OPHDIAT dataset, was fine-tuned on $\mathcal{A}_L$. In practice, fine-tuning consisted of continuing training the combination network for the anomaly detection algorithm using new training and validation subsets ($\mathcal{A}_L$ and $\mathcal{A}_V$).

The anomaly detection algorithm has three parameters: selection of relevant input detectors, the number of hidden layers and the number of neurons in each hidden layer. These parameters were selected in order to maximize the "normal vs anomalous" classification performance in the validation subset.

16.7.5 Evaluation of deep learning algorithms

The anomaly detection algorithm was evaluated on the OPHDIAT and OphtaMaine test subsets. To measure the algorithm's capability to discriminate between "anomalous" and "normal" fundus photographs, ROC curves were computed by varying a cutoff on the combination network probabilistic predictions. Classification performance was summarized by the AUC. It was also assessed in terms of sensitivity and specificity. For this purpose, cutoffs on combination network predictions were selected so that specificity reaches 0.9 on the validation subset. Algorithms thus produce a small percentage of false alarms. Using the selected cutoff, specificity and sensitivity were reported on the test subset.

For OphtaMaine, the anomaly detection algorithm was also compared to the second reader (AAB), in terms of sensitivity and specificity, using labels from the first reader (JBR) as ground truth.

16.8 Results

The CN3 that takes 26 detectors as input showed the best performances on $\mathcal{A}_V$. This CN comprised one hidden layer with 3000 neurons. Fig. 16.6 illustrates ROC curve for anomaly detection on the $\mathcal{O}_T$ subset. In this diabetic population, the anomaly detection algorithm is able to detect anomalous fundus photographs with an AUC of 0.9647. Using the selected cutoff (specificity = 0.9 on $\mathcal{O}_V$), it achieved a specificity of 0.9136 and a sensitivity of 0.9006.

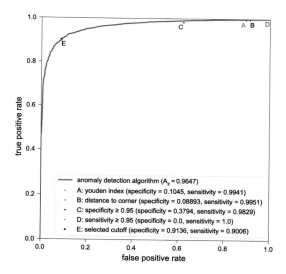

FIGURE 16.6

ROC curve on the $\mathcal{O}_T$ subset for the anomaly detection algorithm. A, B, C, and D points denote the performances of the baseline method using different binary detection thresholds: the Youden's J statistic, the distance to corner, cutoff when specificity is set to higher or equal to 95% and cutoff when sensitivity is set to higher or equal to 95%. The point E denotes the performance of the anomaly detection algorithm using the selected cutoff.

The baseline method performed poorly in detecting anomalies in $\mathcal{O}_T$. As shown in Fig. 16.6, the thresholds obtained using the Youden index and the distance to corner methods yielded poor specificities of 0.1045 and 0.0889 on $\mathcal{O}_T$, respectively. Furthermore, selecting the thresholds so that the specificity is high (≥ 0.95) was expected to produce a small percentage of false alarms but it also produced a poor specificity of 0.3794 on $\mathcal{O}_T$. Similarly, selecting the thresholds so that the sensitivity is high (≥ 0.95) resulted in useless system that outputs 0 of specificity. All these points lie under the ROC curve of the proposed algorithm (or on the curve for the latter), showing that the proposed anomaly detection algorithm outperforms the baseline method.

For each type of anomaly, Fig. 16.7, reports the percentage of images containing this anomaly in $\mathcal{O}_T$ that the anomaly detection algorithm correctly classified as "anomalous" (i.e. the sensitivity per anomaly). These evaluations reveal that the anomaly detection algorithm achieved a high sensitivity for most of the considered anomalies: 24 pathologies or pathological signs were correctly detected with a sensitivity higher than 0.8. It also identified 8 conditions (glaucoma, nevi, retinal pigment epithelium alterations, chorioretinal atrophy, maternally inherited diabetes and deafness, pigmentary migration, bear track dystrophy and macular hole) with a sensitivity ranging between 0.7 and 0.8. However, among the considered anomalies, it showed a low sensitivity (lower than 0.7) for 9 conditions (arteriosclerosis, tilted optic disc, angioid streaks, papilledema, embolus, shunt, pseudovitelliform dystrophy, prethromboses, and telangiectasia). It appears that sensitivity is not significantly correlated with the frequency of an anomaly (p=0.2160).

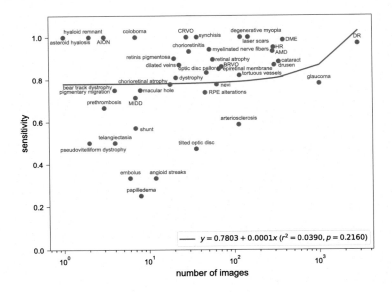

FIGURE 16.7

Sensitivity per pathology versus number of images in log scale using the OPHDIAT test subset.

Fig. 16.8 illustrates performances of the anomaly detection algorithm for screening anomalous fundus photographs in the general population (OphtaMaine's test subset $\mathcal{A}_T$). It displays ROC curves on the test subset of OphtaMaine using the anomaly detection algorithm without and with fine-tuning, respectively. The AUC improved from 0.8308 without fine-tuning to 0.8970 with fine-tuning.

The sensitivity of the anomaly detection algorithm trained on OPHDIAT for recognizing anomalies in $\mathcal{A}_T$ is reported in Fig. 16.9(a). The anomaly detection algorithm detected most of the pathologies with a sensitivity higher than or equal to 0.8 and a specificity of 0.8929. However, among the considered pathologies, it failed to detect the abnormal optic disc, which is the most frequent pathology in

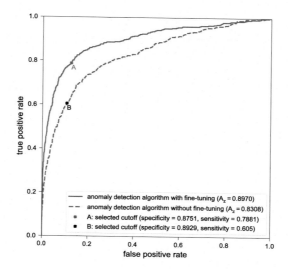

FIGURE 16.8

Receiver operating characteristic for anomaly detection on the OphtaMaine test subset: (a) without fine-tuning, (b) with fine-tuning.

OphtaMaine. It also failed to detect other common signs such as nevi and rare pathologies like tilted optic disc.

The sensitivity of the fine-tuned algorithm for recognizing multiple and rare anomalies in $\mathcal{A}_T$ is depicted in Fig. 16.9(b). The fine-tuned anomaly detection algorithm achieved a specificity of 0.8751. It perfectly detected 13 pathologies (sensitivity higher than 0.9). Moreover, it identified 5 pathologies with a sensitivity ranging between 0.8 and 0.9 (abnormal optic disc, nevi, hemorrhage, Epiretinal Membrane and Macular Epiretinal Membrane (ERM&MEM), and depigmentation). However, it poorly recognized tilted optic disc and tortuous vessels.

Fig. 16.10 compares automatic and human performance in the OphtaMaine's $\mathcal{C}$ subset. Using OphtaMaine's ophthalmologist as reference, the second ophthalmologist achieved a sensitivity of 0.6682 and a specificity of 0.8648. For the same sensitivity (0.6682), the fine-tuned anomaly detection algorithm achieved a specificity of 0.9627, respectively (>0.8648). For the same specificity (0.8648), the fine-tuned anomaly detection algorithm achieved a sensitivity 0.8157, respectively (>0.6682).

We note that without fine tuning, the algorithm achieved a similar performance to AAB: for a specificity of 0.8648, the anomaly detection algorithm achieved a sensitivity of 0.6728. For a sensitivity of 0.6682, it achieved a specificity of 0.8703.

16.9 Discussion

We have presented two meta learning based frameworks for detecting anomalies in fundus photographs. The first one, the anomaly characterization algorithm, recognizes rare conditions in fundus photographs.

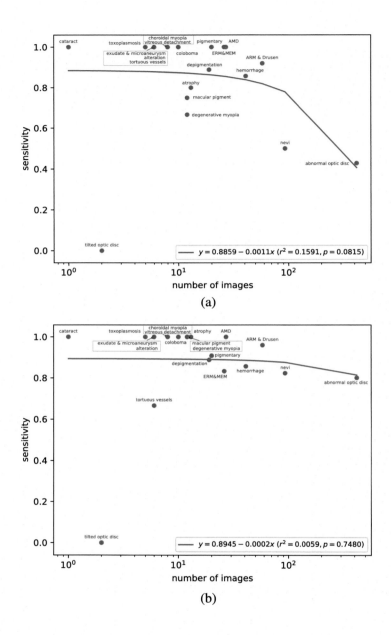

FIGURE 16.9

Sensitivity per pathology versus number of images in log scale using the OphtaMaine test subset for the anomaly detection algorithm: (a) without fine-tuning, (b) with fine-tuning. ARM = Age-related Maculopathy; AMD = Age-related Macular Degeneration; ERM = Epiretinal Membrane; MEM = Macular Epiretinal Membrane.

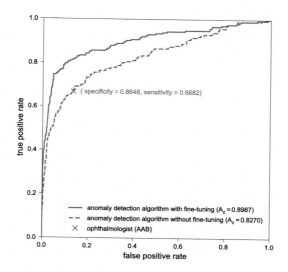

FIGURE 16.10

Receiver operating characteristic curves for anomaly detection on the OphtaMaine $\mathcal{C}$ subset for the anomaly detection algorithm with fine-tuning (solid lines) and without fine-tuning (dashed lines). The cross marker denotes the performance of the ophthalmologist (AAB).

The second one, the anomaly detection algorithm, optimally combines multiple anomaly detectors to predict whether a fundus photograph is normal or anomalous.

Both approaches exploit pretrained convolutional neural networks (CNNs), to improve learning of a new task. The anomaly characterization algorithm, for instance, uses CNNs trained on frequent conditions, to detect rare anomalies in fundus photographs. Similarly, the anomaly detection algorithm employs multiple anomaly-specific detectors (CNNs) to provide the final classification "normal vs anomalous" decision.

Furthermore, both approaches take advantages of the representations learned from CNNs. Indeed, the anomaly characterization algorithm is based on the observation that CNNs tend to cluster similar images in feature space. This observation is further seen for conditions unknown to the CNNs: they are also clustered in feature space (see Fig. 16.3). Thus, to benefit from the rich representation learned by CNNs, a probabilistic framework, based on the t-SNE representation, was proposed. On the other hand, the anomaly detection algorithm also benefits from the learned representation of the trained CNNs. Specifically, in order to optimally integrate the learned features, a merging strategy based on neural network was proposed: a combination network was trained on the features arising from multiple CNNs (anomaly detectors).

The incorporation of t-SNE in our anomaly characterization algorithm for classification purposes is an interesting feature. Specifically, we discovered that decreasing the feature space to two dimensions, which is the standard value for visualization, maximizes classification performance. This is partly due to more reliable kernel density estimations in low-dimensional feature spaces [39]. One advantage is that one can easily browse the image dataset in a 2-D viewer and see how CNNs structure the dataset.

This might be used to show similar visuals to human readers to aid in decision-making [31]. Despite the fact that the probabilistic model is built on the expressionless t-SNE dimension reduction technique, we designed it to be differentiable. This property enables heatmap production for improved visualization via sensitivity analysis [29]. The diseased structures, in particular, are well captured by the CNNs, even for unknown conditions to the CNNs (see Fig. 16.5).

The two proposed approaches were investigated on the OPHDIAT dataset, issued from a diabetic population. The anomaly characterization algorithm achieved good performances: the average area under the ROC curve (AUC) for recognizing 41 conditions on $\mathcal{D}_T$ was 0.9380 (see Table 16.3). When only the rarest conditions were considered, detection performance was similarly good: the average AUC only dropped to 0.9260 when the 30 rarest pathologies were considered (see Table 16.3). The detection performance was poorly correlated with the frequency of a condition: $r^2 = 0.0231$ (or $r^2 = 0.1672$ using a logarithmic scale for frequency), as illustrated in Fig. 16.4. Moreover, the AUC exceeded 0.8 for 37 conditions, showing that the majority of the considered pathologies were well detected. For the "normal vs anomalous" classification task, the anomaly detection algorithm showed good performance on $\mathcal{O}_T$ (AUC: 0.9647). While guaranteeing a high specificity (≈ 0.9), it achieved high sensitivity (> 0.8) for most of the considered anomalies (see Fig. 16.7).

The proposed approaches were compared to baseline frameworks. For the purpose of detecting rare anomalies, our anomaly characterization algorithm was compared with transfer learning, multitask learning and Siamese networks. It appears to significantly outperform traditional approaches such as transfer learning and multitask learning. Interestingly, with similar complexity (one CNN model per condition), it detects rare conditions ($n > 11$) considerably better than transfer learning. This is probably due to the fact that in transfer learning good properties learnt from the initial model (i.e. trained on frequent conditions) may be lost after fine-tuning. Worse, in multitask learning, the detection of frequent conditions, which is trained simultaneously, is negatively impacted. However, there is a more marked contrast when comparing the proposed approach to Siamese networks. Four conditions were better detected using Siamese networks. All these conditions are among the rarest ($n > M_0 = 11$) and three of them were poorly detected (AUC < 0.8) by the proposed solution (see Table 16.3). Indeed, the performance of Siamese networks [15] was shown to be highly independent of the frequency of a condition. However, the proposed solution still significantly outperforms Siamese networks, which have similar complexity (one CNN model per condition). To sum up, the proposed solution is obviously the most relevant ML framework for the target task. Nevertheless, Siamese networks, which use similarity analysis in CNN feature space as well [15], are also an interesting few-shot learning framework.

For the purpose of screening anomalous fundus photographs, the anomaly detection algorithm was compared with a baseline approach that combines multiple anomaly-specific detectors. The results showed that, regardless of the method used to determine the cutoff, the proposed algorithm outperformed the baseline strategy. With the baseline approach, a specificity of 0.3794 was attained at best. Our results demonstrate that (perhaps a few) anomaly-specific detectors produce too many false alarms, invalidating the baseline approach. Unlike the baseline approach, the anomaly detection algorithm is intentionally trained to minimize the overall number of false alarms while maximizing the overall sensitivity. This results in a screening tool for "anomalous fundus photographs" in general which is both sensitive and specific.

Despite promising performances of the anomaly detection algorithm on OPHDIAT, the performances suffered when tested on OphtaMaine. This is due to the test set being greatly different from the training set. On other words, the algorithm misclassifies some examinations due to the variability in pathological characteristics and manifestation, induced by different screened population.

To address this issue, the anomaly detection algorithm was adapted to the general population. The impact of this adaptation on the performances of the algorithm was very beneficial: the AUC improved from 0.8308 to 0.8970. These results showed the interesting impact of fine-tuning the algorithm on detecting anomalies in the general population. Furthermore, on the OphtaMaine's test subset, the fine-tuned anomaly detection algorithm performed well in detecting multiple and rare anomalies. It was able to detect 13 anomalies with a sensitivity > 0.9 and a specificity of 0.8751. It detected not only common anomalies like AMD and degenerative myopia, but also less common ones including coloboma and epiretinal membranes.

The proposed fine-tuning strategy, which requires fewer training samples than re-training, is an effective tool to tackle diverse ocular screening applications. It provides flexibility to meet the needs of clinicians: alert thresholds may differ depending on the aim of screening. It also allows deep learning algorithms to be generalized to the intended screening population. Generally, it enables the algorithm to learn new anomalous characteristics that are unique to the population being studied. In this work, it allowed the algorithm to learn the location, shape and aspect of lesions that were not associated to diabetic patients. It improved the algorithm' sensitivity to pathological signs related to the general population such as abnormal optic disc. In addition, it adapts the algorithm to different screening device types, including portable retinal imaging devices. For all these reasons, this will extend the use of deep learning algorithms and benefit a wider range of patients.

The anomaly detection algorithm achieved human-level performance (see Fig. 16.10). However, the comparison between human and automatic performance revealed that interrater variability among ophthalmologists is high in defining normal fundus images. This is due to the lack of an internationally recognized classification, as contrasted to DR screening. In this specific experiment, this is also linked to mismatch in the readers' background (liberal vs. hospital practice).

One main limitation of this study is that most images were interpreted by a single ophthalmologist. For improving the quality of performance assessment, extensive annotations from multiple experts are desirable. Furthermore, this study suggests that the level of agreement among experts is currently low. One reason is that each ophthalmology department or screening network has its own guideline for classifying data.

In conclusion, the proposed algorithms open new perspectives for ocular pathology screening. The trained detectors of the anomaly characterization algorithm, in particular, might be employed in both traditional and automatic screening settings to generate warnings when rare conditions are detected. For screening ocular anomalies, our anomaly detection algorithm has proven to be efficient in both the diabetic and the general populations. It recognized the majority of the anomalies, including rare anomalies, while ensuring a high specificity. Therefore, ophthalmologists and other graders will save time by automatically discarding normal photographs, lowering the amount of images to review. Finally, the two proposed algorithms can be combined together to form a single screening and diagnosis system. This could be done by firstly applying the anomaly detection algorithm to provide a referral decision, and then using the anomaly characterization algorithm to make the diagnosis for the referred patients. Given the severe shortage of ophthalmologists worldwide, the proposed algorithms are therefore a promising solution for earlier patient care.

Future directions for this work include multicenter training, to ensure that the algorithms can deal with the variety of imaging devices, population characteristics and annotation habits throughout the

World. This is the purpose of the ADMIRE project, which will investigate federated learning in this context.[4] Another future direction is to move from screening / detecting anomalies, to predicting their future evolution. This is notably the purpose of the EviRed project,[5] for DR in particular.

References

[1] R. Bourne, J.D. Steinmetz, S. Flaxman, P.S. Briant, H.R. Taylor, S. Resnikoff, R.J. Casson, A. Abdoli, E. Abu-Gharbieh, A. Afshin, et al., Trends in prevalence of blindness and distance and near vision impairment over 30 years: an analysis for the global burden of disease study, The Lancet Global Health (2020).

[2] R. Caruana, Multitask learning, Machine Learning 28 (1997) 41–75, https://doi.org/10.1023/A:1007379606734.

[3] V. Cheplygina, Cats or CAT scans: transfer learning from natural or medical image source data sets?, Current Opinion in Biomedical Engineering 9 (2019) 21–27, https://doi.org/10.1016/j.cobme.2018.12.005.

[4] J.Y. Choi, T.K. Yoo, J.G. Seo, J. Kwak, T.T. Um, T.H. Rim, Multi-categorical deep learning neural network to classify retinal images: a pilot study employing small database, PLoS ONE 12 (2017) e0187336, https://doi.org/10.1371/journal.pone.0187336.

[5] E. Decencière, G. Cazuguel, X. Zhang, G. Thibault, J.C. Klein, F. Meyer, B. Marcotegui, G. Quellec, M. Lamard, R. Danno, D. Elie, P. Massin, Z. Viktor, A. Erginay, B. Laÿ, A. Chabouis, TeleOphta: machine learning and image processing methods for teleophthalmology, IRBM 34 (2013) 196–203, https://doi.org/10.1016/j.irbm.2013.01.010.

[6] E. Decencière, X. Zhang, G. Cazuguel, B. Lay, B. Cochener, C. Trone, P. Gain, R. Ordonez, P. Massin, A. Erginay, B. Charton, J.C. Klein, Feedback on a publicly distributed database: the Messidor database, Image Analysis & Stereology 33 (2014) 231–234, https://doi.org/10.5566/ias.1155.

[7] J. Devda, R. Eswari, Pathological myopia image analysis using deep learning, Procedia Computer Science 165 (2019) 239–244.

[8] L. Fei-Fei, R. Fergus, P. Perona, One-shot learning of object categories, IEEE Transactions on Pattern Analysis and Machine Intelligence 28 (2006) 594–611, https://doi.org/10.1109/TPAMI.2006.79.

[9] R. Gargeya, T. Leng, Automated identification of diabetic retinopathy using deep learning, Ophthalmology 124 (2017) 962–969.

[10] F. Grassmann, J. Mengelkamp, C. Brandl, S. Harsch, M.E. Zimmermann, B. Linkohr, A. Peters, I.M. Heid, C. Palm, B.H. Weber, A deep learning algorithm for prediction of age-related eye disease study severity scale for age-related macular degeneration from color fundus photography, Ophthalmology 125 (2018) 1410–1420.

[11] S. Guendel, F.C. Ghesu, S. Grbic, E. Gibson, B. Georgescu, A. Maier, D. Comaniciu, Multi-Task Learning for Chest X-Ray Abnormality Classification on Noisy Labels, Technical Report, 2019, arXiv:1905.06362 [cs].

[12] K. He, X. Zhang, S. Ren, J. Sun, Deep residual learning for image recognition, in: Proc. CVPR, Las Vegas, NV, USA, 2016, pp. 770–778.

[13] S. Keel, Z. Li, J. Scheetz, L. Robman, J. Phung, G. Makeyeva, K. Aung, C. Liu, X. Yan, W. Meng, et al., Development and validation of a deep-learning algorithm for the detection of neovascular age-related macular degeneration from colour fundus photographs, Clinical & Experimental Ophthalmology 47 (2019) 1009–1018.

[14] S. Keel, J. Wu, P.Y. Lee, J. Scheetz, M. He, Visualizing deep learning models for the detection of referable diabetic retinopathy and glaucoma, JAMA Ophthalmology 137 (2019) 288–292.

---

[4] https://anr.fr/Projet-ANR-19-LCV2-0005.

[5] https://anr.fr/ProjetIA-18-RHUS-0008.

[15] G. Koch, R. Zemel, R. Salakhutdinov, Siamese neural networks for one-shot image recognition, in: Proc. ICML, University of Toronto, Lille, France, 2015.

[16] B. Lay, R. Danno, G. Quellec, M. Lamard, B. Cochener, A. Erginay, P. Massin, A.L. Guilcher, Using artificial intelligence to detect glaucoma and age related macula degeneration, Investigative Ophthalmology & Visual Science 61 (2020) 1647.

[17] A.Y. Lee, R.T. Yanagihara, C.S. Lee, M. Blazes, H.C. Jung, Y.E. Chee, M.D. Gencarella, H. Gee, A.Y. Maa, G.C. Cockerham, M. Lynch, E.J. Boyko, Multicenter, head-to-head, real-world validation study of seven automated artificial intelligence diabetic retinopathy screening systems, Diabetes Care 44 (2021) 1168–1175, https://doi.org/10.2337/dc20-1877.

[18] F. Li, Z. Liu, H. Chen, M. Jiang, X. Zhang, Z. Wu, Automatic detection of diabetic retinopathy in retinal fundus photographs based on deep learning algorithm, Translational Vision Science & Technology 8 (2019) 4.

[19] F. Li, L. Yan, Y. Wang, J. Shi, H. Chen, X. Zhang, M. Jiang, Z. Wu, K. Zhou, Deep learning-based automated detection of glaucomatous optic neuropathy on color fundus photographs, Graefe's Archive for Clinical and Experimental Ophthalmology (2020) 1–17.

[20] P. Massin, A. Chabouis, A. Erginay, C. Viens-Bitker, A. Lecleire-Collet, T. Meas, P.J. Guillausseau, G. Choupot, B. André, P. Denormandie, Ophdiat©: a telemedical network screening system for diabetic retinopathy in the Île-de-France, Diabetes & Metabolism 34 (2008) 227–234.

[21] T. Mordan, N. Thome, G. Henaff, M. Cord, Revisiting multi-task learning with ROCK: a deep residual auxiliary block for visual detection, in: Proc. NIPS, Montreal, Canada, 2018, pp. 1310–1322.

[22] M. Niemeijer, B. van Ginneken, M.J. Cree, A. Mizutani, G. Quellec, C.I. Sanchez, B. Zhang, R. Hornero, M. Lamard, C. Muramatsu, X. Wu, G. Cazuguel, J. You, A. Mayo, Q. Li, Y. Hatanaka, B. Cochener, C. Roux, F. Karray, M. Garcia, H. Fujita, M.D. Abramoff, Retinopathy online challenge: automatic detection of microaneurysms in digital color fundus photographs, IEEE Transactions on Medical Imaging 29 (2010) 185–195, https://doi.org/10.1109/TMI.2009.2033909.

[23] J.I. Orlando, H. Fu, J.B. Breda, K. van Keer, D.R. Bathula, A. Diaz-Pinto, R. Fang, P.A. Heng, J. Kim, J. Lee, et al., Refuge challenge: a unified framework for evaluating automated methods for glaucoma assessment from fundus photographs, Medical Image Analysis 59 (2020) 101570.

[24] E. Parzen, On estimation of a probability density function and mode, The Annals of Mathematical Statistics 33 (1962) 1065–1076.

[25] J. Perkins Neil, F. Schisterman Enrique, The inconsistency of "optimal" cut-points using two roc based criteria, American Journal of Epidemiology 163 (2006) 670–675.

[26] S. Phasuk, P. Poopresert, A. Yaemsuk, P. Suvannachart, R. Itthipanichpong, S. Chansangpetch, A. Manassakorn, V. Tantisevi, P. Rojanapongpun, C. Tantibundhit, Automated glaucoma screening from retinal fundus image using deep learning, in: 2019 41st Annual International Conference of the IEEE Engineering in Medicine and Biology Society (EMBC), IEEE, 2019, pp. 904–907.

[27] D.M. Powers, Evaluation: from precision, recall and f-measure to roc, informedness, markedness and correlation, arXiv preprint, arXiv:2010.16061, 2020.

[28] T. Pratap, P. Kokil, Computer-aided diagnosis of cataract using deep transfer learning, Biomedical Signal Processing and Control 53 (2019) 101533.

[29] G. Quellec, K. Charrière, Y. Boudi, B. Cochener, M. Lamard, Deep image mining for diabetic retinopathy screening, Medical Image Analysis 39 (2017) 178–193, https://doi.org/10.1016/j.media.2017.04.012.

[30] G. Quellec, M. Lamard, M.D. Abràmoff, E. Decencière, B. Lay, A. Erginay, B. Cochener, G. Cazuguel, A multiple-instance learning framework for diabetic retinopathy screening, Medical Image Analysis 16 (2012) 1228–1240.

[31] G. Quellec, M. Lamard, G. Cazuguel, L. Bekri, W. Daccache, C. Roux, B. Cochener, Automated assessment of diabetic retinopathy severity using content-based image retrieval in multimodal fundus photographs, Investigative Ophthalmology & Visual Science 52 (2011) 8342–8348, https://doi.org/10.1167/iovs.11-7418.

[32] G. Quellec, M. Lamard, P.H. Conze, P. Massin, B. Cochener, Automatic detection of rare pathologies in fundus photographs using few-shot learning, Medical Image Analysis 61 (2020) 101660.

[33] G. Quellec, M. Lamard, A. Erginay, A. Chabouis, P. Massin, B. Cochener, G. Cazuguel, Automatic detection of referral patients due to retinal pathologies through data mining, Medical Image Analysis 29 (2016) 47–64.

[34] G. Quellec, M. Lamard, P.M. Josselin, G. Cazuguel, B. Cochener, C. Roux, Optimal wavelet transform for the detection of microaneurysms in retina photographs, IEEE Transactions on Medical Imaging 27 (2008) 1230–1241, https://doi.org/10.1109/TMI.2008.920619.

[35] G. Quellec, M. Lamard, B. Lay, A.L. Guilcher, A. Erginay, B. Cochener, P. Massin, Instant automatic diagnosis of diabetic retinopathy, Technical Report, 2019, arXiv:1906.11875 [cs, eess].

[36] S. Resnikoff, W. Felch, T.M. Gauthier, B. Spivey, The number of ophthalmologists in practice and training worldwide: a growing gap despite more than 200 000 practitioners, British Journal of Ophthalmology 96 (2012) 783–787.

[37] S. Saha, M. Nassisi, M. Wang, S. Lindenberg, S. Sadda, Z.J. Hu, et al., Automated detection and classification of early amd biomarkers using deep learning, Scientific Reports 9 (2019) 1–9.

[38] R. Sayres, A. Taly, E. Rahimy, K. Blumer, D. Coz, N. Hammel, J. Krause, A. Narayanaswamy, Z. Rastegar, D. Wu, et al., Using a deep learning algorithm and integrated gradients explanation to assist grading for diabetic retinopathy, Ophthalmology 126 (2019) 552–564.

[39] D. Scott, Multivariate Density Estimation: Theory, Practice, and Visualization, John Wiley & Sons, New York, Chicester, 1992.

[40] P. Shyam, S. Gupta, A. Dukkipati, Attentive recurrent comparators, in: Proc. ICML, Sydney, Australia, 2017.

[41] K. Simonyan, A. Vedaldi, A. Zisserman, Deep inside convolutional networks: visualising image classification models and saliency maps, in: ICLR Workshop, Calgary, Canada, 2014.

[42] J. Son, J.Y. Shin, H.D. Kim, K.H. Jung, K.H. Park, S.J. Park, Development and validation of deep learning models for screening multiple abnormal findings in retinal fundus images, Ophthalmology 127 (2020) 85–94.

[43] J.D. Steinmetz, R.R. Bourne, P.S. Briant, S.R. Flaxman, H.R. Taylor, J.B. Jonas, A.A. Abdoli, W.A. Abrha, A. Abualhasan, E.G. Abu-Gharbieh, et al., Causes of blindness and vision impairment in 2020 and trends over 30 years, and prevalence of avoidable blindness in relation to vision 2020: the right to sight: an analysis for the global burden of disease study, The Lancet Global Health 9 (2021) e144–e160.

[44] F. Sung, Y. Yang, L. Zhang, T. Xiang, P.H.S. Torr, T.M. Hospedales, Learning to compare: relation network for few-shot learning, in: Proc. CVPR, Salt Lake City, UT, USA, 2018.

[45] C. Szegedy, S. Ioffe, V. Vanhoucke, A. Alemi, Inception-v4, inception-ResNet and the impact of residual connections on learning, in: Proc. AAAI, San Francisco, CA, USA, 2017, pp. 4278–4284.

[46] C. Szegedy, V. Vanhoucke, S. Ioffe, J. Shlens, Z. Wojna, Rethinking the inception architecture for computer vision, in: Proc. IEEE CVPR, Las Vegas, NV, USA, 2016, pp. 2818–2826.

[47] D.S.W. Ting, L.R. Pasquale, L. Peng, J.P. Campbell, A.Y. Lee, R. Raman, G.S.W. Tan, L. Schmetterer, P.A. Keane, T.Y. Wong, Artificial intelligence and deep learning in ophthalmology, British Journal of Ophthalmology 103 (2019) 167–175.

[48] L. van der Maaten, G. Hinton, Visualizing high-dimensional data using t-SNE, Journal of Machine Learning Research 9 (2008) 2579–2605.

[49] O. Vinyals, C. Blundell, T. Lillicrap, K. Kavukcuoglu, D. Wierstra, Matching networks for one shot learning, in: Proc. NIPS, Barcelona, Spain, 2016, pp. 3637–3645.

[50] Y. Wang, Q. Yao, J. Kwok, L.M. Ni, Generalizing from a Few Examples: A Survey on Few-Shot Learning, Technical Report, 2019, arXiv:1904.05046 [cs].

[51] T.K. Yoo, J.Y. Choi, J.G. Seo, B. Ramasubramanian, S. Selvaperumal, D.W. Kim, The possibility of the combination of oct and fundus images for improving the diagnostic accuracy of deep learning for age-related macular degeneration: a preliminary experiment, Medical & Biological Engineering & Computing 57 (2019) 677–687.

[52] W.J. Youden, Index for rating diagnostic tests, Cancer 3 (1950) 32–35.

[53] Z. Zhang, P. Luo, C.C. Loy, X. Tang, Facial landmark detection by deep multi-task learning, in: D. Fleet, T. Pajdla, B. Schiele, T. Tuytelaars (Eds.), Proc. ECCV, Springer International Publishing, Zurich, Switzerland, 2014, pp. 94–108.

[54] B. Zoph, V. Vasudevan, J. Shlens, Q.V. Le, Learning transferable architectures for scalable image recognition, in: Proc. IEEE CVPR, Salt Lake City, UT, USA, 2018.

Rare disease classification via difficulty-aware meta learning

Xiaomeng Li[a], Lequan Yu[b], Yueming Jin[c], Chi-Wing Fu[d], Lei Xing[e], and Pheng-Ann Heng[d]

[a]*The Hong Kong University of Science and Technology, HKSAR, China*
[b]*The University of Hong Kong, HKSAR, China*
[c]*University College London, London, United Kingdom*
[d]*The Chinese University of Hong Kong, HKSAR, China*
[e]*Stanford University, Palo Alto, CA, United States*

17.1 Introduction

Deep convolutional neural networks have achieved stunning results on various computer-aided diagnosis task [1–4]. One key reason for the success is large amounts of labeled data to support the network training. For example, HAM10000 dataset [5] contains 10,015 dermatoscopic images and cases include actinic keratoses and intraepithelial carcinoma (akiec), basal cell carcinoma (bcc), benign keratosis-like lesions (solar lentigines / seborrheic keratoses and lichen-planus like keratoses, bkl), dermatofibroma (df), melanoma (mel), melanocytic nevi (nv), and vascular lesions (angiomas, angiokeratomas, pyogenic granulomas and hemorrhage, vasc). The Dermofit Image Library [6] consists of 1300 high-resolution images with ten classes of skin lesions. Yet, there are about 7000 known rare diseases [7] that typically catch little attention, and the data is difficult to obtain. These conditions collectively affected about 400 million people worldwide [8] and were generally neglected by the medical imaging community. For example, compared to the common skin lesion melanoma, argyria is a rare skin disorder that causes the skin to change color into a blue or grayish hue. Elastoderma is a rare skin disorder that causes extreme looseness in the skin [9]. Taking retinal diseases as an example, glaucoma, diabetic retinopathy, age-related macular degeneration, and retinopathy of prematurity are relatively common in the clinical practice. In contrast, other retinal diseases, such as fundus pulverulentus and fundus albipunctatus are rare [10]. Hence, developing automatic algorithms for recognizing these diseases is important for rare disease patients. Generally, it is difficult to collect data for these rare diseases and obtain annotations from experienced physicians. This phenomenon raises the following question: *given the extremely low-data regime of rare diseases, can we transfer the inherent knowledge learned from the common diseases to automatically predict the rare disease?* In other words, if we train a model on the metatrain dataset, how could we adapt the model to the new tasks with unseen classes? see examples in Fig. 17.1.

A simple solution is transfer learning, *i.e.*, fine-tuning, where the model is trained on a large dataset and then fine-tuned to another smaller one. However, fine-tuning a model on the few given labeled data *i.e.*, *less than five samples per class* will lead to the overfitting problem; see the training curves shown in Fig. 17.4 in the experiments. Another possible way to solve the overfitting problem is to extract features by a pretrained network and then employ simple classifiers to get predictions, *e.g.*,

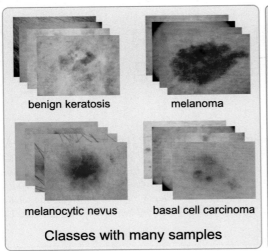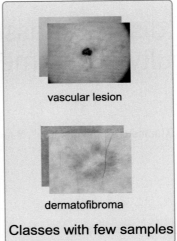

benign keratosis   melanoma   vascular lesion

melanocytic nevus   basal cell carcinoma   dermatofibroma

Classes with many samples   **Classes with few samples**

FIGURE 17.1

The setting of rare disease classification. The metatrain dataset includes classes with many samples; The metatest dataset includes classes with few samples.

support vector machine (SVM) [11] and k-nearest neighbors (kNN). However, a series of experiments in Section 17.4 showed that these methods have limited capacity in classifying rare diseases. Recently, Zhao *et al.* [1] and Mondal *et al.* [3] tackle the low-data regime related issues, *i.e.*, one-shot or few-shot segmentation, in the medical imaging domain. However, both methods rely on the large number of unlabeled images, which are not appropriate for handling rare disease classification since rare disease cases are challenging to collect. Maicas *et al.* [12] present a meta learning method to learn a good initialization on a series of tasks, which can be used to pretrain medical image analysis models. In this regard, developing effective techniques for rare disease diagnosis in low-data regimes is of vital importance.

Meta learning techniques refer to performing model training on a wide range of learning tasks instead of an individual task, such that the model can be quickly adapted to new tasks. In general, meta learning updates a network by equally treating (averaging) the gradient directions from different randomly-sampled tasks. Hence, the meta learning process often stops at a stage where "easy tasks" are well-learned and "difficulty tasks" are still being misclassified. This hinders the meta learning and affects the results on rare disease classification, in which the rare disease samples are unseen in training. This observation motivates us to consider a more effective meta learning optimization. In this book chapter, we present a difficulty-aware meta learning (DAML) method [13], which first trains a meta-classifier on a series of related tasks (*e.g.*, common disease classification), instead of a single individual task, such that the transferable internal representations with the gradient-based learning rule can make rapid progress on the new tasks (*e.g.*, rare disease classification). More importantly, we discover that the contribution of each task sample to the metaobjective is various. To better optimize the metaclassifier, a dynamic modulating function over the learning tasks is formulated, where the function automatically downweights the well-learned tasks and rapidly focuses on the hard tasks. Only training on the four skin lesion classes, our method achieves a stunning result on classifying the other three unseen classes, with an AUC of 83.3% under five samples setting. We also validate our method on several rare disease classification tasks using the public Dermofit Image Library[1] and achieve a high AUC of 82.67% under the five samples setting, demonstrating the potential of our method for real clinical practice.

In this chapter, we first give a comprehensive literature review in Section 17.2, including skin lesion classification/segmentation from dermoscopic images, few-shot learning on skin lesion classification, rare disease diagnosis, and meta learning in medical image analysis. Then, we provide a preliminary study in Section 17.3.1, illustrate the problem setting in Section 17.3.2, describe our approach 17.3.3 and provide the experimental details in Section 17.3.4. We show two case studies in Section 17.4. Finally, we give a detailed discussion in Section 17.5 and conclude this book chapter in Section 17.6.

17.2 Related work

17.2.1 Skin lesion classification and segmentation from dermoscopic images

Dermoscopy is the examination of skin lesions with a dermatoscope device consisting of a high-quality magnifying lens and a (polarizable) illumination system [14]. After the release of many large dermoscopic datasets, developing deep learning algorithms to automatically classify and segment lesions from dermoscopic images is becoming an active research topic. For example, Yu et al. [15] proposed a very deep neural network for melanoma classification and segmentation and achieved the best performance on the classification subtask in ISBI 2016 Skin Lesion Analysis Towards Melanoma Detection Challenge. Codella et al. [16] developed an ensemble of deep learning algorithms for melanoma recognition and segmentation in dermoscopy images from the ISIC-2016 dataset and showed that the method outperformed dermatologists. Perez et al. [17] showed that ensembling CNN architectures will improve the melanoma classification performance. Tschand et al. [18] used popular convolution-based networks such as InceptionV3 and ResNet50 on a combined dataset of 7895 dermoscopic and 5829 close-up lesion images for diagnosis of nonpigmented skin cancers.

For skin lesion segmentation, Yuan et al. [19] developed a 19-layer deep convolutional neural network and achieved the best performance on ISBI 2016 skin lesion analysis towards melanoma detection challenge. They further developed a 29-layer deep neural network for skin lesion segmentation and achieved 0.784 on the online validation dataset. Later on, Li et al. [20] proposed a new dense deconvolutional network for skin lesion segmentation based on residual learning. Al et al. [21] proposed full resolution convolutional networks for skin lesion segmentation. Recently, Lei et al. [22] proposed a generative adversarial network (GAN), consisting of a dense convolution U-Net (UNet-SCDC) based segmentation module and a dual discrimination (DD) module for skin lesion segmentation from ISIC Skin Lesion Challenge Datasets of 2017 and 2018.

Although various deep learning models have been developed for skin lesion classification and segmentation, less attention has been paid to generalizing the model on unseen classes. In other words, how can we transfer the inherent knowledge learned from the common diseases to support the rare

---

[1] https://licensing.eri.ed.ac.uk/i/software/dermofit-image-library.html.

(unseen) disease classification? In this book chapter, we focus on the rare disease prediction problem and present our solutions.

17.2.2 Few-shot learning on skin lesion classification

There has been a growth of interest in few-shot learning on skin lesion classification in recent years. The methods can be broadly classified into two main categories: meta learning-based and transfer-learning-based methods. For meta learning-based methods, some models are built on gradient-based meta learning methods like MAML [23] and Reptile [24]. The goal of meta learning is to train a model on a variety of learning tasks, such that it can solve new learning tasks by using only a small number of training samples. For example, Finn *et al.* [23] present a meta learning method, namely MAML, where the key idea is to train the model's initial parameters such that the model has maximal performance on a new task after the parameters have been updated through one or more gradient steps computed with a small amount of data from that new task. With the remarkable results achieved by MAML on a few-shot learning problem, several researchers considered improving it from different perspectives. For example, considering the skin image is rotation-invariant, Mahajan *et al.* [25] replaced the conventional operation with group equivariant convolutions and demonstrated the effectiveness of the method on few-shot skin lesion classification tasks. Since dermoscopic images have imbalanced class samples and have various difficulties in episodic tasks, Li *et al.* [13] considers the various difficulties in different episodic tasks and adjusts the weights of loss for different tasks so that easier tasks become less important and harder tasks are dominant. Singh *et al.* [26] proposed meta learning-based "MetaMed" for few-shot skin lesion classification, where advanced image augmentation techniques like CutOut [27], MixUp [28], and CutMix [29] are used to alleviate the overfitting problem.

Another category is the metric-learning-based approaches. The main idea is to learn the feature representations and design a distance metric between support and query set to predict the labels. Two representative metrics are cosine similarity in [30] and Euclidean distance in Prototypical Network [31]. To model intra-class variability in dermoscopic images, Prabhu *et al.* [32] proposed a prototypical clustering network for dermatological disease diagnosis, an extension of Prototypical Networks [31] that learns a mixture of "prototype" for each class. Zhu *et al.* [33] also built upon Prototypical Networks, and their proposed network can implicitly generate prototypes for each episode. They set a different temperature for different categories to penalize query samples that are not close enough to their belonging categories to further strengthen the generalization ability of the learned metric. Some other works are not restricted to the specific type of method. They show the general improvement on several FSL models for their proposed techniques. In Zhu *et al.* [34] indicate the incompatibility between cross-entropy loss and episode training, and therefore, they propose the query-relative loss to enhance the behavior further.

Since it is hard to collect enough labeled data on skin lesion conditions to meet the requirement for the pretraining stage, people explore the possibility of cross-domain FSL, e.g., train a model from Imagenet (the source domain) and generalize it to ISIC2018 (the target domain). The benchmark dataset for the cross-domain FSL method is introduced in [35]. They train various FSL models (including both meta learning and transfer-learning-based approaches) on the source domain and test/finetune on the target domain. However, the domain shift problem between source and target domain is hard to deal with. Hence, some works [36–38] try to bring in unlabeled data from the target domain and self-supervised learning strategies to mitigate the performance degradation of few-shot learners due to large domain differences in the pretraining stage.

17.2.3 Rare disease diagnosis

Rare disease diagnosis is a rapidly expanding research and clinical development area, which has an important value in clinical practice. Advancements in data mining and genetic understanding have led to improved identification of rare conditions and possible pathways for improving rare disease diagnosis and treatment. For example, Svenstrup *et al.* [39] reviewed recent initiatives on the use of web search, social media, and data mining in data repositories for medical diagnosis. Whicher *et al.* [40] conducted a landscape review of available methodological approaches to address the challenges of rare disease research. Their goal is to call for methodological approaches that can address the challenges for robust research on rare diseases. With the public available rare disease dataset, *i.e.*, Orphanet dataset, Alves *et al.* [41] used the associations of rare diseases and their symptoms and automatically predicted the most likely rare diseases based on patient's symptoms.

From the genetic preceptive, the rare disease diagnosis and treatment is improved [42], with the advancements in genetic understanding. For example, Baynam *et al.* [42] describes an algorithm that automates the most labor-intensive part of genetic diagnosis: that of matching a patient's genetic sequence and symptoms to a disease described in the scientific literature.

In recent few years, several methods tried to use deep learning algorithms to tackle the rare disease diagnosis problem. For example, Cui *et al.* [43] proposed a complementary pattern augmentation (CO-NAN) framework for rare disease detection from patients' clinical records, which combines ideas from both adversarial training and max-margin classification. The method is evaluated on two rare disease detection tasks, *i.e.*, inflammatory bowel disease (IBD) detection and idiopathic pulmonary fibrosis (IPF) detection.

Yoo *et al.* [44] demonstrated that few-shot learning using a generative adversarial network (GAN) could improve the applicability of deep learning in the optical coherence tomography (OCT) diagnosis of rare diseases. Hu *et al.* [45] proposed a random under-sampled convolutional neural network (RUS-CNN) with medical event embedding to solve these two problems in rare disease diagnosis using Electronic Health Records (EHRs). However, these works analyzed the rare disease diagnosis from genetics, text, or records. Medical imaging is a convenient and important tool during the clinical routine. We are not aware of works diagnose rare diseases from medical imaging.

Actually, many patients are finally diagnosed after a radiologist's suggestion in a radiological report. Although diagnostic imaging cannot be considered a basis for diagnosing most rare diseases, these studies represent an important element in the diagnostic chain. We highlight the success of radiology in diagnosing rare diseases and helping patients get treatment as early as possible.

17.2.4 Meta learning in medical image analysis

Meta learning, or learning to learn, has become a hot topic in recent artificial intelligence. There is a growth of interest in applying meta learning in different medical image analysis problems, such as domain generalization [46–48], medical image registration [49] and few-shot medical image segmentation [50,51] and selective labeling [52].

In 2018, Li *et al.* [53] proposed the first method that adapts the meta learning for domain generalization. The source domain is used as the metatrain dataset, and the target domain is employed as the metatest dataset. Later on, Dou *et al.* [47] designed a derived soft confusion matrix to preserve interclass relationships and a metric-learning component to encourage domain-independent class-specific cohesion feature learning. Inspired by these achievements, researchers started to adapt this method to domain generalization in medical imaging. For example, Liu *et al.* [46] proposed a share-aware meta learning approach to generalize the prostate MRI segmentation to unseen domains. To achieve it, they incorporated the compact shape constraint into the meta learning framework to preserve the complete shape of segmentation masks. To further improve the performance, they employed a contrastive loss to regularize the model to capture contours regardless of domains. Recently, Liu *et al.* [48] combined the semisupervised learning for domain generalization. They proposed to disentangle the representations and combine them to reconstruct the input image to better utilize the unlabeled data.

For medical image registration, Park *et al.* [49] proposed a meta learning approach for nonrigid registration, where the metalearner is trained on a variety of existing registration datasets, and the metatest is performed on the metatest dataset. For few-shot medical image segmentation, Ouyang *et al.* [54] demonstrated that few-shot segmentation with a self-supervised method can be used to eliminate the need of having annotated medical images. They used an adaptive local pooling module in conjunction with prototypical networks to perform segmentation. Khadga *et al.* [50] incorporated implicit model agnostic meta learning for few-shot image segmentation [55]. For selective labeling, Smit *et al.* [52] proposed a meta learning-based selective labeling method for medical images, which consists of a trainable selector that selects medical images using image embeddings obtained from contrastive pre-training, and a nonparametric selector that classifies unseen images using cosine similarity. Jiang *et al.* [56] proposed to extend few-shot learning to medium-shot to evaluate medical classification tasks. They fused the gradient-based and metric-based meta learning together to improve the overall training of the network. Jamal *et al.* [57] proposes to metatrain an unbiased initial model by preventing it from overperforming on some tasks or directly minimizing the inequality of performances across different tasks. The proposed method, namely TAMS, fine-tunes parameters of a metric space to represent medical data in a more semantically meaningful way. However, in the real clinical setting, we have an imbalanced image class, which would cause difficulty in learning a generalized metaclassifier. Among these works, no study tackles the problem of rare disease classification.

17.3 Methodology

We aim to train a neural network using metatrain data (common diseases), such that given new tasks associated with few data samples (metatest data for rare diseases), we can quickly adapt the network model via a few steps of gradient descent to handle the new tasks; see Fig. 17.2 for the pipeline.

17.3.1 Preliminary knowledges

We denote a model as f that maps the input to the output. During meta learning, we consider a distribution over tasks $p(\mathcal{T})$ instead of an individual task. Specifically, in the K-shot setting, the model is trained to learn a new task $\mathcal{T}_i$ drawn from $p(\mathcal{T})$, where the model is trained with K samples. Then, the model feedback the corresponding loss $\mathcal{L}_{\mathcal{T}_i}$ calculated from $\mathcal{T}_i$, and then tested on new samples from $\mathcal{T}_i$. The test error on sampled task $\mathcal{T}_i$ serves as the training error of the meta learning process. When adapting to a new task $\mathcal{T}_i$, the model's parameters ϕ become ϕ_i'. The model f is improved by computing one or more gradient descent updates on task $\mathcal{T}_i$. For example,

$$\phi_i' = \phi - \gamma \nabla_\phi \mathcal{L}_{\mathcal{T}_i}(f_\phi), \tag{17.1}$$

where γ is the step size and may be fixed as parameters or metalearned. The metaoptimization across tasks is performed via stochastic gradient descent (SGD), such that the model parameters are updated as follows:

$$\phi \leftarrow \phi - \alpha \nabla_\phi \sum_{\mathcal{T}_i \sim p(\mathcal{T})} \mathcal{L}_{\mathcal{T}_i}, \qquad (17.2)$$

where α is the metastep size.

17.3.2 Datasets

We employ the ISIC 2018 Skin Lesion Analysis Towards Melanoma Detection Dataset [58,59], which has a total of 10,015 skin lesion images from seven skin diseases, including melanocytic nevus (6705), melanoma (1113), benign keratosis (1099), basal cell carcinoma (514), actinic keratosis (327), vascular lesion (142) and dermatofibroma (115). We simulate the problem by utilizing the four classes with largest amount of cases as common diseases (*i.e.*, metatrain dataset D_{tr}) and the left three classes as the rare diseases (*i.e.*, metatest dataset D_{te}).

Task instance $\mathcal{T}_i$ is randomly sampled from distribution over tasks $p(\mathcal{T})$ and $D_{tr}, D_{te} \in p(\mathcal{T})$. During metatrain stage, learning task $\mathcal{T}_i$ are binary classification tasks and each task consists of two random classes with k samples per class in D_{tr}. During the metatest stage, each test task instance is sampled from D_{te}.

17.3.3 Difficulty-aware meta learning framework

Current model-agnostic metaearning learns the metaclassifier according to the averaged evaluation of tasks sampled from $p(\mathcal{T})$ [23]. However, this meta learning process is easily dominated by well-learned tasks. To improve the effectiveness and emphasize on difficult tasks in the metatraining stage, we propose the difficulty-aware meta learning method. The main framework and metatraining procedure are described in Fig. 17.2 and Algorithm 17.1. We **metatrain** a base model parameters ϕ on a series of learning tasks in D_{tr}. First, task instance $\mathcal{T}_i$ is randomly sampled from $p(\mathcal{T})$ (line 3 in Algorithm 17.1). As mentioned above, the learning task $\mathcal{T}_i$ is a binary classification task that consists of two random classes with k samples per class in D_{tr}. The "adaptation steps" takes ϕ as input and returns parameters ϕ_i' adapted specifically for task instance $\mathcal{T}_i$ by using gradient descent iteratively, with the corresponding cross entropy loss function $\mathcal{L}_{\mathcal{T}_i}$ for $\mathcal{T}_i$ (lines 5-8). The cross-entropy loss for $\mathcal{T}_i$ and the gradient descent are defined in Eq. (17.3) and Eq. (17.4).

$$\mathcal{L}_{\mathcal{T}_i}(f_{\phi_i}) = - \sum_{x_j, y_j \sim \mathcal{T}_i} y_j \log(f_{\phi_i}(x_j)) + (1 - y_j) \log(1 - f_{\phi_i}(x_j)), \qquad (17.3)$$

$$\phi_i' \leftarrow \phi_i - \gamma \nabla_\phi \mathcal{L}_{\mathcal{T}_i}(f_{\phi_i}), \qquad (17.4)$$

where γ is the inner loop adaptation learning rate and ϕ_i' is the adapted model parameters for task $\mathcal{T}_i$.

After the "adaptation steps", the model parameters are trained by optimizing for the performance respect to tasks adapted in the "adaptation steps". Concretely, a dynamically scaled cross-entropy loss **over the learning tasks** is formulated, where it automatically downweights the easy tasks and focuses on hard tasks; as shown in Fig. 17.3. Formally, the difficulty-aware metaoptimization function is defined

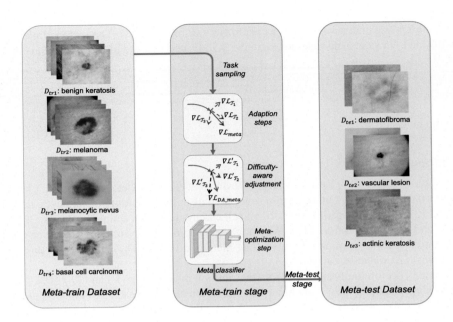

FIGURE 17.2

The pipeline of our proposed difficulty-aware meta learning (DAML) system. The metaclassifier (neural network) is explicitly trained on the metatrain dataset, such that given new tasks with only a few samples, the metaclassifier can rapidly adapt to the new tasks with a high accuracy. Our novel difficulty-aware metaoptimization scheme can dynamically downweight the contribution of easy tasks and focus more to learn from hard tasks.

as

$$\mathcal{L}_{DA\_meta} = \sum_{\mathcal{T}_i \sim p(\mathcal{T})} -\mathcal{L}_{\mathcal{T}_i}{}^{\eta} \log(\max(\epsilon, 1 - \mathcal{L}_{\mathcal{T}_i})), \qquad (17.5)$$

$$\phi \leftarrow \phi - \alpha \nabla_\phi \sum_{\mathcal{T}_i \sim p(\mathcal{T})} \mathcal{L}_{\mathcal{T}_{DA\_meta}}, \qquad (17.6)$$

where $\mathcal{L}_{\mathcal{T}_i}$ is the original cross entropy loss for task $\mathcal{T}_i$, η is a scaling factor and ϵ is a smallest positive integer satisfying $\max(\epsilon, 1 - \mathcal{L}_{\mathcal{T}_i}) > 0$. Then the metaclassifier is updated by performing Eq. (17.6). The whole metatraining procedure can be found in Algorithm 17.1.

Intuitively, our difficulty-aware metaloss dynamically reduces the contribution from easy tasks and focuses on the hard tasks, which in turn increases the importance of optimizing the misclassified tasks. For example, with $\eta = 3$, a task with cross-entropy loss 0.9 would have higher loss in the metaoptimization stage, while a task with lower loss would be given less importance. We analyze the effect of different values for hyperparameter η in the following experiments.

Algorithm 17.1 Meta learning Algorithm.

Require: D_{tr}: Metatrain dataset
Require: α, γ: meta learning rate, inner-loop adaptation learning rate
1: Randomly initialize network weight ϕ
2: **while** not converged **do**
3:      Sample batch of tasks from D_{tr}
4:      **for** task $\mathcal{T}_i$ in batch **do**
5:          **for** number of adaptation steps **do**
6:              Evaluate $\mathcal{L}_{\mathcal{T}_i}\left(f_{\phi_i}\right)$ with respect to k samples using Eq. (17.3).
7:              Compute gradient descent for $\mathcal{T}_i$ using Eq. (17.4).
8:          **end for**
9:          Evaluate $\mathcal{L}_{DA\_meta}\left(f_{\phi_i}\right)$ using Eq. (17.5).
10:     **end for**
11:     Update network weight ϕ using Eq. (17.6).
12: **end while**
13: **return** ϕ;

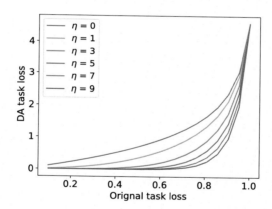

FIGURE 17.3

Visualization of Eq. (17.5). The original task loss could be infinite. For clear visualization, we show the original task loss within [0, 1].

17.3.4 Metatraining details

We employed the 4 conv blocks as the backbone architecture [60], which has 4 modules with a 3x3 conv and 64 filters, followed by a BN, a ReLU, and a 2x2 max-pooling. We used Adam optimizer with a meta learning rate of 0.001 and divide by 10 for every 150 epochs. We totally trained 3000 iterations and the adopted the difficulty-aware optimization at around 1500 iterations. The batch size is 4, consisting of 4 tasks sampled from metatrain dataset. Each task consists of randomly k samples from 2 classes. We query 15 images from each of two classes to adapt parameters for $\mathcal{T}_i$, as the same protocol

Table 17.1 The AUC performance of different methods on skin lesion dataset. # refers to under #-shot test setting. Each result is averaged over 30 runs.

	backbone	#	AUC	#	AUC	#	AUC
ConvFeature + KNN	DenseNet	1	50.00%	3	56.07%	5	62.69%
ConvFeature + SVM	DenseNet	1	61.46%	3	61.68%	5	67.44%
Finetune + Aug	DenseNet	1	58.57%	3	68.05%	5	73.65%
Finetune + Aug	4 Conv Blocks	1	58.49%	3	68.13%	5	75.90%
Relation Net [60]	4 Conv Blocks	1	59.97%	3	62.87%	5	72.40%
MAML [23]	4 Conv Blocks	1	63.77%	3	77.98%	5	81.20%
Task sampling [12]	4 Conv Blocks	1	64.21%	3	78.40%	5	82.05%
DAML (ours)	4 Conv Blocks	1	**67.33%**	3	**79.60%**	5	**83.30%**

in [23,60,61]. During metatest stage, the inference is performed by randomly sampling k samples from 2 classes from metatest dataset, *i.e.*, D_{te}. The final report results are the averaged AUC over 30 runs.

17.4 Experiments and results
17.4.1 Case study 1: ISIC 2018 skin lesion dataset
We conduct experiments on ISIC 2018 skin lesion classification dataset.[2] We first compare our method with some strong baselines, *i.e.*, fine-tuning, feature extraction+classifiers, to validate the effectiveness of our method for classification in the extremely low-data regime. Then, we compare with other related methods to show the effectiveness of our novel difficulty-aware meta learning framework. Next, we analyze the improvement of our proposed difficulty-aware metaoptimization loss, the effect of different scaling factors, as well as the importance of network architecture and data augmentation.

Comparison with Strong Baselines We first show the results of the standard fine-tuning method on rare disease classification for comparison. We report the performance of fine-tuning with two different network architectures: the DenseNet [62] and 4 Conv Blocks [60] in Table 17.1, where the former one is the state-of-the-art classification network and the latter one is the most commonly used architecture in few-shot learning setting in computer vision. Note that we employ the data augmentation technique on both the pretraining and fine-tuning stages, including random scaling, rotation, and mirror flipping. Fig. 17.4 shows the training loss curve and the test AUC performance when performing fine-tuning on few given samples. Each plot is the average over 30 runs. It is observed that when k is large, the fine-tuning could perform well and achieves the AUC at around 97%. However, with a smaller k, the model converges rapidly but the AUC performance reduces devastatingly. For example, the 4 Conv Blocks only achieve 58.49% AUC with $k = 1$. We also employ the pretrained DenseNet as feature extractor and utilize another classifiers, *e.g.*, SVM and KNN, to coduct rare disease classification. As shown in Table 17.1, the performance of these methods is inferior, indicating that these methods have

---
[2] https://challenge2018.isic-archive.com/task3/.

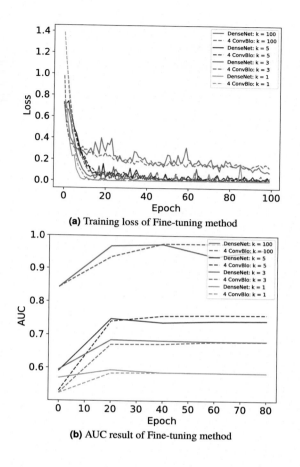

(a) Training loss of Fine-tuning method

(b) AUC result of Fine-tuning method

FIGURE 17.4

The training curve (a) and test AUC (b) when performing fine-tuning on metatest dataset.

limited capacity in tackling the classification task with just a few samples from unseen class. In other aspect, our method achieves 83.30% AUC with $k = 5$ and 79.60% AUC with $k = 3$, demonstrating the effectiveness of our method for disease classification in the extremely low-data regime.

Comparison with Other Methods We also report the performance of the widely used few shot learning approaches, Relation Net [60], MAML [23] and Task sample [12] for the rare disease classification task in Table 17.1. Our method surpasses these three approaches, especially the Relation Net. The reason may be that our metatrain dataset only has four classes, limiting the representation capability of the feature extraction in the metric-based approach. It is worth noting that the meta learning based approaches excel all the baseline methods and metric-based method, demonstrating the promising results of meta learning approach for rare disease classification. Overall, our method further improves the original MAML method, which demonstrates the effectiveness of our difficulty-aware metaoptimiza-

Table 17.2 Ablation study results under 5 samples setting.

Experiments setting	AUC
ResBlocks + 32f + no Aug	75.8%
ConvBlocks + 64f + no Aug	79.3%
ConvBlocks + 64f + Aug	81.2%
ConvBlocks + 64f + Aug, $\eta = 1$	81.7%
ConvBlocks + 64f + Aug, $\eta = 3$	82.4%
ConvBlocks + 64f + Aug, $\eta = 5$	**83.3%**
ConvBlocks + 64f + Aug, $\eta = 7$	83.1%

Table 17.3 Results of our method and other method for rare disease classification on the Public Dermofit Image Library.

	backbone	#	AUC	#	AUC	#	AUC
MAML [23]	4 Conv Blocks	1	63.00%	3	74.03%	5	80.70%
Task sampling [12]	4 Conv Blocks	1	63.20%	3	76.10%	5	81.80%
DAML (ours)	4 Conv Blocks	1	**63.33%**	3	**77.15%**	5	**82.76%**

tion procedure. Maicas *et al.* [12] proposes a meta learning method that addresses the task sampling issue. From Table 17.1, we can see our method achieves better results than task sampling method [12] under all sample settings.

Ablation study of Our Method We provide detailed analysis on the effects of our difficulty-aware metaoptimization loss, network architectures and data augmentation under 5 samples setting, as shown in Table 17.2. First, we analyze the effects of η in our difficulty-aware loss. We found that our method can obviously improve the overall performance of the meta learning and the performance is best when $\eta = 5$. We then explore the importance of network architecture. "conv blocks + 64f + Aug" refers to architectures consisting of 4 conv blocks with 64 feature maps with heavy data augmentation. More complicated networks, *i.e.*, residual blocks, would severely lead to the overfitting problem; as the comparison shown in Table 17.2. Moreover, the heavy data augmentation, *i.e.*, random rotation, flipping, scaling with crop, can only slightly improve the AUC results from 79.3% to 81.2%.

17.4.2 Case study 2: validation on real clinical data

We validated our method for rare diseases classification in the real clinical data from the public Dermofit Image Library.[3] The disease classes we employed are *squamous cell carcinoma*, *haemangioma*, and *pyogenic granuloma*. These skin classes are new cases that are not presented in the ISIC 2018 skin lesion dataset. Table 17.3 shows the results trained on the ISIC 2018 skin lesion dataset and tested on the few-shot cases from the Dermofit Image Library. As shown in Table 17.3, our method outperforms MAML and Task sampling by around 2.0% and 1.0%, respectively. Our method achieves an average

---

[3] https://licensing.eri.ed.ac.uk/i/software/dermofit-image-library.html.

AUC of 82.76%, 77.15%, and 63.33% under 5 samples, 3 samples, and 1 sample setting, demonstrating the potential usage of our method for real clinical applications.

17.5 Discussions

Solutions for rare disease classification Except for the image-based solution presented in this book chapter, there are several methods that solve the rare disease classification problem from different perspectives, such as genetic sequence and symptoms [42], clinical records [43] and EHRs [45]. A promising future direction is to design a neural network to extract features from the multimodal data (including imaging, texts, and reports) for rare disease diagnosis. Another potential solution is to consider developing a powerful feature extractor by incorporating the test sample information [63].

Potentials of our method Our method has the potential to be applied to other related applications such as federated learning. Medical data usually has privacy regulations. Hence, it is often infeasible to collect and share patient data in a centralized data lake. This issue poses challenges for training deep convolutional networks, requiring large numbers of diverse training examples. Federated learning provides a solution, which allows collaborative and decentralized training of neural networks without sharing the patient data. For example, Li *et al.* [64] implemented and evaluated practical federated learning systems for brain tumor segmentation. Our method is also feasible to be tested for federated learning since our method only accesses training data (common dataset) during the training stage and can be fast adapted according to the test data (private dataset) during the inference time. Exploring the applications of our method in federated learning would be a future work of this book chapter.

17.6 Conclusion

In conclusion, this chapter provides a comprehensive literature review on meta learning in medical image analysis, few-shot learning in skin lesion classification, and rare disease diagnosis. Moreover, this chapter presents a difficulty-aware meta learning approach for rare disease diagnosis with two case studies on skin lesion classification datasets. Through dynamically scaling the task difficulty, our method can solve the imbalanced problem in the skin lesion dataset. The method has been validated on skin lesion classification from ISIC 2018 dataset and the Dermofit Image Library. Both application scenarios of rare disease diagnosis have demonstrated highly promising results in classifying unseen disease cases. The proposed frameworks are general and can be extended to other similar scenarios. Finally, we discussed some potential applications of our method.

Acknowledgments

This work was supported by a research grant from HKUST Bridge Gap Fund (BGF.027.2021), a research grant from Key-Area Research and Development Program of Guangdong Province, China (2020B010165004), Hong Kong Innovation and Technology Fund (Project No. ITS/311/18FP & ITS/426/17FP), National Natural

Science Foundation of China (Project No. U1813204), and HKU Seed Fund for Basic Research (Project No. 202009185079).

References

[1] A. Zhao, G. Balakrishnan, F. Durand, J.V. Guttag, A.V. Dalca, Data augmentation using learned transforms for one-shot medical image segmentation, in: IEEE Conference on Computer Vision and Pattern Recognition, 2019.

[2] X. Li, H. Chen, X. Qi, Q. Dou, C.-W. Fu, P.-A. Heng, H-denseunet: hybrid densely connected unet for liver and tumor segmentation from ct volumes, IEEE Transactions on Medical Imaging 37 (12) (2018) 2663–2674.

[3] A.K. Mondal, J. Dolz, C. Desrosiers, Few-shot 3d multi-modal medical image segmentation using generative adversarial learning, arXiv preprint, arXiv:1810.12241, 2018.

[4] F. Isensee, P.F. Jaeger, S.A. Kohl, J. Petersen, K.H. Maier-Hein, nnu-net: a self-configuring method for deep learning-based biomedical image segmentation, Nature Methods 18 (2) (2021) 203–211.

[5] P. Tschandl, C. Rosendahl, H. Kittler, The ham10000 dataset, a large collection of multi-source dermatoscopic images of common pigmented skin lesions, Scientific Data 5 (1) (2018) 1–9.

[6] R. Fisher, J. Rees, Dermofit: a cognitive prosthesis to aid focal skin lesion diagnosis, 2012.

[7] J. Jia, R. Wang, Z. An, Y. Guo, X. Ni, T. Shi, Rdad: a machine learning system to support phenotype-based rare disease diagnosis, Frontiers in Genetics 9 (2018).

[8] M. Khoury, R. Valdez, Rare diseases, genomics and public health: an expanding intersection, Genomics and Health Impact Blog, 2016.

[9] https://www.verywellhealth.com/rare-skin-diseases-5096005. (Accessed 30 July 2021).

[10] A. Skorczyk-Werner, P. Pawłowski, M. Michalczuk, A. Warowicka, A. Wawrocka, K. Wicher, A. Bakunowicz-Łazarczyk, M.R. Krawczyński, Fundus albipunctatus, Journal of Applied Genetics 56 (3) (2015) 317–327.

[11] C. Cortes, V. Vapnik, Support-vector networks, Machine Learning 20 (3) (1995) 273–297.

[12] G. Maicas, A.P. Bradley, J.C. Nascimento, I. Reid, G. Carneiro, Training medical image analysis systems like radiologists, in: International Conference on Medical Image Computing and Computer Assisted Intervention, Springer, 2018, pp. 546–554.

[13] X. Li, L. Yu, Y. Jin, C.-W. Fu, L. Xing, P.-A. Heng, Difficulty-aware meta-learning for rare disease diagnosis, in: International Conference on Medical Image Computing and Computer-Assisted Intervention, Springer, 2020, pp. 357–366.

[14] M. Goyal, T. Knackstedt, S. Yan, S. Hassanpour, Artificial intelligence-based image classification for diagnosis of skin cancer: challenges and opportunities, Computers in Biology and Medicine (2020) 104065.

[15] L. Yu, H. Chen, Q. Dou, J. Qin, P.-A. Heng, Automated melanoma recognition in dermoscopy images via very deep residual networks, IEEE Transactions on Medical Imaging 36 (4) (2016) 994–1004.

[16] N.C. Codella, Q.-B. Nguyen, S. Pankanti, D.A. Gutman, B. Helba, A.C. Halpern, J.R. Smith, Deep learning ensembles for melanoma recognition in dermoscopy images, IBM Journal of Research and Development 61 (4/5) (2017) 5:1–5.15.

[17] F. Perez, S. Avila, E. Valle, Solo or ensemble? Choosing a cnn architecture for melanoma classification, in: Proceedings of the IEEE/CVF Conference on Computer Vision and Pattern Recognition Workshops, 2019.

[18] P. Tschandl, C. Rosendahl, B.N. Akay, G. Argenziano, A. Blum, R.P. Braun, H. Cabo, J.-Y. Gourhant, J. Kreusch, A. Lallas, et al., Expert-level diagnosis of nonpigmented skin cancer by combined convolutional neural networks, JAMA Dermatology 155 (1) (2019) 58–65.

[19] Y. Yuan, M. Chao, Y.-C. Lo, Automatic skin lesion segmentation using deep fully convolutional networks with Jaccard distance, IEEE Transactions on Medical Imaging 36 (9) (2017) 1876–1886.

[20] H. Li, X. He, F. Zhou, Z. Yu, D. Ni, S. Chen, T. Wang, B. Lei, Dense deconvolutional network for skin lesion segmentation, IEEE Journal of Biomedical and Health Informatics 23 (2) (2018) 527–537.

[21] M.A. Al-Masni, M.A. Al-Antari, M.-T. Choi, S.-M. Han, T.-S. Kim, Skin lesion segmentation in dermoscopy images via deep full resolution convolutional networks, Computer Methods and Programs in Biomedicine 162 (2018) 221–231.

[22] B. Lei, Z. Xia, F. Jiang, X. Jiang, Z. Ge, Y. Xu, J. Qin, S. Chen, T. Wang, S. Wang, Skin lesion segmentation via generative adversarial networks with dual discriminators, Medical Image Analysis 64 (2020) 101716.

[23] C. Finn, P. Abbeel, S. Levine, Model-agnostic meta-learning for fast adaptation of deep networks, in: International Conference on Machine Learning, JMLR. org, 2017, pp. 1126–1135.

[24] A. Nichol, J. Achiam, J. Schulman, On first-order meta-learning algorithms, arXiv preprint, arXiv:1803. 02999, 2018.

[25] K. Mahajan, M. Sharma, L. Vig, Meta-dermdiagnosis: few-shot skin disease identification using meta-learning, in: Proceedings of the IEEE/CVF Conference on Computer Vision and Pattern Recognition Workshops, 2020, pp. 730–731.

[26] R. Singh, V. Bharti, V. Purohit, A. Kumar, A.K. Singh, S.K. Singh, Metamed: few-shot medical image classification using gradient-based meta-learning, Pattern Recognition (2021) 108111.

[27] T. DeVries, G.W. Taylor, Improved regularization of convolutional neural networks with cutout, arXiv preprint, arXiv:1708.04552, 2017.

[28] H. Zhang, M. Cisse, Y.N. Dauphin, D. Lopez-Paz, mixup: beyond empirical risk minimization, arXiv preprint, arXiv:1710.09412, 2017.

[29] S. Yun, D. Han, S.J. Oh, S. Chun, J. Choe, Y. Yoo, Cutmix: regularization strategy to train strong classifiers with localizable features, in: Proceedings of the IEEE/CVF International Conference on Computer Vision, 2019, pp. 6023–6032.

[30] O. Vinyals, C. Blundell, T. Lillicrap, D. Wierstra, et al., Matching networks for one shot learning, Advances in Neural Information Processing Systems 29 (2016) 3630–3638.

[31] J. Snell, K. Swersky, R.S. Zemel, Prototypical networks for few-shot learning, arXiv preprint, arXiv:1703. 05175, 2017.

[32] V. Prabhu, A. Kannan, M. Ravuri, M. Chaplain, D. Sontag, X. Amatriain, Few-shot learning for dermatological disease diagnosis, in: Machine Learning for Healthcare Conference, PMLR, 2019, pp. 532–552.

[33] W. Zhu, W. Li, H. Liao, J. Luo, Temperature network for few-shot learning with distribution-aware large-margin metric, Pattern Recognition 112 (2021) 107797.

[34] W. Zhu, H. Liao, W. Li, W. Li, J. Luo, Alleviating the incompatibility between cross entropy loss and episode training for few-shot skin disease classification, in: International Conference on Medical Image Computing and Computer-Assisted Intervention, Springer, 2020, pp. 330–339.

[35] Y. Guo, N.C. Codella, L. Karlinsky, J.V. Codella, J.R. Smith, K. Saenko, T. Rosing, R. Feris, A broader study of cross-domain few-shot learning, in: European Conference on Computer Vision, Springer, 2020, pp. 124–141.

[36] D. Chen, Y. Chen, Y. Li, F. Mao, Y. He, H. Xue, Self-supervised learning for few-shot image classification, in: ICASSP 2021-2021 IEEE International Conference on Acoustics, Speech and Signal Processing (ICASSP), IEEE, 2021, pp. 1745–1749.

[37] C. Medina, A. Devos, M. Grossglauser, Self-supervised prototypical transfer learning for few-shot classification, arXiv preprint, arXiv:2006.11325, 2020.

[38] C.P. Phoo, B. Hariharan, Self-training for few-shot transfer across extreme task differences, arXiv preprint, arXiv:2010.07734, 2020.

[39] D. Svenstrup, H.L. Jørgensen, O. Winther, Rare disease diagnosis: a review of web search, social media and large-scale data-mining approaches, Rare Diseases 3 (1) (2015) e1083145.

[40] D. Whicher, S. Philbin, N. Aronson, An overview of the impact of rare disease characteristics on research methodology, Orphanet Journal of Rare Diseases 13 (1) (2018) 14.

[41] R. Alves, M. Piñol, J. Vilaplana, I. Teixidó, J. Cruz, J. Comas, E. Vilaprinyo, A. Sorribas, F. Solsona, Computer-assisted initial diagnosis of rare diseases, PeerJ 4 (2016) e2211.

[42] G. Baynam, N. Pachter, F. McKenzie, S. Townshend, J. Slee, C. Kiraly-Borri, A. Vasudevan, A. Hawkins, S. Broley, L. Schofield, et al., The rare and undiagnosed diseases diagnostic service–application of massively parallel sequencing in a state-wide clinical service, Orphanet Journal of Rare Diseases 11 (1) (2016) 77.

[43] L. Cui, S. Biswal, L.M. Glass, G. Lever, J. Sun, C. Xiao, Conan: complementary pattern augmentation for rare disease detection, in: Proceedings of the AAAI Conference on Artificial Intelligence, vol. 34, 2020, pp. 614–621.

[44] T.K. Yoo, J.Y. Choi, H.K. Kim, Feasibility study to improve deep learning in oct diagnosis of rare retinal diseases with few-shot classification, Medical & Biological Engineering & Computing 59 (2) (2021) 401–415.

[45] Y. Hu, F. Chen, Y. Cai, Y. Yuan, A random under-sampled deep architecture with medical event embedding: highly imbalanced rare disease classification with ehr data, Network 20 (21) (2019) 22.

[46] Q. Liu, Q. Dou, P.-A. Heng, Shape-aware meta-learning for generalizing prostate mri segmentation to unseen domains, in: International Conference on Medical Image Computing and Computer-Assisted Intervention, Springer, 2020, pp. 475–485.

[47] Q. Dou, D. Coelho de Castro, K. Kamnitsas, B. Glocker, Domain generalization via model-agnostic learning of semantic features, Advances in Neural Information Processing Systems 32 (2019) 6450–6461.

[48] X. Liu, S. Thermos, A. O'Neil, S.A. Tsaftaris, Semi-supervised meta-learning with disentanglement for domain-generalised medical image segmentation, arXiv preprint, arXiv:2106.13292, 2021.

[49] H. Park, G.M. Lee, S. Kim, G.H. Ryu, A. Jeong, S.H. Park, M. Sagong, A meta-learning approach for medical image registration, arXiv preprint, arXiv:2104.10447, 2021.

[50] R. Khadga, D. Jha, S. Ali, S. Hicks, V. Thambawita, M.A. Riegler, P. Halvorsen, Few-shot segmentation of medical images based on meta-learning with implicit gradients, arXiv preprint, arXiv:2106.03223, 2021.

[51] Z. Cao, T. Zhang, W. Diao, Y. Zhang, X. Lyu, K. Fu, X. Sun, Meta-seg: a generalized meta-learning framework for multi-class few-shot semantic segmentation, IEEE Access 7 (2019) 166109–166121.

[52] A. Smit, D. Vrabac, Y. He, A.Y. Ng, A.L. Beam, P. Rajpurkar, Medselect: selective labeling for medical image classification combining meta-learning with deep reinforcement learning, arXiv preprint, arXiv:2103.14339, 2021.

[53] D. Li, Y. Yang, Y.-Z. Song, T.M. Hospedales, Learning to generalize: meta-learning for domain generalization, in: Thirty-Second AAAI Conference on Artificial Intelligence, 2018.

[54] C. Ouyang, C. Biffi, C. Chen, T. Kart, H. Qiu, D. Rueckert, Self-supervision with superpixels: training few-shot medical image segmentation without annotation, in: European Conference on Computer Vision, Springer, 2020, pp. 762–780.

[55] A. Rajeswaran, C. Finn, S. Kakade, S. Levine, Meta-learning with implicit gradients, 2019.

[56] X. Jiang, L. Ding, M. Havaei, A. Jesson, S. Matwin, Task adaptive metric space for medium-shot medical image classification, in: International Conference on Medical Image Computing and Computer-Assisted Intervention, Springer, 2019, pp. 147–155.

[57] M.A. Jamal, G.-J. Qi, Task agnostic meta-learning for few-shot learning, in: Proceedings of the IEEE Conference on Computer Vision and Pattern Recognition, 2019, pp. 11719–11727.

[58] M.A.A. Milton, Automated skin lesion classification using ensemble of deep neural networks in isic 2018: skin lesion analysis towards melanoma detection challenge, arXiv preprint, arXiv:1901.10802, 2019.

[59] X. Li, L. Yu, H. Chen, C.-W. Fu, L. Xing, P.-A. Heng, Transformation-consistent self-ensembling model for semisupervised medical image segmentation, IEEE Transactions on Neural Networks and Learning Systems 32 (2) (2020) 523–534.

[60] F. Sung, Y. Yang, L. Zhang, T. Xiang, P.H. Torr, T.M. Hospedales, Learning to compare: relation network for few-shot learning, in: IEEE Conference on Computer Vision and Pattern Recognition, 2018, pp. 1199–1208.

[61] X. Li, L. Yu, C.-W. Fu, M. Fang, P.-A. Heng, Revisiting metric learning for few-shot image classification, Neurocomputing 406 (2020) 49–58.

[62] G. Huang, Z. Liu, L. Van Der Maaten, K.Q. Weinberger, Densely connected convolutional networks, in: IEEE Conference on Computer Vision and Pattern Recognition, 2017, pp. 4700–4708.

[63] S. Yang, L. Liu, M. Xu, Free lunch for few-shot learning: distribution calibration, arXiv preprint, arXiv: 2101.06395, 2021.

[64] W. Li, F. Milletarì, D. Xu, N. Rieke, J. Hancox, W. Zhu, M. Baust, Y. Cheng, S. Ourselin, M.J. Cardoso, et al., Privacy-preserving federated brain tumour segmentation, in: International Workshop on Machine Learning in Medical Imaging, Springer, 2019, pp. 133–141.

Other meta learning applications

Improved MR image reconstruction using federated learning

18

Pengfei Guo, Puyang Wang, Jinyuan Zhou, Shanshan Jiang, and Vishal M. Patel

Johns Hopkins University, Baltimore, MD, United States

18.1 Introduction

Magnetic resonance imaging (MRI) is one of the most widely used imaging techniques in clinical applications. It is noninvasive and can be customized with different pulse sequences to capture different kinds of tissues. For instance, fat tissues are bright in T_1-weighted images, which can clearly show gray and white matter tissues in the brain. The radiofrequency pulse sequences used to make T_2-weighted images can delineate fluid from cortical tissue [12]. However, to increase the signal-to-noise ratio (SNR), clinical scanning usually involves the usage of multiple saturation frequencies and repeating acquisitions, which results in relatively long scan time. Various compressed sensing (CS) based methods have been proposed in the literature for accelerating the MRI sampling process by under-sampling in the k-space during acquisition [4,22,23]. In recent years, data driven deep learning-based methods have been shown to produce superior performance on MR image reconstruction from partial k-space observations [21,39,40].

However, deep networks usually require large amounts of diversity-rich paired data which can be labor-intensive and prohibitively expensive to collect. In addition, one has to deal with patient privacy issues when storing them, making it difficult to share data with other institutions. Although deidentification [34] might provide a solution, building a large scale centralized dataset at a particular institution is still a challenging task.

The recently introduced federated learning (FL) framework [26,37,16] addresses this issue by allowing collaborative and decentralized training of deep learning-based methods. In particular, there is a server that periodically communicates with each institution to aggregate a global model and then shares it with all institutions. Each institution utilizes and stores its own private data. It is worth noting that instead of directly transferring data for training, the communication in FL algorithms only involves model parameters or update gradients, which resolves the privacy concerns. Hence, FL methods intrinsically facilitate multiinstitutional collaborations between data centers (e.g., hospitals in the context of medical images).

However, the generalizability of models trained with the FL setting can still be suboptimal due to domain shift, which results from the data collected at multiple institutions with different sensors, disease types, and acquisition protocols, etc. This can be clearly seen from Fig. 18.1 where we show fully-sampled (Fig. 18.1(a)) and under-sampled (Fig. 18.1(b)) images from four different datasets.

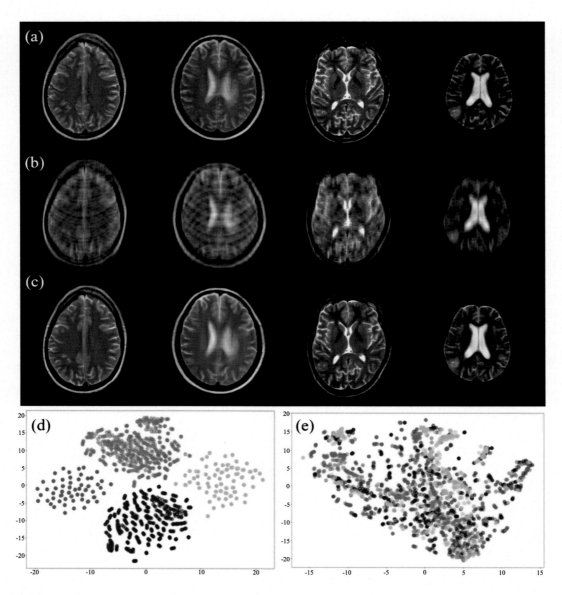

FIGURE 18.1

Top row: (a) ground truth, (b) zero-filled images, and (c) reconstructed images from the fastMRI [14], HPKS [11], IXI [3], and BraTS [27] datasets from left to right, respectively. *Bottom row*: t-SNE plots. The distribution of (d) latent features without cross-site modeling, and (e) latent features corresponding to the proposed cross-site modeling. In each plot, green, blue, yellow, and red dots represent data from fastMRI [14], HPKS [11], IXI [3], and BraTS [27] datasets, respectively.

In Fig. 18.1(d), we visualize latent features corresponding to images from these datasets using t-Distributed Stochastic Neighbor Embedding (t-SNE) plot [24]. As can be seen from Fig. 18.1(d), features from a particular dataset are grouped together in a cluster indicating that each dataset has its own bias. As a result, we can see four different clusters of latent features. In order to make use of these datasets in the FL framework, one needs to align these features and remove the domain shift among the datasets. To circumvent this challenge, recently we proposed a cross-site model for MR image reconstruction in which the learned intermediate latent features among different source sites are aligned with the distribution of the latent features at the target site [7]. Specifically, the proposed method involves two optimization steps. In the first step, local reconstruction networks are trained on private data. In the second step, the intermediate latent features of the target domain data are transferred to other local source entities. An adversarial domain identifier is then trained to align the latent space distribution between the source domain and the target domain. Hence, minimizing the loss of adversarial domain identifier results in the reconstruction network weights being automatically adapted to the target domain. Fig. 18.1(e) and (c) show the distribution of aligned features and the corresponding reconstructed images in four datasets. The proposed cross-site modeling allows us to leverage datasets from various institutions for obtaining improved reconstructions.

18.2 Related work

Reconstruction of MR images from under-sampled k-space data is an ill-posed inverse problem. In order to obtain a regularized solution, some priors are often used. CS-based methods make use of sparsity priors for recovering the image [22,23] from partial k-space observations. In recent years, deep learning-based methods have been shown to produce superior performance on MR image reconstruction [13,19,32,25,41]. Some deep learning-based methods approach the problem by directly learning a mapping from the under-sampled data to the fully-sampled data in the image domain [39,40,15,31]. Methods that learn a mapping in the k-space domain have also been proposed in the literature [1,9].

Federated learning is a decentralized learning framework which allows multiple institutions to collaboratively learn a shared machine learning model without sharing their local training data [2,26,28]. The FL training process consists of the following steps: (1) All institutions locally compute gradients and send locally trained network parameters to the server. (2) The server performs aggregation over the uploaded parameters from K institutions. (3) The server broadcasts the aggregated parameters to K institutions. (4) All institutions update their respective models with aggregated parameters and test the performance of the updated models. The institutions collaboratively learn a machine learning model with the help of a central cloud server [43]. After a sufficient number of local training and update exchanges between the institutions and the server, a global optimal learned model can be obtained.

McMahan *et al.* [26] proposed FedAvg, which learns a global model by averaging model parameters from local entities. FedAvg [26] is one of the most commonly used frameworks for FL. FedProx [35] and Agnostic Federated Learning (AFL) [29] are extensions of FedAvg which attempt to address the learning bias issue of the global models for local entities. Recently, Sheller *et al.* [29] and Li *et al.* [17] proposed medical image segmentation models based on the FL framework. Peng *et al.* [30] proposed the federated adversarial alignment to mitigate the domain shift problem in image classification. In [18], Li *et al.* formulated a privacy-preserving pipeline for multiinstitutional functional MRI classification and investigated different aspects of the communication frequency in federated models and privacy-preserving mechanisms. Although these methods [30,18] achieved promising results to overcome domain shift in classification, due to the differences in network architectures, one cannot directly utilize them for MR image reconstruction.

18.3 Methodology

Similar to [39,40,15,31], the proposed method addresses the MR image reconstruction problem by directly learning a mapping from the under-sampled data to the fully-sampled data in the image domain. The MR image reconstruction process can be formulated as follows

$$x = F^{-1}(F_d y + \epsilon),$$
$$x, y \in \mathbb{C}^N, \tag{18.1}$$

where x denotes the observed under-sampled image, y is the fully-sampled image, and ϵ denotes noise. Here, F and F^{-1} denote the Fourier transform matrix and its inverse, respectively. F_d represents the undersampling Fourier encoding matrix that is defined as the multiplication of the Fourier transform matrix F with a binary undersampling mask matrix. The acceleration factor (AF) controls the ratio of the amount of k-space data required for a fully-sampled image to the amount collected in an accelerated acquisition. The goal is to estimate y from the observed under-sampled image x.

18.3.1 FL-based MRI reconstruction

The proposed FL-MR framework is presented in Fig. 18.2 and Algorithm 18.1. Let $\mathcal{D}^1, \mathcal{D}^2, \ldots, \mathcal{D}^K$ denote the MR image reconstruction datasets from K different institutions. Each local dataset $\mathcal{D}^k$ contains pairs of under-sampled and fully-sampled images. At each institution, a local model is trained using its own data by iteratively minimizing the following loss

$$\mathcal{L}_{\text{recon}} = \sum_{(x,y) \sim \mathcal{D}^k} \| G^k(x) - y \|_1, \tag{18.2}$$

where G^k corresponds to the local model at site k and is parameterized by Θ_{G^k}. $G^k(x)$ corresponds to the reconstructed image $\hat{y}$. After optimization with several local epochs (i.e. P epochs) via

$$\Theta_{G^k}^{(p+1)} \leftarrow \Theta_{G^k}^{(p)} - \gamma \nabla \mathcal{L}_{\text{recon}}, \tag{18.3}$$

each institution can obtain the trained FL-MR reconstruction model with the updated model parameters. Since each institution has its own data which may be collected by a particular sensor, disease type, and acquisition protocol, each $\mathcal{D}^k$ has a certain characteristic. Thus, when a local model is trained using its own data, it introduces a bias and does not generalize well to MR images from another institutions (see Fig. 18.1). One way to overcome this issue would be to train the network on a diverse multidomain dataset by combining data from K institutions as $\mathcal{D} = \{\mathcal{D}^1 \cup \mathcal{D}^2 \cup \cdots \cup \mathcal{D}^K\}$ [8,6,5,36,42]. However, as discussed earlier, due to privacy concerns, this solution is not feasible and impedes multiinstitutional collaborations in practice.

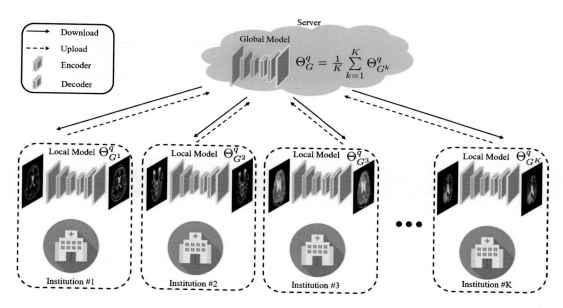

FIGURE 18.2

An overview of the proposed FL-MR framework. Through several rounds of communication between data centers and server, the collaboratively trained global model parameterized by Θ_G^q can be obtained in a data privacy-preserving manner.

Algorithm 18.1: FL-based MRI Reconstruction.

Input: $\mathcal{D} = \{\mathcal{D}^1, \mathcal{D}^2, \ldots, \mathcal{D}^K\}$, datasets from K institution; P, the number of local epochs; Q, the number of global epochs; γ, learning rate; $G^1, G^2, \ldots, G^K$, local models parameterized by $\Theta_{G^1}, \Theta_{G^2}, \ldots, \Theta_{G^K}$; G, the global model parameterized by Θ_G.
Output: well-trained global model G
▷ parameters initialization;
for $q = 1\ to\ Q$ **do**
  for $k = 1\ to\ K$ ***in parallel*** **do**
    ▷ deploy weights to local model;
    for $p = 1\ to\ P$ **do**
      ▷ compute reconstruction loss $\mathcal{L}_{\text{recon}}$ with Eq. (18.2) and update parameters Θ_{G^k};
    end
    ▷ upload weights to server;
  end
  ▷ update global model with Eq. (18.4);
end
return Θ_G^Q

To tackle this limitation and allow various sites to collaboratively train a MR image reconstruction model, we propose the FL-MR framework based on FedAVG [26]. Without accessing private data in each site, the proposed FL-MR method leverages a central server to utilize the information from other institutions by aggregating local model updates. The central server performs the aggregation of model updates by averaging the updated parameters from all local models as follows

$$\Theta_G^q = \frac{1}{K} \sum_{k=1}^{K} \Theta_{G^k}^q, \qquad (18.4)$$

where q represents the q-th global epoch. After Q rounds of communication between local sites and central server, the trained global model parameterized by Θ_G^Q, can leverage multidomain information without directly accessing the private data in each institution.

18.3.2 FL-MR with cross-site modeling

Domain shift among datasets inevitably degrades the performance of machine learning models [20]. Existing works [10,38] achieve superior performance by leveraging adversarial training. However, such methods require direct access to the source and target data, which is not allowed in FL-MR. Since we have multiple source domains and the data are stored in local institutions, training a single model that has access to source domains and target domain simultaneously is not feasible. Inspired by federated adversarial alignment [30] in classification tasks, we propose FL-MR with Cross-site Modeling (FL-MRCM) to address the domain shift problem in FL-based MRI reconstruction. As shown in Fig. 18.3, for a source site $\mathcal{D}_s^k$, we leverage the encoder part of the reconstruction networks (E_s^k) to project input onto the latent space z_s^k. Similarly, we can obtain z_t for the target site $\mathcal{D}_t$. For each ($\mathcal{D}_s^k$, $\mathcal{D}_t$) source-target domain pair, we introduce an adversarial domain identifier C^k to align the latent space distribution between the source domain and the target domain. C^k is trained in an adversarial manner. Specifically, we first train C^k to identify which site the latent features come from. We then train the encoder part of the reconstruction networks to confuse C^k. It should be noted that C^k only has access to the output latent features from E_s^k and E_t, to maintain data sharing regulations. Given the k-th source site data $\mathcal{D}_s^k$ and the target site data $\mathcal{D}_t$, the loss function for C^k can be defined as follows

$$\begin{aligned} \mathcal{L}_{\text{adv}C^k} = & - \mathbb{E}_{x_s^k \sim \mathcal{D}_s^k}[\log C^k(z_s^k)] \\ & - \mathbb{E}_{x_t \sim \mathcal{D}_t}[\log(1 - C^k(z_t))], \end{aligned} \qquad (18.5)$$

where $z_s^k = E_s^k(x_s^k)$ and $z_t = E_t(x_t)$. The loss function for encoders can be defined as follows

$$\mathcal{L}_{\text{adv}E^k} = - \mathbb{E}_{x_s^k \sim \mathcal{D}_s^k}[\log C^k(z_s^k)] - \mathbb{E}_{x_t \sim \mathcal{D}_t}[\log C^k(z_t)]. \qquad (18.6)$$

The overall loss function used for training the k-th source site with data $\mathcal{D}_s^k$ consists of the reconstruction and adversarial losses. It is defined as follows

$$\mathcal{L}_{\mathcal{D}_s^k} = \mathcal{L}_{\text{recon}} + \lambda_{\text{adv}}(\mathcal{L}_{\text{adv}C^k} + \mathcal{L}_{\text{adv}E^k}), \qquad (18.7)$$

where λ_{adv} is a constant which controls the contribution of the adversarial loss. The detailed training

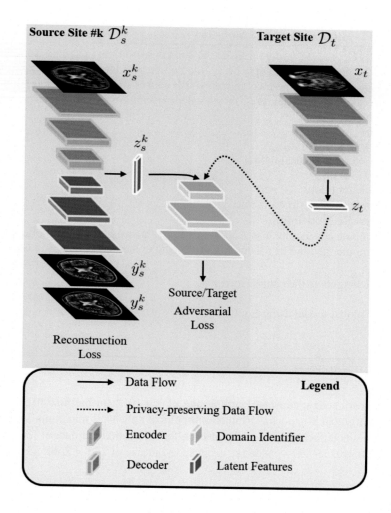

FIGURE 18.3

An overview of the proposed FL-MR framework with cross-site modeling in a source site.

procedure of FL-MRCM in a source site is presented in Algorithm 18.2. Fig. 18.4 shows a global view of proposed FL-MRCM for multiinstitutional collaborations in MR image reconstruction task. For the target site, the decoder part (green block) and the ground truth image are transparent, since they might be not involved during the training.

18.3.3 Training and implementation details

We use U-Net [33] style encoder-decoder architecture for the reconstruction networks. λ_{adv} is set equal to 1. Acceleration factor (AF) is set equal to 4. The network is trained using the Adam optimizer with

---

Algorithm 18.2: FL-MR with Cross-site Modeling.

Input: $\mathcal{D}_s = \{\mathcal{D}_s^1, \mathcal{D}_s^2, \ldots, \mathcal{D}_s^K\}$, data from the K source institutions; $\mathcal{D}_t$, data from the target institution; P, the number of local epochs; Q, the number of global epochs; γ, learning rate; $\Theta_{G_s^1}, \ldots, \Theta_{G_s^K}$, parameters of the local models in the source sites; $\Theta_{C^1}, \ldots, \Theta_{C^K}$, domain identifiers; Θ_G, the global model; Θ_{E_t}, the encoder part of G in the target site.

  ▷ parameters initialization

for $q = 0\ to\ Q$ **do**

    for $k = 0\ to\ K$ ***in parallel*** **do**

        ▷ deploy weights to local model

        for $p = 0\ to\ P$ **do**

            Reconstruction:

            ▷ compute reconstruction loss $\mathcal{L}_{\mathrm{recon}}$ using Eq. (18.2)

            Cross-site Modeling:

            ▷ compute adversarial loss $\mathcal{L}_{\mathrm{adv}C^k}$ and $\mathcal{L}_{\mathrm{adv}E_s^k}$ using Eq. (18.5) and Eq. (18.6)

            ▷ compute the total loss using Eq. (18.7) and update $\Theta_{G_s^k}$, Θ_{C^k}, and Θ_{E_t}

        end

        ▷ upload weights to the central server

    end

    ▷ update the global model using Eq. (18.4)

end

return Θ_G^Q

---

the following hyperparameters: constant learning rate of 1×10^{-4} for the first 40 global epochs then 1×10^{-5} for the last global 10 epochs; 50 maximum global epochs; 2 maximum local epochs; batch size of 16. Hyperparameter selection is performed on the IXI validation dataset [3]. During training, the cross-sectional images are zero-padded or cropped to the size of 256×256.

18.4 Experiments and results

In this section, we present the details of the datasets and various experiments conducted to demonstrate the effectiveness of the proposed framework. Specifically, we conduct experiments under two scenarios. Fig. 18.5 gives an overview of different training and evaluation strategies involved in the two scenarios. In Scenario 1, we analyze the effectiveness of improving the generalizability of the trained models using the proposed methods and other alternative strategies. Thus, the performance of a trained model is evaluated against a dataset that is not directly observed during training. In particular, we choose one dataset at a time to emulate the role of the user institution and consider data from other sites for training. This scenario is common in clinical practice. MRI scanners are usually equipped with accelerated acquisition techniques, so the user institution might not have access to fully-sampled data for training. In Scenario 2, we evaluate the proposed method by training it on the data from all available institutions to demonstrate the benefits of collaboration under the setting of federated learning. Rather

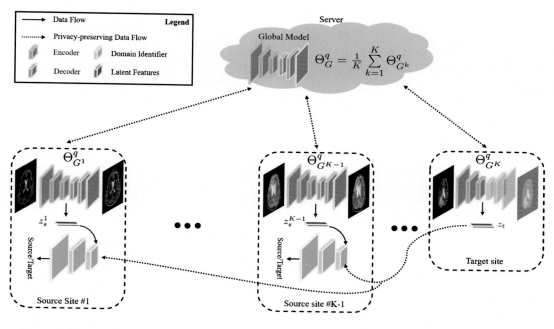

FIGURE 18.4

The overview of the proposed FL-MRCM framework. Through several rounds of communication between data centers and server, the collaboratively trained global model parameterized by Θ_G^q can be obtained in a data privacy-preserving manner.

than assuming that user institution does not have access to fully-sampled data, the training data split of user institution is also involved as a part of collaborations.

18.4.1 Datasets

fastMRI [14] (F for short): T_1-weighted images corresponding to 3443 subjects are used for conducting experiments. In particular, data from 2583 subjects are used for training and remaining data from 860 subjects are used for testing. In addition, T_2-weighted images from 3832 subjects are also used, where data from 2874 subjects are used for training and data from 958 subjects are used for testing. For each subject, approximately 15 axial cross-sectional images that contain brain tissues are provided in this dataset.

HPKS [11] (H for short): This dataset is collected from posttreatment patients with malignant glioma. T_1 and T_2-weighted images from 144 subjects are analyzed, where 116 subjects' data are used for training and 28 subjects' data are used for testing. For each subject, 15 axial cross-sectional images that contain brain tissues are provided in this dataset.

IXI [3] (I for short): T_1-weighted images from 581 subjects are used, where 436 subjects' data are used for training, 55 subjects' data are used for validation, and 90 subjects' data are used for testing. T_2-weighted images from 578 subjects are also analyzed, where 434 subjects' data are used for training,

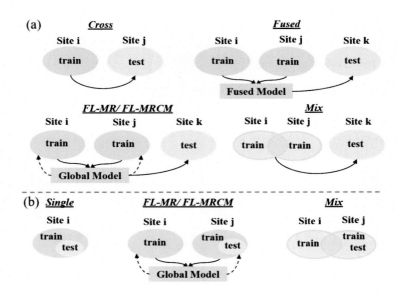

FIGURE 18.5

The schematic of different training strategies in (a) Scenario 1, and (b) Scenario 2. Note that for FL-MRCM, the source sites are the institutions that provide training data and the target site is the institution that provides testing data.

55 subjects' data are used for validation and the remaining 89 subjects' data are used for testing. For each subject, there are approximately 150 and 130 axial cross-sectional images that contain brain tissues for T_1 and T_2-weighted MR sequences, respectively.

BraTS [27] (B for short): T_1 and T_2-weighted images from 494 subjects are used, where 369 subjects' data are used for training and 125 subjects' data are used for testing. For each subject, approximately 120 axial cross-sectional images that contain brain tissues are provided for both MR sequences.

18.4.2 Evaluation of the generalizability

In the first set of experiments (Scenario 1), we analyze the model's generalizability to data from another site. In Table 18.1, we compare the quality of reconstructed images from different methods on four datasets using structural similarity index measure (SSIM) and peak-signal-to-noise ratio (PSNR). We first compare the performance of the proposed framework with models trained with data from a single data center. In this case, we obtain a trained model from one of the institutions and evaluate its performance on another data center in Table 18.1 under the label **Cross**. It is also possible to obtain multiple trained models from several institutions and fuse their outputs, which does not violate privacy regulations. In this case, we fuse the reconstructed images of the trained model from various institutions by calculating the average. The results corresponding to this strategy are shown in Table 18.1 under the label **Fused**. In addition, we can obtain a model that is trained with data from all available data centers,

Table 18.1 Quantitative comparison with models trained by different strategies in Scenario 1.

Methods	Data Centers (Institutions)		T_1-weighted				T_2-weighted			
	Train	Test	SSIM	PSNR	Average		SSIM	PSNR	Average	
					SSIM	PSNR			SSIM	PSNR
Cross	F	B	0.9016	34.65	0.7907	30.02	0.9003	33.09	0.8296	29.51
	H	B	0.6670	29.12			0.8222	31.06		
	I	B	0.8795	33.76			0.8610	31.36		
	B	F	0.7694	28.61			0.7851	27.63		
	H	F	0.8571	31.82			0.8682	29.04		
	I	F	0.8417	31.18			0.8921	30.08		
	B	H	0.5188	25.07			0.5898	26.28		
	F	H	0.8402	28.52			0.8842	30.09		
	I	H	0.6281	27.09			0.8583	29.45		
	B	I	0.8785	30.10			0.7423	27.75		
	F	I	0.9102	31.16			0.8917	29.57		
	H	I	0.7968	29.16			0.8598	28.74		
Fused	F, H, I	B	0.8672	33.98	0.8223	31.27	0.8696	32.73	0.8264	30.17
	B, H, I	F	0.8557	32.03			0.8524	29.19		
	B, F, I	H	0.6615	27.87			0.7394	29.28		
	B, F, H	I	0.9047	31.22			0.8441	29.47		
FL-MR	F, H, I	B	0.9452	35.59	0.8976	32.09	0.916	33.76	0.8997	31.49
	B, H, I	F	0.9099	33.15			0.8991	30.86		
	B, F, I	H	0.8249	28.49			0.8874	31.02		
	B, F, H	I	0.9103	31.11			0.8962	30.32		
FL-MRCM	F, H, I	B	**0.9504**	**35.93**	**0.9108**	**32.51**	**0.9275**	**33.96**	**0.9113**	**31.77**
	B, H, I	F	**0.9149**	**33.31**			**0.9139**	**31.31**		
	B, F, I	H	**0.8581**	**29.24**			**0.8978**	**31.35**		
	B, F, H	I	**0.9197**	**31.54**			**0.9058**	**30.47**		
Mix (Upper Bound)	F, H, I	B	0.9589	36.68	0.9182	32.96	0.9464	34.58	0.9260	32.44
	B, H, I	F	0.9222	33.79			0.9239	31.89		
	B, F, I	H	0.8630	29.19			0.9168	32.14		
	B, F, H	I	0.9286	32.19			0.9169	31.14		

which is denoted by **Mix** in Table 18.1. However, this case compromises subjects' privacy from other institutions, so we treat it as an upper bound.

As it can be seen from Table 18.1, our proposed FL-MR method exhibits better generalization and clearly outperforms other privacy-preserving alternative strategies. FL-MRCM further improves the reconstruction quality in each dataset by mitigating the domain shift. Fig. 18.6 shows the qualitative performance of different methods on T_1 and T_2-weighted images from four datasets. It can be observed that the proposed FL-MRCM method yields reconstructed images with remarkable visual similarity

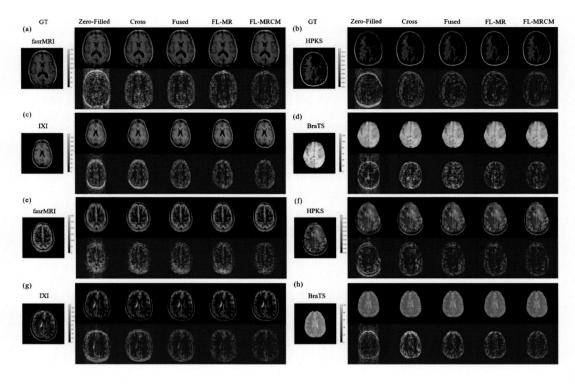

FIGURE 18.6

Qualitative results of different methods that correspond to Scenario 1. For results of T_1-weighted images on, (a) fastMRI [14], (b) HPKS [11], (c) IXI [3], (d) BraTS [27]. For results of T_2-weighted images on, (e) fastMRI [14], (f) HPKS [11], (g) IXI [3], (h) BraTS [27]. The second row of each subfigure shows the absolute image difference between reconstructed images and the ground truth.

to the reference images compared to the other alternatives (see the last column of each subfigure in Fig. 18.6) in four datasets with diverse characteristics.

18.4.3 Evaluation of FL-based collaborations

In the second set of experiments (Scenario 2), we analyze the effectiveness of our method to leverage data from all available institutions in a privacy-preserving manner. Since the goal is to evaluate the benefit of multiinstitution collaborations, we compare the performance of the proposed framework with models trained with data from a single data center and evaluate on its own testing data, which is denoted by **Single** in Table 18.2. Similar to Scenario 1, we obtain a model that is directly trained with all available data, which is denoted by **Mix** in Table 18.2 and we treat it as an upper bound. It can be seen that the proposed FL-MRCM method outperforms the other methods and reaches the upper bound in term of SSIM and PSNR. It is worth noting that the multiinstitution collaborations by the

Table 18.2 Quantitative comparison with models trained by different strategies in Scenario 2.

Methods	Data Centers (Institutions)		T_1-weighted				T_2-weighted			
	Tain	Test	SSIM	PSRN	Average SSIM	PSNR	SSIM	PSNR	Average SSIM	PSNR
Single	B	B	0.9660	37.30	0.9351	33.81	0.9558	34.90	0.9278	32.35
	F	F	0.9494	35.45			0.9404	32.43		
	H	H	0.8855	29.67			0.9001	31.29		
	I	I	0.9396	32.80			0.9151	30.79		
FL-MR	B, F, H, I	B	0.9662	37.37	0.9294	33.92	0.9482	35.34	0.9238	32.64
		F	0.9404	35.25			0.9306	32.19		
		H	0.8732	30.03			0.9021	31.74		
		I	0.9379	33.03			0.9145	31.29		
FL-MRCM	B, F, H, I	B	0.9676	37.57	**0.9381**	**34.14**	0.9630	35.85	**0.9373**	**33.13**
		F	0.9475	35.57			0.9385	32.69		
		H	0.8940	30.27			0.9232	32.44		
		I	0.9432	33.13			0.9244	31.54		
Mix (Upper Bound)	B, F, H, I	B	0.9698	37.62	0.9440	34.35	0.9655	35.83	0.9398	33.14
		F	0.9558	36.15			0.9435	32.82		
		H	0.9047	30.57			0.9236	32.47		
		I	0.9454	33.08			0.9266	31.44		

proposed FL-based method exhibit significant improvement on the smaller dataset. Specifically, on the HPKS [11], FL-MRCM improves SSIM from 0.9001 to 0.9232 and PSNR from 31.29 to 32.44 in T_2-weighted sequences. As shown in Fig. 18.7, the proposed methods have a better ability of suppressing errors around the skull and lesion regions, which is consistent with the quantitative results.

18.4.4 Ablation study

The individual contribution of proposed cross-site modeling is demonstrated by a set of experiments (i.e. the comparison between FL-MR and FL-MRCM) in two scenarios under the setting of FL. Furthermore, we conduct a detailed ablation study to analyze the effectiveness of the proposed cross-site modeling without the FL framework. In this case, we obtain a trained model from one of the available sites and evaluate its performance on the data from another institution to observe the gain purely contributed by the cross-site modeling in Table 18.3. Sample reconstructed images are shown in Fig. 18.8. Experiments with cross-site modeling achieve smaller error. To investigate the performance improvement of the proposed FL-MRCM, we conduct t-test based on the SSIM of the reconstructed images between FL-MRCM and other methods. Averaged p values of each group of experiments in two scenarios are presented in Table 18.4. A p value less than 0.05 is usually considered as statistically significant. The reported performance of FL-MRCM satisfies this criterion. To further demonstrate the performance of the proposed FL-MRCM, we show an example of Bland–Altman plot for fastMRI (the largest dataset) in Fig. 18.9. The y axis represents the SSIM difference of the reconstructed images between FL-MRCM and other methods. We can observe that most points lie in the positive range, which implies that FL-MRCM exhibits better reconstruction performance on most subjects.

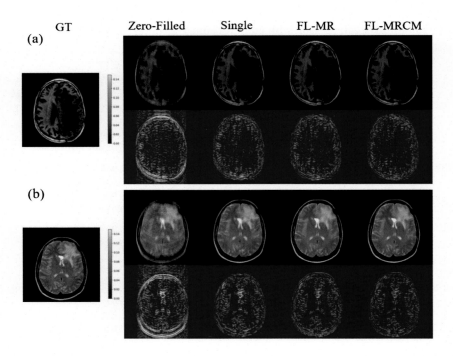

FIGURE 18.7

Qualitative results and error maps corresponding to different methods in Scenario 2 on HPKS [11]. (a) T_1-weighted, and (b) T_2-weighted images.

Table 18.3 Quantitative ablation study of the proposed cross-site modeling on the T_2-weighted images. For experiments with cross-site modeling, the target site is the institution that provides the test data.

Data Centers (Institutions)		w/o Cross-site Modeling				w/Cross-site Modeling			
Train	Test	SSIM	PSNR	Average SSIM	PSNR	SSIM	PSNR	Average SSIM	PSNR
B	F	0.7851	27.63	0.7057	27.22	0.7914	27.85	**0.7525**	**27.32**
B	H	0.5898	26.28			0.6806	26.08		
B	I	0.7423	27.75			0.7856	28.03		
F	B	0.9003	33.09	0.8921	30.92	0.9139	33.84	**0.9027**	**31.58**
F	H	0.8842	30.09			0.8936	30.75		
F	I	0.8917	29.57			0.9004	30.14		
H	B	0.8222	31.06	0.8501	29.61	0.8391	31.54	**0.8582**	**30.07**
H	F	0.8682	29.04			0.8646	29.36		
H	I	0.8598	28.74			0.8709	29.31		
I	B	0.8610	31.36	0.8738	30.30	0.8946	32.11	**0.8949**	**31.06**
I	F	0.8921	30.08			0.9065	30.80		
I	H	0.8583	29.45			0.8837	30.26		

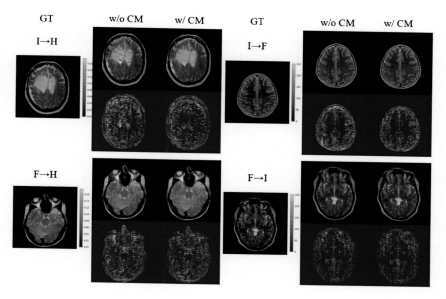

FIGURE 18.8

Qualitative comparisons and error maps on the T_2-weighted images using cross-site modeling (CM). I→H represents the results from the model trained on I and tested on H, etc.

Table 18.4 The p values of t-test among different methods in two scenarios.

| | Scenario 1 | | | Scenario 2 | |
Method	T_1-weighted	T_2-weighted	Method	T_1-weighted	T_2-weighted
Cross	4.11×10^{-27}	2.76×10^{-07}	Single	3.20×10^{-02}	7.92×10^{-03}
Fused	9.51×10^{-20}	1.12×10^{-15}	FL-MR	2.20×10^{-02}	4.34×10^{-07}
FL-MR	5.28×10^{-05}	6.47×10^{-03}	FL-MRCM	-	-
FL-MRCM	-	-	-	-	-

18.5 Conclusion

We presented a FL-based framework to leverage multiinstitutional data for the MR image reconstruction task in a privacy-preserving manner. To address the domain shift issue during collaborations, we introduce a cross-site modeling approach that provides the supervision to align the latent space distribution between the source domain and the target domain in each local entity without directly sharing the data. Through extensive experiments on four datasets with diverse characteristics, it is demonstrated that the proposed method is able to achieve better generalization. In addition, we show the benefits of multiinstitutional collaborations under the FL-based framework in MR image reconstruction task.

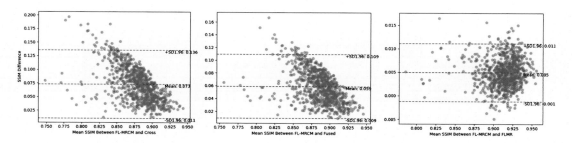

FIGURE 18.9

Bland–Altman plot corresponding to the fastMRI dataset between FL-MRCM and other methods in Scenario 1.

References

[1] Mehmet Akçakaya, Steen Moeller, Sebastian Weingärtner, Kâmil Uğurbil, Scan-specific robust artificial-neural-networks for k-space interpolation (raki) reconstruction: database-free deep learning for fast imaging, Magnetic Resonance in Medicine 81 (1) (2019) 439–453.

[2] Keith Bonawitz, Vladimir Ivanov, Ben Kreuter, Antonio Marcedone, H. Brendan McMahan, Sarvar Patel, Daniel Ramage, Aaron Segal, Karn Seth, Practical secure aggregation for privacy-preserving machine learning, in: Proceedings of the 2017 ACM SIGSAC Conference on Computer and Communications Security, 2017, pp. 1175–1191.

[3] brain development.org.

[4] Emmanuel J. Candès, Justin Romberg, Terence Tao, Robust uncertainty principles: exact signal reconstruction from highly incomplete frequency information, IEEE Transactions on Information Theory 52 (2) (2006) 489–509.

[5] Pengfei Guo, Puyang Wang, Rajeev Yasarla, Jinyuan Zhou, Vishal M. Patel, Shanshan Jiang, Anatomic and molecular mr image synthesis using confidence guided cnns, IEEE Transactions on Medical Imaging (2020).

[6] Pengfei Guo, Puyang Wang, Rajeev Yasarla, Jinyuan Zhou, Vishal M. Patel, Shanshan Jiang, Confidence-guided lesion mask-based simultaneous synthesis of anatomic and molecular mr images in patients with post-treatment malignant gliomas, arXiv preprint, arXiv:2008.02859, 2020.

[7] Pengfei Guo, Puyang Wang, Jinyuan Zhou, Shanshan Jiang, Vishal M. Patel, Multi-institutional collaborations for improving deep learning-based magnetic resonance image reconstruction using federated learning, in: Proceedings of the IEEE/CVF Conference on Computer Vision and Pattern Recognition (CVPR), June 2021, pp. 2423–2432.

[8] Pengfei Guo, Puyang Wang, Jinyuan Zhou, Vishal M. Patel, Shanshan Jiang, Lesion mask-based simultaneous synthesis of anatomic and molecular mr images using a gan, in: International Conference on Medical Image Computing and Computer-Assisted Intervention, Springer, 2020, pp. 104–113.

[9] Yoseo Han, Leonard Sunwoo, Jong Chul Ye, k-space deep learning for accelerated mri, IEEE Transactions on Medical Imaging 39 (2) (2019) 377–386.

[10] Judy Hoffman, Eric Tzeng, Taesung Park, Jun-Yan Zhu, Phillip Isola, Kate Saenko, Alexei Efros, Trevor Darrell, Cycada: cycle-consistent adversarial domain adaptation, in: International Conference on Machine Learning, PMLR, 2018, pp. 1989–1998.

[11] Shanshan Jiang, Charles G. Eberhart, Michael Lim, Hye-Young Heo, Yi Zhang, Lindsay Blair, Zhibo Wen, Matthias Holdhoff, Doris Lin, Peng Huang, et al., Identifying recurrent malignant glioma after treatment using amide proton transfer-weighted mr imaging: a validation study with image-guided stereotactic biopsy, Clinical Cancer Research 25 (2) (2019) 552–561.

[12] Nikolaos L. Kelekis, et al., Hepatocellular carcinoma in North America: a multiinstitutional study of appearance on t1-weighted, t2-weighted, and serial gadolinium-enhanced gradient-echo images, AJR. American Journal of Roentgenology 170 (4) (1998) 1005–1013.

[13] Florian Knoll, Kerstin Hammernik, Chi Zhang, Steen Moeller, Thomas Pock, Daniel K. Sodickson, Mehmet Akcakaya, Deep-learning methods for parallel magnetic resonance imaging reconstruction: a survey of the current approaches, trends, and issues, IEEE Signal Processing Magazine 37 (1) (2020) 128–140.

[14] Florian Knoll, Jure Zbontar, Anuroop Sriram, Matthew J. Muckley, Mary Bruno, Aaron Defazio, Marc Parente, Krzysztof J. Geras, Joe Katsnelson, Hersh Chandarana, et al., fastmri: a publicly available raw k-space and dicom dataset of knee images for accelerated mr image reconstruction using machine learning, Radiology: Artificial Intelligence 2 (1) (2020) e190007.

[15] Dongwook Lee, Jaejun Yoo, Sungho Tak, Jong Chul Ye, Deep residual learning for accelerated mri using magnitude and phase networks, IEEE Transactions on Biomedical Engineering 65 (9) (2018) 1985–1995.

[16] Li Tian, Anit Kumar Sahu, Ameet Talwalkar, Virginia Smith, Federated learning: challenges, methods, and future directions, IEEE Signal Processing Magazine 37 (3) (2020) 50–60.

[17] Wenqi Li, Fausto Milletarì, Daguang Xu, Nicola Rieke, Jonny Hancox, Wentao Zhu, Maximilian Baust, Yan Cheng, Sébastien Ourselin, M. Jorge Cardoso, et al., Privacy-preserving federated brain tumour segmentation, in: International Workshop on Machine Learning in Medical Imaging, Springer, 2019, pp. 133–141.

[18] Xiaoxiao Li, Yufeng Gu, Nicha Dvornek, Lawrence Staib, Pamela Ventola, James S. Duncan, Multi-site fmri analysis using privacy-preserving federated learning and domain adaptation: abide results, arXiv preprint, arXiv:2001.05647, 2020.

[19] Dong Liang, Jing Cheng, Ziwen Ke, Leslie Ying, Deep mri reconstruction: unrolled optimization algorithms meet neural networks, arXiv preprint, arXiv:1907.11711, 2019.

[20] Mingsheng Long, Yue Cao, Jianmin Wang, Michael Jordan, Learning transferable features with deep adaptation networks, in: International Conference on Machine Learning, PMLR, 2015, pp. 97–105.

[21] Alexander Selvikvåg Lundervold, Arvid Lundervold, An overview of deep learning in medical imaging focusing on mri, Zeitschrift für Medizinische Physik 29 (2) (2019) 102–127.

[22] Michael Lustig, David Donoho, John M. Pauly, Sparse mri: the application of compressed sensing for rapid mr imaging, Magnetic Resonance in Medicine: An Official Journal of the International Society for Magnetic Resonance in Medicine 58 (6) (2007) 1182–1195.

[23] Shiqian Ma, Wotao Yin, Yin Zhang, Amit Chakraborty, An efficient algorithm for compressed mr imaging using total variation and wavelets, in: 2008 IEEE Conference on Computer Vision and Pattern Recognition, IEEE, 2008, pp. 1–8.

[24] Laurens van der Maaten, Geoffrey Hinton, Visualizing data using t-sne, Journal of Machine Learning Research 9 (Nov) (2008) 2579–2605.

[25] Morteza Mardani, Enhao Gong, Joseph Y. Cheng, Shreyas Vasanawala, Greg Zaharchuk, Marcus Alley, Neil Thakur, Song Han, William Dally, John M. Pauly, et al., Deep generative adversarial networks for compressed sensing automates mri, arXiv preprint, arXiv:1706.00051, 2017.

[26] Brendan McMahan, Eider Moore, Daniel Ramage, Seth Hampson, Blaise Aguera y Arcas, Communication-efficient learning of deep networks from decentralized data, in: Artificial Intelligence and Statistics, PMLR, 2017, pp. 1273–1282.

[27] Bjoern H. Menze, et al., The multimodal brain tumor image segmentation benchmark (brats), IEEE Transactions on Medical Imaging 34 (10) (2014) 1993–2024.

[28] Payman Mohassel, Peter Rindal, Aby3: a mixed protocol framework for machine learning, in: Proceedings of the 2018 ACM SIGSAC Conference on Computer and Communications Security, 2018, pp. 35–52.

[29] Mehryar Mohri, Gary Sivek, Ananda Theertha Suresh, Agnostic federated learning, arXiv preprint, arXiv:1902.00146, 2019.

[30] Xingchao Peng, Zijun Huang, Yizhe Zhu, Kate Saenko, Federated adversarial domain adaptation, arXiv preprint, arXiv:1911.02054, 2019.

[31] Chen Qin, Jo Schlemper, Jose Caballero, Anthony N. Price, Joseph V. Hajnal, Daniel Rueckert, Convolutional recurrent neural networks for dynamic mr image reconstruction, IEEE Transactions on Medical Imaging 38 (1) (2018) 280–290.

[32] Saiprasad Ravishankar, Jong Chul Ye, Jeffrey A. Fessler, Image reconstruction: from sparsity to data-adaptive methods and machine learning, Proceedings of the IEEE 108 (1) (2019) 86–109.

[33] Olaf Ronneberger, Philipp Fischer, Thomas Brox, U-net: convolutional networks for biomedical image segmentation, in: International Conference on Medical Image Computing and Computer-Assisted Intervention, Springer, 2015, pp. 234–241.

[34] Joachim Roski, George W. Bo-Linn, Timothy A. Andrews, Creating value in health care through big data: opportunities and policy implications, Health Affairs 33 (7) (2014) 1115–1122.

[35] Anit Kumar Sahu, Tian Li, Maziar Sanjabi, Manzil Zaheer, Ameet Talwalkar, Virginia Smith, On the convergence of federated optimization in heterogeneous networks, arXiv preprint, arXiv:1812.06127, 2018, 3.

[36] Veit Sandfort, Ke Yan, Perry J. Pickhardt, Ronald M. Summers, Data augmentation using generative adversarial networks (cyclegan) to improve generalizability in ct segmentation tasks, Scientific Reports 9 (1) (2019) 1–9.

[37] Micah J. Sheller, G. Anthony Reina, Brandon Edwards, Jason Martin, Spyridon Bakas, Multi-institutional deep learning modeling without sharing patient data: a feasibility study on brain tumor segmentation, in: International MICCAI Brainlesion Workshop, Springer, 2018, pp. 92–104.

[38] Eric Tzeng, Judy Hoffman, Trevor Darrell, Kate Saenko, Simultaneous deep transfer across domains and tasks, in: Proceedings of the IEEE International Conference on Computer Vision, 2015, pp. 4068–4076.

[39] Puyang Wang, Eric Z. Chen, Terrence Chen, Vishal M. Patel, Shanhui Sun, Pyramid convolutional rnn for mri reconstruction, arXiv preprint, arXiv:1912.00543, 2019.

[40] Puyang Wang, Pengfei Guo, Jianhua Lu, Jinyuan Zhou, Shanshan Jiang, Vishal M. Patel, Improving amide proton transfer-weighted mri reconstruction using t2-weighted images, in: International Conference on Medical Image Computing and Computer-Assisted Intervention, Springer, 2020, pp. 3–12.

[41] Shanshan Wang, Ziwen Ke, Huitao Cheng, Sen Jia, Leslie Ying, Hairong Zheng, Dong Liang, Dimension: dynamic mr imaging with both k-space and spatial prior knowledge obtained via multi-supervised network training, NMR in Biomedicine (2019) e4131.

[42] Wenjun Yan, Lu Huang, Liming Xia, Shengjia Gu, Fuhua Yan, Yuanyuan Wang, Qian Tao, Mri manufacturer shift and adaptation: increasing the generalizability of deep learning segmentation for mr images acquired with different scanners, Radiology: Artificial Intelligence 2 (4) (2020) e190195.

[43] Qiang Yang, Yang Liu, Tianjian Chen, Yongxin Tong, Federated machine learning: concept and applications, ACM Transactions on Intelligent Systems and Technology (TIST) 10 (2) (2019) 1–19.

Neural architecture search for medical image applications

Viet-Khoa Vo-Ho[a], **Kashu Yamazaki**[a], **Hieu Hoang**[b], **Minh-Triet Tran**[b], **and Ngan Le**[a]

[a]*Department of Computer Science & Computer Engineering, University of Arkansas, Fayetteville, AR, United States*
[b]*Department of Computer Science, VNUHCM-University of Science, HCM, Viet Nam*

19.1 Neural architecture search: background

From the earliest LeNet [38] to the recent deep learning networks, designing network architecture heavily relies on prior knowledge and the experience of researchers. Furthermore, searching for an optimal and effective network architecture are also time consuming and computationally intensive due to the immersive amount of experiments for every architecture. Automated machine learning (AutoML) is recently proposed to align with such demands to automatically design the network architecture instead of relying on human experiences and repeated manual tuning. Neural Architecture Search (NAS) is an instance of hyperparameter optimization that aims to search the optimal network architecture for a given task automatically, instead of handcrafting the building blocks or layers of the model [10].

NAS have already identified more efficient network architectures in general computer vision tasks. MetaQNN [1] and NAS-RL [73] are the two earliest works in the field of NAS. By automating the design of a neural network for the task at hand, NAS has tremendous potential to surpass the human design of deep networks for both visual recognition and natural language processing [43,7,47,57]. This motivated various NAS applications in medical image tasks e.g. classification, segmentation, reconstruction. In a standard problem setup, the outer optimization searches for architectures with good validation performance while the inner optimization trains networks with the specified architecture. However, full evaluation of the inner loop is expensive since it requires a many-shot neural network to be trained. A typical NAS technique contains two stages: the searching stage, which aims to find a good architecture, and the evaluating stage, where the best architecture is trained from scratch and validated on the test data. Corresponding to two stages, there are three primary components: search space $\mathcal{A}$, search strategy, and evaluation strategy. Denote A is single network in $\mathcal{A}$ i.e. $A \in \mathcal{A}$. Let S^{train} and S^{val} are two datasets corresponding to training set and testing set. The performance of the network A, which is trained on S^{train} and evaluated on S^{val}, is measured by function $\mathcal{F}$. In general, NAS can be mathematically formulated as follows:

$$\underset{A}{\operatorname{argmax}} = \mathcal{F}(S^{val}(S^{train}(A))) \tag{19.1}$$

Fig. 19.1 visualize a general NAS architecture with three components i.e. search space, search strategy and evaluation strategy.

Meta Learning With Medical Imaging and Health Informatics Applications. https://doi.org/10.1016/B978-0-32-399851-2.00029-6

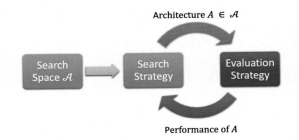

Architecture $A \in \mathcal{A}$

Performance of A

FIGURE 19.1

NAS algorithm with three components: search space, search strategy, and evolution strategy.

19.1.1 Search space

In principle, the search space specifies a set of operations (e.g. convolution, normalization, activation, etc.) and how they are connected, defines which architectures can be represented. Thus, search space design has a key impact on the final performance of the NAS algorithm. In general, the search space defines a set of configurations which can be continuous or discrete hyperparameters [44] in a structured or unstructured fashion. In NAS, search spaces usually involve discrete hyperparameters with a structure that can be captured with a directed acyclic graph (DAG) [48,44]. The most naive approach to design the search space for neural network architectures is to depict network topologies, either CNN or RNN, with a list of sequential layer-wise operations, as can be seen in [1,73]. Because each operation is associated with different layer-specific parameters which were implemented by hard-coded techniques, thus, this network representation strongly depends on expert knowledge.

To deal with too many nodes and edges in an entire architecture as well as to reduce the complexity of NAS search tasks, search spaces are usually defined over some smaller building block and learned metaarchitecture to form a larger architecture [18,58,20]. NASNet [74] is one of the first works to make use of cell-based neural architecture. There are two types of cells in NASNet: normal cells and reduction cells. The former cells aim to extract advanced features while keeping the spatial resolution unchanged whereas the later cells aim to reduce the spatial resolution. A complete network contains many blocks, each block consists of multiple repeated normal cells followed by a reduction cell. An illustration of NASnet is shown in Fig. 19.2 Leveraging NASNet, [44,50,49,70] proposed similar cell-based search space but the reduce cells are eliminated as in Block-QNN [70] and DPPNet [49] and replaced by pooling layers. In order to deal with U-Net-like encoder-decoder architectures, AutoDispNet [52] contains three types of cells: normal, reduction, and upsampling. At the encoder path, it comprises alternate connections of normal cells and reduction cells while the decoder path consists of a stack of multiple upsampling cells. More details of the cells from popular cell-based search spaces are theoretically and experimentally studied in [54]. Instead of stacking one or more identical cells, FPNAS [12] considers stacking more diversity of blocks which aim to the improvement of neural architecture performance. Instead of a graph of operations, [4] consider a neural network as a system with multiple memory blocks which can read and write. Each layer operation is designed to: firstly, read from a subset of memory blocks; secondly, computes results; finally, write the results into another subset of blocks.

Since the size of the search space is exponentially large or even unbounded, incorporating prior knowledge about properties well-suited for task can reduce the size of the search space and simplify

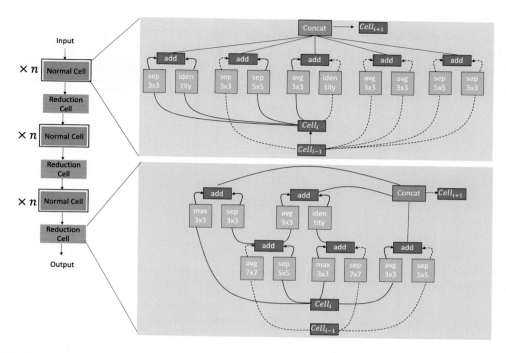

FIGURE 19.2

Left: The overall structure of the *search space* of NASNet with two cells: normal cell and reduction cell. The normal cell is repeated ×n and then connected to a reduction cell. Right: Architecture of the best normal cell and reduction cells.

the search task. This could introduce a human bias, which may prevent the discovery of the optimal architectural building blocks that go beyond the current state-of-the-art.

19.1.2 Search strategy

Given a search space, there are various search methods to select a configuration of network architecture for evaluation. The search strategy defines the way to explore the search space for the sake of finding the high-performance architecture candidates. The most basic search strategies are grid search (i.e. systematically screening the search space) and random search (i.e. randomly selecting architectures from the search space to be tested) [3]. They are quite effective in practice for a small search spaces but they may fail with a large search space. Among hyperparameter optimization search methods, gradient-based approaches [32] and Bayesian optimization [53] based on Gaussian processes or Gaussian distribution has already proven its usefulness, specially in continuous space [31,34]. However, they may not work well with the discrete and high dimensionality space. To apply gradient, gradient-based approaches transform the discrete search problem into a continuous optimization problem. With distribution assumption, Bayesian-based approaches rely on the choice of kernels. By contrast, evolutionary strategies [50,56] are more flexible and can be applied to any search space. However, evolutionary methods require to

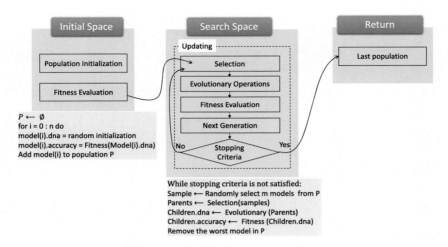

FIGURE 19.3

Top: Flowchart of evolutionary strategy in NAS. Bottom: Pseudo code of evolutionary strategy in NAS.

define a set of possible mutations to apply to different architectures. As an alternation, reinforcement learning is used to train a recurrent neural network controller to generate good architectures [73,48].

The conventional NAS algorithms, which leverage either gradient-based or Bayesian optimization or evolutionary search or reinforcement learning, can be prohibitively expensive as thousands of models are required to be trained in a single experiment.

Compare to RL-based algorithms, gradient-based algorithms are more efficient even gradient-based algorithms require to construct a supernet in advance, which also highly requires expertise. Due to the improper relationship for adapting to gradient-based optimization, both RL-based algorithms and gradient-based are often ill-conditioned architectures. Among all search strategy, evolutionary strategy (ES) NAS is the most popular, which can use some common approaches such as genetic algorithms [55], genetic programming [36], particle swarm optimization [33]. Fig. 19.3 shows an illustration of the flowchart of an ES algorithm which takes place in the initial space and the search space sequentially. ES starts with a population is initialized within the initial space. In the population, each individual represents a solution (i.e., a DNN architecture) for NAS and it is evaluated by fitness process. After the initial population is fitness evaluated, the whole population starts the evolutionary process within the search space. In the evolutionary process, the population is updated by the selection and the evolutionary operators in each iteration, until the stopping criterion is met. Finally, a population that has finished the evolution is obtained.

19.1.3 Evaluation strategy

For each hyperparameter configuration (from search strategy), we need to evaluate its performance. The evaluation can be benchmarked by either fully or partially training a model with the given hyperparameters, and subsequently measuring its quality on a validation set. Full training evaluation is a default method and it is known as the first generation of NAS evaluation strategy, which requires thousands of

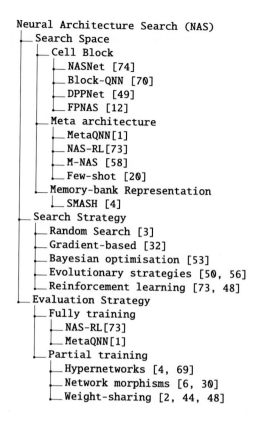

```
Neural Architecture Search (NAS)
 └─Search Space
    ├─Cell Block
    │  ├─NASNet [74]
    │  ├─Block-QNN [70]
    │  ├─DPPNet [49]
    │  └─FPNAS [12]
    ├─Meta architecture
    │  ├─MetaQNN[1]
    │  ├─NAS-RL[73]
    │  ├─M-NAS [58]
    │  └─Few-shot [20]
    └─Memory-bank Representation
       └─SMASH [4]
 └─Search Strategy
    ├─Random Search [3]
    ├─Gradient-based [32]
    ├─Bayesian optimisation [53]
    ├─Evolutionary strategies [50, 56]
    └─Reinforcement learning [73, 48]
 └─Evaluation Strategy
    ├─Fully training
    │  ├─NAS-RL[73]
    │  └─MetaQNN[1]
    └─Partial training
       ├─Hypernetworks [4, 69]
       ├─Network morphisms [6, 30]
       └─Weight-sharing [2, 44, 48]
```

FIGURE 19.4

Summary NAS architecture regarding search space, search strategy, and evaluation strategy.

GPU days to achieve a desired result. To speed up the evaluation process, partial training methods make use of early-stopping. Hypernetworks [4,69], network morphisms [6,30] and weight-sharing [2,44] are common NAS evaluation methods. Among three methods, weight-sharing is less complexity because it does not require training an auxiliary network while network morphism is the most expensive which requires on the order of 100 GPU days.

NAS approaches categorized by search space, search strategy and evaluation strategy are summarized in Fig. 19.4.

19.2 NAS for medical imaging

The recent breakthroughs of Neural Architecture Search (NAS) have motivated various applications in medical images such as segmentation, classification, reconstruction, etc. Starting from NASNet [74], many novel search spaces, search strategy and evaluation strategy has been proposed for biomedical images. The following sections will detail recent efficient NAS for medical imaging applications.

19.2.1 NAS for medical image classification

In image classification, the search space can be divided into either network topology level [62,21], which perform search on the network topology; or cell level [43,44,48,50], which focus on searching optimal cells and apply a predefined network topology. NASNet [74] is considered as one of the first successful NAS architectures for image classification. The overall architecture of NASNet together with its normal cell and reduction cell are shown in Fig. 19.1. In NASNet, the normal cell returns a feature map of the same dimension whereas the reduction cell returns feature map where the feature map height and width is reduced by a factor of two. Both normal cell and reduction cell are searched by a controller, which is fashioned from Recurrent Neural Network (RNN).

In this section, we take the frontier NAS approach [73] developed by Google Brain as an instance to show how to employ NAS into image classification. The network architecture of NAS [73] is shown in Fig. 19.5 (top) where the controller is defined as RNN based on Long Short Term Memory (LSTM) [24] is shown in Fig. 19.5 (bottom). The RNN controller is responsible for generating new architectural hyperparameters of CNNs, and is trained using REINFORCE [61]. In NAS, controller predicts the parameters θ_C corresponding to filter height, filter width, stride height, stride width, and number of filters for one layer and repeats. Every prediction is carried out by a softmax classifier and then fed into the next time step as input. The parameter θ_C is optimized in order to maximize the expected validation accuracy of the proposed architectures. After the controller predicts a set of hyperparameters θ_C, a neural network with the specified configuration is built, i.e. a child model, and trained to convergence on a dataset (CIFAR-10 is used). In this architecture, the child network accuracy R is utilized as a reward to train the controller under a reinforcement learning mechanism. In NAS, each gradient update to the controller parameters θ_C corresponds to training one child network to convergence. An upper threshold on the number of layers in the CNNs is used to stop the process of generating new architectures. Each network proposed by the RNN controller is trained on CIFAR10 dataset for 50 epochs with the use of vast computational resources (450 GPUs for 3-4 days for a single experiment). The search space contains 12,800 architectures.

Based on NAS, many effective NAS approaches on image classification have been proposed such as evolution-based NAS [50] (i.e. using evolution algorithms to simultaneously optimize topology alongside with parameters), ENAS [48] (i.e. sharing of parameters among child models), DARTS [44] (i.e. formulating the task in a differentiable manner to shorten the search within four GPU days), GDAS [16] (i.e. enabling the search speed in four GPU hours), ProxylessNAS [5] (i.e. process on a large-scale target tasks and the target hardware platforms).

Inspired by the successes of NAS in computer vision, i.e. image classification, there are several attempts in medical image classification that employed NAS techniques. Leveraged by [19], which uses the hill climbing algorithm with the network morphism transformation to search for the architectures, Kwasigroch et al., [35] proposed a malignant melanoma detection for skin lesion classification. In this method, the hill-climbing algorithm can be interpreted as a simple evolutionary algorithm with only network morphism operation. Adopt AdaNet framework [11] as the NAS engine, [13] proposed Adanet-NAS to optimize a CNN model for three classes fMRI signal classification.

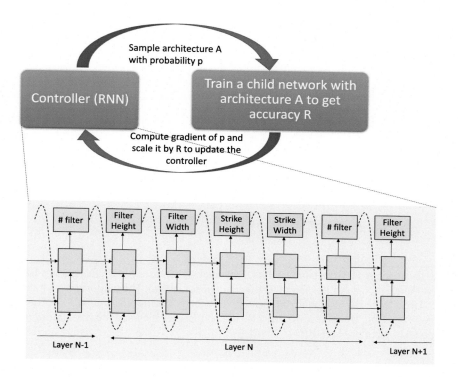

FIGURE 19.5

Top: An overview of Neural Architecture Search. Bottom: NAS Controller by RNN.

19.2.2 NAS for medical image segmentation

Medical image segmentation faces some unique challenges such as lacking annotated data, inhomogeneous intensity, and vast memory usage for processing 3D high resolution images. 3DUnet [51], VNet [45] are first 3D networks designed for medical image segmentation. Later, many other effective CNN-based 3D networks for medical image segmentation such as cascade-Unet [37], UNet++ [71], Densenet [25], H-DenseUNe [39], NN-UNet [27] have been proposed.

In computer vision, NAS has mainly solved image classification and a few recent work recently applied NAS to image segmentation such as FasterSeg [9], Auto-DeepLab [42].

In medical analysis, accurate segmentation of medical images is a crucial step in computer-aided diagnosis, surgical planning and navigation which have been applied in a wide range of clinical applications. Great achievements have been made in medical segmentation thanks to the recent breakthroughs in deep learning, such as 3D-UNet and NN-UNet. However, it remains very difficult to address some challenges such as extremely small object with respect to the whole volume, weak boundary, various location, shape, and appearance. Furthermore, volumetric image segmentation is extremely expensive to train, thus, it is difficult to attain an efficient 3D architecture search. NAS-Unet [60] and V-NAS [72] are two of the first NAS architectures for medical segmentation. NAS-Unet is based on U-like/V-net backbone (i.e. Densenet implementation [28] in NAS-NET and V-net [45] in V-NAS) with two types

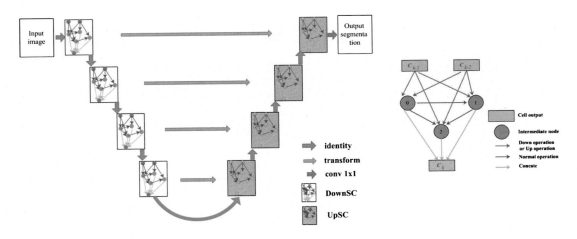

FIGURE 19.6

Left: The U-like backbone of Nas-Unet architecture, the rectangle represents cell architectures need to search. The green arrow merely represents the flow of feature map (input image). The gray arrow is a transform operation belongs to UpSC and is also automatically searched. Right: NAS-Unet cell architecture. The red arrow indicates an down operation, the blue arrow indicates the normal operation and the green arrow represents a concatenate operation. Courtesy of [60].

of cell architectures called DownSC and UpSC as given in Fig. 19.6 (left). NAS-UNet is based on cell-block building search space and the search cell contains three types of primitive operation: Down PO (average pooling, max pooling, down cweight, down dilation conv., down depth conv., and down conv.), Up PO (up cweight, up depth conv., up conv., up dilation conv.), and Normal PO (identity, cweight, dilation conv., depth conv., conv.) as shown in Fig. 19.6 (right). In NAS-Unet, both DownSC and UpSC are simultaneously updated by a differential architecture strategy during the search stage. As given in Fig. 19.6(a), NAS-Unet contains L_1 cells in the encoder path o learn the different level of semantic context information and L_1 cells in the decoder path to restore the spatial information of each probability. Compare to Densenet [25], NAS-Unet replaces the convolution layers with these cells and moves upsampling operation and downsample operation into the cells. Leverage by DARTS [44] NAS-Unet constructs an overparameterized network $C(e_1 = MixO_1, ..., e_E = MixO_E).$, where each edge is a mixed operation that has N parallel paths, denoted as MixO, as shown in Fig. 19.7 (left). The output of a mixed operation $MixO$ is defined based on the output of its N paths: $MixO(x) = \sum_{(i=1)}^{N} w_i o_i(x)$. To save memory during update strategy, NAS-Unet makes use of ProxylessNAS [5] as shown in Fig. 19.7 (right). By using ProxylessNAS, NAS-Unet update of one of architecture parameters by gradient descent at each step. To obtain that objective, NAS-Unet first freezes the architecture parameters and stochastically sample binary gates for each batch of input data. NAS-Unet then updates parameters of active paths via standard gradients descent on the training dataset as shown in Fig. 19.7 (right). These two update steps are performed in an alternative manner.

In additional to NAS-Unet, V-NAS [72] is another NAS cell-blocked-based NAS architecture and based on V-Net [45] network design. In V-NAS, a cell is defined as a fully convolutional module composing of several convolutional (Conv+BN+ReLU) layers, which is then repeated multiple times

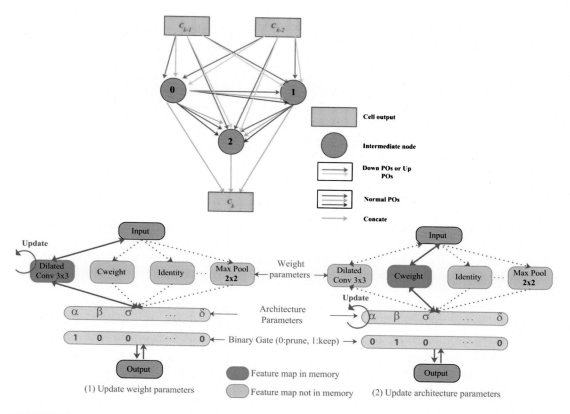

FIGURE 19.7

Top: Overparameterized cCell architecture a NAS-Unet. Each edge associates with N candidate operations from different primitive operation sets. Bottom: Update strategy by ProxylessNAS [5]. Courtesy of [60].

to construct the entire neural network. Corresponding encoder path and decoder path, V-NAS consists of encoder cell and decoder cell which are chosen between 2D, 3D, or Pseudo-3D (P3D) as shown in Fig. 19.8. V-NAS is designed with ResNet-50 in the encoder path and pyramid volumetric pooling (PVP) in the decoder path.

[72] designed a search space consisting of both 2D, 3D, and pseudo-3D (P3D) operations, and let the network itself select between these operations at each layer.

Different from NAS-Unet [60] and V-NAS [72] which search cells and apply it to a U-Net/V-Net like architecture, C2FNAS [68] searches 3D network topology in a U-shaped space and then searches the operation for each cell. The search procedure contains two stages corresponding to macro level (i.e. defining how every cell is connected to each other) and micro-level (assigning an operation to each node). Thus, a network is constructed from scratch in a macro-to-micro manner under two stages which aim to relieve the memory pressure and resolve the inconsistency problem between search stage and deployment stage. MS-NAS [65] applied PC-DARTS [63] and Auto-DeepLab's formulation to 2D

$$\{\text{Encoder}\underbrace{\begin{bmatrix}3 \times 3 \times 1\\1 \times 1 \times 1\end{bmatrix}}_{E_0:\,2D}, \text{Encoder}\underbrace{\begin{bmatrix}3 \times 3 \times 3\\1 \times 1 \times 1\end{bmatrix}}_{E_1:\,3D}, \text{Encoder}\underbrace{\begin{bmatrix}3 \times 3 \times 1\\1 \times 1 \times 3\end{bmatrix}}_{E_2:\,\text{P3D}}\}$$

$$\{\text{Decoder}\underbrace{\begin{bmatrix}3 \times 3 \times 1\\3 \times 3 \times 1\end{bmatrix}}_{D_0:\,2D}, \text{Decoder}\underbrace{\begin{bmatrix}3 \times 3 \times 3\\3 \times 3 \times 3\end{bmatrix}}_{D_1:\,3D}, \text{Decoder}\underbrace{\begin{bmatrix}3 \times 3 \times 1\\1 \times 1 \times 3\end{bmatrix}}_{D_2:\,\text{P3D}}\}$$

FIGURE 19.8

Encoder cell and decoder cell defined in V-NAS [72].

medical images MS-NAS is designed with three types of cells: expanding cells (i.e. expands and up-samples the scale of feature map), contracting cells (i.e. contracts and downsamples the scale of feature map;), and nonscaling cells (i.e. keeps the scale of feature map constant) to automatically determine the network backbone, cell type, operation parameters, and fusion scales. Recently, BiX-NAS [59] searches for the optimal bi-directional architecture by recurrently skipping multiscale features while discarding insignificant ones at the same time.

One of the current limitations of NAS is that it lack of corresponding baseline and sharable experimental protocol. Thus, it is difficult to compare between NAS search algorithms. In this section, we make comparison based on the performance on particular dataset without knowing where is the performance gain come from.

19.2.3 NAS for other medical image applications

Inspired by continuous relaxation of the architecture representation of DARTS [44] with differentiable search, [64] proposed NAS-based reconstruction which searches for the internal structure of the cells. The reconstruction module is a stack of cells as shown in Fig. 19.9 (left) where the first and the last common 3×3 convolutional layer. For each cell, it maps the output tensors of previous two cells to construct its output by concatenating two previous cells with a parameter representing the relaxation of discrete inner cell architectures. The search space contains three operators defined as in Fig. 19.9 (right). The inner structure of cells is search through DARTS [44].

A similar NAS-based MRI reconstruction network introduced by EMR-NAS [26] where the search space contains eight different cells with the same kernel size 3×3 but different dilation rate and the connection between them.

Besides classification, segmentation and reconstruction, lesion detection is another important task in medical analysis. In addition to TruncatedRPN balances positive and negative data for false positive reduction; ElixirNet [29] proposed Auto-lesion Block (ALB) to locate the tiny-size lesion by dilated convolution with flexible receptive fields. The search space for ALB contains 9 operators i.e. 3×1 and 1×3 depthwise-separable conv, 3×3 depthwise-separable conv, 5×5 depthwise-separable conv, 3×3 atrous conv with dilate rate 3, 5×5 atrous conv with dilate rate 5, average pooling, skip connection, no connection, nonlocal. All operations are of stride 1 and the convolved feature maps are padded to preserve their spatial resolution. Among all operators, nonlocal operator aims to encode semantic

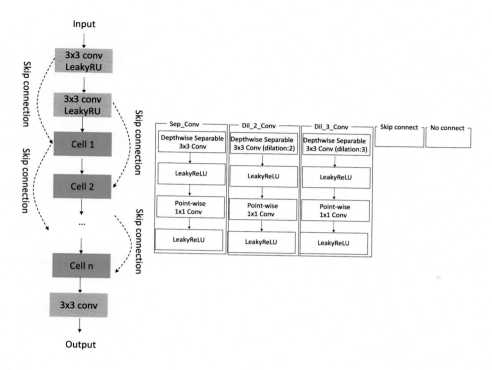

FIGURE 19.9

Left: The reconstruction module used in NAS-based reconstruction [64]. Right: Candidate layer operations in search space.

relation between region proposals which is relevant to the lesion detection. The cell is searched by DARTS [44].

NAS is also employed to localize multiple uterine standard plan (SP) in 3D Ultrasound (US) simultaneously by MultiAgent RL (MARL) framework [66]. In MARL, the optimal agent for each plane is obtained by one-shot NAS [23] to avoid time-consuming. The search strategy is based on GDAS [16] which search by gradient descent and only updates the subgraph sampled from the supernet in each iteration. In MARL, the search space contains 8 cells (5 normal cells and 3 reduce cells) and each agent has its own 4 cells (3 normal cells and 1 reduce cells). The cell search space consists of 10 operations including none, 3×3 conv., 5×5 conv., 3×3 dilated conv., 5×5 dilated conv., 3×3 separable conv., 5×5 separable conv., 3×3 max pooling, 3×3 avg pooling, and skip-connection.

19.3 Future perspectives

Artificially neuron networks (ANN) have made breakthroughs in many medical fields, including recognition, segmentation, detection, reconstruction, etc. Compared with ANN, NAS is still in the initial research stage even NAS has become a popular subject in the area of machine-learning science. Commercial services such as Google's AutoML and open-source libraries such as Auto-Keras make NAS accessible to the broader machine learning environment. At the current stage of development, NAS-based approaches focus on improving image classification accuracy, reducing time consumption during search for a neural architecture. There are some challenges and future perspectives discussed as follows:

Search space: There are various effective search spaces; however, they are based on human knowledge and experience, which inevitably introduce human bias. Balancing between freedom of neural architecture design, search cost and network performance in NAS-based approach is an important future research direction. For example, to reduce the search space as much as possible while also improving network performance, NASNet [74] proposes a modular search space that was later widely adopted. However, this comes at the expense of the freedom of neural architecture design. Thus, general, flexible, and human bias-free search space are critical requirements. To minimize the human bias, AutoML-Zero [20] applies evolution strategy (ES) and designs two-layer neural networks based on basic mathematical operations (cos, sin, mean, st).

Robustness: Even NAS has been proven effective in many datasets, it is still limited when dealing with dataset that contains noise, adversarial attacks or open-set dataset. Some efforts have been proposed to boost the NAS's robustness such as Chen et al. [8] proposed a loss function for noise tolerant. Guoet al. [22] explored the intrinsic impact of network architectures to adversarial attacks.

Learn new data: Most of the existing NAS methods can search an appropriate architecture for a single task. To search for a new architecture on a new task, a suggested solution is combine meta learning into NAS [46,20,40]. For example [40] proposed a transferable neural architecture search to generate a metaarchitecture, which can adapt to new task and new data easily while [20] applied NAS into few-shot learning. On learning new data, a recent work by [41] proposed unsupervised neural architecture search (UnNAS) shows that an architecture searched without labels is competitive with those searched with labels.

Reproducibility: Most of the existing NAS methods have many parameters that need to be set manually at the implementation level which maybe described in the original paper. In addition to the design of the neural architecture, configure nonarchitecture hyperparameters (e.g. initial learning rate, weight decay, drop out ratio, optimizer type, etc) are also time consumption and strongly effect network performance. Jointly search of hyperparameters and architectures has been taken into consideration; however, it just focuses on small data sets and small search spaces. Recent research AutoHAS [17], FBNet [14] show that jointly search of hyperparameters and architectures has great potential. Furthermore, reproduce NAS requires a vast of resource. With the rise of NAS-based techniques, it is now possible to produce state-of-the-art ANNs for many applications with relatively low search time consumption (a few 10 GPU-days rather than 1000 GPU-days). The future NAS-based approach should be able to address various problems across domains i.e. tasks: segmentation, object detection, depth estimation, machine translation, speech recognition, etc; computing platform: server, mobile, IOT and CPU, GPU, TPU; sensor: camera, lidar, radar, microphone; objectives: accuracy, parameter size, MACs, latency, energy. Instead of wasting much time on the model evaluation, some datasets (e.g. NAS-Bench-101 [67], NAS-Bench-201 [15]) support NAS researchers to focus on the design of optimization algorithm.

Comparison: At the current stage of development, there is no corresponding baseline and sharable experimental protocol besides random sampling which has been proven to be a strong baseline. This make it difficult to compare between NAS search algorithms. Instead of blindly stacking certain techniques to increase performance, it is critical to have more ablation experiments on which part of the NAS design leads to performance gains.

Acknowledgment

This material is based upon work supported by the National Science Foundation under Award No. OIA-1946391; partially funded by Gia Lam Urban Development and Investment Company Limited, Vingroup and supported by Vingroup Innovation Foundation (VINIF) under project code VINIF.2019.DA19.

References

[1] Bowen Baker, et al., Designing neural network architectures using reinforcement learning, in: ICLR (Poster), 2017.
[2] Gabriel Bender, et al., Understanding and simplifying one-shot architecture search, in: International Conference on Machine Learning, PMLR, 2018, pp. 550–559.
[3] James Bergstra, Yoshua Bengio, Random search for hyper-parameter optimization, Journal of Machine Learning Research 13 (2) (2012).
[4] Andrew Brock, et al., Smash: one-shot model architecture search through hypernetworks, arXiv preprint, arXiv:1708.05344, 2017.
[5] Han Cai, Ligeng Zhu, Song Han, ProxylessNAS: direct neural architecture search on target task and hardware, in: International Conference on Learning Representations, 2019.
[6] Han Cai, et al., Path-level network transformation for efficient architecture search, in: International Conference on Machine Learning, PMLR, 2018, pp. 678–687.
[7] Liang-Chieh Chen, et al., Searching for efficient multi-scale architectures for dense image prediction, in: Advances in Neural Information Processing Systems, 2018.
[8] Yi-Wei Chen, et al., On robustness of neural architecture search under label noise, Frontiers in Big Data 3 (2020) 2.
[9] Wuyang Chen, et al., FasterSeg: searching for faster real-time semantic segmentation, in: International Conference on Learning Representations, 2020.
[10] Xuelian Cheng, et al., Hierarchical neural architecture search for deep stereo matching, arXiv preprint, arXiv: 2010.13501, 2020.
[11] Corinna Cortes, et al., Adanet: adaptive structural learning of artificial neural networks, in: International Conference on Machine Learning, PMLR, 2017, pp. 874–883.
[12] Jiequan Cui, et al., Fast and practical neural architecture search, in: Proceedings of the IEEE/CVF International Conference on Computer Vision, 2019, pp. 6509–6518.
[13] Haixing Dai, et al., Optimize CNN model for FMRI signal classification via Adanet-based neural architecture search, in: 2020 IEEE 17th International Symposium on Biomedical Imaging (ISBI), IEEE, 2020, pp. 1399–1403.
[14] Xiaoliang Dai, Alvin Wan, Peizhao Zhang, Bichen Wu, Zijian He, Zhen Wei, Kan Chen, et al., FBNetV3: joint architecture-recipe search using predictor pretraining, in: Proceedings of the IEEE/CVF Conference on Computer Vision and Pattern Recognition, 2021, pp. 16276–16285.
[15] Xuanyi Dong, Yi Yang, Nas-bench-201: extending the scope of reproducible neural architecture search, arXiv preprint, arXiv:2001.00326, 2020.
[16] Xuanyi Dong, Yi Yang, Searching for a robust neural architecture in four gpu hours, in: Proceedings of the IEEE/CVF Conference on Computer Vision and Pattern Recognition, 2019, pp. 1761–1770.

[17] Xuanyi Dong, et al., AutoHAS: differentiable hyper-parameter and architecture search, arXiv e-prints, arXiv–2006, 2020.

[18] Thomas Elsken, Jan Hendrik Metzen, Frank Hutter, Neural architecture search: a survey, The Journal of Machine Learning Research 20 (1) (2019) 1997–2017.

[19] Thomas Elsken, Jan-Hendrik Metzen, Frank Hutter, Simple and efficient architecture search for convolutional neural networks, arXiv preprint, arXiv:1711.04528, 2017.

[20] Thomas Elsken, et al., Meta-learning of neural architectures for few-shot learning, in: Proceedings of the IEEE/CVF Conference on Computer Vision and Pattern Recognition, 2020, pp. 12365–12375.

[21] Jiemin Fang, et al., Densely connected search space for more flexible neural architecture search, in: Proceedings of the IEEE/CVF Conference on Computer Vision and Pattern Recognition, 2020, pp. 10628–10637.

[22] Minghao Guo, et al., When nas meets robustness: in search of robust architectures against adversarial attacks, in: Proceedings of the IEEE/CVF Conference on Computer Vision and Pattern Recognition, 2020, pp. 631–640.

[23] Zichao Guo, et al., Single path one-shot neural architecture search with uniform sampling, in: Computer Vision – ECCV 2020, Springer International Publishing, Cham, 2020, pp. 544–560.

[24] Sepp Hochreiter, Jürgen Schmidhuber, Long short-term memory, Neural Computation 9 (8) (1997) 1735–1780.

[25] Gao Huang, et al., Densely connected convolutional networks, in: Proceedings of the IEEE Conference on Computer Vision and Pattern Recognition, 2017, pp. 4700–4708.

[26] Qiaoying Huang, et al., Enhanced MRI reconstruction network using neural architecture search, in: International Workshop on Machine Learning in Medical Imaging, Springer, 2020, pp. 634–643.

[27] Fabian Isensee, et al., Automated design of deep learning methods for biomedical image segmentation, arXiv preprint, arXiv:1904.08128, 2019.

[28] Simon Jégou, et al., The one hundred layers tiramisu: fully convolutional densenets for semantic segmentation, in: Proceedings of the IEEE Conference on Computer Vision and Pattern Recognition Workshops, 2017, pp. 11–19.

[29] Chenhan Jiang, et al., Elixirnet: relation-aware network architecture adaptation for medical lesion detection, in: Proceedings of the AAAI Conference on Artificial Intelligence, vol. 34, no. 07, 2020, pp. 11093–11100.

[30] Haifeng Jin, Qingquan Song, Xia Hu, Efficient neural architecture search with network morphism, arXiv preprint, arXiv:1806.10282, 2018, 9.

[31] Kandasamy Kirthevasan, et al., Gaussian process optimisation with multi-fidelity evaluations, in: Proceedings of the 30th/International Conference on Advances in Neural Information Processing Systems (NIPS'30), 2016.

[32] Kandasamy Kirthevasan, et al., Neural architecture search with Bayesian optimisation and optimal transport, arXiv preprint, arXiv:1802.07191, 2018.

[33] James Kennedy, Russell Eberhart, Particle swarm optimization, in: Proceedings of ICNN'95-International Conference on Neural Networks, vol. 4, IEEE, 1995, pp. 1942–1948.

[34] Aaron Klein, et al., Fast Bayesian optimization of machine learning hyperparameters on large datasets, in: Artificial Intelligence and Statistics, PMLR, 2017, pp. 528–536.

[35] Arkadiusz Kwasigroch, Michał Grochowski, Agnieszka Mikołajczyk, Neural architecture search for skin lesion classification, IEEE Access 8 (2020) 9061–9071.

[36] William B. Langdon, Riccardo Poli, Foundations of Genetic Programming, Springer Science & Business Media, 2013.

[37] Ngan Le, et al., A multi-task contextual atrous residual network for brain tumor detection & segmentation, in: 2020 25th International Conference on Pattern Recognition (ICPR), IEEE, 2021, pp. 5943–5950.

[38] Y. Lecun, et al., Gradient-based learning applied to document recognition, Proceedings of the IEEE 86 (11) (1998) 2278–2324, https://doi.org/10.1109/5.726791.

[39] Xiaomeng Li, et al., H-DenseUNet: hybrid densely connected UNet for liver and tumor segmentation from CT volumes, IEEE Transactions on Medical Imaging 37 (12) (2018) 2663–2674.

[40] Dongze Lian, et al., Towards fast adaptation of neural architectures with meta learning, in: International Conference on Learning Representations, 2019.

[41] Chenxi Liu, et al., Are labels necessary for neural architecture search?, in: European Conference on Computer Vision, Springer, 2020, pp. 798–813.

[42] Chenxi Liu, et al., Auto-deeplab: hierarchical neural architecture search for semantic image segmentation, in: Proceedings of the IEEE/CVF Conference on Computer Vision and Pattern Recognition, 2019, pp. 82–92.

[43] Chenxi Liu, et al., Progressive neural architecture search, in: Proceedings of the European Conference on Computer Vision (ECCV), 2018, pp. 19–34.

[44] Hanxiao Liu, Karen Simonyan, Yiming Yang, Darts: differentiable architecture search, arXiv preprint, arXiv: 1806.09055, 2018.

[45] Fausto Milletari, Nassir Navab, Seyed-Ahmad Ahmadi, V-net: fully convolutional neural networks for volumetric medical image segmentation, in: 2016 Fourth International Conference on 3D Vision (3DV), IEEE, 2016, pp. 565–571.

[46] Ramakanth Pasunuru, Mohit Bansal, Continual and multi-task architecture search, arXiv preprint, arXiv: 1906.05226, 2019.

[47] Juan-Manuel Perez-Rua, Moez Baccouche, Stéphane Pateux, Efficient progressive neural architecture search, in: British Machine Vision Conference 2018, BMVC 2018, BMVA Press, 2018.

[48] Hieu Pham, et al., Efficient neural architecture search via parameters sharing, in: International Conference on Machine Learning, PMLR, 2018, pp. 4095–4104.

[49] A.J. Piergiovanni, et al., Evolving space-time neural architectures for videos, in: Proceedings of the IEEE/CVF International Conference on Computer Vision, 2019, pp. 1793–1802.

[50] Esteban Real, et al., Regularized evolution for image classifier architecture search, in: Proceedings of the AAAI Conference on Artificial Intelligence, vol. 33, no. 01, 2019, pp. 4780–4789.

[51] Olaf Ronneberger, Philipp Fischer, Thomas Brox, U-net: convolutional networks for biomedical image segmentation, in: International Conference on Medical Image Computing and Computer-Assisted Intervention, Springer, 2015, pp. 234–241.

[52] Tonmoy Saikia, et al., Autodispnet: improving disparity estimation with automl, in: Proceedings of the IEEE/CVF International Conference on Computer Vision, 2019, pp. 1812–1823.

[53] Bobak Shahriari, et al., Taking the human out of the loop: a review of Bayesian optimization, Proceedings of the IEEE 104 (1) (2015) 148–175.

[54] Yao Shu, Wei Wang, Shaofeng Cai, Understanding architectures learnt by cell-based neural architecture search, in: International Conference on Learning Representations, 2020.

[55] S.N. Sivanandam, S.N. Deepa, Genetic algorithms, in: Introduction to Genetic Algorithms, Springer, 2008, pp. 15–37.

[56] Xingyou Song, et al., ES-ENAS: combining evolution strategies with neural architecture search at no extra cost for reinforcement learning, arXiv preprint, arXiv:2101.07415, 2021.

[57] Mingxing Tan, et al., Mnasnet: platform-aware neural architecture search for mobile, in: Proceedings of the IEEE/CVF Conference on Computer Vision and Pattern Recognition, 2019, pp. 2820–2828.

[58] Jiaxing Wang, et al., M-nas: meta neural architecture search, in: Proceedings of the AAAI Conference on Artificial Intelligence, vol. 34, no. 04, 2020, pp. 6186–6193.

[59] Xinyi Wang, et al., BiX-NAS: searching efficient bi-directional architecture for medical image segmentation, arXiv preprint, arXiv:2106.14033, 2021.

[60] Yu Weng, et al., Nas-unet: neural architecture search for medical image segmentation, IEEE Access 7 (2019) 44247–44257.

[61] Ronald J. Williams, Simple statistical gradient-following algorithms for connectionist reinforcement learning, Machine Learning 8 (3) (1992) 229–256.

[62] Saining Xie, et al., Exploring randomly wired neural networks for image recognition, in: Proceedings of the IEEE/CVF International Conference on Computer Vision, 2019, pp. 1284–1293.

[63] Yuhui Xu, et al., PC-DARTS: partial channel connections for memory-efficient architecture search, arXiv preprint, arXiv:1907.05737, 2019.

[64] Jiangpeng Yan, et al., Neural architecture search for compressed sensing magnetic resonance image reconstruction, Computerized Medical Imaging and Graphics 85 (2020) 101784.

[65] Xingang Yan, et al., Ms-nas: multi-scale neural architecture search for medical image segmentation, in: International Conference on Medical Image Computing and Computer-Assisted Intervention, Springer, 2020, pp. 388–397.

[66] Xin Yang, et al., Searching collaborative agents for multi-plane localization in 3d ultrasound, Medical Image Analysis (2021) 102119.

[67] Chris Ying, et al., Nas-bench-101: towards reproducible neural architecture search, in: International Conference on Machine Learning, PMLR, 2019, pp. 7105–7114.

[68] Qihang Yu, et al., C2fnas: coarse-to-fine neural architecture search for 3d medical image segmentation, in: Proceedings of the IEEE/CVF Conference on Computer Vision and Pattern Recognition, 2020, pp. 4126–4135.

[69] Chris Zhang, Mengye Ren, Raquel Urtasun, Graph hypernetworks for neural architecture search, arXiv preprint, arXiv:1810.05749, 2018.

[70] Zhao Zhong, et al., Practical block-wise neural network architecture generation, in: Proceedings of the IEEE Conference on Computer Vision and Pattern Recognition, 2018, pp. 2423–2432.

[71] Zongwei Zhou, et al., Unet++: redesigning skip connections to exploit multiscale features in image segmentation, IEEE Transactions on Medical Imaging 39 (6) (2019) 1856–1867.

[72] Zhuotun Zhu, et al., V-nas: neural architecture search for volumetric medical image segmentation, in: 2019 International Conference on 3D Vision (3DV), IEEE, 2019, pp. 240–248.

[73] Barret Zoph, Quoc V. Le, Neural architecture search with reinforcement learning, in: International Conference on Learning Representations ICLR, 2016.

[74] Barret Zoph, et al., Learning transferable architectures for scalable image recognition, in: Proceedings of the IEEE Conference on Computer Vision and Pattern Recognition, 2018, pp. 8697–8710.

Meta learning in the big data regime

Applications to transfer learning and few shot learning

Swami Sankaranarayanan[a] **and Yogesh Balaji**[b]

[a]*MIT, Cambridge, MA, United States*
[b]*NVIDIA, San Jose, CA, United States*

20.1 Introduction

Humans have an amazing ability to learn about concepts with only a few examples - whether fit a new model quickly or update an existing model of the world is open for debate. In either case, humans are able to extrapolate new concepts they perceive to the knowledge base that exists in their brain. Particularly stunning is the amount of generalization that they are able to achieve in this process. Conventional machine learning algorithms rarely display such generalization abilities due to their sensitivity to distortions or distribution shifts.

Meta learning is an approach that aims to mimic this generalization behavior. While applications of meta learning can be varied (such as hyperparameter optimization or learning the types of data augmentations that best increase performance), the aspect that we will be discussing in this chapter relates to its application in large scale settings that involve transfer learning and few shot learning. The key challenges with few shot learning and transfer learning setting are the shift in distribution and quick adaptability. Meta learning can be used to learn the model from collections of few-shot classification tasks, which makes the training objective more consistent with the testing objective.

In this chapter, we demonstrate that while Meta learning is a useful technique for domain adaptation, it can also be extremely useful for regular supervised and semisupervised learning, especially in a teacher student setting [3] and few shot learning settings [2]. These approaches also demonstrate that meta learning techniques when implemented in a scalable and computationally efficient manner can improve performance on conventional supervised learning paradigms as well.

20.2 Metapseudo labels

To understand metapseudo labels, let us begin by describing vanilla pseudo label optimization in Fig. 20.1. Pseudo Labels (PL) train the student model to minimize the cross-entropy loss on unlabeled data.

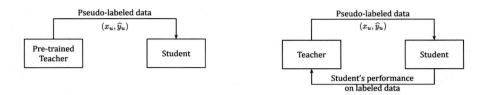

FIGURE 20.1 Metapseudo labels.

The left figure shows training with regular pseudo labels data while the right figure shows the metapseudo labels approach. The key difference is that the teacher network is updated along with the student to generate the pseudo labels in the latter case.

$$\theta_S^{PL} = \underset{\theta_S}{argmin} \quad \mathrm{E}_{x_u} \left[CE(T(x_u; \theta_T), S(x_u; \theta_S)) \right] \tag{20.1}$$

where the pseudo target $T(...)$ is produced by a fully trained *frozen* teacher model with parameters θ_T. Given a well trained teacher, the pseudo labels approach aims to achieve a good initialization of the student parameters to obtain high accuracy over the labeled dataset. The key dependency to note is that the optimal student parameters always depend on the teacher parameters through the pseudo targets. We can express this dependency explicitly as: $\theta_S^{PL}(\theta_T)$. It follows that the final loss on the labeled data also depends on θ_T: $\mathcal{L}_l(\theta_S^{PL}(\theta_T))$. This expression naturally lends itself to the fact that we can further optimize the teacher parameters to make the pseudo targets more accurate, as shown below:

$$\begin{aligned} \underset{\theta_T}{min} \quad & \mathcal{L}_l(\theta_S^{PL}(\theta_T)) \\ \text{s.t.} \quad & \theta_S = \underset{\theta_S}{argmin} \quad \mathcal{L}_u(\theta_S, \theta_T) \end{aligned} \tag{20.2}$$

The top equation aims to optimize the teacher parameters according to the performance of the student on the labeled data, while the bottom equation optimizes the student parameters according to the performance of the teacher on unlabeled data. In the pseudo label (PL) setting, only the bottom equation is employed. By optimizing both student and teacher alternatively, the teacher network is forced to get better along with the student network thus encouraging a symbiotic relationship. The implicit dependency of θ_S^{PL} on (θ_T) is very complicated as computing the gradient $\nabla_{\theta_T}(\theta_S^{PL}(\theta_T))$ requires unrolling the student optimization process ($\underset{\theta_S}{argmin}$).

20.2.1 Approximating pseudo label gradient with meta learning

As described in the previous chapter, we can use Meta learning techniques to approximate the second order gradient from Eq. (20.2). Following the methods described in the previous chapter, we can approximate the bi-level optimization problem as:

$$\theta_S(\theta_T^{PL}) \approx \theta_S - \eta_S \cdot \nabla_{\theta_S} \mathcal{L}_u(\theta_T, \theta_S) \tag{20.3}$$

Plugging this approximation into the optimization in Eq. (20.2) yields:

$$\min_{\theta_T} \quad \mathcal{L}_l(\theta_S - \eta_S \cdot \nabla_{\theta_S} \mathcal{L}_u(\theta_T, \theta_S)) \qquad (20.4)$$

When optimizing Eq. (20.4), the student parameters are held fixed and this way the approximation ignores the higher order dependency thereby allowing us to backpropagate only the first order gradient. One can use either hard or soft pseudo labels from the teacher, using soft labels has the advantage that the objective becomes the entire teacher distribution which is easier to optimize since it becomes fully differentiable. The authors of this work prefer hard pseudo labels since it results in smaller computational graphs and hence faster convergence in large scale settings. In summary, the optimization of Eq. (20.2) can be summarized as an alternating optimization procedure as follows:

- Student: Draw a batch of unlabeled data; obtain teacher predictions; Optimize the student parameters from (20.4) with SGD, holding the teacher parameters fixed.
- Teacher: Draw a batch of labeled data; Optimize the teacher parameters with objective (20.3). Performing updates in this order enables one to reuse the gradient computed for the student update i.e. $(\theta_S - \eta_S \cdot \nabla_{\theta_S} \mathcal{L}_u(\theta_T, \theta_S))$ can be reused from the above step.

This section described an approach to simplify the training of a student teacher network to enable much better performance by adapting the teacher network to the student network at each step. The use of meta learning techniques enabled us to simplify the second order gradient update to a first order update there by making this computationally more feasible for big data setting.

20.2.2 Experimental setup

For evaluating the metapseudo labels approach, the authors consider three standard benchmarks: CIFAR-10-4K, SVHN-1K, and ImageNet-10%, which have been widely used in the literature to fairly benchmark semisupervised learning algorithms. These benchmarks were created by keeping a small fraction of the training set as labeled data while using the rest as unlabeled data. For CIFAR-10, 4000 labeled examples are kept as labeled data while 41,000 examples are used as unlabeled data. The test set for CIFAR-10 is standard and consists of 10,000 examples. For SVHN, 1000 examples are used as labeled data whereas about 603,000 examples are used as unlabeled data. The test set for SVHN is also standard, and has 26,032 examples. Finally, for ImageNet, 128,000 examples are used as labeled data which is approximately 10% of the whole ImageNet training set while the rest of 1.28 million examples are used as unlabeled data. The test set for ImageNet is the standard ILSVRC 2012 version that has 50,000 examples. The image resolutions used are 32x32 for CIFAR-10 and SVHN, and 224x224 for ImageNet.

In all the experiments, the teacher model and the student model share the same architecture but have independent weights. For CIFAR-10-4K and SVHN-1K, a WideResNet-28-2 is used which has 1.45 million parameters. For ImageNet, a ResNet-50 is used which has 25.5 million parameters. These architectures are also commonly used by previous works in this area. During the Metapseudo Labels training phase where the teacher and the student are both trained, the default hyperparameters from previous work are used. After training both the teacher and student with Metapseudo Labels, the student is finetuned on the labeled dataset. For this finetuning phase, SGD is employed with a fixed learning rate of 10^{-5} and a batch size of 512, running for 2000 steps for ImageNet-10% and 1000 steps for CIFAR-10

Method	CIFAR-10-4K (mean ± std)	SVHN-1K (mean ± std)	ImageNet-10% Top-1	ImageNet-10% Top-5
Label Propagation Methods				
Temporal Ensemble [35]	83.63 ± 0.63	92.81 ± 0.27	–	
Mean Teacher [64]	84.13 ± 0.28	94.35 ± 0.47	–	
VAT + EntMin [44]	86.87 ± 0.39	94.65 ± 0.19	–	83.39
LGA + VAT [30]	87.94 ± 0.19	93.42 ± 0.36	–	
ICT [71]	92.71 ± 0.02	96.11 ± 0.04	–	
MixMatch [5]	93.76 ± 0.06	96.73 ± 0.31	–	
ReMixMatch [4]	94.86 ± 0.04	97.17 ± 0.30	–	
EnAET [72]	94.65	97.08	–	
FixMatch [58]	95.74 ± 0.05	97.72 ± 0.38	71.5	89.1
UDA* [76]	94.53 ± 0.18	97.11 ± 0.17	68.07	88.19
Self-Supervised Methods				
SimCLR [8, 9]	–	–	71.7	90.4
MOCOv2 [10]	–	–	71.1	–
PCL [38]	–	–	–	85.6
PIRL [43]	–	–	–	84.9
BYOL [21]	–	–	68.8	89.0
Meta Pseudo Labels	**96.11 ± 0.07**	**98.01 ± 0.07**	**73.89**	**91.38**
Supervised Learning with full dataset*	94.92 ± 0.17	97.41 ± 0.16	76.89	93.27

FIGURE 20.2 Metapseudo labels Results.

Results of Metapseudo labels on CIFAR-10-4K, SVHN-1K, and ImageNet-10%. Higher is better.

and SVHN. Since the amount of labeled examples is limited for all three datasets, no heldout validation set is used. Instead, the model at the final checkpoint is returned.

To ensure a fair comparison, the authors only compare Metapseudo Labels against methods that use the same architectures and do not compare against methods that use larger architectures. Primarily, Metapseudo Labels against two baselines: Supervised Learning with full dataset and Unsupervised Data Augmentation. Supervised Learning with full dataset represents an oracle-like performance because it unfairly makes use of all labeled data. They also compare against UDA because the implementation of Metapseudo Labels uses UDA in training the teacher. Both of these baselines use the same experimental protocols and hence ensure a fair comparison.

20.2.3 Results and discussion

The results with Metapseudo Labels in comparison with other methods are presented in Fig. 20.2. The results show that under strictly fair comparisons, Metapseudo Labels significantly improve over UDA. Interestingly, on CIFAR-10-4K, Metapseudo Labels even exceed the oracle-like supervised learning on full dataset. On ImageNet-10%, Metapseudo Labels outperform the UDA teacher by more than 5% in top-1 accuracy, going from 68.07% to 73.89%. For ImageNet, such relative improvement is very significant.

20.3 Metabaseline

Contemporary meta learning approaches can be complicated to setup and train. The ease of compute or the lack there of is sometime ignore in meta learning. Since meta learning can increase the complexity of the training methodology, it becomes increasingly important to develop techniques that are reproducible and yield consistent improvements. The Metabaseline approach addresses the issue of

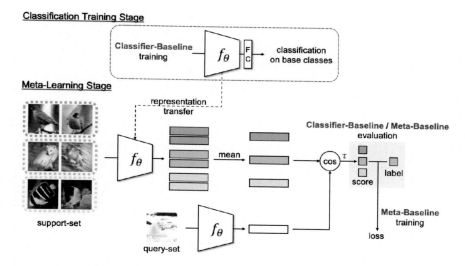

FIGURE 20.3 Metabaseline.

Classifier-Baseline is to train a classification model on all base classes and remove its last FC layer to get the encoder f. Given a few-shot task, it computes the average feature for samples of each class in support-set, then it classifies a sample in query-set by nearest-centroid with cosine similarity as distance. In Metabaseline, it further optimizes a converged Classifier-Baseline on its evaluation metric, and an additional learnable scalar τ is introduced to scale cosine similarity.

complexity in meta learning. The claim is that they provide a simple baseline for meta learning that has been overlooked in prior work. They demonstrate that this new baseline achieves competitive performance on state-of-the-art methods on standard benchmarks and is easy to set up and follow. Specifically, for the few shot learning setting, they point out to a trade-off between the meta learning objective and the whole classification. In this section, we explain the simple Metabaseline approach for few shot learning by starting with a naive classifier baseline and improving it using ideas derived from meta learning. The whole approach is illustrated in Fig. 20.3.

20.3.1 Problem setup

In this section, we explore the few shot learning setting. Let C_{base} be the number of base classes for whom labeled data is available. The goal is to learn the concepts that appear in novel classes C_{novel} with a few samples per class. In a traditional N-way K-shot few-shot classification task, the *support-set* contains N classes with K samples per class, the *query-set* contains samples from the same N classes with Q samples per class, and the goal is to classify the N × Q query images into N classes.

20.3.2 Classifier baseline

This setting refers to the naive baseline where one trains a large classification model on a large labeled base dataset. It refers to training a classifier with classification loss on all base classes and performing few-shot tasks with a cosine similarity based inference procedure. Specifically, the classifier is trained on all base classes with standard cross-entropy loss, then the last FC layer is removed to get the encoder representation f_θ, which maps the input to a feature embedding. Given a few shot task with a support set S, let S_c denote the few shot samples in class c. The average embedding for class c is then computed as follows:

$$w_c = \frac{1}{|S_c|} \sum_{x \in S_c} f_\theta(x) \tag{20.5}$$

Given the average embedding for class c, given a query sample x in a few shot task, one can predict the conditional probability that x belongs to class c as:

$$p(y = c|x) = \frac{exp(\langle f_\theta, w_c \rangle)}{\sum_{c'} exp(\langle f_\theta, w_{c'} \rangle)} \tag{20.6}$$

where $(\langle x, y \rangle)$ represents the cosine similarity between the embeddings x and y. There have been several variants of this naive classifier baseline over the years, but the primary focus has been to train a better classifier that is more amenable to the few shot learning setting. The MetaReg approach described in the previous chapter is an instance of one such approach that used meta learning to train a better classifier which then uses the cosine similarity approach described here for inference.

20.3.3 Metabaseline approach

In this section, we describe the Metabaseline approach that is illustrated in Fig. 20.3. The first stage is training the classifier as described in the above step. The second stage is the meta learning stage, which optimizes the model on the evaluation metric of Classifier-Baseline. Specifically, given the feature encoder f_θ, it samples N-way K-shot tasks (with N × Q query samples) from the training dataset with base classes, C_{base}. To compute the loss for each metastep, it computes the centroids of N classes in support-set as defined in Eq. (20.5), which are then used to compute the predicted probability distribution for each sample in query-set defined in Eq. (20.6). The loss is a cross-entropy loss computed from p and the labels of the samples from the query-set. During training, each training batch can contain several tasks and the average loss is computed for generating the loss gradient.

The authors introduce a trick that stabilizes the training more by learning a scaling factor to scale the cosine similarity appropriately across different metatasks. When we multiply the cosine similarity by a learnable scalar τ, and the probability prediction in training becomes:

$$p(y = c|x) = \frac{exp(\tau \cdot \langle f_\theta, w_c \rangle)}{\sum_{c'} exp(\tau \cdot \langle f_\theta, w_{c'} \rangle)} \tag{20.7}$$

The main objective of the Metabaseline approach is to investigate whether the meta learning objective is still effective over a whole-classification model. As a method, while every component in Metabaseline has been proposed in prior works, the authors claim that none of the prior works studies them as a whole. Therefore, Metabaseline should also be an important baseline that has been overlooked in contemporary approaches.

20.3.4 Experimental setup

In this section, we demonstrate the results of the Metabaseline approach on mini-Imagenet and the large scale Imagenet-800 datasets. The miniImageNet dataset is a common benchmark for few-shot learning. It contains 100 classes sampled from ILSVRC-2012, which are then randomly split to 64, 16, 20 classes as training, validation, and testing set respectively. Each class contains 600 images of size 84 × 84.

For demonstrating efficacy on a real large scale dataset, the model is evaluated on ImageNet-800, which is derived from ILSVRC-2012 1K classes by randomly splitting 800 classes as base classes and 200 classes as novel classes. The base classes contain the images from the original training set, the novel classes contain the images from the original validation set. This larger dataset aims at making the training setting standard as the ImageNet 1K classification task.

The authors use ResNet-12 that follows the most of recent works on miniImageNet. For ImageNet800, they use ResNet-18, ResNet-50. The SGD optimizer is used for the classification training stage, with momentum 0.9, the learning rate starts from 0.1 and the decay factor is 0.1. On miniImageNet, they train for 100 epochs with batch size 128 on 4 GPUs, the learning rate decays at epoch 90. On ImageNet-800, they train 90 epochs with batch size 256 on 8 GPUs, the learning rate decays at epoch 30 and 60. The weight decay is 0.0005 for ResNet-12 and 0.0001 for ResNet-18 or ResNet-50. Standard data augmentation is applied, including random resized crop and horizontal flip. For meta learning stage, they use the SGD optimizer with momentum 0.9. The learning rate is fixed as 0.001. The batch size is 4, i.e. each training batch contains 4 few-shot tasks to compute the average loss. The cosine scaling parameter τ is initialized as 10. They also apply consistent sampling for evaluating the performance. For the novel class split in a dataset, the sampling of testing few-shot tasks follows a deterministic order. Consistent sampling allows to get a better model comparison with the same number of sampled tasks.

20.3.5 Results and discussion

Following the standard-setting, experiments are conducted on miniImageNet and Imagenet-800, the results are shown in Figs. 20.4 and 20.5 respectively. To get a fair comparison to prior works, the authors perform model selection according to the validation set. On both datasets, one can observe that the Metabaseline achieves competitive performance to state-of-the-art methods. Importantly, they highlight that many methods for comparison introduce more parameters and architecture designs (e.g. the self-attention approach), while Metabaseline has the minimum parameters and the simplest design. One can also notice in the results that the simple Classifier-Baseline can achieve competitive performance when compared to meta learning methods, especially in 5-shot tasks.

For a real large scale setting, the authors further evaluate their methods on the larger dataset, ImageNet-800. In this larger-scale experiment, they note that freezing the Batch Normalization layer [9] (set to eval mode) is beneficial. From the results, we can observe that in this large dataset Metabaseline improves Classifier-Baseline in 1-shot, while not improving the performance in 5-shot setting. Compared to results reported from past papers, Metapseudo Labels have achieved the best accuracies among the same model architectures on all the three datasets: CIFAR-10-4K, SVHN-1K, and ImageNet-10%. On CIFAR-10-4K and SVHN-1K, Metapseudo Labels leads to almost 10% relative error reduction. On ImageNet-10%, Metapseudo Labels outperform SimCLR [1] by 2.19% top-1 accuracy.

Model	Backbone	1-shot	5-shot
Matching Networks [29]	ConvNet-4	43.56 ± 0.84	55.31 ± 0.73
Prototypical Networks [24]	ConvNet-4	48.70 ± 1.84	63.11 ± 0.92
Prototypical Networks (re-implement)	ResNet-12	53.81 ± 0.23	75.68 ± 0.17
Activation to Parameter [18]	WRN-28-10	59.60 ± 0.41	73.74 ± 0.19
LEO [22]	WRN-28-10	61.76 ± 0.08	77.59 ± 0.12
Baseline++ [1]	ResNet-18	51.87 ± 0.77	75.68 ± 0.63
SNAIL [13]	ResNet-12	55.71 ± 0.99	68.88 ± 0.92
AdaResNet [15]	ResNet-12	56.88 ± 0.62	71.94 ± 0.57
TADAM [16]	ResNet-12	58.50 ± 0.30	76.70 ± 0.30
MTL [25]	ResNet-12	61.20 ± 1.80	75.50 ± 0.80
MetaOptNet [11]	ResNet-12	62.64 ± 0.61	78.63 ± 0.46
SLA-AG [10]	ResNet-12	62.93 ± 0.63	79.63 ± 0.47
ProtoNets + TRAML [12]	ResNet-12	60.31 ± 0.48	77.94 ± 0.57
ConstellationNet [33]	ResNet-12	**64.89 ± 0.23**	**79.95 ± 0.17**
Classifier-Baseline (ours)	ResNet-12	58.91 ± 0.23	77.76 ± 0.17
Meta-Baseline (ours)	ResNet-12	63.17 ± 0.23	79.26 ± 0.17

FIGURE 20.4 Metabaseline Results.

Results of Metabaseline and other contemporary meta learning approaches on mini-Imagenet.

Model	Backbone	1-shot	5-shot
Classifier-Baseline (ours)	ResNet-18	83.51 ± 0.22	**94.82 ± 0.10**
Meta-Baseline (ours)	ResNet-18	**86.39 ± 0.22**	**94.82 ± 0.10**
Classifier-Baseline (ours)	ResNet-50	86.07 ± 0.21	**96.14 ± 0.08**
Meta-Baseline (ours)	ResNet-50	**89.70 ± 0.19**	**96.14 ± 0.08**

FIGURE 20.5 Metabaseline Imagenet-800 Results.

Results of Metabaseline on the large scale Imagenet-800 dataset.

20.4 Conclusion

In this chapter, we discussed approaches that use meta learning based techniques in conventional supervised learning that result in big performance gains in both large data settings and few shot data settings. These methods push the frontier in meta learning research so that meta learning is not just a bespoke training scheme but a scalable and efficient approach to train generalizable representations aimed both towards accuracy and quick adaptability. It is our hope that this can encourage the reader to pursue meta learning in more safety critical setting yet focusing on keeping the training procedures more approachable, simpler and aimed towards reproducibility.

References

[1] Ting Chen, Simon Kornblith, Mohammad Norouzi, Geoffrey Everest Hinton, A simple framework for contrastive learning of visual representations, 2020.

[2] Yinbo Chen, Zhuang Liu, Huijuan Xu, Trevor Darrell, Xiaolong Wang, Meta-baseline: exploring simple meta-learning for few-shot learning, in: Proceedings of the IEEE/CVF International Conference on Computer Vision, 2021, pp. 9062–9071.

[3] Hieu Pham, Zihang Dai, Qizhe Xie, Quoc V. Le, Meta pseudo labels, in: Proceedings of the IEEE/CVF Conference on Computer Vision and Pattern Recognition, 2021, pp. 11557–11568.

Index

Printed in the United States
by Baker & Taylor Publisher Services